Dear Carolina:

Keep your elbows off
the table!

Love,

Nick

December 2006

A BRIDE'S BOUQUET

"THE RADIANCE OF A TRULY HAPPY BRIDE IS SO BEAUTIFYING THAT EVEN A PLAIN GIRL IS MADE PRETTY, AND A PRETTY ONE. DIVINE." [Page 373.]

ETIQUETTE

IN SOCIETY, IN BUSINESS, IN POLITICS AND AT HOME

BY EMILY POST
(MRS. PRICE POST)

Author of "Purple and Fine Linen," "The Title Market," "Woven in the Tapestry," "The Flight of a Moth," "Letters of a Worldly Godmother," etc., etc.

ILLUSTRATED WITH PRIVATE PHOTOGRAPHS
AND FACSIMILES OF SOCIAL FORMS

FACSIMILE EDITION

APPLEWOOD BOOKS
Bedford, Massachusetts

This edition of *Etiquette* was originally published by Funk & Wagnalls Company in 1922.

Thank you for purchasing an Applewood book. Applewood reprints America's lively classics—books from the past that are still of interest to modern readers. For a free copy of our current catalog, write to:

Applewood Books
P.O. Box 365
Bedford, MA 01730

ISBN 1-55709-991-X

Library of Congress Control Number:

2006920129

10 9 8 7 6 5 4 3 2 1

TO YOU MY FRIENDS
WHOSE IDENTITY IN THESE PAGES
IS VEILED IN FICTIONAL DISGUISE
IT IS BUT FITTING THAT
I DEDICATE THIS BOOK.

Elizabeth L. Post

INTRODUCTION

MANNERS AND MORALS

By

Richard Duffy

Many who scoff at a book of etiquette would be shocked to hear the least expression of levity touching the Ten Commandments. But the Commandments do not always prevent such virtuous scoffers from dealings with their neighbor of which no gentleman could be capable and retain his claim to the title. Though it may require ingenuity to reconcile their actions with the Decalogue—the ingenuity is always forthcoming. There is no intention in this remark to intimate that there is any higher rule of life than the Ten Commandments; only it is illuminating as showing the relationship between manners and morals, which is too often overlooked. The polished gentleman of sentimental fiction has so long served as the type of smooth and conscienceless depravity that urbanity of demeanor inspires distrust in ruder minds. On the other hand, the blunt, unpolished hero of melodrama and romantic fiction has lifted brusqueness and pushfulness to a pedestal not wholly merited. Consequently, the kinship between conduct that keeps us within the law and conduct that makes civilized life worthy to be called such, deserves to be noted with emphasis. The Chinese sage, Confucius, could not tolerate the suggestion that virtue is in itself enough without politeness, for he viewed them as inseparable and "saw courtesies as coming from the heart," maintaining that "when they are practised with all the heart, a moral elevation ensues."

People who ridicule etiquette as a mass of trivial and arbitrary conventions, "extremely troublesome to those

who practise them and insupportable to everybody else,"
seem to forget the long, slow progress of social intercourse in the upward climb of man from the primeval
state. Conventions were established from the first to
regulate the rights of the individual and the tribe. They
were and are the rules of the game of life and must be
followed if we would "play the game." Ages before
man felt the need of indigestion remedies, he ate his
food solitary and furtive in some corner, hoping he
would not be espied by any stronger and hungrier fellow.
It was a long, long time before the habit of eating
in common was acquired; and it is obvious that the
practise could not have been taken up with safety until
the individuals of the race knew enough about one another and about the food resources to be sure that
there was food sufficient for all. When eating in common became the vogue, table manners made their appearance and they have been waging an uphill struggle
ever since. The custom of raising the hat when meeting
an acquaintance derives from the old rule that friendly
knights in accosting each other should raise the visor for
mutual recognition in amity. In the knightly years, it
must be remembered, it was important to know whether
one was meeting friend or foe. Meeting a foe meant
fighting on the spot. Thus, it is evident that the conventions of courtesy not only tend to make the wheels of
life run more smoothly, but also act as safeguards in
human relationship. Imagine the Paris Peace Conference,
or any of the later conferences in Europe, without the
protective armor of diplomatic etiquette!

Nevertheless, to some the very word etiquette is an
irritant. It implies a great pother about trifles, these
conscientious objectors assure us, and trifles are unimportant. Trifles are unimportant, it is true, but then life
is made up of trifles. To those who dislike the word, it
suggests all that is finical and superfluous. It means a
garish embroidery on the big scheme of life; a clog on
the forward march of a strong and courageous nation.
To such as these, the words etiquette and politeness con-

note weakness and timidity. Their notion of a really polite man is a dancing master or a man milliner. They were always willing to admit that the French were the politest nation in Europe and equally ready to assert that the French were the weakest and least valorous, until the war opened their eyes in amazement. Yet, that manners and fighting can go hand in hand appears in the following anecdote:

In the midst of the war, some French soldiers and some non-French of the Allied forces were receiving their rations in a village back of the lines. The non-French fighters belonged to an Army that supplied rations plentifully. They grabbed their allotments and stood about while hastily eating, uninterrupted by conversation or other concern. The French soldiers took their very meager portions of food, improvised a kind of table on the top of a flat rock, and having laid out the rations, including the small quantity of wine that formed part of the repast, sat down in comfort and began their meal amid a chatter of talk. One of the non-French soldiers, all of whom had finished their large supply of food before the French had begun eating, asked sardonically: "Why do you fellows make such a lot of fuss over the little bit of grub they give you to eat?" The Frenchman replied: "Well, we are making war for civilization, are we not? Very well, we are. Therefore, we eat in a civilized way."

To the French we owe the word etiquette, and it is amusing to discover its origin in the commonplace familiar warning—"Keep off the grass." It happened in the reign of Louis XIV, when the gardens of Versailles were being laid out, that the master gardener, an old Scotsman, was sorely tried because his newly seeded lawns were being continually trampled upon. To keep trespassers off, he put up warning signs or tickets—*etiquettes*—on which was indicated the path along which to pass. But the courtiers paid no attention to these directions and so the determined Scot complained to the King in such convincing manner that His Majesty issued an edict commanding everyone at Court to "keep within the *etiquettes*." Gradually the term came to cover all the rules for correct demeanor and deportment in court circles; and thus through the centuries it has grown into use to describe the conventions sanctioned for the purpose of smoothing personal contacts and developing tact and good manners in social intercourse. With the decline of feudal courts and the rise of empires of industry, much of the ceremony of life was discarded for plain and less formal dealing. Trousers and coats supplanted doublets and hose, and the change in costume was not more extreme than the change in social ideas. The court ceased to be the arbiter of manners, though the aristocracy of the land remained the high exemplar of good breeding.

Yet, even so courtly and materialistic a mind as Lord Chesterfield's acknowledged a connection between manners and morality, of which latter the courts of Europe seemed so sparing. In one of the famous "Letters to His Son" he writes: "Moral virtues are the foundation of society in general, and of friendship in particular; but attentions, manners, and graces, both adorn and strengthen them." Again he says: "Great merit, or great failings, will make you respected or despised; but trifles, little attentions, mere nothings, either done or reflected, will make you either liked or disliked, in the general run of the world." For all the wisdom and brilliancy of his worldly knowledge, perhaps no other writer has done so much to bring disrepute on the "manners and graces" as Lord Chesterfield, and this, it is charged, because he debased them so heavily by considering them merely as the machinery of a successful career. To the moralists, the fact that the moral standards of society in Lord Chesterfield's day were very different from those of the present era rather adds to the odium that has become associated with his attitude. His severest critics, however, do concede that he is candid and outspoken, and many admit that his social strategy is widely practised even in these days.

But the aims of the world in which he moved were routed by the onrush of the ideals of democratic equality, fraternity, and liberty. With the prosperity of the newer shibboleths, the old-time notion of aristocracy, gentility, and high breeding became more and more a curio to be framed suitably in gold and kept in the glass case of an art museum. The crashing advance of the industrial age of gold thrust all courts and their sinuous graces aside for the unmistakable ledger balance of the counting-house. This new order of things had been a long time in process, when, in the first year of this century, a distinguished English social historian, the late The Right Honorable G. W. E. Russell, wrote: "Probably in all ages of history men have liked money, but a hundred years ago they did not talk about it in society . . . Birth, breeding, rank, accomplishments, eminence in literature, eminence in art, eminence in public service—all these things still count for something in society. But when combined they are only as the dust of the balance when weighed against the all-prevalent power of money. The worship of the Golden Calf is the characteristic cult of modern society." In the Elizabethan Age of mighty glory, three hundred years before this was said, Ben Jonson had railed against money as "a thin membrane of honor," groaning: "How hath all true reputation fallen since money began to have any!" Now the very fact that the debasing effect of money on the social organism has been so constantly reprehended, from Scriptural days onward, proves the instinctive yearning of mankind for a system of life regulated by good taste, high intelligence and sound affections. But, it remains true that, in the succession of great commercial epochs, coincident with the progress of modern science and invention, *almost* everything can be bought and sold, and so *almost* everything is rated by the standard of money.

Yet, this standard is precisely not the ultimate test of the Christianity on which we have been pluming ourselves through the centuries. Still, no one can get along without money; and few of us get along very well with what we have. At least we think so—because everybody else seems to think that way. We Americans are members of the nation which, materially, is the richest, most prosperous and most promising in the world. This idea is dinned into our heads continually by foreign observers, and publicly we "own the soft impeachment." Privately, each individual American seems driven with the decision that he must live up to the general conception of the nation as a whole. And he does, but in less strenuous moments he might profitably ponder the counsel of Gladstone to his countrymen: "Let us respect the ancient manners and recollect that, if the true soul of chivalry has died among us, with it all that is good in society has died. Let us cherish a sober mind; take for granted that in our best performances there are latent many errors which in their own time will come to light."

America, too, has her ancient manners to remember and respect; but, in the rapid assimilation of new peoples into her economic and social organism, more pressing concerns take up nearly all her time. The perfection of manners by intensive cultivation of good taste, some believe, would be the greatest aid possible to the moralists who are alarmed over the decadence of the younger generation. Good taste may not make men or women really virtuous, but it will often save them from what theologians call "occasions of sin." We may note, too, that grossness in manners forms a large proportion of the offenses that fanatical reformers foam about. Besides grossness, there is also the meaner selfishness. Selfishness is at the polar remove from the worldly manners of the old school, according to which, as Dr. Pusey wrote, others were preferred to self, pain was given to no one, no one was neglected, deference was shown to the weak and the aged, and unconscious courtesy extended to all inferiors. Such was the "beauty" of the old manners, which he felt consisted in "acting upon Christian principle, and if in any case it became soulless, as apart from Christianity, the beautiful form was there, into which the real life might re-enter."

As a study of all that is admirable in American manners, and as a guide to behavior in the simplest as well as the most complex requirements of life day by day, whether we are at home or away from it, there can be no happier choice than the present volume. It is conceived in the belief that etiquette in its broader sense means the technique of human conduct under all circumstances in life. Yet all minutiæ of correct manners are included and no detail is too small to be explained, from the selection of a visiting card to the mystery of eating corn on the cob. Matters of clothes for men and women are treated with the same fullness of information and accuracy of taste as are questions of the furnishing of their houses and the training of their minds to social intercourse. But there is no exaggeration of the minor details at the expense of the more important spirit of personal conduct and attitude of mind. To dwell on formal trivialities, the author holds, is like "measuring the letters of the sign-boards by the roadside instead of profiting by the directions they offer." She would have us know also that "it is not the people who make small technical mistakes or even blunders, who are barred from the paths of good society, but those of sham and pretense whose veneered vulgarity at every step tramples the flowers in the gardens of cultivation." To her mind the structure of etiquette is comparable to that of a house, of which the foundation is ethics and the rest good taste, correct speech, quiet, unassuming behavior, and a proper pride of dignity.

To such as entertain the mistaken notion that politeness implies all give and little or no return, it is well to recall Coleridge's definition of a gentleman: "We feel the gentlemanly character present with us," he said, "whenever, under all circumstances of social intercourse, the trivial, not less than the important, through the whole detail of his manners and deportment, and with the ease of a habit, a person shows respect to others in such a way as at the same time implies, in his own feelings, and habitually, an assured anticipation of reciprocal respect from them to himself. In short, the gentlemanly character arises out of the feeling of equality acting as a habit, yet flexible to the varieties of rank, and modified without being disturbed or superseded by them." Definitions of a gentleman are numerous, and some of them famous; but we do not find such copiousness for choice in definitions of a lady. Perhaps it has been understood all along that the admirable and just characteristics of a gentleman should of necessity be those also of a lady, with the charm of womanhood combined. And, in these days, with the added responsibility of the vote.

Besides the significance of this volume as an indubitable authority on manners, it should be pointed out that as a social document, it is without precedent in American literature. In order that we may better realize the behavior and environment of well-bred people, the distinguished author has introduced actual persons and places in fictional guise. They are the persons and the places of her own world; and whether we can or can not penetrate the incognito of the Worldlys, the Gildings, the Kindharts, the Oldnames, and the others, is of no importance. Fictionally, they are real enough for us to be interested and instructed in their way of living. That they happen to move in what is known as Society is incidental, for, as the author declares at the very outset: "Best Society is not a fellowship of the wealthy, nor does it seek to exclude those who are not of exalted birth; but it is an association of gentlefolk, of which good form in speech, charm of manner, knowledge of the social amenities, and instinctive consideration for the feelings of others, are the credentials by which society the world over recognizes its chosen members."

The immediate fact is that the characters of this book are thoroughbred Americans, representative of various sections of the country and free from the slightest tinge of snobbery. Not all of them are even well-to-do, in the post-war sense; and their devices of economy in household outlay, dress and entertainment are a revelation in the science of ways and means. There are parents, children, relatives and friends all passing before us in the pageant of life from the cradle to the grave. No circumstance, from an introduction to a wedding, is overlooked in this panorama and the spectator has beside him a cicerone in the person of the author who clears every doubt and answers every question. In course, the conviction grows upon him that etiquette is no flummery of poseurs "aping the manners of their betters," nor a code of snobs, who divide their time between licking the boots of those above them and kicking at those below, but a system of rules of conduct based on respect of self coupled with respect of others. Meanwhile, to guard against conceit in his new knowledge, he may at odd moments recall Ben Jonson's lines:

"Nor stand so much on your gentility,
Which is an airy, and mere borrowed thing,
From dead men's dust, and bones: And none of yours
Except you make, or hold it."

CONTENTS

PHOTOGRAPHIC ILLUSTRATIONS

ETIQUETTE

CHAPTER I

WHAT IS BEST SOCIETY?

"Society" is an ambiguous term; it may mean much or nothing. Every human being—unless dwelling alone in a cave—is a member of society of one sort or another, and therefore it is well to define what is to be understood by the term "Best Society" and why its authority is recognized. Best Society abroad is always the oldest aristocracy; composed not so much of persons of title, which may be new, as of those families and communities which have for the longest period of time known highest cultivation. Our own Best Society is represented by social groups which have had, since this is America, widest rather than longest association with old world cultivation. Cultivation is always the basic attribute of Best Society, much as we hear in this country of an "Aristocracy of wealth."

To the general public a long purse is synonymous with high position—a theory dear to the heart of the "yellow" press and eagerly fostered in the preposterous social functions of screen drama. It is true that Best Society is comparatively rich; it is true that the hostess of great wealth, who constantly and lavishly entertains, will shine, at least to the readers of the press, more brilliantly than her less affluent sister. Yet the latter, through her quality of birth, her poise, her inimitable distinction, is often the jewel of deeper water in the social crown of her time.

The most advertised commodity is not always intrinsically the best, but is sometimes merely the product of a company with plenty of money to spend on advertising. In the same way, money brings certain people before the public —sometimes they are persons of "quality," quite as often

1

the so-called "society leaders" featured in the public press do not belong to good society at all, in spite of their many published photographs and the energies of their press-agents. Or possibly they do belong to "smart" society; but if too much advertised, instead of being the "queens" they seem, they might more accurately be classified as the court jesters of to-day.

THE IMITATION AND THE GENUINE

New York, more than any city in the world, unless it be Paris, loves to be amused, thrilled and surprised all at the same time; and will accept with outstretched hand any one who can perform this astounding feat. Do not under-estimate the ability that can achieve it: a scintillating wit, an arresting originality, a talent for entertaining that amounts to genius, and gold poured literally like rain, are the least requirements.

Puritan America on the other hand demanding, as a ticket of admission to her Best Society, the qualifications of birth, manners and cultivation, clasps her hands tight across her slim trim waist and announces severely that New York's "Best" is, in her opinion, very "bad" indeed. But this is because Puritan America, as well as the general public, mis-takes the jester for the queen.

As a matter of fact, Best Society is not at all like a court with an especial queen or king, nor is it confined to any one place or group, but might better be described as an unlimited brotherhood which spreads over the entire surface of the globe, the members of which are invariably people of culti-vation and worldly knowledge, who have not only perfect manners but a perfect manner. Manners are made up of trivialities of deportment which can be easily learned if one does not happen to know them; manner is personality—the outward manifestation of one's innate character and atti-tude toward life. A gentleman, for instance, will never be ostentatious or overbearing any more than he will ever be servile, because these attributes never animate the impulses of a well-bred person. A man whose manners suggest the grotesque is invariably a person of imitation rather than of real position.

Etiquette must, if it is to be of more than trifling use, include ethics as well as manners. Certainly what one is, is of far greater importance than what one appears to be. A knowledge of etiquette is of course essential to one's decent behavior, just as clothing is essential to one's decent appearance; and precisely as one wears the latter without being self-conscious of having on shoes and perhaps gloves, one who has good manners is equally unself-conscious in the observance of etiquette, the precepts of which must be so thoroughly absorbed as to make their observance a matter of instinct rather than of conscious obedience.

Thus Best Society is not a fellowship of the wealthy, nor does it seek to exclude those who are not of exalted birth; but it *is* an association of gentle-folk, of which good form in speech, charm of manner, knowledge of the social amenities, and instinctive consideration for the feelings of others, are the credentials by which society the world over recognizes its chosen members.

CHAPTER II

INTRODUCTIONS

THE CORRECT FORM

The word "present" is preferable on formal occasions to the word "introduce." On informal occasions neither word is expressed, though understood, as will be shown below. The correct formal introduction is:

"Mrs. Jones, may I present Mr. Smith?"
or,
"Mr. Distinguished, may I present Mr. Young?"

The younger person is always presented to the older or more distinguished, but a gentleman is always presented to a lady, even though he is an old gentleman of great distinction and the lady a mere slip of a girl.

No lady is ever, except to the President of the United States, a cardinal, or a reigning sovereign, presented to a man. The correct introduction of either a man or woman:

To the President,
is,
"Mr. President, I have the honor to present Mrs. Jones, of Chicago."

To a Cardinal,
is,
"Your Eminence, may I present Mrs. Jones?"

To a King:

Much formality of presenting names on lists is gone through beforehand; at the actual presentation an "accepted" name is repeated from functionary to equerry and nothing is said to the King or Queen except: "Mrs. Jones."

But a Foreign Ambassador is presented, "Mr. Ambassador, may I present you to Mrs. Jones."

Very few people in polite society are introduced by their formal titles. A hostess says, "Mrs. Jones, may I present the Duke of Overthere?" or "Lord Blank?"; never "his Grace" or "his Lordship." The Honorable is merely Mr. Lordson, or Mr. Holdoffice. A doctor, a judge, a bishop, are addressed and introduced by their titles. The clergy are usually Mister unless they formally hold the title of Doctor, or Dean, or Canon. A Catholic priest is "Father Kelly." A senator is always introduced as Senator, whether he is still in office or not. But the President of the United States, once he is out of office, is merely "Mr." and not "Ex-president."

THE PREVAILING INTRODUCTION AND INFLECTION

In the briefer form of introduction commonly used,

"Mrs. Worldly, Mrs. Norman,"

if the two names are said in the same tone of voice it is not apparent who is introduced to whom; but by accentuating the more important person's name, it can be made as clear as though the words "May I present" had been used.

The more important name is said with a slightly rising inflection, the secondary as a mere statement of fact. For instance, suppose you say, "Are you there?" and then "It is raining!" Use the same inflection exactly and say, "Mrs. Worldly?"—"Mrs. Younger!"

Are you there?—It is raining!
Mrs. Worldly?—Mrs. Younger!

The unmarried lady is presented to the married one, unless the latter is very much the younger. As a matter of fact, in introducing two ladies to each other or one gentleman to another, no distinction is made. "Mrs. Smith; Mrs. Norman." "Mr. Brown; Mr. Green."

The inflection is:

I think—it's going to rain!
Mrs. Smith—Mrs. Norman!

A man is also often introduced, "Mrs. Worldly? Mr. Norman!" But to a very distinguished man, a mother would say:

"Mr. Edison—My daughter, Mary!"

To a young man, however, she should say, "Mr. Struthers, have you met my daughter?" If the daughter is married, she should have added, "My daughter, Mrs. Smartlington." The daughter's name is omitted because it is extremely bad taste (except in the South) to call her daughter "Miss Mary" to any one but a servant, and on the other hand she should not present a young man to "Mary." The young man can easily find out her name afterward.

OTHER FORMS OF INTRODUCTION

Other permissible forms of introduction are:

"Mrs. Jones, do you know Mrs. Norman?

or,

"Mrs. Jones, you know Mrs. Robinson, don't you?" (on no account say "Do you not?" Best Society always says "don't you?")

or,

"Mrs. Robinson, have you met Mrs. Jones?"

or,

"Mrs. Jones, do you know my mother?"

or,

"This is my daughter Ellen, Mrs. Jones."

These are all good form, whether gentlemen are introduced to ladies, ladies to ladies, or gentlemen to gentlemen. In introducing a gentleman to a lady, you may ask Mr. Smith if he has met Mrs. Jones, but you must not ask Mrs. Jones if she has met Mr. Smith!

FORMS OF INTRODUCTIONS TO AVOID

Do *not* say: "Mr. Jones, shake hands with Mr. Smith," or "Mrs. Jones, I want to make you acquainted with Mrs. Smith." *Never* say: "make you acquainted with" and do not, in introducing one person to another, call one of them "my friend." You can say "my aunt," or "my sister," or "my cousin"—but to pick out a particular person as "my friend" is not only bad style but, unless you have only one friend, bad manners—as it implies Mrs. Smith is "my friend" and you are a stranger.

You may very properly say to Mr. Smith "I want you to meet Mrs. Jones," but this is not a form of introduction, nor is it to be said in Mrs. Jones' hearing. Upon leading Mr. Smith up to Mrs. Jones, you say "Mrs. Jones may I present Mr. Smith" or "Mrs. Jones; Mr. Smith." Under no circumstances whatsoever say "Mr. Smith meet Mrs. Jones," or "Mrs. Jones meet Mr. Smith." Either wording is equally preposterous.

Do not repeat "Mrs. Jones? Mrs. Smith! Mrs. Smith? Mrs. Jones!" To say each name once is quite enough.

Most people of good taste very much dislike being asked their names. To say "What is your name?" is always abrupt and unflattering. If you want to know with whom you have been talking, you can generally find a third person later and ask "Who was the lady with the grey feather in her hat?" The next time you see her you can say "How do you do, Mrs. —————" (calling her by name).

WHEN TO SHAKE HANDS

When gentlemen are introduced to each other they always shake hands.

When a gentleman is introduced to a lady, she sometimes puts out her hand—especially if he is some one she has long heard about from friends in common, but to an entire stranger she generally merely bows her head slightly and says: "How do you do!" Strictly speaking, it is always her place to offer her hand or not as she chooses, but if he puts out his hand, it is rude on her part to ignore it. Nothing could be more ill-bred than to treat curtly any overture made in spontaneous friendliness. No thoroughbred lady would ever refuse to shake any hand that is honorable, not even the hand of a coal heaver at the risk of her fresh white glove.

Those who have been drawn into a conversation do not usually shake hands on parting. But there is no fixed rule.

A lady sometimes shakes hands after talking with a casual stranger; at other times she does not offer her hand on parting from one who has been punctiliously presented to her. She may find the former sympathetic and the latter very much the contrary.

Very few rules of etiquette are inelastic and none more so than the acceptance or rejection of the strangers you meet.

There is a wide distance between rudeness and reserve. You can be courteously polite and at the same time extremely aloof to a stranger who does not appeal to you, or you can be welcomingly friendly to another whom you like on sight. Individual temperament has also to be taken into consideration: one person is naturally austere, another genial. The latter shakes hands far more often than the former. As already said, it is unforgivably rude to refuse a proffered hand, but it is rarely necessary to offer your hand if you prefer not to.

WHAT TO SAY WHEN INTRODUCED

Best Society has only one phrase in acknowledgment of an introduction: "How do you do?" It literally accepts no other. When Mr. Bachelor says, "Mrs. Worldly, may I present Mr. Struthers?" Mrs. Worldly says, "How do you do?" Struthers bows, and says nothing. To sweetly echo "Mr. Struthers?" with a rising inflection on "—thers?" is *not* good form. Saccharine chirpings should be classed with crooked little fingers, high hand-shaking and other affectations. All affectations are bad form.

Persons of position do not say: "Charmed," or "Pleased to meet you," etc., but often the first remark is the beginning of a conversation. For instance,

Young Struthers is presented to Mrs. Worldly. She smiles and perhaps says, "I hear that you are going to be in New York all winter?" Struthers answers, "Yes, I am at the Columbia Law School," etc., or since he is much younger than she, he might answer, "Yes, Mrs. Worldly," especially if his answer would otherwise be a curt yes or no. Otherwise he does not continue repeating her name.

TAKING LEAVE OF ONE YOU HAVE JUST MET

After an introduction, when you have talked for some time to a stranger whom you have found agreeable, and you then take leave, you say, "Good-by, I am very glad to have met you," or "Good-by, I hope I shall see you again soon"—or "some.time." The other person answers, "Thank you," or perhaps adds, "I hope so, too." Usually "Thank you" is all that is necessary.

In taking leave of. a group of strangers—it makes no difference whether you have been introduced to them or merely included in their conversation—you bow "good-by" to any who happen to be looking at you, but you do not attempt to attract the attention of those who are unaware that you are turning away.

INTRODUCING ONE PERSON TO A GROUP

This is never done on formal occasions when a great many persons are present. At a small luncheon, for instance, a hostess always introduces her guests to one another.

Let us suppose you are the hostess: your position is not necessarily near, but it is toward the door. Mrs. King is sitting quite close to you, Mrs. Lawrence also near. Miss Robinson and Miss Brown are much farther away.

Mrs. Jones enters. You go a few steps forward and shake hands with her, then stand aside as it were, for a second only, to see if Mrs. Jones goes to speak to any one. If she apparently knows no one, you say,

"Mrs. King, do you know Mrs. Jones?" Mrs. King being close at hand (usually but not necessarily) rises, shakes hands with Mrs. Jones and sits down again. If Mrs. King is an elderly lady, and Mrs. Jones a young one, Mrs. King merely extends her hand and does not rise. Having said "Mrs. Jones" once, you do not repeat it immediately, but turning to the other lady sitting near you, you say, "Mrs. Lawrence," then you look across the room and continue, "Miss Robinson, Miss Brown—Mrs. Jones!" Mrs. Lawrence, if she is young, rises and shakes hands with Mrs. Jones, and the other two bow but do not rise.

At a very big luncheon you would introduce Mrs. Jones

to Mrs. King and possibly to Mrs. Lawrence, so that Mrs. Jones might have some one to talk to. But if other guests come in at this moment, Mrs. Jones finds a place for herself and after a pause, falls naturally into conversation with those she is next to, without giving her name or asking theirs.

A friend's roof is supposed to be an introduction to those it shelters. In Best Society this is always recognized if the gathering is intimate, such as at a luncheon, dinner or house party; but it is not accepted at a ball or reception, or any "general" entertainment. People always talk to their neighbors at table whether introduced or not. It would be a breach of etiquette not to! But if Mrs. Jones and Mrs. Norman merely spoke to each other for a few moments, in the drawing-room, it is not necessary that they recognize each other afterwards.

NEW YORK'S BAD MANNERS

New York's bad manners are often condemned and often very deservedly. Even though the cause is carelessness rather than intentional indifference, the indifference is no less actual and the rudeness inexcusable.

It is by no means unheard of that after sitting at table next to the guest of honor, a New Yorker will meet her the next day with utter unrecognition. Not because the New Yorker means to "cut" the stranger or feels the slightest unwillingness to continue the acquaintance, but because few New Yorkers possess enthusiasm enough to make an effort to remember all the new faces they come in contact with, but allow all those who are not especially "fixed" in their attention, to drift easily out of mind and recognition. It is mortifyingly true; no one is so ignorantly indifferent to everything outside his or her own personal concern as the socially fashionable New Yorker, unless it is the Londoner! The late Theodore Roosevelt was a brilliantly shining exception. And, of course, and happily, there are other men and women like him in this. But there are also enough of the snail-in-shell variety to give color to the very just resentment that those from other and more gracious cities hold against New Yorkers.

Everywhere else in the world (except London), the impulse of self-cultivation, if not the more generous ones of consideration and hospitality, induces people of good breeding to try and make the effort to find out what manner of mind, or experience, or talent, a stranger has; and to remember, at least out of courtesy, anyone for whose benefit a friend of theirs gave a dinner or luncheon. To fashionable New York, however, luncheon was at one-thirty; at three there is something else occupying the moment—that is all.

Nearly all people of the Atlantic Coast dislike general introductions, and present people to each other as little as possible. In the West, however, people do not feel comfortable in a room full of strangers. Whether or not to introduce people therefore becomes not merely a question of propriety, but of consideration for local custom.

NEVER INTRODUCE UNNECESSARILY

The question as to when introductions should be made, or not made, is one of the most elusive points in the entire range of social knowledge. "Whenever necessary to bridge an awkward situation," is a definition that is exact enough, but not very helpful or clear. The hostess who allows a guest to stand, awkward and unknown, in the middle of her drawing-room is no worse than she who pounces on every chance acquaintance and drags unwilling victims into forced recognition of each other, everywhere and on all occasions.

The fundamental rule never to introduce unnecessarily brings up the question:

WHICH ARE THE NECESSARY OCCASIONS?

First, in order of importance, is the presentation of everyone to guests of honor, whether the "guests" are distinguished strangers for whom a dinner is given, or a bride and groom, or a débutante being introduced to society. It is the height of rudeness for anyone to go to an entertainment given in honor of some one and fail to "meet" him. (Even though one's memory is too feeble to remember him afterward!)

INTRODUCTIONS AT A DINNER

The host must always see that every gentleman either knows or is presented to the lady he is to "take in" to dinner, and also, if possible, to the one who is to sit at the other side of him.   If the latter introduction is overlooked, people sitting next each other at table nearly always introduce themselves. A gentleman says, "How do you do, Mrs. Jones.   I am Arthur Robinson."   Or showing her his place card, "I have to introduce myself, this is my name." Or the lady says first, "I am Mrs. Hunter Jones."   And the man answers, "How do you do, Mrs. Jones, my name is Titherington Smith."

It is not unusual, in New York, for those placed next each other to talk without introducing themselves—particularly if each can read the name of the other on the place cards.

OTHER NECESSARY INTRODUCTIONS

Even in New York's most introductionless circles, people always introduce:

A small group of people who are to sit together anywhere.

Partners at dinner.

The guests at a house party.

Everyone at a small dinner or luncheon.

The four who are at the same bridge table.

Partners or fellow-players in any game.

At a dance, when an invitation has been asked for a stranger, the friend who vouched for him should personally present him to the hostess.   "Mrs. Worldly, this is Mr. Robinson, whom you said I might bring."   The hostess shakes hands and smiles and says: "I am very glad to see you, Mr. Robinson."

A guest in a box at the opera always introduces any gentleman who comes to speak to her, to her hostess, unless the latter is engrossed in conversation with a visitor of her own, or unless other people block the distance between so that an introduction would be forced and awkward.

A newly arriving visitor in a lady's drawing-room is not introduced to another who is taking leave. Nor is an animated conversation between two persons interrupted to introduce a third. Nor is any one ever led around a room and introduced right and left.

If two ladies or young girls are walking together and they meet a third who stops to speak to one of them, the other walks slowly on and does not stand awkwardly by and wait for an introduction. If the third is asked by the one she knows, to join them, the sauntering friend is overtaken and an introduction always made. The third, however, must not join them unless invited to do so.

At a very large dinner, people (excepting the gentlemen and ladies who are to sit next to each other at table) are not collectively introduced. After dinner, men in the smoking room or left at table always talk to their neighbors whether they have been introduced or not, and ladies in the drawing-room do the same. But unless they meet soon again, or have found each other so agreeable that they make an effort to continue the acquaintance, they become strangers again, equally whether they were introduced or not.

Some writers on etiquette speak of "correct introductions" that carry "obligations of future acquaintance," and "incorrect introductions," that seemingly obligate one to nothing.

Degrees of introduction are utterly unknown to best society. It makes not the slightest difference so far as any one's acceptance or rejection of another is concerned how an introduction is worded or, on occasions, whether an introduction takes place at all.

Fashionable people in very large cities take introductions lightly; they are veritable ships that pass in the night. They show their red or green signals—which are merely polite sentences and pleasant manners—and they pass on again.

When you are introduced to some one for the second time and the first occasion was without interest and long ago, there is no reason why you should speak of the former meeting.

If some one presents you to Mrs. Smith for the second

time on the same occasion, you smile and say "I have already met Mrs. Smith," but you say nothing if you met Mrs. Smith long ago and she showed no interest in you at that time.

Most rules are elastic and contract and expand according to circumstances. You do not remind Mrs. Smith of having met her before, but on meeting again any one who was brought to your own house, or one who showed you an especial courtesy you instinctively say, "I am so glad to see you again."

INCLUDING SOMEONE IN CONVERSATION WITHOUT AN INTRODUCTION

On occasions it happens that in talking to one person you want to include another in your conversation without making an introduction. For instance: suppose you are talking to a seedsman and a friend joins you in your garden. You greet your friend, and then include her by saying, "Mr. Smith is suggesting that I dig up these cannas and put in delphiniums." Whether your friend gives an opinion as to the change in color of your flower bed or not, she has been made part of your conversation.

This same maneuver of evading an introduction is also resorted to when you are not sure that an acquaintance will be agreeable to one or both of those whom an accidental circumstance has brought together.

INTRODUCTIONS UNNECESSARY

You must never introduce people to each other in public places unless you are certain beyond a doubt that the introduction will be agreeable to both. You cannot commit a greater social blunder than to introduce, to a person of position, some one she does not care to know, especially on shipboard, in hotels, or in other very small, rather public, communities where people are so closely thrown together that it is correspondingly difficult to avoid undesirable acquaintances who have been given the wedge of an introduction.

As said above, introductions in very large cities are unimportant. In New York, where people are meeting new faces daily, seldom seeing the same one twice in a year, it requires a tenacious memory to recognize those one hoped most to see again, and others are blotted out at once.

People in good society rarely ask to be introduced to each other, but if there is a good reason for knowing some one, they often introduce themselves; for instance, Mary Smith says:

"Mrs. Jones, aren't you a friend of my mother's? I am Mrs. Titherington Smith's daughter." Mrs. Jones says:

"Why, my dear child, I am so glad you spoke to me. Your mother and I have known each other since we were children!"

Or, an elder lady asks: "Aren't you Mary Smith? I have known your mother since she was your age." Or a young woman says: "Aren't you Mrs. Worldly?" Mrs. Worldly, looking rather freezingly, politely says "Yes" and waits. And the stranger continues, "I think my sister Millicent Manners is a friend of yours." Mrs. Worldly at once unbends. "Oh, yes, indeed, I am devoted to Millicent! And you must be ——?"

"I'm Alice."

"Oh, of course, Millicent has often talked of you, and of your lovely voice. I want very much to hear you sing some time."

These self-introductions, however, must never presumingly be made. It would be in very bad taste for Alice to introduce herself to Mrs. Worldly if her sister knew her only slightly.

A BUSINESS VISIT NOT AN INTRODUCTION

A lady who goes to see another to get a reference for a servant, or to ask her aid in an organization for charity, would never consider such a meeting as an introduction, even though they talked for an hour. Nor would she offer to shake hands in leaving. On the other hand, neighbors who are continually meeting, gradually become accustomed to say "How do you do?" when they meet, even though they never become acquaintances.

THE RETORT COURTEOUS TO ONE YOU HAVE FORGOTTEN

Let us suppose some one addresses you, and then slightly disconcerted says: "You don't remember me, do you?" The polite thing—unless his manner does not ring true, is to say "Why, of course, I do." And then if a few neutral remarks lead to no enlightening topic, and bring no further memory, you ask at the first opportunity who it was that addressed you. If the person should prove actually to be unknown, it is very easy to repel any further advances. But nearly always you find it is some one you ought to have known, and your hiding the fact of your forgetfulness saves you from the rather rude and stupid situation of blankly declaring: "I don't remember you."

If, after being introduced to you, Mr. Jones calls you by a wrong name, you let it pass, at first, but if he persists you may say: "My name is Simpson, not Simpkin."

At a private dance, young men nowadays introduce their men friends to young women without first asking the latter's permission, because all those invited to a lady's house are supposed to be eligible for presentation to everyone, or they would not be there.

At a public ball young men and women keep very much to their own particular small circle and are not apt to meet outsiders at all. Under these circumstances a gentleman should be very careful not to introduce a youth whom he knows nothing about to a lady of his acquaintance—or at least he should ask her first. He can say frankly: "There is a man called Sliders who has asked to meet you. I don't know who he is, but he seems decent. Shall I introduce him?" The lady can say "Yes"; or, "I'd rather not."

INTRODUCTION BY LETTER

An introduction by letter is far more binding than a casual spoken introduction which commits you to nothing. This is explained fully and example letters are given in the chapter on Letters.

A letter of introduction is handed you unsealed, always. It is correct for you to seal it at once in the presence of its author. You thank your friend for having written it and go on your journey.

If you are a man and your introduction is to a lady, you go to her house as soon as you arrive in her city, and leave the letter with your card at her door. Usually you do not ask to see her; but if it is between four and six o'clock it is quite correct to do so if you choose. Presenting yourself with a letter is always a little awkward. Most people prefer to leave their cards without asking to be received.

If your letter is to a man, you mail it to his house, unless the letter is a business one. In the latter case you go to his office, and send in your card and the letter. Meanwhile you wait in the reception room until he has read the letter and sends for you to come into his private office.

If you are a woman, you mail your letter of social introduction and do nothing further until you receive an acknowledgment. If the recipient of your letter leaves her card on you, you in return leave yours on her. But the obligation of a written introduction is such that only illness can excuse her not asking you to her house—either formally or informally.

When a man receives a letter introducing another man, he calls the person introduced on the telephone and asks how he may be of service to him. If he does not invite the newcomer to his house, he may put him up at his club, or have him take luncheon or dinner at a restaurant, as the circumstances seem to warrant.

Chapter III

GREETINGS

WHAT TO SAY WHEN INTRODUCED

As explained in the foregoing chapter, the correct formal greeting is: "How do you do?" If Mrs. Younger is presented to Mrs. Worldly, Mrs. Worldly says "How do you do?" If the Ambassador of France is presented to her, she says "How do you do?" Mrs. Younger and the Ambassador likewise say "How do you do?" or merely bow.

There are a few expressions possible under other circumstances and upon other occasions. If you have, through friends in common, long heard of a certain lady, or gentleman, and you know that she, or he, also has heard much of you, you may say when you are introduced to her: "I am very glad to meet you," or "I am delighted to meet you at last!" Do not use the expression "pleased to meet you" then or on any occasion. And you must not say you are delighted unless you have reason to be sure that she also is delighted to meet you.

To one who has volunteered to help you in charitable work for instance, you would say: "It is very good of you to help us," or, "to join us."

In business a gentleman says: "Very glad to meet you," or "Delighted to meet you." Or, if in his own office: "Very glad to see you!"

INFORMAL GREETINGS

Informal greetings are almost as limited as formal, but not quite; for besides saying "How do you do?" you can say "Good morning" and on occasions "How are you?" or "Good evening."

On very informal occasions, it is the present fashion to greet an intimate friend with "Hello!" This seem-

18

ingly vulgar salutation is made acceptable by the tone in which it is said. To shout "Hul*low!*" is vulgar, but "Hello, Mary" or "How 'do John," each spoken in an ordinary tone of voice, sound much the same. But remember that the "Hello" is spoken, not called out, and never used except between intimate friends who call each other by the first name.

There are only two forms of farewell: "Good-by" and "Good night." Never say "Au revoir" unless you have been talking French, or are speaking to a French person. Never interlard your conversation with foreign words or phrases when you can possibly translate them into English; and the occasions when our mother tongue will not serve are extremely rare.

Very often in place of the over-worn "How do you do," perhaps more often than not, people skip the words of actual greeting and plunge instead into conversation: "Why, Mary! When did you get back?" or "What is the news with you?" or "What have you been doing lately?" The weather, too, fills in with equal faithfulness. "Isn't it a heavenly day!" or "Horrid weather, isn't it?" It would seem that the variability of the weather was purposely devised to furnish mankind with unfailing material for conversation.

In bidding good-by to a new acquaintance with whom you have been talking, you shake hands and say, "Good-by. I am very glad to have met you." To one who has been especially interesting, or who is somewhat of a personage you say: "It has been a great pleasure to meet you." The other answers: "Thank you."

IN CHURCH

People do not greet each other in church, except at a wedding. At weddings people do speak to friends sitting near them, but in a low tone of voice. It would be shocking to enter a church and hear a babel of voices!

Ordinarily in church if a friend happens to catch your eye, you smile, but never actually bow. If you go to a church not your own and a stranger offers you a seat in her pew, you should, on leaving, turn to her and say: "Thank you." But you do not greet anyone until you are out on the church steps, when you naturally speak to your friends. "Hello" should not be said on this occasion because it is too "familiar" for the solemnity of church surroundings.

SHAKING HANDS

Gentlemen always shake hands when they are introduced to each other. Ladies rarely do so with gentlemen who are introduced to them; but they usually shake hands with other ladies, if they are standing near together. All people who know each other, unless merely passing by, shake hands when they meet.

A gentleman on the street never shakes hands with a lady without first removing his right glove. But at the opera, or at a ball, or if he is usher at a wedding, he keeps his glove on.

PERSONALITY OF A HANDSHAKE

A handshake often creates a feeling of liking or of irritation between two strangers. Who does not dislike a "boneless" hand extended as though it were a spray of sea-weed, or a miniature boiled pudding? It is equally annoying to have one's hand clutched aloft in grotesque affectation and shaken violently sideways, as though it were being used to clean a spot out of the atmosphere. What woman does not wince at the viselike grasp that cuts her rings into her flesh and temporarily paralyzes every finger?

The proper handshake is made briefly; but there should be a feeling of strength and warmth in the clasp, and, as in bowing, one should at the same time look into the countenance of the person whose hand one takes. In giving her hand to a foreigner, a married woman always relaxes her arm and fingers, as it is customary for him to lift her hand to his lips. But by a relaxed hand is not meant a wet rag; a hand should have life even though it be passive. A woman should always allow a man who is only an acquaintance to shake her hand; she should never shake his. To a very old friend she gives a much firmer clasp, but he shakes her hand more than she shakes his. Younger women usually shake the hand of the older; or they both merely clasp hands, give them a dropping movement rather than a shake, and let go.

POLITE GREETINGS FROM YOUNGER TO OLDER

It is the height of rudeness for young people not to go and shake hands with an older lady of their acquaintance when they meet her away from home, if she is a hostess to whose house they have often gone. It is not at all necessary for either young women or young men to linger and enter into a conversation, unless the older lady detains them, which she should not do beyond the briefest minute.

Older ladies who are always dragging young men up to unprepossessing partners, are studiously avoided and with reason; but otherwise it is inexcusable for any youth to fail in this small exaction of polite behavior. If a young man is talking with some one when an older lady enters the room, he bows formally from where he is, as it would be rude to leave a young girl standing alone while he went up to speak to Mrs. Worldly or Mrs. Toplofty. But a young girl passing near an older lady can easily stop for a moment, say "How do you do, Mrs. Jones!" and pass on.

People do not cross a room to speak to any one unless— to show politeness to an acquaintance who is a stranger there; to speak to an intimate friend; or to talk to some one about something in particular.

CHAPTER IV

SALUTATIONS OF COURTESY

WHEN A GENTLEMAN TAKES OFF HIS HAT

A gentleman takes off his hat and holds it in his hand when a lady enters the elevator in which he is a passenger, but he puts it on again in the corridor. A public corridor is like the street, but an elevator is suggestive of a room, and a gentleman does not keep his hat on in the presence of ladies in a house.

This is the rule in elevators in hotels, clubs and apartments. In office buildings and stores the elevator is considered as public a place as the corridor. What is more, the elevators in such business structures are usually so crowded that the only room for a man's hat is on his head. But even under these conditions a gentleman can reveal his innate respect for women by not permitting himself to be crowded too near to them.

When a gentleman stops to speak to a lady of his acquaintance in the street, he takes his hat off with his left hand, leaving his right free to shake hands, or he takes it off with his right and transfers it to his left. If he has a stick, he puts his stick in his left hand, takes off his hat with his right, transfers his hat also to his left hand, and gives her his right. If they walk ahead together, he at once puts his hat on; but while he is standing in the street talking to her, he should remain hatless. There is no rudeness greater than for him to stand talking to a lady with his hat on, and a cigar or cigarette in his mouth.

A gentleman always rises when a lady comes into a room. In public places men do not jump up for every strange woman who happens to approach. But if any woman addresses a remark to him, a gentleman at once

22

rises to his feet as he answers her. In a restaurant, when a lady bows to him, a gentleman merely makes the gesture of rising by getting up half way from his chair and at the same time bowing. Then he sits down again.

When a lady goes to a gentleman's office on business he should stand up to receive her, offer her a chair, and not sit down until after she is seated. When she rises to leave, he must get up instantly and stand until she has left the office.

It is not necessary to add that every American citizen stands with his hat off at the passing of the "colors" and when the national anthem is played. If he didn't, some other more loyal citizen would take it off for him. Also every man should stand with his hat off in the presence of a funeral that passes close or blocks his way.

A GENTLEMAN LIFTS HIS HAT

Lifting the hat is a conventional gesture of politeness shown to strangers only, not to be confused with bowing, which is a gesture used to acquaintances and friends. In lifting his hat, a gentleman merely lifts it slightly off his forehead and replaces it; he does not smile nor bow, nor even look at the object of his courtesy. No gentleman ever subjects a lady to his scrutiny or his apparent observation.

If a lady drops her glove, a gentleman should pick it up, hurry ahead of her—on no account nudge her—offer the glove to her and say: "I think you dropped this!" The lady replies: "Thank you." The gentleman should then lift his hat and turn away.

If he passes a lady in a narrow space, so that he blocks her way or in any manner obtrudes upon her, he lifts his hat as he passes.

If he gets on a street car and the car gives a lurch just as he is about to be seated and throws him against another passenger, he lifts his hat and says "Excuse me!" or "I beg your pardon!" He must *not* say "Pardon *me!*" He must not take a seat if there are ladies standing. But if he is sitting and ladies enter, should they be young, he may with perfect propriety keep his seat. If a very old woman, or a young one carrying a baby, enters the car, a gentleman rises at once, lifts his hat slightly, and says: "Please take my seat." He lifts his hat again when she thanks him.

If the car is very crowded when he wishes to leave it and a lady is directly in his way, he asks: "May I get through, please?" As she makes room for him to pass, he lifts his hat and says: "Thank you!"

If he is in the company of a lady in a street car, he lifts his hat to another gentleman who offers her a seat, picks up something she has dropped, or shows her any civility.

He lifts his hat if he asks anyone a question, and always, if, when walking on the street with either a lady or a gentleman, his companion bows to another person. In other words, a gentleman lifts his hat whenever he says "Excuse me," "Thank you," or speaks to a stranger, or is spoken to by a lady, or by an older gentleman. And no gentleman ever keeps a pipe, cigar or cigarette in his mouth when he lifts his hat, takes it off, or bows.

THE BOW OF CEREMONY

The standing bow, made by a gentleman when he rises at a dinner to say a few words, in response to applause, or across a drawing-room at a formal dinner when he bows to a lady or an elderly gentleman, is usually the outcome of the bow taught little boys at dancing school. The instinct of clicking heels together and making a quick bend over from the hips and neck, as though the human body had two hinges, a big one at the hip and a slight one at the neck, and was quite rigid in between, remains in a modified form through life. The man who as a child came habitually into his mother's drawing-room when there was "company," generally makes a charming bow when grown, which is wholly lacking in self-consciousness. There is no apparent "heel-clicking" but a camera would show that the motion is there.

In every form of bow, as distinct from merely lifting his hat, a gentleman looks at the person he is bowing to. In a very formal standing bow, his heels come together, his knees are rigid and his expression is rather serious.

THE INFORMAL BOW

The informal bow is merely a modification of the above; it is easy and unstudied, but it should suggest the ease of controlled muscles, not the floppiness of a rag doll.

In bowing on the street, a gentleman should never take his hat off with a flourish, nor should he sweep it down to his knee; nor is it graceful to bow by pulling the hat over the face as though examining the lining. The correct bow, when wearing a high hat or derby, is to lift it by holding the brim directly in front, take it off merely high enough to escape the head easily, bring it a few inches forward, the back somewhat up, the front down, and put it on again. To a very old lady or gentleman, to show adequate respect, a sweeping bow is sometimes made by a somewhat exaggerated circular motion downward to perhaps the level of the waist, so that the hat's position is upside down.

If a man is wearing a soft hat he takes it by the crown instead of the brim, lifts it slightly off his head and puts it on again.

The bow to a friend is made with a smile, to a very intimate friend often with a broad grin that fits exactly with the word "Hello"; whereas the formal bow is mentally accompanied by the formal salutation: "How do you do!"

THE BOW OF A WOMAN OF CHARM

The reputation of Southern women for having the gift of fascination is perhaps due not to prettiness of feature more than to the brilliancy or sweetness of their ready smile. That Southern women are charming and "feminine" and lovable is proverbial. How many have noticed that Southern women always bow with the grace of a flower bending in the breeze and a smile like sudden sunshine? The unlovely woman bows as though her head were on a hinge and her smile sucked through a lemon.

Nothing is so easy for any woman to acquire as a charming bow. It is such a short and fleeting duty. Not a bit of trouble really; just to incline your head and spontaneously smile as though you thought "Why, *there* is Mrs. Smith! How glad I am to see her!"

Even to a stranger who does her a favor, a woman of charm always smiles as she says "Thank you!" As a possession for either woman or man, a ready smile is more valuable in life than a ready wit; the latter may sometimes bring enemies, but the former always brings friends.

WHEN TO BOW

Under formal circumstances a lady is supposed to bow to a gentleman first; but people who know each other well bow spontaneously without observing this etiquette.

In meeting the same person many times within an hour or so, one does not continue to bow after the second, or at most third meeting. After that one either looks away or merely smiles. Unless one has a good memory for people, it is always better to bow to some one whose face is familiar than to run the greater risk of ignoring an acquaintance.

THE "CUT DIRECT"

For one person to look directly at another and not acknowledge the other's bow is such a breach of civility that only an unforgivable misdemeanor can warrant the rebuke. Nor without the gravest cause may a lady "cut" a gentleman. But there are no circumstances under which a gentleman may "cut" any woman who, even by courtesy, can be called a lady.

On the other hand, one must not confuse absent-mindedness, or a forgetful memory with an intentional "cut." Anyone who is preoccupied is apt to pass others without being aware of them, and without the least want of friendly regard. Others who have bad memories forget even those by whom they were much attracted. This does not excuse the bad memory, but it explains the seeming rudeness.

A "cut" is very different. It is a direct stare of blank refusal, and is not only insulting to its victim but embarrassing to every witness. Happily it is practically unknown in polite society.

CHAPTER V

ON THE STREET AND IN PUBLIC

WALKING ON THE STREET

A gentleman, whether walking with two ladies or one, takes the curb side of the pavement. He should never sandwich himself between them.

A young man walking with a young woman should be careful that his manner in no way draws attention to her or to himself. Too devoted a manner is always conspicuous, and so is loud talking. Under no circumstances should he take her arm, or grasp her by or above the elbow, and shove her here and there, unless, of course, to save her from being run over! He should not walk along hitting things with his stick. The small boy's delight in drawing a stick along a picket fence should be curbed in the nursery! And it is scarcely necessary to add that no gentleman walks along the street chewing gum or, if he is walking with a lady, puffing a cigar or cigarette.

All people in the streets, or anywhere in public, should be careful not to talk too loud. They should especially avoid pronouncing people's names, or making personal remarks that may attract passing attention or give a clue to themselves.

One should never call out a name in public, unless it is absolutely unavoidable. A young girl who was separated from her friends in a baseball crowd had the presence of mind to put her hat on her parasol and lift it above the people surrounding her so that her friends might find her.

Do not attract attention to yourself in public. This is one of the fundamental rules of good breeding. Shun conspicuous manners, conspicuous clothes, a loud voice, staring at people, knocking into them, talking across anyone—

in a word do not attract attention to yourself. Do not expose your private affairs, feelings or innermost thoughts in public. You are knocking down the walls of your house when you do.

GENTLEMEN AND BUNDLES

Nearly all books on etiquette insist that a "gentleman must offer to carry a lady's bundles." Bundles do not suggest a lady in the first place, and as for gentlemen and bundles!—they don't go together at all. Very neat packages that could never without injury to their pride be designated as "bundles" are different. Such, for instance, might be a square, smoothly wrapped box of cigars, candy, or books. Also, a gentleman might carry flowers, or a basket of fruit, or, in fact, any package that looks tempting. He might even stagger under bags and suitcases, or a small trunk—but carry a "bundle"? Not twice! And yet, many an unknowing woman, sometimes a very young and pretty one, too, has asked a relative, a neighbor, or an admirer, to carry something suggestive of a pillow, done up in crinkled paper and odd lengths of joined string. Then she wonders afterwards in unenlightened surprise why her cousin, or her neighbor, or her admirer, who is one of the smartest men in town, never comes to see her any more!

A GENTLEMAN OFFERS HIS ARM

To an old lady or to an invalid a gentleman offers his arm if either of them wants his support. Otherwise a lady no longer leans upon a gentleman in the daytime, unless to cross a very crowded thoroughfare, or to be helped over a rough piece of road, or under other impeding circumstances. In accompanying a lady anywhere at night, whether down the steps of a house, or from one building to another, or when walking a distance, a gentleman always offers his arm. The reason is that in her thin high-heeled slippers, and when it is too dark to see her foothold clearly, she is likely to trip.

Under any of these circumstances when he proffers his

assistance, he might say: "Don't you think you had better take my arm? You might trip." Or—"Wouldn't it be easier if you took my arm along here? The going is pretty bad." Otherwise the only occasions on which a gentleman offers his arm to a lady are in taking her in at a formal dinner, or taking her in to supper at a ball, or when he is an usher at a wedding. Even in walking across a ballroom, except at a public ball in the grand march, it is the present fashion for the younger generation to walk side by side, never arm in arm. This, however, is merely an instance where etiquette and the custom of the moment differ. Old-fashioned gentlemen still offer their arm, and it is, and long will be, in accordance with etiquette to do so. But etiquette does *not* permit a gentleman to take a lady's arm!

In seeing a lady to her carriage or motor, it is quite correct for a gentleman to put his hand under her elbow to assist her; and in helping her out he should alight first and offer her his hand. He should not hold a parasol over her head unless momentarily while she searches in her wrist-bag for something, or stops perhaps to put on or take off her glove, or do anything that occupies both hands. With an umbrella the case is different, especially in a sudden and driving rain, when she is often very busily occupied in trying to hold "good" clothes out of the wet and a hat on, as well. She may also, under these circumstances, take the gentleman's arm, if the "going" is thereby made any easier.

A LADY NEVER "ON THE LEFT"

The owner always sits on the right hand side of the rear seat of a carriage or a motor, that is driven by a coachman or a chauffeur. If the vehicle belongs to a lady, she should take her own place always, unless she relinquishes it to a guest whose rank is above her own, such as that of the wife of the President or the Governor. If a man is the owner, he must, on the contrary, give a lady the right hand seat. Whether in a private carriage, a car or a taxi, a lady must *never* sit on a gentleman's left; because according to European etiquette, a lady "on the left" is *not* a "lady." Although this etiquette is not strictly observed in America, no gentleman should risk allowing even a single foreigner to misinterpret a lady's position.

AWKWARD QUESTIONS OF PAYMENT

It is becoming much less customary than it used to be for a gentleman to offer to pay a lady's way. If in taking a ferry or a subway, a young woman stops to buy magazines, chocolates, or other trifles, a young man accompanying her usually offers to pay for them. She quite as usually answers: "Don't bother, I have it!" and puts the change on the counter. It would be awkward for him to protest, and bad taste to press the point. But usually in small matters such as a subway fare, he pays for two. If he invites her to go to a ball game, or to a matinée or to tea, he naturally buys the tickets and any refreshment which they may have.

Very often it happens that a young woman and a young man who are bound for the same house party, at a few hours' distance from the place where they both live, take the same train—either by accident or by pre-arrangement. In this case the young woman should pay for every item of her journey. She should not let her companion pay for her parlor car seat or for her luncheon; nor should he, when they arrive at their destination, tip the porter for carrying her bag.

A gentleman who is by chance sitting next to a lady of his acquaintance on a train or boat, should never think of offering to pay for her seat or for anything she may buy from the vendor.

THE "ESCORT"

Notwithstanding the fact that he is met, all dressed in his best store clothes, with his "lady friend" leaning on his arm, in the pages of counterfeit society novels and unauthoritative books on etiquette, there is no such actual person known to good society—at least not in New York or any great city—as an escort. He is not only unknown, but he is impossible.

In good society ladies do not go about under the "care of" gentlemen! It is unheard of for a gentleman to "take" a young girl alone to a dance or to dine or to parties of any description; nor can she accept his sponsorship anywhere whatsoever. A well behaved young girl goes to public dances only when properly chaperoned and to a private dance with her mother or else accompanied by her maid, who waits for her the entire evening in the dressing room. It is not only improper, it is *impossible* for any man to take a lady to a party of any sort, to which she has not been personally invited by the hostess.

A lady may never be under the "protection" of a man *anywhere!* A young girl is not even taken about by her betrothed. His friends send invitations to her on his account, it is true, and, if possible, he accompanies her, but correct invitations must be sent by them to her, or she should not go.

Older ladies are often thoughtless and say to a young man: "Bring your fiancée to see me!" His answer should be: "Indeed, I'd love to any time you telephone her"; or, "I know she'd love to come if you'd ask her." If the lady stupidly persists in casually saying, "Do bring her," he must smile and say lightly: "But I can't bring her without an invitation from you." Or, he merely evades the issue, and does *not* bring her.

THE RESTAURANT CHECK

Everyone has at some time or other been subjected to the awkward moment when the waiter presents the check to the host. For a host to count up the items is suggestive of parsimony, while not to look at them is disconcertingly reckless, and to pay before their faces for what his guests have eaten is embarrassing. Having the check presented to a hostess when gentlemen are among her guests, is more unpleasant. Therefore, to avoid this whole transaction, people who have not charge accounts, should order the meal ahead, and at the same time pay for it in advance, including the waiter's tip. Charge customers should make arrangements to have the check presented to them elsewhere than at table.

IN STORES OR SHOPS

Lack of consideration for those who in any capacity serve you, is always an evidence of ill-breeding, as well as of inexcusable selfishness. Occasionally a so-called "lady" who has nothing whatever to do but drive uptown or down in her comfortable limousine, vents her irritability upon a saleswoman at a crowded counter in a store, because she does not leave other customers and wait immediately upon her. Then, perhaps, when the article she asked for is not to be had, she complains to the floor-walker about the saleswoman's stupidity! Or having nothing that she can think of to occupy an empty hour on her hands, she demands that every sort of material be dragged down from the shelves until, discovering that it is at last time for her appointment, she yawns and leaves.

Of course, on the other hand, there is the genuinely lethargic saleswoman whose mind doesn't seem to register a single syllable that you have said to her; who, with complete indifference to you and your preferences, insists on showing what you distinctly say you do not want, and who caps the climax by drawling "They" are wearing it this season! Does that sort of saleswoman ever succeed in selling anything? Does anyone living buy anything because someone, who knows nothing, tells another, who is often an expert, what an indiscriminating "They" may be doing? That kind of a saleswoman would try to tell Kreisler that "They" are not using violins this season!

There are always two sides to the case, of course, and it is a credit to good manners that there is scarcely ever any friction in stores and shops of the first class. Salesmen and women are usually persons who are both patient and polite, and their customers are most often ladies in fact as well as "by courtesy." Between those before and those behind the counters, there has sprung up in many instances a relationship of mutual goodwill and friendliness. It is, in fact, only the woman who is afraid that someone may encroach upon her exceedingly insecure dignity, who shows neither courtesy nor consideration to any except those whom she considers it to her advantage to please.

REGARD FOR OTHERS

Consideration for the rights and feelings of others is not merely a rule for behavior in public but the very foundation upon which social life is built.

Rule of etiquette the first—which hundreds of others merely paraphrase or explain or elaborate—is:

Never do anything that is unpleasant to others.

Never take more than your share—whether of the road in driving a car, of chairs on a boat or seats on a train, or food at the table.

People who picnic along the public highway leaving a clutter of greasy paper and swill (not a pretty name, but neither is it a pretty object!) for other people to walk or drive past, and to make a breeding place for flies, and furnish nourishment for rats, choose a disgusting way to repay the land-owner for the liberty they took in temporarily occupying his property.

CHAPTER VI

AT THE OPERA, THE THEATER, AND OTHER PUBLIC GATHERINGS

Excepting a religious ceremonial, there is no occasion where greater dignity of manner is required of ladies and gentlemen both, than in occupying a box at the opera. For a gentleman especially no other etiquette is so exacting.

In walking about in the foyer of the opera house, a gentleman leaves his coat in the box—or in his orchestra chair—but he always wears his high hat. The "collapsible" hat is for use in the seats rather than in the boxes, but it can be worn perfectly well by a guest in the latter if he hasn't a "silk" one. A gentleman must always be in full dress, tail coat, white waistcoat, white tie and white gloves whether he is seated in the orchestra or a box. He wears white gloves nowhere else except at a ball, or when usher at a wedding.

As people usually dine with their hostess before the opera, they arrive together; the gentlemen assist the ladies to lay off their wraps, one of the gentlemen (whichever is nearest) draws back the curtain dividing the anteroom from the box, and the ladies enter, followed by the gentlemen, the last of whom closes the curtain again. If there are two ladies besides the hostess, the latter places her most distinguished or older guest in the corner nearest the stage. The seat furthest from the stage is always her own. The older guest takes her seat first, then the hostess takes her place, whereupon the third lady goes forward in the center to the front of the box, and stands until one of the gentlemen places a chair for her between the other two. (The chairs are arranged in three rows, of one on either side with an aisle left between.)

One of the duties of the gentlemen is to see that the curtains at the back of the box remain tightly closed, as the light from the ante-room shining in the faces of others in the audience across the house is very disagreeable to them.

A gentleman never sits in the front row of a box, even though he is for a time alone in it.

AS TO VISITING

It is the custom for a gentleman who is a guest in one box to pay visits to friends in other boxes during the entr'actes. He must visit none but ladies of his acquaintance and must never enter a box in which he knows only the gentlemen, and expect to be introduced to the ladies. If Arthur Norman, for instance, wishes to present a gentleman to Mrs. Gilding in her box at the opera, he must first ask her if he may bring his friend James Dawson. (He would on no account speak of him as Mr. Dawson unless he is an elderly person.) A lady's box at the opera is actually her house, and only those who are acceptable as visitors in her house should ask to be admitted.

But it is quite correct for a gentleman to go into a stranger's box to speak to a lady who is a friend of his, just as he would go to see her if she were staying in a stranger's house. But he should not go into the box of one he does not know, to speak to a lady with whom he has only a slight acquaintance, since visits are not paid quite so casually to ladies who are themselves visitors. Upon a gentleman's entering a box it is obligatory for whoever is sitting behind the lady to whom the arriving gentleman's visit is addressed, to relinquish his chair. Another point of etiquette is that a gentleman must never leave the ladies of his own box alone. Occasionally it happens that the gentlemen in Mrs. Gilding's box, for instance, have all relinquished their places to visitors and have themselves gone to Mrs. Worldly's or Mrs. Jones' or Mrs. Town's boxes. Mrs. Gilding's guests must, from the vantage point of the Worldly, Jones or Town boxes, keep a watchful eye on their hostess and instantly return to her support when they see her visitors about to leave, even though the ladies whom they are momentarily visiting be left to themselves. It is of course the duty of the other gentlemen who came to the opera with Mrs. Worldly, Mrs. Jones or Mrs. Town to hurry to them.

A gentleman must never stay in any box that he does not belong in, after the lowering of the lights for the curtain. Nor, in spite of cartoons to the contrary, does good taste permit conversation during the performance or during the overture. Box holders arriving late or leaving before the final curtain do so as quietly as possible and always without speaking.

A "BRILLIANT OPERA NIGHT"

A "brilliant opera night," which one often hears spoken of (meaning merely that all the boxes are occupied, and that the ladies are more elaborately dressed than usual) is generally a night when a leader of fashion such as Mrs. Worldly, Mrs. Gilding, or Mrs. Toplofty, is giving a ball; and most of the holders of the parterre boxes are in ball dresses, with an unusual display of jewels. Or a house will be particularly "brilliant" if a very great singer is appearing in a new rôle, or if a personage be present, as when Marshal Joffre went to the Metropolitan.

AFTER THE PERFORMANCE

One gentleman, at least, must wait in the carriage lobby until all the ladies in his party have driven away. *Never* under any circumstances may "the last" gentleman leave a lady standing alone on the sidewalk. It is the duty of the hostess to take all unattended ladies home who have not a private conveyance of their own, but the obligation does not extend to married couples or odd men. But if a married lady or widow has ordered her own car to come for her, the odd gentleman waits with her until it appears. It is then considerate for her to offer him a "lift," but it is equally proper for her to thank him for waiting and drive off alone.

AT THE THEATER

New Yorkers of highest fashion almost never occupy a box at the theater. At the opera the world of fashion is to be seen in the parterre boxes (not the first tier), and in boxes at some of the horse shows and at many public charity balls and entertainments, but those in boxes at the theater are usually "strangers" or "outsiders."

No one can dispute that the best theater seats are those in the center of the orchestra. A box in these days of hatlessness has nothing to recommend it except that the people can sit in a group and gentlemen can go out between the acts easily, but these advantages hardly make up for the disadvantage to four or at least three out of the six box occupants who see scarcely a slice of the stage.

WILL YOU DINE AND GO TO THE PLAY?

There is no more popular or agreeable way of entertaining people than to ask them to "dine and go to the play." The majority do not even prefer to have "opera" substituted for "play," because those who care for serious music are a minority compared with those who like the theater.

If a bachelor gives a small theater party he usually takes his guests to dine at the Fitz-Cherry or some other fashionable and "amusing" restaurant, but a married couple living in their own house are more likely to dine at home, unless they belong to a type prevalent in New York which is "restaurant mad." The Gildings, in spite of the fact that their own chef is the best there is, are much more apt to dine in a restaurant before going to a play—or if they don't dine in a restaurant, they go to one for supper afterwards. But the Normans, if they ask people to dine and go to the theater, invariably dine at home.

A theater party can of course be of any size, but six or eight is the usual number, and the invitations are telephoned: "Will Mr. and Mrs. Lovejoy dine with Mr. and Mrs. Norman at seven-thirty on Tuesday and go to the play?"

Or "Will Mr. and Mrs. Oldname dine with Mr. Club-win Doe on Saturday at the Toit d'Or and go to the play?"

When Mr. and Mrs. Oldname "accept with pleasure" a second message is given: "Dinner will be at 7.30."

Mrs. Norman's guests go to her house. Mr. Doe's guests meet him in the foyer of the Toit d'Or. But the guests at both dinners are taken to the theater by their host. If a dinner is given by a hostess who has no car of her own, a guest will sometimes ask: "Don't you want me to have the car come back for us?" The hostess can either say to an intimate friend "Why, yes, thank you very much," or to a more formal acquaintance, "No, thank you just the same—I have ordered taxis." Or she can accept. There is no rule beyond her own feelings in the matter.

Mr. Doe takes his guests to the theater in taxis. The Normans, if only the Lovejoys are dining with them, go in Mrs. Norman's little town car, but if there are to be six or eight, the ladies go in her car and the gentlemen follow in a taxi. (Unless Mrs. Worldly or Mrs. Gilding are in the party and order their cars back.)

TICKETS BOUGHT IN ADVANCE

Before inviting anyone to go to a particular play, a hostess must be sure that good tickets are to be had. She should also try to get seats for a play that is new; since it is dull to take people to something they have already seen. This is not difficult in cities where new plays come to town every week, but in New York, where the same ones run for a year or more, it is often a choice between an old good one or a new one that is poor. If intimate friends are coming, a hostess usually asks them what they want to see and tries to get tickets accordingly.

It is really unnecessary to add that one must *never* ask people to go to a place of public amusement and then stand in line to get seats at the time of the performance.

GOING DOWN THE AISLE OF A THEATER

The host, or whichever gentleman has the tickets, (if there is no host, the hostess usually hands them to one of the gentlemen before leaving her house), goes down the aisle first and gives the checks to the usher, and the others follow in the order in which they are to sit and which the hostess must direct. It is necessary that each knows who follows whom, particularly if a theater party arrives after the curtain has gone up. If the hostess "forgets," the guests always ask before trooping down the aisle "How do you want us to sit?" For nothing is more awkward and stupid than to block the aisle at the row where their seats are, while their hostess "sorts them"; and worse yet, in her effort to be polite, sends the ladies to their seats first and then lets the gentlemen stumble across them to their own places. Going down the aisle is not a question of precedence, but a question of seating. The one who is to sit eighth from the aisle, whether a lady or a gentleman, goes first, then the seventh, then the sixth, and if the gentleman with the checks is fifth, he goes in his turn and the fourth follows him.

If a gentleman and his wife go to the theater alone, the question as to who goes down the aisle first depends on where the usher is. If the usher takes the checks at the head of the aisle, she follows the usher. Otherwise the gentleman goes first with the checks. When their places are shown him, he stands aside for his wife to take her place first and then he takes his. A lady never sits in the aisle seat if she is with a gentleman.

GOOD MANNERS AT THE THEATER

In passing across people who are seated, always face the stage and press as close to the backs of the seats you are facing as you can. Remember also not to drag anything across the heads of those sitting in front of you. At the moving pictures, especially when it is dark and difficult to see, a coat on an arm passing behind a chair can literally devastate the hair-dressing of a lady occupying it.

If you are obliged to cross in front of some one who gets up to let you pass, say "Thank you," or "Thank you very much" or "I am very sorry."   Do *not* say "Pardon *me!*" or "Beg pardon!"   Though you can say "I beg your pardon."   That, however, would be more properly the expression to use if you brushed your coat over their heads, or spilled water over them, or did something to them for which you should actually *beg* their pardon. But "Beg pardon," which is an abbreviation, is one of the phrases never said in best society.

Gentlemen who want to go out after every act should always be sure to get aisle seats.   There are no greater theater pests than those who come back after the curtain has gone up and temporarily snuff out the view of everyone behind, as well as annoy those who are obliged to stand up and let them by.

Between the acts nearly all gentlemen go out and smoke at least once, but those wedged in far from the aisle, who file out every time the curtain drops are utterly lacking in consideration for others.   If there are five acts, they should at most go out for two entr'actes and even then be careful to come back before the curtain goes up.

VERY INCONSIDERATE TO GIGGLE AND TALK

Nothing shows less consideration for others than to whisper and rattle programmes and giggle and even make audible remarks throughout a performance.   Very young people love to go to the theater in droves called theater parties and absolutely ruin the evening for others who happen to sit in front of them.   If Mary and Johnny and Susy and Tommy want to talk and giggle, why not arrange chairs in rows for them in a drawing-room, turn on a phonograph as an accompaniment and let them sit there and chatter!

If those behind you insist on talking it is never good policy to turn around and glare.   If you are young they pay no attention, and if you are older—most young people think an angry older person the funniest sight on earth! The small boy throws a snowball at an elderly gentleman for no other reason! The only thing you can do is to say amiably: "I'm sorry, but I can't hear anything while you talk." If they still persist, you can ask an usher to call the manager.

The sentimental may as well realize that every word said above a whisper is easily heard by those sitting directly in front, and those who tell family or other private affairs might do well to remember this also.

As a matter of fact, comparatively few people are ever anything but well behaved. Those who arrive late and stand long, leisurely removing their wraps, and who insist on laughing and talking are rarely encountered; most people take their seats as quietly and quickly as they possibly can, and are quite as much interested in the play and therefore as attentive and quiet as you are. A very annoying person at the "movies" is one who reads every "caption" out loud.

PROPER THEATER CLOTHES

At the evening performance in New York a lady wears a dinner dress; a gentleman a dinner coat, often called a Tuxedo. Full dress is not correct, but those going afterwards to a ball can perfectly well go to the theater first if they do not make themselves conspicuous. A lady in a ball dress and many jewels should avoid elaborate hair ornamentation and must keep her wrap, or at least a sufficiently opaque scarf, about her shoulders to avoid attracting people's attention. A gentleman in full dress is not conspicuous.

And on the subject of theater dress it might be tentatively remarked that prinking and "making up" in public are all part of an age which can not see fun in a farce without bedroom scenes and actors in pajamas, and actresses running about in negligés with their hair down. An audience which night after night watches people dressing and undressing probably gets into an unconscious habit of dressing or prinking itself. In other days it was always thought that so much as to adjust a hat-pin or glance in a glass was lack of breeding. Every well brought up young woman was taught that she must finish dressing in her bedchamber. But to-day young women in theaters, restaurants, and other public places, are continually studying their reflection in little mirrors and patting their hair and powdering their noses and fixing this or adjusting that in a way that in Mrs. Oldname's girlhood would have absolutely barred them from good society; nor can Mrs. Worldly or Mrs. Oldname be imagined "preening" and "prinking" anywhere. They dress as carefully and as beautifully as possible, but when they turn away from the mirrors in their dressing rooms they never look in a glass or "take note of their appearance" until they dress again. And it must be granted that Lucy Gilding, Constance Style, Celia Lovejoy, Mary Smartlington and the other well-bred members of the younger set do not put finishing touches on their faces in public—as yet!

THE COURTESY OF SENDING TICKETS EARLY

Most people are at times "obliged" to take tickets for various charity entertainments—balls, theatricals, concerts or pageants—to which, if they do not care to go themselves, they give away their tickets. Those who intend giving tickets should remember that a message, "Can you use two tickets for the Russian ballet to-night?" sent at seven o'clock that same evening, after the Lovejoys have settled themselves for an evening at home (Celia having decided not to curl her hair and Donald having that morning sent his only dinner coat to be re-faced) can not give the same pleasure that their earlier offer would have given. An opera box sent on the morning of the opera is worse, since to find four music-loving people to fill it on such short notice at the height of the season is an undertaking that few care to attempt.

A BIG THEATER PARTY

A big theater party is one of the favorite entertainments given for a débutante. If fifty or more are to be asked, invitations are sometimes engraved.

Mrs. Toplofty

requests the pleasure of

[Name of guest is written on this line.]

company at the theater and a small dance afterward

in honor of her great-niece

Miss Millicent Gilding

on Tuesday the sixth of January

at half-past eight o'clock

R. s. v. p.

But—and usually—the "general utility" invitation (see page 118) is filled in, as follows:

To meet Miss Millicent Gilding

Mrs. Toplofty

requests the pleasure of

Miss Rosalie Gray's

company at *the Theater and at a dance*
on *Tuesday the sixth of January*
    at *8. 15*

R. s. v. p.

Or notes in either wording above are written by hand.

All those who accept have a ticket sent them. Each ticket sent a débutante is accompanied by a visiting card on which is written:

> "Be in the lobby of the Comedy Theater at
> 8.15. Order your motor to come for you
> at 010 Fifth Avenue at 1 A. M."

On the evening of the theater party, Mrs. Toplofty herself stands in the lobby to receive the guests. As soon as any who are to sit next to each other have arrived, they are sent into the theater; each gives her (or his) ticket to an usher and sits in the place alloted to her (or him). It is well for the hostess to have a seat plan for her own use in case thoughtless young people mix their tickets all up and hand them to an usher in a bunch! And yet— if they do mix themselves to their own satisfaction, she would better "leave them" than attempt to disturb a plan that may have had more method in it than madness.

When the last young girl has arrived, Mrs. Toplofty goes into the theater herself (she does not bother to wait for any boys), and in this one instance she very likely sits in a stage box so as to "keep her eye on them," and with her she has two or three of her own friends.

After the theater, big motor busses drive them all either to the house of the hostess or to a hotel for supper and to dance. If they go to a hotel, a small ballroom must be engaged and the dance is a private one; it would be considered out of place to take a lot of very young people to a public cabaret.

Carelessly chaperoned young girls are sometimes, it is true, seen in very questionable places because some of the so-called dancing restaurants are perfectly fit and proper for them to go to; many other places however, are not, and for the sake of general appearances it is safer to make it a rule that no *very* young girl should go anywhere after the theater except to a private house or a private dance or ball.

Older people, on the other hand, very often go for a supper to one of the cabarets for which New York is famous (or infamous?), or perhaps go to watch a vaudeville performance at midnight, or dance, or do both together.

Others, if they are among the great majority of "quiet" people, go home after the theater, especially if they have dined with their hostess (or host) before the play.

DON'T BE LATE

When you are dining before going to the opera or theater you must arrive on the stroke of the hour for which you are asked; it is one occasion when it is inexcusable to be late.

In accepting an invitation for lunch or dinner after which you are going to a game, or any sort of performance, you must not be late! Nothing is more unfair to others who are keen about whatever it is you are going to see, than to make them miss the beginning of a performance through your thoughtless selfishness.

For this reason box-holders who are music-lovers do not ask guests who have the "late habit" to dine before the opera, because experience has taught them they will miss the overture and most of the first act if they do. Those, on the other hand, who care nothing for music and go to the opera to see people and be seen, seldom go until most if not all of the first act is over. But these in turn might give music-loving guests their choice of going alone in time for the overture and waiting for them in the box at the opera, or having the pleasure of dining with their hostess but missing most of the first part.

AT GAMES, THE CIRCUS OR ELSEWHERE

Considerate and polite behavior by each member of an audience is the same everywhere. At out-door games, or at the circus, it is not necessary to stop talking. In fact, a good deal of noise is not out of the way in "rooting" at a match, and a circus band does not demand silence in order to appreciate its cheerful blare. One very great annoyance in open air gatherings is cigar smoke when blown directly in one's face, or worse yet the smoke from a smouldering cigar. It is almost worthy of a study in air currents to discover why with plenty of space all around, a tiny column of smoke will make straight for the nostrils of the very one most nauseated by it!

The only other annoyance met with at ball games or parades or wherever people occupy seats on the grand-stand, is when some few in front get excited and insist on standing up. If those in front stand—those behind naturally have to! Generally people call out "down in front." If they won't stay "down," then all those behind have to stay "up." Also umbrellas and parasols entirely blot out the view of those behind.

CHAPTER VII

CONVERSATION

NEED OF RECIPROCITY

Ideal conversation should be a matter of equal give and take, but too often it is all "take." The voluble talker— or chatterer—rides his own hobby straight through the hours without giving anyone else, who might also like to say something, a chance to do other than exhaustedly await the turn that never comes. Once in a while—a very long while—one meets a brilliant person whose talk is a delight; or still more rarely a wit who manipulates every ordinary topic with the agility of a sleight-of-hand performer, to the ever increasing rapture of his listeners.

But as a rule the man who has been led to believe that he is a brilliant and interesting talker has been led to make himself a rapacious pest. No conversation is possible between others whose ears are within reach of his ponderous voice; anecdotes, long-winded stories, dramatic and pathetic, stock his repertoire; but worst of all are his humorous yarns at which he laughs uproariously though every one else grows solemn and more solemn.

There is a simple rule, by which if one is a voluble chatterer (to be a good talker necessitates a good mind) one can at least refrain from being a pest or a bore. And the rule is merely, to stop and think.

"THINK BEFORE YOU SPEAK"

Nearly all the faults or mistakes in conversation are caused by not thinking. For instance. a first rule for behavior in society is: "Try to do and say those things only which will be agreeable to others." Yet how many people, who really know better, people who are perfectly capable of intelligent understanding if they didn't

48

let their brains remain asleep or locked tight, go night after night to dinner parties, day after day to other social gatherings, and absent-mindedly prate about this or that without ever taking the trouble to *think* what they are saying and to whom they are saying it! Would a young mother describe twenty or thirty cunning tricks and sayings of the baby to a bachelor who has been helplessly put beside her at dinner if she *thought?* She would know very well, alas! that not even a very dear friend would really care for more than a *hors d'oeuvre* of the subject, at the board of general conversation.

The older woman is even worse, unless something occurs (often when it is too late) to make her wake up and realize that she not only bores her hearers but prejudices everyone against her children by the unrestraint of her own praise. The daughter who is continually lauded as the most captivating and beautiful girl in the world, seems to the wearied perceptions of enforced listeners annoying and plain. In the same way the "magnificent" son is handicapped by his mother's—or his father's—overweening pride and love in exact proportion to its displayed intensity. On the other hand, the neglected wife, the unappreciated husband, the misunderstood child, takes on a glamor in the eyes of others equally out of proportion. That great love has seldom perfect wisdom is one of the great tragedies in the drama of life. In the case of the overloving wife or mother, some one should love her enough to make her *stop and think* that her loving praise is not merely a question of boring her hearers but of handicapping unfairly those for whom she would gladly lay down her life—and yet few would have the courage to point out to her that she would far better lay down her tongue.

The cynics say that those who take part in social conversation are bound to be either the bores or the bored; and that which you choose to be, is a mere matter of selection. And there must be occasions in the life of everyone when the cynics seem to be right; the man of affairs who, sitting next to an attractive looking young woman, is regaled throughout dinner with the detailed accomplishments of the young woman's husband; the woman of intellect who must listen with interest to the droolings of an especially prosy man who holds forth on the super-everything of his own possessions, can not very well consider that the evening was worth dressing, sitting up, and going out for.

People who talk too easily are apt to talk too much, and at times imprudently, and those with vivid imagination are often unreliable in their statements. On the other hand the "man of silence" who never speaks except when he has something "worth while" to say, is apt to wear well among his intimates, but is not likely to add much to the gaiety of a party.

Try not to repeat yourself; either by telling the same story again and again or by going back over details of your narrative that seemed especially to interest or amuse your hearer. Many things are of interest when briefly told and for the first time; *nothing* interests when too long dwelt upon; little interests that is told a second time. The exception is something very pleasant that you have heard about A. or more especially A.'s child, which having already told A. you can then tell B., and later C. in A.'s presence. Never do this as a habit, however, and never drag the incident into the conversation merely to flatter A., since if A. is a person of taste, he will be far more apt to resent than be pleased by flattery that borders on the fulsome.

Be careful not to let amiable discussion turn into contradiction and argument. The tactful person keeps his prejudices to himself and even when involved in a discussion says quietly "No. I don't think I agree with you" or "It seems to me thus and so." One who is well-bred never says "You are wrong!" or "Nothing of the kind!" If he finds another's opinion utterly opposed to his own, he switches to another subject for a pleasanter channel of conversation.

When some one is talking to you, it is inconsiderate to keep repeating "What did you say?" Those who are deaf are often obliged to ask that a sentence be repeated. Otherwise their irrelevant answers would make them appear half-witted. But countless persons with perfectly good hearing say "What?" from force of habit and careless inattention.

THE GIFT OF HUMOR

The joy of joys is the person of light but unmalicious humor. If you know any one who is gay, beguiling and amusing, you will, if you are wise, do everything you can to make him prefer your house and your table to any other; for where he is, the successful party is also. What he says is of no matter, it is the twist he gives to it, the intonation, the personality he puts into his quip or retort or observation that delights his hearers, and in his case the ordinary rules do not apply.

Eugene Field could tell a group of people that it had rained to-day and would probably rain tomorrow, and make everyone burst into laughter—or tears if he chose—according to the way it was said. But the ordinary rest of us must, if we would be thought sympathetic, intelligent or agreeable, "go fishing."

GOING FISHING FOR TOPICS

The charming talker is neither more nor less than a fisherman. (Fisherwoman rather, since in America women make more effort to be agreeable than men do.) Sitting next to a stranger she wonders which "fly" she had better choose to interest him. She offers one topic; not much of a nibble. So she tries another or perhaps a third before he "rises" to the bait.

THE DOOR SLAMMERS

There are people whose idea of conversation is contradiction and flat statement. Finding yourself next to one of these, you venture:

"Have you seen any good plays lately?"

"No, hate the theater."

"Which team are you for in the series?"

"Neither. Only an idiot could be interested in base-ball."

"Country must have a good many idiots!" mockingly.

"Obviously it has." Full stop. In desperation you veer to the personal.

"I've never seen Mrs. Bobo Gilding as beautiful as she is to-night."

"Nothing beautiful about her. As for the name 'Bobo,' it's asinine."

"Oh, it's just one of those children's names that stick sometimes for life."

"Perfect rot. Ought to be called by his name," etc.

Another, not very different in type though different in method, is the self-appointed instructor whose proper place is on the lecture platform, not at a dinner table.

"The earliest coins struck in the Peloponnesus were stamped on one side only; their alloy——" etc.

Another is the expounder of the obvious: "Have you ever noticed," says he, deeply thinking, "how people's tastes differ?"

Then there is the vulgarian of fulsome compliment: "Why are you so beautiful? It is not fair to the others——" and so on.

TACTLESS BLUNDERERS

Tactless people are also legion. The means-to-be-agree-able elderly man says to a passée acquaintance, "Twenty years ago you were the prettiest woman in town"; or in the pleasantest tone of voice to one whose only son has married. "Why is it, do you suppose, that young wives always dislike their mothers-in-law?"

If you have any ambition to be sought after in society you must not talk about the unattractiveness of old age to the elderly, about the joys of dancing and skating to the lame, or about the advantages of ancestry to the self-made. It is also dangerous, as well as needlessly un-kind, to ridicule or criticize others, especially for what they can't help. If a young woman's familiar or other-wise lax behavior deserves censure, a casual unflattering remark may not add to your own popularity if your listener is a relative, but you can at least, without being shamefaced, stand by your guns. On the other hand to say needlessly "What an ugly girl!" or "What a half-wit that boy is!" can be of no value except in drawing attention to your own tactlessness.

The young girl who admired her own facile adjectives said to a casual acquaintance: "How *can* you go about with that moth-eaten, squint-eyed, bag of a girl!" "Because," answered the youth whom she had intended to dazzle, "the lady of your flattering epithets happens to be my sister."

It is scarcely necessary to say that one whose tactless remarks ride rough-shod over the feelings of others, is not welcomed by many.

THE BORE

A bore is said to be "one who talks about himself when you want to talk about yourself!" which is superficially true enough, but a bore might more accurately be described as one who is interested in what does not interest you, and insists that you share his enthusiasm, in spite of your disinclination. To the bore life holds no dullness; every subject is of unending delight. A story told for the thousandth time has not lost its thrill; every tiresome detail is held up and turned about as a morsel of delectableness; to him each pea in a pod differs from another with the entrancing variety that artists find in tropical sunsets.

On the other hand, to be bored is a bad habit, and one only too easy to fall into. As a matter of fact, it is impossible, almost, to meet anyone who has not *something* of interest to tell you if you are but clever enough yourself to find out what it is. There are certain always delightful people who refuse to be bored. Their attitude is that no subject need ever be utterly uninteresting, so long as it is discussed for the first time. Repetition alone is deadly dull. Besides, what is the matter with trying to be agreeable yourself? Not *too* agreeable. Alas!

it is true: "Be polite to bores and so shall you have bores always round about you." Furthermore, there is no reason why you should be bored when you can be otherwise. But if you find yourself sitting in the hedgerow with nothing but weeds, there is no reason for shutting your eyes and seeing nothing, instead of finding what beauty you may in the weeds. To put it cynically, life is too short to waste it in drawing blanks. Therefore, it is up to you to find as many pictures to put on your blank pages as possible.

A FEW IMPORTANT DETAILS OF SPEECH IN CONVERSATION

Unless you wish to stamp yourself a person who has never been out of "provincial" society, never speak of your husband as "Mr." except to an inferior. Mrs. Worldly for instance in talking with a stranger would say "my husband," and to a friend, meaning one not only whom she calls by her first name, but anyone on her "dinner list," she says, "Dick thought the play amusing" or "Dick said——". This does not give her listener the privilege of calling him "Dick." The listener in return speaks of her own husband as "Tom" even if he is seventy—unless her hearer is a very young person (either man or woman), when she would say "my husband." Never "Mr. Older." To call your husband Mr. means that you consider the person you are talking to, beneath you in station. Mr. Worldly in the same way speaks of Mrs. Worldly as "my wife" to a gentleman, or "Edith" in speaking to a lady. *Always.*

In speaking about other people, one says "Mrs.," "Miss" or "Mr." as the case may be. It is bad form to go about saying "Edith Worldly" or "Ethel Norman" to those who do not call them Edith or Ethel, and to speak thus familiarly of one whom you do not call by her first name, is unforgivable. It is also effrontery for a younger person to call an older by her or his first name, without being asked to do so. Only a very underbred, thick-skinned person would attempt it.

Also you must not take your conversation "out of the

drawing-room." Operations, ills or personal blemishes, details and appurtenances of the dressing-room, for instance, are neither suitable nor pleasant topics, nor are personal jokes in good taste.

THE "OMNISCIENCE" OF THE VERY RICH

Why a man, because he has millions, should assume that they confer omniscience in all branches of knowledge, is something which may be left to the psychologist to answer, but most of those thrown much in contact with millionaires will agree that an attitude of infallibility is typical of a fair majority.

A professor who has devoted his life to a subject modestly makes a statement. "You are all wrong," says the man of millions, "It is this way——". As a connoisseur he seems to think that because he can pay for anything he fancies, he is accredited expert as well as potential owner. Topics he does not care for are "bosh," those which he has a smattering of, he simply appropriates; his prejudices are, in his opinion, expert criticism; his taste impeccable; his judgment infallible; and to him the world is a pleasance built for his sole pleasuring. But to the rest of us who also have to live in it with as much harmony as we can, such persons are certainly elephants at large in the garden. We can sometimes induce them to pass through gently, but they are just as likely at any moment to pull up our fences and push the house itself over on our defenseless heads.

There are countless others of course, very often the richest of all, who are authoritative in all they profess, who are experts and connoisseurs, who are human and helpful and above everything respecters of the garden enclosure of others.

DANGERS TO BE AVOIDED

In conversation the dangers are very much the same as those to be avoided in writing letters. Talk about things which you think will be agreeable to your hearer. Don't dilate on ills, misfortune, or other unpleasantnesses. The one in greatest danger of making enemies is the man or woman of brilliant wit. If sharp, wit is apt to produce a feeling of mistrust even while it stimulates. Furthermore the applause which follows every witty sally becomes in time breath to the nostrils, and perfectly well-intentioned people, who mean to say nothing unkind, in the flash of a second "see a point," and in the next second, score it with no more power to resist than a drug addict can resist a dose put into his hand!

The mimic is a joy to his present company, but the eccentric mannerism of one is much easier to imitate than the charm of another, and the subjects of the habitual mimic are all too apt to become his enemies.

You need not, however, be dull because you refrain from the rank habit of a critical attitude, which like a weed will grow all over the place if you let it have half a chance. A very good resolve to make and keep, if you would also keep any friends you make, is never to speak of anyone without, in imagination, having them overhear what you say. One often hears the exclamation "I would say it to her face!" At least be very sure that this is true, and not a braggart's phrase and then—nine times out of ten think better of it and refrain. Preaching is all very well in a text-book, schoolroom or pulpit, but it has no place in society. Society is supposed to be a pleasant place; telling people disagreeable things to their faces or behind their backs is *not* a pleasant occupation.

Do not be too apparently clever if you would be popular. The cleverest woman is she who, in talking to a man, makes *him* seem clever. This was Mme. Recamier's great charm.

A FEW MAXIMS FOR THOSE WHO TALK TOO MUCH—
AND EASILY!

The faults of commission are far more serious than those of omission; regrets are seldom for what you left unsaid.

The chatterer reveals every corner of his shallow mind; one who keeps silent can not have his depth plumbed.

Don't pretend to know more than you do. To say you
have read a book and then seemingly to understand
nothing of what you have read, proves you a half-wit.
Only the very small mind hesitates to say "I don't know."

Above all, stop and *think* what you are saying! This
is really the first, last and only rule. If you "stop" you
can't chatter or expound or flounder ceaselessly, and if
you *think,* you will find a topic and a manner of presenting
your topic so that your neighbor will be interested rather
than long-suffering.

Remember also that the sympathetic (not apathetic) listener is the delight of delights. The person who looks
glad to see you, who is seemingly eager for your news,
or enthralled with your conversation; who looks at you
with a kindling of the face, and gives you spontaneous
and undivided attention, is the one to whom the palm for
the art of conversation would undoubtedly be awarded.

Chapter VIII

WORDS, PHRASES AND PRONUNCIATION

PHRASES AVOIDED IN GOOD SOCIETY

It is difficult to explain why well-bred people avoid certain words and expressions that are admitted by etymology and grammar. So it must be merely stated that they have and undoubtedly always will avoid them. Moreover, this choice of expression is not set forth in any printed guide or book on English, though it is followed in all literature.

To liken Best Society to a fraternity, with the avoidance of certain seemingly unimportant words as the sign of recognition, is not a fantastic simile. People of the fashionable world invariably use certain expressions and instinctively avoid others; therefore when a stranger uses an "avoided" one he proclaims that he "does not belong," exactly as a pretended Freemason proclaims himself an "outsider" by giving the wrong "grip"—or whatever it is by which Brother Masons recognize one another.

People of position are people of position the world over —and by their speech are most readily known. Appearance on the other hand often passes muster. A "show-girl" may be lovely to look at as she stands in a seemingly unstudied position and in perfect clothes. But let her say "My Gawd!" or "Wouldn't that jar you!" and where is her loveliness then?

And yet, and this is the difficult part of the subject to make clear, the most vulgar slang like that quoted above, is scarcely worse than the attempted elegance which those unused to good society imagine to be the evidence of cultivation.

People who say "I come," and "I seen it," and "I done it" prove by their lack of grammar that they had little education in their youth.   Unfortunate, very; but they may at the same time be brilliant, exceptional characters, loved by everyone who knows them, because they are what they seem and nothing else.   But the caricature "lady" with the comic picture "society manner" who says "Pardon *me*" and talks of "retiring," and "residing," and "desiring," and "being acquainted with," and "attending" this and that with "her escort," and curls her little finger over the handle of her teacup, and prates of "culture," does *not* belong to Best Society, and *never* will!   The offense of pretentiousness is committed oftener perhaps by women than by men, who are usually more natural and direct.   A genuine, sincere, kindly American man—or woman—can go anywhere and be welcomed by everyone, provided of course, that he is a man of ability and intellect.   One finds him all over the world, neither aping the manners of others nor treading on the sensibilities of those less fortunate than himself.

Occasionally too, there appears in Best Society a provincial in whose conversation is perceptible the influence of much reading of the Bible.   Such are seldom if ever stilted or pompous or long-worded, but are invariably distinguished for the simplicity and dignity of their English.

There is no better way to cultivate taste in words, than by constantly reading the best English.   None of the words and expressions which are taboo in good society will be found in books of proved literary standing.   But it must not be forgotten that there can be a vast difference between literary standing and popularity, and that many of the "best sellers" have no literary merit whatsoever.

To be able to separate best English from merely good English needs a long process of special education, but to recognize bad English one need merely skim through a page of a book, and if a single expression in the left-hand column following can be found (unless purposely quoted in illustration of vulgarity) it is quite certain that the author neither writes best English nor belongs to Best Society.

NEVER SAY:	CORRECT FORM:
In our residence we retire early (or arise)	At our house we go to bed early (or get up)
I desire to purchase	I should like to buy
Make you acquainted with	(See Introductions)
Pardon *me!*	I beg your pardon. Or, Excuse me! Or, sorry!
Lovely food	Good food
Elegant home	Beautiful house—or place
A stylish dresser	She dresses well, or she wears lovely clothes
Charmed! or Pleased to meet you!	How do you do!
Attended	Went to
I trust I am not trespassing	I hope I am not in the way (unless trespassing on private property is actually meant)
Request (meaning ask)	Used only in the third person in formal written invitations.
Will you accord me permission?	Will you let me? or May I?
Permit me to assist you	Let me help you
Brainy	Brilliant or clever
I presume	I suppose
Tendered him a banquet	Gave him a dinner
Converse	Talk

NEVER SAY:	CORRECT FORM:
Partook of liquid refreshment	Had something to drink
Perform ablutions	Wash
A song entitled	Called (proper if used in legal sense)
I will ascertain	I will find out
Residence or mansion	House, or big house
In the home	In some one's house or At home
Phone, photo, auto	Telephone, photograph, automobile

"Tintinnabulary summons," meaning bell, and "Bovine continuation," meaning cow's tail, are more amusing than offensive, but they illustrate the theory of bad style that is pretentious.

As examples of the very worst offenses that can be committed, the following are offered:

"Pray, accept my thanks for the flattering ovation you have tendered me."

"Yes," says the preposterous bride, "I am the recipient of many admired and highly prized gifts."

"Will you permit me to recall myself to you?"

Speaking of bridesmaids as "pretty servitors," "dispensing hospitality," asking any one to "step this way."

Many other expressions are provincial and one who seeks purity of speech should, if possible, avoid them, but as "offenses" they are minor:

Reckon, guess, calculate, or figure, meaning think.

Allow, meaning agree.

Folks, meaning family.

Cute, meaning pretty or winsome.

Well, I declare! 'Pon my word!

Box party, meaning sitting in a box at the theater.

Visiting with, meaning talking to.

There are certain words which have been singled out and misused by the undiscriminating until their value is destroyed. Long ago "elegant" was turned from a word denoting the essence of refinement and beauty, into gaudy trumpery. "Refined" is on the verge. But the pariah of the language is culture! A word rarely used by those who truly possess it, but so constantly misused by those who understand nothing of its meaning, that it is becoming a synonym for vulgarity and imitation. To speak of the proper use of a finger bowl or the ability to introduce two people without a blunder as being "evidence of culture of the highest degree" is precisely as though evidence of highest education were claimed for who ever can do sums in addition, and read words of one syllable. Culture in its true meaning is widest possible education, *plus* especial refinement and taste.

The fact that slang is apt and forceful makes its use irresistibly tempting. Coarse or profane slang is beside the mark, but "flivver," "taxi," the "movies," "deadly" (meaning dull), "feeling fit," "feeling blue," "grafter," a "fake," "grouch," "hunch" and "right o!" are typical of words that it would make our spoken language stilted to exclude.

All colloquial expressions are little foxes that spoil the grapes of perfect diction, but they are very little foxes; it is the false elegance of stupid pretentiousness that is an annihilating blight which destroys root and vine.

In the choice of words, we can hardly find a better guide than the lines of Alexander Pope:

"In words, as fashions, the same rule will hold;
Alike fantastic, if too new, or old:
Be not the first by whom the new are tried,
Nor yet the last to lay the old aside."

PRONUNCIATION

Traits of pronunciation which are typical of whole sections of the country, or accents inherited from European parents must not be confused with crude pronunciations that have their origin in illiteracy. A gentleman of Irish blood may have a brogue as rich as plum cake, or another's accent be soft Southern or flat New England, or rolling Western; and to each of these the utterance of the others may sound too flat, too soft, too harsh, too refined, or drawled, or clipped short, but not uncultivated.

To a New York ear, which ought to be fairly unbiased since the New York accent is a composite of all accents, English women chirrup and twitter. But the beautifully modulated, clear-clipped enunciation of a cultivated Englishman, one who can move his jaws and not swallow his words whole, comes as near to perfection in English as the diction of the Comédie Française comes to perfection in French.

The Boston accent is very crisp and in places suggestive of the best English but the vowels are so curiously flattened that the speech has a saltless effect. There is no rhyming word as flat as the way they say "heart"—"haht." And "bone" and "coat"—"bawn," "cawt," to rhyme with awe!

Then South, there is too much salt—rather too much sugar. Every one's mouth seems full of it, with "I" turned to "ah" and every staccato a drawl. But the voices are full of sweetness and music unknown north of the Potomac.

The Pennsylvania burr is perhaps the mother of the Western one. It is strong enough to have mothered all the r's in the wor-r-rld! Philadelphia's "haow" and "caow" for "how" and "cow," and "me" for "my" is quite as bad as the "water-r" and "thot" of the West.

N'Yawk is supposed to say "yeh" and "Omurica" and "Toosdeh," and "puddin'." Probably five per cent. of it does, but as a whole it has no accent, since it is a composite of all in one.

In best New York society there is perhaps a generally accepted pronunciation which seems chiefly an elimination of the accents of other sections. Probably that is what all people think of their own pronunciation. Or do they not know whether their inflection is right or wrong? Nothing should be simpler to determine. If they pronounce according to a standard dictionary, they are correct; if they don't, they have an "accent" or are ignorant; it is for them to determine which. Such differences as between saying wash or wawsh, ad*vert*isement or adver*tise*ment are of small importance. But no one who makes the least pretence of being a person of education says: kep for kept, genelmun or gempmun or laydee, vawde-vil, or eye-talian.

HOW TO CULTIVATE AN AGREEABLE SPEECH

First of all, remember that while affectation is odious, crudeness must be overcome. A low voice is always pleasing, not whispered or murmured, but low in pitch. Do not talk at the top of your head, nor at the top of your lungs. Do not slur whole sentences together; on the other hand, do not pronounce as though each syllable were a separate tongue and lip exercise.

As a nation we do not talk so much too fast, as too loud. Tens of thousands twang and slur and shout and burr! Many of us drawl and many others of us race tongues and breath at full speed, but, as already said, the speed of our speech does not matter so much. Pitch of voice matters very much and so does pronunciation—enunciation is not so essential—except to one who speaks in public.

Enunciation means the articulation of whatever you have to say distinctly and clearly. Pronunciation is the proper sounding of consonants, vowels and the accentuation of each syllable.

There is no better way to cultivate a perfect pronunciation, apart from association with cultivated people, than by getting a small pronouncing dictionary of words in ordinary use, and reading it word by word, marking and studying any that you use frequently and mispronounce. When you know them, then read any book at random slowly aloud to yourself, very carefully pronouncing each word. The consciousness of this exercise may make you stilted in conversation at first, but by and by the "sense" or "impulse" to speak correctly will come.

This is a method that has been followed by many men handicapped in youth through lack of education, who have become prominent in public life, and by many women, who likewise handicapped by circumstances, have not only made possible a creditable position for themselves, but have then given their children the inestimable advantage of learning their mother tongue correctly at their mother's knee.

CHAPTER IX

ONE'S POSITION IN THE COMMUNITY

THE CHOICE

First of all, it is necessary to decide what one's personal idea of position is, whether this word suggests merely a social one, comprising a large or an exclusive acquaintance and leadership in social gaiety, or position established upon the foundation of communal consequence, which may, or may not, include great social gaiety. In other words, you who are establishing yourself, either as a young husband or a stranger, would you, if you could have your wish granted by a genie, choose to have the populace look upon you askance and in awe, because of your wealth and elegance, or would you wish to be loved, not as a power conferring favors which belong really to the first picture, but as a fellow-being with an understanding heart? The granting of either wish is not a bit beyond the possibilities of anyone. It is merely a question of depositing securities of value in the bank of life.

THE BANK OF LIFE

Life, whether social or business, is a bank in which you deposit certain funds of character, intellect and heart; or other funds of egotism, hard-heartedness and unconcern; or deposit—nothing! And the bank honors your deposit, and no more. In other words, you can draw nothing out but what you have put in.

If your community is to give you admiration and honor, it is merely necessary to be admirable and honorable. The more you put in, the more will be paid out to you. It is too trite to put on paper! But it is astonishing, isn't

65

it, how many people who are depositing nothing whatever, expect to be paid in admiration and respect?

A man of really high position is always a great citizen first and above all. Otherwise he is a hollow puppet whether he is a millionaire or has scarcely a dime to bless himself with. In the same way, a woman's social position that is built on sham, vanity, and selfishness, is like one of the buildings at an exposition; effective at first sight, but bound when slightly weather-beaten to show stucco and glue.

It would be very presumptuous to attempt to tell any man how to acquire the highest position in his community, especially as the answer is written in his heart, his intellect, his altruistic sympathy, and his ardent civic pride. A subject, however, that is not so serious or over-aweing, and which can perhaps have directions written for it, is the lesser ambition of acquiring a social position.

TAKING OR ACQUIRING A SOCIAL POSITION

A bride whose family or family-in-law has social position has merely to take that which is hers by inheritance; but a stranger who comes to live in a new place, or one who has always lived in a community but unknown to society, have both to acquire a standing of their own. For example:

THE BRIDE OF GOOD FAMILY

The bride of good family need do nothing on her own initiative. After her marriage when she settles down in her own house or apartment, everyone who was asked to her wedding breakfast or reception, and even many who were only bidden to the church, call on her. She keeps their cards, enters them in a visiting or ordinary alphabetically indexed blank book, and within two weeks she returns each one of their calls.

As it is etiquette for everyone when calling for the first time on a bride, to ask if she is in, the bride, in returning her first calls, should do likewise. As a matter of fact, a bride assumes the intimate visiting list of both her own and her husband's families, whether they call on her or not. By and by, if she gives a general tea or ball, she can invite whom, among them, she wants to. She should not, however, ask any mere acquaintances of her family to her house, until they have first invited her and her husband to theirs. But if she would like to invite intimate friends of her own or of her husband, or of her family, there is no valid reason why she should not do so.

Usually when a bride and groom return from their wedding trip, all their personal friends and those of their respective parents, give "parties" for them. And from being seen at one house, they are invited to another. If they go nowhere, they do not lose position but they are apt to be overlooked until people remember them by seeing them. But it is not at all necessary for young people to entertain in order to be asked out a great deal; they need merely be attractive and have engaging manners to be as popular as heart could wish. But they must make it a point to be considerate of everyone and never fail to take the trouble to go up with a smiling "How do you do" to every older lady who has been courteous enough to invite them to her house. That is not "toadying," it is being merely polite. To go up and gush is a very different matter, and to go up and gush over a prominent hostess who has never invited them to her house, *is* toadying and of a very cheap variety.

A really well-bred person is as charming as possible to all, but effusive to none, and shows no difference in manner either to the high or to the lowly when they are of equally formal acquaintance.

THE BRIDE WHO IS A STRANGER

The bride who is a stranger, but whose husband is well known in the town to which he brings her, is in much the same position as the bride noted above, in that her husband's friends call on her; she returns their visits, and many of them invite her to their house. But it then devolves upon her to make herself liked, otherwise she will find herself in a community of many acquaintances but no friends. The best ingredients for likeableness are a happy expression of countenance, an unaffected manner, and a sympathetic attitude. If she is so fortunate as to possess these attributes her path will have roses enough. But a young woman with an affected pose and bad or conceited manners, will find plenty of thorns. Equally unsuccessful is she with a chip-on-her-shoulder who, coming from New York for instance, to live in Bright-meadows, insists upon dragging New York sky-scrapers into every comparison with Brightmeadows' new six-storied building. She might better pack her trunks and go back where she came from. Nor should the bride from Brightmeadows who has married a New Yorker, flaunt Brightmeadows standards or customs, and tell Mrs. Worldly that she does not approve of a lady's smoking! Maybe she doesn't and she may be quite right, and she should not under the circumstances smoke herself; but she should not make a display of intolerance, or she, too, had better take the first train back home, since she is likely to find New York very, very lonely.

HOW TOTAL STRANGERS ACQUIRE SOCIAL STANDING

When new people move into a community, bringing letters of introduction to prominent citizens, they arrive with an already made position, which ranks in direct proportion to the standing of those who wrote the introductions. Since, however, no one but "persons of position" are eligible to letters of importance, there would be no question of acquiring position—which they have—but merely of adding to their acquaintance.

As said in another chapter, people of position are people of position the world over, and all the cities strung around the whole globe are like so many chapter-houses of a brotherhood, to which letters of introduction open the doors.

However, this is off the subject, which is to advise

those who have no position, or letters, how to acquire the former. It is a long and slow road to travel, particularly long and slow for a man and his wife in a big city. In New York people could live in the same house for generations, and do, and not have their next door neighbor know them even by sight. But no other city, except London, is as unaware as that. When people move to a new city, or town, it is usually because of business. The husband at least makes business acquaintances, but the wife is left alone. The only thing for her to do is to join the church of her denomination, and become interested in some activity; not only as an opening wedge to acquaintanceships and possibly intimate friendships, but as an occupation and a respite from loneliness. Her social position is gained usually at a snail's pace—nor should she do anything to hurry it. If she is a real person, if she has qualities of mind and heart, if she has charming manners, sooner or later a certain position will come, and in proportion to her eligibility.

One of the ladies with whom she works in church, having gradually learned to like her, asks her to her house. Nothing may ever come of this, but another one also inviting her, may bring an introduction to a third, who takes a fancy to her. This third lady also invites her where she meets an acquaintance she has already made on one of the two former occasions, and this acquaintance in turn invites her. By the time she has met the same people several times, they gradually, one by one, offer to go and see her, or ask her to come and see them. One inviolable rule she must not forget: it is fatal to be pushing or presuming. She must remain dignified always, natural and sympathetic when anyone approaches her, but she should not herself approach any one more than half way. A smile, the more friendly the better, is never out of place, but after smiling, she should pass on! Never grin weakly, and —— cling!

If she is asked to go to see a lady, it is quite right to go. But not again, until the lady has returned the visit, or asked her to her house. And if admitted when making a first visit, she should remember not to stay more than twenty minutes at most, since it is always wiser to make others sorry to have her leave than run the risk of having the hostess wonder why her visitor doesn't know enough to go!

THE ENTRANCE OF AN OUTSIDER

The outsider enters society by the same path, but it is steeper and longer because there is an outer gate of reputation called "They are not people of any position" which is difficult to unlatch. Nor is it ever unlatched to those who sit at the gate rattling at the bars, or plaintively peering in. The better, and the only way if she has not the key of birth, is through study to make herself eligible. Meanwhile, charitable, or civic work, will give her interest and occupation as well as throw her with ladies of good breeding, by association with whom she can not fail to acquire some of those qualities of manner before which the gates of society always open.

WHEN POSITION HAS BEEN ESTABLISHED

When her husband belongs to a club, or perhaps she does too, and the neighbors are friendly and those of social importance have called on her and asked her to their houses, a newcomer does not have to stand so exactly on the chalk line of ceremony as in returning her first visits and sending out her first invitations.

After people have dined with each other several times, it is not at all important to consider whether an invitation is owed or paid several times over. She who is hospitably inclined can ask people half a dozen times to their once if she wants to, and they show their friendliness by coming. Nor need visits be paid in alternate order. Once she is really accepted by people she can be as friendly as she chooses.

When Mrs. Oldname calls on Mrs. Stranger the first time, the latter may do nothing but call in return; it would be the height of presumption to invite one of conspicuous prominence until she has first been invited by her. Nor may the Strangers ask the Oldnames to dine after being merely invited to a tea. But when Mrs. Oldname asks Mrs. Stranger to lunch, the latter might then invite the former to dinner, after which, if they accept, the Strangers can continue to invite them on occasion, whether they are invited in turn or not; especially if the Strangers are continually entertaining, and the Oldnames are not. But on no account must the Strangers' parties be arranged solely for the benefit of any particular fashionables.

The Strangers can also invite to a party any children whom their own children know at school, and Mrs. Stranger can quite properly go to fetch her own children from a party to which their schoolmates invited them.

MONEY NOT ESSENTIAL TO SOCIAL POSITION

Bachelors, unless they are very well off, are not expected to give parties; nor for that matter are very young couples. All hostesses go on asking single men and young people to their houses without it ever occurring to them that any return other than politeness should be made.

There are many couples, not necessarily in the youngest set either, who are tremendously popular in society in spite of the fact that they give no parties at all. The Lovejoys, for instance, who are clamored for everywhere, have every attribute—except money. With fewer clothes perhaps than any fashionable young woman in New York, she can't compete with Mrs. Bobo Gilding or Constance Style for "smartness" but, as Mrs. Worldly remarked: "What would be the use of Celia Lovejoy's beauty if it depended upon continual variation in clothes?"

The only "entertaining" the Lovejoys ever do is limited to afternoon tea and occasional welsh-rarebit suppers. But they return every bit of hospitality shown them by helping to make a party "go" wherever they are. Both are amusing, both are interesting, both do everything well. They can't afford to play cards for money, but they both play a very good game and the table is delighted to "carry them," or they play at the same table against each other.

This, by the way, is another illustration of the conduct of a gentleman; if young Lovejoy played for money he would win undoubtedly in the long run because he plays unusually well, but to use card-playing as a "means of making money" would be contrary to the ethics of a gentleman, just as playing for more than can be afforded turns a game into "gambling."

AN ELUSIVE POINT ESSENTIAL TO SOCIAL SUCCESS

The sense of whom to invite with whom is one of the most important, and elusive, points in social knowledge. The possession or lack of it is responsible more than anything else for the social success of one woman, and the failure of another. And as it is almost impossible, without advice, for any stranger anywhere to know which people like or dislike each other, the would-be hostess must either by means of natural talent or more likely by trained attention, read the signs of liking or prejudice much as a woodsman reads a message in every broken twig or turned leaf.

One who can read expression, perceives at a glance the difference between friendliness and polite aloofness. When a lady is unusually silent, strictly impersonal in conversation, and entirely unapproachable, something is not to her liking. The question is, what? Or usually, whom? The greatest blunder possible would be to ask her what the matter is. The cause of annoyance is probably that she finds someone distasteful and it should not be hard for one whose faculties are not asleep to discover the offender and if possible separate them, or at least never ask them together again.

CHAPTER X

CARDS AND VISITS

USEFULNESS OF CARDS

Who was it that said—in the Victorian era probably, and a man of course—"The only mechanical tool ever needed by a woman is a hair-pin"? He might have added that with a hair-pin and a visiting card, she is ready to meet most emergencies.

Although the principal use of a visiting card, at least the one for which it was originally invented—to be left as an evidence of one person's presence at the house of another—is going gradually out of ardent favor in fashionable circles, its usefulness seems to keep a nicely adjusted balance. In New York, for instance, the visiting card has entirely taken the place of the written note of invitation to informal parties of every description. Messages of condolence or congratulation are written on it; it is used as an endorsement in the giving of an order; it is even tacked on the outside of express boxes. The only employment of it which is not as flourishing as formerly is its being left in quantities and with frequency at the doors of acquaintances. This will be explained further on.

A CARD'S SIZE AND ENGRAVING

The card of a lady is usually from about 2¾ to 3½ inches wide, by 2 to 2¾ inches high, but there is no fixed rule. The card of a young girl is smaller and more nearly square in shape. (About 2 inches high by 2½ or 2⅝ inches long, depending upon the length of the name.) Young girls use smaller cards than older ladies. A gentleman's card is long and narrow, from 2⅞ to 3¼ inches long, and from 1¼ to 1⅝ inches high. All visiting cards are engraved on white unglazed bristol board, which may be of medium thickness or thin, as one fancies.

73

A few years ago there was a fad for cards as thin as writing paper, but one seldom sees them in America now. The advantage of a thin card is that a greater quantity may be carried easily.

The engraving most in use to-day is shaded block. Script is seldom seen, but it is always good form and so is plain block, but with the exception of old English all ornate lettering should be avoided. All people who live in cities should have the address in the lower right corner, engraved in smaller letters than the name. In the country, addresses are not important, as every one knows where every one else lives. People who have town and country houses usually have separate cards, though not necessarily a separate plate.

ECONOMICAL ENGRAVING

The economically inclined can have several varieties of cards printed from one plate. The cards would vary somewhat in size in order to "center" the wording.

Example:

The plate:

Mr. and Mrs. Gilding
Miss Gilding

00 FIFTH AVENUE
GOLDEN HALL

may be printed.

Miss Gilding's name should never appear on a card with both her mother's and father's, so her name being out of line under the "Mr. and Mrs." engraving makes no difference.

or

Mr. and Mrs. Gilding

GOLDEN HALL

or

Mrs. Gilding
Miss Gilding

oo FIFTH AVENUE

or

Mrs. Gilding

GOLDEN HALL

The personal card is in a measure an index of one's character. A fantastic or garish note in the type effect, in the quality or shape of the card, betrays a lack of taste in the owner of the card.

It is not customary for a married man to have a club address on his card, and it would be serviceable only in giving a card of introduction to a business acquaintance, under social rather than business circumstances, or in paying a formal call upon a political or business associate. Unmarried men often use no other address than that of a club; especially if they live in bachelor's quarters, but young men who live at home use their home address.

CORRECT NAMES AND TITLES

To be impeccably correct, initials should not be engraved on a visiting card. A gentleman's card should read: Mr. John Hunter Titherington Smith, but since names are sometimes awkwardly long, and it is the American custom to cling to each and every one given in baptism, he asserts his possessions by representing each one with an initial, and engraves his cards Mr. John H. T. Smith, or Mr. J. H. Titherington Smith, as suits his fancy. So, although, according to high authorities, he should drop a

name or two and be Mr. Hunter Smith, or Mr. Titherington Smith, it is very likely that to the end of time
the American man, and necessarily his wife, who must
use the name as he does, will go on cherishing initials.

And a widow no less than a married woman should
always continue to use her husband's Christian name, or
his name and another initial, engraved on her cards. She
is Mrs. John Hunter Titherington Smith, or, to compromise, Mrs. J. H. Titherington Smith, but she is *never*
Mrs. Sarah Smith; at least not anywhere in good society.
In business and in legal matters a woman is necessarily
addressed by her own Christian name, because she uses it
in her signature. But no one should ever address an
envelope, except from a bank or a lawyer's office, "Mrs.
Sarah Smith." When a widow's son, who has the name
of his father, marries, the widow has Sr. added to her
own name, or if she is the "head" of the family, she very
often omits all Christian names, and has her card engraved
"Mrs. Smith," and the son's wife calls herself Mrs. John
Hunter Smith. Smith is not a very good name as an
example, since no one could very well claim the distinction
of being *the* Mrs. Smith. It, however, illustrates the
point.

For the daughter-in-law to continue to use a card with
Jr. on it when her husband no longer uses Jr. on his,
is a mistake made by many people. A wife always bears
the name of her husband. To have a man and his mother
use cards engraved respectively Mr. J. H. Smith and
Mrs. J. H. Smith and the son's wife a card engraved Mrs.
J. H. Smith, Jr., would announce to whomever the three
cards were left upon, that Mr. and Mrs. Smith and *their*
daughter-in-law had called.

The cards of a young girl after she is sixteen have
always "Miss" before her name, which must be her real
and never a nick-name: Miss Sarah Smith, not Miss
Sally Smith.

The fact that a man's name has "Jr." added at the
end in no way takes the place of "Mr." His card should
be engraved Mr. John Hunter Smith, Jr., and his wife's

Mrs. John Hunter Smith, Jr. Some people have the "Jr." written out, "junior." It is not spelled with a capital J if written in full.

A boy puts Mr. on his cards when he leaves school, though many use cards without Mr. on them while in college. A doctor, or a judge, or a minister, or a military officer have their cards engraved with the abbreviation of their title: Dr. Henry Gordon; Judge Horace Rush; The Rev. William Goode; Col. Thomas Doyle.

The double card reads: Dr. and Mrs. Henry Gordon; Hon. and Mrs., etc.

A woman who has divorced her husband retains the legal as well as the social right to use her husband's full name, in New York State at least. Usually she prefers, if her name was Alice Green, to call herself Mrs. Green Smith; not Mrs. Alice Smith, and on no account Mrs. Alice Green—unless she wishes to give the impression that she was the guilty one in the divorce.

CHILDREN'S CARDS

That very little children should have visiting cards is not so "silly" as might at first thought be supposed. To acquire perfect manners, and those graces of deportment that Lord Chesterfield so ardently tried to instil into his son, training can not begin early enough, since it is through lifelong familiarity with the niceties of etiquette that much of the distinction of those to the manner born is acquired.

Many mothers think it good training for children to have their own cards, which they are taught not so much to leave upon each other after "parties," as to send with gifts upon various occasions.

At the rehearsal of a wedding, the tiny twin flower girls came carrying their wedding present for the bride between them, to which they had themselves attached their own small visiting cards. One card was bordered and engraved in pink, and the other bordered and engraved in blue, and the address on each read *"Chez Maman."*

And in going to see a new baby cousin each brought a small 1830 bouquet, and sent to their aunt their cards, on which, after seeing the baby, one had printed "He is very little," and the other, "It has a red face." This shows that if modern society believes in beginning social training in the nursery, it does not believe in hampering a child's natural expression.

SPECIAL CARDS AND WHEN TO USE THEM

The double card, reading Mr. and Mrs., is sent with a wedding present, or with flowers to a funeral, or with flowers to a débutante, and is also used in paying formal visits.

The card on which a débutante's name is engraved under that of her mother, is used most frequently when no coming-out entertainment has been given for the daughter. Her name on her mother's card announces, wherever it is left, that the daughter is "grown" and "eligible" for invitations. In the same way a mother may leave her son's card with her own upon any of her own friends—especially upon those likely to entertain for young people. This is the custom if a young man has been away at school and college for so long that he has not a large acquaintance of his own. It is, however, correct under any circumstances when formally leaving cards to leave those of all sons and daughters who are grown.

THE P. P. C. CARD

This is merely a visiting card, whether of a lady or a gentleman, on which the initials P. P. C. (*pour prendre congé*—to take leave) are written in ink in the lower left corner. This is usually left at the door, or sent by mail to acquaintances, when one is leaving for the season, or for good. It never takes the place of a farewell visit when one has received especial courtesy, nor is it in any sense a message of thanks for especial kindness. In either of these instances, a visit should be paid or a note of farewell and thanks written.

CARDS OF NEW OR TEMPORARY ADDRESS

In cities where there is no Social Register or other printed society list, one notifies acquaintances of a change of address by mailing a visiting card.

Cards are also sent, with a temporary address written in ink, when one is in a strange city and wishes to notify friends where one is stopping.

It is also quite correct for a lady to mail her card with her temporary address written on it to any gentleman whom she would care to see, and who she is sure would like to see her.

WHEN CARDS ARE SENT

When not intending to go to a tea or a wedding reception (the invitation to which did not have R. s. v. p. on it and require an answer), one should mail cards to the hostess so as to arrive on the morning of the entertainment. To a tea given for a débutante cards are enclosed in one envelope and addressed:

Mrs. Gilding
Miss Gilding

00 Fifth Avenue
New York

For a wedding reception, cards are sent to Mr. and Mrs. ————, the mother and father of the bride, and another set of cards sent to Mr. and Mrs. ————, the bride and bridegroom.

THE VISIT OF EMPTY FORM

Not so many years ago, a lady or gentleman, young girl or youth, who failed to pay her or his "party call" after having been invited to Mrs. Social-Leader's ball was left out of her list when she gave her next one. For the old-fashioned hostess kept her visiting list with the precision of a bookkeeper in a bank; everyone's credit was entered or cancelled according to the presence of her or his cards in the card receiver. Young people who liked to be asked to her house were apt to leave an extra one at the door, on occasion, so that theirs should not be among the missing when the new list for the season was made up—especially as the more important old ladies were very quick to strike a name off, but seldom if ever known to put one back.

But about twenty years ago the era of informality set in and has been gaining ground ever since. In certain cities old-fashioned hostesses, it is said, exclude delinquents. But New York is too exotic and intractable, and the too exacting hostess is likely to find her tapestried rooms rather empty, while the younger world of fashion flocks to the crystal-fountained ballroom of the new Spendeasy Westerns. And then, too, life holds so many other diversions and interests for the very type of youth which of necessity is the vital essence of all social gaiety. Society can have distinction and dignity without youth— but not gaiety. The country with its outdoor sports, its freedom from exacting conventions, has gradually deflected the interest of the younger fashionables, until at present they care very little whether Mrs. Toplofty and Mrs. Social-Leader ask them to their balls or not. They are glad enough to go, of course, but they don't care enough for invitations to pay dull visits and to live up to the conventions of "manners" that old-fashioned hostesses demand. And as these "rebels" are invariably the most attractive and the most eligible youths, it has become almost an issue; a hostess must in many cases either invite none but older people and the few young girls and men whose mothers have left cards for them, or ignore convention and invite the rebels.

In trying to find out where the present indifference started, many ascribe it to Bobo Gilding, to whom entering a great drawing-room was more suggestive of the daily afternoon tea ordeal of his early nursery days, than a voluntary act of pleasure. He was long ago one of the first to rebel against old Mrs. Toplofty's exactions of party calls, by saying he did not care in the least whether his great-aunt Jane Toplofty invited him to her stodgy old ball or not. And then Lucy Wellborn (the present Mrs. Bobo Gilding) did not care much to go either if none of her particular men friends were to be there. Little she cared to dance the cotillion with old Colonel Bluffington or to go to supper with that odious Hector Newman.

And so, beginning first with a few. gilded youths, then including young society, the habit has spread until the obligatory paying of visits by young girls and men has almost joined the once universal "day at home" as belonging to a past age. Do not understand by this that visits are never paid on other occasions. Visits to strangers, visits of condolence, and of other courtesies are still paid, quite as punctiliously as ever. But within the walls of society itself, the visit of formality is decreasing. One might almost say that in certain cities society has become a family affair. Its walls are as high as ever, higher perhaps to outsiders, but among its own members, such customs as keeping visiting lists and having days at home, or even knowing who owes a visit to whom, is not only unobserved but is unheard of.

But because punctilious card-leaving, visiting, and "days at home" have gone out of fashion in New York, is no reason why these really important observances should not be, or are not, in the height of fashion elsewhere. Nor, on the other hand, must anyone suppose because the younger fashionables in New York pay few visits and never have days at home, that they are a bit less careful about the things which they happen to consider essential to good-breeding.

The best type of young men pay few, if any, party calls, because they work and they exercise, and whatever time is left over, if any, is spent in their club or at the house of a young woman, not tête-a-tête, but invariably playing bridge. The Sunday afternoon visits that the youth of another generation used always to pay, are unknown in this, because every man who can, spends the week-end in the country.

It is scarcely an exaggeration to say that not alone men, but many young married women of highest social position, except to send with flowers or wedding presents, do not use a dozen visiting cards a year. But there are circumstances when even the most indifferent to social obligations must leave cards.

WHEN CARDS MUST BE LEFT

Etiquette absolutely demands that one leave a card within a few days after taking a first meal in a lady's house; or if one has for the first time been *invited* to lunch or dine with strangers, it is inexcusably rude not to leave a card upon them, whether one accepted the invitation or not.

One must also unfailingly return a first call, even if one does not care for the acquaintance. Only a real "cause" can excuse the affront to an innocent stranger that the refusal to return a first call would imply. If one does not care to continue the acquaintance, one need not pay a second visit.

Also a card is always left with a first invitation. Supposing Miss Philadelphia takes a letter of introduction to Mrs. Newport—Mrs. Newport, inviting Miss Philadelphia to her house, would not think of sending her invitation without also leaving her card. Good form demands that a visit be paid before issuing a *first invitation*. Sometimes a note of explanation is sent asking that the formality be waived, but it is *never* disregarded, except in the case of an invitation from an older lady to a young girl. Mrs. Worldly, for instance, who has known Jim Smartlington always, might, instead of calling on Mary Smith, to whom his engagement is announced, write her a note, asking her to lunch or dinner. But in inviting Mrs. Greatlake of Chicago she would leave her card with her invitation at Mrs. Greatlake's hotel.

It seems scarcely necessary to add that anyone not

entirely heartless must leave a card on, or send flowers to, an acquaintance who has suffered a recent bereavement. One should also leave cards of inquiry or send flowers to sick people.

INVITATION IN PLACE OF RETURNED VISIT

Books on etiquette seem agreed that sending an invitation does not cancel the obligation of paying a visit—which may be technically correct—but fashionable people, who are in the habit of lunching or dining with each other two or three times a season, pay no attention to visits whatever. Mrs. Norman calls on Mrs. Gilding. Mrs. Gilding invites the Normans to dinner. They go. A short time afterward Mrs. Norman invites the Gildings—or the Gildings very likely again invite the Normans. Some evening at all events, the Gildings dine with the Normans. Someday, if Mrs. Gilding happens to be leaving cards, she may leave them at the Normans—or she may not. Some people leave cards almost like the "hares" in a paper chase; others seldom if ever do. Except on the occasions mentioned in the paragraph before this, or unless there is an illness, a death, a birth, or a marriage, people in society invite each other to their houses and don't leave cards at all. Nor do they ever consider whose "turn" it is to invite whom.

"NOT AT HOME"

When a servant at a door says "Not at home," this phrase means that the lady of the house is "Not at home to visitors." This answer neither signifies nor implies—nor is it intended to—that Mrs. Jones is out of the house. Some people say "Not receiving," which means actually the same thing, but the "not at home" is infinitely more polite; since in the former you know she is in the house but won't see you, whereas in the latter case you have the pleasant uncertainty that it is quite possible she is out.

To be told "Mrs. Jones is at home but doesn't want to see you," would certainly be unpleasant. And to "beg

to be excused"—except in a case of illness or bereavement
—has something very suggestive of a cold shoulder.   But
"not at home" means that she is not sitting in the drawing
room behind her tea tray; that and nothing else.   She
may be out or she may be lying down or otherwise occupied.   Nor do people of the world find the slightest
objection if a hostess, happening to recognize the visitor
as a particular friend, calls out, "Do come in!   I *am* at
home to *you!*"   Anyone who talks about this phrase as
being a "white lie" either doesn't understand the meaning
of the words, or is going very far afield to look for
untruth.   To be consistent, these over-literals should also
exact that when a guest inadvertently knocks over a tea
cup and stains a sofa, the hostess instead of saying "It is
nothing at all!   Please don't worry about it," ought for
the sake of truth to say, "See what your clumsiness has
done!   You have ruined my sofa!"   And when someone
says "How are you?" instead of answering "Very well,
thank you," the same truthful one should perhaps take
an hour by the clock and mention every symptom of
indisposition that she can accurately subscribe to.

While "not at home" is merely a phrase of politeness,
to say "I am *out*" after a card has been brought to you
is both an untruth and an inexcusable rudeness.   Or to
have an inquiry answered, "I don't know, but I'll see,"
and then to have the servant, after taking a card, come
back with the message "Mrs. Jones is out" can not fail
to make the visitor feel rebuffed.   Once a card has been
admitted, the visitor *must* be admitted also, no matter how
inconvenient receiving her may be.   You may send a
message that you are dressing but will be very glad to
see her if she can wait ten minutes.   The visitor can
either wait or say she is pressed for time.   But if she
does not wait, then *she* is rather discourteous.

Therefore, it is of the utmost importance always to
leave directions at the door such as, "Mrs. Jones is not at
home."   "Miss Jones will be home at five o'clock," "Mrs.
Jones will be home at 5.30," or Mrs. Jones "is at home"
in the library to intimate friends, but "not at home" in

the drawing-room to acquaintances. It is a nuisance to be obliged to remember either to turn an "in" and "out" card in the hall, or to ring a bell and say, "I am going out," and again, "I have come in." But whatever plan or arrangement you choose, no one at your front door should be left in doubt and then repulsed. It is not only bad manners, it is bad housekeeping.

THE OLD-FASHIONED DAY AT HOME

It is doubtful if the present generation of New Yorkers knows what a day at home is! But their mothers, at least, remember the time when the fashionable districts were divided into regular sections, wherein on a given day in the week, the whole neighborhood was "at home." Friday sounds familiar as the day for Washington Square! And was it Monday for lower Fifth Avenue? At all events, each neighborhood on the day of its own, suggested a local fête. Ladies in visiting dresses with trains and bonnets and nose-veils and tight gloves, holding card cases, tripped demurely into this house, out of that, and again into another; and there were always many broughams and victorias slowly "exercising" up and down, and very smart footmen standing with maroon or tan or fur rugs over their arms in front of Mrs. Wellborn's house or Mrs. Oldname's, or the big house of Mrs. Toplofty at the corner of Fifth Avenue. It must have been enchanting to be a grown person in those days! Enchanting also were the C-spring victorias, as was life in general that was taken at a slow carriage pace and not at the motor speed of to-day. The "day at home" is still in fashion in Washington, and it is ardently to be hoped that it also flourishes in many cities and towns throughout the country or that it will be revived, for it is a delightful custom—though more in keeping with Europe than America, which does not care for gentle paces once it has tasted swift. A certain young New York hostess announced that she was going to stay home on Saturday afternoons. But the men went to the country and the women to the opera, and she gave it up.

There are a few old-fashioned ladies, living in old-fashioned houses, and still staying at home in the old-fashioned way to old-fashioned friends who for decades have dropped in for a cup of tea and a chat. And there are two maiden ladies in particular, joint chatelaines of an imposingly beautiful old house where, on a certain afternoon of the week, if you come in for tea, you are sure to meet not alone those prominent in the world of fashion, but a fair admixture of artists, scientists, authors, inventors, distinguished strangers—in a word Best Society in its truest sense. But days at home such as these are not easily duplicated; for few houses possess a "salon" atmosphere, and few hostesses achieve either the social talent or the wide cultivation necessary to attract and interest so varied and brilliant a company.

MODERN CARD LEAVING: A QUESTIONABLE ACT OF POLITENESS

The modern New York fashion in card-leaving is to dash as fast as possible from house to house, sending the chauffeur up the steps with cards, without ever asking if anyone is home. Some butlers announce "Not at home" from force of habit even when no question is asked. There are occasions when the visitors *must ask* to see the hostess (see page 88); but cards are left without asking whether a lady is at home under the following circumstances:

Cards are left on the mother of the bride, after a wedding, also on the mother of the groom.

Cards are also left after any formal invitation. Having been asked to lunch or dine with a lady whom you know but slightly you should leave your card whether you accepted the invitation or not, within three days if possible, or at least within a week, of the date for which you were invited. It is not considered necessary (in New York at least) to ask if she is at home; promptness in leaving your card is, in this instance, better manners than delaying your "party call" and asking if she is at home. This matter of asking at the door is one that depends upon the customs of each State and city, but as it is always wiser to err on the side of politeness, it is the better policy, if in doubt, to ask "Is Mrs. Blank at home?" rather than to run the risk of offending a lady who may like to see visitors.

A card is usually left with a first invitation to a stranger who has brought a letter of introduction, but it is more polite—even though not necessary—to ask to be received. Some ladies make it a habit to leave a card on everyone on their visiting list once a season.

It is correct for the mother of a débutante to leave her card as well as her daughter's on every lady who has invited the daughter to her house, and a courteous hostess returns all of these pasteboard visits. But neither visit necessitates closer or even further acquaintance.

VISITS WHICH EVERYONE MUST PAY

Paying visits differs from leaving cards in that you must ask to be received. A visit of condolence should be paid at once to a friend when a death occurs in her immediate family. A lady does not call on a gentleman, but writes him a note of sympathy.

In going to inquire for sick people, you should ask to be received, and it is always thoughtful to take them gifts of books or fruit or flowers.

If a relative announces his engagement, you must at once go to see his fiancée. Should she be out, you do not ask to see her mother. You do, however, leave a card upon both ladies and you ask to see her mother if received by the daughter.

A visit of congratulation is also paid to a new mother and a gift invariably presented to the baby.

MESSAGES WRITTEN ON CARDS

"With sympathy" or "With deepest sympathy" is written on your visiting card with flowers sent to a funeral. This same message is written on a card and left at the door of a house of mourning, if you do not know the family well enough to ask to be received.

"To inquire" is often written on a card left at the house of a sick person, but not if you are received.

In going to see a friend who is visiting a lady whom you do not know, whether you should leave a card on the hostess as well as on your friend depends upon the circumstances: if the hostess is one who is socially prominent and you are unknown, it would be better taste not to leave a card on her, since your card afterward found without explanation might be interpreted as an uncalled-for visit made in an attempt for a place on her list. If, on the other hand, she is the unknown person and you are the prominent one, your card is polite, but unwise unless you mean to include her name on your list. But if she is one with whom you have many interests in common, then you may very properly leave a card for her.

In leaving a card on a lady stopping at a hotel or living in an apartment house, you should write her name in pencil across the top of your card, to insure its being given to her, and not to some one else.

At the house of a lady whom you know well and whom you are sorry not to find at home, it is "friendly" to write "Sorry not to see you!" or "So sorry to miss you!"

Turning down a corner of a visiting card is by many intended to convey that the visit is meant for all the ladies in the family. Other people mean merely to show that the card was left at the door in person and not sent in an envelope. Other people turn them down from force of habit and mean nothing whatever. But whichever the reason, more cards are bent or dog-eared than are left flat.

ENGRAVED CARDS ANNOUNCING ENGAGEMENT, BAD FORM

Someone somewhere asked whether or not to answer an engraved card announcing an engagement. The answer can have nothing to do with etiquette, since an engraved announcement is unknown to good society. (For the proper announcement of an engagement see page 304.)

WHEN PEOPLE SEE THEIR FRIENDS

Five o'clock is the informal hour when people are "at home" to friends. The correct hour for leaving cards and paying formal visits is between 3.30 and 4.30. One should hesitate to pay a visit at the "tea hour" unless one is sure of one's welcome among the "intimates" likely to be found around the hostess's tea-table.

Many ladies make it their practise to be home if possible at five o'clock, and their friends who know them well come in at that time. (For the afternoon tea-table and its customs, see page 171.)

INFORMAL VISITING OFTEN ARRANGED BY TELEPHONE

For instance, instead of ringing her door-bell, Mrs. Norman calls Mrs. Kindhart on the telephone: "I haven't seen you for weeks! Won't you come in to tea, or to lunch—just you." Mrs. Kindhart answers, "Yes, I'd love to. I can come this afternoon"; and five o'clock finds them together over the tea-table.

In the same way young Struthers calls up Millicent Gilding, "Are you going to be in this afternoon?" She says, "Yes, but not until a quarter of six." He says, "Fine, I'll come then." Or she says, "I'm so sorry, I'm playing bridge with Pauline—but I'll be in tomorrow!" He says, "All right, I'll come to-morrow."

The younger people rarely ever go to see each other without first telephoning. Or since even young people seldom meet except for bridge, most likely it is Millicent Gilding who telephones the Struthers youth to ask if he can't possibly get uptown before five o'clock to make a fourth with Mary and Jim and herself.

HOW A FIRST VISIT IS MADE

In very large cities, neighbors seldom call on each other. But if strangers move into a neighborhood in a small town or in the country, or at a watering-place, it is not only unfriendly but uncivil for their neighbors not to call on them. The older residents always call on the newer. And the person of greatest social prominence should make the first visit, or at least invite the younger or less prominent one to call on her; which the younger should promptly do.

Or two ladies of equal age or position may either one say, "I wish you would come to see me." To which the other replies "I will with pleasure." More usually the first one offers "I should like to come to see you, if I may." And the other, of course, answers "I shall be delighted if you will."

The first one, having suggested going to see the second, is bound in politeness to do so, otherwise she implies that the acquaintance on second thought seems distasteful to her.

Everyone invited to a wedding should call upon the bride on her return from the honeymoon. And when a man marries a girl from a distant place, courtesy absolutely demands that his friends and neighbors call on her as soon as she arrives in her new home.

ON OPENING THE DOOR TO A VISITOR

On the hall table in every house, there should be a small silver, or other card tray, a pad and a pencil. The nicest kind of pad is one that when folded, makes its own envelope, so that a message when written need not be left open. There are all varieties and sizes at all stationers.

When the door-bell rings, the servant on duty, who can easily see the chauffeur or lady approaching, should have the card tray ready to present, on the palm of the left hand. A servant at the door must never take the cards in his or her fingers.

CORRECT NUMBER OF CARDS TO LEAVE

When the visitor herself rings the door-bell and the message is "not at home," the butler or maid proffers the card tray on which the visitor lays a card of her own and her daughter's for each lady in the house and a card of her husband's and son's for each lady and gentleman. But three is the greatest number ever left of any one card.   In calling on Mrs. Town, who has three grown daughters and her mother living in the house, and a Mrs. Stranger staying with her whom the visitor was invited to a luncheon to meet, a card on each would need a packet of six.   Instead, the visitor should leave three— one for Mrs. Town, one for all the other ladies of the house, and one for Mrs. Stranger.   In asking to be received, her query at the door should be "Are any of the ladies at home?"   Or in merely leaving her cards she should say "For all of the ladies."

WHEN THE CALLER LEAVES

The butler or maid must stand with the front door open until a visitor re-enters her motor, or if she is walking, until she has reached the sidewalk.   It is bad manners ever to close the door in a visitor's face.

When a chauffeur leaves cards, the door may be closed as soon as he turns away.

WHEN THE LADY OF THE HOUSE IS AT HOME

When the door is opened by a waitress or a parlor-maid and the mistress of the house is in the drawing-room, the maid says "This way, please," and leads the way. She goes as quickly as possible to present the card tray. The guest, especially if a stranger, lags in order to give the hostess time to read the name on the card.

The maid meanwhile moves aside, to make room for the approaching visitor, who goes forward to shake hands with the hostess.   If a butler is at the door, he reads the card himself, picking it up from the tray, and opening the door of the drawing-room announces: "Mrs. Soandso," after which he puts the card on the hall table.

The duration of a formal visit should be in the neighborhood of twenty minutes.   But if other visitors are announced, the first one—on a very formal occasion— may cut her visit shorter.   Or if conversation becomes especially interesting, the visit may be prolonged five minutes or so.   On no account must a visitor stay an hour! A hostess always rises when a visitor enters, unless the visitor is a very young woman or man and she herself elderly, or unless she is seated behind the tea-table so that rising is difficult. She should, however, always rise and go forward to meet a lady much older than herself; but she never rises from her tea-table to greet a man, unless he is quite old.

If the lady of the house is "at home" but upstairs, the servant at the door leads the visitor into the reception room, saying "Will you take a seat, please?" and then carries the card to the mistress of the house.

On an exceptional occasion, such as paying a visit of condolence or inquiring for a convalescent, when the question as to whether he will be received is necessarily doubtful, a gentleman does not take off his coat or gloves, but waits in the reception room with his hat in his hand. When the servant returning says either "Will you come this way, please?" or "Mrs. Town is not well enough to see any one, but Miss Alice will be down in a moment," the visitor divests himself of his coat and gloves, which the servant carries, as well as his hat, out to the front hall.

As said before, few men pay visits without first telephoning. But perhaps two or three times during a winter a young man, when he is able to get away from his office in time, will make a tea-time visit upon a hostess who has often invited him to dinner or to her opera box. Under ordinary circumstances, however, some woman member of his family leaves his card for him after a dinner or a dance, or else it is not left at all.

A gentleman paying visits, always asks if the hostess is at home. If she is, he leaves his hat and stick in the hall and also removes and leaves his gloves—and rubbers should he be wearing them. If the hour is between five and half-past, the hostess is inevitably at her tea-table, in the library, to which, if he is at all well known to the servant at the door, he is at once shown without being first asked to wait in the reception room. A gentleman entering a room in which there are several people who are strangers, shakes hands with his hostess and slightly bows to all the others, whether he knows them personally or not. He, of course, shakes hands with any who are friends, and with all men to whom he is introduced, but with a lady only if she offers him her hand.

HOW TO ENTER A DRAWING-ROOM

To know how to enter a drawing-room is supposed to be one of the supreme tests of good breeding. But there should be no more difficulty in entering the drawing-room of Mrs. Worldly than in entering the sitting-room at home. Perhaps the best instruction would be like that in learning to swim. "Take plenty of time, don't struggle and don't splash about!" Good manners socially are not unlike swimming—not the "crawl" or "overhand," but smooth, tranquil swimming. (Quite probably where the expression "in the swim" came from anyway!) Before actually entering a room, it is easiest to pause long enough to see where the hostess is. Never start forward and then try to find her as an afterthought. The place to pause is on the threshold—not half-way in the room. The way *not* to enter a drawing-room is to dart forward and then stand awkwardly bewildered and looking about in every direction. A man of the world stops at the entrance of the room for a scarcely perceptible moment, until he perceives the most unencumbered approach to the hostess, and he thereupon walks over to her. When he greets his hostess he pauses slightly, the hostess smiles and offers her hand; the gentleman smiles and shakes hands, at the same time bowing. A lady shakes hands with the hostess and with every one she knows who is nearby. She bows to acquaintances at a distance and to strangers to whom she is introduced.

HOW TO SIT GRACEFULLY

Having shaken hands with the hostess, the visitor, whether a lady or a gentleman, looks about quietly, without hurry, for a convenient chair to sit down upon, or drop into. To sit gracefully one should not perch stiffly on the edge of a straight chair, nor sprawl at length in an easy one. The perfect position is one that is easy, but dignified. In other days, no lady of dignity ever crossed her knees, held her hands on her hips, or twisted herself sideways, or even *leaned back in her chair!* To-day all these things are done; and the only etiquette left is on the subject of how not to exaggerate them. No lady should cross her knees so that her skirts go up to or above them; neither should her foot be thrust out so that her toes are at knee level. An arm a-kimbo is *not* a graceful attitude, nor is a twisted spine! Everyone, of course, leans against a chair back, except in a box at the opera and in a ballroom, but a lady should never throw herself almost at full length in a reclining chair or on a wide sofa when she is out in public. Neither does a gentleman in paying a formal visit sit on the middle of his backbone with one ankle supported on the other knee, and both as high as his head.

The proper way for a lady to sit is in the center of her chair, or slightly sideways in the corner of a sofa. She may lean back, of course, and easily; her hands relaxed in her lap, her knees together, or if crossed, her foot must not be thrust forward so as to leave a space between the heel and her other ankle. On informal occasions she can lean back in an easy chair with her hands on the arms. In a ball dress a lady of distinction never leans back in a chair; one can not picture a beautiful and high-bred woman, wearing a tiara and other ballroom jewels, leaning against anything. This is, however, not so much a rule of etiquette as a question of beauty and fitness.

A gentleman, also on very formal occasions, should sit in the center of his chair; but unless it is a deep lounging one, he always leans against the back and puts a hand or an elbow on its arms.

POSTSCRIPTS ON VISITS

A lady never calls on another under the sponsorship of a gentleman—unless he is her husband or father. A young girl can very properly go with her fiancé to return visits paid to her by members or friends of his family; but she should not pay an initial visit unless to an invalid who has written her a note asking her to do so.

If, when arriving at a lady's house, you find her motor

at the door, you should leave your card as though she were not at home. If she happens to be in the hall, or coming down the steps, you say "I see you are going out, and I won't keep you!"

If she insists on your coming in, you should stay only a moment. Do not, however, fidget and talk about leaving. Sit down as though your leaving immediately were not on your mind, but after two or three minutes say "Good-by" and go.

A young man may go to see a young girl as often as he feels inclined and she cares to receive him. If she continually asks to be excused, or shows him scant attention when he is talking to her, or in any other way indicates that he annoys or bores her, his visits should cease.

It is very bad manners to invite one person to your house and leave out another with whom you are also talking. You should wait for an opportunity when the latter is not included in your conversation.

In good society ladies do not kiss each other when they meet either at parties or in public.

It is well to remember that nothing more blatantly stamps an ill-bred person than the habit of patting, nudging or taking hold of people. "Keep your hands to yourself!" might almost be put at the head of the first chapter of every book on etiquette.

Be very chary of making any such remarks as "I am afraid I have stayed too long," or "I must apologize for hurrying off," or "I am afraid I have bored you to death talking so much." All such expressions are self-conscious and stupid. If you really think you are staying too long or leaving too soon or talking too much—don't!

AN INVALID'S VISIT BY PROXY

It is not necessary that an invalid make any attempt to return the visits to her friends who are attentive enough to go often to see her. But if a stranger calls on her—particularly a stranger who may not know that she is always confined to the house, it is correct for a daughter or sister or even a friend to leave the invalid's card for her and even to pay a visit should she find a hostess "at home." In this event the visitor by proxy lays her own card as well as that of the invalid on the tray proffered her. Upon being announced to the hostess, she naturally explains that she is appearing in place of her mother (or whatever relation the invalid is to her) and that the invalid herself is unable to make any visits.

A lady never pays a party call on a gentleman. But if the gentleman who has given a dinner has his mother (or sister) staying with him and if the mother (or sister) chaperoned the party, cards should of course be left upon her.

Having risen to go, *go!* Don't stand and keep your hostess standing while you say good-by, and make a last remark last half an hour!

Few Americans are so punctilious as to pay their dinner calls within twenty-four hours; but it is the height of correctness and good manners.

When a gentleman, whose wife is away, accepts some one's hospitality, it is correct for his wife to pay the party call with (or for) him, since it is taken for granted that she would have been included had she been at home.

In other days a hostess thought it necessary to change quickly into a best dress if important company rang her door-bell. A lady of fashion to-day receives her visitors at once in whatever dress she happens to be wearing, since not to keep them waiting is the greater courtesy.

CHAPTER XI

INVITATIONS, ACCEPTANCES AND REGRETS

THE FORMAL INVITATION

As an inheritance from the days when Mrs. Brown presented her compliments and begged that Mrs. Smith would do her the honor to take a dish of tea with her, we still—notwithstanding the present flagrant disregard of old-fashioned convention—send our formal invitations, acceptances and regrets, in the prescribed punctiliousness of the third person.

All formal invitations, whether they are to be engraved or to be written by hand (and their acceptances and regrets) are invariably in the third person, and good usage permits of no deviation from this form.

WEDDING INVITATIONS

The invitation to the ceremony is engraved on the front sheet of white note-paper. The smartest, at present, is that with a raised margin—or plate mark. At the top of the sheet the crest (if the family of the bride has the right to use one) is embossed without color. Otherwise the invitation bears no device. The engraving may be in script, block, shaded block, or old English. The invitation to the ceremony should always request "the honour" of your "presence," and never the "pleasure" of your "company." (Honour is spelled in the old-fashioned way, with a "u" instead of "honor.")

Enclosed in Two Envelopes

Two envelopes are never used except for wedding invitations or announcements; but wedding invitations and all accompaning cards are always enclosed first in an inner envelope that has no mucilage on the flap, and is superscribed "Mr. and Mrs. Jameson Greatlake," without address. This is enclosed in an outer envelope which is sealed and addressed:

Mr. and Mrs. Jameson Greatlake,

24 Michigan Avenue,

Chicago.

To those who are only "asked to the church" no house invitation is enclosed.

THE CHURCH INVITATION

The proper form for an invitation to a church ceremony is:

(Form No. 1.)

Mr. and Mrs. John Huntington Smith

request the honour of your presence

at the marriage of their daughter

Mary Katherine

to

Mr. James Smartlington

on Tuesday the first of November

at twelve o'clock

at St. John's Church

in the City of New York

(Form No. 2.)

Mr. and Mrs. John Huntington Smith

request the honour of

Miss Pauline Town's

presence at the marriage of their daughter

Mary Katherine

to

Mr. James Smartlington

on Tuesday the first of November

at twelve o'clock

at St. John's Church

(The size of invitations is 5⅛ wide by 7⅜ deep.)

(When the parents issue the invitations for a wedding at a house other than their own.)

Mr. and Mrs. Richard Littlehouse

request the honour of

presence at the marriage of their daughter

Betty

to

Mr. Frederic Robinson

on Saturday the fifth of November

at four o'clock

at the house of Mr. and Mrs. Sterlington

Tuxedo Park

New York

R. s. v. p.

No variation is permissible in the form of a wedding invitation. Whether fifty guests are to be invited or five thousand, the paper, the engraving and the wording, and the double envelope are precisely the same.

Church Card of Admittance

In cities or wherever the general public is not to be admitted, a card of about the size of a small visiting card is enclosed with the church invitation:

**Please present this card
at St. John's Church
on Tuesday the first of November**

Cards to Reserved Pews

To the family and very intimate friends who are to be seated in especially designated pews:

**Please present this to an usher
Pew No........ ..
on Thursday the ninth of May**

Engraved pew cards are ordered only for very big weddings where twenty or more pews are to be reserved. The more usual custom—at all small and many big weddings— is for the mother of the bride, and the mother of the bridegroom each to write on her personal visiting card:

Pew No. 7

Mrs. John Huntington Smith

FOUR WEST THIRTY-SIXTH STREET

A card for the reserved enclosure but no especial pew is often inscribed "Within the Ribbons."

INVITATION TO THE HOUSE

The invitation to the breakfast or reception following the church ceremony is engraved on a card to match the paper of the church invitation and is the size of the latter after it is folded for the envelope:

Mr. and Mrs. John Huntington Smith
request the pleasure of

Mr. Mrs. James Greatlake's

company on Tuesday the first of November
at half after four o'clock
at Four West Thirty-sixth Street

R. s. v. p.

CEREMONY AND RECEPTION INVITATION IN ONE

Occasionally, especially for a country wedding, the invitation to the breakfast or the reception is added to the one to the ceremony:

Mr. and Mrs. Alexander Chatterton

request the honour of

Mr & Mrs Worldly's

presence at the marriage of their daughter

Hester

to

Mr. James Town, junior

on Tuesday the first of June

at three o'clock

at St. John's Church

and afterwards at Sunnylawn

Ridgefield

R. s. v. p.

Or the invitation reads "at twelve o'clock, at St. John's Church, and afterwards at breakfast at Sunnylawn"; but "afterwards to the reception at Sunnylawn" is wrong.

THE INVITATION TO A HOUSE WEDDING

Is precisely the same except that "at Sunnylawn" or "at Four West Thirty-sixth Street" is put in place of "at St. John's Church," and an invitation to stay on at a house, to which the guest is already invited, is not necessary.

The Train Card

If the wedding is to be in the country, a train card is enclosed:

> A special train will leave Grand Central Station at 12:45 P.M., arriving at Ridgefield at 2:45. Returning, train will leave Ridgefield at 5:10 P.M., arriving New York at 7.02 P.M.
>
> *Show this card at the gate.*

INVITATION TO RECEPTION AND NOT TO CEREMONY

It sometimes happens that the bride prefers none but her family at the ceremony, and a big reception. This plan is chosen where the mother of the bride or other very near relative is an invalid. The ceremony may take place at a bedside, or it may be that the invalid can go down to the drawing-room with only the immediate families, and is unequal to the presence of many people.

Under these circumstances the invitations to the breakfast or reception are sent on sheets of note paper like that used for church invitations, but the wording is:

Mr. and Mrs. Grantham Jones

request the pleasure of your company

at the wedding breakfast of their daughter

Muriel

and

Mr. Burlingame Ross, Jr.

on Saturday the first of November

at one o'clock

at Four East Thirty-Eighth Street

**The favor of an
answer is requested**

The "pleasure of your company" is requested in this case instead of the "honour of your presence."

If a wedding is to be so small that no invitations are engraved, the notes of invitation should be personally written by the bride:

Sally Dear:

Our wedding is to be on Thursday the tenth at half-past twelve, Christ Church Chantry. Of course we want you and Jack and the children! And we want all of you to come afterward to Aunt Mary's, for a bite to eat and to wish us luck.

Affectionately,

Helen.

or

Dear Mrs. Kindhart:

Dick and I are to be married at Christ Church Chantry at noon on Thursday the tenth. We both want you and Mr. Kindhart to come to the church and afterward for a very small breakfast to my Aunt's—Mrs. Slade—at Two Park Avenue. With much love from us both,

Affectionately,

Helen.

WEDDING ANNOUNCEMENTS

If no general invitations were issued to the church, an announcement engraved on note paper like that of the invitation to the ceremony, is sent to the entire visiting list of both the bride's and the groom's family:

Mr. and Mrs. Maynard Barnes

have the honour to announce

the marriage of their daughter

Priscilla

to

Mr. Eben Hoyt Leaming

on Tuesday the twenty-sixth of April

One thousand nine hundred and twenty-two

in the City of New York

THE SECOND MARRIAGE

INVITATIONS

Invitations to the marriage of a widow—if she is very young—are sent in the name of her parents exactly as were the invitations to her first wedding, excepting that her name instead of being merely Priscilla is now written Priscilla Barnes Leaming, thus:

Mr. and Mrs. Maynard Barnes
request the honour of your presence
at the marriage of their daughter
Priscilla Barnes Leaming

to

etc.

ANNOUNCEMENTS

For a young widow's marriage are also the same as for a first wedding:

Mr. and Mrs. Maynard Barnes
have the honour to announce
the marriage of their daughter
Priscilla Barnes Leaming
to
Mr. Worthington Adams

etc.

But the announcement of the marriage of a widow of maturer years is engraved on note paper and reads:

Mrs. Priscilla Barnes Leaming

and

Mr. Worthington Adams

have the honour to announce their marriage

on Monday the second of November

at Saratoga Springs

New York

CARDS OF ADDRESS

If the bride and groom wish to inform their friends of their future address (especially in cities not covered by the Social Register), it is customary to enclose a card with the announcement:

Mr. and Mrs. Worthington Adams
will be at home
after the first of December
at Twenty-five Alderney Place

Or merely their visiting card with their new address in the lower right corner:

Mr. and Mrs. Worthington Adams

25 ALDERNEY PLACE

INVITATION TO WEDDING ANNIVERSARY

For a wedding anniversary celebration, the year of the wedding and the present year are usually stamped across the top of an invitation. Sometimes the couple's initials are added.

1898-1922

Mr. and Mrs. Alvin Johnson

request the pleasure of

[signature]

company at the

Twenty-fifth Anniversary of their marriage

on Wednesday the first of June

at nine o'clock

Twenty-four Austin Avenue

R. s. v. p.

ANSWERING A WEDDING INVITATION

An invitation to the church only requires no answer whatever. An invitation to the reception or breakfast is answered on the first page of a sheet of note paper, and although it is written "by hand" the spacing of the words must be followed as though they were engraved. This is the form of acceptance:

Mr. and Mrs. Robert Gilding, Jr.,

accept with pleasure

Mr. and Mrs. John Huntington Smith's

kind invitation for

Tuesday the first of June

The regret reads:

Mr. and Mrs. Richard Brown

regret that they are unable to accept

Mr. and Mrs. John Huntington Smith's

kind invitation for

Tuesday the first of June

OTHER FORMAL INVITATIONS

All other formal invitations are engraved (never printed) on cards of thin white matte Bristol board, either plain or plate-marked like those for wedding reception cards. Note paper such as that used for wedding invitations is occasionally, but rarely, preferred.

Monograms, addresses, personal devices are not used on engraved invitations.

The size of the card of invitation varies with personal preference from four and a half to six inches in width, and from three to four and a half inches in height. The most graceful proportion is three units in height to four in width.

The lettering is a matter of personal choice, but the plainer the design, the better. Scrolls and ornate trimmings are bad taste always. Punctuation is used only after each letter of the R.s.v.p. and it is absolutely correct to use small letters for the s.v.p. Capitals R.S.V.P. are permissible; but fastidious people prefer "R.s.v.p."

INVITATION TO A BALL

The word "ball" is never used excepting in an invitation to a public one, or at least a semi-public one, such as may be given by a committee for a charity or a club, or association of some sort.

For example:

The Committee of the Greenwood Club

request the pleasure of your company

at a Ball

to be held in the Greenwood Clubhouse

on the evening of November the seventh

at ten o'clock.

for the benefit of

The Neighborhood Hospital

Tickets five dollars

Invitations to a private ball, no matter whether the ball is to be given in a private house, or whether the hostess has engaged an entire floor of the biggest hotel in the world, announce merely that Mr. and Mrs. Somebody will be "At Home," and the word "dancing" is added almost as though it were an afterthought. in the lower left corner, the words "At Home" being slightly larger than those of the rest of the invitation. When both "At" and "Home" are written with a capital letter, this is the most punctilious and formal invitation that it is possible to send. It is engraved in script usually, on a card of white Bristol board about five and a half inches wide and three and three-quarters of an inch high. Like the wedding invitation it has an embossed crest without color, or nothing.

The precise form is:

Mr. and Mrs. Titherington de Puyster

At Home

On Monday the third of January

at ten o'clock

One East Fiftieth Street

The favour of an answer
is requested   *Dancing*

or

Mr. and Mrs. Davis Jefferson

At Home

On Monday the third of January

at ten o'clock

Town and Country Club

Kindly send reply to
Three Mt. Vernon Square   *Dancing*

(If preferred, the above invitations may be engraved in block or shaded block type.)

BALL FOR DÉBUTANTE DAUGHTER

Very occasionally an invitation is worded

Mr. and Mrs. Davis Jefferson

Miss Alice Jefferson

At Home

if the daughter is a débutante and the ball is for her, but it is not strictly correct to have any names but those of the host and his wife above the words "At Home."

The proper form of invitation when the ball is to be given for a débutante, is as follows:

Mr. and Mrs. de Puyster

request the pleasure of

Miss Rosalie Gray's

company at a dance in honour of their daughter

Miss Alice de Puyster

on Monday evening, the third of January

at ten o'clock

One East Fiftieth Street

R.s.v.p.

or

Mr. and Mrs. Titherington de Puyster
Miss Alice de Puyster
request the pleasure of

Mr & Mrs Greatlakes

company on Monday evening the third of January
at ten o'oclock
One East Fiftieth Street

Dancing
R. s. v. p.

The form most often used by fashionable hostesses in
New York and Newport is:

Mr. and Mrs. Gilding

request the pleasure of

company at a small dance

on Monday the first of January

at Ought Ought Fifth Avenue

Even if given for a débutante daughter, her name does not appear, and it is called a "small dance," whether it is really small or big. The request for a reply is often omitted, since everyone is supposed to know that an answer is necessary. But if the dance, or dinner, or whatever the entertainment is to be, is given at one address and the hostess lives at another, both addresses are always given:

Mr. and Mrs. Sidney Oldname

request the pleasure of

company at a dance

on Monday evening the sixth of January

at ten o'clock

The Fitz-Cherry

Kindly send response to
Brookmeadows
L. I.

If the dance is given for a young friend who is not a relative, Mr. and Mrs. Oldname's invitations should

request the pleasure of

company at a dance in honour of

Miss Rosalie Grey

WHEN AND HOW ONE MAY ASK FOR AN INVITATION
FOR A STRANGER

One may never ask for an invitation for oneself anywhere! And one may not ask for an invitation to a luncheon or a dinner for a stranger. But an invitation for any general entertainment may be asked for a stranger —especially for a house-guest.

Example:

Dear Mrs. Worldly,

A young cousin of mine, David Blakely from Chicago, is staying with us.

May Pauline take him to your dance on Friday? If it will be inconvenient for you to include him, please do not hesitate to say so frankly.

Very sincerely yours,

Caroline Robinson Town.

Answer:

Dear Mrs. Town,

I shall be delighted to have Pauline bring Mr. Blakely on the tenth.
Sincerely yours,

Edith Worldly.

Or

A man might write for an invitation for a friend. But a very young girl should not ask for an invitation for a man—or anyone—since it is more fitting that her mother ask for her. An older girl might say to Mrs. Worldly, "My cousin is staying with us, may I bring him to your dance?" Or if she knows Mrs. Worldly very well she might send a message by telephone: "Miss Town would like to know whether she may bring her cousin, Mr. Michigan, to Mrs. Worldly's dance."

CARD OF GENERAL INVITATION

Invitations to important entertainments are nearly always especially engraved, so that nothing is written except the name of the person invited; but, for the hostess who entertains constantly, a card which is engraved in blank, so that it may serve for dinner, luncheon, dance, garden party, musical, or whatever she may care to give, is indispensable.

The spacing of the model shown below, the proportion of the words, and the size of the card, are especially good.

Mrs. Stevens

requests the pleasure of

company at

on

at   **o'clock**

Two Elm Place

The blank which may be used only for dinner:

Mr. and Mrs. Huntington Jones

request the pleasure of

company at dinner

on

at eight o'clock

at Two Thousand Fifth Avenue

(*For type and spacing follow model on p.* 118.)

INVITATIONS TO RECEPTIONS AND TEAS

Invitations to receptions and teas differ from invitations to balls in that the cards on which they are engraved are usually somewhat smaller, the words "At Home" with capital letters are changed to "will be at home" with small letters, and the time is not set at the hour. Also, except on very unusual occasions, a man's name does not appear. The name of the débutante for whom the tea is given is put under that of her mother, and sometimes under that of her sister or the bride of her brother.

Mrs. James Town

Mrs. James Town, junior

Miss Pauline Town

will be at home

On Tuesday the eighth of December

from four until six o'clock

Two Thousand Fifth Avenue.

Mr. Town's name would probably appear with that of his wife if he were an artist, and the reception was given in his studio to view his pictures, or if a reception were given to meet a distinguished guest such as a bishop or a governor, in which case "In honour of the Right Reverend William Powell," or "To meet His Excellency the Governor," is at the top of the invitation.

THE FORMAL INVITATION WHICH IS WRITTEN

When the formal invitation to dinner or lunch is written instead of engraved, note paper stamped with house or personal device is used. The wording and spacing must follow the engraved models exactly.

350 PARK AVENUE

Mr. and Mrs. John Kindhart

request the pleasure of

Mr. and Mrs. Robert Gilding Jr.'s

company at dinner

on Tuesday the sixth of December

at eight o'clock.

It must *not* be written:

350 PARK AVENUE
TELEPHONE 7572 PLAZA

The foregoing example has four faults:

(1) Letters in the third person must follow the prescribed form. This does not. (2) The writing is crowded against the margin. (3) The telephone number should be used only for business and informal notes and letters. (4) The full name John should be used instead of the initial "J." "Mr. and Mrs." is better form than "Mr. & Mrs."

RECALLING AN INVITATION

If for illness or other reason invitations have to be recalled the following forms are correct. They are always printed instead of engraved, there being no time for engraving.

Owing to sudden illness

Mr. and Mrs. John Huntington Smith

are obliged to recall their invitations

for Tuesday the tenth of June.

The form used when the invitation is postponed:

Mr. and Mrs. John Huntington Smith

regret exceedingly

that owing to the illness of Mrs. Smith

their dance is temporarily postponed.

When a wedding is broken off after the invitations have been issued:

Mr. and Mrs. Benjamin Nottingham

announce

that the marriage of their daughter

Mary Katharine

and

Mr. Jerrold Atherton

will not take place

FORMAL ACCEPTANCE OR REGRET

Acceptances or regrets are always written. An engraved form to be filled in is vulgar—nothing could be in worse taste than to flaunt your popularity by announcing that it is impossible to answer your numerous invitations without the time-saving device of a printed blank. If you have a dozen or more invitations a day, if you have a hundred, hire a staff of secretaries if need be, but answer "by hand."

The formal acceptance to an invitation, whether it is to a dance, wedding breakfast or a ball, is identical:

Mr. and Mrs. Donald Lovejoy
accept with pleasure
Mr. and Mrs. Smith's
kind invitation for dinner
on Monday the tenth of December
at eight o'clock

The formula for regret:

Mr. Clubwin Doe
regrets extremely that a previous engagement
prevents his accepting
Mr. and Mrs. Smith's
kind invitation for dinner
on Monday the tenth of December

or

Mr. and Mrs. Timothy Kerry
regret that they are unable to accept
Mr. and Mrs. Smith's
kind invitation for dinner
on Monday the tenth of December

In accepting an invitation the day and hour must be repeated, so that in case of mistake it may be rectified and prevent one from arriving on a day when one is not expected. But in declining an invitation it is not necessary to repeat the hour.

VISITING CARD INVITATIONS

With the exception of invitations to house-parties, din-ners and luncheons, the writing of notes is past. For an informal dance, musical, picnic, for a tea to meet a guest, or for bridge, a lady uses her ordinary visiting card:

> To meet
> Miss Millicent Gilding
>
> MRS. JOHN KINDHART
>
> Tues. Jan. 7.
> Dancing at 10. o'ck.
>
> 350 PARK AVENUE

or

> Wed. Jan. 8.
> Bridge at 4. o'ck.
>
> MRS. JOHN KINDHART
>
> R.s.v.p.   350 PARK AVENUE

Answers to invitations written on visiting cards are always formally worded in the third person, precisely as though the invitation had been engraved.

INVITATIONS IN THE SECOND PERSON

The informal dinner and luncheon invitation is not spaced according to set words on each line, but is written merely in two paragraphs. Example:

Dear Mrs. Smith:

Will you and Mr. Smith dine with us on Thursday, the seventh of January, at eight o'clock?

Hoping so much for the pleasure of seeing you,

Very sincerely,

Caroline Robinson Town.

THE INFORMAL NOTE OF ACCEPTANCE OR REGRET

Dear Mrs. Town:

It will give us much pleasure to dine with you on Thursday the seventh, at eight o'clock.

Thanking you for your kind thought of us,

Sincerely yours,

Margaret Smith.

Wednesday.

or

Dear Mrs. Town:

My husband and I will dine with you on Thursday the seventh, at eight o'clock, with greatest pleasure.

Thanking you so much for thinking of us,

Always sincerely,

Margaret Smith.

or

Dear Mrs. Town:

We are so sorry that we shall be unable to dine with you on the seventh, as we have a previous engagement.

With many thanks for your kindness in thinking of us,

Very sincerely,

Ethel Norman.

INVITATION TO COUNTRY HOUSE

To an intimate friend:

Dear Sally:

Will you and Jack (and the baby and nurse, of course) come out the 28th (Friday), and stay for ten days? Morning and evening trains take only forty minutes, and it won't hurt Jack to commute for the weekdays between the two Sundays! I am sure the country will do you and the baby good, or at least it will do me good to have you here.

With much love, affectionately,

Ethel Norman.

To a friend of one's daughter:

Dear Mary:

Will you and Jim come on Friday the first for the Worldly dance, and stay over Sunday? Muriel asks me to tell you that Helen and Dick, and also Jimmy Smith are to be here and she particularly hopes that you will come, too.

The three-twenty from New York is the best train—much. Though there is a four-twenty and a five-sixteen, in case Jim is not able to take the earlier one.

Very sincerely,

Alice Jones.

Confirming a verbal invitation:

Dear Helen:

This note is merely to remind you that you and Dick are coming here for the Worldly dance on the sixth. Mother is expecting you on the three-twenty train, and will meet you here at the station.

Affectionately,

Muriel.

Invitation to a house party at a camp:

Dear Miss Strange:

Will you come up here on the sixth of September and stay until the sixteenth? It would give us all the greatest pleasure.

There is a train leaving Broadway Station at 8.03 A. M. which will get you to Dustville Junction at 5 P. M. and here in time for supper.

It is only fair to warn you that the camp is very primitive; we have no luxuries, but we can make you fairly comfortable if you like an outdoor life and are not too exacting. Please do not bring a maid or any clothes that the woods or weather can ruin. You will need nothing but outdoor things: walking boots (if you care to walk), a bathing suit (if you care to swim in the lake), and something comfortable rather than smart for evening (if you care to dress for supper). But on no account bring evening, or any *good* clothes!

Hoping so much that camping appeals to you and that we shall see you on the evening of the sixth,

Very sincerely yours,

Martha Kindhart.

THE INVITATION BY TELEPHONE

Custom which has altered many ways and manners has taken away all opprobrium from the message by telephone, and with the exception of those of a very small minority of letter-loving hostesses, all informal invitations are sent and answered by telephone. Such messages, however, follow a prescribed form:

"Is this Lenox 0000? Will you please ask Mr. and Mrs. Smith if they will dine with Mrs. Grantham Jones next Tuesday the tenth at eight o'clock? Mrs. Jones' telephone number is Plaza, one two ring two."

The answer:

"Mr. and Mrs. Huntington Smith regret that they will be unable to dine with Mrs. Jones on Tuesday the tenth, as they are engaged for that evening.

Or

"Will you please tell Mrs. Jones that Mr. and Mrs. Huntington Smith are very sorry that they will be unable to dine with her next Tuesday, and thank her for asking them."

Or

"Please tell Mrs. Jones that Mr. and Mrs. Huntington Smith will dine with her on Tuesday the tenth, with pleasure."

The formula is the same, whether the invitation is to dine or lunch, or play bridge or tennis, or golf, or motor, or go on a picnic.

"Will Mrs. Smith play bridge with Mrs. Grantham Jones this afternoon at the Country Club, at four o'clock?"

"Hold the wire please * * * Mrs. Jones will play bridge with pleasure at four o'clock."

In many houses, especially where there are several grown sons or daughters, a blank form is kept in the pantry:

Will

               with M

on   the

at   o'clock.   Telephone number

         Accept

         Regret

These slips are taken to whichever member of the family has been invited, who crosses off "regret" or "accept" and hands the slip back for transmission by the butler, the parlor-maid or whoever is on duty in the pantry.

If Mr. Smith and Mrs. Jones are themselves telephoning there is no long conversation, but merely:

Mrs. Jones:

"Is that you Mrs. Smith (or Sarah)? This is Mrs. Jones (or Alice). Will you and your husband (or John) dine with us to-morrow at eight o'clock?"

Mrs. Smith:

"I'm so sorry we can't. We are dining with Mabel."

Or

"We have people coming here."

Invitations to a house party are often as not telephoned:

"Hello, Ethel? This is Alice. Will you and Arthur come on the sixteenth for over Sunday?"

"The sixteenth? That's Friday. We'd love to!"

"Will you take the 3:20 train? etc."

"A GEM OF A HOUSE MAY BE NO SIZE AT ALL, BUT ITS LINES ARE HONEST, AND ITS PAINTING AND WINDOW CURTAINS IN GOOD TASTE. . . . AND ITS BELL IS ANSWERED PROMPTLY BY A TRIM MAID WITH A LOW VOICE AND QUIET, COURTEOUS MANNER." [Page 131.]

CHAPTER XII

THE WELL-APPOINTED HOUSE

Every house has an outward appearance to be made as presentable as possible, an interior continually to be set in order, and incessantly to be cleaned. And for those that dwell within it there are meals to be prepared and served; linen to be laundered and mended; personal garments to be brushed and pressed; and perhaps children to be cared for. There is also a door-bell to be answered in which manners as well as appearance come into play.

Beyond these fundamental necessities, luxuries can be added indefinitely, such as splendor of architecture, of gardening, and of furnishing, with every refinement of service that executive ability can produce. With all this genuine splendor possible only to the greatest establishments, a little house can no more compete than a diamond weighing but half a carat can compete with a stone weighing fifty times as much. And this is a good simile, because the perfect little house may be represented by a corner cut from precisely the same stone and differing therefore merely in size (and value naturally), whereas the house in bad taste and improperly run may be represented by a diamond that is off color and full of flaws; or in some instances, merely a piece of glass that to none but those as ignorant as its owner, for a moment suggests a gem of value.

A gem of a house may be no size at all, but its lines are honest, and its painting and window curtains in good taste. As for its upkeep, its path or sidewalk is beautifully neat, steps scrubbed, brasses polished, and its bell answered promptly by a trim maid with a low voice and quiet courteous manner; all of which contributes to the impression of "quality" even though it in nothing suggests the luxury of a palace whose opened bronze door reveals a row of powdered footmen.

But the "mansion" of bastard architecture and crude

paint, with its brass indifferently clean, with coarse lace behind the plate glass of its golden-oak door, and the bell answered at eleven in the morning by a butler in an ill-fitting dress suit and wearing a mustache, might as well be placarded: "Here lives a vulgarian who has never had an opportunity to acquire cultivation." As a matter of fact, the knowledge of how to make a house distinguished both in appearance and in service, is a much higher test than presenting a distinguished appearance in oneself and acquiring presentable manners. There are any number of people who dress well, and in every way appear well, but a lack of breeding is apparent as soon as you go into their houses. Their servants have not good manners, they are not properly turned out, the service is not well done, and the decorations and furnishings show lack of taste and inviting arrangement.

The personality of a house is indefinable, but there never lived a lady of great cultivation and charm whose home, whether a palace, a farm-cottage or a tiny apartment, did not reflect the charm of its owner. Every visitor feels impelled to linger, and is loath to go. Houses without personality are a series of rooms with furniture in them. Sometimes their lack of charm is baffling; every article is "correct" and beautiful, but one has the feeling that the decorator made chalk-marks indicating the exact spot on which each piece of furniture is to stand. Other houses are filled with things of little intrinsic value, often with much that is shabby, or they are perhaps empty to the point of bareness, and yet they have that "inviting" atmosphere, and air of unmistakable quality which is an unfailing indication of high-bred people.

"BECOMING" FURNITURE

Suitability is the test of good taste always. The manner to the moment, the dress to the occasion, the article to the place, the furniture to the background. And yet to combine many periods in one and commit no anachronism, to put something French, something Spanish, something Italian, and something English into an American house and

"THE PERSONALITY OF A HOUSE IS INDEFINABLE, BUT THERE NEVER LIVED A LADY OF GREAT CULTIVATION AND CHARM WHOSE HOME, WHETHER A PALACE, A FARM-COTTAGE OR A TINY APARTMENT, DID NOT REFLECT THE CHARM OF ITS OWNER."

[Page 132.]

have the result the perfection of American taste—is a feat of legerdemain that has been accomplished time and again.

A woman of great taste follows fashion in house furnishing, just as she follows fashion in dress, in general principles only. She wears what is becoming to her own type, and she puts in her house only such articles as are becoming to it.

That a quaint old-fashioned house should be filled with quaint old-fashioned pieces of furniture, in size proportionate to the size of the rooms, and that rush-bottomed chairs and rag-carpets have no place in a marble hall, need not be pointed out. But to an amazing number of persons, proportion seems to mean nothing at all. They will put a huge piece of furniture in a tiny room so that the effect is one of painful indigestion; or they will crowd things all into one corner—so that it seems about to capsize; or they will spoil a really good room by the addition of senseless and inappropriately cluttering objects, in the belief that because they are valuable they must be beautiful, regardless of suitability. Sometimes a room is marred by "treasures" clung to for reasons of sentiment.

THE BLINDNESS OF SENTIMENT

It is almost impossible for any of us to judge accurately of things which we have throughout a lifetime been accustomed to. A chair that was grandmother's, a painting father bought, the silver that has always been on the dining table—are all so part of ourselves that we are sentiment-blind to their defects.

For instance, the portrait of a Colonial officer, among others, has always hung in Mrs. Oldname's dining-room. One day an art critic, whose knowledge was better than his manners, blurted out, "Will you please tell me why you have that dreadful thing in this otherwise perfect room?" Mrs. Oldname, somewhat taken back, answered rather wonderingly: "Is it dreadful?—Really? I have a feeling of affection for him and his dog!"

The critic was merciless. "If you call a cotton-flannel effigy, a dog! And as for the figure, it is equally false and lifeless! It is amazing how any one with your taste can bear looking at it!" In spite of his rudeness, Mrs. Old-name saw that what he said was quite true, but not until the fact had been pointed out to her. Gradually she grew to dislike the poor officer so much that he was finally relegated to the attic. In the same way most of us have belongings that have "always been there" or perhaps "treasures" that we love for some association, which are probably as bad as can be, to which habit has blinded us, though we would not have to be told of their hideousness were they seen by us in the house of another.

It is not to be expected that all people can throw away every esthetically unpleasing possession, with which nearly every house twenty-five years ago was filled, but those whose pocket-book and sentiment will permit, would add greatly to the beauty of their houses by sweeping the bad into the ash can! Far better have stone-ware plates that are good in design than expensive porcelain that is horrible in decoration.

The only way to determine what is good and what is horrible is to study what is good in books, in museums, or in art classes in the universities, or even by studying the magazines devoted to decorative art.

Be very careful though. Do not mistake modern eccentricities for "art." There are frightful things in vogue to-day —flamboyant colors, grotesque, triangular and oblique designs that can not possibly be other than bad, because aside from striking novelty, there is nothing good about them. By no standard can a room be in good taste that looks like a perfume manufacturer's phantasy or a design reflected in one of the distorting mirrors that are mirth-provokers at county fairs.

TO DETERMINE AN OBJECT'S WORTH

In buying an article for a house one might formulate for oneself a few test questions:

First, is it useful? Anything that is really useful has a reason for existence.

Second, has it *really* beauty of form and line and color?

(Texture is not so important.)   Or is it merely striking, or amusing?

Third, is it entirely suitable for the position it occupies?

Fourth, if it were eliminated would it be missed? Would something else look as well or better, in its place? Or would its place look as well empty? A truthful answer to these questions would at least help in determining its value, since an article that failed in any of them could not be "perfect."

Fashion affects taste—it is bound to. We abominate Louis the Fourteenth and Empire styles at the moment, because curves and super-ornamentation are out of fashion; whether they are really bad or not, time alone can tell. At present we are admiring plain silver and are perhaps exacting that it be too plain? The only safe measure of what is good, is to choose that which has best endured. The "King" and the "Fiddle" pattern for flat silver, have both been in use in houses of highest fashion ever since they were designed, so that they, among others, must have merit to have so long endured.

In the same way examples of old potteries and china and glass, at present being reproduced, are very likely good, because after having been for a century or more in disuse, they are again being chosen. Perhaps one might say that the "second choice" is "proof of excellence."

SERVICE

The subject of furnishings is however the least part of this chapter—appointments meaning decoration being of less importance (since this is not a book on architecture or decoration!), than appointments meaning *service*.

But before going into the various details of service, it might be a good moment to speak of the unreasoning indignity cast upon the honorable vocation of a servant.

There is an inexplicable tendency, in this country only, for working people in general to look upon domestic service as an unworthy, if not altogether degrading vocation. The cause may perhaps be found in the fact that this same scorning public having for the most part little opportunity to know high-class servants, who are to be found only in high-class families, take it for granted that ignorant "servant girls" and "hired men" are representative of their kind. Therefore they put upper class servants in the same category—regardless of whether they are uncouth and illiterate, or persons of refined appearance and manner who often have considerable cultivation, acquired not so much at school as through the constant contact with ultra refinement of surroundings, and not infrequently through the opportunity for world-wide travel.

And yet so insistently has this obloquy of the word "servant" spread that every one sensitive to the feelings of others avoids using it exactly as one avoids using the word "cripple" when speaking to one who is slightly lame. Yet are not the best of us "servants" in the Church? And the highest of us "servants" of the people and the State?

To be a slattern in a vulgar household is scarcely an elevated employment, but neither is working in a sweat-shop, or belonging to a calling that is really degraded; which is otherwise about all that equal lack of ability would procure. On the other hand, consider the vocation of a lady's maid or *"courier"* valet and compare the advantages these enjoy (to say nothing of their never having to worry about overhead expenses), with the opportunities of those who have never been out of the "factory" or the "store" or further away than the adjoining town in their lives. As for a nurse, is there any vocation more honorable? No character in E. F. Benson's "Our Family Affairs" is more beautiful or more tenderly drawn than that of "Beth," who was not only nurse to the children of the Archbishop of Canterbury but one of the most dearly beloved of the family's members—her place was absolutely next to their mother's in the very heart of the household always.

Two years ago, Anna, who had for a lifetime been Mrs. Gilding's personal maid, died. Every engagement of that seemingly frivolous family was cancelled, even the invitations for their ball.   Not one of the family but mourned for what she truly was, their humble but nearest friend. Would it have been so much better, so much more dignified, for these two women, who lived long useful years in closest association with every cultivating influence of life, to have lived on in their native villages and worked in a factory, or to have had a little store of their own?   Does this false idea of dignity—since it *is* false—go so far as that?

HOW MANY SERVANTS FOR CORRECT SERVICE?

It stands to reason that one may expect more perfect service from a "specialist" than from one whose functions are multiple.   But small houses that have a double equip-ment—meaning an alternate who can go in the kitchen, and two for the dining-room—can be every bit as well run. so far as essentials go, as the palaces of the Gildings and the Worldlys, though of course not with the same impres-siveness. But good service is badly handicapped if, when the waitress goes out, there is no one to open the door, or when the cook goes out, there is no one to prepare a meal.

For what one might call "complete" service, (meaning service that is adequate for constant entertaining and can stand comparison with the most luxurious establishments, three are the minimum—a cook, a butler (or waitress) and a housemaid. The reason why luncheons and dinners can not be "perfectly" given with a waitress alone is because two persons are necessary for the exactions of modern stand-ards of service. Yet one alone can, on occasion, manage very well, if attention is paid to ordering an especial menu for single-handed service—described on page 233. Aside from the convenience of a second person in the dining-room, a house can not be run very comfortably and smoothly without alternating shifts in staying in and going out.   The waitress being on "duty" to answer bell and telephone and serve tea one afternoon, and the housemaid taking her place the next. They also alternate in going out every other evening after dinner.

It should be realized that above the number necessary for essentials, each additional chambermaid, parlor-maid, footman, scullery maid or useful man, is made necessary by the size of the house and by the amount of entertaining usual, rather than (as is often supposed) for the mere reason of show.   The seemingly superfluous number of footmen at Golden Hall and Great Estates are, aside from standing on parade at formal parties, needed actually to do the immense amount of work that houses of such size entail; whereas a small apartment can be fairly well looked after by one alone.

All house employees and details of their several duties, manners, and appearances, are enumerated below.   Beginning with the greatest and most complicated establishments possible, the employee of highest rank is:

THE SECRETARY WHO IS ALSO COMPANION

The position of companion, which is always one of social equality with her employer, exists only when the lady of the house is an invalid, or very elderly, or a widow, or a young girl.   (In the latter case the "companion" is a "chaperon.")

Her secretarial duties consist in writing impersonal letters and notes and probably paying bills; she may have occasional invitations to send out, and to answer, though a lady needing a companion is not apt to be greatly interested in social activities. The companion never performs the services of a maid—but she occasionally does the housekeeping.   Otherwise her duties can not very well be set down, because they vary with individual requirements.   One lady likes continually to travel and merely wants a companion, (usually a poor relative or friend) to go with her.   Another who is a semi-invalid never leaves her room, and the duties of her companion are almost those of a trained nurse. The average requirement is in being personally agreeable, tactful, intelligent, and—companionable!

A companion dresses as any other lady does; according to the occasion, her personal taste, her age, and her means.

VARIED SOCIAL STANDING OF THE PRIVATE SECRETARY

The private secretary to a diplomat, since he must first pass the diplomatic examination in order to qualify, is invariably a young man of education, if not of birth, and his social position is always that of a member of his "chief's" family.

The position of an ordinary private secretary is sometimes that of an upper servant; or, on the other hand, his own social position may be much higher than that of his employer.   A secretary who either has position of his own or is given position by his employer, is in every way treated as a member of the family; he is present at all general entertainments; and quite as often as not at lunches and dinners.   The duties of a private secretary are naturally to attend to all correspondence, take shorthand notes of speeches or conversations, file papers and documents and in every way serve as extra eyes and hands and supplementary brain for his employer.

THE SOCIAL SECRETARY

The position of social secretary is an entirely clerical one, and never confers any "social privileges" unless the secretary is also "companion."

Her duties are to write all invitations, acceptances, and regrets; keep a record of every invitation received and every one sent out, and to enter in an engagement book every engagement made for her employer, whether to lunch, dinner, to be fitted, or go to the dentist.   She also writes all impersonal notes, takes longer letters in shorthand, and writes others herself after being told their purport.   She also audits all bills and draws the checks for them; the checks are filled in and then presented to her employer to be signed, after which they are put in their envelopes, sealed and sent. When the receipted bills are returned, the secretary files them according to her own method, where they can at any time be found by her if needed for reference.   In many cases it is she (though it is most often the butler) who telephones invitations and other messages.

Occasionally a social secretary is also a social manager; devises entertainments and arranges all details such as the decorations of the house for a dance, or a programme of entertainment following a very large dinner. The social secretary very rarely lives in the house of her employer; more often than not she goes also to one or two other houses—since there is seldom work enough in one to require her whole time.

Miss Brisk, who is Mrs. Gilding's secretary, has little time for any one else. She goes every day for from two to sometimes eight or nine hours in town, and at Golden Hall lives in the house. Usually a secretary can finish all there is to do in an average establishment in about an hour, or at most two, a day, with the addition of five or six hours on two or three other days each month for the paying of bills.

Supposing she takes three positions; she goes to Mrs. A. from 8.30 to 10 every day, and for three extra hours on the 10th and 11th of every month. To Mrs. B. from 10.30 to 1 (her needs being greater) and for six extra hours on the 12th, 13th and 14th of every month. And to Mrs. C. every day at 3 o'clock for an indefinite time of several hours or only a few minutes.

Her dress is that of any business woman. Conspicuous clothes are out of keeping as they would be out of keeping in an office; which, however, is no reason why she should not be well dressed. Well-cut tailor-made suits are the most appropriate with a good-looking but simple hat; as good shoes as she can possibly afford, and good gloves and immaculately clean shirt waists, represent about the most dignified and practical clothes. But why describe clothes! Every woman with good sense enough to qualify as a secretary has undoubtedly sense enough to dress with dignity.

THE HOUSEKEEPER

In a very big house the housekeeper usually lives in the house. Smaller establishments often have a "visiting housekeeper" who comes for as long as she is needed each morning. The resident housekeeper has her own bedroom and bath and sitting-room always. Her meals are brought to her by an especial kitchen-maid, called in big houses the "hall girl," or occasionally the butler details an under footman to that duty.

In an occasional house all the servants, the gardener as well as the cook and butler and nurses, come under the housekeeper's authority; in other words, she superintends the entire house exactly as a very conscientious and skilled mistress would do herself, if she gave her whole time and attention to it. She engages the servants, and if necessary, dismisses them; she sees the cook, orders meals, goes to the market, or at least supervises the cook's market orders, and likewise engages and apportions the work of the men servants.

Ordinarily, however, she is in charge of no one but the housemaids, parlor-maids, useful man and one of the scullery maids. The cook, butler, nurses and lady's maid do not come under her supervision. But should difficulties arise between herself and them it would be within her province to ask for their dismissal which would probably be granted; since she would not ask without grave cause that involved much more than her personal dislike. A good housekeeper is always a woman of experience and tact, and often a lady; friction is, therefore, extremely rare.

THE ORGANIZATION OF A GREAT HOUSE

The management of a house of greatest size, is divided usually into several distinct departments, each under its separate head. The housekeeper has charge of the appearance of the house and of its contents; the manners and looks of the housemaids and parlor-maids, as well as their work in cleaning walls, floors, furniture, pictures, ornaments, books, and taking care of linen.

The butler has charge of the pantry and dining-room. He engages all footmen, apportions their work and is responsible for their appearance, manners and efficiency.

The cook is in charge of the kitchen, under-cook and kitchen-maids.

The nurse and the personal maid and cook are under the direction of the lady of the house. The butler and the valet as well as the chauffeur and gardener are engaged by the gentleman of the house.

THE BUTLER

The butler is not only the most important servant in every big establishment, but it is by no means unheard of for him to be in supreme command, not only as steward, but as house-keeper as well.

At the Worldly's for instance, Hastings who is actually the butler, orders all the supplies, keeps the household accounts and engages not only the men servants but the house-maids, parlor-maids and even the chef.

But normally in a great house, the butler has charge of his own department only, and his own department is the dining-room and pantry, or possibly the whole parlor floor. In all smaller establishments the butler is always the valet —and in many great ones he is valet to his employer, even though he details a footman to look after other gentlemen of the family or visitors.

In a small house the butler works a great deal with his hands and not so much with his head. In a great establishment, the butler works very much with his head, and with his hands not at all.

At Golden Hall where guests come in dozens at a time (both in the house and the guest annex), his stewardship— even though there is a housekeeper—is not a job which a small man can fill. He has perhaps thirty men under him at big dinners, ten who belong under him in the house always; he has the keys to the wine cellar and the combination of the silver safe. (The former being in this day by far the greater responsibility!) He also chooses the china and glass and linen as well as the silver to be used each day, oversees the setting of the table, and the serving of all food.

When there is a house party every breakfast tray that leaves the pantry is first approved by him.

At all meals he stands behind the chair of the lady of the house—in other words, at the head of the table. In occasional houses, the butler stands at the opposite end as he is supposed to be better able to see any directions given him. At Golden Hall the butler stands behind Mr. Gilding but at Great Estates Hastings invariably stands behind Mrs. Worldly's chair so that at the slightest turn of her head, he need only take a step to be within reach of her voice. (The husband by the way is "head of the house," but the wife is "head of the table.")

At tea time, he oversees the footmen who place the tea-table, put on the tea cloth and carry in the tea tray, after which Hastings himself places the individual tables.

When there is "no dinner at home" he waits in the hall and assists Mr. Worldly into his coat, and hands him his hat and stick, which have previously been handed to the butler by one of the footmen.

The Butler in a Smaller House

In a smaller house, the butler also takes charge of the wines and silver, does very much the same as the butler in the bigger house, except that he has less overseeing of others and more work to do himself. Where he is alone, he does all the work—naturally. Where he has either one foot-man or a parlor-maid, he passes the main courses at the table and his assistant passes the secondary dishes.

He is also valet not only for the gentleman of the house but for any gentleman guests as well.

What the Butler Wears

The butler never wears the livery of a footman and on no account knee breeches or powder. In the early morning he wears an ordinary sack suit—black or very dark blue—with a dark, inconspicuous tie. For luncheon or earlier, if he is on duty at the door, he wears black trousers, with gray stripes, a double-breasted, high-cut, black waistcoat, and black swallowtail coat without satin on the revers, a white stiff-bosomed shirt with standing collar, and a black four-in-hand tie.

In fashionable houses, the butler does not put on his

dress suit until six o'clock.   The butler's evening dress differs from that of a gentleman in a few details only: he has
no braid on his trousers, and the satin on his lapels (if any)
is narrower, but the most distinctive difference is that a
butler wears a black waistcoat and a white lawn tie, and a
gentleman always wears a white waistcoat with a white tie,
or a white waistcoat and a black tie with a dinner coat, but
never the reverse.

Unless he is an old-time colored servant in the South
a butler who wears a "dress suit" in the daytime is either
a hired waiter who has come in to serve a meal, or he has
never been employed by persons of position; and it is unnecessary to add that none but vulgarians would employ a butler (or any other house servant) who wears a mustache!
To have him open the door collarless and in shirt-sleeves
is scarcely worse!

A butler never wears gloves, nor a flower in his buttonhole.   He sometimes wears a very thin watch chain in the
daytime but none at night.   He never wears a scarf-pin, or
any jewelry that is for ornament alone.   His cuff-links
should be as plain as possible, and his shirt studs white
enamel ones that look like linen.

THE HOUSE FOOTMEN

All house servants who assist in waiting on the table
come under the direction of the butler, and are known as
footmen.   One who never comes into the dining-room is
known as a useful man.   The duties of the footmen (and
useful man) include cleaning the dining-room, pantry, lower
hall, entrance vestibule, sidewalk, attending to the furnace,
carrying coal to the kitchen, wood to all the open fireplaces
in the house, cleaning the windows, cleaning brasses, cleaning all boots, carrying everything that is heavy, moving furniture for the parlor-maids to clean behind it, valeting all
gentlemen, setting and waiting on table, attending the front
door, telephoning and writing down messages, and—incessantly and ceaselessly, cleaning and polishing silver.

In a small house, the butler polishes silver, but in a very
big house one of the footmen is silver specialist, and does

nothing else. Nothing! If there is to be a party of any
sort he puts on his livery and joins the others who line the
hall and bring dishes to the table. But he does not assist in setting the table or washing dishes or in cleaning anything whatsoever—except silver.

The butler also usually answers the telephone—if not, it
is answered by the first footman. The first footman is deputy butler.

The footmen also take turns in answering the door. In
houses of great ceremony like those of the Worldlys' and
the Gildings', there are always two footmen at the door if
anyone is to be admitted. One to open the door and the
other to conduct a guest into the drawing-room. But if
formal company is expected, the butler himself is in the
front hall with one or two footmen at the door.

The Footmen's Livery

People who have big houses usually choose a color for
their livery and never change it. Maroon and buff, for
instance, are the colors of the Gildings; all their motor
cars are maroon with buff lines and cream-colored or maroon
linings. The chauffeurs and outside footmen wear maroon
liveries. The house footmen, for everyday, wear ordinary
footmen's liveries, maroon trousers and long-tailed coats
with brass buttons and maroon-and-buff striped waistcoats.

For gala occasions, Mrs. Gilding adds as many caterer's
men as necessary, but they all are dressed in her full-dress
livery, consisting of a "court" coat which comes together
at the neck in front, and then cuts away to long tails at the
back. The coat is of maroon broadcloth with frogs and
epaulets of black braiding. There is a small standing collar of buff cloth, and a falling cravat of pleated cream-colored lace worn in front. The waistcoat is of buff satin, the
breeches of black satin, cream-colored stockings, pumps,
and the hair is powdered. It is first pomaded and then thickly
powdered. Wigs are never worn.

Mrs. Worldly however compromises between the "court"
footman and the ordinary one, and puts her footmen in

green cloth coats cut like the everyday liveries, with silver buttons on which the crest is raised in relief, but adds black velvet collars, and black satin waistcoats in place of the everyday striped ones. Black satin knee breeches, black silk stockings, and pumps with silver buckles, and their ordinary hair, cut short.

The powdered footman's "court" livery is, as a matter of fact, very rarely seen. Three or four houses in New York, and one or two otherwhere, would very likely include them all. Knee breeches are more usual, but even those are seen in none but very lavish houses.

To choose servants who are naturally well-groomed is more important than putting them in smart liveries. Men must be close shaven and have their hair well cut. Their linen must be immaculate, their shoes polished, their clothes brushed and in press, and their finger nails clean and well cared for. If a man's fingers are indelibly stained he would better wear white cotton gloves.

THE COOK

The kitchen is always in charge of the cook. In a small house, or in an apartment, she is alone and has all the cooking, cleaning of kitchen and larder, to do, the basement or kitchen bell to answer, and the servants' table to set and their dishes to wash as well as her kitchen utensils. In a bigger house, the kitchen-maid lights the kitchen fire, and does all cleaning of kitchen and pots and pans, answers the basement bell, sets the servants' table and washes the servants' table dishes. In a still bigger house, the second cook cooks for the servants always, and for the children sometimes, and assists the cook by preparing certain plainer portions of the meals, the cook preparing all dinner dishes, sauces and the more elaborate items on the menu. Sometimes there are two or more kitchen-maids who merely divide the greater amount of work between them.

In most houses of any size, the cook does all the marketing. She sees the lady of the house every morning, and submits menus for the day. In smaller houses, the lady does the ordering of both supplies and menus.

How a Cook Submits the Menu

In a house of largest size—at the Gildings for instance, the chef writes in his "book" every evening, the menus for the next day, whether there is to be company or not. (None, of course, if the family are to be out for all meals.) This "book" is sent up to Mrs. Gilding with her breakfast tray. It is a loose-leaf blank book of rather large size. The day's menu sheet is on top, but the others are left in their proper sequence underneath, so that by looking at her engagement book to see who dined with her on such a date, and then looking at the menu for that same date, she knows —if she cares to—exactly what the dinner was.

If she does not like the chef's choice, she draws a pencil through and writes in something else. If she has any orders or criticisms to make, she writes them on an envelope pad, folds the page, and seals it and puts the "note" in the book.

If the menu is to be changed, the chef re-writes it, if not the page is left as it is, and the book put in a certain place in the kitchen.

The butler always goes into the kitchen shortly after the book has come down, and copies the day's menus on a pad of his own. From this he knows what table utensils will be needed.

This system is not necessary in medium sized or small houses, but where there is a great deal of entertaining it is much simpler for the butler to be able to go and "see for himself" than to ask the cook and—forget. And ask again, and the cook forget, and then—disturbance!—because the butler did not send down the proper silver dishes or have the proper plates ready, or had others heated unnecessarily.

THE KITCHEN-MAID

The kitchen-maids are under the direction of the cook, except one known colloquially as the "hall girl" who is supervised by the housekeeper. She is evidently a survival of the "between maid" of the English house. Her sobriquet comes from the fact that she has charge of the servants' hall, or dining-room, and is in fact the waitress for them. She also takes care of the housekeeper's rooms, and carries all her meals up to her. If there is no housekeeper, the hall girl is under the direction of the cook.

THE PARLOR-MAID

The parlor-maid keeps the drawing-room and library in order. The useful man brings up the wood for the fireplaces, but the parlor-maid lays the fire. In some houses the parlor-maid takes up the breakfast trays; in other houses, the butler does this himself and then hands them to the lady's maid, who takes them into the bedrooms. The windows and the brasses are cleaned by the useful man and heavy furniture moved by him so she can clean behind them.

The parlor-maid assists the butler in waiting at table, and washing dishes, and takes turns with him in answering the door and the telephone.

In huge houses like the Worldlys' and the Gildings', the footmen assist the butler in the dining-room and at the door —and there is always a "pantry maid" who washes dishes and cleans the pantry.

THE HOUSEMAID

The housemaid does all the chamber work, cleans all silver on dressing-tables, polishes fixtures in the bathroom— in other words takes care of the bedroom floors.

In a bigger house, the head housemaid has charge of the linen and does the bedrooms of the lady and gentleman of the house and a few of the spare rooms. The second housemaid does the nurseries, extra spare rooms, and the servants' floor. The bigger the establishment, the more housemaids, and the work is further divided. The housemaid is by many people called the chambermaid.

UNIFORMS

In all houses of importance and fashion, the parlor-maid and the housemaids, and the waitress (where there is no butler), are all dressed alike. Their "work" dresses are of plain cambric and in whatever the "house color" may be, with large white aprons with high bibs, and Eton collars, but no cuffs (as they must be able to unbutton their sleeves and turn them up.) Those who serve in the dining-room must always dress before lunch, and the afternoon dresses vary according to the taste—and purse—of the lady of the house. Where no uniforms are supplied, each maid is supposed to furnish herself with a plain black dress for afternoon, on which she wears collars and cuffs of embroidered muslin usually (always supplied her), and a small afternoon apron, with or without shoulder straps, and with or without a cap.

In very "beautifully done" houses (all the dresses of the maids are furnished them), the color of the uniforms is chosen to harmonize with the dining-room. At the Gildings', Jr., for instance, where there are no men servants because Mr. Gilding does not like them, but where the house is as perfect as a picture on the stage, the waitress and parlor-maid wear in the blue and yellow dining-room, dresses of Nattier blue taffeta with aprons and collars and cuffs of plain hemstitched cream-colored organdie, that is as transparent as possible; blue stockings and patent leather slippers with silver buckles, their hair always beautifully smooth. Sometimes they wear caps and sometimes not, depending upon the waitress' appearance. Twenty years ago, every maid in a lady's house wore a cap except the personal maid, who wore (and still does) a velvet bow, or nothing. But when every little slattern in every sloppy household had a small mat of whitish Swiss pinned somewhere on an untidy head, and was decked out in as many yards of embroidery ruffling on her apron and shoulders as her person could carry, fashionable ladies began taking caps and trimmings off, and exacting instead that clothes be good in cut and hair be neatly arranged.

A few ladies of great taste dress their maids according to individual becomingness; some faces look well under a cap, others look the contrary. A maid whose hair is rather fluffy—especially if it is dark—looks pretty in a cap, particularly of the coronet variety. No one looks well in a doily laid flat, but fluffy fair hair with a small mat tilted up against a knot of hair dressed high can look very smart. A young woman whose hair is straight and rebellious to order, can be made to look tidy and even attractive in a headdress that encircles the whole head. A good one for this purpose has a very narrow ruche from 9 to 18 inches long on either side of a long black velvet ribbon. The ruche goes part way, or all the way, around the head, and the velvet ribbon ties, with streamers hanging down the back. On the other hand, many extremely pretty young women with hair worn flat do not look well in caps of any description—except "Dutch" ones which are, in most houses, too suggestive of fancy dress. If no caps are worn the hair must be fault-lessly smooth and neat; and of course where two or more maids are seen together, they must be alike. It would not do to have one wear a cap and the other not.

THE LADY'S MAID

A first class lady's maid is required to be a hairdresser, a good packer and an expert needlewoman. Her first duty is to keep her lady's clothes in order and to help her dress, and undress. She draws the bath, lays out underclothes, always brushes her lady's hair and usually dresses it, and gets out the dress to be worn, as well as the stockings, shoes, hat, veil, gloves, wrist bag, parasol, or whatever accessories go with the dress in question.

As soon as the lady is dressed, everything that has been worn is taken to the sewing room and each article is gone over, carefully brushed if of woolen material, cleaned if silk. Everything that is mussed is pressed, everything that can be suspected of not being immaculate is washed or cleaned with cleaning fluid, and when in perfect order is replaced where it belongs in the closet. Underclothes as mended are put in the clothes hamper. Stockings are looked over for rips or small holes, and the maid usually washes very fine stockings herself, also lace collars or small pieces of lace trimming.

Some maids have to wait up at night, no matter how late, until their ladies return; but as many, if not more, are never asked to wait longer than a certain hour.

But the maid for a débutante in the height of the season, between the inevitable "go fetching" at this place and that, and mending of party dresses danced to ribbons and soiled by partner's hands on the back, and slippers "walked on" until there is quite as much black part as satin or metal, has no sinecure.

Why Two Maids?

In very important houses where mother and daughters go out a great deal there are usually two maids, one for the mother and one for the daughters. But even in moderate households it is seldom practical for a débutante and her mother to share a maid—at least during the height of the season. That a maid who has to go out night after night for weeks and even months on end, and sit in the dressing-rooms at balls until four and five and even six in the morning, is then allowed to go to bed and to sleep until luncheon is merely humane. And it can easily be seen that it is more likely that she will need the help of a seamstress to re-furbish dance-frocks, than that she will have any time to devote to her young lady's mother—who in "mid-season," therefore, is forced to have a maid of her own, ridiculous as it sounds, that two maids for two ladies should be neces-sary! Sometimes this is overcome by engaging an especial maid "by the evening" to go to parties and wait, and bring the débutante home again. And the maid at home can then be "maid for two."

Dress of a Lady's Maid

A lady's maid wears a black skirt, a laundered white waist, and a small white apron, the band of which buttons in the back.

In traveling, a lady's maid always wears a small black silk apron and some maids wear black taffeta ones always. In the afternoon, she puts on a black waist with white collar and cuffs. Mrs. Gilding, Jr., puts her maid in black taffeta with embroidered collar and cuffs. For "company occa-sions," when she waits in the dressing-room, she wears light gray taffeta with a very small embroidered mull apron with a narrow black velvet waist-ribbon, and collar and cuffs of mull to match—which is extremely pretty, but also extremely extravagant.

THE VALET

The valet (pronounced val-et not vallay) is what Beau Brummel called a gentleman's gentleman. His duties are exactly the same as those of the lady's maid—except that he does not sew! He keeps his employer's clothes in perfect order, brushes, cleans and presses everything as soon as it has been worn—even if only for a few moments. He lays out the clothes to be put on, puts away everything that is a personal belonging. Some gentlemen like their valet to help them dress; run the bath, shave them and hold each article in readiness as it is to be put on. But most gentlemen merely like their clothes "laid out" for them, which means that trousers have belts or braces attached, shirts have cuff links and studs; and waistcoat buttons are put in.

The valet also unpacks the bags of any gentleman guests when they come, valets them while there, and packs them when they go. He always packs for his own gentleman, buys tickets, looks after the luggage, and makes himself generally useful as a personal attendant, whether at home or when traveling.

At big dinners, he is required (much against his will) to serve as a footman—in a footman's, not a butler's, livery.

The valet wears no livery except on such occasions. His "uniform" is an ordinary business suit, dark and inconspicuous in color, with a black tie.

In a bachelor's quarters a valet is often general factotum; not only valeting but performing the services of cook, butler, and even housemaid.

THE NURSE

Everybody knows the nurse is either the comfort or the torment of the house. Everyone also knows innumerable young mothers who put up with inexcusable crankiness from a crotchety middle-aged woman because she was "so wonderful" to the baby. And here let it be emphasized that such an one usually turns out to have been not wonderful to the baby at all.   That she does not actually abuse a help-less infant is merely granting that she is not a "monster."

Devotion must always be unselfish; the nurse who is *really* "wonderful" to the baby is pretty sure to be a person who is kind generally.   In ninety-nine cases out of a hun-dred the sooner a domineering nurse—old or young—is got rid of, the better.   It has been the experience of many a mother whose life had been made perfectly miserable through her belief that if she dismissed the tyrant the baby would suffer, that in the end—there *is* always an end!—the baby was quite as relieved as the rest of the family when the "right sort" of a kindly and humane person took the tyrant's place.

It is unnecessary to add that one can not be too particular in asking for a nurse's reference and in never failing to get a personal one from the lady she is leaving.   Not only is it necessary to have a sweet-tempered, competent and clean person, but her moral character is of utmost importance, since she is to be the constant and inseparable companion of the children whose whole lives are influenced by her example, especially where busy parents give only a small portion of time to their children.

COURTESY TO ONE'S HOUSEHOLD

In a dignified house, a servant is never spoken to as Jim, Maisie, or Katie, but always as James or Margaret or Katherine, and a butler is called by his last name, nearly always.   The Worldly's butler, for instance, is called Hast-ings, not John.   In England, a lady's maid is also called by her last name, and the cook, if married, is addressed as Mrs. and the nurse is always called "Nurse."   A chef is usually called "Chef" or else by his last name.

Always abroad, and every really well-bred lady or gentle-man here, says "please" in asking that something be brought her or him.   "Please get me the book I left on the table in my room!" Or "Please give me some bread!" Or "Some bread, please."   Or one can say equally politely and omit the please, "I'd like some toast," but it is usual and in-stinctive to every lady or gentleman to add "please."

In refusing a dish at the table, one must say "No, thank you," or "No, thanks," or else one shakes one's head. A head can be shaken politely or rudely. To be courteously polite, and yet keep one's walls up is a thing every thorough-bred person knows how to do—and a thing that everyone who is trying to become such must learn to do.

A rule can't be given because there isn't any. As said in another chapter, a well-bred person always lives within the walls of his personal reserve, a vulgarian has no walls —or at least none that do not collapse at the slightest touch. But those who think they appear superior by being rude to others whom fortune has placed below them, might as well, did they but know it, shout their own unexalted origin to the world at large, since by no other method could it be more widely published.

THE HOUSE WITH LIMITED SERVICE

The fact that you live in a house with two servants, or in an apartment with only one, need not imply that your house lacks charm or even distinction, or that it is not completely the home of a lady or gentleman. But, as explained in the chapter on Dinners, if you have limited service you must devise systematic economy of time and labor or you will have disastrous consequences.

Every person, after all, has only one pair of hands, and a day has only so many hours, and one thing is inevitable, which young housekeepers are apt to forget, a few can not do the work of many, and do it in the same way. It is all very well if the housemaid can not get into young Mrs. Gilding's room until lunch time, nor does it matter if its confusion looks like the aftermath of a cyclone. The house-maid has nothing to do the rest of the day but put that one room and bath in order. But in young Mrs. Gaily's small house where the housemaid is also the waitress, who is supposed to be "dressed" for lunch, it does not have to be pointed out that she can not sweep, dust, tidy up rooms, wash out bathtubs, polish fixtures, and at the same time be dressed in afternoon clothes. If Mrs. Gaily is out for lunch, it is true the chambermaid-waitress need not be dressed to wait on table, but her thoughtless young mistress would not be amiable if a visitor were to ring the doorbell in the early afternoon and have it opened by a maid in a rumpled "working" dress.

Supposing the time to put the bedroom in order is from ten to eleven each morning: it is absolutely necessary that Mrs. Gaily take her bath before ten so that even if she is not otherwise "dressed" she can be out of her bedroom and bath at ten o'clock promptly.   She can go elsewhere while her room is done up and then come back and finish dressing later.   In this case she must herself "tidy" any disorder that she makes in dressing; put away her négligé and slippers and put back anything out of place.   On the days when Mr. Gaily does not go to the office he too must get up and out so that the house can be put in order.

THE ONE MAID ALONE

But where one maid alone cooks, cleans, waits on table, and furthermore serves as lady's maid and valet, she must necessarily be limited in the performance of each of these duties in direct proportion to their number.   Even though she be eagerly willing, quality must give way before quantity produced with the same equipment, or if quality is necessary then quantity must give way.   In the house of a fashionable gay couple like the Lovejoys' for instance, the time spent in "maiding" or "valeting" has to be taken from cleaning or cooking.   Besides cleaning and cooking, the one maid in their small apartment can press out Mrs. Lovejoy's dresses and do a little mending, but she can not sit down and spend one or two hours going over a dress in the way a specialist maid can.   Either Mrs. Lovejoy herself must do the sewing or the housework, or one or the other must be left undone.

THE MANAGEMENT OF SERVANTS

It is certainly a greater pleasure and incentive to work for those who are appreciative than for those who continually find fault.   Everyone who did war work can not fail to remember how easy it was to work for, or with, some people, and how impossible to get anything done for others.

And just as the "heads" of work-rooms or "wards" or "canteens" were either stimulating or dispiriting, so must they and their types also be to those who serve in their households.

This, perhaps, explains why some people are always having a "servant problem"; finding servants difficult to get, more difficult to keep, and most difficult to get efficient work from. It is a question whether the "servant problem" is not more often a mistress problem. It must be! Because, if you notice, those who have woes and complaints are invariably the same, just as others who never have any trouble are also the same. It does not depend on the size of the house; the Lovejoys never have any trouble, and yet their one maid of all work has a far from "easy" place, and a vacancy at Brookmeadows is always sought after, even though the Oldnames spend ten months of the year in the country. Neither is there any friction at the Golden Hall or Great Estates, even though the latter house is run by the butler— an almost inevitable cause of trouble. These houses represent a difference in range of from one alone, to nearly forty on the household payroll.

THOSE WHO HAVE PERSISTENT "TROUBLE"

It might be well for those who have trouble to remember a few rules which are often overlooked: Justice must be the foundation upon which every tranquil house is constructed. Work must be as evenly divided as possible; one servant should not be allowed liberties not accorded to all.

It is not just to be too lenient, any more than it is just to be unreasonably strict. To allow impertinence or sloppy work is inexcusable, but it is equally inexcusable to show causeless irritability or to be overbearing or rude. And there is no greater example of injustice than to reprimand those about you because you happen to be in a bad humor, and at another time overlook offenses that are greater because you are in an amiable mood.

There is also no excuse for "correcting" either a servant or a child before people.

And when you do correct, do not forget to make allow-

"THE PERFECT MISTRESS SHOWS ALL THOSE IN HER EMPLOY THE CONSIDERATION AND TRUST DUE THEM AS HON-ORABLE SELF-RESPECTING AND CONSCIENTIOUS HUMAN BEINGS."

[Page 157.]

ances, if there be any reason why allowance should be made.

If you live in a palace like Golden Hall, or any completely equipped house of important size, you overlook *nothing!* There is no more excuse for delinquency than there is in the Army. If anything happens, such as illness of one servant, there is another to take his (or her) place. A huge household is a machine and it is the business of the engineers —in other words, the secretary, housekeeper, chef or butler, to keep it going perfectly.

But in a little house, it may not be fair to say "Selma, the silver is dirty!" when there is a hot-air furnace and you have had company to every meal, and you have perhaps sent her on errands between times, and she has literally not had a moment. If you don't know whether she has had time or not, you could give her the benefit of the doubt and say (trustfully, not haughtily) "You have not had time to clean the silver, have you?" This—in case she has really been unable to clean it—points out just as well the fact that it is not shining, but is not a criticism. Carelessness, on the other hand, when you know she has had plenty of time, should never be overlooked.

Another type that has "difficulties" is the distrustful— sometimes actually suspicious—person who locks everything tight and treats all those with whom she comes in contact as though they were meddlesomely curious at least, or at worst, dishonest. It is impossible to overstate the misfortune of this temperament. The servant who is "watched" for fear she "won't work," listened to for fear she may be gossiping, suspected of wanting to take a liberty of some sort, or of doing something else she shouldn't do, is psychologically encouraged, almost driven, to do these very things.

The perfect mistress expects perfect service, but it never occurs to her that perfect service will not be voluntarily and gladly given. She, on her part, shows all of those in her employ the consideration and trust due them as honorable, self-respecting and conscientious human beings. If she has reason to think they are not all this, a lady does not keep them in her house.

ETIQUETTE OF SERVICE

The well-trained high-class servant is faultlessly neat in appearance, reticent in manner, speaks in a low voice, walks and moves quickly but silently, and is unfailingly courteous and respectful. She (or he) always knocks on a door, even of the library or sitting-room, but opens it without waiting to hear "Come in," as knocking on a downstairs door is merely politeness. At a bedroom door she would wait for permission to enter. In answering a bell, she asks "Did you ring, sir?" or if especially well-mannered she asks "Did Madam ring?"

A servant always answers "Yes, Madam," or "Very good, sir," *never* "Yes," "No," "All right," or "Sure."

Young people in the house are called "Miss Alice" or "Mr. Ollie," possibly "Mr. Oliver," but they are generally called by their familiar names with the prefix of Miss or Mister. Younger children are called Miss Kittie and Master Fred, but never by the nurse, who calls them by their first names until they are grown—sometimes always.

All cards and small packages are presented on a tray.

TIME "OUT" AND "IN"

No doubt in the far-off districts there are occasional young women who work long and hard and for little compensation, but at least in all cities, servants have their definite time out. Furthermore, they are allowed in humanely run houses to have "times in" when they can be at home to friends who come to see them. In every well-appointed house of size there is a sitting-room which is furnished with comfortable chairs and sofa if possible, a good droplight to read by, often books, and always magazines (sent out as soon as read by the family). In other words, they have an inviting room to use as their own exactly as though they were living at home. If no room is available, the kitchen has a cover put on the table, a droplight, and a few restful chairs are provided.

THE MAIDS' MEN FRIENDS

Are maids allowed to receive men friends? Certainly they are! Whoever in remote ages thought it was better to forbid "followers" the house, and have Mary and Selma slip out of doors to meet them in the dark, had very distorted notions to say the least. And any lady who knows so little of human nature as to make the same rule for her maids to-day is acting in ignorant blindness of her own duties to those who are not only in her employ but also under her protection.

A pretty young woman whose men friends come in occasionally and play cards with the others, or dance to a small and not loud phonograph in the kitchen, is merely being treated humanly. Because she wears a uniform makes her no less a young girl, with a young girl's love of amusement, which if not properly provided for her "at home" will be sought for in sinister places.

This responsibility is one that many ladies who are occupied with charitable and good works elsewhere often overlook under their own roof. It does not mean that the kitchen should be a scene of perpetual revelry and mirth that can by any chance disturb the quiet of the neighborhood or even the family. Unseemly noise is checked at once, much as it would be if young people in the drawing-room became disturbing. Continuous company is not suitable either, and those who abuse privileges naturally must have them curtailed, but the really high-class servant who does not appreciate kindness and requite it with considerate and proper behavior is rare.

SERVICE IN FORMAL ENTERTAINING

ON THE SIDEWALK AND IN THE HALL

For a wedding, or a ball, and sometimes for teas and big dinners, there is an awning from curb to front door. But usually, especially in good weather, a dinner or other moderate sized evening entertainment is prepared for by stretching a carpet (a red one invariably!) down the front steps and across the pavement to the curb's edge. At all important functions there is a chauffeur (or a caterer's man) on the sidewalk to open the door of motors, and a footman or waitress stationed inside the door of the house to open it on one's approach. This same servant, or more often another stationed in the hall beyond, directs arriving guests to the dressing-rooms.

DRESSING-ROOMS

Houses especially built for entertaining, have two small rooms on the ground floor, each with its lavatory, and off of it, a rack for the hanging of coats and wraps. In most houses, however, guests have to go upstairs where two bedrooms are set aside, one as a ladies', and the other as a gentlemen's coat room.

At an afternoon tea in houses where dressing-rooms have not been installed by the architect, the end of the hall, if it is wide, is sometimes supplied with a coat rack (which may be rented from a caterer) for the gentlemen. Ladies are in this case supposed to go into the drawing-room as they are, or go upstairs to the bedroom put at their disposal and in charge of a lady's maid or housemaid.

If the entertainment is very large, checks are always given to avoid confusion in the dressing-rooms exactly as in public "check rooms." In the ladies' dressing-room—whether downstairs or up—there must be an array of toilet necessities such as brushes and combs; well-placed mirrors, hairpins, powder with stacks of individual cotton balls, or a roll of cotton in a receptacle from which it may be pulled. In the lavatory there must be fresh soap and plenty of small hand towels. The lady's personal maid and one or two assistants if necessary, depending upon the size of the party, but one and all of them as neatly dressed as possible, assist ladies off and on with their wraps, and give them coat checks.

A lady's maid should always look the arriving guests over —not boldly nor too apparently, but with a quick glance for anything that may be amiss. If the drapery of a dress is caught up on its trimming, or a fastening undone, it is her duty to say: "Excuse me, madam (or miss), but there is a hook undone"—or "the drapery of your gown is caught—shall I fix it?" Which she does as quietly and quickly as possible. If there is a rip of any sort, she says: "I think there is a thread loose, I'll just tack it. It will only be a moment."

The well-bred maid instinctively makes little of a guest's accident, and is as considerate as the hostess herself. Employees instinctively adopt the attitude of their employer.

In the gentlemen's coat room of a perfectly appointed house the valet's attitude is much the same. If a gentleman's coat should have met with any accident, the valet says: "Let me have it fixed for you, sir, it'll only take a moment!" And he divests the gentleman of his coat and takes it to a maid and asks her please to take a stitch in it. Meanwhile he goes back to his duties in the dressing-room until he is sure the coat is finished, when he gets it and politely helps the owner into it.

In a small country house where dressing-room space is limited, the quaint tables copied from old ones are very useful, screened off at the back of the downstairs hall, or in a very small lavatory. They look, when shut, like an ordinary table, but when the top is lifted a mirror, the height of the table's width, swings forward and a series of small compartments and trays both deep and shallow are laid out on either side. The trays of course are kept filled with hairpins, pins and powder, and the compartments have sunburn lotion and liquid powder, brush, comb and whiskbroom, and whatever else the hostess thinks will be useful.

THE ANNOUNCEMENT OF GUESTS

The butler's duty is to stand near the entrance to the reception or drawing-room, and as each guest arrives (unless they are known to him) he asks: "What name, please?" He then leads the way into the room where the hostess is receiving, and says distinctly: "Mr. and Mrs. Jones." If Mrs. Jones is considerably in advance of her husband, he says: "Mrs. Jones!" then waits for Mr. Jones to approach before announcing: "Mr. Jones!"

At a very large party such as a ball, or a very big tea

or musical, he does not leave his place, but stands just outside the drawing-room, and the hostess stands just within, and as the guests pass through the door, he announces
each one's name.

It is said to be customary in certain places to have waitresses announce people. But in New York guests are never
announced if there are no men servants. At a very large
function such as a ball or tea, a hostess who has no butler at
home, always employs one for the occasion. If, for instance,
she is giving a ball for her daughter, and all the sons and
daughters of her own acquaintance are invited, the chances
are that not half or even a quarter of her guests are known
to her by sight, so that their announcement is not a mere
matter of form but of necessity.

THE ANNOUNCEMENT OF DINNER

When the butler on entering the room to announce
dinner, happens to catch the attention of the hostess, he
merely bows. Otherwise he approaches within speaking
distance and says, "Dinner is served." He never says,
"Dinner is ready."

At a large dinner where it is quite a promenade to circle
the table in search of one's name, the butler stands just within the dining-room and either reads from a list or says from
memory "right" or "left" as the case may be, to each gentleman and lady on approaching. In a few of the smartest
houses a leaf has been taken from the practise of royalty
and a table plan arranged in the front hall, which is shown
to each gentleman at the moment when he takes the envelope
enclosing the name of his partner at dinner. This table
plan is merely a diagram made in leather with white name
cards that slip into spaces corresponding to the seats at
the table. On this a gentleman can see exactly where he
sits and between whom; so that if he does not know the lady
who is to be on his left as well as the one he is to "take in,"
he has plenty of time before going to the table to ask his
host to present him.

At the end of the evening, the butler is always at the
front door—and by that time, unless the party is very large,

he should have remembered their names, if he is a perfect butler, and as Mr. and Mrs. Jones appear he opens the door and calls down to the chauffeur "Mr. Jones' car!" And in the same way "Mr. Smith's car!" "Miss Gilding's car!" When a car is at the door, the chauffeur runs up the steps and says to the butler: "Miss Gilding's car" or "Mrs. Jones' car." The butler then announces to either Mr. or Mrs. Jones, "Your car, sir," or "Your car, madam," and holds the door open for her to go out, or he may say, "Your car, Miss," if the Gilding car comes first.

DINING-ROOM SERVICE AT PRIVATE ENTERTAINMENTS

Supper at a ball in a great house (big enough for a ball) is usually in charge of the butler, who by "supper time" is free from his duties of "announcing" and is able to look after the dining-room service. The sit-down supper at a ball is served exactly like a dinner—or a wedding breakfast; and the buffet supper of a dance is like the buffet of a wedding reception.

At a large tea where the butler is on duty "announcing" at the same time that other guests are going into the dining-room for refreshments, the dining-room service has to be handed over to the first footman and his assistants or a capable waitress is equally able to meet the situation. She should have at least two maids with her, as they have to pour all cups of tea and bouillon and chocolate as well as to take away used cups and plates and see that the food on the table is replenished.

At a small tea where ladies perform the office of pouring, one man or maid in the dining-room is plenty, to bring in more hot water or fresh cups, or whatever the table hostesses have need of.

FORMAL SERVICE WITHOUT MEN SERVANTS

Many, and very fastidious, people, who live in big houses and entertain constantly, have neither men servants nor employ a caterer, ever. Efficient women take men's places equally well, though two services are omitted. Women never (in New York at least) announce guests or open the doors of motors. But there is no difference whatsoever in the details of the pantry, dining-room, hall or dressing-room, whether the services are performed by men or women. (No women, of course, are ever on duty in the gentlemen's dressing-rooms.)

At an evening party, the door is opened by the waitress, assisted by the parlor-maid who directs the way to the dressing-rooms. The guests, when they are ready to go in the drawing-room, approach the hostess unannounced. A guest who may not be known by sight does not wait for her hostess to recognize her but says at once, "How do you do, Mrs. Eminent, I'm Mrs. Joseph Blank"; or a young girl says, "I am Constance Style" (not "Miss Style," unless she is beyond the "twenties") ; or a married woman merely announces herself as "Mrs. Town." She does not add her husband's name as it is taken for granted that the gentleman following her is Mr. Town.

CHAPTER XIII

TEAS AND OTHER AFTERNOON PARTIES

TEAS

Except at a wedding, the function strictly understood by the word "reception" went out of fashion, in New York at least, during the reign of Queen Victoria, and its survivor is a public or semi-public affair presided over by a committee, and is a serious, rather than a merely social event.

The very word "reception" brings to mind an aggregation of personages, very formal, very dressed up, very pompous, and very learned, among whom the ordinary mortal can not do other than wander helplessly in the labyrinth of the specialist's jargon. Art critics on a varnishing day reception, are sure to dwell on the effect of a new technique, and the comment of most of us, to whom a painting ought to look like a "picture," is fatal. Equally fatal to meet an explorer and not know where or what he explored; or to meet a celebrated author and not have the least idea whether he wrote detective stories or expounded Taoism. On the other hand it is certainly discouraging after studying up on the latest Cretan excavations in order to talk intelligently to Professor Diggs, to be pigeon-holed for the afternoon beside Mrs. Newmother whose interest in discovery is limited to "a new tooth in baby's head."

Yet the difference between a reception and a tea is one of atmosphere only, like the difference in furnishing twin houses. One is enveloped in the heavy gloom of the mid-Victorian period, the other is light and alluring in the fashion of to-day.

A "tea," even though it be formal, is nevertheless friendly and inviting. One does not go in "church" clothes nor with ceremonious manner; but in an informal and every-day spirit, to see one's friends and be seen by them.

165

THE AFTERNOON TEA WITH DANCING

The afternoon tea with dancing is usually given to "bring out" a daughter, or to present a new daughter-in-law. The invitations are the same whether one hundred or two thousand are sent out. For instance:

Mrs. Grantham Jones

Miss Muriel Jones

will be at home

on Tuesday, the third of December

from four until seven o'clock

The Fitz-Cherry

Dancing

As invitations to formal teas of this sort are sent to the hostess' "general" visiting list, and very big houses are comparatively few, a ballroom is nearly always engaged at a hotel. Many hotels have a big and a small ballroom, and unless one's acquaintance is enormous the smaller room is preferable.

Too much space for too few people gives an effect of emptiness which always is suggestive of failure; also one must not forget that an undecorated room needs more people to make it look "trimmed" than one in which the floral decoration is lavish. On the other hand, a "crush" is very disagreeable, even though it always gives the effect of "success."

The arrangements are not as elaborate as for a ball. At most a screen of palms behind which the musicians sit (unless they sit in a gallery), perhaps a few festoons of green here and there, and the débutante's own flowers banked on tables where she stands to receive, form as much decoration as is ever attempted.

Whether in a public ballroom or a private drawing-room, the curtains over the windows are drawn and the lights lighted as if for a ball in the evening. If the tea is at a private house there is no awning unless it rains, but there is a chauffeur or coachman at the curb to open motor doors, and a butler, or caterer's man, to open the door of the house before any one has time to ring.

Guests as they arrive are announced either by the hostess' own butler or a caterer's "announcer." The hostess receives everyone as at a ball; if she and her daughter are for the moment standing alone, the new arrival, if a friend, stands talking with them until a newer arrival takes his or her place.

After "receiving" with her mother or mother-in-law for an hour or so, as soon as the crowd thins a little, the débutante or bride may be allowed to dance.

The younger people, as soon as they have shaken hands with the hostess, dance. The older ones sit about, or talk to friends or take tea.

At a formal tea, the tea-table is exactly like that at a wedding reception, in that it is a large table set as a buffet, and is always in charge of the caterer's men, or the hostess' own butler or waitress and assistants. It is never presided over by deputy hostesses.

THE MENU IS LIMITED

Only tea, bouillon, chocolate, bread and cakes are served. There can be all sorts of sandwiches, hot biscuits, crumpets, muffins, sliced cake and little cakes in every variety that a cook or caterer can devise—whatever can come under the head of "bread and cake" is admissible; but nothing else, or it becomes a "reception," and not a "tea." At the end of the table or on a separate table near by, there are bowls or pitchers of orangeade or lemonade or "punch" (meaning in these days something cold that has fruit juice in it) for the dancers, exactly as at a ball.

Guests go to the table and help themselves to their own selection of bread and cakes. The chocolate, already poured into cups and with whipped cream on top, is passed on a tray by a servant. Tea also poured into cups, not mixed but accompanied by a small pitcher of cream, bowl of sugar, and dish of lemon, is also passed on a tray. A guest taking her plate of food in one hand and her tea or chocolate in the other, finds herself a chair somewhere, if possible, near a table, so that she can take her tea without discomfort.

AFTERNOON TEAS WITHOUT DANCING

Afternoon teas without dancing are given in honor of visiting celebrities or new neighbors or engaged couples, or to "warm" a new house; or, most often, for a house-guest from another city.

The invitation is a visiting card of the hostess with "to meet Mrs. So-and-So" across the top of it and "Jan. 10, Tea at 4 o'clock" in the lower corner, opposite the address.

At a tea of this description, tea and chocolate may be passed on trays or poured by two ladies, as will be explained below.

Unless the person for whom the tea is given is such a celebrity that the "tea" becomes a "reception," the hostess does not stand at the door, but merely near it so that any-one coming in may easily find her. The ordinary afternoon tea given for one reason or another is, in winter, merely and literally, being at home on a specified afternoon with the blinds and curtains drawn, the room lighted as at night, a fire burning and a large tea-table spread in the dining-room or a small one near the hearth. An afternoon tea in summer is the same, except that artificial light is never used, and the table is most often on a veranda.

"DO COME IN FOR A CUP OF TEA"

This is Best Society's favorite form of invitation. It is used on nearly every occasion whether there is to be music or a distinguished visitor, or whether a hostess has merely an inclination to see her friends. She writes on her personal visiting card: "Do come in on Friday for a cup of tea and hear Ellwin play, or Farrish sing, or to meet Senator West, or Lady X." Or even more informally: "I have not seen you for so long."

Invitations to a tea of this description are never "general." A hostess asks either none but close friends, or at most her "dining" list; sometimes this sort of a "tea" is so small that she sits behind her own tea-table—exactly as she does every afternoon.

But if the tea is of any size, from twenty upwards, the table is set in the dining-room and two intimate friends of the hostess "pour" tea at one end, and chocolate at the other. The ladies who "pour" are always especially invited beforehand and always wear afternoon dresses, with hats, of course, as distinguished from the street clothes of other guests. As soon as a hostess decides to give a tea, she selects two friends for this duty who are, in her opinion, decorative in appearance and also who (this is very important) can be counted on for gracious manners to everyone and under all circumstances.

It does not matter if a guest going into the dining-room for a cup of tea or chocolate does not know the deputy hostesses who are "pouring." It is perfectly correct for a stranger to say "May I have a cup of tea?"

The one pouring should answer very responsively, "Certainly! How do you like it? Strong or weak?"

If the latter, she deluges it with hot water, and again watching for the guest's negative or approval, adds cream or lemon or sugar. Or, preferring chocolate, the guest perhaps goes to the other end of the table and asks for a cup of chocolate. The table hostess at that end also says "Certainly," and pours out chocolate. If she is surrounded with people, she smiles as she hands it out, and that is all. But if she is unoccupied and her momentary "guest by courtesy" is alone, it is merest good manners on her part to make a few pleasant remarks. Very likely when asked for chocolate she says: "How nice of you! I have been feeling very neglected at my end. Everyone seems to prefer tea." Whereupon the guest ventures that people are afraid of chocolate because it is so fattening or so hot. After an observation or two about the weather, or the beauty of the china or how good the little cakes look, or the sandwiches taste, the guest finishes her chocolate.

If the table hostess is still unoccupied the guest smiles and slightly nods "Good-by," but if the other's attention has been called upon by someone else, she who has finished her chocolate, leaves unnoticed.

If another lady coming into the dining-room is an acquaintance of one of the table hostesses, the new visitor draws up a chair, if there is room, and drinks her tea or chocolate at the table. But as soon as she has finished, she should give her place up to a newer arrival. Or perhaps a friend appears, and the two take their tea together over in another part of the room, or at vacant places farther down the table. The tea-table is not set with places; but at a table where ladies are pouring, and especially at a tea that is informal, a number of chairs are usually ready to be drawn up for those who like to take their tea at the table.

In many cities, strangers who find themselves together in the house of a friend in common, always talk. In New York smart people always do at dinners or luncheons, but never at a general entertainment. Their cordiality to a stranger would depend largely upon the informal, or intimate, quality of the tea party; it would depend on who the stranger might be, and who the New Yorker. Mrs. Worldly would never dream of speaking to anyone—no matter whom—if it could be avoided. Mrs. Kindhart on the other hand, talks to everyone, everywhere and always. Mrs. Kindhart's position is as good as Mrs. Worldly's every bit, but perhaps she can be more relaxed; not being the conspicuous hostess that Mrs. Worldly is, she is not so besieged

"THE AFTERNOON TEA-TABLE IS THE SAME IN ITS SERVICE WHETHER IN THE TINY BANDBOX HOUSE OF THE NEWEST BRIDE, OR IN THE DRAWING-ROOM OF MRS. WORLDLY OF GREAT ES-TATES." [Page 171.]

by position-makers and invitation-seekers. Perhaps Mrs. Worldly, finding that nearly every one who approaches her wants something, has come instinctively to avoid each new approach.

THE EVERY-DAY AFTERNOON TEA TABLE

The every-day afternoon tea table is familiar to everyone; there is not the slightest difference in its service whether in the tiny bandbox house of the newest bride, or in the drawing-room of Mrs. Worldly of Great Estates, except that in the little house the tray is brought in by a woman— often a picture in appearance and appointment—instead of a butler with one or two footmen in his wake. In either case a table is placed in front of the hostess. A tea-table is usually of the drop-leaf variety because it is more easily moved than a solid one. There are really no "correct" dimensions; any small table is suitable. It ought not to be so high that the hostess seems submerged behind it, nor so small as to be overhung by the tea tray and easily knocked over. It is usually between 24 and 26 inches wide and from 27 to 36 inches long, or it may be oval or oblong. A double-decked table that has its second deck above the main table is not good because the tea tray perched on the upper deck is neither graceful nor convenient. In proper serving, not only of tea but of cold drinks of all sorts, even where a quantity of bottles, pitchers and glasses need space, everything should be brought on a tray and not trundled in on a tea-wagon!

A cloth must always be first placed on the table, before putting down the tray. The tea cloth may be a yard, a yard and a half, or two yards square. It may barely cover the table, or it may hang half a yard over each edge. A yard and a quarter is the average size. A tea cloth can be colored, but the conventional one is of white linen, with little or much white needlework or lace, or both.

On this is put a tray big enough to hold everything except the plates of food. The tray may be a massive silver one that requires a footman with strong arms to lift it, or it may be of Sheffield or merely of effectively lacquered tin.

In any case, on it should be: a kettle which ought to be already boiling, with a spirit lamp under it, an empty tea-pot, a caddy of tea, a tea strainer and slop bowl, cream pitcher and sugar bowl, and, on a glass dish, lemon in slices. A pile of cups and saucers and a stack of little tea plates, all to match, with a napkin (about 12 inches square, hem-stitched or edged to match the tea cloth) folded on each of the plates, like the filling of a layer cake, complete the paraphernalia. Each plate is lifted off with its own napkin. Then on the tea-table, back of the tray, or on the shelves of a separate "curate," a stand made of three small shelves, each just big enough for one good-sized plate, are always two, usually three, varieties of cake and hot breads.

THINGS PEOPLE EAT AT TEA

The top dish on the "curate" should be a covered one, and holds hot bread of some sort; the two lower dishes may be covered or not, according to whether the additional food is hot or cold; the second dish usually holds sandwiches, and the third cake. Or perhaps all the dishes hold cake; little fancy cakes for instance, and pastries and slices of layer cakes. Many prefer a simpler diet, and have bread and butter, or toasted crackers, supplemented by plain cookies. Others pile the "curate" until it literally staggers, under pastries and cream cakes and sandwiches of pâté de foie gras or mayonnaise. Others, again, like marmalade, or jam, or honey on bread and butter or on buttered toast or muffins. This necessitates little butter knives and a dish of jam added to the already overloaded tea tray.

Selection of afternoon tea food is entirely a matter of whim, and new food-fads sweep through communities. For a few months at a time, everyone, whether in a private house or a country club, will eat nothing but English muffins and jam, then suddenly they like only toasted cheese crackers, or Sally Lunn, or chocolate cake with whipped cream on top. The present fad of a certain group in New York is bacon and toast sandwiches and fresh hot gingerbread. Let it be hoped for the sake of the small household that it will die out rather than become epidemic, since the gingerbread must be baked every afternoon, and the toast and bacon are two other items that come from a range.

Sandwiches for afternoon tea as well as for all collations, are made by buttering the end of the loaf, spreading on the "filling" and then cutting off the prepared slice as thin as possible. A second slice, unspread, makes the other side of the sandwich. When it is put together, the crust is either cut off leaving a square and the square again divided diagonally into two triangular sandwiches, or the sandwich is cut into shape with a regular cutter. In other words, a "party" sandwich is not the sort of sandwich to eat—or order—when hungry!

The tea served to a lady who lives alone and cares for only one dish of eatables would naturally eliminate the other two. But if a visitor is "received," the servant on duty should, without being told, at once bring in at least another dish and an additional cup, saucer, plate and napkin.

Afternoon tea at a very large house party or where especially invited people are expected for tea, should include two plates of hot food such as toast or hot biscuits split open and buttered, toasted and buttered English muffins, or crumplets, corn muffins or hot gingerbread. Two cold plates should contain cookies or fancy cakes, and perhaps a layer cake. In hot weather, in place of one of the hot dishes, there should be pâté or lettuce sandwiches, and always a choice of hot or iced tea, or perhaps iced coffee or chocolate frappé, but rarely if ever, anything else.

THE ETIQUETTE OF TEA SERVING AND DRINKING

As tea is the one meal of intimate conversation, a servant never comes to the room at tea-time unless rung for, to bring fresh water or additional china or food, or to take away used dishes. When the tray and curate are brought in, individual tables, usually glass topped and very small and low, are put beside each of the guests, and the servant then withdraws. The hostess herself "makes" the tea and pours it. Those who sit near enough to her put out their hands for their cup-and-saucer. If any ladies are sitting farther off, and a gentleman is present, he, of course, rises and takes the tea from the hostess to the guest.   He also then passes the curate, afterward putting it back where it belongs and resuming his seat.   If no gentleman is present, a lady gets up and takes her own tea which the hostess hands her, carries it to her own little individual table, comes back, takes a plate and napkin, helps herself to what she likes and goes to her place.

If the cake is very soft and sticky or filled with cream, small forks must be laid on the tea-table.

As said above, if jam is to be eaten on toast or bread, there must be little butter knives to spread it with.   Each guest in taking her plate helps herself to toast and jam and a knife and carries her plate over to her own little table. She then carries her cup of tea to her table and sits down comfortably to drink it.   If there are no little tables, she either draws her chair up to the tea-table, or manages as best she can to balance plate, cup and saucer on her lap— a very difficult feat!

In fact, the hostess who, providing no individual tables, expects her guest to balance knife, fork, jam, cream cake, plate and cup and saucer, all on her knees, should choose her friends in the circus rather than in society.

THE GARDEN PARTY

The garden party is merely an afternoon tea out of doors. It may be as elaborate as a sit-down wedding breakfast or as simple as a miniature strawberry festival.   At an elaborate one (in the rainy section of our country) a tent or marquise with sides that can be easily drawn up in fine weather and dropped in rain, and with a good dancing floor, is often put up on the lawn or next to the veranda, so that in case of storm people will not be obliged to go out of doors.   The orchestra is placed within or near open sides of the tent, so that it can be heard on the lawn and veranda as well as where they are dancing.   Or instead of a tea with dancing, if most of the guests are to be older, there may be a concert or other form of professional entertainment.

On the lawn there are usually several huge bright-colored umbrella tents, and under each a table and a group of chairs, and here and there numerous small tables and chairs.   For, although the afternoon tea is always put in the dining-room footmen or maids carry varieties of food out on large trays to the lawn, and the guests hold plates on their knees and stand glasses on tables nearby.

At a garden party the food is often much more prodigal than at a tea in town.   Sometimes it is as elaborate as at a wedding reception.   In addition to hot tea and chocolate, there is either iced coffee or a very melted café parfait, or frosted chocolate in cups.   There are also pitchers of various drinks that have rather mysterious ingredients, but are all very much iced and embellished with crushed fruits and mint leaves.   There are often berries with cream, especially in strawberry season, on an estate that prides itself on those of its own growing, as well as the inevitable array of fancy sandwiches and cakes.

At teas and musicales and all entertainments where the hostess herself is obliged to stand at the door, her husband or a daughter (if the hostess is old enough, and lucky enough to have one) or else a sister or a very close friend, should look after the guests, to see that any who are strangers are not helplessly wandering about alone, and that elderly ladies are given seats if there is to be a performance, or to show any other courtesies that devolve upon a hostess.

THE ATMOSPHERE OF HOSPITALITY

The atmosphere of hospitality is something very intangible, and yet nothing is more actually felt—or missed. There are certain houses that seem to radiate warmth like an open wood fire, there are others that suggest an arrival by wireless at the North Pole, even though a much brighter actual fire may be burning on the hearth in the drawing-room of the second than of the first.   Some people have the gift of hospitality; others whose intentions are just as kind and whose houses are perfection in luxury of appointments, seem to petrify every approach.   Such people appearing at a picnic color the entire scene with the blue light of their austerity. Such people are usually not masters, but slaves, of etiquette. Their chief concern is whether this is correct, or whether that is properly done, or is this person or that such an one as they care to know? They seem, like *Hermione* (Don Marquis's heroine), to be anxiously asking themselves, "Have I failed to-day, or have I not?"

Introspective people who are fearful of others, fearful of themselves, are never successfully popular hosts or hostesses. If you for instance, are one of these, if you are *really* afraid of knowing some one who might some day prove unpleasant, if you are such a snob that you can't take people at their face value, then why make the effort to bother with people at all? Why not shut your front door tight and pull down the blinds and, sitting before a mirror in your own drawing-room, order tea for two?

"THE PERFECT EXAMPLE OF A FORMAL DINNER TABLE OF WEALTH, LUXURY AND TASTE, WHICH INVOLVES NO EFFORT ON THE PART OF THE HOSTESS OF A GREAT HOUSE BEYOND DECIDING UPON THE DATE AND THE PRINCIPAL GUESTS WHO ARE TO FORM THE NUCLEUS OF THE PARTY."

[Page 177.]

CHAPTER XIV

FORMAL DINNERS

NOT FOR THE NOVICE TO ATTEMPT

If the great world of society were a university which issued degrees to those whom it trains to its usages, the *magna cum laude* honors would be awarded without question, not to the hostess who may have given the most marvelous ball of the decade, but to her who knows best every component detail of preparation and service, no less than every inexorable rule of etiquette, in formal dinner-giving.

To give a perfect dinner of ceremony is the supreme accomplishment of a hostess! It means not alone perfection of furnishing, of service, of culinary skill, but also of personal charm, of tact. The only other occasion when a hostess must have equal—and possibly even greater ability —is the large and somewhat formal week-end party, which includes a dinner or two as by no means its least formidable features.

There are so many aspects to be considered in dinner giving that it is difficult to know whether to begin upstairs or down, or with furnishing, or service, or people, or manners! One thing is certain, no novice should ever begin her social career by attempting a formal dinner, any more than a pupil swimmer, upon being able to take three strokes alone, should attempt to swim three miles out to sea. The former will as surely drown as the latter.

HOW A DINNER IS GIVEN IN A GREAT HOUSE

When Mrs. Worldly gives a dinner, it means no effort on her part whatsoever beyond deciding upon the date and the principal guests who are to form the nucleus; every further detail is left to her subordinates—even to the completion of her list of guests. For instance, she decides that she will have an "older" dinner, and finding that the tenth is available for herself, she tells her secretary to send out invitations for that date. She does not have especial cards engraved but uses the dinner blank described in the chapter on Invitations. She then looks through her "dinner list" and orders her secretary to invite the Oldworlds, the Eminents, the Learneds, the Wellborns, the Highbrows, and the Onceweres. She also picks out three or four additional names to be substituted for those who regret. Then turning to the "younger married" list she searches for a few suitable but "amusing" or good-looking ones to give life to her dinner which might otherwise be heavy. But her favorites do not seem appropriate. It will not do to ask the Bobo Gildings, not because of the difference in age but because Lucy Gilding smokes like a furnace and is miserable unless she can play bridge for high stakes, and, just as soon as she can bolt through dinner, sit at a card table; while Mrs. Highbrow and Mrs. Oncewere quite possibly disapprove of women's smoking and are surely horrified at "gambling." The Smartlings won't do either, for the same reason, nor the Gaylies. She can't ask the Newell Riches either, because Mrs. Oldworld and Mrs. Wellborn both dislike vulgarity too much to find compensation in qualities which are merely amusing. So she ends by adding her own friends the Kindharts and the Normans, who "go" with everyone, and a few somewhat younger people, and approves her secretary's suggestions as to additional names if those first invited should "regret."

The list being settled, Mrs. Worldly's own work is done. She sends word to her cook that there will be twenty-four on the tenth; the menu will be submitted to her later, which she will probably merely glance at and send back. She never sees or thinks about her table, which is in the butler's province.

On the morning of the dinner her secretary brings her the place cards, (the name of each person expected, written on a separate card) and she puts them in the order in which they are to be placed on the table, very much as though playing solitaire. Starting with her own card at one end and her husband's at the other, she first places the lady of honor on

"DETAIL OF PLACE SET AT A FORMAL DINNER TABLE OF A GREAT HOUSE." [Page 179.]

his right, the second in importance on his left. Then on either side of herself, she puts the two most important gentlemen. The others she fits in between, trying to seat side by side those congenial to each other.

When the cards are arranged, the secretary attends to putting the name of the lady who sits on each gentleman's right in the envelope addressed to him. She then picks up the place cards still stacked in their proper sequence, and takes them to the butler who will put them in the order arranged on the table after it is set.

Fifteen minutes before the dinner hour, Mrs. Worldly is already standing in her drawing-room. She has no personal responsibility other than that of being hostess. The whole machinery of equipment and service runs seemingly by itself. It does not matter whether she knows what the menu is. Her cook is more than capable of attending to it. That the table shall be perfect is merely the every-day duty of the butler. She knows without looking that one of the chauffeurs is on the sidewalk; that footmen are in the hall; that her own maid is in the ladies' dressing-room, and the valet in that of the gentlemen; and that her butler is just outside the door near which she is standing.

So with nothing on her mind (except a jewelled ornament and perfectly "done" hair) she receives her guests with the tranquillity attained only by those whose household—whether great or small—can be counted on to run like a perfectly coordinated machine.

HOW A DINNER CAN BE BUNGLED

This is the contrasting picture to the dinner at the Worldly's—a picture to show you particularly who are a bride how awful an experiment in dinner giving can be.

Let us suppose that you have a quite charming house, and that your wedding presents included everything necessary to set a well-appointed table. You have not very experienced servants, but they would all be good ones with a little more training.

You have been at home for so few meals you don't quite know how experienced they are. Your cook at least makes good coffee and eggs and toast for breakfast, and the few other meals she has cooked seemed to be all right, and she is such a nice clean person!

So when your house is "in order" and the last pictures and curtains are hung, the impulse suddenly comes to you to give a dinner! Your husband thinks it is a splendid idea. It merely remains to decide whom you will ask. You hesitate between a few of your own intimates, or older people, and decide it would be such fun to ask a few of the hostesses whose houses you have almost lived at ever since you "came out." You decide to ask Mrs. Toplofty, Mr. Clubwin Doe, the Worldlys, the Gildings, and the Kindharts and the Wellborns. With yourselves that makes twelve. You can't have more than twelve because you have only a dozen of everything; in fact you decide that twelve will be pretty crowded, but that it will be safe to ask that number because a few are sure to "regret." So you write notes (since it is to be a formal dinner), and—they all accept! You are a little worried about the size of the dining-room, but you are overcome by the feeling of your popularity. Now the thing to do is to prepare for a dinner. The fact that Nora probably can't make fancy dishes does not bother you a bit. In your mind's eye you see delicious plain food passed; you must get Sigrid a dress that properly fits her, and Delia, the chambermaid (who was engaged with the understanding that she was to serve in the dining-room when there was company), has not yet been at table, but she is a very willing young person who will surely look well.

Nora, when you tell her who are coming, eagerly suggests the sort of menu that would appear on the table of the Worldlys or the Gildings. You are thrilled at the thought of your own kitchen producing the same. That it may be the same in name only, does not occur to you. You order flowers for the table, and candy for your four compotiers. You pick out your best tablecloth, but you find rather to your amazement that when the waitress asks you about setting the table, you have never noticed in detail how the places are laid. Knives and spoons go on the right of the plate, of course, and forks on the left, but which goes next to the plate, or whether the wine glasses should stand nearer or beyond the goblet you can only guess. It is quite simple, however, to give directions in serving; you just tell the chambermaid that she is to follow the waitress, and pass the sauces and the vegetables. And you have already explained carefully to the latter that she must not deal plates around the table like a pack of cards, or ever take them off in piles either. (*That* much at least you do know.) You also make it a point above everything that the silver must be very clean; Sigrid seems to understand, and with the optimism of youth, you approach the dinner hour without misgiving. The table, set with your wedding silver and glass, looks quite nice. You are a little worried about the silver—it does look rather yellow, but perhaps it is just a shadow. Then you notice there are a great many forks on the table! You ask your husband what is the matter with the forks? He does not see anything wrong. You need them all for the dinner you ordered, how can there be less? So you straighten a candlestick that was out of line, and put the place cards on.

Then you go into the drawing-room. You don't light the fire until the last moment, because you want it to be burning brightly when your guests arrive. Your drawing-room looks a little stiff somehow, but an open fire more than anything else makes a room inviting, and you light it just as your first guest rings the bell. As Mr. Clubwin Doe enters, the room looks charming, then suddenly the fire smokes, and in the midst of the smoke your other guests arrive. Every one begins to cough and blink. They are very polite, but the smoke, growing each moment denser, is not to be overlooked. Mrs. Toplofty takes matters in her own hands and makes Mr. Doe and your husband carry the logs, smoke and all, and throw them into the yard. The room still thick with smoke is now cheerlessly fireless, and another factor beginning to distress you is that, although everyone has arrived, there is no sign of dinner. You wait, at first merely eager to get out of the smoke-filled drawing-rom. Gradually you are becoming nervous—what can have happened? The dining-room door might be that of a tomb for all the evidence of life behind it. You become really alarmed. Is dinner never going to be served? Everyone's eyes are red from the smoke, and conversation is getting weaker and weaker. Mrs. Toplofty—evidently despairing—sits down. Mrs. Worldly also sits, both hold their eyes shut and say nothing. At last the dining-room door opens, and Sigrid instead of bowing slightly and saying in a low tone of voice, "Dinner is served," stands stiff as a block of wood, and fairly shouts: "Dinner's all ready!"

You hope no one heard her, but you know very well that nothing escaped any one of those present. And between the smoke and the delay and your waitress' manners, you are already thoroughly mortified by the time you reach the table. But you hope that at least the dinner will be good. For the first time you are assailed with doubt on that score. And again you wait, but the oyster course is all right. And then comes the soup. You don't have to taste it to see that it is wrong. It looks not at all as "clear" soup should! Its color, instead of being glass-clear amber. is greasy-looking brown. You taste it, fearing the worst, and the worst is realized. It tastes like dish-water—and is barely tepid. You look around the table; Mr. Kindhart alone is trying to eat it.

In removing the plates, Delia, the assistant, takes them up by piling one on top of the other, clashing them together as she does so. You can feel Mrs. Worldly looking with almost hypnotized fascination—as her attention might be drawn to a street accident against her will. Then there is a wait. You wait and wait, and looking in front of you, you notice the bare tablecloth without a plate. You know instantly that the service is wrong, but you find yourself puzzled to know how it should have been done. Finally Sigrid comes in with a whole dozen plates stacked in a pile, which she proceeds to deal around the table. You at least know that to try to interfere would only make matters worse. You hold your own cold fingers in your lap knowing that you must sit there, and that you can do nothing.

The fish which was to have been a *mousse* with Hollandaise sauce, is a huge mound, much too big for the platter, with a narrow gutter of water around the edge and the center dabbed over with a curdled yellow mess. You realize that not only is the food itself awful, but that the quantity is too great for one dish. You don't know what to do next; you know there is no use in apologizing, there is no way of dropping through the floor, or waking yourself up. You have collected the smartest and the most critical people around your table to put them to torture such as they will never forget. Never! You have to bite your lips to keep from crying. Whatever possessed you to ask these people to your horrible house?

Mr. Kindhart, sitting next to you, says gently, "Cheer up, little girl, it doesn't really matter!" And then you know to the full how terrible the situation is. The meal is endless; each course is equally unappetizing to look at, and abominably served. You notice that none of your guests eat anything. They can't.

You leave the table literally sick, but realizing fully that the giving of a dinner is not as easy as you thought. And in the drawing-room, which is now fireless and freezing, but at least smokeless, you start to apologize and burst into tears!

As you are very young, and those present are all really fond of you, they try to be comforting, but you know that it will be years (if ever) before any of them will be willing to risk an evening in your house again. You also know that without malice, but in truth and frankness, they will tell everyone: "Whatever you do, don't dine with the Newweds unless you eat your dinner before you go, and wear black glasses so no sight can offend you."

When they have all gone, you drag yourself miserably upstairs, feeling that you never want to look in that drawing-room or dining-room again. Your husband, remembering the trenches, tries to tell you it was not so bad! But you *know!* You lie awake planning to let the house, and to discharge each one of your awful household the next morning, and then you realize that the fault is not a bit more theirs than yours.

If you had tried the chimney first, and learned its peculiarities; if you yourself had known every detail of cooking and service, of course you would not have attempted to give the dinner in the first place; not at least until, through giving little dinners, the technique of your household had become good enough to give a big one.

On the other hand, supposing that you had had a very experienced cook and waitress; dinner would, of course, not have been bungled, but it would have lacked something, somewhere, if you added nothing of your own personality to its perfection. It is almost safe to make the statement that no dinner is ever really well done unless the hostess herself knows every smallest detail thoroughly. Mrs. Worldly pays seemingly no attention, but nothing escapes her. She can walk through a room without appearing to look either to the right or left, yet if the slightest detail is amiss, an ornament out of place, or there is one dull button on a footman's livery, her house telephone is rung at once!

Having generalized by drawing two pictures, it is now time to take up the specific details to be considered in giving a dinner.

DETAILED DIRECTIONS FOR DINNER GIVING

The requisites at every dinner, whether a great one of 200 covers, or a little one of six, are as follows:

Guests. People who are congenial to one another. This is of first importance.

Food. A suitable menu perfectly prepared and dished. (Hot food to be *hot*, and cold, *cold*.)

Table furnishing. Faultlessly laundered linen, brilliantly polished silver, and all other table accessories suitable to the occasion and surroundings.

Service. Expert dining-room servants and enough of them.

Drawing-room. Adequate in size to number of guests and inviting in arrangement.

A cordial and hospitable host.

A hostess of charm. Charm says everything—tact, sympathy, poise and perfect manners—always.

And though for all dinners these requisites are much the same, the necessity for perfection increases *in* proportion to the formality of the occasion.

TASTE IN SELECTION OF PEOPLE

The proper selection of guests is the first essential in all entertaining, and the hostess who has a talent for assembling the right people has a great asset. Taste in house furnishings or in clothes or in selecting a cook, is as nothing compared to taste in people! Some people have this "sense" —others haven't. The first are the great hosts and hostesses; the others are the mediocre or the failures.

It is usually a mistake to invite great talkers together. Brilliant men and women who love to talk want hearers, not rivals. Very silent people should be sandwiched between good talkers, or at least voluble talkers. Silly people should never be put anywhere near learned ones, nor the dull near the clever, unless the dull one is a young and pretty woman with a talent for listening, and the clever, a man with an admiration for beauty, and a love for talking.

Most people think two brilliant people should be put together. Often they should, but with discretion. If both are voluble or nervous or "temperamental," you may create a situation like putting two operatic sopranos in the same part and expecting them to sing together.

The endeavor of a hostess, when seating her table, is to put those together who are likely to be interesting to each other. Professor Bugge might bore *you* to tears, but Mrs. Entomoid would probably delight in him; just as Mr. Stocksan Bonds and Mrs. Rich would probably have interests in common. Making a dinner list is a little like making a Christmas list. You put down what *they* will (you hope) like, not what you like. Those who are placed between congenial neighbors remember your dinner as delightful— even though both food and service were mediocre; but ask people out of their own groups and seat them next to their pet aversions, and wild horses could not drag them to your house again!

HOW A DINNER LIST IS KEPT

Nearly every hostess keeps a dinner list—apart from her general visiting list—of people with whom she is accustomed to dine, or to invite to dinner or other small entertainments. But the prominent hostess, if she has grown daughters and continually gives parties of all sorts and sizes and ages, usually keeps her list in a more complete and "ready reference" order.

Mrs. Gilding, for instance, has guest lists separately indexed. Under the general heading "Dinners," she has older married, younger married, girls, men. Her luncheon list is taken from her dinner list. "Bridge" includes especially good players of all ages; "dances," young married people, young girls, and dancing men. Then she has a cross-index list of "Important Persons," meaning those of real distinction who are always the foundation of all good society; "Amusing," usually people of talent—invaluable for house parties; and "New People," including many varieties and unassorted. Mrs. Gilding exchanges invitations with a number of these because they are interesting or amusing, or because their parties are diverting and dazzling. And Mrs. Gilding herself, being typical of New York's Cavalier element rather than its Puritan strain, personally prefers diversion to edification. Needless to say, "Boston's Best," being ninety-eight per cent. Puritan, has no "new" list. Besides her list of "New People," she has a short "frivolous" list of other Cavaliers like herself, and a "Neutral" list, which is the most valuable of all because it comprises those who "go" with everyone. Besides her own lists she has a "Pantry" list, a list that is actually made out for the benefit of the butler, so that on occasions he can invite guests to "fill in." The "Pantry" list comprises only intimate friends who belong on the "Neutral" list and fit in everywhere; young girls and young and older single men.

Allowing the butler to invite guests at his own discretion is not quite as casual as it sounds. It is very often an unavoidable expedient. For instance, at four o'clock in the afternoon, Mr. Blank telephones that he cannot come to dinner that same evening. Mrs. Gilding is out; to wait until she returns will make it too late to fill the place. Her butler who has been with her for years knows quite as well as Mrs. Gilding herself exactly which people belong in the same group. The dinner cards being already in his possession, he can see not only who is expected for dinner but the two ladies between whom Mr. Blank has been placed, and he thereupon selects some one on the "Pantry" list who is suitable for Mr. Blank's place at the table, and telephones the invitation. Perhaps he calls up a dozen before he finds one disengaged. When Mrs. Gilding returns he says, "Mr. Blank telephoned he would not be able to come for dinner as he was called to Washington. Mr. Bachelor will be happy to come in his place." Married people are seldom on this list, because the butler need not undertake to fill any but an odd place—that of a gentleman particularly. Otherwise two ladies would be seated together.

ASKING SOMEONE TO FILL A PLACE

Since no one but a fairly intimate friend is ever asked to fill a place, this invitation is always telephoned. A very young man is asked by the butler if he will dine with Mrs. Gilding that evening, and very likely no explanation is made; but if the person to be invited is a lady or an older gentleman (except on such occasions as noted above), the hostess herself telephones:

"Can you do me a great favor and fill a place at dinner tonight?" The one who receives this invitation is rather bound by the rules of good manners to accept if possible

IMPORTANCE OF DINNER ENGAGEMENTS

Dinner invitations must be answered immediately; engraved or written ones by return post, or those which were telephoned, by telephone and at once! Also, nothing but

serious illness or death or an utterly unavoidable accident
can excuse the breaking of a dinner engagement.

To accept a dinner at Mrs. Nobody's and then break the
obligation upon being invited to dine with the Worldlys,
proclaims anyone capable of such rudeness an unmitigated
snob, whom Mrs. Worldly would be the first to cut from
her visiting list if she knew of it.   The rule is: "Don't accept an invitation if you don't care about it."   Having declined the Nobody invitation in the first place, you are then
free to accept Mrs. Worldly's, or to stay at home.   There
are times, however, when engagements between very
close friends or members of the family may perhaps be
broken, but only if made with the special stipulation: "Come
to dinner with us alone Thursday if nothing better turns
up!"   And the other answers, "I'd love to—and you let me
know too, if you want to do anything else."   Meanwhile if
one of them is invited to something unusually tempting,
there is no rudeness in telephoning her friend, "Lucy has
asked us to hear Galli-Curci on Thursday!" and the other
says, "Go, by all means!   We can dine Tuesday next week
if you like, or come Sunday for supper."   This privilege of
intimacy can, however, be abused.   An engagement, even
with a member of one's family, ought never to be broken
twice within a brief period, or it becomes apparent that the
other's presence is more a fill-in of idle time than a longed-
for pleasure.

THE MENU

It may be due to the war period, which accustomed everyone to going with very little meat and to marked reduc-
tion in all food, or it may be, of course, merely vanity that
is causing even grandparents to aspire to svelte figures, but
whatever the cause, people are putting much less food on
their tables than formerly.   The very rich, living in the
biggest houses with the most imposing array of servants, sit
down to three, or at most four, courses when alone, or when
intimate friends who are known to have moderate appetites,
are dining with them.

Under no circumstances would a private dinner, no matter how formal, consist of more than:

1. Hors d'oeuvre
2. Soup
3. Fish
4. Entree
5. Roast
6. Salad
7. Dessert
8. Coffee

The menu for an informal dinner would leave out the entrée, and possibly either the hors d'oeuvre or the soup.

As a matter of fact, the marked shortening of the menu is in informal dinners and at the home table of the well-to-do. Formal dinners have been as short as the above schedule for twenty-five years. A dinner interlarded with a row of extra entrées, Roman punch, and hot dessert is unknown except at a public dinner, or in the dining-room of a parvenu. About thirty-five years ago such dinners are said to have been in fashion!

THE BALANCED MENU

One should always try to choose well-balanced dishes; an especially rich dish balanced by a simple one. Timbale with a very rich sauce of cream and pâté de foie gras might perhaps be followed by French chops, broiled chicken or some other light, plain meat. An entrée of about four broiled mushrooms on a small round of toast should be followed by boned capon or saddle of mutton or spring lamb. It is equally bad to give your guests very peculiar food unless as an extra dish. Some people love highly flavored Spanish or Indian dishes, but they are not appropriate for a formal dinner. At an informal dinner an Indian curry or Spanish enchillada for one dish is delicious for those who like it, and if you have another substantial dish such as a plain roast which practically everyone is able to eat, those who don't like Indian food can make their dinner of the other course.

It is the same way with the Italian dishes. One hating

garlic and onions would be very wretched if onions were put in each and every course, and liberally. With Indian curry, a fatally bad selection would be a very peppery soup, such as croute au pot filled with pepper, and fish with green peppers, and then the curry, and then something casserole filled again with peppers and onions and other throat-searing ingredients, finishing with an endive salad. Yet more than one hostess has done exactly this. Or equally bad is a dinner of flavorless white sauces from beginning to end; a creamed soup, boiled fish with white sauce, then vol au vent of creamed sweetbreads, followed by breast of chicken and mashed potatoes and cauliflower, palm root salad, vanilla ice cream and lady-cake. Each thing is good in itself but dreadful in the monotony of its combination.

Another thing: although a dinner should not be long, neither should it consist of samples, especially if set before men who are hungry!

The following menu might seem at first glance a good dinner, but it is one from which the average man would go home and forage ravenously in the ice box:

A canapé (good, but merely an appetizer)

Clear soup (a dinner party helping, and no substance)

Smelts (one apiece)

Individual croutards of sweetbreads (holding about a dessert-spoonful)

Broiled squab, small potato croquette, and string beans

Lettuce salad, with about one small cracker apiece

Ice cream

The only thing that had any sustaining quality, barring the potato which was not more than a mouthful, was the last, and very few men care to make their dinner of ice cream. If instead of squab there had been filet of beef cut in generous slices, and the potato croquettes had been more numerous, it would have been adequate. Or if there had been a thick cream soup, and a fish with more substance —such as salmon or shad, or a baked thick fish of which he could have had a generous helping—the squab would have been adequate also. But many women order trimmings rather than food; men usually like food.

THE DINNER TABLE OF YESTERDAY

All of us old enough to remember the beginning of this century can bring to mind the typical (and most fashionable) dinner table of that time. Occasionally it was oblong or rectangular, but its favorite shape was round, and a thick white damask cloth hung to the floor on all sides. Often as not there was a large lace centerpiece, and in the middle of it was a floral mound of roses (like a funeral piece, exactly), usually red. The four compotiers were much scrolled and embossed, and the four candlesticks, also scrolled, but not to match, had shades of perforated silver over red silk linings, like those in restaurants to-day. And there was a gas droplight thickly petticoated with fringed red silk. The plates were always heavily "jewelled" and hand painted, and enough forks and knives and spoons were arrayed at each "place" for a dozen courses. The glasses numbered at least six, and the entire table was laden with little dishes—and spoons! There were olives, radishes, celery and salted nuts in glass dishes; and about ten kinds of sugar-plums in ten different styles of ornate and bumpy silver dishes; and wherever a small space of tablecloth showed through, it was filled with either a big "Apostle" spoon or little Dutch ones criss-crossed.

Bread was always rolled in the napkin (and usually fell on the floor) and the oysters were occasionally found already placed on the table when the guests came in to dinner! Loading a table to the utmost of its capacity with useless implements which only in rarest instances had the least value, would seem to prove that quantity without quality must have been thought evidence of elegance and generous hospitality! And the astounding part of the bad taste epidemic was that few if any escaped. Even those who had inherited colonial silver and glass and china of consummate beauty, sent it dust-gathering to the attic and cluttered their tables with stuffy and spurious lumber.

But to-day the classic has come into its own again! As though recovering from an illness, good taste is again demanding severe beauty of form and line, and banishing everything that is useless or superfluous. During the last twenty years most of us have sent an army of lumpy dishes to the melting-pot, and junky ornaments to the ash heap along with plush table covers, upholstered mantel-boards and fern dishes! To-day we are going almost to the extreme of bareness, and putting nothing on our tables not actually needed for use.

THE DINING-ROOM

It is scarcely necessary to point out that the bigger and more ambitious the house, the more perfect its appointments must be. If your house has a great Georgian dining-room, the table should be set with Georgian or an *earlier* period English silver. Furthermore, in a "great" dining-room, all the silver should be real! "Real" meaning nothing so trifling as "sterling," but genuine and important "period" pieces made by Eighteenth Century silversmiths, such as de Lamerie or Crespell or Buck or Robertson, or perhaps one of their predecessors. Or if, like Mrs. Oldname, you live in an old Colonial house, you are perhaps also lucky enough to have inherited some genuine American pieces made by Daniel Rogers or Paul Revere! Or if you are an ardent admirer of Early Italian architecture and have built yourself a Fifteenth Century stone-floored and frescoed or tapestry-hung dining room, you must set your long refectory table with a "runner" of old hand-linen and altar embroidery, or perhaps Thirteenth Century damask and great cisterns or ewers and beakers in high-relief silver and gold; or in Callazzioli or majolica, with great bowls of fruit and church candlesticks of gilt, and even follow as far as is practicable the crude table implements of that time. It need not be pointed out that Twentieth Century appurtenances in a Thirteenth or Fifteenth Century room are anachronisms. But because the dining-table in the replica of a palace (whether English, Italian, Spanish or French) may be equipped with great "standing cups" and candelabra so heavy a man can scarcely lift one, it does not follow that all the rest of us who live in medium or small houses, should attempt anything of the sort. Nothing could be more out of proportion—and therefore in worse taste. Nor is it necessary, in order to have a table that is inviting, to set it with any of the completely exquisite things which all people of taste long for, but which are possessed (in quantity at least) only through wealth, inheritance, or "collector's luck."

A PLEASING DINING-ROOM AT LIMITED COST

Enchanting dining-rooms and tables have been achieved with an outlay amounting to comparatively nothing.

There is a dining-room in a certain small New York house that is quite as inviting as it is lacking in expensiveness. Its walls are rough-plastered "French gray." Its table is an ordinary drop-leaf kitchen one painted a light green that is almost gray; the chairs are wooden ones, somewhat on the Windsor variety, but made of pine and painted like the table, and the side tables or consoles are made of a cheap round pine table which has been sawed in half, painted gray-green, and the legless sides fastened to the walls. The glass curtains are point d'esprit net with a deep flounce at the bottom and outside curtains are (expensive) watermelon pink changeable taffeta. There is a gilt mirror over a cream (absolutely plain) mantel and over each console a picture of a conventional bouquet of flowers in a flat frame the color of the furniture, with the watermelon color of the curtains predominating in a neutral tint background. The table is set with a rather coarse cream-colored linen drawn-work centerpiece (a tea cloth actually) big enough to cover all but three inches of table edge. In the middle of the table is a glass bowl with a wide turn-over rim, holding deep pink flowers (roses or tulips) standing upright in glass flower holders as though growing. In midwinter, when real flowers are too expensive, porcelain ones take their place—unless there is a lunch or dinner party. The compotiers are glass urns and the only pieces of silver used are two tall Sheffield candelabra at night, without shades, the salts and peppers and the necessary spoons and forks. The knives are "ivory" handled.

SETTING THE TABLE

Everything on the table must be geometrically spaced; the centerpiece in the actual center, the "places" at equal distances, and all utensils balanced; beyond this one rule you may set your table as you choose.

If the tablecloth is of white damask, which for dinner is always good style, a "felt" must be put under it. (To say that it must be smooth and white, in other words perfectly laundered, is as beside the mark as to say that faces and hands should be clean!) If the tablecloth has lace insertions, it must on no account be put over satin or over a color. In a very "important" dining-room and on a very large table, a cloth of plain and finest quality damask with no trimming other than a monogram (or crest) embroidered on either side, is in better taste than one of linen with elaborations of lace and embroidery. Damask is the old-fashioned but essentially conservative (and safely best style) tablecloth, especially suitable in a high-ceilinged room that is either English, French, or of no special period, in decoration. Lace tablecloths are better suited to an Italian room—especially if the table is a refectory one. Handkerchief linen tablecloths embroidered and lace-inserted are also, strangely enough, suited to all quaint, low-ceilinged, old-fashioned but beautifully appointed rooms; the reason being that the lace cloth is put over a bare table. The lace cloth must also go over a refectory table without felt or other lining.

Very high-studded rooms (unless Italian) on the other hand, seem to need the thickness of damask. To be sure, one does see in certain houses—at the Gildings' for instance—an elaborate lace and embroidery tablecloth put on top of a plain one which in turn goes over a felt, but this combination is always somewhat overpowering, whereas lace over a bare table is light and fragile.

Another thing—very ornate, large, and arabesqued designs, no matter how marvellous as examples of workmanship, inevitably produce a vulgar effect.

All needlework, whether to be used on the table or on a

bed, must, in a beautifully finished house, be fine rather than striking. Coarse linen, coarse embroideries, all sorts of Russian drawn-work, Italian needlework or mosaic (but avoiding big scrolled patterns), are in perfect keeping— and therefore in good taste—in a cottage, a bungalow or a house whose furnishings are not too fine.

But whatever type of cloth is used, the middle crease must be put on so that it is an absolutely straight and unwavering line down the exact center from head to foot. If it is an embroidered one, be sure the embroidery is "right side out." Next goes the centerpiece which is always the chief ornament. Usually this is an arrangement of flowers in either a bowl or a vase, but it can be any one of an almost unlimited variety of things; flowers or fruit in any arrangement that taste and ingenuity can devise; or an ornament in silver that needs no flowers, such as a covered cup; or an epergne, which, however, necessitates the use of fruit, flowers or candy. Mrs. Wellborn, for instance, whose heirlooms are better than her income, rarely uses flowers, but has a wonderful old centerpiece that is ornament enough in itself. The foundation is a mirror representing a lake, surrounded by silver rocks and grass. At one side, jutting into the lake, is a knoll with a group of trees sheltering a stag and doe. The ornament is entirely of silver, almost twenty inches high, and about twenty inches in diameter across the "lake."

The Normans have a full-rigged silver ship in the center of their table and at either end rather tall lanterns, Venetian really, but rather appropriate to the ship; and the salt cellars are very tall ones (about ten inches high), of sea shells supported on the backs of dolphins.

However, to go back to table setting: A cloth laid straight; then a centerpiece put in the middle; then four candlesticks at the four corners, about half-way between the center and the edge of the table, or two candelabra at either end halfway between the places of the host and hostess and the centerpiece. Candles are used with or without shades. Fashion at the moment, says "without," which means that, in order to bring the flame well above people's eyes, candle-

sticks or candelabra must be high and the candles as long
as the proportion can stand.   Longer candles can be put in
massive candlesticks than in fragile ones.   But whether
shaded or not, there are candles on all dinner tables always!
The center droplight has gone out entirely.   Electroliers
in candlesticks were never good style, and kerosene lamps
in candlesticks—horrible!   Fashion says, "Candles! prefer-
ably without shades, but shades if you insist, and few or
many—but candles!"

Next comes the setting of the places.   (If it is an exten-
sion table, leaves have, of course, been put in; or if it is sta-
tionary, guests have been invited according to its size.)
The distance between places at the table must never be so
short that guests have no elbow room, and that the servants
can not pass the dishes properly; when the dining-room
chairs are very high backed and are placed so close as to
be almost touching, it is impossible for them not to risk
spilling something over some one.   On the other hand, to
place people a yard or more apart so that conversation has
to be shouted into the din made by everyone else's shouting,
is equally trying.   About two feet from plate center to plate
center is ideal.   If the chairs have narrow and low backs,
people can sit much closer together, especially at a small
round table, the curve of which leaves a spreading wedge
of space between the chairs at the back even if the seats
touch at the front corners.   But on the long straight sides
of a rectangular table in a very large—and impressive—
dining-room there should be at least a foot of space between the chairs.

SETTING THE PLACES

The necessary number of plates, with the pattern or initials right side up, are first put around the table at equal
distances (spaced with a tape measure if the butler or
waitress has not an accurate eye).   Then on the left of each
plate, handle towards the edge of the table, and prongs up,
is put the salad fork, the meat fork is put next, and then the
fish fork.   The salad fork, which will usually be the third

used, is thus laid nearest to the plate. If there is an entrée, the fork for this course is placed between the fish fork and that for the roast and the salad fork is left to be brought in later. On the right of the plate, and nearest to it, is put the steel meat knife, then the silver fish knife, the edge of each toward the plate. Then the soup spoon and then the oyster fork or grape fruit spoon. Additional forks and knives are put on the table during dinner.

In putting on the glasses, the water goblet is at the top and to the right of the knives, and the wine glasses are either grouped to the right of the goblet, or in a straight line slanting down from the goblet obliquely towards the right. (Butter plates are never put on a dinner table.) A dinner napkin folded square and flat is laid on each "place" plate; very fancy foldings are not in good taste, but if the napkin is very large, the sides are folded in so as to make a flattened roll a third the width of its height. (Bread should *not* be put in the napkin—not nowadays.) The place cards are usually put above the plate on the table-cloth, but some people put them on top of the napkin because they are more easily read.

When the places have been set, four silver dishes (or more on a very big table), either bowl or basket or paten shaped, are put at the four corners, between the candlesticks (or candelabra) and the centerpiece; or wherever there are four equally spaced vacancies on the table. These dishes, or compotiers, hold candy or fruit, chosen less for taste than for decorative appearance.

On a very large table the four compotiers are filled with candy, and two or four larger silver dishes or baskets are filled with fruit and put on alternately with the candy dishes. Flowers are also often put in two or four smaller vases, in addition to a larger and dominating one in the center.

Peppers and salts should be put at every other place. For a dinner of twelve there should be six salt cellars at least, if not six pepper pots.

Olives and radishes are served from the side table, but salted nuts are often put on the dinner table either in two big silver dishes, or in small individual ones.

HAVE SILVER THAT SHINES OR NONE

Lots of people who would not dream of using a wrinkled tablecloth or chipped glass or china, seem perfectly blind to dirty silver—silver that is washed clean of food of course, but so dull that it looks like jaundiced pewter.

Don't put any silver on your table if you can't have it cleaned. Infinitely rather have every ornament of glass or china—and if knives and forks have crevices in the design of their handles that are hard to clean, buy plain plated ones, or use tin! Anything is better than yellow-faced dirty-finger-nailed silver. The first thing to ask in engaging a waitress is, "Can you clean silver?" If she can't, she would better be something else.

Of course no waitress and no single-handed butler can keep silver the way it is kept in such houses as the Worldlys', nor is such perfection expected. The silver polishing of perfection in huge houses is done by such an expert that no one can tell whether a fork has that moment been sent from the silversmiths or not. It is not merely polished until it is bright, but burnished so that it is new! Every piece of silver in certain of the great establishments, or in smaller ones that are run like a great one, is never picked up by a servant except with a rouged chamois. No piece of silver is ever allowed by the slightest chance to touch another piece. Every piece is washed separately. The footman who gathers two or three forks in a bunch will never do it a second time, and keep his place. If the ring of a guest should happen to scratch a knife handle or a fork, the silver-polisher may have to spend an entire day using his thumb or a silver buffer, and rub and rub until no vestige of a scratch remains.

Perfection such as this is attainable only in a great house where servants are specialists of super-efficiency; but in every perfectly run house, where service is not too limited, every piece of silver that is put on the table, at every meal, is handled with a rouged chamois and given a quick wipe-off as it is laid on the dining table. No silver should ever be picked up in the fingers as that always leaves a mark.

And the way "moderate" households, which are nevertheless perfectly run for their size and type, have burnished silver, is by using not more than they can have cleaned.

In view of the present high cost of living (including wages) and the consequent difficulty, with a reduced number of servants, of keeping a great quantity of silver brilliant, even the most fashionable people are more and more using only what is essential, and in occasional instances, are taking to china! People who are lucky enough to have well-stored attics these days are bringing treasures out of them.

But services of Swansea or Lowestoft or Spode, while easily cleaned, are equally easily broken, so that genuine Eighteenth Century pieces are more apt to see a cabinet than a dinner table.

But the modern manufacturers are making enchanting "sets" that are replicas of the old. These tea sets with cups and saucers to match and with a silver kettle and tray, are seen almost as often as silver services in simple houses in the country, as well as in the small apartment in town.

DON'TS IN TABLE SETTING!

Don't put ribbon trimmings on your table. Satin bands and bows have no more place on a lady's table than have chop-house appurtenances. Pickle jars, catsup bottles, toothpicks and crackers are not private-house table ornaments. Crackers are passed with oyster stew and with salad, and any one who wants "relishes" can have them in his own house (though they insult the cook!). At all events, pickles and tomato sauces and other cold meat condiments are never presented at table in a bottle, but are put in glass dishes with small serving spoons. Nothing is ever served from the jar or bottle it comes in except certain kinds of cheese, Bar-le-Duc preserves (only sometimes) and wines. Pickles, jellies, jams, olives, are all put into small glass dishes.

Saucers for vegetables are contrary to all etiquette. The only extra plates ever permitted are the bread and butter plates which are put on at breakfast and lunch and supper above and to the left of the forks, but *never* at dinner.

The crescent-shaped salad plate, made to fit at the side of the place plate, is seen rarely in fashionable houses. When two plates are made necessary by the serving of game or broiled chicken or squab, for which the plate should be very hot, at the same time as the salad which is cold, the crescent-shaped plate is convenient in that it takes little room.

A correct and very good serving dish for a family of two, is the vegetable dish that has a partition dividing it into two or even three divisions, so that a small quantity of two or three vegetables can be passed at the same time.

Napkin rings are unknown in fashionable houses outside of the nursery. But in large families where it is impossible to manage such a wash as three clean napkins a day entail, napkin rings are probably necessary. In most moderately run houses, a napkin that is unrumpled and spotless after a meal, is put aside and used again for breakfast; but to be given a napkin that is not perfectly clean is a horrid thought. Perhaps though, the necessity for napkin rings results in the achievement of the immaculate napkin—which is quite a nice thought.

CORRECT SERVICE OF DINNER

Whether there are two at table or two hundred, plates are changed and courses presented in precisely the same manner.

For faultless service, if there are many "accompanied" dishes, two servants are necessary to wait on as few as two persons. But two can also efficiently serve eight; or with unaccompanied dishes an expert servant can manage eight alone, and with one assistant, he can perfectly manage twelve.

In old-fashioned times people apparently did not mind waiting tranquilly through courses and between courses, even though meat grew cold long before the last of many vegetables was passed, and they waited endlessly while a slow talker and eater finished his topic and his food. But people of to-day do not like to wait an unnecessary second. The moment fish is passed them, they expect the cucumbers or sauce, or whatever should go with the fish, to follow immediately. And when the first servant hands the meat course, they consider that they should not be expected to wait a moment for a second servant to hand the gravy or jelly or whatever goes with the meat. No service is good in this day unless swift—and, of course, soundless.

A late leader of Newport society who had a world-wide reputation for the brilliancy of her entertainments, had an equally well-known reputation for rapidly served dinners. "Twenty minutes is quite long enough to sit at table— ever!" is what she used to say, and what her household had to live up to. She had a footman to about every two guests and any one dining with her had to cling to the edge of his plate or it would be whisked away! One who looked aside or "let go" for a second found his plate gone! That was extreme; but, even so, better than a snail-paced dinner!

THE DINNER HOUR

In America the dinner hour is not a fixture, since it varies in various sections of the country. The ordinary New York hour when "giving a dinner" is eight o'clock, half past eight in Newport. In New York, when dining and going to the opera, one is usually asked for seven-fifteen, and for seven-thirty before going to a play. Otherwise only "quiet" people dine before eight. But invitations should, of course, be issued for whatever hour is customary in the place where the dinner is given.

THE BUTLER IN THE DINING-ROOM

When the dinner guests enter the dining-room, it is customary for the butler to hold out the chair of the mistress of the house. This always seems a discourtesy to the guests. And an occasional hostess insists on having the chair of the guest of honor held by the butler instead of her own. If there are footmen enough, the chair of each lady is held for her; otherwise the gentleman who takes her in to dinner helps her to be seated. Ordinarily where there are two servants, the head one holds the chair of the hostess and the second, the chair on the right of the host. The hostess always seats herself as quickly as possible so that the butler may be free to assist a guest to draw her chair up to the table.

In a big house the butler always stands throughout a meal back of the hostess' chair, except when giving one of the men under him a direction, or when pouring wine. He is not supposed to leave the dining-room himself or ever to handle a dish. In a smaller house where he has no assistant, he naturally does everything himself; when he has a second man or parlor-maid, he passes the principal dishes and the assistant follows with the accompanying dishes or vegetables.

So-called "Russian" service is the only one known in New York which merely means that nothing to eat is ever put on the table except ornamental dishes of fruit and candy. The meat is carved in the kitchen or pantry, vegetables are passed and returned to the side table. Only at breakfast or possibly at supper are dishes of food put on the table.

THE EVER-PRESENT PLATE

From the setting of the table until it is cleared for dessert, a plate must remain at every cover. Under the first two courses there are always two plates. The plate on which oysters or hors d'oeuvres are served is put on top of the place plate. At the end of the course the used plate is removed, leaving the place plate. The soup plate is also put on top of this same plate. But when the soup plate is removed, the underneath plate is removed with it, and a hot plate immediately exchanged for the two taken away. The place plate merely becomes a hot fish plate, but it is there just the same.

The Exchange Plate

If the first course had been a canapé or any cold dish that was offered in bulk instead of being brought on separate plates, it would have been eaten on the place plate, and an exchange plate would have been necessary before the soup could be served. That is, a clean plate would have been exchanged for the used one, and the soup plate then put on top of that. The reason for it is that a plate with food on it can never be exchanged for a plate that has had food on it; a clean one must come between.

If an entrée served on individual plates follows the fish, clean plates are first exchanged for the used ones until the whole table is set with clean plates. Then the entrée is put at each place in exchange for the clean plate. Although dishes are always presented at the left of the person served, plates are removed and replaced at the right.

Glasses are poured and additional knives placed at the right, but forks are put on as needed from the left.

May the Plates for Two Persons Be Brought in Together?

The only plates that can possibly be brought into the dining-room one in each hand are for the hors d'oeuvres, soup and dessert. The first two plates are placed on others which have not been removed, and the dessert plates need merely be put down on the tablecloth. But the plates of every other course have to be exchanged and therefore each individual service requires two hands. Soup plates, two at a time, would better not be attempted by any but the expert and sure-handed, as it is in placing one plate, while holding the other aloft that the mishap of "soup poured down some one's back" occurs! If only one plate of soup is brought in at a time, that accident at least cannot happen. In the same way the spoon and fork on the dessert plate can easily fall off, unless it is held level. "Two plates at a time" therefore is not a question of etiquette, but of the servant's skill.

Plate Removed When Fork Is Laid Down

Once upon a time it was actually considered impolite to remove a single plate until the last guest at the table had finished eating! In other days people evidently did not mind looking at their own dirty plates indefinitely, nor could they have minded sitting for hours at table. Good service to-day requires the removal of each plate as soon as the fork is laid upon it; so that by the time the last fork is put down, the entire table is set with clean plates and is ready for the next course.

DOUBLE SERVICE AND THE ORDER OF TABLE PRECEDENCE

At every well-ordered dinner, there should be a double service for ten or twelve persons; that is, no hot dish should, if avoidable, be presented to more than six, or nine at the outside. At a dinner of twelve, for instance, two dishes each holding six portions, are garnished exactly alike and presented at opposite ends of the table. One to the lady on the right of the host, and the other to the lady at the opposite end of the table. The services continue around to the right, but occasional butlers direct that after serving the "lady of honor" on the right of the host, the host is skipped and the dish presented to the lady on his left, after which the dish continues around the table to the left, to ladies and gentlemen as they come. In this event the second service starts opposite the lady of honor and also skips the first gentleman, after which it goes around the table to the left, skips the lady of honor and ends with the host. The first service when it reaches the other end of the table skips the lady who was first served and ends with the gentleman who was skipped.

It is perhaps more polite to the ladies to give them preference, but it is complicated, and leaves another gentleman as well as the host, sitting between two ladies who are eating while he is apparently forgotten. The object (which is to prevent the lady who is second in precedence from being served last) can be accomplished by beginning the first service from the lady on the right of the host and continuing on the right 6 places; the second service begins with the lady on the left of the host and continues on the left five places, and then comes back to the host. The best way of all, perhaps, is to vary the "honor" by serving the entrée and salad courses first to the lady on the left instead of to the lady on the right and continue the service of these two courses to the left.

A dinner of eighteen has sometimes two services, but if *very* perfect, three. Where there are three services they start with the lady of honor and the sixth from her on either side and continue to the right.

FILLING GLASSES

As soon as the guests are seated and the first course put in front of them, the butler goes from guest to guest on the right hand side of each, and asks "Apollinaris or plain water!" and fills the goblet accordingly. In the same way he asks later before pouring wine: "Cider, sir?" "Grape fruit cup, madam?" Or in a house which has the remains of a cellar, "Champagne?" or "Do you care for whisky and soda, sir?"

But the temperature and service of wines which used to be an essential detail of every dinner have now no place at all. Whether people will offer frappéd cider or some other iced drink in the middle of dinner, and a warmed something else to take the place of claret with the fish, remains to be seen. A water glass standing alone at each place makes such a meager and untrimmed looking table that most people put on at least two wine glasses, sherry and champagne, or claret and sherry, and pour something pinkish or yellowish into them. A rather popular drink at present is an equal mixture of white grape-juice and ginger ale with mint leaves and much ice. Those few who still have cellars, serve wines exactly as they used to, white wine, claret, sherry and Burgundy warm, champagne ice cold; and after dinner, green mint poured over crushed ice in little glasses, and other liqueurs of room temperature. Whisky is always poured at the table over ice in a tall tumbler, each gentleman "saying when" by putting his hand out. The glass is then filled with soda or Apollinaris.

As soon as soup is served the parlor-maid or a footman passes a dish or a basket of dinner rolls. If rolls are not available, bread cut in about two-inch-thick slices, is cut cross-ways again in three. An old-fashioned silver cake basket makes a perfect modern bread-basket. Or a small wicker basket that is shallow and inconspicuous will do. A guest helps himself with his fingers and lays the roll or bread on the tablecloth, always. No bread plates are ever on a table where there is no butter, and no butter is ever served at a dinner. Whenever there is no bread left at any one's place at table, more should be passed. The glasses should also be kept filled.

PRESENTING DISHES

Dishes are presented held flat on the palm of the servant's right hand; every hot one must have a napkin placed as a pad under it. An especially heavy meat platter can be steadied if necessary by holding the edge of the platter with the left hand, the fingers protected from being burned by a second folded napkin.

Each dish is supplied with whatever implements are needed for helping it; a serving spoon (somewhat larger than an ordinary tablespoon) is put on all dishes and a fork of large size is added for fish, meat, salad and any vegetables or other dishes that are hard to help. String beans, braised celery, spinach en branche, etc., need a fork and spoon. Asparagus has various special lifters and tongs, but most people use the ordinary spoon and fork, putting the spoon underneath and the fork, prongs down, to hold the stalks on the spoon while being removed to the plate. Corn on the cob is taken with the fingers, but is *never* served at a dinner party. A galantine or mousse, as well as peas, mashed potatoes, rice, etc., are offered with a spoon only.

THE SERVING TABLE

The serving table is an ordinary table placed in the corner of the dining-room near the door to the pantry, and behind a screen, so that it may not be seen by the guests at table. In a small dining-room where space is limited, a set of shelves like a single bookcase is useful.

The serving table is a halfway station between the dinner table and the pantry. It holds stacks of cold plates, extra forks and knives, and the finger bowls and dessert plates. The latter are sometimes put out on the sideboard, if the serving table is small or too crowded.

At little informal dinners all dishes of food after being passed are left on the serving table in case they are called upon for a second helping. But at formal dinners, dishes are never passed twice, and are therefore taken direct to the pantry after being passed.

CLEARING TABLE FOR DESSERT

At dinner always, whether at a formal one, or whether a member of the family is alone, the salad plates, or the plates of whatever course precedes dessert, are removed, leaving the table plateless. The salt cellars and pepper pots are taken off on the serving tray (without being put on any napkin or doily, as used to be the custom), and the crumbs are brushed off each place at table with a folded napkin onto a tray held under the table edge. A silver crumb scraper is still seen occasionally when the tablecloth is plain, but its hard edge is not suitable for embroidery and lace, and ruinous to a bare table, so that a napkin folded to about the size and thickness of an iron-holder is the crumb-scraper of to-day.

DESSERT

The captious say "dessert means the fruit and candy which come after the ices." "Ices" is a misleading word too, because suggestive of the individual "ices" which flourished at private dinners in the Victorian age, and still survive at public dinners, suppers at balls, and at wedding breakfasts, but which are seen at not more than one private dinner in a thousand—if that.

In the present world of fashion the "dessert" is ice-cream, served in one mold; not ices (a lot of little frozen images). And the refusal to call the "sweets" at the end of the dinner, which certainly include ice cream and cake, "dessert," is at least not the interpretation of either good usage or good society. In France, where the word "dessert" originated, "ices" were set apart from dessert merely because French chefs delight in designating each item of a meal as a separate course.   But chefs and cook-books notwithstanding, dessert means everything sweet that comes at the end of a meal.   And the great American dessert is ice cream—or pie.   Pie, however, is not a "company" dessert.   Ice cream on the other hand is the inevitable conclusion of a formal dinner.   The fact that the spoon which is double the size of a teaspoon is known as nothing but a dessert spoon, is offered in further proof that "dessert" is "spoon" and not "finger"*food!

Dessert Service

There are two, almost equally used, methods of serving dessert.   The first or "hotel method," also seen in many fashionable private houses, is to put on a china plate for ice cream or a first course, and the finger bowl on a plate by itself, afterwards.   In the "private house" service, the entire dessert paraphernalia is put on at once.

In detail: In the two-course, or hotel, service, the "dessert" plate is of china, or if of glass, it must have a china one under it.   A china dessert plate is just a fairly deep medium sized plate and it is always put on the table with a "dessert" spoon and fork on it.   After the inevitable ice cream has been eaten, a fruit plate with a finger bowl on it, is put on in exchange.   A doily goes under the finger bowl, and a fruit knife and fork on either side.

In the single course, or private house, service, the ice cream plate is of glass and belongs under the finger bowl which it matches.   The glass plate and finger bowl in turn are put on the fruit plate with a doily between, and the dessert spoon and fork go on either side of the finger bowl (instead of the fruit knife and fork).   This arrangement of plates is seen in such houses as the Worldlys' and the Oldnames', and in fact in most very well done houses.   The finger bowls and glass plates that match make a prettier service than the finger bowl on a china plate by itself; also it eliminates a change—but not a removal—of plates.   In this service, a guest lifts the finger bowl off and eats his ice cream on the glass plate, after which the glass plate is removed and the china one is left for fruit.

Some people think this service confusing because an occasional guest, in lifting off the finger bowl, lifts the glass plate too, and eats his dessert on his china plate. It is merely necessary for the servants to notice at which place the china plate has been used and to bring a clean one; otherwise a "cover" is left with a glass plate or a bare tablecloth for fruit. Also any one taking fruit must have a fruit knife and fork brought to him. Fruit is passed immediately after ice-cream; and chocolates, conserves, or whatever the decorative sweets may be, are passed last.

This single service may sound as though it were more complicated than the two-course service, but actually it is less. Few people use the wrong plate and usually the ice-cream plates having others under them can be taken away two at a time. Furthermore, scarcely any one takes fruit, so that the extra knives and forks are few, if any.

Before finishing dessert, it may be as well to add in detail, that the finger bowl doiley is about five or six inches in diameter; it may be round or square, and of the finest and sheerest needlework that can be found (or afforded). It must always be cream or white. Colored embroideries look well sometimes on a country lunch table but not at dinner. No matter where it is used, the finger bowl is less than half filled with cold water; and at dinner parties, a few violets, sweet peas, or occasionally a gardenia, is put in it. (A slice of lemon is never seen outside of a chophouse where eating with the fingers may necessitate the lemon in removing grease. Pretty thought!)

Black coffee is never served at a fashionable dinner table, but is brought afterwards with cigarettes and liqueurs into the drawing-room for the ladies, and with cigars, cigarettes and liqueurs into the smoking room for the gentlemen.

If there is no smoking-room, coffee and cigars are brought to the table for the gentlemen after the ladies have gone into the drawing-room.

PLACE CARDS

The place cards are usually about an inch and a half high by two inches long, sometimes slightly larger.　People of old family have their crest embossed in plain white; occasionally an elderly hostess, following a lifelong custom, has her husband's crest stamped in gold.　Nothing other than a crest must ever be engraved on a place card; and usually they are plain, even in the houses of old families.

Years ago "hand-painted" place cards are said to have been in fashion.　But excepting on such occasions as a Christmas or a birthday dinner, they are never seen in private houses to-day.

MENU CARDS

Small, standing porcelain slates, on which the menu is written, are seen on occasional dinner tables.　Most often there is only one which is placed in front of the host; but sometimes there is one between every two guests.

SEATING THE TABLE

As has already been observed, the most practical way to seat the table is to write the names on individual cards first, and then "place" them as though playing solitaire; the guest of honor on the host's right, the second lady in rank on his left; the most distinguished or oldest gentleman on the right of the hostess, and the other guests filled in between.

WHO IS THE GUEST OF HONOR?

The guest of honor is the oldest lady present, or a stranger whom you wish for some reason to honor.　A bride at her first dinner in your house, after her return from her honeymoon, takes, if you choose to have her, precedence over older people.　Or if a younger woman has been long away she, in this instance of welcoming her home, takes precedence over her elders. The guest of honor is always led in to dinner by the host and placed on his right, the second in importance sits on his left and is taken in to dinner by the gentleman on whose right she sits. The hostess is always the last to go into the dining-room at a formal dinner.

THE ENVELOPES FOR THE GENTLEMEN

In an envelope addressed to each gentleman is put a card on which is written the name of the lady he is to take down to dinner. This card just fits in the envelope, which is an inch or slightly less high and about two inches long. When the envelopes are addressed and filled, they are arranged in two neat rows on a silver tray and put in the front hall. The tray is presented to each gentleman just before he goes into the drawing-room, on his arrival.

THE TABLE DIAGRAM

A frame made of leather, round or rectangular, with small openings at regular intervals around the edge in which names written on cards can be slipped, shows the seating of the table at a glance. In a frame holding twenty-four cards, twelve guests would be indicated by leaving every other card place blank, or for eight, only one in three is filled. This diagram is shown to each gentleman upon his arrival, so that he can see who is coming for dinner and where he himself is placed. At a dinner of ten or less this diagram is especially convenient as "envelopes" are used only at formal dinners of twelve and over.

WHEN THE HOSTESS SITS AT THE SIDE

When the number of guests is a multiple of four, the host and hostess never sit opposite each other. It would bring two ladies and two gentlemen together if they did. At a table which seats two together at each end, the fact that the host is opposite a gentleman and the hostess opposite a lady is not noticeable; nor is it ever noticeable at a round table. But at a narrow table which has room for only one at the end, the hostess invariably sits in the seat next to that which is properly her own, putting in her place a gentleman at the end. The host usually keeps his seat rather than the hostess because the seat of honor is on his right; and in the etiquette governing dinners, the host and not the hostess is the more important personage!

When there are only four, they keep their own places, otherwise the host and hostess would sit next to each other. At a dinner of eight, twelve, sixteen, twenty, etc., the host keeps his place, but at supper for eight or twelve, the hostess keeps *her* place and the host moves a place to the right or left because the hostess at supper pours coffee or chocolate. And although the host keeps his seat at a formal dinner in honor of the lady he takes in, at a little dinner of eight, where there is no guest of honor, the host does not necessarily keep his seat at the expense of his wife unless he carves, in which case he must have the end place; just as at supper she has the end place in order to pour.

SIDEWALK, HALL, AND DRESSING ROOMS

One can be pretty sure on seeing a red velvet carpet spread down the steps of a house (or up! since there are so many sunken American basement entrances) that there are people for dinner. The carpet is kept rolled, or turned under near the foot (or top) of the steps until a few minutes before the dinner hour when it is spread across the width of the pavement by the chauffeur or whoever is on duty on the sidewalk. Very big or formal dinners often have an awning, especially at a house where there is much entertaining and which has an awning of its own; but at an ordinary house, for a dinner of twelve or so, the man on the pavement must, if it is raining, shelter each arriving guest under his coachman's umbrella from carriage to door. If it does not rain, he merely opens the doors of vehicles. Checks are never given at dinners, no matter how big; every motor is called by address at the end of the evening. The Worldly car is not shouted for as "Worldly!" but "xox Fifth Avenue!" The typical coachman of another day used to tell you "carriages are ordered for ten-fifteen." Carriages were nearly always ordered for that hour, though with slow and long dinners no one ever actually left until the horses had exercised for at least an hour! But the chauffeur of to-day opens the door in silence—unless there is to be a concert or amateur theatricals, when he, like the coachman says, "Motors are ordered for twelve o'clock," or whatever hour he is told to say.

In this day of telephone and indefinite bridge games, many people prefer to have their cars telephoned for, when they are ready to go home. Those who do not play bridge leave an eight o'clock dinner about half past ten, or at least order their cars for that hour.

In all modern houses of size there are two rooms on the entrance floor, built sometimes as dressing-rooms and nothing else, but more often they are small reception rooms, each with a lavatory off of it. In the one given to the ladies, there is always a dressing-table with toilet appointments on it, and the lady's maid should be on duty to give whatever service may be required; when there is no dressing-room on the ground floor, the back of the hall is arranged with coat-hangers and an improvised dressing-table for the ladies, since modern people—in New York at least—never go upstairs to a bedroom if they can help it. In fact, nine ladies out of ten drop their evening cloaks at the front door, handing them to the servant on duty, and go at once without more ado to the drawing-room. A lady arriving in her own closed car can't be very much blown about, in a completely air tight compartment and in two or three minutes of time!

Gentlemen also leave their hats and coats in the front part of the hall. A servant presents to each a tray of envelopes, and if there is one, the table diagram. Envelopes are not really necessary when there is a table diagram, since every gentleman knows that he "takes in" the lady placed on his right! But at very big dinners in New York or Washington, where many people are sure to be strangers to one another, an absent-minded gentleman might better, perhaps, have his partner's name safely in his pocket.

ANNOUNCING GUESTS

A gentleman always falls behind his wife in entering the drawing-room. If the butler knows the guests, he merely announces the wife's name first and then the husband's. If he does not know them by sight he asks whichever is nearest to him, "What name, please?" And whichever one is asked, answers: "Mr. and Mrs. Lake."

The butler then precedes the guests a few steps into the room where the hostess is stationed, and standing aside says in a low tone but very distinctly: "Mrs. Lake," a pause and then, "Mr. Lake." Married people are usually announced separately as above, but occasionally people have their guests announced "Mr. and Mrs.———."

ANNOUNCING PERSONS OF RANK

All men of high executive rank are not alone announced first, but take precedence of their wives in entering the room. The President of the United States is announced simply, "The President and Mrs. Harding." His title needs no qualifying appendage, since he and he solely, is *the* President. He enters first, and alone, of course; and then Mrs. Harding follows. The same form precisely is used for "The Vice-President and Mrs. Coolidge." A governor is sometimes in courtesy called "Excellency" but the correct announcement would be "the Governor of New Jersey and Mrs. Edwards." He enters the room and Mrs. Edwards follows. "The Mayor and Mrs. Thompson" observe the same etiquette; or in a city other than his own he would be announced "The Mayor of Chicago and Mrs. Thompson."

Other announcements are "The Chief Justice and Mrs. Taft," "The Secretary of State and Mrs. Hughes." "Senator and Mrs. Washington," but in this case the latter enters the room first, because his office is not executive.

According to diplomatic etiquette an Ambassador and his wife should be announced, "Their Excellencies the Ambassador and Ambassadress of Great Britain." The Ambassador enters the room first. A Minister Plenipotentiary is announced "The Minister of Sweden." He enters a moment later and "Mrs. Ogren" follows. But a First Secretary and his wife are announced, if they have a title of their own, "Count and Countess European," or "Mr. and Mrs. American."

The President, the Vice-President, the Governor of a State, the Mayor of a city, the Ambassador of a foreign Power—in other words, all executives—take precedence over their wives and enter rooms and vehicles first. But Senators, Representatives, Secretaries of legations and all other officials who are not executive, allow their wives to precede them, just as they would if they were private individuals.

Foreigners who have hereditary titles are announced by them: "The Duke and Duchess of Overthere." "The Marquis and Marchioness of Landsend," or "Sir Edward and Lady Blank," etc. Titles are invariably translated into English, "Count and Countess Lorraine," not "M. le Comte et Mme. la Comtesse Lorraine."

HOW A HOSTESS RECEIVES AT A FORMAL DINNER

On all occasions of formality, at a dinner as well as at a ball, the hostess stands near the door of her drawing-room, and as guests are announced, she greets them with a smile and a hand-shake and says something pleasant to each. What she says is nothing very important, charm of expression and of manner can often wordlessly express a far more gracious welcome than the most elaborate phrases (which as a matter of fact should be studiously avoided). Unless a woman's loveliness springs from generosity of heart and sympathy, her manners, no matter how perfectly practised, are nothing but cosmetics applied to hide a want of inner beauty; precisely as rouge and powder are applied in the hope of hiding the lack of a beautiful skin. One device is about as successful as the other; quite pleasing unless brought into comparison with the real.

Mrs. Oldname, for instance, usually welcomes you with some such sentences as, "I am very glad to see you" or "I am so glad you could come!" Or if it is raining, she very likely tells you that you were very unselfish to come out in the storm. But no matter what she says or whether anything at all, she takes your hand with a firm pressure and her smile is really a *smile* of welcome, not a mechanical exercise of the facial muscles. She gives you always—even if only for the moment—her complete attention; and you go into her drawing-room with a distinct feeling that you are under the roof, not of a mere acquaintance, but of a friend. Mr. Oldname who stands never very far from his wife, always comes forward and, grasping your hand, accentuates his wife's more subtle but no less vivid welcome. And either you join a friend standing near, or he presents you, if you are a man, to a lady; or if you are a lady, he presents a man to you.

Some hostesses, especially those of the Lion-Hunting and the New-to-Best-Society variety are much given to explanations, and love to say "Mrs. Jones, I want you to meet Mrs. Smith. Mrs. Smith is the author of 'Dragged from the Depths,' a most enlightening work of psychic insight." Or to a good-looking woman, "I am putting you next to the Assyrian Ambassador—I want him to carry back a flattering impression of American women!"

But people of good breeding do not over-exploit their distinguished guests with embarrassing hyperbole, or make personal remarks. Both are in worst possible taste. Do not understand by this that explanations can not be made; it is only that they must not be embarrassingly made to their faces. Nor must a "specialist's" subject be forced upon him, like a pair of manacles, by any exploiting hostess who has captured him. Mrs. Oldname might perhaps, in order to assist conversation for an interesting but reticent person, tell a lady just before going in to dinner, "Mr. Traveler who is sitting next to you at the table, has just come back from two years alone with the cannibals." This is not to exploit her "Traveled Lion" but to give his neighbor a starting point for conversation at table. And although personal remarks are never good form, it would be permissible for an older lady in welcoming a very young one, especially a débutante or a bride, to say, "How lovely you look, Mary dear, and what an adorable dress you have on!"

But to say to an older lady, "That is a very handsome string of pearls you are wearing," would be objectionable.

THE DUTY OF THE HOST

The host stands fairly near his wife so that if any guest seems to be unknown to all of the others, he can present him to some one. At formal dinners introductions are never general and people do not as a rule speak to strangers, except those next to them at table or in the drawing-room after dinner. The host therefore makes a few introductions if necessary. Before dinner, since the hostess is standing (and no gentleman may therefore sit down) and as it is awkward for a lady who is sitting, to talk with a gentleman who is standing, the ladies usually also stand until dinner is announced.

WHEN DINNER IS ANNOUNCED

It is the duty of the butler to "count heads" so that he may know when the company has arrived. As soon as he has announced the last person, he notifies the cook. The cook being ready, the butler, having glanced into the dining-room to see that windows have been closed and the candles on the table lighted, enters the drawing-room, approaches the hostess, bows, and says quietly, "Dinner is served."

The host offers his arm to the lady of honor and leads the way to the dining-room. All the other gentlemen offer their arms to the ladies appointed to them, and follow the host, in an orderly procession, two and two; the only order of precedence is that the host and his partner lead, while the hostess and her partner come last. At all formal dinners, place cards being on the table, the hostess does not direct people where to sit. If there was no table diagram in the hall, the butler, standing just within the dining-room door, tells each gentleman as he approaches "Right" or "Left."

"R" or "L" is occasionally written on the lady's name card in the envelopes given to the gentlemen, or if it is such a big dinner that there are many separate tables, the tables are numbered with standing placards (as at a public dinner) and the table number written on each lady's name card.

THE MANNERS OF A HOSTESS

First of all, a hostess must show each of her guests equal and impartial attention. Also, although engrossed in the person she is talking to, she must be able to notice anything amiss that may occur. The more competent her servants, the less she need be aware of details herself, but the hostess giving a formal dinner with uncertain dining-room efficiency has a far from smooth path before her. No matter what happens, if all the china in the pantry falls with a crash, she must not appear to have heard it. No matter what goes wrong she must cover it as best she may, and at the same time cover the fact that she is covering it. To give hectic directions, merely accentuates the awkwardness. If a dish appears that is unpresentable, she as quietly as possible orders the next one to be brought in. If a guest knocks over a glass and breaks it, even though the glass be a piece of genuine Steigel, her only concern must seemingly be that her guest's place has been made uncomfortable. She says, "I am so sorry, but I will have it fixed at once!" The broken glass is *nothing!* And she has a fresh glass brought (even though it doesn't match) and dismisses all thought of the matter.

Both the host and hostess must keep the conversation going, if it lags, but this is not as definitely their duty at a formal, as at an informal dinner. It is at the small dinner that the skilful hostess has need of what Thackeray calls the "showman" quality. She brings each guest forward in turn to the center of the stage. In a lull in the conversation she says beguilingly to a clever but shy man, "John, what was that story you told me——" and then she repeats briefly an introduction to a topic in which "John" particularly shines. Or later on, she begins a narrative and breaks off suddenly, turning to some one else, *"You tell them!"*

These examples are rather bald, and overemphasize the method in order to make it clear. Practise and the knowledge of human nature, or of the particular temperament with which she is trying to deal, can alone tell her when she may lead or provoke this or that one to being at his best, to his own satisfaction as well as that of the others who may be present. Her own character and sympathy are the only real "showman" assets, since no one "shows" to advantage except in a congenial environment.

THE LATE GUEST

A polite hostess waits twenty minutes after the dinner hour, and then orders dinner served. To wait more than twenty minutes, or actually fifteen after those who took the allowable five minutes grace, would be showing lack of consideration to many for the sake of one. When the late guest finally enters the dining-room, the hostess rises, shakes hands with her, but does not leave her place at table. She doesn't rise for a gentleman. It is the guest who must go up to the hostess and apologize for being late. The hostess must never take the guest to task, but should say something polite and conciliatory such as, "I was sure you would not want us to wait dinner!" The newcomer is usually served with dinner from the beginning unless she is considerate enough to say to the butler, "Just let me begin with this course."

Old Mrs. Toplofty's manners to late guests are an exception: on the last stroke of eight o'clock in winter and half after eight in Newport, dinner is announced. She waits for no one! Furthermore, a guest arriving after a course has been served, does not have to protest against disarranging the order of dinner since the rule of the house is that a course which has passed a chair is not to be returned. A guest missing his "turn" misses that course. The result is that everyone dining with Mrs. Toplofty arrives on the stroke of the dinner hour; which is also rather necessary, as she is one of those who like the service to be rushed through at top speed, and anyone arriving half an hour late would find dinner over.

It would be excellent discipline if there were more hostesses like her, but no young woman could be so autocratic and few older ones care (or dare) to be. Nothing shows selfish want of consideration more than being habitually late for dinner. Not only are others, who were themselves considerate, kept waiting, but dinner is dried and ruined for everyone else through the fault of the tardy one. And though expert cooks know how to keep food from becoming uneatable, no food can be so good as at the moment for which it is prepared, and the habitually late guest should be made to realize how unfairly she is meeting her hostess' generosity by destroying for every one the hospitality which she was invited to share.

On the other hand, before a formal dinner, it is the duty of the hostess to be dressed and in her drawing-room fifteen, or ten minutes at least, before the hour set for dinner. For a very informal dinner it is not important to be ready ahead of time, but even then a late hostess is an inconsiderate one.

ETIQUETTE OF GLOVES AND NAPKIN

Ladies always wear gloves to formal dinners and take them off at table. Entirely off. It is hideous to leave them on the arm, merely turning back the hands. Both gloves and fan are supposed to be laid across the lap, and one is supposed to lay the napkin folded once in half across the lap too, on top of the gloves and fan, and all three are supposed to stay in place on a slippery satin skirt on a little lap, that more often than not slants downward.

It is all very well for etiquette to say "They stay there," but every woman knows they don't! And this is quite a nice question: If you obey etiquette and lay the napkin on top of the fan and gloves loosely across your satin-covered knees, it will depend merely upon the heaviness and position of the fan's handle whether the avalanche starts right, left or forward, onto the floor. There is just *one* way to keep these four articles (including the lap as one) from disintegrating, which is to put the napkin cornerwise across your knees and tuck the two side corners under like a lap robe, with the gloves and the fan tied in place as it were. This ought not to be put in a book of etiquette, which should say you must do nothing of the kind, but it is either do that or have the gentleman next you groping under the table at the end of the meal; and it is impossible to imagine that etiquette should wish to conserve the picture of "gentlemen on all fours" as the concluding ceremonial at dinners.

THE TURNING OF THE TABLE

The turning of the table is accomplished by the hostess, who merely turns from the gentleman (on her left probably) with whom she has been talking through the soup and the fish course, to the one on her right. As she turns, the lady to whom the "right" gentleman has been talking, turns to the gentleman further on, and in a moment everyone at table is talking to a new neighbor. Sometimes a single couple who have become very much engrossed, refuse to change partners and the whole table is blocked; leaving one lady and one gentleman on either side of the block, staring alone at their plates. At this point the hostess has to come to the rescue by attracting the blocking lady's attention and saying, "Sally, you cannot talk to Professor Bugge any longer! Mr. Smith has been trying his best to attract your attention."

"Sally" being in this way brought awake, is obliged to pay attention to Mr. Smith, and Professor Bugge, little as he may feel inclined, must turn his attention to the other side. To persist in carrying on their own conversation at the expense of others, would be inexcusably rude, not only to their hostess but to every one present.

At a dinner not long ago, Mr. Kindhart sitting next to Mrs. Wellborn and left to himself because of the assiduity of the lady's farther partner, slid his own name-card across and in front of her, to bring her attention to the fact that it was "his turn."

ENEMIES MUST BURY HATCHETS

One inexorable rule of etiquette is that you must talk to your next door neighbor at a dinner table. You *must,* that is all there is about it!

Even if you are placed next to some one with whom you have had a bitter quarrel, consideration for your hostess, who would be distressed if she knew you had been put in a disagreeable place, and further consideration for the rest of the table which is otherwise "blocked," exacts that you give no outward sign of your repugnance and that you make a pretence at least for a little while, of talking together.

At dinner once, Mrs. Toplofty, finding herself next to a man she quite openly despised, said to him with apparent placidity, "I shall not talk to you—because I don't care to. But for the sake of my hostess I shall say my multiplication tables. Twice one are two, twice two are four ——" and she continued on through the tables, making him alternate them with her. As soon as she politely could she turned again to her other companion.

MANNERS AT TABLE

It used to be an offense, and it still is considered impolite, to refuse dishes at the table, because your refusal implies that you do not like what is offered you. If this is true, you should be doubly careful to take at least a little on your plate and make a pretence of eating some of it, since to refuse course after course can not fail to distress your hostess. If you are "on a diet" and accepted the invitation with that stipulation, your not eating is excusable; but even then to sit with an empty plate in front of you throughout a meal makes you a seemingly reproachful table companion for those of good appetite sitting next to you.

ATTACKING A COMPLICATED DISH

When a dinner has been prepared by a chef who prides himself on being a decorative artist, the guest of honor and whoever else may be the first to be served have quite a problem to know which part of an intricate structure is to be eaten, and which part is scenic effect!

The main portion is generally clear enough; the uncertainty is in whether the flowers are eatable vegetables and whether the things that look like ducks are potatoes, or trimming. If there are six or more, the chances are they are edible, and that one or two of a kind are embellishments only. Rings around food are nearly always to be eaten; platforms under food seldom, if ever, are. Anything that looks like pastry is to be eaten; and anything divided into separate units should be taken on your plate complete. You should not try to cut a section from anything that has already been divided into portions in the kitchen. Aspics and desserts are, it must be said, occasionally Chinese puzzles, but if you do help yourself to part of the decoration, no great harm is done.

Dishes are *never* passed from hand to hand at a dinner, not even at the smallest and most informal one. Sometimes people pass salted nuts to each other, or an extra sweet from a dish near by, but not circling the table.

LEAVING THE TABLE

At the end of dinner, when the last dish of chocolates has been passed and the hostess sees that no one is any longer eating, she looks across the table, and catching the eye of one of the ladies, slowly stands up. The one who happens to be observing also stands up, and in a moment everyone is standing. The gentlemen offer their arms to their partners and conduct them back to the drawing-room or the library or wherever they are to sit during the rest of the evening.

Each gentleman then slightly bows, takes leave of his partner, and adjourns with the other gentlemen to the smoking-room, where after-dinner coffee, liqueurs, cigars and cigarettes are passed, and they all sit where they like and with whom they like, and talk.

It is perfectly correct for a gentleman to talk to any other who happens to be sitting near him, whether he knows him or not. The host on occasions—but it is rarely necessary—starts the conversation if most of the guests are inclined to keep silent, by drawing this one or that into discussion of a general topic that everyone is likely to take part in. At the end of twenty minutes or so, he must take the opportunity of the first lull in the conversation to suggest that they join the ladies in the drawing-room.

In a house where there is no smoking-room, the gentlemen do not conduct the ladies to the drawing-room, but stay where they are (the ladies leaving alone) and have their coffee, cigars, liqueurs and conversation sitting around the table.

In the drawing-room, meanwhile, the ladies are having coffee, cigarettes, and liqueurs passed to them. There is not a modern New York hostess, scarcely even an old-fashioned one, who does not have cigarettes passed after dinner.

At a dinner of ten or twelve, the five or six ladies are apt to sit in one group, or possibly two sit by themselves, and three of four together, but at a very large dinner they inevitably fall into groups of four or five or so each. In any case, the hostess must see that no one is left to sit alone. If one of her guests is a stranger to the others, the hostess draws a chair near one of the groups and offering it to her single guest sits beside her. After a while when this particular guest has at least joined the outskirts of the conversation of the group, the hostess leaves her and joins another group where perhaps she sits beside some one else who has been somewhat left out. When there is no one who needs any especial attention, the hostess nevertheless sits for a time with each of the different groups in order to spend at least a part of the evening with all of her guests.

WHEN THE GENTLEMEN RETURN TO THE DRAWING-ROOM

When the gentlemen return to the drawing-room, if there is a particular lady that one of them wants to talk to, he naturally goes directly to where she is, and sits down beside her. If, however, she is securely wedged in between two other ladies, he must ask her to join him elsewhere. Supposing Mr. Jones, for instance, wants to talk to Mrs. Bobo Gilding, who is sitting between Mrs. Stranger and Miss Stiffleigh: Mr. Jones saunters up to Mrs. Gilding—

he must not look too eager or seem too directly to prefer her to the two who are flanking her position, so he says rather casually, "Will you come and talk to me?" Whereupon she leaves her sandwiched position and goes over to another part of the room, and sits down where there is a vacant seat beside her. Usually, however, the ladies on the ends, being accessible, are more apt to be joined by the first gentleman entering than is the one in the center, whom it is impossible to reach. Etiquette has always decreed that gentlemen should not continue to talk together after leaving the smoking-room, as it is not courteous to those of the ladies who are necessarily left without partners.

At informal dinners, and even at many formal ones, bridge tables are set up in an adjoining room, if not in the drawing-room. Those few who do not play bridge spend a half hour (or less) in conversation and then go home, unless there is some special diversion.

MUSIC OR OTHER ENTERTAINMENT AFTER DINNER

Very large dinners of fifty or over are almost invariably followed by some sort of entertainment. Either the dinner is given before a ball or a musicale or amateur theatricals, or professionals are brought in to dance or sing.

In this day when conversation is not so much a "lost" as a "wilfully abandoned" art, people in numbers can not be left to spend an evening on nothing but conversation. Grouped together by the hundred and with bridge tables absent, the modern fashionables in America, and in England, too, are as helpless as children at a party without something for them to do, listen to, or look at!

VERY BIG DINNERS

A dinner of sixty, for instance, is always served at separate tables; a center one of twenty people, and four corner tables of ten each. Or if less, a center table of twelve and four smaller tables of eight. A dinner of thirty-six or less is seated at a single table.

But whether there are eighteen, eighty, or one or two hundred, the setting of each individual table and the service is precisely the same. Each one is set with centerpiece, candles, compotiers, and evenly spaced plates, with the addition of a number by which to identify it; or else each table is decorated with different colored flowers, pink, yellow, orchid, white. Whatever the manner of identification, the number or the color is written in the corner of the ladies' name cards that go in the envelopes handed to each arriving gentleman at the door: "pink," "yellow," "orchid," "white," or "center table."

In arranging for the service of dinner the butler details three footmen, usually, to each table of ten, and six footmen to the center table of twenty. There are several houses (palaces really) in New York that have dining-rooms big enough to seat a hundred or more easily. But sixty is a very big dinner, and even thirty does not "go" well without an entertainment following it.

Otherwise the details are the same in every particular as well as in table setting: the hostess receives at the door; guests stand until dinner is announced; the host leads the way with the guest of honor. The hostess goes to table last. The host and hostess always sit at the big center table and the others at that table are invariably the oldest present. No one resents being grouped according to "age," but many do resent a segregation of ultra fashionables. You must never put all the prominent ones at one table, unless you want forever to lose the acquaintance of those at every other.

After dinner, the gentlemen go to the smoking-room and the ladies sit in the ballroom, where, if there is to be a theatrical performance, the stage is probably arranged. The gentlemen return, the guests take their places, and the performance begins. After the performance the leave-taking is the same as at all dinners or parties.

TAKING LEAVE

That the guest of honor must be first to take leave was in former times so fixed a rule that everyone used to sit on and on, no matter how late it became, waiting for her whose duty it was, to go! More often than not, the guest of honor was an absent-minded old lady, or celebrity, who very likely was vaguely saying to herself, "Oh, my! are these people never going home?" until by and by it dawned upon her that the obligation was her own!

But to-day, although it is still the obligation of the guest who sat on the host's right to make the move to go, it is not considered ill-mannered, if the hour is growing late, for another lady to rise first. In fact, unless the guest of honor is one *really*, meaning a stranger or an elderly lady of distinction, there is no actual precedence in being the one first to go. If the hour is very early when the first lady rises, the hostess, who always rises too, very likely says: "I *hope* you are not thinking of going!"

The guest answers, "We don't want to in the least, but Dick has to be at the office so early!" or "I'm sorry, but I must. Thank you so much for asking us."

Usually, however, each one merely says, "Good night, thank you so much." The hostess answers, "I am so glad you could come!" and she then presses a bell (not one that any guest can hear!) for the servants to be in the dressing-rooms and hall. When one guest leaves, they all leave—except those at the bridge tables. They all say, "Good night" to whomever they were talking with and shake hands, and then going up to their hostess, they shake hands and say, "Thank you for asking us," or "Thank you so much."

"Thank you so much; good night," is the usual expression. And the hostess answers, "It was so nice to see you again," or "I'm glad you could come." But most usually of all she says merely, "Good night!" and suggests friendliness by the tone in which she says it—an accent slightly more on the "good" perhaps than on the "night."

In the dressing-room, or in the hall, the maid is waiting to help the ladies on with their wraps, and the butler is at the door. When Mr. and Mrs. Jones are ready to leave, he goes out on the front steps and calls, "Mr. Jones' car!" The Jones' chauffeur answers, "Here," the butler says to either Mr. or Mrs. Jones, "Your car is at the door!" and they go out.

The bridge people leave as they finish their games; sometimes a table at a time or most likely two together. (Husbands and wives are never, if it can be avoided, put at the same table.)   Young people in saying good night say, "Good night, it has been too wonderful!" or "Good night, and thank you *so* much."   And the hostess smiles and says, "So glad you could come!" or just "Good night!"

THE LITTLE DINNER

The little dinner is thought by most people to be the very pleasantest social function there is.   It is always informal, of course, and intimate conversation is possible, since strangers are seldom, or at least very carefully, included.   For younger people, or others who do not find great satisfaction in conversation, the dinner of eight and two tables of bridge afterwards has no rival in popularity.   The formal dinner is liked by most people now and then (and for those who don't especially like it, it is at least salutary as a spine stiffening exercise), but for night after night, season after season, the little dinner is to social activity what the roast course is to the meal.

The service of a "little" dinner is the same as that of a big one.   As has been said, proper service in properly run houses is never relaxed, whether dinner is for eighteen or for two alone.   The table appointments are equally fine and beautiful, though possibly not quite so rare.   Really priceless old glass and china can't be replaced because duplicates do not exist and to use it three times a day would be to court destruction; replicas, however, are scarcely less beautiful and can be replaced if chipped.   The silver is identical; the food is equally well prepared, though a course or two is eliminated; the service is precisely the same.   The clothes that fashionable people wear every evening they are home alone, are, if not the same, at least as beautiful of their kind.   Young Gilding's lounge suit is quite as "handsome" as his dinner clothes, and he tubs and shaves and changes his linen when he puts it on.   His wife wears a tea gown, which is classified as a negligé rather in irony, since it is apt to be more elaborate and gorgeous (to say nothing of dignified) than half of the garments that masquerade these days as evening dresses!   They wear these informal

A DINNER SERVICE WITHOUT SILVER—"THE LITTLE DINNER IS THOUGHT BY MOST PEOPLE TO BE THE VERY PLEASANTEST SOCIAL FUNCTION THERE IS."

[Page 228.]

clothes only if very intimate friends are coming to dinner alone. "Alone" may include as many as eight!—but never includes a stranger.

Otherwise, at informal dinners, the host wears a dinner coat and the hostess a simple evening dress, or perhaps an elaborate one that has been seen by everyone and which goes on at little dinners for the sake of getting some "wear out of it." She never, however, receives formally standing, though she rises when a guest comes into the room, shakes hands and sits down again. When dinner is announced, gentlemen do not offer their arms to the ladies. The hostess and the other ladies go into the dining-room together, not in a procession, but just as they happen to come. If one of them is much older than the others, the younger ones wait for her to go ahead of them, or one who is much younger goes last. The men stroll in the rear. The hostess on reaching the dining-room goes to her own place where she stands and tells everyone where she or he is to sit. "Mary, will you sit next to Jim, and Lucy on his other side; Kate, over there, Bobo, next to me," etc.

CARVING ON THE TABLE

Carving is sometimes seen at "home" dinner tables. A certain type of man always likes to carve, and such a one does. But in forty-nine houses out of fifty, in New York at least, the carving is done by the cook in the kitchen—a roast while it is still in the roasting pan, and close to the range at that, so that nothing can possibly get cooled off in the carving. After which the pieces are carefully put together again, and transferred to an intensely hot platter. This method has two advantages over table carving; quicker service, and hotter food. Unless a change takes place in the present fashion, none except cooks will know anything about carving, which was once considered an art necessary to every gentleman. The boast of the high-born Southerner, that he could carve a canvas-back holding it on his fork, will be as unknown as the driving of a four-in-hand.

Old-fashioned butlers sometimes carve in the pantry, but in the most modern service *all* carving is done by the cook. Cold meats are, in the English service, put whole on the sideboard and the family and guests cut off what they choose themselves. In America cold meat is more often sliced and laid on a platter garnished with finely chopped meat jelly and water cress or parsley.

THE "STAG" OR "BACHELOR" DINNER

A man's dinner is sometimes called a "stag" or a "bachelor" dinner; and as its name implies, is a dinner given by a man and for men only. A man's dinner is usually given to celebrate an occasion of welcome or farewell. The best-known bachelor dinner is the one given by the groom just before his wedding. Other dinners are more apt to be given by one man (or a group of men) in honor of a noted citizen who has returned from a long absence, or who is about to embark on an expedition or a foreign mission. Or a young man may give a dinner in honor of a friend's twenty-first birthday; or an older man may give a dinner merely because he has a quantity of game which he has shot and wants to share with his especial friends.

Nearly always a man's dinner is given at the host's club or his bachelor quarters or in a private room in a hotel. But if a man chooses to give a stag dinner in his own house, his wife (or his mother) should *not* appear. For a wife to come downstairs and receive the guests for him, can not be too strongly condemned as out of place. Such a maneuver on her part, instead of impressing his guests with her own grace and beauty, is far more likely to make them think what a "poor worm" her husband must be, to allow himself to be hen-pecked. And for a mother to appear at a son's dinner is, if anything, worse. An essential piece of advice to every woman is: No matter how much you may want to say "How do you do" to your husband's or your son's friends—*don't!*

CHAPTER XV

DINNER GIVING WITH LIMITED EQUIPMENT

THE SERVICE PROBLEM

People who live all the year in the country are not troubled with formal dinner giving, because (excepting on great estates) formality and the country do not go together.

For the one or two formal dinners which the average city dweller feels obliged to give every season, nothing is easier than to hire professionals; it is also economical, since nothing is wasted in experiment. A cook equal to the Gildings' chef can be had to come in and cook your dinner at about the price of two charwomen; skilled butlers or waitresses are to be had in all cities of any size at comparatively reasonable fees.

The real problem is in giving the innumerable casual and informal dinners for which professionals are not only expensive, but inappropriate. The problem of limited equipment would not present great difficulty if the tendency of the age were toward a slower pace, but the opposite is the case; no one wants to be kept waiting a second at table, and the world of fashion is growing more impatient and critical instead of less.

The service of a dinner can however be much simplified and shortened by choosing dishes that do not require accessories.

DISHES THAT HAVE ACCOMPANYING CONDIMENTS

Nothing so delays the service of a dinner as dishes that must immediately be followed by necessary accessories. If there is no one to help the butler or waitress, no dish must be included on the menu—unless you are only one or two at table, or unless your guests are neither critical nor "modern"—that is not complete in itself.

231

For instance, fish has nearly always an accompanying dish. Broiled fish, or fish meunière, has ice-cold cucumbers sliced as thin as Saratoga chips, with a very highly seasoned French dressing, or a mixture of cucumbers and tomatoes. Boiled fish always has mousseline, Hollandaise, mushroom or egg sauce, and round scooped boiled potatoes sprinkled with parsley. Fried fish must always be accompanied by tartar sauce and pieces of lemon, and a boiled fish even if covered with sauce when served, is usually followed by additional sauce.

Many meats have condiments. Roast beef is never served at a dinner party—it is a family dish and generally has Yorkshire pudding or roast potatoes on the platter with the roast itself, and is followed by pickles or spiced fruit.

Turkey likewise, with its chestnut stuffing and accompanying cranberry sauce, is not a "company" dish, though excellent for an informal dinner. Saddle of mutton is a typical company dish—all mutton has currant jelly. Lamb has mint sauce—or mint jelly.

Partridge or guinea hen must have two sauce boats— presented on one tray—browned bread-crumbs in one, and cream sauce in the other.

Apple sauce goes with barnyard duck.

The best accompaniment to wild duck is the precisely timed 18 minutes in a quick oven! And celery salad, which goes with all game, need not be especially hurried.

Salad is always the accompaniment of "tame game," aspics, cold meat dishes of all sorts, and is itself "accompanied by" crackers and cheese or cheese soufflé or cheese straws.

SPECIAL MENUS OF UNACCOMPANIED DISHES

One person can wait on eight people if dishes are chosen which need no supplements. The fewer the dishes to be passed, the fewer the hands needed to pass them. And yet many housekeepers thoughtlessly order dishes within the list above, and then wonder why the dinner is so hopelessly slow, when their waitress is usually so good!

The following suggestions are merely offered in illustration; each housekeeper can easily devise further for herself. It is not necessary to pass anything whatever with melon or grapefruit, or a macédoine of fruit, or a canapé. Oysters, on the other hand, have to be followed by tabasco and buttered brown bread. Soup needs nothing with it (if you do not choose split pea which needs croutons, or petite marmite which needs grated cheese). Fish dishes which are "made" with sauce in the dish, such as sole au vin blanc, lobster Newburg, crab ravigote, fish mousse, especially if in a ring filled with plenty of sauce, do not need anything more. Tartar sauce for fried fish can be put in baskets made of hollowed-out lemon rind—a basket for each person—and used as a garnishing around the dish.

Filet mignon, or fillet of beef, both of them surrounded by little clumps of vegetables share with chicken casserole in being the life-savers of the hostess who has one waitress in her dining-room. Another dish, but more appropriate to lunch than to dinner, is of French chops banked against mashed potatoes, or purée of chestnuts, and surrounded by string beans or peas. None of these dishes requires any following dish whatever, not even a vegetable.

Fried chicken with corn fritters on the platter is almost as good as the two beef dishes, since the one green vegetable which should go with it, can be served leisurely, because fried chicken is not quickly eaten. And a ring of aspic with salad in the center does not require accompanying crackers as immediately as plain lettuce.

Steak and broiled chicken are fairly practical since neither needs gravy, condiment, or sauce—especially if you have a divided vegetable dish so that two vegetables can be passed at the same time.

If a hostess chooses not necessarily the above dishes but others which approximately take their places, she need have no fear of a slow dinner, if her one butler or waitress is at all competent.

THE POSSIBILITIES OF THE PLAIN COOK

In giving informal or little dinners, you need never worry because you cannot set the dishes of a "professional" dinner-party cook before your friends or even strangers; so long as the food that you are offering is good of its kind.

It is by no means necessary that your cook should be able to make the "clear" soup that is one of the tests of the perfect cook (and practically never produced by any other); nor is it necessary that she be able to construct comestible mosaics and sculptures. The essential thing is to prevent her from attempting anything she can't do well. If she can make certain dishes that are pretty as well as good to taste, so much the better. But remember, the more pretentious a dish is, the more it challenges criticism.

If your cook can make neither clear nor cream soup, but can make a delicious clam chowder, better far to have a clam chowder! On no account let her attempt clear green turtle, which has about as good a chance to be perfect as a suprême of boned capon—in other words, none whatsoever! And the same way throughout dinner. Whichever dishes your own particular Nora or Selma or Marie can do best, those are the ones you must have for your dinners. Another thing: it is not important to have variety. Because you gave the Normans chicken casserole the last time they dined with you is no reason why you should not give it to them again—if that is the "specialty of the house" as the French say. A late, and greatly loved, hostess whose Sunday luncheons at a huge country house just outside of Washington were for years one of the outstanding features of Washington's smartest society, had the same lunch exactly, week after week, year after year. Those who went to her house knew just as well what the dishes would be as they did where the dining-room was situated. At her few enormous and formal dinners in town, her cook was allowed to be magnificently architectural, but if you dined with her alone, the chances were ten to one that the Sunday chicken and pancakes would appear before you.

DO NOT EXPERIMENT FOR STRANGERS

Typical dinner-party dishes are invariably the temptation no less than the downfall of ambitious ignorance. Never let an inexperienced cook *attempt a new dish* for company, no matter how attractive her description of it may sound. Try it yourself, or when you are having family or most intimate friends who will understand if it turns out all wrong that it is a "trial" dish. In fact, it is a very good idea to share the testing of it with some one who can help you in suggestions, if they are needed for its improvement. Or supposing you have a cook who is rather poor on all dinner dishes, but makes delicious bread and cake and waffles and oyster stew and creamed chicken, or even hash! You can make a specialty of asking people to "supper." Suppers are necessarily informal, but there is no objection in that. Formal parties play a very small rôle anyway compared to informal ones. There are no end of people, and the smartest ones at that, who entertain only in the most informal possible way. Mrs. Oldname gives at most two formal dinners a year; her typical dinners and suppers are for eight.

PROPER DISHING

The "dishing" is quite as important as the cooking; a smear or thumb-mark on the edge of a dish is like a spot on the front of a dress!

Water must not be allowed to collect at the bottom of a dish (that is why a folded napkin is always put under boiled fish and sometimes under asparagus). And dishes must be hot; they cannot be too hot! Meat juice that has started to crust is nauseating. Far better have food too hot to eat and let people take their time eating it than that others should suffer the disgust of cold victuals! Sending in cold food is one of the worst faults (next to not knowing how to cook) that a cook can have.

PROFESSIONAL OR HOME DINING ROOM SERVICE

Just as it is better to hire a professional dinner-party cook than to run the risk of attempting a formal dinner with your own Nora or Selma unless you are very sure she is adequate, in the same way it is better to have a professional waitress as captain over your own, or a professional butler over your own inexperienced one, than to have your meal served in spasms and long pauses. But if your waitress, assisted by the chambermaid, perfectly waits on six, you will find that they can very nicely manage ten, even with accompanied dishes.

BLUNDERS IN SERVICE

If an inexperienced servant blunders, you should pretend, if you can, not to know it. Never attract anyone's attention to anything by apologizing or explaining, unless the accident happens to a guest. Under ordinary circumstances "least said, soonest mended" is the best policy.

If a servant blunders, it makes the situation much worse to take her to task, the cause being usually that she is nervous or ignorant. Speak, if it is necessary to direct her, very gently and as kindly as possible; your object being to restore confidence, not to increase the disorder. Beckon her to you and tell her as you might tell a child you were teaching: "Give Mrs. Smith a tablespoon, not a teaspoon." Or, "You have forgotten the fork on that dish." Never let her feel that you think her stupid, but encourage her as much as possible and when she does anything especially well, tell her so.

THE ENCOURAGEMENT OF PRAISE

Nearly all people are quick to censure but rather chary of praise. Admonish of course where you must, but censure only with justice, and don't forget that whether of high estate or humble, we all of us like praise—sometimes. When a guest tells you your dinner is the best he has ever eaten, remember that the cook cooked it, and tell her it was praised. Or if the dining-room service was silent and quick and perfect, then tell those who served it how well it was done. If you are entertaining all the time, you need not commend your household after every dinner you give, but if any especial willingness, attentiveness, or tact is shown, don't forget that a little praise is not only merest justice but is beyond the purse of no one.

CHAPTER XVI

LUNCHEONS, BREAKFASTS AND SUPPERS

THE INVITATIONS

Although the engraved card is occasionally used for an elaborate luncheon, especially for one given in honor of a noted person, formal invitations to lunch in very fashionable houses are nearly always written in the first person, and rarely sent out more than a week in advance. For instance:

Dear Mrs. Kindhart (or Martha):

Will you lunch with me on Monday the tenth at half after one o'clock?

Hoping so much to see you,

Sincerely (or affectionately),

Jane Toplofty.

If the above lunch were given in honor of somebody— Mrs. Eminent, for instance—the phrase "to meet Mrs. Eminent" would have been added immediately after the word "o'clock." At a very large luncheon for which the engraved card might be used, "To meet Mrs. Eminent" would be written across the top of the card of invitation.

Informal invitations are telephoned nearly always.

Invitation to a stand-up luncheon (or breakfast; it is breakfast if the hour is twelve or half after, and lunch if at one, or one-thirty), is either telephoned or written on an ordinary visiting card:

Sat. Oct. 2,
Luncheon at 1 o'clock

Mr. and Mrs. Gilding

GOLDEN HALL

If R.s.v.p. is added in the lower corner, the invitation should be answered, otherwise the hostess is obliged to guess how many to provide for.

Or, if the hostess prefers, a personal note is always courteous:

> Dear Mrs. Neighbor:
>
> We are having a stand-up luncheon on Saturday, October Second, at one o'clock, and hope that you and your husband and any guests who may be staying with you will come,
>
> > Very sincerely yours,
> >
> > > Alice Toplofty Gilding.
>
> Golden Hall
> Sept. 27.

A personal note always exacts a reply—which may however be telephoned, unless the invitation was worded in the formal third person. A written answer is more polite, if the hostess is somewhat of a stranger to you.

THE FORMAL LUNCHEON OF TO-DAY

Luncheon, being a daylight function, is never so formidable as a dinner, even though it may be every bit as formal and differ from the latter in minor details only. Luncheons are generally given by, and for, ladies, but it is not unusual, especially in summer places or in town on Saturday or Sunday, to include an equal number of gentlemen.

But no matter how large or formal a luncheon may be, there is rarely a chauffeur on the sidewalk, or a carpet or an awning. The hostess, instead of receiving at the door, sits usually in the center of the room in some place that has an unobstructed approach from the door. Each guest coming into the room is preceded by the butler to within a short speaking distance of the hostess, where he announces the new arrival's name, and then stands aside. Where there is a waitress instead of a butler, guests greet the hostess unannounced. The hostess rises, or if standing takes a step forward, shakes hands, says "I'm so glad to see you," or "I am delighted to see you," or "How do you do!" She then waits for a second or two to see if the guest who has just come in speaks to anyone; if not, she makes the necessary introduction.

When the butler or waitress has "counted heads" and knows the guests have arrived, he or she enters the room, bows to the hostess and says, "Luncheon is served."

If there is a guest of honor, the hostess leads the way to the dining-room, walking beside her. Otherwise, the guests go in twos or threes, or even singly, just as they happen to come, except that the very young make way for their elders, and gentlemen stroll in with those they happen to be talking to, or, if alone, fill in the rear. The gentlemen *never* offer their arms to ladies in going in to a luncheon—unless there should be an elderly guest of honor, who might be taken in by the host, as at a dinner. But the others follow informally.

THE TABLE

Candles have no place on a lunch or breakfast table; and are used only where a dining-room is unfortunately without daylight. Also a plain damask tablecloth (which must always be put on top of a thick table felt) is correct for dinner but not for luncheon. The traditional lunch table is "bare"—which does not mean actually bare at all, but that it has a centerpiece, either round or rectangular or square, with place mats to match, made in literally unrestricted varieties of linen, needlework and lace. The centerpiece is anywhere from 30 inches to a yard and a half square, on a square or round table, and from half a yard to a yard wide by length in proportion to the length of a rectangular table. The place mats are round or square or rectangular to match, and are put at the places.

Or if the table is a refectory one, instead of centerpiece and doilies, the table is set with a runner not reaching to the edge at the side, but falling over both ends. Or there may be a tablecloth made to fit the top of the table to within an inch or two of its edge. Occasionally there is a real cloth that hangs over like a dinner cloth, but it always has lace or open-work and is made of fine linen so that the table shows through.

The decorations of the table are practically the same as for dinner: flowers, or a silver ornament or epergne in the center, and flower dishes or compotiers or patens filled with ornamental fruit or candy at the corners. If the table is very large and rather bare without candles, four vases or silver bowls of flowers, or ornamental figures are added.

If the center ornament is of porcelain, four porcelain figures to match have at least a logical reason for their presence, or a bisque "garden" set of vases and balustrades, with small flowers and vines put in the vases to look as though they were growing, follows out the decoration. Most people, however, like a sparsely ornamented table.

The places are set as for dinner, with a place plate, three forks, two knives and a small spoon. The lunch napkin, which should match the table linen, is much smaller than the dinner napkin, and is not folded quite the same: it is folded like a handkerchief, in only four folds (four thicknesses). The square is laid on the place plate diagonally, with the monogrammed (or embroidered) corner pointing down toward the edge of the table. The upper corner is then turned sharply under in a flat crease for about a quarter of its diagonal length; then the two sides are rolled loosely under, making a sort of pillow effect laid sideways; with a straight top edge and a pointed lower edge, and the monogram displayed in the center.

Another feature of luncheon service, which is always omitted at dinner, is the bread and butter plate.

The Bread and Butter Plate

The butter plate has been entirely dispossessed by the bread and butter plate, which is part of the luncheon service always—as well as of breakfast and supper. It is a very small plate about five and a half to six and a half inches in diameter, and is put at the left side of each place just beyond the forks. Butter is sometimes put on the plate by the servant (as in a restaurant) but usually it is passed. Hot breads are an important feature of every luncheon; hot crescents, soda biscuits, bread biscuits, dinner rolls, or corn bread, the latter baked in small pans like pie plates four inches in diameter. Very thin bread that is roasted in the oven until it is curled and light brown (exactly like a large Saratoga chip), is often made for those who don't eat butter, and is also suitable for dinner. This "double-baked" bread, toast, and one or two of the above varieties, are all put in an old-fashioned silver cake-basket, or actual basket of wicker, and passed as often as necessary. Butter is also passed (or helped) throughout the meal until the table is cleared for dessert. Bread and butter plates are always removed with the salt and pepper pots.

THE SERVICE OF LUNCHEON

The service is identical with that of dinner. Carving is done in the kitchen and no food set on the table except ornamental dishes of fruit, candy and nuts. The plate service is also the same as at dinner. The places are never left plateless, excepting after salad, when the table is cleared and crumbed for dessert. The dessert plates and finger bowls are arranged as for dinner. Flowers are usually put in the finger bowls, a little spray of any sweet-scented flower, but "corsage bouquets" laid at the places with flower pins complete are in very bad taste.

Five courses at most (not counting the passing of a dish of candy or after-dinner coffee as a course), or more usually four actual courses, are thought sufficient in the smartest houses. Not even at the Worldlys' or the Gildings' will you ever see a longer menu than:

1. Fruit, or soup in cups
2. Eggs
3. Meat and vegetables
4. Salad
5. Dessert

or

1. Fruit
2. Soup
3. Meat and vegetables
4. Salad
5. Dessert

or

1. Fruit
2. Soup
3. Eggs
4. Fowl or "tame" game with salad
5. Dessert

An informal lunch menu is seldom more than four courses and would eliminate either No. 1 or No. 2 or No. 5.

The most popular fruit course is a macédoine or mixture of fresh orange, grape fruit, malaga grapes, banana, and perhaps a peach or a little pineapple; in fact, any sort of fruit cut into very small pieces, with sugar and maraschino, or rum, for flavor—or nothing but sugar—served in special bowl-shaped glasses that fit into long-stemmed and much larger ones, with a space for crushed ice between; or it can just as well be put in champagne or any bowl-shaped glasses, after being kept as cold as possible in the ice-box until sent to the table.

If the first course is grape fruit, it is cut across in half, the sections cut free and all dividing skin and seeds taken out with a sharp vegetable knife, and sugar put in it and left standing for an hour or so.   A slice of melon is served plain.

Soup at luncheon, or at a wedding breakfast or a ball supper, is never served in soup plates, but in two-handled cups, and is eaten with a teaspoon or a bouillon spoon.   It is limited to a few varieties: either chicken, or clam broth, with a spoonful of whipped cream on top; or bouillon, or green turtle, or strained chicken, or tomato broth; or in summer, cold bouillon or broth.

Lunch party egg dishes must number a hundred varieties. (See any cook book!)   Eggs that are substantial and "rich," such as eggs Benedict, or stuffed with pâté de foie gras and a mushroom sauce, should then be "balanced" by a simple meat, such as broiled chicken and salad, combining meat and salad courses in one.   On the other hand, should you have a light egg course, like "eggs surprise," you could have meat and vegetables, and plain salad; or an elaborate salad and no dessert.   Or with fruit and soup, omit eggs, especially if there is to be an aspic with salad.

The menu of an informal luncheon, if it does not leave out a course, at least chooses simpler dishes.   A bouillon or broth, shirred eggs or an omelette; or scrambled eggs on toast which has first been spread with a pâté or meat purée; then chicken or a chop with vegetables, a salad of plain lettuce with crackers and cheese, and a pudding or pie or any other "family" dessert.   Or broiled chicken, chicken croquettes, or an aspic, is served with the salad in very hot weather.   While cold food is both appropriate and palatable, no meal should ever be chosen without at least one course of hot food.   Many people dislike cold food, and it disagrees with others, but if you offer your guests soup, or even tea or chocolate, it would then do to have the rest of the meal cold.

LUNCHEON BEVERAGES

It is an American custom—especially in communities where the five o'clock tea habit is neither so strong nor so universal as in New York, for the lady of a house to have the tea set put before her at the table, not only when alone, but when having friends lunching informally with her, and to pour tea, coffee, or chocolate. And there is certainly not the slightest reason why, if she is used to these beverages and would feel their omission, she should not "pour out" what she chooses. In fact, although tea is never served hot at formal New York luncheons, iced tea is customary in all country houses in summer; and chocolate, not poured by the hostess, but brought in from the pantry and put down at the right of each plate, is by no means unusual at informal lunch parties.

Iced tea at lunch in summer is poured at the table by a servant from a glass pitcher, and is prepared like a "cup" with lemon and sugar, and sometimes with cut up fresh fruit and a little squeezed fruit juice. Plain cold tea may be passed in glasses, and lemon and sugar separately. At an informal luncheon, cold coffee, instead of tea, is passed around in a glass pitcher, on a tray that also holds a bowl of powdered sugar and a pitcher of cold milk, and another of as thick as possible cream. The guests pour their coffee to suit themselves into tall glasses half full of broken ice, and furnished with very long-handled spoons.

If tea or coffee or chocolate are not served during the meal, there is always a cup of some sort: grape or orange juice (in these days) with sugar and mint leaves, and ginger ale or carbonic water.

If dessert is a hot pudding or pastry, the "hotel service" of dessert plates should be used. The glass plate is particularly suitable for ice cream or any cold dessert, but is apt to crack if intensely hot food is put on it.

DETAILS OF ETIQUETTE AT LUNCHEONS

Gentlemen leave their coats, hats, sticks, in the hall; ladies leave heavy outer wraps in the hall, or dressing-room, but always go into the drawing-room with their hats and gloves on. They wear their fur neck pieces and carry their muffs in their hands, if they choose, or they leave them in the hall or dressing-room. But fashionable ladies *never* take off their hats. Even the hostess herself almost invariably wears a hat at a formal luncheon in her own house, though there is no reason why she should not be hatless if she prefers, or if she thinks she is prettier without! Guests, however, do not take off their hats at a lunch party even in the country. They take off their gloves at the table, or sooner if they choose, and either remove or turn up, their veils. The hostess does not wear gloves, ever. It is also very unsuitable for a hostess to wear a face veil in her own house, unless there is something the matter with her face, that must not be subjected to view! A hostess in a veil does not give her guests the impression of "veiled beauty," but the contrary. Guests, on the other hand, may with perfect fitness keep their veils on throughout the meal, merely fastening the lower edge up over their noses. They must *not* allow a veil to hang loose, and carry food under and behind it, nor must they eat with gloves on. A veil kept persistently over the face, and gloves kept persistently over the hands, means one thing: Ugliness behind. So unless you have to—don't!

The wearing of elaborate dresses at luncheons has gone entirely out of fashion; and yet one does once in a while see an occasional lady—rarely a New Yorker—who outshines a bird of paradise and a jeweler's window; but New York women of distinction wear rather simple clothes—simple meaning untrimmed, not inexpensive. Very conspicuous clothes are chosen either by the new rich, to assure themselves of their own elegance—which is utterly lacking—or by the muttons dressed lamb-fashion, to assure themselves of their own youth—which alas, is gone!

Gentlemen at luncheon in town on a Sunday wear cutaway coats; in other words, what they wear to church. On a Saturday, they wear their business suits, sack coat with either stiff or pleated-bosom shirts, and a starched collar. In the country, they wear country clothes.

WHAT THE SERVANTS WEAR

A butler wears his "morning" clothes; cutaway coat, gray striped trousers, high black waistcoat, black tie. A "hired waiter" wears a dress suit, but never a butler in a "smart" house; he does not put on his evening clothes until

"AT AN INFORMAL DINNER THE TABLE
APPOINTMENTS ARE EQUALLY FINE
AND BEAUTIFUL, THOUGH POSSIBLY
NOT QUITE SO RARE."   [Page 228.]

after six o'clock. In a smart house, the footmen wear their dress liveries, and a waitress and other maids wear their best uniforms.

THE GUESTS LEAVE

The usual lunch hour is half past one. By a quarter to three the last guest is invariably gone, unless, of course, it is a bridge luncheon, or for some other reason they are staying longer. From half an hour to three-quarters at the table, and from twenty minutes to half an hour's conversation afterwards, means that by half past two (if lunch was prompt) guests begin leaving. Once in a while, especially at a mixed lunch where perhaps talented people are persuaded to become "entertainers" the audience stays on for hours! But such parties are so out of the usual that they have nothing to do with the ordinary procedure, which is to leave about twenty minutes after the end of the meal.

The details for leaving are also the same as for dinners. One lady rises and says good-by, the hostess rises and shakes hands and rings a bell (if necessary) for the servant to be in the hall to open the door. When one guest gets up to go, the others invariably follow. They say "Good-by" and "Thank you so much."

Or, at a little luncheon, intimate friends often stay on indefinitely; but when lunching with an acquaintance one should never stay a moment longer than the other guests. The guest who sits on and on, unless earnestly pressed to do so, is wanting in tact and social sense. If a hostess invites a stranger who might by any chance prove a barnacle, she can provide for the contingency by instructing her butler or waitress to tell her when her car is at the door. She then says: "I had to have the car announced, because I have an appointment at the doctor's. Do wait while I put on my things—I shall be only a moment! And I can take you wherever you want to go!" This expedient should not be used when a hostess has leisure to sit at home, but on the other hand, a guest should never create an awkward situation for her hostess by staying too long.

In the country where people live miles apart, they naturally stay somewhat longer than in town.

Or two or three intimate friends who perhaps (especially in the country) come to spend the day, are not bound by rules of etiquette but by the rules of their own and their hostess' personal preference. They take off their hats or not as they choose, and they bring their sewing or knitting and sit all day, or they go out and play games, and in other ways behave as house-guests rather than visitors at luncheon. The only rule about such an informal gathering as this is, that no one should ever go and spend the day and make herself at home unless she is in the house of a really very intimate friend or relative, or unless she has been especially and specifically invited to do that very thing.

THE STAND-UP LUNCHEON

This is nothing more nor less than a buffet lunch. It is popular because it is a very informal and jolly sort of party —an indoor picnic really—and never attempted except among people who know each other well.

The food is all put on the dining table and every one helps himself. There is always bouillon or oyster stew or clam chowder. The most "informal" dishes are suitable for this sort of a meal, as for a picnic. There are two hot dishes and a salad, and a dessert which may be, but seldom is, ice cream.

Stand-up luncheons are very practical for hostesses who have medium sized houses, or when an elastic number of guests are expected at the time of a ball game, or other event that congregates a great many people.

A hunt breakfast is usually a stand-up luncheon. It is a "breakfast" by courtesy of half an hour in time. At twelve-thirty it is breakfast, at one o'clock it is lunch.

Regular weekly stand-up luncheons are given by hospitable people who have big places in the country and encourage their friends to drive over on some especial day when they are "at home"—Saturdays or Sundays generally —and intimate friends drop in uninvited, but always prepared for. On such occasions, luncheon is made a little more comfortable by providing innumerable individual tables to which people can carry the plates, glasses or cups and sit down in comfort.

SUPPERS

Supper is the most intimate meal there is, and since none but family or closest friends are ever included, invitations are invariably by word of mouth.

The atmosphere of a luncheon is often formal, but informal luncheons and suppers differ in nothing except day and evening lights, and clothes. Strangers are occasionally invited to informal luncheons, but only intimate friends are bidden to supper.

THE SUPPER TABLE

The table is set, as to places and napery, exactly like the lunch table, with the addition of candlesticks or candelabra as at dinner. Where supper differs from the usual lunch table is that in front of the hostess is a big silver tea-tray with full silver service for tea or cocoa or chocolate or breakfast coffee, most often chocolate or cocoa and either tea or coffee. At the host's end of the table there is perhaps a chafing dish—that is, if the host fancies himself a cook!

A number of people whose establishments are not very large, have very informal Sunday night suppers on their servants' Sundays out, and forage for themselves. The table is left set, a cold dish of something and salad are left in the icebox; the ingredients for one or two chafing dish specialties are also left ready. At supper time a member of the family, and possibly an intimate friend or two, carry the dishes to the table and make hot toast on a toaster.

This kind of supper is, in fact as well as spirit, an indoor picnic; thought to be the greatest fun by the Kindharts, but little appreciated by the Gildings, which brings it down, with so many other social customs, to a mere matter of personal taste.

Chapter XVII

BALLS AND DANCES

A ball is the only social function in America to which such qualifying words as splendor and magnificence can with proper modesty of expression be applied. Even the most elaborate wedding is not quite "a scene of splendor and magnificence" no matter how luxurious the decorations or how costly the dress of the bride and bridesmaids, because the majority of the wedding guests do not complete the picture. A dinner may be lavish, a dance may be beautiful, but a ball alone is prodigal, meaning, of course, a private ball of greatest importance.

On rare occasions, a great ball is given in a private house, but since few houses are big enough to provide dancing space for several hundred and sit-down supper space for a greater number still, besides smoking-room, dressing-room and sitting-about space, it would seem logical to describe a typical ball as taking place in the ballroom suite built for the purpose in nearly all hotels.

A HOSTESS PREPARES TO GIVE A BALL

The hostess who is not giving the ball in her own house goes first of all to see the manager of the hotel (or of whatever suitable assembly rooms there may be) and finds out which evenings are available. She then telephones—probably from the manager's office—and engages the two best orchestras for whichever evening both the orchestras and the ballroom are at her disposal. Of the two, music is of more importance than rooms. With perfect music the success of a ball is more than three-quarters assured; without it, the most beautiful decorations and most delicious supper are as flat as a fallen soufflé. You cannot give a ball or a dance that is anything but a dull promenade if you have dull music.

To illustrate the importance that prominent hostesses attach to music: a certain orchestra in New York to-day is forced to dash almost daily, not alone from party to party, but from city to city. Time and again its leader has conducted the music at a noon wedding in Philadelphia, and a ball in Boston; or a dancing tea in Providence and a ball that evening in New York; because Boston, Providence, New York and Philadelphia hostesses all at the present moment clamor for this one especial orchestra. The men have a little more respite than the leader since it is his "leading" that every one insists upon. Tomorrow another orchestra will probably make the daily tour of various cities' ballrooms.

At all balls, there must be two orchestras, so that each time one finishes playing the other begins. At very dignified private balls, dancers should not stand in the middle of the floor and clap as they do in a dance hall or cabaret if the music ends. On the other hand, the music should not end.

Having secured the music and engaged the ballroom, reception rooms, dressing-rooms and smoking-room, as well as the main restaurant (after it is closed to the public), the hostess next makes out her list and orders and sends out her invitations.

INVITATIONS

The fundamental difference between a ball and a dance is that people of all ages are asked to a ball, while only those of approximately one age are asked to a dance. Once in a while a ball is given to which the hostess invites every person on her visiting list. Mr. and Mrs. Titherington de Puyster give one every season, which although a credit to their intentions is seldom a credit to their sense of beauty!

Snobbish as it sounds and *is*, a brilliant ball is necessarily a collection of brilliantly fashionable people, and the hostess who gathers in all the oddly assorted frumps on the outskirts of society cannot expect to achieve a very distinguished result.

Ball invitations properly include all of the personal friends of the hostess no matter what their age, and all her better-known social acquaintances—meaning every one she would be likely to invite to a formal dinner. She does not usually invite a lady with whom she may work on a charitable committee, even though she may know her well, and like her. The question as to whether an outsider may be invited is not a matter of a hostess' own inclination so much as a question whether the "outsider" would be agreeable to all the "insiders" who are coming. If the co-worker is in everything a lady and a fitting ornament to society, the hostess might very possibly ask her.

If the ball to be given is for a débutante, all the débutantes whose mothers are on the "general visiting list" are asked as well as all young dancing men in these same families. In other words the children of all those whose names are on the general visiting list of a hostess are selected to receive invitations, but the parents on whose standing the daughters and sons are asked, are rarely invited.

When a List is Borrowed

A lady who has a débutante daughter, but who has not given any general parties for years—or ever, and whose daughter, having been away at boarding-school or abroad, has therefore very few acquaintances of her own, must necessarily in sending out invitations to a ball take the list of young girls and men from a friend or a member of her family. This of course could only be done by a hostess whose position is unquestioned, but having had no occasion to keep a young people's list, she has not the least idea who the young people of the moment are, and takes a short-cut as above. Otherwise she would send invitations to children of ten and spinsters of forty, trusting to their being of suitable age.

To take a family or intimate friend's list is also important to the unaccustomed hostess, because to leave out any of the younger set who "belong" in the groups which are included, is not the way to make a party a success. Those who don't find their friends go home, or stay and are bored, and the whole party sags in consequence. So that if a hostess knows the parents personally of, let us say, eighty per cent. of young society, she can quite properly include the twenty per cent. she does not know, so that the hundred per cent. can come together. In a small community it is rather cruel to leave out any of the young people whose friends are all invited. In a very great city on the other hand, an habitual hostess does not ask any to her house whom she does not know, but she can of course be as generous as she chooses in allowing young people to have invitations for friends.

Asking for an Invitation to a Ball

It is always permissible to ask a hostess if you may "bring" a dancing man who is a stranger to her. It is rather difficult to ask for an invitation for an extra girl, and still more difficult to ask for older people, because the hostess has no ground on which she can refuse without being rude; she can't say there is no room since no dance is really limited, and least of all a ball. Men who dance are always an asset, and the more the better; but a strange young girl hung around the neck of the hostess is about as welcome as a fog at a garden party. If the girl is to be brought and "looked after" by the lady asking for the invitation—who has herself been already invited—that is another matter, and the hostess can not well object. Or if the young girl is the fiancée of the man whose mother asks for the invitation, that is all right too; since he will undoubtedly come with her and see that she is not left alone. Invitations for older people are never asked for unless they are rather distinguished strangers and unquestionably suitable.

Invitations are never asked for persons whom the hostess already knows, since if she had cared to invite them she would have done so. It is, however, not at all out of the way for an intimate friend to remind her of some one who in receiving no invitation has more than likely been overlooked. If the omission was intentional, nothing need be said; if it was an oversight, the hostess is very glad to repair her forgetfulness.

Invitations for Strangers

An invitation that has been asked for a stranger is sent direct and without comment. For instance, when the Greatlakes of Chicago came to New York for a few weeks, Mrs. Norman asked both Mrs. Worldly and Mrs. Gilding to send them invitations; one to a musicale and the other to a ball. The Greatlakes received these invitations without Mrs. Norman's card enclosed or any other word of explanation, as it was taken for granted that Mrs. Norman would tell the Greatlakes that it was through her that the invitations were sent. The Greatlakes said "Thank you very much for asking us" when they bid their hostess good night, and they also left their cards immediately on the Worldlys and Gildings after the parties—but it was also the duty of Mrs. Norman to thank both hostesses—verbally—for sending the invitations.

DECORATIONS

So far as good taste is concerned, the decorations for a ball cannot be too lavish or beautiful. To be sure they should not be lavish if one's purse is limited, but if one's purse is really limited, one should not give a ball! A small dance or a dancing tea would be more suitable.

Ball decorations have on occasions been literally astounding, but as a rule no elaboration is undertaken other than hanging greens and flowers over the edge of the gallery, if there is a gallery, banking palms in corners, and putting up sheaves of flowers or trailing vines wherever most effective.

In any event the hostess consults her florist, but if the decorations are to be very important, an architect or an artist is put in charge, with a florist under him.

THE BALL BEAUTIFUL

Certain sounds, perfumes, places, always bring associated pictures to mind: Restaurant suppers; Paris! Distinguished-looking audiences; London! The essence of charm in society; Rome! Beguiling and informal joyousness; San Francisco! Recklessness; Colorado Springs! The afternoon visit; Washington! Hectic and splendid gaiety; New York! Beautiful balls; Boston!

There are three reasons (probably more) why the balls in Boston have what can be described only by the word "quality." The word "elegance" before it was misused out of existence expressed it even better.

First: Best Society in Boston having kept its social walls intact, granting admission only to those of birth and breeding, has therefore preserved a quality of unmistakable cultivation. There are undoubtedly other cities, especially in the South, which have also kept their walls up and their traditions intact—but Boston has been the wise virgin as well, and has kept her lamp filled.

Second: Boston hostesses of position have never failed to demand of those who would remain on their lists, strict obedience to the tenets of ceremonies and dignified behavior; nor ceased themselves to cultivate something of the "grand manner" that should be the birthright of every thoroughbred lady and gentleman.

Third: Boston's older ladies and gentlemen always dance at balls, and they neither rock around the floor, nor take their dancing violently. And the fact that older ladies of distinction dance with dignity, has an inevitable effect upon younger ones, so that at balls at least, dancing has not degenerated into gymnastics or contortions.

The extreme reverse of a "smart" Boston ball is one—no matter where—which has a roomful of people who deport themselves abominably, who greet each other by waving their arms aloft, who dance like Apaches or jiggling music-box figures, and who scarcely suggest an assemblage of even decent—let alone well-bred—people.

SUPPER

A sit-down supper that is served continuously for two or three hours, is the most elaborate ball supper. Next in importance is the sit-down supper at a set time. Third, the buffet supper which is served at dances but not at balls.

At the most fashionable New York balls, supper service begins at one and continues until three and people go when

they feel like it. The restaurant is closed to the public at
one o'clock; the entrance is then curtained or shut off from
the rest of the hotel. The tables are decorated with flowers
and the supper service opened for the ball guests. Guests
sit where they please, either "making up a table," or a man
and his partner finding a place wherever there are two
vacant chairs. At a private ball guests do not pay for anything or sign supper checks, or tip the waiter, since the
restaurant is for the time being the private dining-room of
the host and hostess.

At a sit-down supper at a set hour, the choice of menu
is unlimited, but suppers are never as elaborate now as they
used to be. Years ago few balls were given without terrapin, and a supper without champagne was as unheard of.
In fact, champagne was the heaviest item of expenditure
always. Decorations might be very limited, but champagne was as essential as music! Cotillion favors were also
an important item which no longer exists; and champagne
has gone its way with nectar, to the land of fable, so that if
you eliminate elaborate decorations, ball-giving is not half
the expense it used to be.

FOR A SIT-DOWN SUPPER THAT IS CONTINUOUS

When the service of supper continues for several hours,
it is necessary to select food that can be kept hot indefinitely
without being spoiled. Birds or broiled chicken, which
should be eaten the moment they are cooked, are therefore
unsuitable. Dishes prepared in sauce keep best, such as
lobster Newburg, sweetbreads and mushrooms, chicken à
la King, or creamed oysters. Pâtés are satisfactory as
the shells can be heated in a moment and hot creamed
chicken or oysters poured in. Of course all cold dishes and
salads can stand in the pantry or on a buffet table
all evening.

The menu for supper at a ball is entirely a matter of the
hostess' selection, but whether it is served at one time or
continuously, the supper menu at an important ball includes:

1. Bouillon or green turtle (clear) in cups.

2. Lobster a la Newburg (or terrapin or oyster pâté or another hot dish of shell-fish or fowl).
3. A second choice hot dish of some sort, squab, chicken and peas (if supper is served at a special hour) or croquettes and peas if continuous.
4. Salad, which includes every variety known, with or without an aspic.
5. Individual ices, fancy cakes.
6. Black coffee in little cups.

Breakfast served at about four in the morning and consisting of scrambled eggs with sausages or bacon and breakfast coffee and rolls is an occasional custom at both dances and balls.

There is always an enormous glass bowl of punch or orangeade—sometimes two or three bowls each containing a different iced drink—in a room adjoining the ballroom. And in very cold climates it is the thoughtful custom of some hostesses to have a cup of hot chocolate or bouillon offered each departing guest. This is an especially welcome attention to those who have a long drive home.

A DANCE

A dance is merely a ball on a smaller scale, fewer people are asked to it and it has usually, but not necessarily, simpler decorations.

But the real difference is that invitations to balls always include older people—as many if not more than younger ones—whereas invitations to a dance for a débutante, for instance, include none but very young girls, young men and the merest handful of the hostess' most intimate friends.

Supper may equally be a simple buffet or an elaborate sit-down one, depending upon the size and type of the house.

Or a dance may equally well as a ball be given in the "banquet" or smaller ballroom of a hotel, or in the assembly or ballroom of a club.

A formal dance differs from an informal one merely in elaboration, and in whether the majority of those present are strangers to one another; a really informal dance is one to which only those who know one another well are invited.

DETAILS OF PREPARATION FOR A BALL OR DANCE IN A PRIVATE HOUSE

There is always an awning and a red carpet down the steps (or up), and a chauffeur to open the carriage doors and a policeman or detective to see that strangers do not walk uninvited into the house. If there is a great crush, there is a detective in the hall to "investigate" anyone who does not have himself announced to the hostess.

All the necessary appurtenances such as awning, red carpet, coat hanging racks, ballroom chairs, as well as crockery, glass, napkins, waiters and food are supplied by hotels or caterers. (Excepting in houses like the Gildings,' where footmen's liveries are kept purposely, the caterer's men are never in footmen's liveries.)

Unless a house has a ballroom the room selected for dancing must have all the furniture moved out of it; and if there are adjoining rooms and the dancing room is not especially big, it adds considerably to the floor space to put no chairs around it. Those who dance seldom sit around a ballroom anyway, and the more informal grouping of chairs in the hall or library is a better arrangement than the wainscot row or wall-flower exposition grounds. The floor, it goes without saying, must be smooth and waxed, and no one should attempt to give a dance whose house is not big enough.

ETIQUETTE IN THE BALLROOM

New York's invitations are usually for "ten o'clock" but first guests do not appear before ten-thirty and most people arrive at about eleven or after. The hostess, however, must be ready to receive on the stroke of the hour specified in her invitations, and the débutante or any one the ball may be given for, must also be with her.

It is not customary to put the débutante's name on the formal "At Home" invitation, and it is even occasionally omitted on invitations that "request the pleasure of———" so that the only way acquaintances can know the ball is being given for the daughter is by seeing her standing beside her mother.

Mr. and Mrs. Robert Gilding

request the pleasure of

[Name of guest is written here]

company on Tuesday, the twenty-seventh of December

at ten o'clock

at the Fitz-Cherry

Dancing

R.s.v.p.
Twenty-three East Laurel Street

The hostess never leaves her post, wherever it is she is standing, until she goes to supper. If, as at the Ritz in New York, the ballroom opens on a foyer at the head of a stairway, the hostess always receives at this place. In a private house where guests go up in an elevator to the dressing rooms, and then walk down to the ballroom floor, the hostess receives either at the foot of the stairway, or just outside the ballroom.

THE HOSTESS AT A BALL

Guests arriving are announced, as at a dinner or afternoon tea, and after shaking hands with the hostess, they must pass on into the ballroom. It is not etiquette to linger beside the hostess for more than a moment, especially if later arrivals are being announced. A stranger ought never go to a ball alone, as the hostess is powerless to "look after" any especial guests; her duty being to stand in one precise place and receive. A stranger who is a particular friend of the hostess would be looked after by the host; but a stranger who is invited through another guest should be looked after by that other.

A gentleman who has received an invitation through a friend is usually accompanied by the friend who presents him. Otherwise when the butler announces him to the hostess, he bows, and says "Mrs. Norman asked you if I might come." And the hostess shakes hands and says "How do you do, I am very glad to see you." If other young men or any young girls are standing near, the hostess very likely introduces him. Otherwise, if he knows no one, he waits among the stags until his own particular sponsor appears.

After supper, when she is no longer receiving, the hostess is free to talk with her friends and give her attention to the roomful of young people who are actually in her charge.

When her guests leave she does not go back to where she received, but stands wherever she happens to be, shakes hands and says "Good night." There is one occasion when it is better not to bid one's hostess good night, and that is, if one finds her party dull and leaves again immediately; in this one case it is more polite to slip away so as to attract the least attention possible, but late in the evening it is inexcusably ill mannered not to find her and say "Good night" and "Thank you."

The duty of seeing that guests are looked after, that shy youths are presented to partners, that shyer girls are not left on the far wall-flower outposts, that the dowagers are taken in to supper, and that the elderly gentlemen are provided with good cigars in the smoking-room, falls to the host and his son or son-in-law, or any other near male member of the family.

MASQUERADE VOUCHERS

Vouchers or tickets of admission like those sent with invitations to assembly or public balls should be enclosed in invitations to a masquerade; it would be too easy otherwise for dishonest or other undesirable persons to gain admittance. If vouchers are not sent with the invitations, or better yet, mailed afterwards to all those who have accepted, it is necessary that the hostess receive her guests singly in a small private room and request each to unmask before her.

HOW TO WALK ACROSS A BALLROOM

If you analyze the precepts laid down by etiquette you will find that for each there is a perfectly good reason. Years ago a lady never walked across a ballroom floor without the support of a gentleman's arm, which was much easier than walking alone across a very slippery surface in high-heeled slippers. When the late Ward McAllister classified New York society as having four hundred people who were "at ease in a ballroom," he indicated that the ballroom was the test of the best manners. He also said at a dinner—after his book was published and the country had already made New York's "Four Hundred" a theme for cartoons and jests—that among the "Four hundred who were at ease," not more than ten could gracefully cross a ballroom floor alone. If his ghost is haunting the ballrooms of our time, it is certain the number is still further reduced. The athletic young woman of to-day strides across the ballroom floor as though she were on the golf course; the happy-go-lucky one ambles—shoulders stooped, arms swinging, hips and head in advance of chest; others trot, others shuffle, others make a rush for it. The young girl who could walk across a room with the consummate grace of Mrs. Oldname (who as a girl of eighteen was one of Mr. McAllister's ten) would have to be very assiduously sought for.

How does Mrs. Oldname walk? One might answer by describing how Pavlowa dances. Her body is perfectly balanced, she holds herself straight, and yet in nothing suggests a ramrod. She takes steps of medium length, and, like all people who move and dance well, walks from the hip, not the knee. On no account does she swing her arms, nor does she rest a hand on her hip! Nor when walking, does she wave her hands about in gesticulation.

Some one asked her if she had ever been *taught* to cross a ballroom floor. As a matter of fact, she had. Her grandmother, who was a Toplofty, made all her grandchildren walk daily across a polished floor with sand-bags on their heads. And the old lady directed the drill herself. No shuffling of feet and no stamping, either; no waggling of hips, no swinging of arms, and not a shoulder stooped. Furthermore, they were taught to enter a room and to sit for an indefinite period in self-effacing silence while their elders were talking.

Older gentlemen still give their arms to older ladies in all "promenading" at a ball, since the customs of a lifetime are not broken by one short and modern generation. Those of to-day walk side by side, except in going down to supper when supper is at a set hour.

At public balls when there is a grand march, ladies take gentlemen's arms.

DISTINCTION VANISHED WITH COTILLION

The glittering display of tinsel satin favors that used to be the featured and gayest decoration of every ballroom, is gone; the cotillion leader, his hands full of "seat checks," his manners a cross between those of Lord Chesterfield and a traffic policeman, is gone; and much of the distinction that used to be characteristic of the ballroom is gone with the cotillion. There is no question that a cotillion was prettier to look at than a mob scene of dancers crowding each other for every few inches of progress.

The reason why cotillions were conducive to good manners was that people were on exhibition, where now they are unnoticed components of a general crowd. When only a sixth, at most, of those in the room danced while others had nothing to do but watch them, it was only natural that those "on exhibition" should dance as well as they possibly could, and since their walking across the room and asking others to dance by "offering a favor" was also watched, grace of deportment and correct manners were not likely to deteriorate, either.

The cotillion was detested and finally banned by the majority who wanted to dance ceaselessly throughout the evening. But it was of particular advantage to the very young girl who did not know many men, as well as to what might be called the helpless type. Each young girl, if she had a partner, had a place where she belonged and where she sat throughout the evening. And since no couple could dance longer than the few moments allowed by the "figure," there was no chance of anyone's being "stuck"; so that the average girl had a better chance of being asked to dance than now—when, without programmes, and without cotillions, there is nothing to relieve the permanency of a young man's attachment to an unknown young girl once he asks her to dance.

THE ORDEAL BY BALLROOM

Instead of being easier, it would seem that time makes it increasingly difficult for any but distinct successes to survive the ordeal by ballroom. Years ago a débutante was supposed to flutter into society in the shadow of mamma's protecting amplitude; to-day she is packed off by herself and with nothing to relieve her dependence upon whoever may come near her. To liken a charming young girl in the prettiest of frocks to a spider is not very courteous; and yet the rôle of spider is what she is forced by the exigencies of ballroom etiquette to play. She *must* catch a fly, meaning a trousered companion, so as not to be left in placarded disgrace; and having caught him she must hang on to him until another takes his place.

There should be drastic revision of ballroom customs. There is a desperate need of what in local dancing classes was called the "Dump," where without rudeness a gentleman could leave a lady as soon as they had finished dancing.

There used to be a chaperon into whose care a young girl could be committed; there used to be the "dance card" or programme (still in vogue at public balls) that allotted a certain dance to a certain gentleman and lady equally. There used to be the cotillion which, while cruel, at least committed its acts of cruelty with merciful dispatch. When the cotillion began, the girl who had no partner—went home. She had to. Now, once she has acquired a companion, he is planted beside her until another takes his place. It is this fact and no other which is responsible for the dread that the average young girl feels in facing the ordeal of a ballroom, and for the discourteous unconcern shown by dancing men who under other conditions would be friendly.

The situation of a young girl, left cruelly alone, draws its own picture, but the reason for the callous and ill-mannered behavior of the average dancing man, may perhaps need a word of explanation.

For instance: Jim Smartlington, when he was a senior at college, came down to the Toploftys' ball on purpose to see Mary Smith. Very early, before Mary arrived, he saw a Miss Blank, a girl he had met at a dinner in Providence, standing at the entrance of the room. Following a casual impulse of friendliness he asked her to dance. She danced badly. No one "cut in" and they danced and danced, sat down and danced again. Mary arrived. Jim walked Miss Blank near the "stag" line and introduced several men, who bowed and slid out of sight with the dexterity of eels who recognized a hook. From half-past ten until supper at half-past one, Jim was "planted." He was then forced to tell her he had a partner for supper, and left her at the door of the dressing-room. There was no other place to "leave her." He felt like a brute and a cad, even though he had waited nearly three hours before being able to speak to the girl he had come purposely to see.

There really is something to be said on the man's side; especially on that of one who has to get up early in the morning and who, only intending to see one or two particular friends and then go home, is forced because of an impulse of courtesy not only to spend an endless and exhausting evening, but to be utterly unfit for his work next day.

One is equally sorry for the girl! But in the example above her stupid handling of the situation not only spoiled one well-intentioned man's evening, but completely "finished" herself so far as her future chances for success were concerned. Not alone her partner but every brother-stag who stood in the doorway mentally placarded her "Keep off." It is suicidal for a girl to make any man spend an entire evening with her. If at the end of two dances, there is no intimate friend she can signal to, or an older lady she can insist on being left with, she should go home; and if the same thing happens several times, she should not go to balls.

For the reasons given above, there is little that a hostess or host can do, unless a promise of "release" is held out, and that in itself is a deplorable situation; a humiliation that no young girl's name should be submitted to. And yet there it is! It is only necessary for a hostess to say "I want to introduce you to a charming——" And she is already speaking to the air.

Boston hostesses solve the problem of a young girl's success in a ballroom in a way unknown in New York, by having ushers.

USHERS

Each hostess chooses from among the best known young men in society, who have perfect address and tact, a number to act as ushers. They are distinguished by white boutonnières, like those worn by ushers at a wedding, and they are deputy hosts. It is their duty to see that wall-flowers are not left decorating the seats in the ballroom and it is also their duty to relieve a partner who has too long been planted beside the same "rosebud."

The ushers themselves have little chance to follow their own inclinations, and unless the "honor" of being chosen by a prominent hostess has some measure of compensation, the appointment—since it may not be refused—is a doubtful pleasure. An usher has the right to introduce anyone to anyone without knowing either principal personally and without asking any lady's permission. He may also ask a lady (if he has a moment to himself) to dance with him, whether he has ever met her or not, and he can also leave her promptly, because any "stag" called upon by an usher must dance. The usher in turn must release every "stag" he calls upon by substituting another; and the second by a third and so on. In order to make a ball "go," meaning to keep everyone dancing, the ushers have on occasions to spend the entire evening in relief work.

At a ball where there are ushers, a girl standing or sitting alone would at once be rescued by one of them, and a rotation of partners presented to her. If she is "hopeless" —meaning neither pretty nor attractive nor a good dancer—even the ushers are in time forced to relieve her partners and take her to a dowager friend of the hostess, beside whom she will be obliged to sit until she learns that she must seek her popularity otherwise than at balls.

On the other hand, on an occasion when none of her friends happen to be present, the greatest belle of the year can spend an equally deadly evening.

THE DANCE PROGRAM

The program or dance-card of public balls and college class dances, has undeniable advantages. A girl can give as many dances as she chooses to whomever she chooses; and a man can be sure of having not only many but uninterrupted dances with the one he most wants to be with—provided "she" is willing. Why the dance-card is unheard of at private balls in New York is hard to determine, except that fashionable society does not care to take its pleasure on schedule! The gilded youth likes to dance when the impulse moves him; he also likes to be able to stay or leave when he pleases. In New York there are often two or three dances given on the same evening, and he likes to drift from one to the other just as he likes to drift from one partner to another, or not dance at all if he does not want to. A man who writes himself down for the tenth jazz must be eagerly appearing on the stroke of the first bar. Or if he does not engage his partners busily at the opening of the evening, he can not dance at all—he may not want to, but he hates not being able to.

So again we come back to the present situation and the problem of the average young girl whose right it is, because of her youth and sweetness, to be happy and young—and not to be terrified, wretched and neglected. The one and only solution seems to be for her to join a group.

THE FLOCK-SYSTEM OF THE WISE FLEDGLINGS

If a number of young girls and young men come together —better yet, if they go everywhere together, always sit in a flock, always go to supper together, always dance with one another—they not only have a good time but they are sure to be popular with drifting odd men also. If a man knows that having asked a girl to dance, one of her group will inevitably "cut in," he is eager to dance with her. Or if he can take her "to the others" when they have danced long enough, he is not only delighted to be with her for a while but to sit with her "and the others" off and on throughout that and every other evening, because since there are always "some of them together" he can go again the moment he chooses.

Certain groups of clever girls sit in precisely the same place in a ballroom, to the right of the door, or the left, or in a corner. One might almost say they form a little club; they dance as much as they like, but come back "home" between whiles. They all go to supper together, and whether individuals have partners or not is scarcely noticeable, nor even known by themselves.

No young girl, unless she is a marked favorite, should ever go to a ball alone. If her especial "flock" has not as yet been systematized, she must go to a dinner before every dance, so as to go, and stay, with a group. If she is not asked to dinner, her mother must give one for her; or she must have at least one dependable beau—or better, two —who will wait for her and look out for her.

MAID GOES WITH HER

A young girl who goes to a ball without a chaperon (meaning of course a private ball), takes a maid with her who sits in the dressing-room the entire evening. Not only is it thought proper to have a maid waiting, but nothing can add more to the panic of a partnerless girl than to feel she has not even a means of escape by going home; she can always call a taxi as long as her maid is with her, and go. Otherwise she either has to stay in the ballroom or sit forlorn among the visiting maids in the dressing-room.

WHAT MAKES A YOUNG GIRL A BALLROOM SUCCESS

Much of the above is so pessimistic one might suppose that a ballroom is always a chamber of torture and the young girl taken as an example above, a very drab and distorted caricature of what "a real young girl" should be and is. But remember, the young girl who is a "belle of the ballroom" needs no advice on how to manage a happy situation; no thought spent on how to make a perfect time better. The ballroom is the most wonderful stage-setting there is for the girl who is a ballroom success. And for this, especial talents are needed just as they are for art or sport or any other accomplishment.

The great ballroom success, first and foremost, dances well. Almost always she is pretty. Beauty counts enormously at a ball. The girl who is beautiful and dances well is, of course, the ideal ballroom belle. But—this for encouragement—these qualities can in a measure at least be acquired. All things being more or less equal, the girl who dances best has the most partners. Let a daughter of Venus or the heiress of Midas dance badly, and she might better stay at home.

To dance divinely is an immortal gift, but to dance well can (except in obstinate cases, as the advertisements say) be taught. Let us suppose therefore, that she dances well, that she has a certain degree of looks, that she is fairly intelligent. The next most important thing, after dancing well, is to be unafraid, and to look as though she were having a good time. Conversational cleverness is of no account in a ballroom; some of the greatest belles ever known have been as stupid as sheep, but they have had happy dispositions and charming and un-self-conscious manners. There is one thing every girl who would really be popular should learn, in fact, she must learn—self-unconsciousness! The best advice might be to follow somewhat the precepts of mental science and make herself believe that a good time exists in her own mind. If she can become possessed with the idea that she is having a good time and look as though she were, the psychological effect is astonishing.

"CUTTING IN"

When one of the "stags" standing in the doorway sees a girl dance past whom he wants to dance with, he darts forward, lays his hand on the shoulder of her partner, who relinquishes his place in favor of the newcomer, and a third in turn does the same to him. Or, the one who was first dancing with her, may "cut in on" the partner who took her from him, after she has danced once around the ballroom. This seemingly far from polite maneuver, is considered correct behavior in best society in Boston, New York, Philadelphia, Buffalo, Pittsburgh, Chicago, San Francisco, and therefore most likely in all parts of America. (Not in London, nor on the Continent.)

At dances organized during the War in the canteens for soldiers and sailors on furlough, the men refused to "cut in" because they thought it was rude and undoubtedly it is, except that custom has made it acceptable. If, however, it still seems "rude" to the young men of Othertown to "cut in," then they should not do so.

SITTING OUT DANCES

On the other hand, if a girl is sitting in another room, or on the stairs with a man alone, a second one should not interrupt, or ask her to dance. If she is sitting in a group, he can go up and ask her, "Don't you want to dance some of this?" She then either smiles and says, "Not just now —I am very tired," or if she likes him, she may add, "Come and sit with us!"

To refuse to dance with one man and then immediately dance with another is an open affront to the first one— excusable only if he was intoxicated or otherwise actually offensive so that the affront was both intentional and justifiable. But under ordinary circumstances, if she is "dancing," she must dance with everyone who asks her; if she is "not dancing," she must not make exceptions.

An older lady can very properly refuse to dance and then perhaps dance briefly with her son or husband, without hurting her guest's proper pride, but having refused to dance with one gentleman she must not change her mind and dance later with another.

A young girl who is dancing may not refuse to change partners when another "cuts in." This is the worst phase of the "cutting in" custom; those who particularly want to dance together are often unable to take more than a dozen steps before being interrupted. Once in a while a girl will shake her head "No" to a "stag" who darts toward her. But that is considered rude. A few others have devised dancing with their eyes shut as a signal that they do not want to be "cut in on." But this is neither customary nor even a generally known practise.

It is always the privilege of the girl to stop dancing; a man is supposed to dance on and on, until she—or the music—stops.

ASKING FOR A DANCE

When a gentleman is introduced to a lady he says, "May I have some of this?" or "Would you care to dance?"

A lady never asks a gentleman to dance, or to go to supper with her, though she may if she is older, or if she is a young girl who is one of a "flock," she may say "Come and sit at our table!" This however would not imply that in sitting at "their" table he is supposed to sit next to her.

In asking a lady to go to supper, a gentleman should say "Will you go to supper with me?" Or "May I take you to supper?" He should never say, "Have you a partner?" as she is put in an awkward position in having to admit that she has none.

A BALL IS NOT A DANCING SCHOOL

Since a girl may not without rudeness refuse to dance with a man who "cuts in," a man who does not know how to dance is inexcusably inconsiderate if he "cuts in" on a good dancer and compels a young girl to become instructress for his own pleasure with utter disregard of hers. If at home, or elsewhere, a young girl volunteers to "teach" him, that is another matter, but even so, the ballroom is no place to practise—unless he is very sure that his dancing is not so bad as to be an imposition on his teacher.

THE MOST ELABORATE DINNER-DANCE EVER GIVEN IN NEW YORK

"The scene represents the palace and garden at Versailles. There were only four tables. Singers appeared on the balcony during dinner, other performers danced, sang and juggled on the pathways. After the dinner the pathways of grass were taken up to permit dancing by the guests."

[Page 271.]

NOVELTIES AND INNOVATIONS

Formal occasions demand strict conventions. At an important wedding, at a dinner of ceremony, at a ball, it is not only bad form but shocking to deviate from accepted standards of formality. "Surprize" is an element that must be avoided on all dignified occasions. Those therefore, who think it would be original and pleasing to spring surprizes on their guests at an otherwise conventional and formal entertainment, should save their ideas for a children's party where surprizes not only belong, but are delightedly appreciated. To be sure, one might perhaps consider that scenic effects or unusual diversions, such as one sees at a costume ball or a "period" dinner, belong under the head of "surprize." But in the first place such entertainments are not conventional; and in the second, details that are in accordance with the period or design of the ball or dinner are "conventions" after all.

On the other hand, in the country especially, nothing can be more fun or more appropriate than a barn dance, or an impromptu play, or a calico masquerade, with properties and clothes made of any old thing and in a few hours— even in a few minutes.

Music need not be an orchestra but it must be *good,* and the floor must be adequate and smooth. The supper is of secondary importance. As for manners, even though they may be "unrestrained," they can be meticulously perfect for all that! There is no more excuse for rude or careless or selfish behavior at a picnic than at a ball.

PUBLIC BALLS

A public ball is a ball given for a benefit or charity. A committee makes the arrangements and tickets are sold to the public, either by being put on sale at hotels or at the house of the secretary of the committee. A young girl of social position does not go to a public ball without a chaperon. To go in the company of one or more gentlemen would be an unheard-of breach of propriety.

SUBSCRIPTION DANCES AND BALLS

These are often of greater importance in a community than any number of its private balls. In Boston and Phil- adelphia for instance, a person's social standing is depend- ent upon whether or not she or he is "invited to the As- semblies." The same was once true in New York when the Patriarch and Assembly Balls were the dominating en- tertainments. In Baltimore too, a man's social standing is non-existent if he does not belong to the "Monday Ger- mans," and in many other cities membership in the subscrip- tion dances or dancing classes or sewing circles distinctly draws the line between the inside somebodies and the outside nobodies.

Subscription dances such as these are managed and all invitations are issued by patronesses who are always ladies of unquestioned social prominence. Usually these patron- esses are elected for life, or at least for a long period of years. When for one reason or another a vacancy occurs, a new member is elected by the others to fill her place. No outsider may ever ask to become a member. Usually a number of names are suggested and voted on at a meeting, and whoever wins the highest number of votes is elected.

The expenses of balls such as Assemblies, are borne by the patronesses collectively, but other types of dances are paid for by subscribers who are invited to "take tickets"— as will be explained.

How Subscription Dances Are Organized

Whether in city, town or village, the organization is the same: A small group of important ladies decide that it would be agreeable to have two or three balls—or maybe only one—a season. This original group then suggests ad- ditional names until they have all agreed upon a list suf- ficient in size to form a nucleus. These then are invited to join, and all of them at another meeting decide on the final size of the list and whom it is to include. The list may be a hundred, or it may stay at the original group of a half dozen or so. Let us for example say the complete list is fifty. Fifty ladies, therefore, the most prominent possible, are the patronesses or managers, or whatever they choose to call themselves. They also elect a chairman, a vice-chairman, a secretary, and a treasurer. They then elect seven or eight others who are to constitute the managing committee. The other thirty-eight or forty are merely "members" who will pay their dues and have the right to a certain number of tickets for each of the balls. These tickets, by the way, are never actually sent by the members themselves, who merely submit the names of the guests they have chosen to the committee on invitations. This is the only practical way to avoid duplication. Otherwise, let us say that Mrs. Oldname, Mrs. Worldly, Mrs. Norman and Mrs. Gilding each send their two tickets to the young Smartlingtons, which would mean that the Smartlingtons would have to return three, and those three invitations would start off on a second journey perhaps to be returned again.

On the other hand, if each patroness sends in a list, the top names which have not yet been entered in the "invitation book" are automatically selected, and the committee notify her to whom her invitations went.

There is also another very important reason for the sending in of every name to the committee: exclusiveness. Otherwise the balls would all too easily deteriorate into the character of public ones. Every name must be approved by the committee on invitations, who always hold a special meeting for the purpose, so that no matter how willing a certain careless member would be to include Mr. and Mrs. Unsuitable, she is powerless to send them tickets if they are not approved of.

As a matter of fact there is rarely any question of withholding invitations, since a serious objection would have to be sustained against one to warrant such an action on the part of the committee.

Number of Invitations Issued

With fifty members, each might perhaps be allowed, besides her own ticket, two ladies' invitations and four gentlemen's. That would make three hundred and fifty invitations available altogether. The founders can of course decide on whatever number they choose. Patronesses can also exchange tickets. One who might want to ask a double number of guests to the "First Assembly" can arrange with another to exchange her "Second Assembly" invitations for "First" ones. Also it often happens that the entire list sent in by a member has already been included, and not wanting to use her tickets, she gives them to another member who may have a débutante daughter and therefore be in need of extra ones.

Bachelor Balls (like the "Monday Germans" of Baltimore) are run by the gentlemen instead of the ladies. Otherwise they are the same as the Assemblies.

Other Forms of Subscription Dances

Other forms are somewhat different in that instead of dividing the expenses between members who jointly issue invitations to few or many guests, the committee of ten, we will say, invites either all the men who are supposed to be eligible or all the young girls, to subscribe to a certain number of tickets.

For instance, dances known usually as Junior Assemblies or the Holiday Dances are organized by a group of ladies —the mothers, usually, of débutantes. The members of the organization are elected just as the others are, for life. But they are apt after a few years, when their daughters are "too old," to resign in favor of others whose daughters are beginning to be grown. The débutantes of highest social position are invited to become members. Each one pays "dues" and has the privilege of asking two men to each dance. Mothers are not expected to go to these dances unless they are themselves patronesses. Sometimes young women go to these dances until they marry; often they are for débutantes, but most often they are for girls the year before they "come out," and for boys who are in college.

Patronesses Receive

At a subscription dance where patronesses take the place of a hostess, about four of these ladies are especially selected by the ball committee to receive. They always stand in line and bow to each person who is announced, but do not shake hands. The guest arriving also bows to the hostesses collectively (not four times). A lady, for instance, is announced: she takes a few steps toward the "receiving line" and makes a slight courtesy; the ladies receiving make a courtesy in unison, and the guest passes on. A gentleman bows ceremoniously, the way he was taught in dancing school, and the ladies receiving incline their heads.

CHAPTER XVIII

THE DEBUTANTE

HOW A YOUNG GIRL IS PRESENTED TO SOCIETY

Any one of various entertainments may be given to present a young girl to society. The favorite and most elaborate of these, but possible only to parents of considerable wealth and wide social acquaintance, is a ball. Much less elaborate, but equal in size, and second in favor to-day, is an afternoon tea with dancing. Third, and gaining in popularity, is a small dance, which presents the débutante to the younger set and a few of her mother's intimate friends. Fourth, is a small tea without music. Fifth, the mere sending out of the mother's visiting card with the daughter's name engraved below her own, announces to the world that the daughter is eligible for invitations.

A BALL FOR A DÉBUTANTE

A ball for a débutante differs in nothing from all other balls excepting that the débutante "receives" standing beside the hostess, and furthest from the entrance, whether that happens to be on the latter's right or left. The guests as they mount the stairs or enter the ballroom and are "announced," approach the hostess first, who, as she shakes hands with each, turns to the débutante and says "Mrs. Worldly, my daughter." Or "Cynthia, I want to present you to Mrs. Worldly." ("Want to" is used on this occasion because "may I" is too formal for a mother to say to her child.) A friend would probably know the daughter; in any event the mother's introduction would be, "You remember Cynthia, don't you?"

Each arriving guest always shakes hands with the débutante as well as with the hostess, and if there is a queue

276

of people coming at the same time, there is no need of saying anything beyond "How do you do?" and passing on as quickly as possible. If there are no others entering at the moment, each guest makes a few pleasant remarks. A stranger, for instance, would perhaps comment on how lovely, and many, the débutante's bouquets are, or express a hope that she will enjoy her winter, or talk for a moment or two about the "gaiety of the season" or "the lack of balls," or anything that shows polite interest in the young girl's first glimpse of society. A friend of her mother might perhaps say "You look too lovely, Cynthia dear, and your dress is enchanting!"

Personal compliments, however, are proper only from a close friend. No acquaintance, unless she is quite old, should ever make personal remarks. An old lady or gentleman might very forgivably say "You don't mind, my dear, if I tell you how sweet I think you look," or "What a pretty frock you have on." But it is bad taste for a young woman to say to another "What a handsome dress you have on!" and worst of all to add "Where did you get it?" The young girl's particular friends are, of course, apt to tell her that her dress is wonderful, or more likely, "simply divine."

It is customary in most cities to send a débutante a bouquet at her "coming out" party. They may be "bouquets" really, or baskets, or other decorative flowers, and are sent by relatives, friends of the family, her father's business associates, as well as by young men admirers. These "bouquets" are always banked near and if possible, around the place the débutante stands to receive. If she has great quantities, they are placed about the room wherever they look most effective. The débutante usually holds one of the bouquets while receiving, but she should remember that her choice of this particular one among the many sent her is somewhat pointed to the giver, so that unless she is willing to acknowledge one particular beau as "best" it is wiser to carry one sent by her father, or brother, especially if either send her one of the tiny 1830 bouquets that have been for a year or two in fashion, and are no weight to hold.

These bouquets are about as big around as an ordinary saucer, and just as flat on top as a saucer placed upside down. The flowers chosen are rosebuds or other compact flowers, massed tightly together, and arranged in a precise pattern; for instance, three or four pink rosebuds are put in the center, around them a row of white violets, around these a single row of the pink roses, surrounded again by violets, and so on for four or five rows. The bouquet is then set in stiff white lace paper, manufactured for the purpose, the stems wrapped in white satin ribbon, with streamers of white and pink ribbons about a quarter of an inch wide and tied to hang twenty inches or so long. The colors and patterns in which these little bouquets may be made are unlimited.

THE DÉBUTANTE RECEIVES

At a ball, where the guests begin coming about half past ten, the débutante must stand beside the hostess and "receive" until at least twelve o'clock—later if guests still continue to arrive.

At all coming-out parties, the débutante invites a few of her best girl friends to receive with her. Whether the party is in the afternoon or evening, these young girls wear evening dresses and come early and stay late. Their being asked to "receive" is a form of expression merely, as they never stand in line, and other than wearing pretty clothes and thus adding to the picture, they have no "duties" whatsoever.

AT SUPPER

The débutante goes to supper with a partner who has surely spoken for the privilege weeks or even months beforehand. But the rest of her own table is always made up by herself; that is, it includes the young girls who are her most intimate friends, and their supper partners. Her table is usually in the center of the dining-room, but there is no especial decoration to distinguish it, except that it is often somewhat larger than the other tables surrounding it, and a footman or waiter is detailed to tell any who may attempt to take it, that it is "reserved."

After supper the débutante has no duties and is free to enjoy herself.

The afternoon tea with dancing is described in the chapter on Teas and needs no further comment, since its etiquette is precisely the same as that for a ball. The débutante's bouquets are arranged as effectively as possible, and she receives with her mother, or whoever the hostess may be, until the queue of arriving guests thins out, after which she need be occupied with nothing but her own good time, and that of her friends.

Those of smaller means, or those who object to hotel rooms, ask only younger people, and give the tea in their own house. Where there are two rooms on a floor—drawing-room in front, dining-room back, and a library on the floor above, the guests are received in the drawing-room, but whether they dance in the dining-room or up in the library, depends upon which room is the larger. In either case the furniture is moved out. If possible the smallest room should be used to receive in, the largest to dance in, and the tea-table should be set in the medium one.

HOW MANY GUESTS MAY ONE ASK?

A hostess should never try to pack her house beyond the limits of its capacity. This question of how many invitations may safely be sent out is one which each hostess must answer for herself, since beyond a few obvious generalities no one can very well advise her.

Taking a hostess of "average" social position, who is bringing out a daughter of "average" attractiveness and popularity, it would be safe to say that every débutante and younger man asked to a party of any kind where there is dancing, will accept, but that not more than from half to one-third of the older people asked will put in an appearance.

LAVISH PARTIES GIVING WAY TO SIMPLE ONES

A ball, by the way, is always a general entertainment, meaning that invitations are sent to the entire dinner list— not only actual but potential—of the host and hostess, as well as to the younger people who are either themselves friends of the débutante, or daughters and sons of the friends and acquaintances of the hostess.

A dance differs from a ball in that it is smaller, less elaborate and its invitations are limited to the contemporaries of the débutante, or at most the youngest married set.

Invitations to a tea are even more general and should include a hostess' entire visiting list, irrespective of age or even personal acquaintance. The old-fashioned visiting list of the young hostess included the entire list of her mother, plus that of her mother-in-law, to which was added all the names acquired in her own social life. It can easily be seen that this list became a formidable volume by the time her daughter was old enough to "come out," and yet this entire list was supposed to be included in all "general" invitations!

In the present day, however, at least in New York, there is a growing tendency to eliminate these general or "impersonal" invitations. In smartest society, it is not even considered necessary that a "general" entertainment be given to introduce a daughter. In New York last winter there were scarcely a dozen private balls all told. Many of the most fashionable (and richest) hostesses gave dances limited to young girls of their daughters' ages and young dancing men. Even at many of the teas-with-dancing none but young people were asked.

Anyone who likes to sit on the bank and watch the tides of fashion rise and fall, cannot fail to notice that big and lavish entertainments are dwindling, and small and informal ones increasing. It is equally apparent, contrary to popular opinion, that extravagance of expenditure is growing less and less. It is years since any one has given such a ball, for instance, as the Venetian fête the Gildings gave to bring out their eldest daughter, when the entire first floor of the Fitz-Cherry was turned into a replica of Venice—

canals, gondolas, and all. Or the Persian ball of the Van-styles where the whole house was hung, as a background for Oriental costumes, with copper-gold draperies, against which stood at intervals Maxfield Parrish cypress trees. Or the moonlight dance of the Worldlys which was not a fancy dress one, but for which the ballroom was turned into a garden scene, lighted by simulated moonlight that would have added to the renown of Belasco.

Such entertainments as these seem almost "out of key" with the attitude of to-day. For although fancy-dress and elaborate parties are occasionally given, they are not usually given for débutantes, nor on the scale of those mentioned above.

THE DÉBUTANTE'S DRESS

At a ball, the débutante wears her very prettiest ball dress. Old-fashioned sentiment prefers that it be white, and of some diaphanous material, such as net or gauze or lace. It ought not to look overelaborate, even though it is spangled with silver or crystal or is made of sheer lace. It should suggest something light and airy and gay and, above all, young. For a young girl to whom white is unbecoming, a color is perfectly suitable as long as it is a pale shade. She should not wear strong colors such as red, or Yale blue, and on no account black! Her mother, of course, wears as handsome a ball dress as possible, and "all her jewels."

At an afternoon tea the débutante wears an evening dress—a very simple evening dress, but an evening dress all the same. Usually a very pale color, and quite un-trimmed, such as she might wear at home for dinner. Her mother wears an afternoon dress, not an evening one. Both mother and daughter wear long gloves, and neither they, nor the young girls receiving, wear hats.

To describe the details of clothes is futile. Almost before this page comes from the printer, the trend may quite likely change. But the tendency of the moment is toward greater simplicity—in effect at all events.

IN CONFIDENCE TO A DÉBUTANTE

Let us pretend a worldly old godmother is speaking, and let us suppose that you are a young girl on the evening of your coming-out ball. You are excited, of course you are! It is your evening, and you are a sort of little princess! There is music, and there are lights, and there are flowers everywhere—a great ballroom massed with them, tables heaped with bouquets—all for you! You have on an especially beautiful dress—one that was selected from among many others, just because it seemed to you the prettiest. Even your mother and married sister who, *"en grande tenue,"* have always seemed to you dazzling figures, have for the moment become, for all their brocades and jewels, merely background; and you alone are the center of the picture. Up the wide staircase come throngs of fashionables—who mean "the world." They are coming on purpose to bow to you! You can't help feeling that the glittering dresses, the tiaras, the ropes of pearls and chains of diamonds of the "dowagers," the stiff white shirt-fronts and boutonnières and perfectly fitting coats of the older gentlemen, as well as the best clothes of all the younger people, were all put on for you.

You shake hands and smile sweetly to a number of older ladies and shake hands with an equal number of gentlemen, all very politely and properly. Then suddenly, half way up the stairs you see Betty and Anne and Fred and Ollie. Of course your attention is drawn to them. You are vaguely conscious that the butler is shouting some stupid name you never heard of—that you don't care in the least about. Your mother's voice is saying "Mrs. zzzzzz———,"

Impatiently you give your hand to someone—you haven't the slightest idea who it is. So far as your interest is concerned, you might as well be brushing away annoying flies. Your smiles are directed to Betty and Anne. As they reach the top of the stairs you dart forward and enter into an excited conversation, deliberately overlooking a lady and gentleman who, without trying further to attract your attention, pass on. Later in the winter you will perhaps wonder why you alone among your friends are never asked to Great Estates. The lady and gentleman of whom you are so rudely unaware, happen to be Mr. and Mrs. Worldly, and you have entirely forgotten that you are a hostess, and furthermore that you have the whole evening, beginning at supper, when you can talk to these friends of yours! You can dance with Fred and Ollie and Jimmy all the rest of the evening; you can spend most of your time with them for the rest of your life if you and they choose. But when you are out in public, above all at a party which is for *you,* your duty in commonest civility is to overcome your impulses, and behave as a grown-up person—and a well-bred grown-up person at that!

It takes scarcely more than ten seconds to listen to the name that is said to you, to look directly and attentively at the one to whom the name belongs, to put out your hand firmly as you would take hold of something you like, (not something that you feel an aversion to), and with a smile say "How do you do." At your ball your mother says "Mrs. Worldly, my daughter." You look directly at Mrs. Worldly, put out your hand, say "How do you do, Mrs. Worldly." And she passes on. It takes no longer to be cordial and attentive than to be distrait and casual and rude, yet the impression made in a few seconds of actual time may easily gain or lose a friend for life. When no other guests are arriving, you can chatter to your own friends as much as you like, but as you turn to greet another stranger, you must show pleasure, not annoyance, in giving him your attention.

A happy attitude to cultivate is to think in your own mind that new people are all packages in a grab-bag, and that you can never tell what any of them may prove to be until you know what is inside the outer wrappings of casual appearances. To be sure, the old woman of the fairy tale, who turns out to be a fairy in disguise, is not often met with in real life, but neither is her approximate counterpart an impossibility.

As those who have sent you flowers approach, you must thank them; you must also write later an additional note of thanks to older people. But to your family or your own intimate friends, the verbal thanks—if not too casually made—are sufficient.

A FEW DON'TS FOR DÉBUTANTES

Don't think that because you have a pretty face, you need neither brains nor manners. Don't think that you can be rude to anyone and escape being disliked for it.

Whispering is always rude. Whispering and giggling at the same time have no place in good society. Everything that shows lack of courtesy toward others is rude.

If you would be thought a person of refinement, don't nudge or pat or finger people. Don't hold hands or walk arm-about-waist in public. Never put your hand on a man, except in dancing and in taking his arm if he is usher at a wedding or your partner for dinner or supper. Don't allow anyone to paw you. Don't hang on anyone for support, and don't stand or walk with your chest held in, and your hips forward, in imitation of a reversed letter S.

Don't walk across a ballroom floor swinging your arms. Don't talk or laugh loud enough to attract attention, and on no account force yourself to laugh. Nothing is flatter than laughter that is lacking in mirth. If you only laugh because something is irresistibly funny, the chances are your laugh will be irresistible too. In the same way a smile should be spontaneous, because you *feel* happy and pleasant; nothing has less allure than a mechanical grimace, as though you were trying to imitate a tooth-paste advertisement.

WHERE ARE THE "BELLES" OF YESTERDAY?

In olden days and until a comparatively short while ago, a young girl's social success was invariably measured by her popularity in a ballroom. It was the girl who had the most partners, who least frequently sat "against the wall," who carried home the greatest quantity of the baubles known as "favors," who was that evening's and usually the season's belle.

But to-day although ballroom popularity is still important as a test by which a young girl's success is measured, it is by no means the beginning and end that it used to be.

As repeated several times in this book, the day of the belle is past; beaux belong to the past too. To-day is the day of woman's equality with man, and if in proving her equality she has come down from a pedestal, her pedestal was perhaps a theatrical "property" at best and not to be compared for solid satisfaction with the level ground of the entirely real position she now occupies.

A girl's popularity in a ballroom is of importance to be sure, but not greatly more so than the dancing popularity of a youth.

There was a time when "wall-flowers" went to balls night after night where they either sat beside a chaperon or spent the evening in the dressing-room in tears. To-day a young girl who finds she is not a ballroom success avoids ballrooms and seeks her success otherwise. She does not sit in a corner and hope against hope that her "luck will turn" and that Prince Charming will surely some evening discover her. She sizes up the situation exactly as a boy might size up his own chances to "make" the crew or the football team.

TO-DAY'S SPECIALISTS IN SUCCESS

The girl of to-day soon discovers, if she does not know it already, that to be a ballroom belle it is necessary first of all to dance really well. A girl may be as beautiful as a young Diana or as fascinating as Circe, but if she is heavy or steps on her first partner's toes, never again will he ask her to dance. And the news spreads in an instant.

The girl of to-day therefore knows she must learn to dance well, which is difficult, since dancers are born, not made; or she must go to balls for supper only, or not go to balls at all, *unless*—she plays a really good game of bridge! In which case, her chances for popularity at the bridge tables, which are at all balls to-day, are quite as good as though she were a young Pavlowa in the ballroom.

Or perhaps she skates, or hunts, or plays a wonderful game of tennis or golf, each one of which opens a vista leading to popularity, and the possibilities for a "good time" which was after all the mainspring of old-fashioned ballroom success.

And since the day of femininity that is purely ornamental and utterly useless is gone by, it is the girl who does things well who finds life full of interests and of friends and of happiness. The old idea also has passed that measures a girl's popular success by the number of trousered figures around her. It is quality, not quantity, that counts; and the girl who surrounds herself with indiscriminate and possibly "cheap" youths does not excite the envy but the derision of beholders. To the highest type of young girl to-day it makes very little difference whether, in the inevitable "group" in which she is perpetually to be found, there are more men than girls or the opposite.

This does not mean that human nature has changed—scarcely! There always are and doubtless always will be any number of women to whom admiration and flirtation is the very breath of their nostrils, who love to parade a beau just as they love to parade a new dress. But the tendencies of the time do not encourage the flirtatious attitude. It is not considered a triumph to have many love affairs, but rather an evidence of stupidity and bad taste.

FRANKNESS OF TO-DAY

A young man playing tennis with a young girl a generation ago would have been forced patiently to toss her gentle balls and keep his boredom to himself, or he would have held her chin in his hand, while he himself stood shivering for hours in three feet of water, and tried his best to disguise his opinion as to the hopelessness of her ever learning to swim.

To-day he would frankly tell her she had better play tennis for a year or two with a "marker" or struggle at swimming by herself, and any sensible girl would take that advice!

FOR WHAT SHE REALLY IS

Instead of depending upon beauty, upon sex-appeal, the young girl who is "the success of to-day" depends chiefly upon her actual character and disposition. It is not even so necessary to do something well as to refrain from doing things badly. If she is not good at sports, or games, or dancing, then she must find out what she *is* good at and do that! If she is good for nothing but to look in the glass and put rouge on her lips and powder her nose and pat her hair, life is going to be a pretty dreary affair. In other days beauty was worshiped for itself alone, and it has votaries of sorts to-day. But the best type of modern youth does not care for beauty, as his father did; in fact, he doesn't care a bit for it, if it has nothing to "go with it," any more than he cares for butter with no bread to spread it on. Beauty *and* wit, *and* heart, *and* other qualifications or attributes is another matter altogether.

A gift of more value than beauty, is charm, which in a measure is another word for sympathy, or the power to put yourself in the place of others; to be interested in whatever interests them, so as to be pleasing to them, if possible, but not to occupy your thoughts in futilely wondering what they think about you.

Would you know the secret of popularity? It is unconsciousness of self, altruistic interest, and inward kindliness, outwardly expressed in good manners.

CHAPTER XIX

THE CHAPERON AND OTHER CONVENTIONS

A GLOOMY WORD

Of course there are chaperons and chaperons! But it must be said that the very word has a repellent school-teacherish sound. One pictures instinctively a humorless tyrant whose "correct" manner plainly reveals her true purpose, which is to take the joy out of life. That she can be —and often is—a perfectly human and sympathetic person, whose unselfish desire is merely to smooth the path of one who is the darling of her heart, in nothing alters the feeling of gloom that settles upon the spirit of youth at the mention of the very word "chaperon."

FREEDOM OF THE CHAPERONED

As a matter of fact the only young girl who is really "free," is she whose chaperon is never very far away. She need give conventionality very little thought, and not bother about her P's and Q's at all, because her chaperon is always a strong and protective defense; but a young girl who is unprotected by a chaperon is in the position precisely of an unarmed traveler walking alone among wolves—his only defense is in not attracting their notice.

To be sure the time has gone by when the presence of an elderly lady is indispensable to every gathering of young people. Young girls for whose sole benefit and protection the chaperon exists (she does not exist for her own pleasure, youthful opinion to the contrary notwithstanding), have infinitely greater freedom from her surveillance than had those of other days, and the typical chaperon is seldom seen with any but very young girls, too young to have married friends. Otherwise a young married woman, a bride perhaps scarcely out of her teens, is, on all ordinary occasions, a perfectly suitable chaperon, especially if her husband is present. A very young married woman gadding about without her husband is not a proper chaperon.

There are also many occasions when a chaperon is unnecessary! It is considered perfectly correct for a young girl to drive a motor by herself, or take a young man with her, if her family know and approve of him, for any short distance in the country. She may play golf, tennis, go to the Country Club, or Golf Club (if near by), sit on the beach, go canoeing, ride horseback, and take part in the normal sports and occupations of country life. Young girls always go to private parties of every sort without their own chaperon, but the fact that a lady issues an invitation means that either she or another suitable chaperon will be present.

THE BEST CHAPERON HERSELF

Ethically the only chaperon is the young girl's own sense of dignity and pride; she who has the right attributes of character needs no chaperon—ever. If she is wanting in decency and proper pride, not even Argus could watch over her! But apart from ethics, there are the conventions to think of, and the conventions of propriety demand that every young woman must be protected by a chaperon, because otherwise she will be misjudged.

THE RESIDENT CHAPERON

No young girl may live alone. Even though she has a father, unless he devotes his entire time to her, she must also have a resident chaperon who protects her reputation until she is married or old enough to protect it herself—which is not until she has reached a fairly advanced age, of perhaps thirty years or over if she is alone, or twenty-six or so if she lives in her father's house and behaves with such irreproachable circumspection that Mrs. Grundy is given no chance to set tongues wagging.

It goes without saying that a chaperon is always a lady, often one whose social position is better than that of her charge; occasionally she is a social sponsor as well as a moral one.   Her position, if she is not a relative, is very like that of a companion.   Above all, a chaperon must have dignity, and if she is to be of any actual service, she must be kind of heart and have intelligent sympathy and tact. To have her charge not only care for her, but be happy with her, is the only possible way such a relationship can endure.

Needless to say a chaperon's own conduct must be irreproachable and her knowledge of the world such as can only be gained by personal experience; but she need not be an old lady!   She can perfectly well be reasonably young, and a spinster.

Very often the chaperon "keeps the house," but she is never called a "housekeeper."   Nor is she a "secretary" though she probably draws the checks and audits the bills.

It is by no means unusual for mothers who are either very gay or otherwise busy, and cannot give most of their time to their grown and growing daughters, to put them in charge of a resident chaperon.   Often their governess—if she is a woman of the world—gives up her autocracy of the schoolroom and becomes social guardian instead.

THE DUTIES OF A CHAPERON

It is unnecessary to say that a chaperon has no right to be inquisitive or interfering unless for a very good reason. If an objectionable person—meaning one who can not be considered a gentleman—is inclined to show the young girl attentions, it is of course her duty to cut the acquaintance short at the beginning before the young girl's interest has become aroused.   For just such a contingency as this it is of vital importance that confidence and sympathy exist between the chaperon and her charge.   No modern young girl is likely to obey blindly unless she values the opinions of one in whose judgment and affection she has learned to believe.

WHEN INVITATIONS ARE SENT OUT BY A CHAPERON

Usually if a young girl is an orphan, living with a chaperon, a ball or formal party would be given in the name of an aunt or other near relative. If her father is alive, the invitations go out in his name of course, and he receives with her. But if it should happen that she has no near family at all, or if her chaperon is her social sponsor, the chaperon's name can be put on invitations. For example:

Miss Abigail Titherington

Miss Rosalie Gray

will be at home

on Saturday the fifth of December

from four until six o'clock

The Fitz-Cherry

Rosalie has no very near relatives and Miss Titherington has brought her up.

In sending out the invitations for a dinner (a young girl would not be giving a formal dinner) Rosalie telephones her friends "Will you dine with me (or us) next Monday?" or, "On the sixteenth?" It is not necessary to mention Miss Titherington because it is taken for granted that she will be present.

It is also not considered proper for a young girl ever to be alone as hostess. When she invites young girls and men to her house, Miss Titherington either "receives" them or comes into the room while they are there. If the time is afternoon, very likely she pours tea and when everyone has been helped, she goes into another room. She does not stay with them ever, but she is never very far away.

The chaperon (or a parent) should never go to bed until the last young man has left the house. It is an unforgivable breach of decorum to allow a young girl to sit up late at night with a young man—or a number of them. On returning home from a party, she must not invite or allow a man to "come in for a while." Even her fiancé must bid her good night at the door if the hour is late, and some one ought always to sit up, or get up, to let her in. No young girl ought to let herself in with a latch-key.

In old-fashioned days no lady had a latch-key. And it is still fitting and proper for a servant to open the door for her.

A young girl may not, even with her fiancé, lunch in a road house without a chaperon, or go on a journey that can by any possibility last over night. To go out with him in a small sail-boat sounds harmless enough, but might result in a questionable situation if they are becalmed, or if they are left helpless in a sudden fog. The Maine coast, for example, is particularly subject to fogs that often shut down without warning and no one going out on the water can tell whether he will be able to get back within a reasonable time or not. A man and a girl went out from Bar Harbor and did not get back until next day. Everyone knew the fog had come in as thick as pea-soup and that it was impossible to get home; but to the end of time her reputation will suffer for the experience.

A FEW PRECEPTS OF CONVENTION

At a dinner party given for young people in a private house, a somewhat older sister would be a sufficient chaperon. Or the young hostess' mother after receiving the guests may, if she chooses, dine with her husband elsewhere than in the dining-room, the parents' roof being supposedly chaperonage enough.

In going to tea in a college man's room, or in a bachelor's apartment, the proper chaperon should be a lady of fairly mature years. To see two or three apparently young people going into a bachelor's quarters would be open to criticism. There are many places which are unsuitable for young girls to go to whether they are chaperoned or not. No well brought up young girl should be allowed to go to supper at a cabaret until she is married, or has passed the age when "very young" can be applied to her.

CONVENTIONS THAT CHANGE WITH LOCALITY

In New York, for instance, no young girl of social standing may, without being criticized, go alone with a man to the theater. Absolutely no lady (unless middle-aged—and even then she would be defying convention) can go to dinner or supper in a restaurant alone with a gentleman. A lady, not young, who is staying in a very dignified hotel, can have a gentleman dine with her. But any married woman, if her husband does not object, may dine alone in her own home with any man she pleases or have a different one come in to tea every day in the week without being criticized.

A very young girl may motor around the country alone with a man, with her father's consent, or sit with him on the rocks by the sea or on a log in the woods; but she must not sit with him in a restaurant. All of which is about as upside down as it can very well be. In a restaurant they are not only under the surveillance of many eyes, but they can scarcely speak without being overheard, whereas short-distance motoring, driving, riding, walking or sitting on the seashore has no element of protection certainly. Again, though she may not lunch with him in a restaurant, she is sometimes (not always) allowed to go to a moving picture matinée with him! Why sitting in the dark in a moving picture theater is allowed, and the restaurant is tabu is very mysterious.

Older girls and young married women are beginning to lunch with men they know well in some of the New York restaurants, but not in others. In many cities it would be scandalous for a young married woman to lunch with a man not her husband, but quite all right for a young girl and man to lunch at a country club. This last is reasonable because the room is undoubtedly filled with people they

know—who act as potential chaperons. Nearly everywhere it is thought proper for them to go to a dancing club
for tea, if the "club" is managed by a chaperon.

As said above, interpretation of what is proper shifts
according to locality. Even in Victorian days it was proper
in Baltimore for a young girl to go to the theater alone
with a man, and to have him see her home from a ball was
not only permitted but absolutely correct.

"MRS. GRUNDY"

Of course every one has his own portrait of Mrs.
Grundy, and some idea of the personality she shows to him;
but has any one ever tried to ferret out that disagreeable
old woman's own position; to find out where she lives and
why she has nothing to do but meddle in affairs which do
not concern her. Is she a lady? One would imagine she
is not. One would also imagine that she lives in a solid
well-repaired square brown stone house with a cupola used
as a conning tower and equipped with periscope and tel-
escope and wireless. Furthermore, her house is situated
on a bleak hill so that nothing impedes her view and that
of her two pets, a magpie and a jackal. And the business
in life of all three of them is to track down and destroy the
good name of every woman who comes within range, especially if she is young and pretty—and unchaperoned!

The pretty young woman living alone, must literally follow Cinderella's habits. To be out of the house late at
night or sitting up, except to study, are imprudences she can
not allow herself. If she is a widow her conduct must be
above criticism, but if she is young and pretty and divorced,
she must literally live the life of a Puritan spinster of
Salem. The magpie never leaves her window sill and the
jackal sits on the doormat, and the news of her every going
out and coming in, of every one whom she receives, when
they come, how long they stay and at what hour they go, is
spread broadcast.

No unprotected woman can do the least thing that is unconventional without having Mrs. Grundy shouting to everyone the worst possible things about her.

THE BACHELOR GIRL

The bachelor girl is usually a worker; she is generally either earning her living or studying to acquire the means of earning her living. Her days are therefore sure to be occupied, and the fact that she has little time for the gaiety of life, and that she is a worker, puts her in a somewhat less assailable position. She can on occasion go out alone with a man (not a married one), but the theater she goes to must be of conventional character, and if she dines in a restaurant it is imperative that a chaperon be in the party; and the same is true in going to supper at night. No one could very well criticize her for going to the opera or a concert with a man when neither her nor his behavior hints a lack of reserve.

But a girl whose personal dignity is unassailable is not apt to bring censure upon herself, even though the world judges by etiquette, which may often be a false measure. The young woman who wants really to be free from Mrs. Grundy's hold on her, must either live her own life, caring nothing for the world's opinion or the position it offers, or else be chaperoned.

THE BACHELOR HOST AND THE CHAPERON

Barring the one fact that a chaperon must be on hand before young or "single" women guests arrive, and that she may not leave until after those whom she has chaperoned have left, there is no difference whatsover in an entertainment given at the house of a bachelor and one given by a hostess. A bachelor can give dinners or theater parties or yachting parties or house parties or any parties that a hostess can give.

It is unnecessary to say no lady may dine alone in a gentleman's rooms, or house; nor may she dine with a number of gentlemen (unless one of them is her husband, in which case she is scarcely "alone"). But it is perfectly correct for two or more ladies to dine at a gentleman's rooms if one of the ladies is elderly or the husband of one is present.

A bachelor entertaining in bachelor's quarters, meaning that he has only a man servant, must be much more punctilious, and must arrange to have the chaperon bring any young woman guests with her, since no young girls could be seen entering bachelor's quarters alone, and have their "good name" survive. If he has a large establishment, including women servants, and if furthermore he is a man whose own reputation is unblemished, the chaperon may be met at his house. But since it is more prudent for young women to arrive under her care, why run the unnecessary risk of meeting Mrs. Grundy's jackal on the doorstep?

At the house of a bachelor such as described above, the chaperon could be a husbandless young married woman, or in other words, the most careless chaperon possible, without ever giving Mrs. Grundy's magpie cause for ruffling a feather. But no young woman could dine or have tea, no matter how well chaperoned, in the "rooms" of a man of morally bad reputation without running a very unpleasant risk of censure.

A BACHELOR'S HOUSE PARTIES

Bachelors frequently have house parties at their country places. A married lady whose husband is with her is always the chaperon unless the host's mother or sister may be staying—or living— in his house.

There is always something unusually alluring about a bachelor's entertaining. Especially his house parties. Where do all bachelors get those nice and so very respectable elderly maid servants? They can't all have been their nurses! And a bachelor's house has a something about it that is very comfortable but entirely different from a lady's house, though it would be difficult to define wherein the difference lies. He is perhaps more attentive than a hostess, at least he meets his guests at the station if they come by train, or, if they motor to his house, he goes out on the front steps to greet them as they drive up.

A possible reason why bachelors seem to make such good hosts is that only those who have a talent for it make the attempt. There is never any obligation on a gentleman's part to invite ladies to stay with him, whereas it is part of every lady's duty at least occasionally to be a hostess, whether she has talent, or even inclination, for the position or not.

A gentleman can return the courtesies of hostesses to him by occasionally sending flowers, or books, or candy, and by showing them polite attention when he meets them out.

If a bachelor lives in a house of his own, especially in a country community, he is under the same obligations as any other householder to return the hospitality shown by his neighbors to him.

INVITATIONS

The bachelor's invitations are the same as those sent out by a hostess. There is absolutely no difference. His butler or waitress telephones "Will Mr. and Mrs. Norman dine with Mr. Bachelor on Wednesday?" Or he writes a note or uses the engraved dinner card. In giving an informal dance it is quite correct, according to New York fashion, for him to write on his visiting card:

> *Monday January 2ᵈ*
> *At 10 o'clock*
> MR. FREDERICK BACHELOR
>
> *Small dance*   2 PORMANTO PLACE

Or an artist sends his card with his studio address and

Saturday April 7.
at 4. o'ck.

MR. ANTHONY DAUBER

To hear Tonini play.   PARK STUDIO

No invitation of a gentleman mentions that there will be a chaperon because that is taken for granted. No gentleman invites ladies of position to a party unless one or many chaperons are to be present.

A very young girl never goes even to an unmarried doctor's or a clergyman's (unless the latter is very elderly) without a chaperon, who in this instance may be a semi-elderly maid.

A lady having her portrait painted always takes a woman friend, or her maid, who sits in the studio, or at least within sight or hearing.

Chapter XX

ENGAGEMENTS

COURTSHIP

So long as Romance exists and Lochinvar remains young manhood's ideal, love at first sight and marriage in a week is within the boundaries of possibility. But usually (and certainly more wisely) a young man is for some time attentive to a young woman before dreaming of marriage. Thus not only have her parents plenty of time to find out what manner of man he is, and either accept or take means to prevent a serious situation; but the modern young woman herself is not likely to be "carried away" by the personality of anyone whose character and temperament she does not pretty thoroughly understand and weigh.

In nothing does the present time more greatly differ from the close of the last century, than in the unreserved frankness of young women and men towards each other. Those who speak of the domination of sex in this day are either too young to remember, or else have not stopped to consider, that mystery played a far greater and more dangerous rôle when sex, like a woman's ankle, was carefully hidden from view, and therefore far more alluring than to-day when both are commonplace matters.

In cities twenty-five years ago, a young girl had beaux who came to see her one at a time; they in formal clothes and manners, she in her "company best" to "receive" them, sat stiffly in the "front parlor" and made politely formal conversation. Invariably they addressed each other as Miss Smith and Mr. Jones, and they "talked off the top" with about the same lack of reservation as the ambassador of one country may be supposed to talk to him of another. A young man was said to be "devoted" to this young girl or that, but as a matter of fact each was acting a rôle, he of an admirer and she of a siren, and each was actually an utter stranger to the other.

299

FRIENDSHIP AND GROUP SYSTEM

To-day no trace of stilted artificiality remains. The tête-a-tête of a quarter of a century ago has given place to the continual presence of a group. A flock of young girls and a flock of young men form a little group of their own— everywhere they are together. In the country they visit the same houses or they live in the same neighborhood, they play golf in foursomes, and tennis in mixed doubles. In winter at balls they sit at the same table for supper, they have little dances at their own homes, where scarcely any but themselves are invited; they play bridge, they have tea together, but whatever they do, they stay in the pack. In more than one way this group habit is excellent; young women and men are friends in a degree of natural and entirely platonic intimacy undreamed of in their parents' youth. Having the habit therefore of knowing her men friends well, a young girl is not going to imagine a stranger, no matter how perfect he may appear to be, anything but an ordinary human man after all. And in finding out his bad points as well as his good, she is aided and abetted, encouraged or held in check, by the members of the group to which she belongs.

Suppose, for instance, that a stranger becomes attentive to Mary; immediately her friends fix their attention upon him, watching him. Twenty-five years ago the young men would have looked upon him with jealousy, and the young women would have sought to annex him. To-day their attitude is: "Is he good enough for Mary?" And, eagle-eyed, protective of Mary, they watch him. If they think he is all right he becomes a member of the group. It may develop that Mary and he care nothing for each other, and he may fall in love with another member, or he may drift out of the group again or he may stay in it and Mary herself marry out of it. But if he is not liked, her friends will not be bashful about telling Mary exactly what they think, and they will find means usually—unless their prejudice is without foundation—to break up the budding "friendship" far better than any older person could do. If she is really in love with him and determined to marry in spite of their frankly given opinion, she at least makes her decision with her eyes open.

There are also occasions when a young woman is persuaded by her parents into making a "suitable marriage"; there are occasions when a young woman persists in making a marriage in opposition to her parents; but usually a young man either belongs in or joins her particular circle of intimate friends, and one day, it may be to their own surprize, though seldom to that of their intimates, they find that each is the only one in the world for the other, and they become engaged.

FIRST DUTY OF THE ACCEPTED SUITOR

If a young man and his parents are very close friends it is more than likely he will already have told them of the seriousness of his intentions. Very possibly he has asked his father's financial assistance, or at least discussed ways and means, but as soon as he and she have definitely made up their minds that they want to marry each other, it is the immediate duty of the man to go to the girl's father or her guardian, and ask his consent. If her father refuses, the engagement cannot exist. The man must then try, through work or other proof of stability and seriousness, to win the father's approval. Failing in that, the young woman is faced with dismissing him or marrying in opposition to her parents. There are, of course, unreasonable and obdurate parents, but it is needless to point out that a young woman assumes a very great risk who takes her future into her own hands and elopes. But even so, there is no excuse for the most unfilial act of all—deception. The honorable young woman who has made up her mind to marry in spite of her parents' disapproval, announces to them, if she can, that on such and such a day her wedding will take place. If this is impossible, she at least refuses to give her word that she will not marry. The height of dishonor is to "give her word" and then break it.

THE APPROVED ENGAGEMENT

Usually, however, when the young man enters the study or office of her father, the latter has a perfectly good idea of what he has come to say and, having allowed his attentions, is probably willing to accept his daughter's choice; and the former after announcing that the daughter has accepted him, goes into details as to his financial standing and prospects. If the finances are not sufficiently stable, the father may tell him to wait for a certain length of time before considering himself engaged, or if they are satisfactory to him, he makes no objection to an immediate announcement. In either case, the man probably hurries to tell the young woman what her father has said, and if he has been very frequently at the house, very likely they both tell her mother and her immediate family, or, more likely still, she has told her mother first of all.

HIS PARENTS CALL ON HERS

As soon as the young woman's father accepts the engagement, etiquette demands that the parents of the bridegroom-elect call at once (within twenty-four hours) upon the parents of the bride-to-be. If illness or absence prevents one of them, the other must go alone. If the young man is an orphan, his uncle, aunt or other nearest relative should go in the parents' place. Not even deep mourning can excuse the failure to observe this formality.

THE ENGAGEMENT RING

It is doubtful if he who carries a solitaire ring enclosed in a little square box and produces it from his pocket upon the instant that she says "Yes," exists outside of the moving pictures! As a matter of fact, the accepted suitor usually consults his betrothed's taste—which of course may be gratified or greatly modified, according to the length of his purse—or he may, without consulting her, buy what ring he chooses. A solitaire diamond is the conventional emblem of "the singleness and endurability of the one love in his life," and the stone is supposed to be "pure and flawless" as the bride herself, and their future together—or sentiments equally beautiful. There is also sentiment for a sapphire's "depth of true blue." Pearls are supposed to mean tears; emeralds, jealousy; opals, the essence of bad luck; but the ruby stands for warmth and ardor: all of which it is needless to say is purest unfounded superstition.

In the present day, precious stones having soared far out of reach of all but the really rich, fashion rather prefers a large semi-precious one to a microscopic diamond. "Fashion," however, is merely momentary and local, and the great majority will probably always consider a diamond the only ring to have.

It is not obligatory, or even customary, for the girl to give the man an engagement present, but there is no impropriety in her doing so if she wants to, and any of the following articles would be suitable: A pair of cuff links, or waist-coat buttons, or a watch chain, or a key chain, or a cigarette case. Probably because the giving of an engagement ring is his particular province, she very rarely gives him a ring or, in fact, any present at all.

The engagement ring is worn for the first time "in public" on the day of the announcement.

BEFORE ANNOUNCEMENT

Usually a few days before the formal announcement— and still earlier for letters written abroad or to distant States—both young people write to their aunts, uncles, and cousins, and to their most intimate friends, of their engagement, asking them not to tell anyone until the determined date.

As soon as they receive the news, all the relatives of the groom-elect must call on the bride. She is not "welcomed by the family" until their cards, left upon her in person, assure her so. She must, of course, return all of these visits, and as soon as possible.

If his people are in the habit of entertaining, they should very soon ask her with her fiancé to lunch or to dinner, or after the engagement is publicly announced, give a dinner or tea or dance in her honor. If, on the other hand, they are very quiet people, their calling upon her is sufficient in itself to show their welcome.

In case of a recent death in either immediate family, the engagement cannot be publicly announced until the first period of mourning is past. (It is entirely dignified for a private wedding to take place at the bedside of a very ill parent, or soon after a deep bereavement. In that case there is, of course, no celebration, and the service is read in the presence of the immediate families only.)

The announcement is invariably made by the parents of the bride-elect. It is a breach of etiquette for a member of the young man's family to tell of the engagement until the formal announcement has been arranged for.

ANNOUNCEMENT OF ENGAGEMENT

On the evening before the day of the announcement, the bride's mother either sends a note, or has some one call the various daily papers by telephone, and says: "I am speaking for Mrs. John Huntington Smith. Mr. and Mrs. Smith are announcing the engagement of their daughter, Mary, to Mr. James Smartlington, son of Mr. and Mrs. Arthur Brown Smartlington, of 2000 Arcade Avenue."

If either the Huntington Smiths or the Arthur Smartlingtons are socially prominent, reporters will be sent to get further information. Photographs and details, such as entertainments to be given, or plans for the wedding, will probably be asked for. The prejudices of old-fashioned people against giving personal news to papers is rapidly being overcome and not even the most conservative any longer object to a dignified statement of facts, such as Mrs. Smith's telephone message.

It is now considered entirely good form to give photographs to magazines and newspapers, but one should never send them unless specially requested.

On the eve of the announcement, a dinner is sometimes given by the young girl's parents, and the news is told by her father, who at about salad course or dessert, proposes the health of his daughter and future son-in-law.

HOW A HEALTH IS PROPOSED

The host after directing that all glasses at the table be filled, rises, lifts his own glass and says: "I propose we drink to the health of my daughter Mary and the young man she has decided to add permanently to our family, James Smartlington."

Or:

"A standing toast: To my Mary and to her—Jim!"

Or:

"I want you to drink the happiness of a young pair whose future welfare is close to the hearts of all of us: Mary (holding up his glass and looking at her) and Jim!" (holding it up again and looking at him). Every one except Mary and Jim rises and drinks a swallow or two (of whatever the champagne substitute may be). Every one then congratulates the young couple, and Jim is called upon for a "speech"!

Generally rather "fussed," Jim rises and says something like: "I—er—we—thank you all very much indeed for all your good wishes," and sits down. Or if he is an earnest rather than a shy youth, perhaps he continues: "I don't have to tell you how lucky *I* am, the thing for me to do is to prove, if I can, that Mary has not made the mistake of her life in choosing me, and I hope that it won't be very long before we see you all at our own table with Mary at the head of it and I, where I belong, at the foot."

Or:

"I can't make a speech and you know it. But I certainly am lucky and I know it."

WHEN NO SPEECH IS MADE

The prevailing custom in New York and other big cities is for the party to be given on the afternoon or evening of the day of announcement. The engagement in this case is never proclaimed to the guests as an assembled audience. The news is "out" and everyone is supposed to have heard it. Those who have not, can not long remain ignorant, as the groom-elect is either receiving with his fiancée or brought forward by her father and presented to every one he does not know. Everybody congratulates him and offers the bride-to-be good wishes for her happiness.

A dinner or other entertainment given to announce an engagement is by no means necessary. "Quiet people" very often merely write notes of announcement and say they will be at home on such an afternoon at tea time. The form and detail are exactly the same as on an habitual day at home except that the bride and groom-elect both receive as well as her mother.

PARTIES FOR THE ENGAGED COUPLE

If the families and friends of the young couple are at all in the habit of entertaining, the announcement of an engagement is the signal always for a shower of invitations.

The parents of the groom-elect are sure to give a dance, or a "party" of one kind or another "to meet" their daughter-to-be. If the engagement is a short one, their life becomes a veritable dashing from this house to that, and every meal they eat seems to be one given for them by some one. It is not uncommon for a bride-elect to receive a few engagement presents. (These are entirely apart from wedding presents which come later.) A small afternoon teacup and saucer used to be the typical engagement gift, but it has gone rather out of vogue, along with harlequin china in general. Engagement presents are usually personal trifles sent either by her own very intimate friends or by members of her fiancé's family as especial messages of welcome to her—and as such are very charming. But any general fashion that necessitates giving engagement as well as wedding presents may well be looked upon with alarm by those who have only moderately filled pocketbooks!

ENGAGED COUPLE IN PUBLIC

There is said to be still preserved somewhere in Massachusetts a whispering reed through the long hollow length of which lovers were wont to whisper messages of tenderness to each other while separated by a room's length and the inevitable chaperonage of the fiancée's entire family.

From those days to these is a far cry, but even in this era of liberty and naturalness of impulse, running the gauntlet of people's attention and criticism is no small test of the good taste and sense of a young couple.

The hall-mark of so-called "vulgar people" is unrestricted display of uncontrolled emotions. No one should ever be made to feel like withdrawing in embarrassment from the over-exposed privacy of others. The shrew who publicly berates her husband is no worse than the engaged pair who snuggle in public. Every one supposes that lovers kiss each other, but people of good taste wince at being forced to play audience at love scenes which should be private. Furthermore, such cuddling gives little evidence of the deeper caring—no matter how ardent the demonstration may be.

Great love is seldom flaunted in public, though it very often shows itself in pride—that is a little obvious, perhaps. There is a quality of protectiveness in a man's expression as it falls on his betrothed, as though she were so lovely a breath might break her; and in the eyes of a girl whose love is really deep, there is always evidence of that most beautiful look of championship, as though she thought: "No one else can possibly know how wonderful he is!"

This underlying tenderness and pride which is at the base of the attitude of each, only glints beneath the surface of perfect comradeship. Their frank approval of whatever the other may do or say is very charming; and even more so is their obvious friendliness toward all people, of wanting the whole world beautiful for all because it is so beautiful to them. That is love—as it should be! And its evidence is a very sure sign-post pointing to future happiness.

ETIQUETTE OF ENGAGED PEOPLE

It is unnecessary to say that an engaged man shows no attention whatever to other women. It should be plain to every one, even though he need not behave like a moon-calf, that "one" is alone in his thoughts.

Often it so happens that engaged people are very little together, because he is away at work, or for other reasons. Rather than sit home alone, she may continue to go out in society, which is quite all right, but she must avoid being with any one man more than another and she should remain visibly within the general circle of her group. It always gives gossip a chance to see an engaged girl sitting out dances with any particular man, and slander is never far away if any evidence of ardor creeps into their regard, even if it be merely "manner," and actually mean nothing at all.

IN THE BACKWATERS OF LONG ENGAGEMENT

Unless the engaged couple are both so young, or by temperament so irresponsible, that their parents think it best for them to wait until time is given a chance to prove the stability of their affection, no one can honestly advocate a long-delayed marriage.

Where there is no money, it is necessary to wait for better finances. But the old argument that a long engagement was wise in that the young couple were given opportunity to know each other better, has little sense to-day when all young people know each other thoroughly well.

A long engagement is trying to everyone—the man, the

girl, both families, and all friends. It is an unnatural state, like that of waiting at the station for a train, and in a measure it is time wasted. The minds of the two most concerned are centered upon each other; to them life seems to consist in saying the inevitable good-by.

Her family think her absent-minded, distrait, aloof and generally useless. His family never see him. Their friends are bored to death with them—not that they are really less devoted or loyal, but her men friends withdraw, naturally refraining from "breaking in." He has no time between business and going to see her to stop at his club or wherever friends of his may be. Her girl friends do see her in the daytime, but gradually they meet less and less because their interests and hers no longer focus in common. Gradually the stream of the social world goes rushing on, leaving the two who are absorbed in each other to drift forgotten in a backwater. He works harder, perhaps, than ever, and she perhaps occupies herself in making things for her trousseau or her house, or otherwise preparing for the more contented days which seem so long in coming.

Once they are married, they no longer belong in a backwater, but find themselves again sailing in midstream. It may be on a slow-moving current, it may be on a swift,— but their barge sails in common with all other craft on the river of life.

Should a Long Engagement Be Announced?

Whether to announce an engagement that must be of long duration is not a matter of etiquette but of personal preference. On the general principle that frankness is always better than secretiveness, the situation is usually cleared by announcing it. On the other hand, as illustrated above, the certain knowledge of two persons' absorption in each other always creates a marooned situation. When it is only supposed, but not known, that a man and girl particularly like each other, their segregation is not nearly so marked.

MEETING OF KINSMEN

At some time before the wedding, it is customary for the two families to meet each other. That is, the parents of the groom dine or lunch at the house of the parents of the bride to meet the aunts, uncles and cousins. And then the parents of the bride are asked with the same purpose to the house of the groom-elect.

It is not necessary that any intimacy ensue, but it is considered fitting and proper that all the members of the families which are to be allied should be given an opportunity to know one another—at least by sight.

THE ENGAGED COUPLE AND THE CHAPERON

The question of a chaperon differs with locality. In Philadelphia and Baltimore, custom permits any young girl to go alone with a young man approved by her family to the theater, or to be seen home from a party. In New York or Boston, Mrs. Grundy would hold up her hands and run to the neighbors at once with the gossip.

It is perhaps sufficient to say that if a man is thought worthy to be accepted by a father as his daughter's husband, he should also be considered worthy of trust no matter where he finds himself alone with her. It is not good form for an engaged couple to dine together in a restaurant, but it is all right for them to lunch, or have afternoon tea; and few people would criticize their being at the opera or the theater—unless the performance at the latter was of questionable propriety. They should take a chaperon if they motor to road-houses for meals—and it goes without saying that they cannot go on a journey alone that can possibly last over night.

GIFTS WHICH MAY AND THOSE WHICH MAY NOT BE ACCEPTED

The fiancée of a young man who is "saving in order to marry," would be lacking in taste as well as good sense were she to encourage or allow him extravagantly to send her flowers and other charming, but wasteful, presents.

But on the other hand, if the bridegroom-elect has plenty of means, she may not only accept flowers but anything he chooses to select, except wearing apparel or a motor car or a house and furniture—anything that can be classified as "maintenance."

It is perfectly suitable for her to drive his car, or ride his horse, and she may select furniture for their house, which he may buy or have built. But, if she would keep her self-respect, the car must not become hers nor must she live in the house or use its furniture until she is given his name. He may give her all the jewels he can afford, he may give her a fur scarf, but not a fur coat. The scarf is an ornament, the coat is wearing apparel. If she is very poor, she may have to be married in cheese-cloth, or even in the dress she wears usually, but her wedding dress and the clothes she wears away, must not be supplied by the groom or his family. There is one exception: if his mother, for instance, has some very wonderful family lace, or has kept her own wedding dress and has no daughter herself, and it would please her to have her son's wife wear her lace or dress, it is proper for the bride to consent. But it would be starting life on a false basis, and putting herself in a category with women of another class, to be clothed by any man, whether he is soon to be her husband or not.

If the engagement should be so unfortunate as to be broken off, the engagement ring and all other gifts of value must be returned.

CHAPTER XXI

FIRST PREPARATIONS BEFORE A WEDDING

To begin with, before deciding the date of the wedding, the bride's mother must find out definitely on which day the clergyman who is to perform the ceremony is disengaged, and make sure that the church is bespoken for no other service. If it is to be an important wedding, she must also see that the time available for the church is also convenient to the caterer.

Sundays, and days in Lent, are not chosen for weddings, and Friday being a "fast" day in Catholic and very "high" Episcopal churches, weddings on that day, if not forbidden, are never encouraged. But the superstition that Friday and the month of May are unlucky, is too stupid to discuss.

Having settled upon a day and hour, the next step is to decide the number of guests that can be provided for, which is determined by the size of the church and the house, and the type of reception intended.

THE INVITATIONS

The bride-elect and her mother then go to the stationer and decide details, such as size and texture of paper and style of engraving, for the invitations. The order is given at once for the engraving of all the necessary plates, and probably for the full number of house invitations, especially if to a sit-down breakfast where the guests are limited. There are also ordered a moderate number of general church invitations or announcements, which can be increased later when the lists are completed and the definite number of guests more accurately known.

HER MOTHER CONSULTS HIS MOTHER

The bride's mother then consults with the groom, or more likely, with his mother, as to how the house-list is to be divided between them. This never means a completely doubled list, because, if the two families live in the same city, many names are sure to be in duplicate. If the groom's people live in another place, invitations to the house can be liberally sent, as the proportion of guests who will take a long trip seldom go beyond those of the immediate family and such close friends as would be asked to the smallest of receptions.

Usually if Mrs. Smith tells Mrs. Smartlington that two hundred can be included at the breakfast, Mrs. Smith and Mrs. Smartlington will each make a list of one hundred and fifty, certain that one hundred will be in duplicate.

Invitations to a big church wedding are always sent to the entire visiting list, and often the business acquaintances of both families, no matter how long the combined number may be, or whether they can by any chance be present or not. Even people· in deep mourning are included as well as those who live thousands of miles away, as the invitations not merely proffer hospitality but are messengers carrying the news of the marriage.

After a house wedding, or a private ceremony where invitations were limited to relatives and closest personal friends of the young couple, general announcements are sent out to the entire visiting list.

HOW THE WEDDING LIST IS COMPILED

Those who keep their visiting list in order have comparatively little work. But those who are not in the habit of entertaining on a general scale, and yet have a large unassorted visiting list, will have quite a piece of work ahead of them, and cannot begin making it soon enough.

In the cities where a Social Register or other Visiting Book is published, people of social prominence find it easiest to read. it through, marking "XX" in front of the names to be asked to the house, and another mark, such as a dash, in front of those to be asked to the church only, or to have announcements sent them. Other names which do not appear in the printed list may be written as "thought of" at the top or bottom of pages. In country places and smaller cities, or where a published list is not available, or of sufficient use, the best assistant is the telephone book.

List-making should be done over as long a period and for as short sessions as possible, in order that each name as it is read may bring to memory any other that is similar. Long reading at a time robs the repetition of names of all sense, so that nothing is easier than to pass over the name of a friend without noticing it.

A word of warning: To leave out old friends because they are neither rich nor fashionable and to include comparative strangers because they are of great social importance, not alone shows a want of loyalty and proper feeling, but is to invite the contempt of those very ones whom such snobbery seeks to propitiate.

Four lists, therefore, are combined in sending out wedding invitations; the bride and the groom make one each of their own friends, to which is added the visiting list of the bride's family (made out by her mother, or other near relative) and the visiting list of the groom's family made out by his mother, or a relative. Each name is clearly marked, of course, whether for "house" or "church" invitation.

When the four lists are completed, it is the duty of some one to arrange them into a single one by whatever method seems most expedient. When lists are very long, the compiling is usually done by a professional secretary, who also addresses the envelopes, encloses the proper number of cards, and seals, stamps and posts the invitations. The address of a professional secretary can always be furnished by the stationer. Very often, especially where lists do not run into inordinate length, the envelopes are addressed and the invitations sent out by the bride herself and some of her friends who volunteer to help her.

THE MOST ELABORATE WEDDING POSSIBLE

This is the huge wedding of the daughter of ultra rich and prominent people in a city such as New York, or, more probably, a high-noon wedding out of town. The details would in either case be the same, except that the "country setting" makes necessary the additional provision of a special train which takes the guests to a station where they are met by dozens of motors and driven to the church. Later they are driven to the house, and later again, to the returning special train.

Otherwise, whether in the city or the country, the church (if Protestant) is decorated with masses of flowers in some such elaborateness as standards, or arches, or hanging garlands in the church itself, as well as the floral embellishment of the chancel. The service is conducted by a bishop or other distinguished clergyman, with assistant clergymen, and accompanied by a full choral service, possibly with the addition of a celebrated opera soloist. The costumes of the bride and her maids are chosen with painstaking attention to perfection, and with seeming disregard of cost.

Later, at the house, there is not only a floral bower under which the bridal couple receive, but every room has been turned into a veritable woodland or garden, so massed are the plants and flowers. An orchestra—or two, so that the playing may be without intermission—is hidden behind palms in the hall or wherever is most convenient. A huge canopied platform is built on the lawn or added to the veranda (or built out over the yard of a city house), and is decorated to look like an enclosed formal garden. It is packed with small tables, each seating four, six, or eight, as the occasion may require.

THE AVERAGE FASHIONABLE WEDDING

The more usual fashionable wedding is merely a modification of the one outlined above. The chancel of the church is decorated exactly the same, but except in summer when garden flowers are used, there is very little attempted in the body of the church other than sprays of flowers at the ends of the ten to twenty reserved pews, or possibly only at the ends of the first two pews and the two that mark the beginning of the ribboned section. There is often a choral service and a distinguished officiating clergyman.

The costumes of bride and bridesmaids are usually the same in effect, though they may be less lavish in detail.

The real difference begins at the breakfast, where probably a hundred guests are invited, or two hundred at most, instead of from five hundred to a thousand, and except for the canopied background against which the bride and groom receive, there is very little floral decoration of the house. If a tent is built, it is left as it is—a tent—with perhaps some standard trees at intervals to give it a decorated appearance. The tables, even that of the bride, their garniture, the service, and the food are all precisely the same, the difference being in the smaller number of guests provided for.

A SMALL WEDDING

A small wedding is merely a further modification of the two preceding ones. Let us suppose it is a house wedding in a moderate-sized house.

A prayer bench has been placed at the end of the drawing-room or living-room. Back of it is a screen or bower of palms or other greens. One decoration thus serves for chancel and background at the reception. A number of small tables in the dining-room may seat perhaps twenty or even fifty guests, besides the bride's table placed in another room. If the bride has no attendants, she and the groom choose a few close friends to sit at the table with them.

Or, at a smaller wedding, there is a private marriage in a little chapel, or the clergyman reads the service at the house of the bride in the presence of her parents and his and a small handful of guests, who all sit down afterwards at one table for a wedding breakfast.

Or there may be a greater number of guests and a simpler collation, such as a stand-up afternoon tea, where the refreshments are sandwiches, cakes, tea and chocolate.

BREACH OF ETIQUETTE FOR GROOM TO GIVE WEDDING

No matter whether a wedding is to be large or tiny, there is one unalterable rule: the reception must be either at the house of the bride's parents or grandparents or other relative of hers, or else in assembly rooms rented by her family. Never under any circumstances should a wedding reception be given at the house of the groom's family. They may give a ball or as many entertainments of whatever description they choose for the young couple after they are married, but the wedding breakfast and the trousseau of the bride must be furnished by her own side of the house!

When a poor girl marries, her wedding must be in keeping with the means of her parents. It is not only inadvisable for them to attempt expenditure beyond what they can afford, but they would lay themselves open to far greater criticism through inappropriate lavishness, than through meagerness of arrangement—which need not by any means lack charm because inexpensive.

WEDDING OF A CINDERELLA

Some years ago there was a wedding when a girl who was poor married a man who was rich and who would gladly have given her anything she chose, the beauty of which will be remembered always by every witness in spite of, or maybe because of, its utter lack of costliness.

It was in June in the country. The invitations were by word of mouth to neighbors and personal notes to the groom's relatives at a distance. The village church was decorated by the bride, her younger sisters, and some neighbors, with dogwood, than which nothing is more bridelike or beautiful. The shabbiness of her father's little cottage was smothered with flowers and branches cut in a neighboring wood. Her dress, made by herself, was of tarlatan covered with a layer or two of tulle, and her veil was of tulle fastened with a spray, as was her girdle, of natural bridal wreath and laurel leaves. Her bouquet was of trailing bridal wreath and white lilacs. She was very young, and divinely beautiful, and fresh and sweet. The tulle for her dress and veil and her thin silk stockings and white satin slippers represented the entire outlay of any importance for her costume. A little sister in smock of pink sateen and a wreath and tight bouquet of pink laurel clusters, toddled after her and "held" her bouquet—after first laying her own on the floor!

The collation was as simple as the dresses of the bride and bridesmaid. A home-made wedding cake, "professionally" iced and big enough for every one to take home a thick slice in waxed paper piled near for the purpose, and a white wine cup, were the most "pretentious" offerings. Otherwise there were sandwiches, hot biscuits, cocoa, tea and coffee, scrambled eggs and bacon, ice cream and cookies, and the "music" was a victrola, loaned for the occasion. The bride's "going away" dress was of brown Holland linen and her hat a plain little affair as simple as her dress; again her only expenditure was on shoes, stockings and gloves. Later on, she had all the clothes that money could buy, but in none of them was she ever more lovely than in her fashionless wedding dress of tarlatan and tulle, and the plain little frock in which she drove away. Nor are any of the big parties that she gives to-day more enjoyable, though perfect in their way, than her wedding on a June day, a number of years ago.

THE WEDDING HOUR

The fashionable wedding hour in New York is either noon, or else in the afternoon at three, three-thirty or four o'clock, with the reception always a half hour later. High noon, which means that the breakfast is at one o'clock, and four o'clock in the afternoon, with the reception at half after, are the conventional hours.

THE EVENING WEDDING

In San Francisco and generally throughout the West altogether smart weddings are celebrated at nine o'clock in the evening. The details are precisely the same as those of morning or afternoon. The bride and bridesmaids wear dresses that are perhaps more elaborate and "evening" in model, and the bridegroom as well as all men present wear evening clothes, of course. If the ceremony is in a church, the women should wear wraps and an ornament or light scarf of some sort over their hair, as ball dresses are certainly not suitable, besides which church regulations forbid the uncovering of women's heads in consecrated places of worship.

THE MORNING WEDDING

To some, nine o'clock in the morning may sound rather eccentric for a wedding, but to people of the Atlantic Coast it is not a bit more so than an evening hour—less so, if anything, because morning is unconventional anyway and etiquette, never being very strong at that hour, is not defied, but merely left quiescent.

If, for any reason, such as taking an early morning train or ship—an early morning wedding might be a good suggestion. The bride should, of course, not wear satin and lace; she could wear organdie (let us hope the nine o'clock wedding is in summer!), or she could wear very simple white crêpe de chine. Her attendants could wear the simplest sort of morning dresses with garden hats; the groom a sack suit or flannels. And the breakfast—really breakfast —could consist of scrambled eggs and bacon and toast and coffee—and griddle cakes!

The above is not written in ridicule; the hour would be "unusual," but a simple early morning wedding where every one is dressed in morning clothes, and where the breakfast suggests the first meal of the day—could be perfectly adorable! The evening wedding on the other hand, lays itself open to criticism because it is a function—a function is formal, and the formal is always strictly in the province of that austere and inflexible lawmaker, Etiquette. And Etiquette at this moment says: "Weddings on the Atlantic seaboard are celebrated not later than four-thirty o'clock in the afternoon!"

WEDDING PRESENTS

And now let us return to the more particular details of the wedding of our especial bride.

The invitations are mailed about three weeks before the wedding. As soon as they are out, the presents to the bride begin coming in, and she should enter each one carefully in her gift book. There are many published for the purpose, but an ordinary blank book, nicely bound, as she will probably want to keep it, about eight to ten inches square, will answer every purpose. The usual model spreads across the double page, as follows:

Present received date	Article	Sent by	Sender's Address	Where Bought	Date of thanks written
May 20	Silver Dish	Mr. and Mrs. White	1 Elinore Place	Tiffany's	May 20
May 21	12 Plates	Mr. and Mrs. Green	2 North Street	Collamore's	May 21

All gifts as they arrive should be put in a certain room, or part of a room, and never moved away until the description is carefully entered. It will be found a great help to put down the addresses of donors as well as their names so that the bride may not have to waste an unnecessary moment of the overcrowded time which must be spent at her desk.

THE BRIDE'S THANKS

The bride who is happy in receiving a great number of presents spends every spare moment in writing her notes of thanks, which must always be written by her personally. Telephoning won't do at all, and neither will a verbal "Thank you so much," as she meets people here and there. She must write a separate letter for each present—a by no means small undertaking! A bride of this year whose presents, because of her family's great prominence, ran far into the hundreds, never went to bed a single night before her wedding until a note of thanks was checked against every present received that day. To those who offered to help her through her overwhelming task, she, who is supposed to be very spoiled, answered: "If people are kind enough to go out and buy a present for me, I think the least I can do is to write at once and thank them." That her effort was appreciated was evident by everyone's commenting on her prompt and charming notes.

Notes of thanks can be very short, but they should be written with as little delay as possible. When a present is sent by a married couple, the bride writes to the wife and thanks both: "Thank you for the lovely present you and Mr. Jones sent me."

ARRANGING THE PRESENTS

Not so much in an effort to parade her possessions as to do justice to the kindness of the many people who have sent them, a bride should show her appreciation of their gifts by placing each one in the position of greatest advantage. Naturally, all people's tastes are not equally pleasing to the taste of the bride—nor are all pocketbooks equally filled. Very valuable presents are better put in close contrast with others of like quality—or others entirely different in character. Colors should be carefully grouped. Two presents, both lovely in themselves, can be made completely destructive to each other if the colors are allowed to clash.

Usually china is put on one table, silver on another, glass on another, laces and linens on another. But pieces that jar together must be separated as far apart as possible and perhaps even moved to other surroundings. A crudely designed piece of silverware should not be left among beautiful examples, but be put among china ornaments, or other articles that do not reveal its lack of fineness by too direct comparison. For the same reason imitation lace should not be put next to real, nor stone-ware next to Chinese porcelain. To group duplicates is another unfortunate arrangement. Eighteen pairs of pepper pots or fourteen sauceboats in a row might as well be labeled: "Look at this stupidity! What can she do with all of us?" They are sure to make the givers feel at least a little chagrined at their choice.

CARDS WITH PRESENTS

When Mrs. Smith orders a present sent to a bride, she encloses a card reading: "Mr. & Mrs. John Huntington Smith." Nearly every married woman has a plate engraved with both names, but if she hasn't, then she encloses Mr. Smith's card with hers.

Some people write "All good wishes" or "With best wishes," but most people send cards without messages.

DELAYED PRESENTS

If because of illness or absence, a present is not sent until after the wedding, a short note should accompany it, giving the reason for the delay.

WHEN THE PRESENTS ARE SHOWN

There is absolutely no impropriety in showing the presents at the wedding reception. They are always shown at country weddings, and, more often than not, at the most fashionable town houses. The only reason for not showing them, is lack of room in an apartment house. In a town house, an upstairs library, or even a bedroom, from which all the furniture has been removed, is suitable. Tables covered with white damask (plain) tablecloths are put like counters around the sides, and down the center of the room. The cards that were sent with the gifts are sometimes removed, but there is no impropriety in leaving them on, and it certainly saves members of the family from repeating many times who sent this one, and who sent that!

If the house is small so that there is no room available for this display at the wedding, the presents are shown on the day before, and intimate friends are especially asked to come in for tea, and to view them. This is not done if they are to be displayed at the wedding.

Very intimate friends seldom need to be asked; the chances are they will come in often, to see what has come since they were in last!

Wedding presents are all sent to the bride, and are, according to law, her personal property. Articles are marked with her present—not her future—initials. Mary Smith who is going to marry Jim Smartlington is fortunate as M. S. stands for her future as well as her present name. But in the case of Muriel Jones who is to marry Ross, not a piece of linen or silver in "Ross house" will be marked otherwise than "M. J." It is one of the most senseless customs: all her life which will be as Muriel Ross, she uses linen and silver marked with a "J." Later on many people who go to her house—especially as Ross comes from

California where she will naturally be living—will not know what "J" stands for, and many even imagine that the linen and plate have been acquired at auction! Sounds impossible? It has happened more than once.

Occasional brides who dislike the confusing initials, especially ask that presents be marked with their marriage name.

The groom receives few presents. Even those who care about him in particular and have never met his bride, send their present to her, unless they send two presents, one in courtesy to her and one in affection to him. Occasionally some one does send the groom a present, addressed to him and sent to his house. Rather often friends of the groom pick out things particularly suitable for him, such as cigar or cigarette boxes, or rather masculine looking desk sets, etc., which are sent to her but are obviously intended for his use.

EXCHANGING WEDDING PRESENTS

Some people think it discourteous if a bride changes the present chosen for her. All brides exchange some presents, and no friends should allow their feelings to be hurt, unless they are very close to the bride and have chosen the present with particular sentiment. A bride never changes the presents chosen for her by her or the groom's family—unless especially told that she may do so. But to keep twenty-two salt cellars and sixteen silver trays when she has no pepper-pots or coffee spoons or platters or vegetable dishes, would be putting "sentiment" above "sense."

THE TROUSSEAU

A trousseau, according to the derivation of the word, was "a little trusse or bundle" that the bride carried with her to the house of her husband. In modern times the "little bundle" often requires the services of a van to transport.

The wrappers and underclothes of a young girl are usually very simple, but when she is to be a bride, her mother buys her, as lavishly as she can, and of the prettiest possible assortment of lace trimmed lingerie, tea gowns, bed sacques and caps, whatever may be thought especially becoming. The various undress garments which are to be worn in her room or at the breakfast table, and for the sole admiration of her husband, are of far greater importance than the dresses and hats to be worn in public.

In Europe it is the custom to begin collecting linen for a girl's trousseau as soon as she is born, but the American bride cares nothing for dozens upon dozens of stout linen articles. She much prefers gossamer texture lavishly embellished with equally perishable lace. Everything must be bought for beauty; utility is not considered at all. No stout hand-woven underwear trimmed with solidly stitched needlework! Modern Miss Millions demands handkerchief linen and Valenciennes lace of a quality that used to be put as trimming on a ball gown, and Miss Small-purse asks for chiffon and less expensive but even more sheer and perishable laces. Not long ago a stocking was thought fine if it could be run through a wedding ring; to-day no stocking is considered "fit to put on" for town or evening wear unless several together can slip through the measure once the test for one.

THE MOST EXTRAVAGANT TROUSSEAU

The most lavish trousseau imaginable for the daughter of the very rich might be supposed to comprise:

House Linen

One to six dozen finest quality embroidered or otherwise "trimmed" linen sheets with large embroidered monogram.

One to six dozen finest quality linen sheets, plain hemstitched, large monogram.

One to six dozen finest quality linen under-sheets, narrow hem and small monogram.

Two pillow cases and also one "little" pillow case (for small down pillow) to match each upper sheet.

One to two dozen blanket covers (these are of thin washable silk in white or in colors to match the rooms) edged with narrow lace and breadths put together with lace insertion.

Six to twelve blankets.

Three to twelve wool or down-filled quilts.

Two to ten dozen finest quality, extra large, face towels, with Venetian needlework or heavy hand-made lace insertion (or else embroidered at each end), and embroidered monogram.

Five to ten dozen finest quality hemstitched and monogrammed but otherwise plain, towels.

Five to ten dozen little hand towels to match the large ones.

One to two dozen very large bath towels, with embroidered monogram, either white or in color to match the border of towels.

Two to four dozen smaller towels to match.

One tablecloth, six or eight yards long, of finest but untrimmed damask with embroidered monogram on each side, or four corners. Three dozen dinner napkins to match. (Lace inserted and richly embroidered tablecloths of formal dinner size are not in the best taste.)

One tablecloth five to six yards long with two dozen dinner napkins to match.

One to four dozen damask tablecloths two and a half to three yards long, and one dozen dinner napkins to match each tablecloth. All tablecloths and napkins to have embroidered monogram or initials.

Two to six medium sized cut-work, mosaic or Italian lace-work tablecloths, with lunch napkins to match.

Two to six centerpieces, with doilies and lunch napkins to match.

Four to a dozen tea cloths, of filet lace or drawn work or Russian embroidery, with tiny napkins to match. Table pieces and tea-cloths have monograms if there is any plain linen where a monogram can be embroidered, otherwise monograms or initials are put on the napkins only.

One or two dozen damask tablecloths, plain, with monogram, and a dozen napkins to match each.

In addition to the above, there are two to four dozen

servants' sheets and pillow cases (cotton); six to twelve woolen blankets, six to twelve wool filled quilts, four to six dozen towels, and one or two dozen bath towels; six to twelve white damask (cotton or linen and cotton mixed) tablecloths and six to twelve dozen napkins, all marked with machine embroidery.

Two to six dozen kitchen and pantry towels and dishcloths complete the list.

Personal Trousseau

How many dresses can a bride wear? It all depends—is she to be in a big city for the winter season, or at a watering place for the summer? Is she going to travel, or live quietly in the country? It is foolish to get more "outside" clothes than she has immediate use for; fashions change too radically. The most extravagant list for a bride who is to "go out" continually in New York or Newport, would perhaps include a dozen evening dresses, two or three evening wraps, of varying weights. For town there would be from two to four street costumes, a fur coat, another long coat, a dozen hats and from four to ten house dresses. In this day of week-ends in the country, no trousseau, no matter how town-bred the bride, is complete without one or two "country" coats, of fur, leather or woolen materials; several homespun, tweed or tricot suits or dresses; skirts with shirt-waists and sweaters in endless variety; low or flat heeled shoes; woolen or woolen and silk mixture stockings; and sport hats.

If the season is to be spent "out of town"—even in Newport or Palm Beach—the most extravagant bride will find little use for any but country clothes, a very few frocks for Sunday, and possibly a lot of evening dresses. Of course, if she expects to run to town a great deal for lunch, or if she is to travel, she chooses her clothes accordingly.

So much for the outer things. On the subject of the under things, which being of first importance are saved for the last, one can dip into any of the women's magazines devoted to fashion and fashionables, and understand at first sight that the furnishings which may be put upon the person of one young female would require a catalogue as long and as varied as a seedsman's. An extravagant trousseau contains every article illustrated—and more besides—in quality *never* illustrated—and by the dozens! But it must not for a moment be supposed that every fashionable bride has a trousseau like this—especially the household linen which requires an outlay possible only to parents who are very rich and also very indulgent.

THE MODERATE TROUSSEAU

The moderate trousseau simple cuts the above list into a fraction in quantity and also in quality. There is nothing of course that takes the place of the smooth fineness of really beautiful linen—it can no more be imitated than can a diamond, and its value is scarcely less. The "linen" of a really modest trousseau in this day of high prices must of necessity be "cotton." Fortunately, however, many people dislike the chill of linen sheets, and also prefer cotton-face towels, because they absorb better, and cotton is made in attractive designs and in endless variety.

For her personal trousseau, a bride can have everything that is charming and becoming at comparatively little expense. She who knows how to do fine sewing can make things beautiful enough for any one, and the dress made or hat trimmed at home is often quite as pretty on a lovely face and figure as the article bought at exorbitant cost at an establishment of reputation. Youth seldom needs expensive embellishment. Certain things such as footwear and gloves have to be bought, and are necessary. The cost, however, can be modified by choosing dresses that one-color slippers look well with.

In cities such as New York, Washington or Boston, it has never been considered very good taste to make a formal display of the trousseau. A bride may show an intimate friend or two a few of her things, but her trousseau is never spread out on exhibition. There can, however, be no objection to her so doing, if it is the custom of the place in which she lives.

WHAT THE BRIDESMAIDS WEAR

The costumes of the bridesmaids, slippers, stockings, dresses, bouquets, gloves and hats, are selected by the bride, without considering or even consulting them as to their taste or preferences. The bridesmaids are always dressed exactly alike as to texture of materials and model of making, but sometimes their dresses differ in color. For instance, two of them may wear pale blue satin slips covered with blue chiffon and cream lace fichus, and cream-colored "picture" hats trimmed with orchids. The next two wear orchid dresses, cream fichus, and cream hats trimmed with pale blue hydrangeas. The maid of honor likewise wears the same model, but her dress is pink chiffon over pink satin and her cream hat is trimmed with both orchids and hydrangeas. The bouquets would all be alike of orchids and hydrangeas. Their gloves all alike of cream-colored suede, and their slippers, blue, orchid, and pink, with stockings to match. Usually the bridesmaids are all alike in color as well as outline, and the maid of honor exactly the same but in reverse colors. Supposing the bridesmaids to wear pink dresses with blue sashes and pink hats trimmed in blue, and their bouquets are of larkspur—the maid of honor wears the same dress in blue, with pink sash, blue hat trimmed with pink, and carries pink roses.

At Lucy Gilding's wedding, her bridesmaids were dressed in deep shades of burnt orange and yellow, wood-colored slippers and stockings, skirts that shaded from brown through orange to yellow; yellow leghorn hats trimmed with jonquils, and jonquil bouquets. The maid of honor wore yellow running into cream, and her hat, tho of the same shape of leghorn, was trimmed with cream feathers, and she carried a huge cream feather fan.

As in the case of the wedding dress, it is foolish to enter into descriptions of clothes morethan to indicate that they are of light and fragile materials, more suitable to evening than to daytime. Flower girls and pages are dressed in quaint old-fashioned dresses and suits of satin with odd old-fashioned bonnets—or whatever the bride fancies as being especially "picturesque."

If a bridesmaid is in mourning, she wears colors on that one day, as bridesmaids' dresses are looked upon as uniforms, not individual costumes. Nor does she put a black band on her arm. A young girl in deepest mourning should not be a bridesmaid—unless at the very private wedding of a bride or groom also in mourning. In this case she would most likely be the only attendant and wear all white.

As a warning against the growing habit of artifice, it may not be out of place to quote one commentary made by a man of great distinction who, having seen nothing of the society of very young people for many years, "had to go" to the wedding of a niece. It was one of the biggest weddings of the spring season in New York. The flowers were wonderful, the bridesmaids were many and beautiful, the bride lovely. Afterwards the family talked long about the wedding, but the distinguished uncle said nothing. Finally, he was asked point blank: "Don't you think the wedding was too lovely? Weren't the bridesmaids beautiful?"

"No," said the uncle, "I did not think it was lovely at all. Every one of the bridesmaids was so powdered and painted that there was not a sweet or fresh face among them—I can see a procession just like them any evening on the musical comedy stage! One expects make-up in a theater, but in the house of God it is shocking!"

It is unnecessary to add—if youth, the most beautiful thing in the world, would only appreciate how beautiful it is, and how opposite is the false bloom that comes in boxes and bottles! Shiny noses, colorless lips, sallow skins hide as best they may, and with some excuse, behind powder or lip-stick; but to rouge a rose——!

THE COST OF BEING A BRIDESMAID

With the exception of parasols, or muffs or fans, which are occasionally carried in place of bouquets and presented by the bride, every article worn by the bridesmaids, flower girls or pages, although chosen by the bride, must be paid for by the wearers.

It is perhaps an irrefutable condemnation of the modern wedding display that many a young girl has had to refuse the joy of being in the wedding party because a complete bridesmaid outfit costs a sum that parents of moderate means are quite unable to meet for popular daughters. And it is seldom that the bride is herself in a position to give six or eight complete costumes, much as she may want all of her most particular friends with her on her day of days. Very often a bride tries especially to choose clothes that will not be expensive, but New York prices are New York prices, and the chic which is to make the wedding a perfect picture is the thing of all others that has to be paid for.

Even though one particular girl may be able to dress herself very smartly in homemade clothes of her own design and making, those same clothes duplicated eight times seldom turn out well. Why this is so, is a mystery. When a girl looks smart in inferior clothes, the merit is in her, not in the clothes—and in a group of six or eight, five or seven will show a lack of "finish," and the tender-hearted bride who, for the sake of their purses sends her bridesmaids to an average "little woman" to have their clothes made, and to a little hat-place around the corner, is apt to have a rather dowdy little flock fluttering down the aisle in front of her.

HOW MANY BRIDESMAIDS?

This question is answered by: How many friends has she whom she has "always promised" to have with her on that day? Has she a large circle of intimates or only one or two? Her sister is always maid of honor; if she has no sister, she chooses her most intimate friend.

A bride may have a veritable procession: eight or ten bridesmaids, a maid of honor, flower girls and pages. That is, if she follows the English custom, where every younger relative even including the little boys as pages, seems always to be brought into a perfect May-pole procession of ragged ages and sizes.

Or she may have none at all. She almost always has at least one maid, or matron, of honor, as the picture of her father standing holding her bouquet and stooping over to adjust the fall of her dress, would be difficult to witness with gravity.

At an average New York wedding, there are four or six bridesmaids—half of the "maids" may be "matrons," if most of the bride's "group" of friends have married before her. It is, however, not suitable to have young married women as bridesmaids, and then have an unmarried girl as maid of honor.

BEST MAN AND USHERS

The bridegroom always has a best man—his brother if he has one, or his best friend. The number of his ushers is in proportion to the size of the church and the number of guests invited. At a house wedding, ushers are often merely "honorary" and he may have many or none—according to the number of his friends.

As ushers and bridesmaids are chosen only from close friends of the bride and groom, it is scarcely necessary to suggest how to word the asking! Usually they are told that they are expected to serve at the time the engagement is announced, or at any time as they happen to meet. If school or college friends who live at a distance are among the number, letters are necessary. Such as:

"Mary and I are to be married on the tenth of November, and, of course, you are to be an usher." Usually he adds: "'My dinner is to be on the seventh at eight o'clock at——,'" naming the club or restaurant.

It is unheard of for a man to refuse—unless a bridegroom, for snobbish reasons, asks some one who is not really a friend at all.

BRIDE'S USHER AND GROOM'S BRIDESMAID

A brother of the bride, or if she has no brother, then her "favorite cousin" is always asked by the groom to be usher out of compliment to her.

The bride returns the compliment by asking the sister of the groom who is nearest her own age, to be bridesmaid, or if he has no sister, she asks a cousin or even occasionally shows her courtesy by asking the groom to name a particular friend of his. The bride in asking her does not say:

"Will you be one of my bridesmaids because Jim wants me to ask you." If the bridesmaid is not a particular friend of the bride, she knows perfectly that it is on Jim's account that she has been asked. It is the same with the bride's usher. The groom merely asks him as he asks all of the others.

When a foreigner marries an American girl, his own friends being too distant to serve, the ushers are chosen from among the friends of the bride.

BRIDEGROOM HAS NO TROUSSEAU

A whole outfit of new clothes is never considered necessary for a bridegroom, but shabby ones are scarcely appropriate. Whatever his wardrobe may stand in need of should be bought, if possible. He should have, not necessarily new, plenty of good shirts of all kinds, handkerchiefs, underwear, pajamas, socks, ties, gloves, etc., and a certain number of fresh, or as good as new, suits of clothes.

There was a wedding not long ago which caused quite a lot of derisive comment because the groom's mother provided him with a complete and elaborate trousseau from London, enormous trunks full of every sort of raiment imaginable. That part of it all was very nice; her mistake was in inviting a group of friends in to see the finery. The son was so mortified by this publicity that he appeared at the wedding in clothes conspicuously shabby, in order to counteract the "Mama's-darling-little-newly-wed" effect that the publicity of her generous outlay had produced.

It is proper and fitting for a groom to have as many new clothes as he needs, or pleases, or is able to get—but they are never shown to indiscriminate audiences, they are not featured, and he does not go about looking "dressed up."

THE WEDDING CLOTHES OF THE BRIDEGROOM

If he does not already possess a well fitting morning coat (often called a cutaway) he must order one for his wedding. The frock coat is out of fashion at the moment. He must also have dark striped gray trousers. At many smart weddings, especially in the spring, a groom (also his best man) wears a white piqué high double-breasted waistcoat, because the more white that can be got into an otherwise sombre costume the more wedding-like it looks; conventionally he wears a black one to match his coat, like the ushers. The white edge to a black waistcoat is not, at present, very good form.   As to his tie, he may choose an "Ascot" of black and white or gray patterned silk.   Or he may wear a "four-in-hand" matching those selected for the ushers, of black silk with a narrow single, or broken white stripe at narrow or wide intervals.   At one of the ultra smart weddings in New York last spring, after the London fashion, the groom and all the men of the wedding party wore bow ties of black silk with small white dots.

White buckskin gloves are the smartest, but gray suede are the most conventional.   White kid is worn only in the evening.   It is even becoming the fashion for ushers at small country weddings not to wear gloves at all!   But at every wedding, great or small, city or country, etiquette demands that the groom, best man, and ushers, all wear high silk hats, and that the groom carry a walking stick.

Very particular grooms have the soles of their shoes blacked with "water-proof" shoe polish so that when they kneel, their shoes look dark and neat.

WHAT THE BEST MAN WEARS

The best man wears precisely what the groom wears, with only one small exception: the groom's boutonnière is slightly different and more elaborate.   The groom and best man often wear ties that are different from those worn by the ushers, and occasionally white waistcoats.   Otherwise the two principal men are dressed like the ushers.

WHAT THE USHERS WEAR

It is of greatest importance that in dress each usher be an exact counterpart of his fellows, if the picture is to be perfect.

Everyone knows what a ragged-edged appearance is produced by a company of recruits whose uniforms are odd lots. An after-effect of army training was evident at one or two smart New York weddings where the grooms were in each case ex-officers and their ushers turned out in military uniformity. Each of these grooms sent typewritten instructions to his ushers, covering every detail of the "equipment" exacted. Few people may have reasoned why, but scarcely any one failed to notice "what smart looking men all the ushers were." It is always just such attention to detail that produces a perfectly finished result. The directions sent by one of the grooms was as follows:

"Wedding rehearsal on Tuesday, St. Bartholomew's at 5 P. M.

Wedding on Wednesday at 4 P. M.

Please wear:

Black calfskin low shoes.

Plain black silk socks.

Gray striped trousers (the darkest you have).

Morning coat and single-breasted black waistcoat.

White dress shirt (see that cuffs show three-quarters of an inch below coat sleeves).

Stand-up wing collar.

Tie and gloves are enclosed.

Boutonnière will be at the church.

Be at the church yourself at three o'clock, sharp."

THE HEAD USHER

Usually there is no "head usher," but in certain localities courtesy designates the usher who is selected to take the bride's mother up the aisle as the "head," or "first" usher.

Very occasionally, too, a nervous groom appoints an especially "reliable" friend head usher so as to be sure that all details will be carried out—including the prompt and proper appearance at the church of the other ushers. Usually, the ushers divide the arangements among themselves. The groom decides who goes on which aisle. One of them volunteers or is asked to look out for the bride's coming and to notify the groom, another is especially detailed to take the two mothers up the aisle. But very often this arrangement is arbitrarily decided by height. If one mother is very tall and the other very short, they generally go up with different ushers, the tallest being chosen for the taller lady, and one of medium height for the shorter.

THE BRIDESMAIDS' LUNCHEON

In many sections of America, especially in the country and in small towns, brides make an especial feature of asking their bridesmaids to a farewell luncheon. The table is elaborately decorated (invariably in pink with bridesmaids' roses), there is a bride's cake (lady cake) and there are favors in the cake, and mottoes, and altogether it is a "lovely party." In New York there is nothing like that at all. If the bride chooses to give a luncheon to her bridesmaids on whatever day suits her best, there is no objection to her doing so, or in fact, to her inviting whom she pleases to whatever sort of a party her mother is willing she should give. It is not a question of approved etiquette but of her own inclination seconded by the consent of her mother!

If her mother "keeps open house," probably they lunch with her many times before the wedding; if, on the other hand, it is not the habit of the family to have "people running in for meals," it is not necessary that she ask them to lunch at all. But whether they lunch often or never, the chances are that they are in and out of her house every day, looking at new presents as they come, perhaps helping her to write the descriptions in the gift book, and in arranging them in the room where they are to be displayed.

The bride usually goes to oversee the last fittings of the bridesmaids' dresses in order to be sure that they are as she wants them. This final trying-on should be arranged for several days at least before the wedding, so there may be sufficient time to make any alterations that are found necessary. Often the bride tries on her wedding dress at the same time so that she may see the effect of the whole wedding picture as it will be, or if she prefers, she tries on her dress at another hour alone.

Usually her bridesmaids lunch quite informally with her, or come in for tea, the day before the wedding, and on that day the bride gives them each "her present" which is always something to wear. It may be the muffs they are to carry, or parasols, if they have been chosen instead of bouquets. The typical "bridesmaid's present" is a bangle, a breast pin, a hat pin, which, according to the means of the bride, may have great or scarcely any intrinsic value.

BRIDESMAIDS AND USHERS' DINNER

If a wedding is being held in the country, or where most of the bridesmaids or ushers come from a distance, and they are therefore stopping at the bride's house, or with her neighbors, there is naturally a "dinner" in order to provide for the visitors. But where the wedding is in the city—especially when all the members of the bridal party live there also—the custom of giving a dinner has gone rather out of fashion.

If the bridal party is asked to dine at the house of the bride on the evening before the wedding, it is usually with the purpose of gathering a generally irresponsible group of young people together, and seeing that they go to the church for rehearsal, which is of all things the most important. More often the rehearsal is in the afternoon, after which the young people go to the bride's house for tea, allowing her parents to have her to themselves on her last evening home, and giving her a chance to go early to bed so as to be as pretty as possible on the morrow.

THE BACHELOR DINNER

Popularly supposed to have been a frightful orgy, and now arid as the Sahara desert and quite as flat and dreary, the bachelor dinner was in truth more often than not, a sheep in wolf's clothing.

It is quite true that certain big clubs and restaurants had rooms especially constructed for the purpose, with walls of stone and nothing breakable within hitting distance, which certainly does rather suggest frightfulness. As a matter of fact, "an orgy" was never looked upon with favor by any but silly and wholly misguided youths, whose idea of a howling good time was to make a howling noise; chiefly by singing at the top of their lungs and—breaking crockery. A boisterous picture, but scarcely a vicious one! Especially as quantities of the cheapest glassware and crockery were always there for the purpose.

The breaking habit originated with drinking the bride's health and breaking the stem of the wine glass, so that it "might never serve a less honorable purpose." A perfectly high-minded sentiment! And this same time-honored custom is followed to this day. Toward the latter end of the dinner the groom rises, and holding a filled champagne glass aloft says: "To the bride!" Every man rises, drinks the toast standing, and then breaks the delicate stem of the glass. The impulse to break more glass is natural to youth, and probably still occurs. It is not hard to understand. The same impulse is seen at every county fair where enthusiastic youths (and men) delight in shooting, or throwing balls, at clay pipes and ducks and—crockery!

Aside from toasting the bride and its glass-smashing result, the groom's farewell dinner is exactly like any other "man's dinner," the details depending upon the extravagance or the frugality of the host, and upon whether his particular friends are staid citizens of sober years or mere boys full of the exuberance of youth. Usually there is music of some sort, or "Neapolitans" or "coons" who sing, or two or three instrumental pieces, and the dinner party itself does the singing. Often the dinner is short and all go to the theater.

GIFTS PRESENTED TO USHERS

The groom's presents to his ushers are always put at their places at the bachelor dinner. Cuff links are the most popular gift; scarf-pins in localities where they are still fashionable. Silver or gold pencils, belt buckles, key-rings in gold, key-chains in silver, cigarette cases, bill-folders, card-cases, or other small and personal articles are suitable.

The present to the best man is approximately the same, or slightly handsomer than the gift to the ushers.

THE REHEARSAL

The bride always directs her wedding rehearsal, but never herself takes part in it, as it is supposed to be bad luck. Some one else—anyone who happens to be present—is appointed understudy.

Nearly always a few especial friends happen in, generally those who are primed with advice as to how everything should be done, but the opinion of the bride or the bride's mother is final.

VITAL IMPORTANCE OF REHEARSAL

Most of us are familiar with the wedding service, and its form seems simple enough. But, unless one has by experience learned to take care of seemingly non-existent details, the effect (although few may be able to say why) is hitchy and disjointed, and all the effort spent in preparation is wasted. It is not that gauche happenings are serious offenses, no matter how awkward the incident. Even were the wedding party to get hopelessly entangled, no "crime" would have been committed; but any detail that destroys the smoothness of the general impression is fatal to dignity—and dignity is the qualification necessary above all else in ceremonial observances.

HOW THE PROCESSION IS DRILLED

The organist must always be at the rehearsal, as one of the most important details is marking the time of the wedding march. Witnesses of most weddings can scarcely imagine that a wedding march is a *march* at all; more often than not, the heads of ushers and bridesmaids bob up and down like something boiling in a pan. A perfectly drilled wedding procession, like a military one, should move forward in perfect step, rising and falling in a block or unit. To secure perfection of detail, the bars of the processional may be counted so that the music comes to an end at precisely the moment the bride and groom stand side by side at the chancel steps.   This is not difficult; it merely takes time and attention.

A wedding rehearsal should proceed as follows:

First of all, it is necessary to determine the exact speed at which the march is to be played.   The ushers are asked to try it out.   They line up at the door, walk forward two and two.   The audience, consisting of the bride and her mother, and the bridesmaids, decides whether the pace "looks well."   It must not be fast enough to look brisk, or so slow as to be funereal.   At one wedding the ushers counted two beats as one and the pace was so slow that they all wabbled in trying to keep their balance.   The painfulness to everyone may be imagined.   On the other hand it is unsuitable to "trot" up the aisle of a church.

The "audience" having decided the speed, and the organist having noted the tempo, the entire procession, including the bridesmaids and a substitute, instead of the real bride, on her father's arm, go out into the vestibule and make their entry.   Remember, the father is an important factor in the ceremony, and must take part in the rehearsal.

The procession is arranged according to height, the two shortest ushers leading—unless others of nearly the same height are found to be more accurate pacemakers.   The bridesmaids come directly after the ushers, two and two, also according to height, the shortest in the lead.   After the bridesmaids, the maid (or matron) of honor walks alone; flower girls come next (if there are any) and last of all, the understudy bride leaning on the arm of the father, with pages (if she has any) holding up her train.   Each pair in the procession follows the two directly in front by four paces or beats of time.   In the vestibule, every one in the procession must pay attention to the feet directly in front, the pacemakers can follow the army sergeant's example and say very softly "left, left!"   At the end the bride counts eight beats before she and the father put "left foot" forward.   The whole trick is starting; after that they just walk naturally to the beat of the music, but keeping the ones in front as nearly as possible at the same distance.

At the foot of the chancel, the ushers divide. In a small church, the first two go up the chancel steps and stand at the top; one on the right, the other on the left. The second two go to a step or two below the first. If there are more, they stand below again. Chalk marks can be made on the chancel floor if necessary, but it ought not to be difficult, except for very little children who are flower girls or pages, to learn their position.

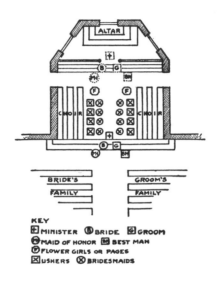

Or in a big church they go up farther, some of them lining the steps, or all of them in front of the choir stalls. The bridesmaids also divide, half on either side, and always stand in front of the ushers. The maid of honor's place is on the left at the foot of the steps, exactly opposite the best man. Flower girls and pages are put above or below the bridesmaids wherever it is thought "the picture" is best.

The grouping of the ushers and bridesmaids in the chancel or lining the steps also depends upon their number and the size of the church. In any event, the bridesmaids stand in front of the ushers; half of them on the right and half on the left. They never stand all on the bride's side, and the ushers on the groom's.

ENTRANCE OF THE BRIDEGROOM

The clergyman who is to perform the marriage comes into the chancel from the vestry. At a few paces behind him follows the groom, who in turn is followed by the best man. The groom stops at the foot of the chancel steps and takes his place at the right, as indicated in the accompanying diagram. His best man stands directly behind him. The ushers and bridesmaids always pass in front of him and take their places as noted above. When the bride approaches, the groom takes only a step to meet her.

A more effective greeting of the bride is possible if the door of the vestry opens into the chancel so that on following the clergyman, the groom finds himself at the top instead of the foot of the chancel steps. He goes forward to the right-hand side (his left), his best man behind him, and waits where he is until his bride approaches, when he goes down the steps to meet her—which is perhaps more gallant than to stand at the head of the aisle, and wait for her to join him.

The real bride watches carefully how the pseudo bride takes her left hand from her father's arm, shifts her fan, or whatever represents her bouquet, from her right hand to her left, and gives her right hand to the groom. In the proper maneuver the groom takes her right hand in his own right hand and draws it through his left arm, at the same time turning toward the chancel. If the service is undivided, and all of it is to be at the altar, this is necessary as the bride always goes up to the altar leaning on the arm of the groom.

If, however, the betrothal is to be read at the foot of the chancel (which is done at most weddings now) he may merely take her hand in his left one and stand as they are.

THE ORGANIST'S CUE

The organist stops at the moment the bride and groom have assumed their places. That is the cue to the organist as to the number of bars necessary for the procession. After the procession has practised "marching" two or three times, everything ought to be perfect. The organist, having count‐ed up the necessary bars of music, can readily give the leading ushers their "music cue"—so that they can start on the measure that will allow the procession and the organ to end together. The organist can, and usually does, stop off short, but there is a better finish if the bride's giving her hand to the groom and taking the last step that brings her in front of the chancel is timed so as to fall precisely on the last bars of the processional.

No words of the service are ever rehearsed, although all the "positions" to be taken are practised.

The pseudo bride takes the groom's left arm and goes slowly up the steps to the altar.

The best man follows behind and to the right of the groom, and the maid of honor (or "first" bridesmaid) leaves her companions and advances behind and to the left of the bride. The pseudo bride (in pantomime) gives her bouquet to the maid of honor; the best man (also in pan‐tomime) hands the ring to the groom, this merely to see that they are at a convenient distance for the services they are to perform. The recessional is played, and the pro‐cession goes out in reversed order. Bride and groom first, then bridesmaids, then ushers, again all taking pains to fall into step with the leaders.

On no account must the bridesmaids walk either up or down the aisle with the ushers! Once in a while the maid of honor takes the arm of the best man and together they follow the bride and groom out of the church. But it gives the impression of a double wedding and spoils the picture.

OBLIGATIONS OF THE BRIDEGROOM

In order that the first days of their life together may be as perfect as possible, the groom must make prepara‐tions for the wedding trip long ahead of time, so that best accommodations can be reserved. If they are to stop first at a hotel in their own city, or one near by, he should go days or even weeks in advance and personally select the rooms. It is much better frankly to tell the proprietor, or room clerk, at the same time asking him to "keep the secret." Everyone takes a friendly interest in a bridal couple, and the chances are that the proprietor will try to reserve the prettiest rooms in the house, and give the best service.

If their first stop is to be at a distance, then he must engage train seats or boat stateroom, and write to the hotel of their destination far enough in advance to receive a written reply, so that he may be sure of the accommodations they will find.

EXPENSE OF THE WEDDING TRIP

Just as it is contrary to all laws of etiquette for the bride to accept any part of her trousseau or wedding reception from the groom, so it is unthinkable for the bride to defray the least fraction of the cost of the wedding journey, no matter though she have millions in her own right, and he be earning ten dollars a week. He must save up his ten dollars as long as necessary, and the trip can be as short as they like, but convention has no rule more rigid than that the wedding trip shall be a responsibility of the groom.

There are two modifications of this rule: a house may be put at their disposal by a member of her family, or, if she is a widow, they may go to one of her own, provided it is not one occupied by her with her late husband. It is also quite all right for them to go away in a motor belonging to her, but driven by him, and all garage expenses belong to him; or if her father or other member of the family offers the use of a yacht or private railway car, the groom may accept but he should remember that the incidental and unavoidable expense of such a "gift" is sometimes greater than the cost of railway tickets.

BUYING THE WEDDING RING

It is quite usual for the bride to go with the groom when he buys the wedding ring, the reason being that as it stays for life on her finger, she should be allowed to choose the width and weight she likes and the size she finds comfortable.

THE GROOM'S PRESENT TO THE BRIDE

He is a very exceptional and enviable man who is financially able to take his fiancée to the jeweler's and let her choose what she fancies. Usually the groom buys the handsomest ornament he can afford—a string of pearls if he has great wealth, or a diamond pendant, brooch or bracelet, or perhaps only the simplest bangle or charm—but whether it is of great or little worth, it must be something for her personal adornment.

FURTHER OBLIGATIONS OF THE GROOM

Gifts must be provided for his best man and ushers, as well as their ties, gloves and boutonnières, a bouquet for his bride, and the fee for the clergyman, which may be a ten dollar gold piece or one or two new one hundred dollar bills, according to his wealth and the importance of the wedding. Whatever the amount, it is enclosed in an envelope and taken in charge by the best man who hands it to the clergyman in his vestry-room immediately after the ceremony.

Chapter XXII

THE DAY OF THE WEDDING

No one is busier than the best man on the day of the wedding. His official position is a cross between trained nurse, valet, general manager and keeper.

Bright and early in the morning he hurries to the house of the groom, generally before the latter is up. Very likely they breakfast together; in any event, he takes the groom in charge precisely as might a guardian. He takes note of his patient's general condition; if he is normal and "fit," so much the better. If he is "up in the air" or "nervous" the best man must bring him to earth and jolly him along as best he can.

BEST MAN AS EXPRESSMAN

His first actual duty is that of packer and expressman; he must see that everything necessary for the journey is packed, and that the groom does not absent-mindedly put the furnishings of his room in his valise and leave his belongings hanging in the closet. He must see that the clothes the groom is to "wear away" are put into a special bag to be taken to the house of the bride (where he, as well as she, must change from wedding into traveling clothes). The best man becomes expressman if the first stage of the wedding journey is to be to a hotel in town. He puts all the groom's luggage into his own car or a taxi, drives to the bride's house, carries the bag with the groom's traveling suit in it to the room set aside for his use—usually the dressing-room of the bride's father or the bedroom of her brother. He then collects, according to pre-arrangement, the luggage of the bride and drives with the entire equipment of both bride and groom to the hotel where rooms have already been engaged, sees it all into the rooms, and makes sure that everything is as it should be.

If he is very thoughtful, he may himself put flowers about the rooms. He also registers for the newly-weds, takes the room key, returns to the house of the groom, gives him the key and assures him that everything at the hotel is in readiness. This maneuver allows the young couple when they arrive to go quietly to their rooms without attracting the notice of any one, as would be the case if they arrived with baggage and were conspicuously shown the way by a bell-boy whose manner unmistakably proclaims "Bride and Groom!"

Or, if they are going at once by boat or train, the best man takes the baggage to the station, checks the large pieces, and fees a porter to see that the hand luggage is put in the proper stateroom or parlor car chairs. If they are going by automobile, he takes the luggage out to the garage and personally sees that it is bestowed in the car.

BEST MAN AS VALET

His next duty is that of valet. He must see that the groom is dressed and ready early, and plaster him up if he cuts himself shaving. If he is wise in his day he even provides a small bottle of adrenaline for just such an accident, so that plaster is unnecessary and that the groom may be whole. He may need to find his collar button or even to point out the "missing" clothes that are lying in full view. He must also be sure to ask for the wedding ring and the clergyman's fee, and put them in his own waistcoat pocket. A very careful best man carries a duplicate ring, in case of one being lost during the ceremony.

BEST MAN AS COMPANION-IN-ORDINARY

With the bride's and groom's luggage properly bestowed, the ring and fee in his pocket, the groom's traveling clothes at the bride's house, the groom in complete wedding attire, and himself also ready, the best man has nothing further to do but be gentleman-in-waiting to the groom until it is time to escort him to the church, where he becomes chief of staff.

AT THE HOUSE OF THE BRIDE

Meanwhile, if the wedding is to be at noon, dawn will not have much more than broken before the house—at least below stairs—becomes bustling.

Even if the wedding is to be at four o'clock, it will still be early in the morning when the business of the day begins. But let us suppose it is to be at noon; if the family is one that is used to assembling at an early breakfast table, it is probable that the bride herself will come down for this last meal alone with her family. They will, however, not be allowed to linger long at the table. The caterer will already be clamoring for possession of the dining-room—the florist will by that time already have dumped heaps of wire and greens into the middle of the drawing-room, if not beside the table where the family are still communing with their eggs. The door-bell has long ago begun to ring. At first there are telegrams and special delivery letters, then as soon as the shops open, come the last-moment wedding presents, notes, messages and the insistent clamor of the telephone.

Next, excited voices in the hall announce members of the family who come from a distance. They all want to kiss the bride, they all want rooms to dress in, they all want to talk. Also comes the hairdresser to do the bride's or her mother's or aunt's or grandmother's hair, or all of them; the manicure, the masseuse—any one else that may have been thought necessary to give final beautifying touches to any or all of the female members of the household. The dozen and one articles from the caterer are meantime being carried in at the basement door; made dishes, and dishes in the making, raw materials of which others are to be made; folding chairs, small tables, chinaware, glassware, napery, knives, forks and spoons—it is a struggle to get in or out of the kitchen or area door.

The bride's mother consults the florist for the third and last time as to whether the bridal couple had not better receive in the library because of the bay window which lends itself easily to the decoration of a background, and because the room, is, if anything, larger than the drawing-room. And for the third time, the florist agrees about the advantage of the window but points out that the library has only one narrow door and that the drawing-room is much better, because it has two wide ones and guests going into the room will not be blocked in the doorway by others coming out.

The best man turns up and wants the bride's luggage.

The head usher comes to ask whether the Joneses to be seated in the fourth pew are the tall dark ones or the blond ones, and whether he had not better put some of the Titheringtons who belong in the eighth pew also in the seventh, as there are nine Titheringtons and the Eminents in the seventh pew are only four.

A bridesmaid-elect hurries up the steps, runs into the best man carrying out the luggage; much conversation and giggling and guessing as to where the luggage is going. Best man very important, also very noble and silent. Bridesmaid shrugs her shoulders, dashes up to the bride's room and dashes down again.

More presents arrive. The furniture movers have come and are carting lumps of heaviness up the stairs to the attic and down the stairs to the cellar. It is all very like an ant-hill. Some are steadily going forward with the business in hand, but others who have become quite bewildered, seem to be scurrying aimlessly this way and that, picking something up only to put it down again.

THE DRAWING-ROOM

Here, where the bride and groom are to receive, one can not tell yet what the decoration is to be. Perhaps it is a hedged-in garden scene, a palm grove, a flowering recess, a screen and canopy of wedding bells—but a bower of foliage of some sort is gradually taking shape.

THE DINING-ROOM

The dining-room, too, blossoms with plants and flowers. Perhaps its space and that of a tent adjoining is filled with little tables, or perhaps a single row of camp chairs stands flat against the walls, and in the center of the room, the dining table pulled out to its farthest extent, is being decked with trimmings and utensils which will be needed later when the spaces left at intervals for various dishes shall be occupied. Preparation of these dishes is meanwhile going on in the kitchen.

THE KITCHEN

The caterer's chefs in white cook's caps and aprons are in possession of the situation, and their assistants run here and there, bringing ingredients as they are told; or perhaps the caterer brings everything already prepared, in which case the waiters are busy unpacking the big tin boxes and placing the *bain-marie* (a sort of fireless cooker receptacle in a tank of hot water) from which the hot food is to be served. Huge tubs of cracked ice in which the ice cream containers are buried are already standing in the shade of the areaway or in the back yard.

LAST PREPARATIONS

Back again in the drawing-room, the florist and his assistants are still tying and tacking and arranging and adjusting branches and garlands and sheaves and bunches, and the floor is a litter of twigs and strings and broken branches. The photographer is asking that the central decoration be finished so he can group his pictures, the florist assures him that he is as busy as possible.

The house is as cold as open windows can make it, to keep the flowers fresh, and to avoid stuffiness. The doorbell continues its ringing, and the parlor maid finds herself a contestant in a marathon, until some one decides that card envelopes and telegrams had better be left in the front hall.

A first bridesmaid arrives. She at least is on time. All decoration activity stops while she is looked at and admired. Panic seizes some one! The time is too short, nothing will be ready! Some one else says the bridesmaid is far too early, there is no end of time.

Upstairs everyone is still dressing. The father of the bride (one would suppose him to be the bridegroom at least) is trying on most of his shirts, the floor strewn with discarded collars! The mother of the bride is hurrying into her wedding array so as to be ready for any emergency, as well as to superintend the finishing touches to her daughter's dress and veil.

THE WEDDING DRESS

Everyone knows what a wedding dress is like. It may be of any white material, satin, brocade, velvet, chiffon or entirely of lace. It may be embroidered in pearls, crystals or silver; or it may be as plain as a slip-cover—anything in fact that the bride fancies, and made in whatever fashion or period she may choose.

As for her veil in its combination of lace or tulle and orange blossoms, perhaps it is copied from a head-dress of Egypt or China, or from the severe drapery of Rebecca herself, or proclaim the knowing touch of the Rue de la Paix. It may have a cap, like that of a lady in a French print, or fall in clouds of tulle from under a little wreath, such as might be worn by a child Queen of the May.

The origin of the bridal veil is an unsettled question.

Roman brides wore "yellow veils," and veils were used in the ancient Hebrew marriage ceremony. The veil as we use it may be a substitute for the flowing tresses which in old times fell like a mantle modestly concealing the bride's face and form; or it may be an amplification of the veil which medieval fashion added to every head-dress.

In olden days the garland rather than the veil seems to have been of greatest importance. The garland was the "coronet of the good girl," and her right to wear it was her inalienable attribute of virtue.

Very old books speak of three ornaments that every virtuous bride must wear, "a ring on her finger, a brooch on her breast and a garland on her head."

A bride who had no dowry of gold was said nevertheless to bring her husband great treasure, if she brought him a garland—in other words, a virtuous wife.

At present the veil is usually mounted by a milliner on a made foundation, so that it need merely be put on—but every young girl has an idea of how she personally wants her wedding veil and may choose rather to put it together herself or have it done by some particular friend, whose taste and skill she especially admires.

If she chooses to wear a veil over her face up the aisle and during the ceremony, the front veil is always a short separate piece about a yard square, gathered on an invisible band, and pinned with a hair pin at either side, after the long veil is arranged. It is taken off by the maid of honor when she gives back the bride's bouquet at the conclusion of the ceremony.

The face veil is a rather old-fashioned custom, and is appropriate only for a very young bride of a demure type; the tradition being that a maiden is too shy to face a congregation unveiled, and shows her face only when she is a married woman.

Some brides prefer to remove their left glove by merely pulling it inside out at the altar. Usually the under seam of the wedding finger of her glove is ripped for about two inches and she need only pull the tip off to have the ring put on. Or, if the wedding is a small one, she wears no gloves at all.

Brides have been known to choose colors other than white. Cloth of silver is quite conventional and so is very deep cream, but cloth of gold suggests the habiliment of a widow rather than that of a virgin maid—of which the white and orange blossoms, or myrtle leaf, are the emblems.

If a bride chooses to be married in traveling dress, she has no bridesmaids, though she often has a maid of honor. A "traveling" dress is either a "tailor made" if she is going directly on a boat or train, or a morning or afternoon dress—whatever she would "wear away" after a big wedding.

But to return to our particular bride; everyone seemingly is in her room, her mother, her grandmother, three aunts, two cousins, three bridesmaids, four small children, two friends, her maid, the dressmaker and an assistant. Every little while, the parlor-maid brings a message or a package. Her father comes in and goes out at regular intervals, in sheer nervousness. The rest of the bridesmaids gradually appear and distract the attention of the audience so that the bride has moments of being allowed to dress undisturbed. At last even her veil is adjusted and all present gasp their approval: "How sweet!" "Dearest, you are too lovely!" and "Darling, how wonderful you look!"

Her father reappears: "If you are going to have the pictures taken, you had better all hurry!"

"Oh, Mary," shouts some one, "what have you on that is

> Something old, something new,
> Something borrowed, something blue,
> And a lucky sixpence in your shoe!"

"Let me see," says the bride, " 'old,' I have old lace; 'new,' I have lots of new! 'Borrowed,' and 'blue'?" A chorus of voices: "Wear my ring," "Wear my pin," "Wear mine! It's blue!" and some one's pin which has a blue stone in it, is fastened on under the trimming of her dress and serves both needs. If the lucky sixpence (a dime will do) is produced, she must at least pay discomfort for her "luck."

Again some one suggests the photographer is waiting and time is short. Having pictures taken before the ceremony is a dull custom, because it is tiring to sit for one's photograph at best, and to attempt anything so delaying as posing at the moment when the procession ought to be starting, is as trying to the nerves as it is exhausting, and more than one wedding procession has consisted of very "dragged out" young women in consequence.

At a country wedding it is very easy to take the pictures out on the lawn at the end of the reception and just before the bride goes to dress. Sometimes in a town house, they are taken in an up-stairs room at that same hour; but usually the bride is dressed and her bridesmaids arrive at her house fully half an hour before the time necessary to leave for the church, and pictures of the group are taken as well as several of the bride alone—with special lights—against the background where she will stand and receive.

PROCESSION TO CHURCH

Whether the pictures are taken before the wedding or after, the bridesmaids always meet at the house of the bride, where they also receive their bouquets. When it is time to go to the church, there are several carriages or motors drawn up at the house. The bride's mother drives away in the first, usually alone, or she may, if she chooses, take one or two bridesmaids in her car, but she must reserve room for her husband who will return from church with her. The maid of honor, bridesmaids and flower girls go in the next vehicles, which may be their own or else are supplied by the bride's family; and last of all, comes the bride's carriage, which always has a wedding appearance. If it is a brougham, the horses' headpieces are decorated with white flowers·and the coachman wears a white bouton nière; if it is a motor, the chauffeur wears a small bunch of white flowers on his coat, and white gloves, and has all the tires painted white to give the car a wedding appear. ance. The bride drives to the church with her father only. Her carriage arrives last of the procession, and stands without moving, in front of the awning, until she and her husband (in place of her father) return from the ceremony and drive back to the house for the breakfast or reception.

If she has no father, this part is taken by an uncle, a brother, a cousin, her guardian, or other close male connection of her family.

If it should happen that the bride has neither father nor very near male relative, or guardian, she walks up the aisle alone. At the point in the ceremony when the clergyman asks who gives the bride, if the betrothal is read at the chancel steps, her mother goes forward and performs the office in exactly the same way that her father would have done.

If the entire ceremony is at the altar, the mother merely stays where she is standing in her proper place at the end of the first pew on the left, and says very distinctly, "I do."

AT THE CHURCH

Meanwhile, about an hour before the time for the ceremony, the ushers arrive at the church and the sexton turns his guardianship over to them. They leave their hats in the vestry, or coat room. Their boutonnières, sent by the groom, should be waiting in the vestibule. They should be in charge of a boy from the florist's, who has nothing else on his mind but to see that they are there, that they are fresh and that the ushers get them. Each man puts one in his buttonhole, and also puts on his gloves. The head usher decides (or the groom has already told them) to which ushers are apportioned the center, and to which the side aisles. If it is a big church with side aisles and gallery, and there are only six ushers, four will be put in the center aisle, and two in the side. Guests who choose to sit up in the gallery find places for themselves.

Often, at a big wedding, the sexton or one of his assistants guards the entrance to the gallery and admission is reserved by cards for the employees of both families, but usually the gallery is open to those who care to go up. An usher whose "place" is in the side aisle may escort occasional personal friends of his own down the center aisle if he happens to be unoccupied at the moment of their entrance. Those of the ushers who are the most likely to recognize the various close friends and members of each family are invariably detailed to the center aisle. A brother of the bride, for instance, is always chosen for this aisle because he is best fitted to look out for his own relatives and to place them according to their near or distant kinship. A second usher should be either a brother of the groom or a near relative who would be able to recognize the family and close friends of the groom.

The first six to twenty pews on both sides of the center aisle are fenced off with white ribbons into a reserved enclosure. The parents of the bride always sit in the first pew on the left (facing the chancel); the parents of the groom always sit in the first pew on the right. The right hand side of the church is the groom's side always, the left is that of the bride.

A CHURCH WEDDING

"In the city or country the church is decorated with masses of flowers, greens and sprays of flowers at the ends of the six to twenty reserved pews."

SEATING THE GUESTS

It is the duty of the ushers to show all guests to their places. An usher offers his arm to each lady as she arrives, whether he knows her personally or not. If the vestibule is very crowded and several ladies are together, he sometimes gives his arm to the older and asks the others to follow. But this is not done unless the crowd is great and the time short.

If the usher thinks a guest belongs in front of the ribbons though she fails to present her card, he always asks at once "Have you a pew number?" If she has, he then shows her to her place. If she has none, he asks whether she prefers to sit on the bride's side or the groom's and gives her the best seat vacant in the unreserved part of the church. He generally makes a few polite remarks as he takes her up the aisle. Such as:

"I am so sorry you came late, all the good seats are taken further up." Or "Isn't it lucky they have such a beautiful day?" or "Too bad it is raining." Or, perhaps the lady is first in making a similar remark or two to him.

Whatever conversation there is, is carried on in a low voice, not, however, whispered or solemn. The deportment of the ushers should be natural but at the same time dignified and quiet in consideration of the fact that they are in church. They must not trot up and down the aisles in a bustling manner; yet they must be fairly agile, as the vestibule is packed with guests who have all to be seated as expeditiously as possible.

The guests without reserved cards should arrive first in order to find good places; then come the reserved seat guests; and lastly, the immediate members of the families, who all have especial places in the front pews held for them.

It is not customary for one who is in deep mourning to go to a wedding, but there can be little criticism of an intimate friend who takes a place in the gallery of the church from which she can see the ceremony and yet be apart from the wedding guests. At a wedding that is necessarily small because of mourning, the women of the family usually lay aside black for that one occasion and wear white.

In Front of the Ribbons

There are two ways in which people "in front of the ribbons" are seated. The less efficient way is by means of a typewritten list of those for whom seats are reserved and of the pews in which they are to be seated, given to each usher, who has read it over for each guest who arrives at the church. From every point of view, the typewritten list is bad; first, it wastes time, and as everyone arrives at the same moment, and every lady is supposed to be taken personally up the aisle "on the arm" of an usher, the time consumed while each usher looks up each name on several gradually rumpling or tearing sheets of paper is easily imagined. Besides which, one who is at all intimate with either family can not help feeling in some degree slighted when, on giving one's name, the usher looks for it in vain.

The second, and far better method, is to have a pew card sent, enclosed with the wedding invitation, or an inscribed visiting card sent by either family. A guest who has a card with "Pew No. 12" on it, knows, and the usher knows, exactly where she is to go. Or if she has a card saying "Reserved" or "Before the ribbons" or any special mark that means in the reserved section but no especial pew, the usher puts her in the "best position available" behind the first two or three numbered rows that are saved for the immediate family, and in front of the ribbons marking the reserved enclosure.

It is sometimes well for the head usher to ask the bride's mother if she is sure she has allowed enough pews in the reserved section to seat all those with cards. Arranging definite seat numbers has one disadvantage; one pew may have every seat occupied and another may be almost empty. In that case an usher can, just before the procession is to form, shift a certain few people out of the crowded pews into the others. But it would be a breach of etiquette for people to re-seat themselves, and no one should be seated after the entrance of the bride's mother.

THE BRIDEGROOM WAITS

Meanwhile, about fifteen minutes before the wedding hour, the groom and his best man—both in morning coats, top-hats, boutonnières and white buckskin (but remember not shiny) gloves, walk or drive to the church and enter the side door which leads to the vestry. There they sit, or in the clergyman's study, until the sexton or an usher comes to say that the bride has arrived.

THE PERFECTLY MANAGED WEDDING

At a perfectly managed wedding, the bride arrives exactly one minute (to give a last comer time to find place) after the hour. Two or three servants have been sent to wait in the vestibule to help the bride and bridesmaids off with their wraps and hold them until they are needed after the ceremony. The groom's mother and father also are waiting in the vestibule. As the carriage of the bride's mother drives up, an usher goes as quickly as he can to tell the groom, and any brothers or sisters of the bride or groom, who are not to take part in the wedding procession and have arrived in their mother's carriage, are now taken by ushers to their places in the front pews. The moment the entire wedding party is at the church, the doors between the vestibule and the church are *closed*. No one is seated after this, except the parents of the young couple. The proper procedure should be carried out with military exactness, and is as follows:

The groom's mother goes down the aisle on the arm of the head usher and takes her place in the first pew on the right; the groom's father follows alone, and takes his place beside her; the same usher returns to the vestibule and immediately escorts the bride's mother; he should then have time to return to the vestibule and take his place in the procession. The beginning of the wedding march should sound just as the usher returns to the head of the aisle. To repeat: *No other person should be seated after the mother of the bride.* Guests who arrive later must stand in the vestibule or go into the gallery.

The sound of the music is also the cue for the clergyman to enter the chancel, followed by the groom and his best man. The two latter wear gloves but have left their hats and sticks in the vestry-room.

The groom stands on the right hand side at the head of the aisle, but if the vestry opens into the chancel, he sometimes stands at the top of the first few steps. He removes his right glove and holds it in his left hand. The best man remains always directly back and to the right of the groom. and does *not* remove his glove.

HERE COMES THE BRIDE

The description of the procession is given in detail on a preceding page in the "Wedding Rehearsal" section.

Starting on the right measure and keeping perfect time, the ushers come, two by two, four paces apart; then the bridesmaids (if any) at the same distance exactly; then the maid of honor alone; then the flower girls (if any); then, at a *double distance,* the bride on her father's right arm. She is dressed always in white, with a veil of lace or tulle. Usually she carries a bridal bouquet of white flowers, either short, or with streamers (narrow ribbons with little bunches of blossoms on the end of each) or trailing vines, or maybe she holds a long sheaf of stiff flowers such as lilies on her arm. Or perhaps she carries a prayer book instead of a bouquet.

THE GROOM COMES FORWARD TO MEET THE BRIDE

As the bride approaches, the groom waits at the foot of the steps (unless he comes down the steps to meet her). The bride relinquishes her father's arm, changes her bouquet from her right to her left, and gives her right hand to the groom. The groom, taking her hand in his right puts it through his left arm—just her finger tips should rest near the bend of his elbow—and turns to face the chancel as he does so. It does not matter whether she takes his arm or whether they stand hand in hand at the foot of the chancel in front of the clergyman.

HER FATHER GIVES HER AWAY

Her father has remained where she left him, on her left and a step or two behind her.   The clergyman stands a step or two above them, and reads the betrothal.   When he says "Who giveth this woman to be married?" the father goes forward, still on her left, and half way between her and the clergyman, but not in front of either, the bride turns slightly toward her father, and gives him her right hand, the father puts her hand into that of the clergyman and says at the same moment: "I do!"   He then takes his place next to his wife at the end of the first pew on the left.

THE MARRIAGE CEREMONY

A soloist or the choir then sings while the clergyman slowly ascends to the altar, before which the marriage is performed.   The bride and groom follow slowly, the fingers of her right hand on his left arm.

The maid of honor, or else the first bridesmaid, moves out of line and follows on the left hand side until she stands immediately below the bride.   The best man takes the same position exactly on the right behind the groom.   At the termination of the anthem, the bride hands her bouquet to the maid of honor (or her prayer-book to the clergyman) and the bride and groom plight their troth.

When it is time for the ring, the best man produces it from his pocket.   If in the handling from best man to groom, to clergyman, to groom again, and finally to the bride's finger, it should slip and fall, the best man must pick it up if he can without searching; if not, he quietly produces the duplicate which all careful best men carry in the other waistcoat pocket, and the ceremony proceeds. The lost ring—or the unused extra one—is returned to the jeweler's next day.   Which ring, under the circumstances, the bride keeps, is a question as hard to answer as that of the Lady or the Tiger.   Would she prefer the substitute ring that was actually the one she was married with?   Or the one her husband bought and had marked for her? Or would she prefer not to have a substitute ring and have the whole wedding party on their knees searching? She alone can decide. Fortunately, even if the clergyman is very old and his hand shaky, a substitute is seldom necessary.

The wedding ring must not be put above the engagement ring. On her wedding day a bride either leaves her engagement ring at home when she goes to church or wears it on her right hand.

AFTER THE CEREMONY

At the conclusion of the ceremony, the minister congratulates the new couple. The organ begins the recessional. The bride takes her bouquet from her maid of honor (who removes the veil if she wore one over her face). She then turns toward her husband—her bouquet in her right hand —and puts her left hand through his right arm, and they descend the steps.

The maid of honor, handing her own bouquet to a second bridesmaid, follows a short distance after the bride, at the same time stooping and straightening out the long train and veil. The bride and groom go on down the aisle. The best man disappears into the vestry room. At a perfectly conducted wedding he does not walk down the aisle with the maid of honor. The maid of honor recovers her bouquet and walks alone. If a bridesmaid performs the office of maid of honor, she takes her place among her companion bridesmaids who go next; and the ushers go last.

The best man has meanwhile collected the groom's belongings and dashed out of the side entrance and around to the front to give the groom his hat and stick.

Sometimes the sexton takes charge of the groom's hat and stick and hands them to him at the church door as he goes out. But in either case the best man always hurries around to see the bride and groom into their carriage, which has been standing at the entrance to the awning since she and her father alighted from it.

All the other conveyances are drawn up in the reverse

order from that in which they arrived.   The bride's carriage leaves first, next come those of the bridesmaids, next the bride's mother and father, next the groom's mother and father, then the nearest members of both families, and finally all the other guests in the order of their being able to find their conveyances.

The best man goes back to the vestry, where he gives the fee to the clergyman, collects his own hat, and coat if he has one, and goes to the bride's house.

As soon as the recessional is over, the ushers hurry back and escort to the door all the ladies who were in the first pews, according to the order of precedence; the bride's mother first, then the groom's mother, then the other occupants of the first pew on either side, then the second and third pews, until all members of the immediate families have left the church.   Meanwhile it is a breach of etiquette for other guests to leave their places.   At some weddings, just before the bride's arrival, the ushers run ribbons down the whole length of the center aisle, fencing the congregation in. As soon as the occupants of the first pews have left, the ribbons are removed and all the other guests go out by themselves, the ushers having by that time hurried to the bride's house to make themselves useful at the reception.

AT THE HOUSE

An awning makes a covered way from the edge of the curb to the front door.   At the lower end the chauffeur (or one of the caterer's men) stands to open the carriage doors and give return checks to the chauffeurs and their employers.   Inside the house the florist has finished, an orchestra is playing in the hall or library, everything is in perfect order.   The bride and groom have taken their places in front of the elaborate setting of flowering plants that has been arranged for them.

The bride stands on her husband's right and her bridesmaids are either grouped beyond her or else divided, half on her side and half on the side of the groom, forming a crescent with bride and groom in the center.

USHERS AT THE HOUSE

At a small wedding the duty of ushers is personally to take guests up to the bride and groom. But at a big reception where guests outnumber ushers fifty or a hundred to one, being personally conducted is an honor accorded only to the very old, the very celebrated or the usher's own best friends. All the other guests stand in a long congested line by themselves. The bride's mother takes her place somewhere near the entrance of the room, and it is for her benefit that her own butler or one furnished by the caterer, asks each guest his name and then repeats it aloud. The guests shake hands with the hostess, and making some polite remark about the "beautiful wedding" or "lovely bride," continue in line to the bridal pair.

WEDDING CONVERSATION

What you should say in congratulating a bridal couple depends on how well you know one, or both of them. But remember it is a breach of good manners to congratulate a bride on having secured a husband.

If you are unknown to both of them, and in a long queue, it is not even necessary to give your name. You merely shake hands with the groom, say a formal word or two such as "Congratulations!"; shake hands with the bride, say "I wish you every happiness!" and pass on.

If you know them fairly well, you may say to him "I hope your good luck will stay with you always!" or "I certainly do congratulate you!" and to her "I hope your whole life will be one long happiness," or, if you are much older than she, "You look too lovely, dear Mary, and I hope you will always be as radiant as you look to-day!" Or, if you are a woman and a relative or really close friend, you kiss the groom, saying, "All the luck in the world to you, dear Jim, she certainly is lovely!" Or, kissing the bride, "Mary, darling, every good wish in the world to you!"

To all the above, the groom and bride answer merely "Thank you."

A man might say to the groom "Good luck to you, Jim, old man!" Or, "She is the most lovely thing I have ever seen!" And to her, "I hope you will have every happiness!" Or "I was just telling Jim how lucky I think he is! I hope you will both be very happy!" Or, if a very close friend, also kissing the bride, "All the happiness you can think of isn't as much as I wish you, Mary dear!" But it cannot be too much emphasized that promiscuous kissing among the guests is an offense against good taste.

To a relative, or old friend of the bride, but possibly a stranger to the groom, the bride always introduces her husband saying, "Jim, this is Aunt Kate!" Or, "Mrs. Neighbor, you know Jim, don't you?" Or formally, "Mrs. Faraway, may I present my husband?"

The groom on the approach of an old friend of his, says, "Mary, this is cousin Carrie." Or, "Mrs. Denver, do you know Mary?" Or, "Hello, Steve, let me introduce you to my wife; Mary, this is Steve Michigan." Steve says "How do you do, Mrs. Smartlington!" And Mary says, "Of course, I have often heard Jim speak of you!"

The bride with a good memory thanks each arriving person for the gift sent her: "Thank you so much for the lovely candlesticks," or "I can't tell you how much I love the dishes!" The person who is thanked says, "I am so glad you like it (or them)," or "I am so glad! I hoped you might find it useful." Or "I didn't have it marked, so that in case you have a duplicate, you can change it."

Conversation is never a fixed grouping of words that are learned or recited like a part in a play; the above examples are given more to indicate the sort of things people in good society usually say. There is, however, one rule: Do not launch into long conversation or details of *yourself*, how you feel or look or what happened to you, or what *you* wore when you were married! Your subject must not deviate from the young couple themselves, their wedding, their future.

Also be brief in order not to keep those behind waiting longer than necessary. If you have anything particular to tell them, you can return later when there is no longer a line. But even then, long conversation, especially concerning yourself, is out of place.

PARENTS OF THE GROOM

The groom's mother always receives either near the bride's mother or else continuing the line beyond the bridesmaids, and it is proper for every guest to shake hands with her too, whether they know her or not, but it is not necessary to say anything. The bride's father sometimes stands beside his wife but he usually circulates among his guests just as he would at a ball or any other party where he is host.

The groom's father is a guest and it is not necessary for strangers to speak to him, unless he stands beside his wife and, as it were, "receives," but there is no impropriety in any one telling him how well they know and like his son or his new daughter-in-law.

The guests, as soon as they have congratulated the bride and groom, go out and find themselves places (if it is to be a sit-down breakfast) at a table.

DETAILS OF A SIT-DOWN BREAKFAST

Unless the house is remarkable in size, there is usually a canopied platform built next to the veranda or on the lawn or over the yard of a city house. The entire space is packed with little tables surrounding the big one reserved for the bridal party, and at a large breakfast a second table is reserved for the parents of the bride and groom and a few close, and especially invited, friends.

Place cards are not put on any of the small tables. All the guests, except the few placed at the two reserved tables, sit with whom they like; sometimes by pre-arrangement, but usually where they happen to find friends—and room!

The general sit-down breakfast—except in great houses like a few of those in Newport—is always furnished by a caterer, who brings all the food, tables, chairs, napery, china and glass, as well as the necessary waiters. The butler and footmen belonging in the house may assist or oversee, or detail themselves to other duties.

Small *menu* cards printed in silver are put on all the tables. Sometimes these cards have the crest of the bride's father embossed at the top, but usually the entwined initials of the bride and groom are stamped in silver to match the wedding cake boxes.

Example:

SS

Bouillon

Lobster Newburg

Suprême of Chicken

Peas

Aspic of Foie Gras

Celery Salad

Ices

Coffee

Instead of bouillon, there may be caviar or melon, or grape fruit, or a purée, or clam broth. For lobster Newburg may be soft-shell crabs or oyster pâté, or other fish. Or the bouillon may be followed by a dish such as sweetbreads and mushrooms, or chicken pâtés, or broiled chicken (a half of a chicken for each guest) or squab, with salad such as whole tomatoes filled with celery. Or the chicken or squab may be the second course, and an aspic with the salad, the third. Individual ices are accompanied by little cakes of assorted variety. There used always to be champagne; a substitute is at best "a poor thing," and what the prevailing one is to be, is as yet not determined. Orange juice and ginger ale, or white grape juice and ginger ale with sugar and mint leaves are two attempts at a satisfying cup that have been offered lately.

THE BRIDE'S TABLE

The feature of the wedding breakfast is always the bride's table. Placed sometimes in the dining-room, sometimes on the veranda or in a room apart, this table is larger and more elaborately decorated than any of the others. There are white garlands or sprays or other arrangement of white flowers, and in the center as chief ornament is an elaborately iced wedding cake. On the top it has a bouquet of white or silver flowers, or confectioner's quaint dolls representing the bride and groom. The top is usually made like a cover so that when the time comes for the bride to cut it, it is merely lifted off. The bride always cuts the cake, meaning that she inserts the knife and makes one cut through the cake, after which each person cuts herself or himself a slice. If there are two sets of favors hidden in the cake, there is a mark in the icing to distinguish the bridesmaids' side from that of the ushers. Articles, each wrapped in silver foil, have been pushed through the bottom of the cake at intervals; the bridesmaids find a ten-cent piece for riches, a little gold ring for "first to be married," a thimble or little parrot or cat for "old maid," a wish-bone for the "luckiest." On the ushers' side, a button or dog is for the bachelor, and a miniature pair of dice as a symbol of lucky chance in life. The ring and ten-cent piece are the same.

If a big piece of the wedding cake is left, the bride's mother has it wrapped in tin foil and put in a sealed tin box and kept for the bride to open on her first anniversary.

The evolution of the wedding cake began in ancient Rome where brides carried wheat ears in their left hands. Later, Anglo-Saxon brides wore the wheat made into chaplets, and gradually the belief developed that a young girl who ate of the grains of wheat which became scattered on the ground, would dream of her future husband. The next step was the baking of a thin dry biscuit which was broken over the bride's head and the crumbs divided amongst the guests. The next step was in making richer cake; then icing it, and the last instead of having it broken over her head, the bride broke it herself into small pieces for the guests. Later she cut it with a knife.

THE TABLE OF THE BRIDE'S PARENTS

The table of the bride's parents differs from other tables in nothing except in its larger size, and the place cards for those who have been invited to sit there. The groom's father always sits on the right of the bride's mother, and the groom's mother has the place of honor on the host's right. The other places at the table are occupied by distinguished guests who may or may not include the clergyman who performed the ceremony. If a bishop or dean performed the ceremony, he is always included at this table and is placed at the left of the hostess, and his wife, if present, sits at the bride's father's left. Otherwise only especially close friends of the bride's parents are invited to this table.

THE WEDDING CAKE

In addition to the big cake on the bride's table, there are at all weddings, near the front door so that the guests may each take one as they go home, little individual boxes of wedding cake, "black" fruit cake. Each box is made of white moiré or gros-grain paper, embossed in silver with the last initial of the groom intertwined with that of the bride and tied with white satin ribbon. At a sit-down breakfast the wedding cake boxes are sometimes put, one at each place, on the tables so that each guest may be sure of receiving one, and other "thoughtless" ones prevented from carrying more than their share away.

THE STANDING BREAKFAST OR RECEPTION

The standing breakfast differs from the sit-down breakfast in service only. Instead of numerous small tables at which the guests are served with a course luncheon, a single long one is set in the dining-room. (The regular table pulled out to its farthest extent.) It is covered with a plain white damask cloth—or it may be of embroidered linen and lace insertion. In the center is usually a bowl or vase or other centerpiece, of white flowers. On it are piles of plates, stacks of napkins and rows of spoons and forks at intervals, making four or possibly six piles altogether. Always there are dishes filled with little fancy cakes, chosen as much for looks as for taste. There is usually a big urn at one end filled with bouillon and one

at the other filled with chocolate or tea. In four evenly
spaced places are placed two cold dishes such as an
aspic of chicken, or ham mousse, or a terrine de foie gras,
or other aspic. The hot dishes may be a boned capon,
vol-au-vent of sweetbread and mushrooms, creamed oysters,
chicken à la King, or chicken croquettes; or there may
be cold cuts, or celery salad, in tomato aspic. Whatever
the choice may be, there are two or three cold dishes and
at least two hot. Whatever there is, must be selected with
a view to its being easily eaten with a fork while the plate
is held in the other hand! There are also rolls and biscuits, pâté de foie gras or lettuce and tomato sandwiches,
the former made usually of split "dinner" rolls with pâté
between, or thin sandwiches rolled like a leaf in which a
moth has built a cocoon. Ices are brought in a little later,
when a number of persons have apparently finished their
"first course." Ice cream is quite as fashionable as individual "ices." It is merely that caterers are less partial to
it because it has to be cut.

After-dinner coffee is put on a side table, as the champagne used to be. From now on there will probably be a
bowl or pitchers of something with a lump of ice in it that
can be ladled into glasses and become whatever those
gifted with imagination may fancy.

Unless the wedding is very small, there is always a
bride's table, decorated exactly as that described for a
sit-down breakfast, and placed usually in the library, but
there is no especial table for the bride's mother and her
guests—or for anyone else.

THE BRIDAL PARTY EAT

By the time the sit-down breakfast has reached its
second course and the queue of arriving guests has
dwindled and melted away, the bride and groom decide that
it is time they too go to breakfast. Arm in arm they
lead the way to their own table followed by the ushers and
bridesmaids. The bride and groom always sit next to
each other, she on his right; the maid of honor (or
matron) is on his left, and the best man is on the right

of the bride. Around the rest of the table come bridesmaids and ushers alternately. Sometimes one or two
others—sisters of the bride or groom or intimate friends,
who were not included in the wedding party, are asked to
the table, and when there are no bridesmaids this is
always the case.

The decoration of the table, the service, the food, is
exactly the same whether the other guests are seated or
standing. At dessert, the bride cuts the cake, and the
bridesmaids and ushers find the luck pieces.

DANCING AT THE WEDDING

On leaving their table, the bridal party join the dancing
which by now has begun in the drawing-room where the
wedding group received. The bride and groom dance at
first together, and then each with bridesmaids or ushers
or other guests. Sometimes they linger so long that those
who had intended staying for the "going away" grow
weary and leave—which is often exactly what the young
couple want! Unless they have to catch a train, they
always stay until the "crowd thins" before going to dress
for their journey. At last the bride signals to her bridesmaids and leaves the room. They all gather at the foot
of the stairs; about half way to the upper landing as
she goes up, she throws her bouquet, and they all try to
catch it. The one to whom it falls is supposed to be the
next married. If she has no bridesmaids, she sometimes
collects a group of other young girls and throws her
bouquet to them.

INTO TRAVELING CLOTHES

The bride goes up to the room that has always been
hers, followed by her mother, sisters and bridesmaids,
who stay with her while she changes into her traveling
clothes. A few minutes after the bride has gone upstairs,
the groom goes to the room reserved for him, and changes
into the ordinary sack suit which the best man has taken
there for him before the ceremony. He does *not* wear
his top hat nor his wedding boutonnière. The groom's

clothes should be "apparently" new, but need not actually be so. The bride's clothes, on the other hand, are always brand new—every article that she has on.

THE GOING-AWAY DRESS

A bride necessarily chooses her going-away dress according to the journey she is to make. If she is starting off in an open motor, she wears a suitably small motor hat and a wrap of some sort over whatever dress (or suit) she chooses. If she is going on a train or boat, she wears a "traveling" dress, such as she would choose under ordinary circumstances. If she is going to a near-by hotel or a country house put at her disposal, she wears the sort of dress and hat suitable to town or country occasion. She should not dress as though about to join a circus parade or the ornaments on a Christmas tree, unless she wants to be stared at and commented upon in a way that no one of good breeding can endure.

The average bride and groom of good taste and feeling try to be as inconspicuous as possible. On one occasion, in order to hide the fact that they were "bride and groom," a young couple "went away" in their oldest clothes and were very much pleased with their cleverness, until, pulling out his handkerchief, the groom scattered rice all over the floor of the parlor car. The bride's lament after this was—"Why had she not worn her prettiest things?"

The groom, having changed his clothes, waits upstairs, in the hall generally, until the bride emerges from her room in her traveling clothes. All the ushers shake hands with them both. His immediate family, as well as hers, have gradually collected—any that are missing must unfailingly be sent for. The bride's mother gives her a last kiss, her bridesmaids hurry down-stairs to have plenty of rice ready and to tell everyone below as they descend "They are coming!" A passage from the stairway and out of the front door, all the way to the motor, is left free between two rows of eager guests, their hands full of rice. Upon the waiting motor the ushers have tied everything they can lay their hands on in the way of white ribbons and shoes and slippers.

HERE THEY COME!

At last the groom appears at the top of the stairs, a glimpse of the bride behind him. It surely is running the gauntlet! They seemingly count "one, two, three, go!" With shoulders hunched and collars held tight to their necks, they run through shrapnel of rice, down the stairs, out through the hall, down the outside steps, into the motor. slam the door, and are off!

The wedding guests stand out on the street or roadway looking after them for as long as a vestige can be seen— and then gradually disperse.

Occasionally young couples think it clever to slip out of the area-way, or over the roofs, or out of the cellar and across the garden. All this is supposed to be in order to avoid being deluged with rice and having labels of "newly wed" or large white bows and odd shoes and slippers tied to their luggage.

Most brides, however, agree with their guests that it is decidedly "spoil sport" to deprive a lot of friends (who have only their good luck at heart) of the perfectly legitimate enjoyment of throwing emblems of good luck after them. If one white slipper among those thrown after the motor lands right side up, on top of it, and stays there, greatest good fortune is sure to follow through life.

There was a time when the "going away carriage" was always furnished by the groom, and this is still the case if it is a hired conveyance, but nowadays when nearly everyone has a motor, the newly married couple—if they have no motor of their own—are sure to have one lent them by the family of one of them. Very often they have two motors and are met by a second car at an appointed place, into which they change after shaking themselves free of rice. The white ribboned car returns to the house, as well as the decorated and labeled luggage, which was all empty—their real luggage having been bestowed safely by the best man that morning in their hotel or boat or train. Or, it may be that they choose a novel journey, for there is, of course, no regulation vehicle. They can go off in a limousine, a pony cart, a yacht, a canoe, on horseback or by airplane. Fancy alone limits the mode of travel, suggests the destination, or directs the etiquette of a honeymoon.

BRIDE'S FIRST DUTY OF THOUGHT FOR GROOM'S PARENTS

At the end of the wedding there is one thing the bride must not forget. As soon as she is in her traveling dress, she must send a bridesmaid or someone out into the hall and ask her husband's parents to come and say good-by to her. If his parents have not themselves come upstairs to see their son, the bride must have them sent for at once!

It is very easy for a bride to forget this act of thoughtfulness and for a groom to overlook the fact that he can not stop to kiss his mother good-by on his way out of the house, and many a mother seeing her son and new daughter rush past without even a glance from either of them, has returned home with an ache in her heart.

It sounds improbable, doesn't it? One naturally exclaims, "But how stupid of her, why didn't she go upstairs? Why didn't her son send for her?" Usually she does, or he does. But often the groom's parents are strangers; and if by temperament they are shy or retiring people they hesitate to go upstairs in an unknown house until they are invited to. So they wait, feeling sure that in good time they will be sent for. Meanwhile the bride "forgets" and it does not occur to the groom that unless he makes an effort while upstairs there will be no opportunity in the dash down to the carriage to recognize them—or anyone.

FLIPPANCY VS. RADIANCE

A completely beautiful wedding is not merely a combination of wonderful flowers, beautiful clothes, smoothness of detail, delicious food. These, though all necessary, are external attributes. The spirit, or soul of it, must have something besides; and that "something" is in the behavior and in the expression of the bride and groom.

The most beautiful wedding ever imagined could be turned from sacrament to circus by the indecorous behavior of the groom and the flippancy of the bride. She, above all, must not reach up and wig-wag signals while she is receiving, any more than she must wave to people as she goes up and down the aisle of the church. She must not cling to her husband, stand pigeon-toed, or lean against him or the wall, or any person, or thing. She must not run her arm through his and let her hand flop on the other side; she must not swing her arms as though they were dangling rope; she must not switch herself this way and that, nor must she "hello" or shout. No matter how young or "natural" and thoughtless she may be, she *must,* during the ceremony and the short time that she stands beside her husband at the reception, assume that she has dignity.

It is not by chance that the phrase "happy pair" is one of the most trite in our language, for happiness above all is the inner essential that must dominate a perfect wedding. An unhappy looking bride, an unwilling looking groom, turns the greatest wedding splendor into sham; without love it is a sacrament inadvisedly entered into, and the sight of a tragic-faced bride strikes chill to the heart.

The radiance of a truly happy bride is so beautifying that even a plain girl is made pretty, and a pretty one, divine. There is something glad yet sweet, shy yet triumphant, serious yet—radiant! There is no other way to put it. And a happy groom looks first of all protective—he, too, may have the quality of radiance, but it is different—more directly glad. They both look as though there were sunlight behind their eyes, as though their mouths irresistibly turned to smiles. No other quality of a bride's expression is so beautiful as radiance; that visible proof of perfect happiness which endears its possessor to all beholders and gives to the simplest little wedding complete beauty.

THE HOUSE WEDDING

A house wedding involves slightly less expenditure but has the disadvantage of limiting the number of guests. The ceremony is exactly the same as that in a church, excepting that the procession advances through an aisle of white satin ribbons from the stairs down which the bridal party descends, to the improvised altar. A small space near the altar is fenced off with other ribbons, for the family. There is a low rail of some sort back of which the clergyman stands, and something for the bride and groom to kneel on during the prayers of the ceremony. The prayer bench is usually about six or eight inches high, and between three and four feet long; at the back of it an upright on either end supports a crosspiece—or altar rail. It can be made in roughest fashion by any carpenter, or amateur, as it is entirely hidden under leaves and flowers. On the kneeling surface of the bench are placed cushions rather than flowers, because the latter stain. All caterers have the necessary standards to which ribbons are tied, like the wires to telegraph poles. The top of each standard is usually decorated with a spray of white flowers.

At a house wedding the bride's mother stands at the door of the drawing-room—or wherever the ceremony is to be— and receives people as they arrive. But the groom's mother merely takes her place near the altar with the rest of the immediate family. The ushers are purely ornamental, unless the house is so large that "pews" have been installed, and the guests are seated as in a church. Otherwise the guests stand wherever they can find places behind the aisle ribbons. Just before the bride's entrance, her mother goes forward and stands in the reserved part of the room. The ushers go up to the top of the stairway. The wedding march begins and the ushers come down two and two, followed by the bridesmaids, exactly as in a church, the bride coming last on her father's arm. The clergyman and the groom and best man have, if possible, reached the altar by another door. If the room has only one door, they go up the aisle a few moments before the bridal procession starts.

The chief difference between a church and house wedding is that the bride and groom do not take a single step together. The groom meets her at the point where the service is read. After the ceremony, there is no recessional. The clergyman withdraws, an usher removes the prayer bench, and the bride and groom merely turn where they stand, and

"AN ATTRACTIVE ALTAR ARRANGEMENT FOR A HOUSE WEDDING." [Page 374.]

receive the congratulations of their guests, unless, of course, the house is so big that they receive in another room.

When there is no recessional, the groom always kisses the bride before they turn to receive their guests—it is against all tradition for any one to kiss her before her husband does.

There are seldom many bridal attendants at a house wedding, two to four ushers, and one to four bridesmaids, unless the house is an immense one.

In the country a house wedding includes one in a garden, with a wedding procession under the trees, and tables out on the lawn—a perfect plan for California or other rainless States, but difficult to arrange on the Atlantic seaboard where rain is too likely to spoil everything.

THE WEDDING IN ASSEMBLY ROOMS

Those whose houses are very small and yet who wish to have a general reception, sometimes give the wedding breakfast in a hotel or assembly rooms. The preparations are identical with those in a private house, the decorations and menu may be lavish or simple. Although it is perfectly good form to hold a wedding reception in a ballroom, a breakfast in a private house, no matter how simple, has greater distinction than the most elaborate collation in a public establishment. Why this is so, is hard to determine. It is probably that without a "home" atmosphere, though it may be a brilliant entertainment, the sentiment is missing.

THE SECOND MARRIAGE

The detail of a spinster's wedding is the same whether she marries a bachelor or a widower, the difference being that a widower does not give a "bachelor" dinner.

The marriage of a widow is the same as that of a maid except that she cannot wear white or orange blossoms, which are emblems of virginity, nor does she have bridesmaids. Usually a widow chooses a very quiet wedding, but there is no reason why she should not have a "big wedding" if she cares to, except that somber ushers and a bride in traveling dress, or at best a light afternoon one with a hat, does not make an effective processional—unless she is beautiful enough to compensate for all that is missing.

A wedding in very best taste for a widow would be a ceremony in a small church or chapel, a few flowers or palms in the chancel the only decoration, and two to four ushers. There are no ribboned-off seats, as only very intimate friends are asked. The bride wears an afternoon street dress and hat. Her dress for a church ceremony should be more conventional than if she were married at home, where she could wear a semi-evening gown and substitute a headdress for a hat. She could even wear a veil if it is colored and does not suggest the bridal white one.

A celebrated beauty wore for her second wedding in her own house, a dress of gold brocade, with a Russian court headdress and a veil of yellow tulle down the back. Another wore a dress of gray and a Dutch cap of silver lace, and had her little girl in quaint cap and long dress, to match her own, as maid of honor.

A widow has never more than one attendant and most often none. There may be a sit-down breakfast afterwards, or the simplest afternoon tea; in any case, the breakfast is, if possible, at the bride's own house, and the bridal pair may either stay where they are and have their guests take leave of them, or themselves drive away afterwards.

Very intimate friends send presents for a second marriage but general acquaintances are never expected to.

SUMMARY OF EXPENSES

All the expenses of a wedding belong to the bride's parents; the invitations are issued by them, the reception is at their house, and the groom's family are little more than ordinary guests. The cost of a wedding varies as much as the cost of anything else that one has or does. A big fashionable wedding can total far up in the thousands and even the simplest entails considerable outlay, which can, however, be modified by those who are capable of doing things themselves instead of employing professional service at every point.

THE PARENTS OF THE BRIDE PROVIDE

1. Engraved invitations and cards.

2. The service of a professional secretary who compiles a single list from the various ones sent her, addresses the envelopes, both inner and outer; encloses the proper number of cards, seals, stamps and mails all the invitations. (This item can be omitted and the work done by the family.)

3. The biggest item of expense—the trousseau of the bride, which may consist not alone of wearing apparel of endless variety and lavish detail, but household linen of finest quality (priceless in these days) and in quantity sufficient for a lifetime; or it may consist of the wedding dress, and even that a traveling one, and one or two others, with barest essentials and few accessories.

4. Awnings for church and house. This may be omitted at the house in good weather, at the church, and also in the country.

5. Decorations of church and house. Cost can be eliminated by amateurs using garden or field flowers.

6. Choir, soloists and organist at church. (Choir and soloists unnecessary.)

7. Orchestra at house. (This may mean fifty pieces with two leaders or it may mean a piano, violin and drum, or a violin, harp and guitar.)

8. Carriages or motors for the bridal party from house to church and back.

9. The collation, which may be the most elaborate sit-down luncheon or the simplest afternoon tea.

10. Boxes of wedding cake.

11. Champagne—used to be one of the biggest items, as a fashionable wedding without plenty of it was unheard of. Perhaps though, pocketbooks may have less relief on account of its omission than would at first seem probable, since what is saved on the wine bill is made up for on the additional food necessary to make the best wineless menu seem other than meagre.

12. The bride's presents to her bridesmaids. (May be jewels of value or trinkets of trifling cost.)

13. A wedding present to the bride from each member of her family—not counting her trousseau which is merely part of the wedding.

14. The bride gives a "wedding present" or a "wedding" ring or both to the groom, if she especially wants to. (Not necessary nor even customary.)

THE GROOM'S EXPENSES ARE

1. The engagement ring—as handsome as he can possibly afford.

2. A wedding present—jewels if he is able, always something for her personal adornment.

3. His bachelor dinner.

4. The marriage license.

5. A personal gift to his best man and each of his ushers.

6. To each of the above he gives their wedding ties, gloves and boutonnières.

7. The bouquet carried by the bride. In many cities it is said to be the custom for the bride to send boutonnières to the ushers and for the groom to order the bouquets of the bridesmaids. In New York's smart world, the bridesmaids' bouquets are looked upon as part of the decorative arrangement, all of which is in the province of the bride's parents.

8. The wedding ring.

9. The clergyman's fee.

10. From the moment the bride and groom start off on their wedding trip, all the expenditure becomes his.

WEDDING ANNIVERSARIES

1 year, paper
5 years, wood
10 years, tin
15 years, crystal
20 years, china
25 years, silver
50 years, gold
75 years, diamond

Wedding anniversaries are celebrated in any number of ways. The "party" may be one of two alone or it may be a dance. Most often it is a dinner, and occasionally, an afternoon tea.

In Germany a silver wedding is a very important event and a great celebration is made of it, but in America it is not very good form to ask any but intimate friends and family to an anniversary party—especially as those bidden are supposed to send presents. These need not, however, be of value; in fact the paper, wooden and tin wedding presents are seldom anything but jokes. Crystal is the earliest that is likely to be taken seriously by the gift-bearers. Silver is always serious, and the golden wedding a quite sacred event.

Most usually this last occasion is celebrated by a large family dinner to which all the children and grandchildren are bidden. Or the married couple perhaps choose an afternoon at home and receive their friends and neighbors, who are, of course, supposed to brings presents made of gold.

CHAPTER XXIII

CHRISTENINGS

A child can, of course, be christened without making a festivity of it at all—just as two people can be married with none but the clergyman and two witnesses—but nearly every mother takes this occasion to see her friends and show her baby to them.

Invitations to a christening are never formal, because none but the family and a very few intimate friends are supposed to be asked. In this day invitations are nearly all sent over the telephone, except to those who are at a distance, or else friends are asked verbally when seen; but it is both correct and polite to write notes. Such as:

Dear Mrs. Kindhart:

The baby is to be christened here at home, next Sunday at half past four, and we hope you and Mr. Kindhart—and the children if they care to—will come.

Affectionately,

Lucy Gilding.

If a telephone message is sent, the form is:

"Mr. and Mrs. Gilding, Jr. would like Mr. and Mrs. Norman to come to the baby's christening on Sunday at half past four, at their house."

ASKING THE GODPARENTS

Before setting the date for the christening, the god-mothers (two for a girl and one for a boy) and the god-fathers (two for a boy and one for a girl) have, of course, already been chosen.

If a godfather (or mother) after having given his consent is abroad or otherwise out of reach at the time of the christening, a proxy takes part in the ceremony instead, and without thereby becoming a godfather. Since god-parents are always most intimate friends, it is natural to ask them when they come to see the mother and the baby (which they probably do often) or to write them if at a distance. Sometimes they are asked at the same time that the baby's arrival is announced to them, occasionally even before.

The Gilding baby, for instance, supposedly sent the fol-lowing telegram:

Mrs. Richard Worldly,
  Great Estates.
  I arrived last night and my mother and father were very glad to see me, and I am now eagerly waiting to see you.
                    Your loving godson,
                      Robert Gilding, 3d.

But more usually a godparent at a distance is telegraphed:

John Strong,
  Equitrust, Paris.
  It's a boy. Will you be godfather?
                      Gilding.

But in any case a formally worded request is out of place. Do *not* write:
"My husband and I sincerely hope that you will consent to be our son's godmother," etc. Any one so slightly known as this wording implies would not be asked to fill so close a position as that of godmother without great presumption on your part.

You must never ask any one to be a godmother or god-father whom you do not know intimately well, as it is a responsibility not lightly to be undertaken and impossible to refuse. Godparents should, however, be chosen from among friends rather than relatives, since the sole advantage of godparents is that they add to the child's relatives, so that if it should be left alone in the world, its godparents become its protectors. But where a child is born with plenty of relatives who can be called upon for advice and affection and assistance in event of his or her becoming an orphan, godparents are often chosen from among them. Nothing could be more senseless, however, than choosing grandparents, since the relationship is as close as can be anyway, and the chances that the parents will outlive their own parents make such a choice still more unsuitable.

In France, the godmother is considered, next to the parents and grandparents, the nearest relative a child can have. In some European countries, the Queen or another who is above the parents in rank, assumes a special protectorate over her godchild. In this instance the godmother appoints herself.

In America a similar situation cannot very well exist; though on rare occasions an employer volunteers to stand as godfather for an employee's child. Godparents must, of course, give the baby a present, if not before, at least at the christening. The standard "gift" is a silver mug, a porringer, or a knife, fork and spoon, marked usually with the baby's name and that of the giver.

Robert Gilding, 3d
From his godfather
John Strong

Or the presents may be anything else they fancy. In New England a very rich godfather sometimes gives the baby a bond which is kept with interest intact until a girl is eighteen or a boy twenty-one.

TIME OF CHRISTENING

In other days of stricter observances a baby was baptized in the Catholic and high Episcopal church on the first or at least second Sunday after its birth. But to-day the christening is usually delayed at least until the young mother is up and about again; often it is put off for months and in some denominations children need not be christened until they are several years old. The most usual age is from two to six months.

If the family is very high church or the baby is delicate and its christening therefore takes place when it is only a week or two old, the mother is carried into the drawing-room and put on a sofa near the improvised font. She is dressed in a becoming negligé and perhaps a cap, and with lace pillows behind her and a cover equally decorative over her feet. The guests in this event are only the family and the fewest possible intimate friends.

THE CHRISTENING IN CHURCH

In arranging for the ceremony the clergyman, of course, is consulted and the place and hour arranged. If it is to be in church, it can take place at the close of the regular service on Sunday, but if a good deal is to be made of the christening, a week day is chosen and an hour when the church is not being otherwise used.

The decorations, if any at all, consist of a few palms or some flowering plants grouped around the font, and the guests invited for the christening take places in the pews which are nearest to the font, wherever that happens to be.

As soon as the clergyman appears, the baby's coat and cap are taken off (in any convenient pew, not necessarily the nearest one), and the godmother, holding the baby in her arms, stands directly in front of the clergyman. The other godparents stand beside her and other relatives and friends nearby.

The godmother who is holding the baby must be sure to pronounce its name distinctly—in fact it is a wise precaution if it is a long or an unusual one, to show the name printed on a slip of paper to the clergyman beforehand—as more than one baby has been given a name not intended for it. And whatever name the clergyman pronounces is fixed for life. The little Town girl who was to have been called Marian is actually Mary Ann!

As soon as the ceremony is over, the godmother hands the baby back to its nurse, who puts on its cap and coat, and it is then driven with all its relatives and friends to the house of its parents or grandparents, where a lunch or an afternoon tea has been arranged.

HOUSE CHRISTENING

Unless forbidden by the church to which the baby's parents belong, the house christening is by far the easier, safer and prettier. Easier, because the baby does not have to have wraps put on and off and be taken out and brought in; safer, because it is not apt to catch cold; and prettier, for a dozen reasons.

The baby in the first place looks much prettier in a dress that has not been crushed by having a coat put over it and taken off and put on and off again. In the second place, a baby brought down from the nursery without any fussing is generally "good," whereas one that has been dressed and undressed and taken hither and yon is apt to be upset and therefore to cry. If it cries in church it just has to cry! In a house it can be taken into another room and be brought back again after it has been made "more comfortable." It is trying to a young mother who is proud of her baby's looks, to go to no end of trouble to get exquisite clothes for it, and ask all her friends in, and then have it look exactly like a tragedy mask carved in a beet! And you can scarcely expect a self-respecting baby who is hauled and mauled and taken to a strange place and handed to a strange person who pours cold water on it—not to protest. And alas! it has only one means.

The arrangements made for a house christening are something like those made for a house wedding—only much simpler. The drawing-room or wherever the ceremony is to be performed is often decorated with pots of pale pink roses, or daisies, or branches of dogwood or white lilacs. Nothing is prettier than the blossoms of fruit trees (if they can be persuaded to keep their petals on) or any other spring flowers. In summer there are all the garden flowers. In autumn, cosmos and white chrysanthemums, or at any season, baby's breath and roses.

The "font" is always a bowl—of silver usually—put on a small high table. A white napkin on the table inevitably suggests a restaurant rather than a ritual and is therefore unfortunate, and most people of taste prefer to have the table covered with old church brocade and an arrangement of flowers either standing behind or laid upon it so that the stems are toward the center and covered by the base of the bowl.

If the clergyman is to wear vestments, a room must be put at his disposal.

At the hour set for the ceremony, the clergyman enters the room first and takes his place at the font. The guests naturally make way, forming an open aisle. If not, the baby's father or another member of the family clears an aisle. The godmother carries the baby and follows the clergyman; the other two godparents walk behind her, and all three stand near the font. At the proper moment the clergyman takes the baby, baptizes it and hands it back to the godmother, who holds it until the ceremony is over.

THE CHRISTENING DRESS

The christening dress is always especially elaborate and beautiful. Often it is one that was worn by the baby's mother, father, or even its grand or great-grandparent. Baby clothes should be as sheer as possible and as soft. The ideal dress is of mull with much or little valenciennes lace (real) and finest hand embroidery. But however much or little its trimming, it must be exquisite in texture. In fact, everything for a baby ought to be hand-made. It can be as plain as a charity garment, but of fine material and tiny hand stitches. If the baby is very little, it is usually laid on a lace trimmed pillow. (This lace, too, must be valenciennes.)

The godmother or godmothers should wear the sort of clothes that they would wear at an afternoon tea. The godfather or fathers should wear formal afternoon clothes. The other guests wear ordinary afternoon clothes and the mother—unless on the sofa—wears a light-colored afternoon dress. She should not wear black on this occasion.

As soon as the ceremony is performed, the clergyman goes to the room that was set apart for him, changes into his ordinary clothes and then returns to the drawing-room to be one of the guests at luncheon or tea. The god-mother hands the baby to the nurse, or maybe to its mother, and everyone gathers around to admire it. And the party becomes exactly like every informal afternoon tea.

The only difference between an ordinary informal tea and a christening is that a feature of the latter is a christening cake and caudle. The christening cake is generally a white "lady" cake elaborately iced, sometimes with the baby's initials, and garlands of pink sugar roses. And although according to cook-books caudle is a gruel, the actual "caudle" invariably served at christenings is a hot eggnog, drunk out of little punch cups. One is supposed to eat the cake as a sign that one partakes of the baby's hospitality, and is therefore its friend, and to drink the caudle to its health and prosperity. But by this time the young host (or hostess) is peacefully asleep in the nursery.

Chapter XXIV

FUNERALS

At no time does solemnity so possess our souls as when we stand deserted at the brink of darkness into which our loved one has gone. And the last place in the world where we would look for comfort at such a time is in the seeming artificiality of etiquette; yet it is in the moment of deepest sorrow that etiquette performs its most vital and real service.

All set rules for social observance have for their object the smoothing of personal contacts, and in nothing is smoothness so necessary as in observing the solemn rites accorded our dead.

It is the time-worn servitor, Etiquette, who draws the shades, who muffles the bell, who keeps the house quiet, who hushes voices and footsteps and sudden noises; who stands between well-meaning and importunate outsiders and the retirement of the bereaved; who decrees that the last rites shall be performed smoothly and with beauty and gravity, so that the poignancy of grief may in so far as possible be assuaged.

FIRST DETAILS

As soon as death occurs, some one (the trained nurse usually) draws the blinds in the sick-room and tells a servant to draw all the blinds of the house.

If they are not already present, the first act of some one at the bedside is to telephone or telegraph the immediate members of the family, the clergyman and the sexton of the church to which the family belong, and possibly one or two closest friends, whose competence and sympathy can be counted on—as there are many things which must be done for the stricken family as well as for the deceased. (The sexton of nearly every Protestant church is also un-

387

dertaker. If he is not, then an outside funeral director is sent for.)

If the illness has been a long one, it may be that the family has become attached to the trained nurse and no one is better fitted than she to turn her ministrations from the one whom she can no longer help, to those who have now very real need of just such care as she can give.

If the death was sudden, or the nurse unsympathetic or for other reasons unavailable, then a relative or a near friend of practical sympathy is the ideal attendant in charge.

CONSIDERATION FOR THE FAMILY

Persons under the shock of genuine affliction are not only upset mentally but are all unbalanced physically. No matter how calm and controlled they seemingly may be, no one can under such circumstances be normal. Their disturbed circulation makes them cold, their distress makes them unstrung, sleepless. Persons they normally like, they often turn from. No one should ever be forced upon those in grief, and all over-emotional people, no matter how near or dear, should be barred absolutely. Although the knowledge that their friends love them and sorrow for them is a great solace, the nearest afflicted must be protected from any one or anything which is likely to overstrain nerves already at the threatening point, and none have the right to feel hurt if they are told they can neither be of use nor be received. At such a time, to some people companionship is a comfort, others shrink from dearest friends. One who is by choice or accident selected to come in contact with those in new affliction should, like a trained nurse, banish all consciousness of self; otherwise he or she will be or no service—and service is the only gift of value that can be offered.

FIRST AID TO THE BEREAVED

First of all, the ones in sorrow should be urged if possible to sit in a sunny room and where there is an open fire. If they feel unequal to going to the table, a very little food should be taken to them on a tray. A cup of tea or coffee or bouillon, a little thin toast, a poached egg, milk if they like it hot, or milk toast. Cold milk is bad for one who is already over-chilled. The cook may suggest something that appeals usually to their taste—but very little should be offered at a time, for although the stomach may be empty, the palate rejects the thought of food, and digestion is never in best order.

It sounds paradoxical to say that those in sorrow should be protected from all contacts, and yet that they must be constantly asked about arrangements and given little time to remain utterly undisturbed. They must think of people they want sent for, and they must decide the details of the funeral; when they would like it held, and whether in church or at the house, whether they want special music or flowers ordered, and where the interment is to be.

ON DUTY AT DOOR

A friend or a servant is always stationed in the hall to open the door, receive notes and cards, and to take messages. In a big house the butler in his day clothes should answer the bell, with the parlor-maid to assist him, until a footman can procure a black livery and take his or her place. A parlor-maid or waitress at the door should wear either a black or gray dress, with her plainest white apron, collar and cuffs.

MEMBER OF FAMILY IN CHARGE

A close friend or male member of the family should be —if not at the door—as near the front hall as possible to see the countless people with whom details have to be arranged, to admit to a member of the family anyone they may want to see, and to give news to, or take messages from, others.

As people come to the house to enquire and offer their services, he gives them commissions the occasion requires. The first friend who hurries to the house (in answer to the telephone message which announced the death) is asked to break the news to an invalid connection of the family, or he may be sent to the florist to order the bell hung, or to the station to meet a child arriving from school.

NOTICE TO PAPERS

The sexton (or other funeral director) sends the notices to the daily papers announcing the death, and the time and place of the funeral. The form is generally selected by a member of the family from among those appearing in that day's newspapers. These notices are paid for by the sexton and put on his bill.

With the exception of the telephone messages or telegrams to relatives and very intimate friends, no other notices are sent out. Only those persons who are expected to go to the house at once have messages sent to them; all others are supposed to read the notice in the papers. When the notice reads "funeral private" and neither place nor time is given, very intimate friends are supposed to ask for these details at the house; others understand they are not expected.

HANGING THE BELL

As a rule the funeral director hangs crepe streamers on the bell; white ones for a child, black and white for a young person, or black for an older person. This signifies to the passerby that it is a house of mourning so that the bell will not be rung unnecessarily nor long.

If they prefer, the family sometimes orders a florist to hang a bunch of violets or other purple flowers on black ribbon streamers, for a grown person; or white violets, white carnations—any white flower without leaves—on the black ribbon for a young woman or man; or white flowers on white gauze or ribbon for a child.

CHECKING EXPENSES IN ADVANCE

It is curious that long association with the sadness of death seems to have deprived an occasional funeral director of all sense of moderation. Whether the temptation of "good business" gradually undermines his character—knowing as he does that bereaved families ask no questions—or whether his profession is merely devoid of taste, he will, if not checked, bring the most ornate and expensive casket in his establishment; he will perform every rite that his professional ingenuity for expenditure can devise; he will employ every attendant he has; he will order vehicles numerous enough for the cortège of a president; he will even, if thrown in contact with a bewildered chief-mourner, secure a pledge for the erection of an elaborate mausoleum.

Some one, therefore, who has the family's interest at heart and knows their taste and purse, should go personally to the establishment of the undertaker, and not only select the coffin, but go carefully into the specification of all other details, so that everything necessary may be arranged for, and unnecessary items omitted.

This does not imply that a family that prefers a very elaborate funeral should not be allowed to have one; but the great majority of people have moderate, rather than unlimited means, and it is not unheard of that a small estate is seriously depleted by vulgarly lavish and entirely inappropriate funeral expenses. One would be a poor sort who for the sake of friends would not willingly endure a little troublesome inquiry, rather than witness a display of splurge and bad taste and realize at the same time that the friends who might have been protected will be deluged with bills which it cannot but embarrass them to pay.

HONORARY PALLBEARERS

The member of the family who is in charge will ask either when they come to the house, or by telephone or telegraph if they are at a distance, six or eight men who are close friends of the deceased to be the pallbearers. When a man has been prominent in public life, he may have twelve or more from among his political or business associates as well as his lifelong social friends. Near relatives are never chosen, as their place is with the women of the family. For a young woman, her own friends or those of her family are chosen. It is a service that may not under any circumstances except serious ill-health, be refused.

The one in charge will tell the pallbearers where they are to meet. It used to be customary for them to go to the house on the morning of the funeral and drive to the church behind the hearse, but as everything tending to a conspicuous procession is being gradually done away with, it is often preferred to have them wait in the vestibule of the church.

Honorary pallbearers serve only at church funerals. They do not carry the coffin for the reason that, being unaccustomed to bearing such a burden, one of them might possibly stumble, or at least give an impression of uncertainty or awkwardness that might detract from the solemnity of the occasion. The sexton's assistants are trained for this service, so as to prevent in so far as is humanly possible a blundering occurrence.

MOURNING FOR FUNERAL

Among those who come to the house there is sure to be a woman friend of the family whose taste and method of expenditure is similar to theirs. She looks through the clothes they have, to see if there is not a black dress or suit that can be used, and makes a list of only the necessary articles which will have to be procured.

All dressmaking establishments give precedence to mourning orders and will fill a commission within twenty-four hours. These first things are made invariably without bothering the wearer with fitting. Alterations, if required, are made later.

Or the mourning departments of the big stores and specialty shops are always willing to send a selection on approval, so that a choice can be made by the family in the privacy of their own rooms. Nearly always acquaintances who are themselves in mourning offer to lend crepe veils, toques and wraps, so that the garments which must be bought at first may be as few as possible. Most women have a plain black suit, or dress, the trimming of which can quickly be replaced with crepe by a maid or a friend.

Most men are of standard size and can go to a clothier and buy a ready-made black suit. Otherwise they must borrow, or wear what they have, as no tailor can make a suit in twenty-four hours.

"SITTING UP" NO LONGER CUSTOMARY

Unless the deceased was a prelate or personage whose lying-in-state is a public ceremony, or unless it is the especial wish of the relatives, the solemn vigil through long nights by the side of the coffin is no longer essential as a mark of veneration or love for the departed.

Nor is the soulless body dressed in elaborate trappings of farewell grandeur. Everything to-day is done to avoid unnecessary evidence of the change that has taken place. In case of a very small funeral the person who has passed away is sometimes left lying in bed in night clothes, or on a sofa in a wrapper, with flowers, but no set pieces, about the room, so that an invalid or other sensitive bereft one may say farewell without ever seeing the all too definite finality of a coffin. In any event the last attentions are paid in accordance with the wish of those most nearly concerned.

EXTRA WORK FOR SERVANTS

Kindness of heart is latent in all of us, and servants, even if they have not been long with a family, rise to the emergency of such a time as that of a funeral, which always puts additional work upon them and often leaves them to manage under their own initiative. The house is always full of people, family and intimate friends occupy all available accommodation, but it is a rare household which does not give sympathy as generously below stairs as above; and he or she would be thought very heartless by their companions who did not willingly and helpfully assume a just share of the temporary tax on energy, time and consideration.

CHURCH FUNERAL

The church funeral is the more trying, in that the family have to leave the seclusion of their house and face a congregation. On the other hand, many who find solemnity only in a church service with the added beauty of choir and organ, prefer to take their heartrending farewell in the House of God.

ARRANGING AND RECORDING FLOWERS

An hour before the time for the service, if the family is Protestant, one or two woman friends go to the church to arrange the flowers which are placed about the chancel. Unless they have had unusual practise in such arrangement they should, if possible, have the assistance of a florist, as effective grouping and fastening of heavy wreaths and sprays is apt to overtax the ingenuity of novices, no matter how perfect their usual taste may be.

Whoever takes charge of the flowers must be sure to collect carefully all the notes and cards. They should always take extra pencils in case the points break, and write on the outside of each envelope a description of the flowers that the card was sent with.

"Spray of Easter lilies and palm branches tied with white ribbon."
"Wreath of laurel leaves and gardenias."
"Long sheaf of pink roses and white lilacs."

These descriptions will afterwards help identify and recall the flowers when notes of thanks are sent.

As the appointed time for the funeral draws near, the organ plays softly, the congregation gradually fills the church. The first pews on either side of the center aisle are left empty.

THE PROCESSIONAL

At the appointed time the funeral procession forms in the vestibule. If there is to be a choral service the minister and the choir enter the church from the rear, and precede the funeral cortège. Directly after the choir and clergy come the pallbearers, two by two, then the coffin covered with flowers and then the family—the chief mourner comes first, leaning upon the arm of her closest male relative. Usually each man is escort for a woman, but two women or two men may walk together according to the division of the family. If the deceased is one of four sons where there is no daughter, the mother and father walk immediately behind the body of their child, followed by the two elder sons and behind them the younger, with the nearest woman relative. If there is a grandmother, she walks with the eldest son and the younger two follow together. If it is a family of daughters who are following their father, the eldest daughter may walk with her mother, or the mother may walk with her brother, or a son-in-law. Although the arrangement of the procession is thus fixed, those in affliction should be placed next to the one whose nearness may be of most comfort to them. A younger child who is calm and soothing would better be next to his mother than an older who is of more nervous temperament.

At the funeral of a woman, her husband sometimes walks alone, but usually with his mother or his daughter. A very few intimate friends walk at the rear of the family, followed by the servants of the household. At the chancel the choir take their accustomed places, the minister stands at the foot of the chancel steps, the honorary pallbearers take their places in the front pews on the left, and the coffin is set upon a stand previously placed there for the purpose. The bearers of the coffin walk quietly around to inconspicuous stations on a side aisle. The family occupy the front pews on the right, the rest of the procession fill vacant places on either side. The service is then read.

THE RECESSIONAL

Upon the conclusion of the service, the procession moves out in the same order as it came in excepting that the choir remain in their places and the honorary pallbearers go first. Outside the church, the coffin is put into the hearse, the family getting into carriages or motors waiting immediately behind, and the flowers are put into a covered vehicle. (It is very vulgar to fill open landaus with displayed floral offerings and parade through the streets.)

FEW GO TO THE BURIAL

If the burial is in the churchyard or otherwise within walking distance, the congregation naturally follows the family to the graveside.   Otherwise, the general congregation no longer expects, nor wishes, to go to the interment which (excepting at a funeral of public importance) is witnessed only by the immediate family and the most intimate friends, who are asked if they "care to go."   The long line of carriages that used to stand at the church ready to be filled with a long file of mere acquaintances is a barbarous thing of the past.

HOUSE FUNERAL

Many people prefer a house funeral—it is simpler, more private, and obviates the necessity for those in sorrow to face people.   The nearest relatives may stay apart in an adjoining room or even upon the upper floor, where they can hear the service but remain in unseen seclusion.

Ladies keep their wraps on.   Gentlemen wear their overcoats or carry them on their arms and hold their hats in their hands.

MUSIC

To many people there is lack of solemnity in a service outside of a church and lacking the accompaniment of the organ.   It is almost impossible to introduce orchestral music that does not sound either dangerously suggestive of the gaiety of entertainment or else thin and flat.   A quartet or choral singing is beautiful and appropriate, if available, otherwise there is usually no music at a house funeral.

HOUSE ARRANGEMENT

Some authorities say that only the flowers sent by very close friends should be shown at a house funeral, and that it is ostentatious to make a display.   But when people, or societies, have been kind enough to send flowers, it would certainly be wanting in appreciation, to say the least, to relegate their offerings to the back yard—or wherever it is that the cavilers would have them hid!

In a small house where flowers would be overpowering, it is customary to insert in the death notice: "It is requested that no flowers be sent," or "Kindly omit flowers."

Arrangement for the service is usually made in the drawing-room, and the coffin is placed in front of the mantel, or between the windows, but always at a distance from the door, usually on stands brought by the funeral director, who also brings enough camp chairs to fill the room without crowding. A friend, or a member of the family, collects the cards and arranges the flowers behind and at the side and against the stands of the coffin. If there is to be a blanket or pall of smilax or other leaves with or without flowers, fastened to a frame, or sewed on thin material and made into a covering, it is always ordered by the family. Otherwise, the wreaths to be placed on the coffin are chosen from among those sent by the family.

THE SERVICE

As friends arrive, they are shown to the room where the ceremony is to be held, but they take their own places. A room must be apportioned to the minister in which to put on his vestments. At the hour set for the funeral the immediate family, if they feel like being present, take their places in the front row of chairs. The women wear small hats or toques and long crepe veils over their faces, so that their countenances may be hidden. The minister takes his stand at the head of the coffin and reads the service.

At its conclusion the coffin is carried out to the hearse, which, followed by a small number of carriages, proceeds to the cemetery.

It is very rare nowadays for any but a small group of relatives and intimate men friends to go to the cemetery, and it is not thought unloving or slighting of the dead for no women at all to be at the graveside. If any women are to be present and the interment is to be in the ground, some one should order the grave lined with boughs and green branches—to lessen the impression of bare earth.

DISTANT COUNTRY FUNERAL

In the country where relatives and friends arrive by train, carriages or motors must be provided to convey them to the house or church or cemetery. If the clergyman has no conveyance of his own, he must always be sent for, and if the funeral is in a house, a room must be set apart for him in which to change his clothes.

It is unusual for a family to provide a "special car." Sometimes the hour of the funeral is announced in the papers as taking place on the arrival of a certain train, but everyone who attends is expected to pay his own railway fare and make, if necessary, his own arrangements for lunch.

Only when the country place where the funeral is held is at a distance from town and a long drive from the railway station, a light repast of bouillon, rolls and tea and sandwiches may be spread on the dining-room table. Otherwise refreshments are never offered—except to those of the family, of course, who are staying in the house.

HOUSE RESTORED TO ORDER

While the funeral cortège is still at the cemetery, some one who is in charge at home must see that the mourning emblem is taken off the bell, that the windows are opened, the house aired from the excessive odor of flowers, and the blinds pulled up. Any furniture that has been displaced should be put back where it belongs, and unless the day is too hot a fire should be lighted in the library or principal bedroom to make a little more cheerful the sad home-coming of the family. It is also well to prepare a little hot tea or broth, and it should be brought them upon their return without their being asked if they would care for it. Those who are in great distress want no food, but if it is handed to them, they will mechanically take it, and something warm to start digestion and stimulate impaired circulation is what they most need.

MOURNING

A generation or two ago the regulations for mourning were definitely prescribed, definite periods according to the precise degree of relationship of the mourner. One's real feelings, whether of grief or comparative indifference, had nothing to do with the outward manifestation one was obliged, in decency, to show. The tendency to-day is toward sincerity. People do not put on black for aunts, uncles and cousins unless there is a deep tie of affection as well as of blood.

Many persons to-day do not believe in going into mourning at all. There are some who believe, as do the races of the East, that great love should be expressed in rejoicing in the re-birth of a beloved spirit instead of selfishly mourning their own earthly loss. But many who object to manifestations of grief, find themselves impelled to wear mourning when their sorrow comes and the number of those who do not put on black is still comparatively small.

PROTECTION OF MOURNING

If you see acquaintances of yours in deepest mourning, it does not occur to you to go up to them and babble trivial topics or ask them to a dance or dinner. If you pass close to them, irresistible sympathy compels you merely to stop and press their hand and pass on. A widow, or mother, in the newness of her long veil, has her hard path made as little difficult as possible by everyone with whom she comes in contact, no matter on what errand she may be bent. A clerk in a store will try to wait on her as quickly and as attentively as possible. Acquaintances avoid stopping her with long conversation that could not but torture and distress her. She meets small kindnesses at every turn, which save unnecessary jars to supersensitive nerves.

Once in a great while, a tactless person may have no better sense than to ask her abruptly for whom she is in mourning! Such people would not hesitate to walk over the graves in a cemetery! And fortunately, such encounters are few.

Since many people, however, dislike long mourning veils

and all crepe generally, it is absolutely correct to omit both if preferred, and to wear an untrimmed coat and hat of plainest black with or without a veil.

A WORD OF ECONOMY

In the first days of stress, people sometimes give away every colored article they possess and not until later are they aware of the effort necessary, to say nothing of the expense, of getting an entire new wardrobe.　Therefore it is well to remember:

Dresses and suits can be dyed without ripping.　Any number of fabrics—all woolens, soft silks, canton crepe, georgette and chiffon, dye perfectly.　Buttonholes have sometimes to be re-worked, snaps or hooks and eyes changed to black, a bit of trimming taken off or covered with dull braid, silk or crepe, and the clothes look every bit as well as though newly ordered.

Straw hats can be painted with an easily applied stain sold in every drug and department store for the purpose. If you cannot trim hats yourself, a milliner can easily imitate, or, if necessary, simplify the general outline of the trimming as it was, and a seamstress can easily cover dyed trimmings on dresses with crepe or dull silk.　Also tan shoes—nearly all footwear made of leather—can be dyed black and made to look like new by any first class shoemaker.

MOURNING MATERIALS

Lustreless silks, such as crepe de chine, georgette, chiffon, grosgrain, peau de soie, dull finish charmeuse and taffeta, and all plain woolen materials, are suitable for deepest mourning.　Uncut velvet is as deep mourning as crepe, but cut velvet is not mourning at all!　Nor is satin or lace. The only lace permissible is a plain or hemstitched net known as "footing."

Fancy weaves in stockings are not mourning, nor is bright jet or silver.　A very perplexing decree is that clothes entirely of white are deepest mourning but the addition of a black belt or hat or gloves produces second mourning.

Patent leather and satin shoes are not mourning.

People in second mourning wear all combinations of black and white as well as clothes of gray and mauve. Many of the laws for materials seem arbitrary, and people interpret them with greater freedom than they used to, but never under any circumstances can one who is not entirely in colors wear satin embroidered in silver or trimmed with jet and lace! With the exception of wearing a small string of pearls and a single ring, especially if it is an engagement ring, jewelry with deepest mourning is never in good taste.

WHEN A VEIL IS NOT WORN

Nor should a woman ever wear a crepe veil to the theater or restaurant, or any public place of amusement. On the other hand, people left long to themselves and their own thoughts grow easily morbid, and the opera or concert or an interesting play may exert a beneficial relaxation. Gay restaurants with thumping strident musical accompaniment or entertainments of the cabaret variety, need scarcely be commented upon. But to go to a matinee with a close friend or relative is becoming more and more usual—and the picture theaters where one may sit in the obscurity and be diverted by the story on the silver screen which, requiring no mental effort, often diverts a sad mind for an hour or so, is an undeniable blessing. An observer would have to be much at a loss for material who could find anything to criticise in seeing a family together under such circumstances.

One generally leaves off a long veil, however, for such an occasion and drives bareheaded, if it be evening, or substitutes a short black face veil over one's hat on entering and leaving a building in the daytime.

MOURNING FOR COUNTRY WEAR

Except for church, crepe veils and clothes heavily trimmed with crepe are not appropriate in the country— ever! Mourning clothes for the summer consist of plain black serge or tweed, silk or cotton material, all black with white organdy collar and cuffs, and a veil-less hat with a brim. Or one may dress entirely in dull materials of white.

A WIDOW'S MOURNING

A widow used never to wear any but woolen materials, made as plain as possible, with deep-hemmed turn-back cuffs and collar of white organdy. On the street she wore a small crepe bonnet with a little cap-border of white crepe or organdy and a long veil of crepe or nun's veiling to the bottom edge of her skirt, over her face as well as down her back. At the end of three months the front veil was put back from over her face, but the long veil was worn two years at least, and frequently for life. These details are identical with those prescribed to-day excepting that she may wear lustreless silks as well as wool, the duration of mourning may be shorter, and she need never wear her veil over her face except at the funeral unless she chooses.

A widow of mature years who follows old-fashioned conventions wears deep mourning with crepe veil two years, black the third year and second mourning the fourth. But shorter periods of mourning are becoming more and more the custom and many consider three or even two years conventional.

THE VERY YOUNG WIDOW

The young widow should wear deep crepe for a year and then lighter mourning for six months and second mourning for six months longer. There is nothing more utterly captivating than a sweet young face under a widow's veil, and it is not to be wondered at that her own loneliness and need of sympathy, combined with all that is appealing to sympathy in a man, results in the healing of her heart. She should, however, *never* remain in mourning for her first husband after she has decided she can be consoled by a second.

There is no reason why a woman (or a man) should not find such consolation, but she should keep the intruding attraction away from her thoughts until the year of respect is up, after which she is free to put on colors and make happier plans.

MOURNING WORN BY A MOTHER

A mother who has lost a grown child wears the same mourning as that prescribed for a widow excepting the white cap ruche. Some mothers wear mourning for their children always, others do not believe in being long in black for a spirit that was young, and, for babies or very young children, wear colorless clothes of white or gray or mauve.

A DAUGHTER OR SISTER

A daughter or sister wears a long veil over her face at the funeral. The length of the veil may be to her waist or to the hem of her skirt, and it is worn for from three months to a year, according to her age and feelings. An older woman wears deep black for her parents, sisters and brothers for a year, and then lightens her mourning during the second year. A young girl, if she is out in society or in college, may wear a long veil for her parents or her betrothed, if she wants to, or she wears a thin net veil edged with crepe and the corners falling a short way down her back—or none at all.

Very young girls of from fourteen to eighteen wear black for three months and then six months of black and white. They never wear veils of any sort, nor are their clothes trimmed in crepe. Children from eight to fourteen wear black and white and gray for six months for a parent, brother, sister or grandparent. Young children are rarely put into mourning, though their clothes are often selected to avoid vivid color. They usually wear white with no black except a hair ribbon for the girls and a necktie for the boys. Very little children in black are too pitiful.

EXTREME FASHION INAPPROPRIATE

Fancy clothes in mourning are always offenses against good taste, because as the word implies, a person is in *mourning*. To have the impression of "fashion" dominant is contrary to the purpose of somber dress; it is a costume for the spirit, a covering for the visible body of one whose soul seeks the background. Nothing can be in worse taste than crepe which is gathered and ruched and puffed and pleated and made into waterfalls, and imitation ostrich feathers as a garnishing for a hat. The more absolutely plain, the more appropriate and dignified is the mourning dress. A "long veil" is a shade pulled down—a protection —it should never be a flaunting arrangement to arrest the amazed attention of the passerby.

The necessity for dignity can not be overemphasized.

BAD TASTE IN MOURNING

Mourning observances are all matters of fixed form, and any deviation from precise convention is interpreted by the world at large as signifying want of proper feeling.

How often has one heard said of a young woman who was perhaps merely ignorant of the effect of her inappropriate clothes or unconventional behavior: "Look at her! And her dear father scarcely cold in his grave!" Or "Little she seems to have cared for her mother—and such a lovely one she had, too." Such remarks are as thoughtless as are the actions of the daughter, but they point to an undeniable condition. Better far not wear mourning at all, saying you do not believe in it, than allow your unseemly conduct to indicate indifference to the memory of a really beloved parent; better that a young widow should go out in scarlet and yellow on the day after her husband's funeral than wear weeds which attract attention on account of their flaunting bad taste and flippancy. One may not, one must not, one *can not* wear the very last cry of exaggerated fashion in crepe, nor may one be boisterous or flippant or sloppy in manner, without giving the impression to all beholders that one's spirit is posturing, tripping, or dancing on the grave of sacred memory.

This may seem exaggerated, but if you examine the expressions, you will find that they are essentially true.

Draw the picture for yourself: A slim figure, if you like, held in the posture of the caterpillar slouch, a long length of stocking so thin as to give the effect of shaded skin above high-heeled slippers with sparkling buckles of bright jet, a short skirt, a scrappy, thin, low-necked, short-sleeved blouse through which white underclothing shows various edgings of lace and ribbons, and on top of this, a painted face under a long crepe veil! Yet the wearer of this costume may in nothing but appearance resemble the unmentionable class of women she suggests; as a matter of fact she is very likely a perfectly decent young person and really sad at heart, and her clothes and "make up" not different from countless others who pass unnoticed because their colored clothing suggests no mockery of solemnity.

MOURNING WEAR FOR MEN

The necessity of business and affairs which has made withdrawal into seclusion impossible, has also made it customary for the majority of men to go into mourning by the simple expedient of putting a black band on their hat or on the left sleeve of their usual clothes and wearing only white instead of colored linen.

A man never under any circumstances wears crepe. The band on his hat is of very fine cloth and varies in width according to the degree of mourning from two and a half inches to within half an inch of the top of a high hat. On other hats the width is fixed at about two and a half or three inches. The sleeve band, from three and a half to four and a half inches in width, is of dull broadcloth on overcoats or winter clothing, and of serge on summer clothes. The sleeve band of mourning is sensible for many reasons, the first being that of economy. Men's clothes do not come successfully from the encounter with dye vats, nor lend themselves to "alterations," and an entire new wardrobe is an unwarranted burden to most.

Except for the one black suit bought for the funeral and kept for Sunday church, or other special occasion, only wealthy men or widowers go to the very considerable expense of getting a new wardrobe. Widowers—especially if they are elderly—always go into black (which includes very dark gray mixtures) with a deep black band on the hat, and of course, black ties and socks and shoes and gloves.

CONVENTIONS OF MOURNING FOR MEN

Although the etiquette is less exacting, the standards of social observance are much the same for a man as for a woman. A widower should not be seen at any general entertainment, such as a dance, or in a box at the opera, for a year; a son for six months; a brother for three—at least! The length of time a father stays in mourning for a child is more a matter of his own inclination.

MOURNING LIVERY

Coachmen and chauffeurs wear black liveries in town. In the country they wear gray or even their ordinary whipcord with a black band on the left sleeve.

The house footman is always put into a black livery with dull buttons and a black and white striped waistcoat. Maids are not put into mourning with the exception of a lady's maid or nurse who, through many years of service, has "become one of the family," and who personally desires to wear mourning as though for a relative of her own.

ACKNOWLEDGMENT OF SYMPATHY

In the case of a very prominent person where messages of condolence, many of them impersonal, mount into the thousands, the sending of engraved cards to strangers is proper, such as:

Mr. W. Joe Bonds
wishes gratefully to acknowledge
your kind expression of sympathy

or

Senator and Mrs. Michigan

wish to express their appreciation of

Miss Millicent Gilding's

sympathy in their recent bereavement

Under no circumstances should such cards be sent to intimate friends, or to those who have sent flowers or written personal letters.

When some one with real sympathy in his heart has taken the trouble to select and send flowers, or has gone to the house and offered what service he might, or has in a spirit of genuine regard, written a personal letter, the receipt of words composed by a stationer and dispatched by a professional secretary is exactly as though his outstretched hand had been pushed aside.

A family in mourning is in retirement from all social activities. There is no excuse on the score of their "having no time." Also no one expects a long letter, nor does any one look for an early reply. A personal word on a visiting card is all any one asks for. The envelope may be addressed by some one else.

It takes but a moment to write "Thank you," or "Thank you for all sympathy," or "Thank you for your kind offers and sympathy." Or, on a sheet of letter paper:

"Thank you, dear Mrs. Smith, for your beautiful flowers and your kind sympathy."

Or:

"Your flowers were so beautiful! Thank you for them and for your loving message."

Or:

"Thank you for your sweet letter. I know you meant it and I appreciate it."

Many, many such notes can be written in a day. If the list is overlong, or the one who received the flowers and messages is in reality so prostrated that she (or he) is unable to perform the task of writing, then some member of her immediate family can write for her:

"Mother (or father) is too ill to write and asks me to thank you for your beautiful flowers and kind message."

Most people find a sad comfort as well as pain, in the reading and replying to letters and cards, but they should not sit at it too long; it is apt to increase rather than assuage their grief. Therefore, no one expects more than a word—but that word should be *seemingly personal.*

OBLIGATIONS OF PRESENCE AT FUNERALS

Upon reading the death notice of a mere acquaintance you may leave your card at the house, if you feel so inclined, or you may merely send your card.

Upon the death of an intimate acquaintance or friend you should go at once to the house, write, "With sympathy" on your card and leave it at the door. Or you should write a letter to the family; in either case, you send flowers addressed to the nearest relative. On the card accompanying the flowers, you write, "With sympathy," "With deepest sympathy," or "With heartfelt sympathy," or "With love and sympathy." If there is a notice in the papers "requesting no flowers be sent," you send them only if you are a very intimate friend.

Or if you prefer, send a few flowers with a note, immediately after the funeral, to the member of the family who is particularly your friend.

If the notice says "funeral private" you do not go unless you have received a message from the family that you are expected, or unless you are such an intimate friend that you know you are expected without being asked. Where a general notice is published in the paper, it is proper and fitting that you should show sympathy by going to the funeral, even though you had little more than a visiting acquaintance with the family. You should *not* leave cards nor go to a funeral of a person with whom you have not in any way been associated or to whose house you have never been asked.

But it is heartless and delinquent if you do not go to the funeral of one with whom you were associated in business or other interests, or to whose house you were often invited, or where you are a friend of the immediate members of the family.

You should wear black clothes if you have them, or if not, the darkest, the least conspicuous you possess. Enter the church as quietly as possible, and as there are no ushers at a funeral, seat yourself where you approximately belong. Only a very intimate friend should take a position far up on the center aisle. If you are merely an acquaintance you should sit inconspicuously in the rear somewhere, unless the funeral is very small and the church big, in which case you may sit on the end seat of the center aisle toward the back.

Chapter XXV

THE COUNTRY HOUSE AND ITS HOSPITALITY

The difference between the great house with twenty to fifty guest rooms, all numbered like the rooms in a hotel, and the house of ordinary good size with from four to six guest rooms, or the farmhouse or small cottage which has but one "best" spare chamber, with perhaps a "man's room" on the ground floor, is much the same as the difference between the elaborate wedding and the simplest—one merely of degree and not of kind.

To be sure, in the great house, week-end guests often include those who are little more than acquaintances of the host and hostess, whereas the visitor occupying the only "spare" room is practically always an intimate friend. Excepting, therefore, that people who have few visitors never ask any one on their general list, and that those who fill an enormous house time and time again necessarily do, the etiquette, manners, guest room appointments and the people who occupy them, are precisely the same. Popular opinion to the contrary, a man's social position is by no means proportionate to the size of his house, and even though he lives in a bungalow, he may have every bit as high a position in the world of fashion as his rich neighbor in his palace—often much better!

We all of us know a Mr. Newgold who would give many of the treasures in his marble palace for a single invitation to Mrs. Oldname's comparatively little house, and half of all he possesses for the latter's knowledge, appearance, manner, instincts and position—none of which he himself is likely ever to acquire, though his children may! But in our description of great or medium or small houses, we are considering those only whose owners belong equally to best society and where, though luxuries vary from the greatest to the least, house appointments are in essentials alike.

410

This is a rather noteworthy fact: all people of good position talk alike, behave alike and live alike. Ill-mannered servants, incorrect liveries or service, sloppily dished food, carelessness in any of the details that to well-bred people constitute the decencies of living, are no more tolerated in the smallest cottage than in the palace. But since the biggest houses are those which naturally attract most attention, suppose we begin our detailed description with them.

HOUSE PARTY OF MANY GUESTS

Perhaps there are ten or perhaps there are forty guests, but if there were only two or three, and the house a little instead of a big one, the details would be precisely the same.

A week-end means from Friday afternoon or from Saturday lunch to Monday morning. The usual time chosen for a house party is over a holiday, particularly where the holiday falls on a Friday or Monday, so that the men can take a Saturday off, and stay from Friday to Tuesday, or Thursday to Monday.

On whichever day the party begins, everyone arrives in the neighborhood of five o'clock, or a day later at lunch time. Many come in their own cars, the others are met at the station—sometimes by the host or a son, or, if it is to be a young party, by a daughter. The hostess herself rarely, if ever, goes to the station, not because of indifference or discourtesy but because other guests coming by motor might find the house empty.

It is very rude for a hostess to be out when her guests arrive. Even some one who comes so often as to be entirely at home, is apt to feel dispirited upon being shown into an empty house. Sometimes a guest's arrival unwelcomed can not be avoided; if, for instance, a man invited for tennis week or a football or baseball game, arrives before the game is over but too late to join the others at the sport.

When younger people come to visit the daughters, it is not necessary that their mother stay at home, since the daughters take their mother's place. Nor is it necessary that she receive the men friends of her son, unless the latter for some unavoidable reason, is absent.

No hostess must ever fail to send a car to the station or boat landing for every one who is expected. If she has not conveyances enough of her own, she must order public ones and have the fares charged to herself.

GREETING OF THE HOST

The host always goes out into the front hall and shakes hands with every one who arrives. He asks the guests if they want to be shown to their rooms, and, if not, sees that the gentlemen who come without valets give their keys to the butler or footman, and that the ladies without maids of their own give theirs to the maid who is on duty for the purpose.

Should any of them feel dusty or otherwise "untidy" they naturally ask if they may be shown to their rooms so that they can make themselves presentable. They should not, however, linger longer than necessary, as their hostess may become uneasy at their delay. Ladies do not—in fashionable houses—make their first appearance without a hat. Gentlemen, needless to say, leave theirs in the hall when they come in.

Travel in the present day, however, whether in parlor car or closed limousines, or even in open cars on macadam roads, obviates the necessity for an immediate removing of "travel stains," so that instead of seeking their rooms, the newcomers usually go directly into the library or out on the veranda or wherever the hostess is to be found behind the inevitable tea tray.

GREETING OF THE HOSTESS

As soon as her guests appear in the doorway, the hostess at once rises, goes forward smiling, shakes hands and tells them how glad she is that they have safely come, or how glad she is to see them, and leads the way to the tea-table. This is one of the occasions when everyone is always introduced. Good manners also demand that the places nearest the hostess be vacated by those occupying them, and that the newly arrived receive attention from the hostess, who sees that they are supplied with tea, sandwiches, cakes and whatever the tea-table affords.

After tea, people either sit around and talk, or, more likely nowadays, they play bridge. About an hour before dinner the hostess asks how long every one needs to dress, and tells them the time. If any need a shorter time than she must allow for herself, she makes sure that they know the location of their rooms, and goes to dress.

A ROOM FOR EVERY GUEST

It is almost unnecessary to say that in no well-appointed house is a guest, except under three circumstances, put in a room with any one else. The three exceptions are:

1. A man and wife, if the hostess is sure beyond a doubt that they occupy similar quarters when at home.

2. Two young girls who are friends and have volunteered, because the house is crowded, to room together in a room with two beds.

3. On an occasion such as a wedding, a ball, or an intercollegiate athletic event, young people don't mind for one night (that is spent for the greater part "up") how many are doubled; and house room is limited merely to cot space, sofas, and even the billiard table.

But she would be a very clumsy hostess, who, for a week-end, filled her house like a sardine box to the discomfort and resentment of every one.

In the well-appointed house, every guest room has a bath adjoining for itself alone, or shared with a connecting room and used only by a man and wife, two women or two men. A bathroom should never (if avoidable) be shared by a woman and a man. A suitable accommodation for a man and wife is a double room with bath and a single room next.

THE GUEST ROOM

The perfect guest room is not necessarily a vast chamber decorated in an historically correct period. Its perfection is the result of nothing more difficult to attain than painstaking attention to detail, and its possession is within the reach of every woman who has the means to invite people to her house in the first place. The ideal guest room is never found except in the house of the ideal hostess, and it is by no means "idle talk" to suggest that every hostess be obliged to spend twenty-four hours every now and then in each room that is set apart for visitors. If she does not do this actually, she should do so in imagination. She should occasionally go into the guest bathroom and draw the water in every fixture, to see there is no stoppage and that the hot water faucets are not seemingly jokes of the plumber. If a man is to occupy the bathroom, she must see that the hook for a razor strop is not missing, and that there is a mirror by which he can see to shave both at night and by daylight. Even though she can see to powder her nose, it would be safer to make her husband bathe and shave both a morning and an evening in each bathroom and then listen carefully to what he says about it!

Even though she has a perfect housemaid, it is not unwise occasionally to make sure herself that every detail has been attended to; that in every bathroom there are plenty of bath towels, face towels, a freshly laundered wash rag, bath mat, a new cake of unscented bath soap in the bathtub soap rack, and a new cake of scented soap on the washstand.

It is not expected, but it is often very nice to find violet water, bath salts, listerine, talcum powder, almond or other hand or sunburn lotion, in decorated bottles on the washstand shelf; but to cover the dressing-table in the bedroom with brushes and an array of toilet articles is more of a nuisance than a comfort. A good clothes brush and whiskbroom are usually very acceptable, as strangely enough, guests almost invariably forget them.

A comforting adjunct to a bathroom that is given to a woman is a hot water bottle with a woolen cover, hanging

"THE IDEAL GUEST ROOM IS NEVER FOUND EXCEPT IN THE HOUSE OF THE IDEAL HOSTESS; AND IT IS BY NO MEANS IDLE TALK TO SUGGEST THAT EVERY HOSTESS BE OBLIGED TO SPEND TWENTY-FOUR HOURS EVERY NOW AND THEN IN EACH ROOM SET APART FOR VISITORS."

[Page 414.]

on the back of the door. Even if the water does not run sufficiently hot, a guest seldom hesitates to ring for that, whereas no one ever likes to ask for a hot water bag—no matter how much she might long for it. A small bottle of Pyro is also convenient for one who brings a curling lamp.

In the bedroom the hostess should make sure (by sleeping in it at least once) that the bed is comfortable, that the sheets are long enough to tuck in, that there are enough pillows for one who sleeps with head high. There must also be plenty of covers. Besides the blankets there should be a wool-filled or an eiderdown quilt, in coloring to go with the room.

There should be a night light at the head of the bed. Not just a decorative glow-worm effect, but a light that is really good to lie in bed and read by. And always there should be books; chosen more to divert than to engross. The sort of selection appropriate for a guest room might best comprise two or three books of the moment, a light novel, a book of essays, another of short stories, and a few of the latest magazines. Spare-room books ought to be especially chosen for the expected guest. Even though one can not choose accurately for the taste of another, one can at least guess whether the visitor is likely to prefer transcendental philosophy or detective stories, and supply either accordingly.

There should be a candle and a box of matches—even though there is electric light it has been known to go out! And some people like to burn a candle all night. There must also be matches and ash receivers on the desk and a scrap-basket beside it.

In hot weather, every guest should have a palm leaf fan, and in August, even though there are screens, a fly killer.

In big houses with a swimming pool, bath-robes are supplied and often bathing suits. Otherwise dressing-gowns are not part of any guest room equipment.

A comfortable sofa is very important (if the room is big enough) with a sofa pillow or two, and with a light-weight quilt or afghan across the end of it.

The hostess should do her own hair in each room to see if the dressing-table is placed where there is a good light over it, both by electric and by daylight. A very simple expedient in a room where massive furniture and low windows make the daylight dressing-table difficult, is the European custom of putting an ordinary small table directly in the window and standing a good sized mirror on it. Nothing makes a more perfect arrangement for a woman.

And the pincushion! It is more than necessary to see that the pins are usable and not rust to the head. There should be black ones and white ones, long and short; also safety pins in several sizes. Three or four threaded needles of white thread, black, gray and tan silk are an addition that has proved many times welcome. She must also examine the writing desk to be sure that the ink is not a cracked patch of black dust at the bottom of the well, and the pens solid rust and the writing paper textures and sizes at odds with the envelopes. There should be a fresh blotter and a few stamps. Also thoughtful hostesses put a card in some convenient place, giving the post office schedule and saying where the mail bag can be found. And a calendar, and a clock that *goes!* Is there anything more typical of the average spare room than the clock that is at a standstill?

There must be plenty of clothes hangers in the closets. For women a few hat stands, and for men trouser hangers and the coat hangers that have a bar across the shoulder piece.

It is unnecessary to add that every bureau drawer should be looked into to see that nothing belonging to the family is filling the space which should belong to the guest, and that the white paper lining the bottom is new. Curtains and sofa pillows must, of course, be freshly laundered; the furniture, floor, walls and ceiling unmarred and in perfect order.

When bells are being installed in new houses they should be on cords and hung at the side of the bed. Light switches should be placed at the side of the door going into the room and bathroom. It is scarcely practical to change the wiring in old houses; but it can at least be seen that the bells work.

People who like strong perfumes often mistakenly think they are giving pleasure in filling all the bed-room drawers with pads heavily scented. Instead of feeling pleasure, some people are made almost sick! But all people (hay-fever patients excepted) love flowers, and vases of them beautify rooms as nothing else can. Even a shabby little room, if dustlessly clean and filled with flowers, loses all effect of shabbiness and is "inviting" instead.

In a hunting country, there should be a bootjack and boot-hooks in the closet.

Guest rooms should have shutters and dark shades for those who like to keep the morning sun out. The rooms should also, if possible, be away from the kitchen end of the house and the nursery.

A shortcoming in many houses is the lack of a news-paper, and the thoughtful hostess who has the morning paper sent up with each breakfast tray, or has one put at each place on the breakfast table, deserves a halo.

At night a glass and a thermos pitcher of water should be placed by the bed. In a few very specially appointed houses, a small glass-covered tray of food is also put on the bed table, fruit or milk and sandwiches, or whatever is marked on the guest card.

THE GUEST CARD

A clever device was invented by Mrs. Gilding whose palatially appointed house is run with the most painstaking attention to every one's comfort. On the dressing-table in each spare room at Golden Hall is a card pad with a pencil attached to it. But if the guest card is used, a specimen is given below.

Needless to say the cards are used only in huge houses that, because of their size, are necessarily run more like a clubhouse than as a "home."

In every house, the questions below are asked by the hostess, though the guests may not readily perceive the fact. At bedtime she always asks: "Would you like to come down to breakfast, or will you have it in your room?" If the

guest says, in her room, she is then asked what she would
like to eat.   She is also asked whether she cares for milk
or fruit or other light refreshment at bedtime, and if there
is a special book she would like to take up to her room
   The guest card mentioned above is as follows:

PLEASE FILL THIS OUT BEFORE GOING DOWN TO DINNER:

What time do you want to be awakened? ....
Or, will you ring? ....
Will you breakfast upstairs? ....
Or down? ....

UNDERSCORE YOUR ORDER:

Coffee, tea, chocolate, milk,
Oatmeal, hominy, shredded wheat,
Eggs, how cooked?
Rolls, muffins, toast,
Orange, pear, grapes, melon.

AT BEDTIME WILL YOU TAKE

Hot or cold milk, cocoa, orangeade,
Sandwiches, meat, lettuce, jam,
Cake, crackers,
Oranges, apples, pears, grapes.

   Besides this list, there is a catalogue of the library with
a card, clipped to the cover, saying:
   "Following books for room No. X." Then four or
six blank lines and a place for the guest's signature.

AT THE DINNER HOUR

   Every one goes down to dinner as promptly as possible
and the procedure is exactly that of all dinners. If it is
a big party, the gentlemen offer their arms to the ladies the
host or hostess has designated. At the end of the evening,
it is the custom that the hostess suggest going upstairs,
rather than the guests who ordinarily depart after dinner. But etiquette is not very strictly followed in this, and
a reasonable time after dinner, if any one is especially tired
he or she quite frankly says: "I wonder if you would
mind very much if I went to bed?" The hostess al-

ways answers: "Why, no, certainly not! I hope you will find everything in your room! If not, will you ring?"

It is not customary for the hostess to go upstairs with a guest, so long as others remain in her drawing-room. If there is only one lady, or a young girl, the hostess accompanies her to her room, and asks if everything has been thought of for her comfort.

HOW GUESTS ARE ASKED AND RECEIVED

Many older ladies adhere to former practise and always write personal notes of invitation. All others write or telegraph to people at a distance, and send telephone messages to those nearby.

When a house is to be filled with friends of daughters or sons of the house, the young people in the habit of coming to the house, or young men, whether making a first visit or not, do not need any invitation further than one given them verbally by a daughter, or even a son. But a married couple, or a young girl invited for the first time, should have the verbal invitation of daughter or son seconded by a note or at least a telephone message sent by the mother herself.

Every one is always asked for a specified time. Even a near relative comes definitely for a week, or a month, or whatever period is selected. This is because other plans have to be made by the owners of the house, such as inviting another group of guests, or preparing to go away themselves.

WHO ARE ASKED ON HOUSE PARTIES

Excepting when strangers bring influential letters of introduction, or when a relative or very intimate friend recently married is invited with her new husband or his bride, only very large and general house parties include any one who is not an intimate friend.

At least seventy per cent of American house parties are young people, either single or not long married, and, in any event, all those asked to any one party—unless the hostess is a failure (or a genius)—belong to the same social group. Perhaps a more broad-minded attitude prevails among young people in other parts of the country, but wilfully narrow-minded Miss Young New York is very chary of accepting an invitation until she finds out who among her particular friends are also invited. If Mrs. Stranger asks her for a week-end, no matter how much she may like Mrs. Stranger personally, she at once telephones two or three of her own group. If some of them are going, she "accepts with pleasure," but if not, the chances are she "regrets." If, on the other hand, she is asked by the Gildings, she accepts at once. Not merely because Golden Hall is the ultimate in luxury, but because Mrs. Gilding has a gift for entertaining, including her selection of people, amounting to genius. On the other hand, Miss Young New York would accept with equal alacrity the invitation of the Jack Littlehouses, where there is no luxury at all. Here in fact, a guest is quite as likely as not to be pressed into service as auxiliary nurse, gardener or chauffeur. But the personality of the host and hostess is such that there is scarcely a day in the week when the motors of the most popular of the younger set are not parked at the Littlehouse door.

PEOPLE WE LOVE TO STAY WITH

We enjoy staying with certain people usually for one of two reasons. First, because they have wonderful, luxurious houses, filled with amusing people; and visiting them is a period crammed with continuous and delightful experience, even though such a visit has little that suggests any personal intercourse or friendship with one's hostess. The other reason we love to visit a certain house is, on the contrary, entirely personal to the host or hostess. We love the house because we love its owner. Nowhere do we feel so much at home, and though it may have none of the imposing magnificence of the great house, it is often far more charming.

Five flunkeys can not do more towards a guest's comfort than to take his hat and stick and to show him the way to the drawing-room. A very smart young New Yorker who is also something of a wag, says that when going to a very magnificent house, he always tries to wear sufficient articles so that he shall have one to bestow upon each footman, Some one saw him, upon entering a palace that is a counterpart of the Worldlys,' quite solemnly hand his hat to the first footman, his stick to the second, his coat to the third, his muffler to the fourth, his gloves to the fifth, and his name to the sixth, as he entered the drawing-room. Needless to say he did this as a matter of pure amusement to himself. Of course six men servants, or more, do add to the impressiveness of a house that is a palace and are a fitting part of the picture. And yet a neat maid servant at the door can divest a guest of his hat and coat, and lead the way to the sitting-room, with equal facility.

Having several times mentioned Golden Hall, the palatial country house of the Gildings, suppose we join the guests and see what the last word in luxury and lavish hospitality is.

Golden Hall is not an imaginary place, except in name. It exists within a hundred miles of New York. The house is a palace, the grounds are a park. There is not only a long wing of magnificent guest rooms in the house, occupied by young girls or important older people, but there is also a guest annex, a separate building designed and run like the most luxurious country club. The second floor has nothing but bedrooms, with bath for each. The third floor has bachelor rooms, and rooms for visiting valets. Visiting maids are put in a separate third floor wing. On the ground floor there is a small breakfast room; a large living-room filled with books, magazines, a billiard and pool table; beyond the living-room is a fully equipped gymnasium; and beyond that a huge, white marble, glass-walled natatorium. The swimming pool is fifty feet by one hundred; on three sides is just a narrow shelf-like walkway, but the fourth is wide and is furnished as a room with lounging chairs upholstered in white oilcloth. Opening out of this are perfectly equipped Turkish and Russian baths in charge of the best Swedish masseur and masseuse procurable.

In the same building are two squash courts, a racquet

court, a court tennis court, and a bowling alley. But the feature of the guest building is a glass-roofed and enclosed riding ring—not big enough for games of polo, but big enough for practise in winter,—built along one entire side of it.

The stables are full of polo ponies and hunters, the garage full of cars, the boathouse has every sort of boat— sailboats, naphtha launches, a motor boat and even a shell. Every amusement is open-heartedly offered, in fact, especially devised for the guests.

At the main house there is a ballroom with a stage at one end. An orchestra plays every night. New moving pictures are shown and vaudeville talent is imported from New York. This is the extreme of luxury in entertaining. As Mrs. Toplofty said at the end of a bewilderingly lavish party: "How are any of us ever going to amuse any one after *this?* I feel like doing my guest rooms up in moth balls."

No one, however, has discovered that invitations to Mrs. Toplofty's are any less welcome. Besides, excitement-loving youth and exercise-devotees were never favored guests at the Hudson Manor anyway.

THE SMALL HOUSE OF PERFECTION

It matters not in the slightest whether the guest room's carpet is Aubusson or rag, whether the furniture is antique, or modern, so long as it is pleasing of its kind. On the other hand, because a house is little is no reason that it can not be as perfect in every detail—perhaps more so —as the palace of the multiest millionaire!

The attributes of the perfect house can not be better represented than by Brook Meadows Farm, the all-the-year home of the Oldnames. Nor can anything better illustrate its perfection than an incident that actually took place there.

A great friend of the Oldnames, but not a man who went at all into society, or considered whether people had position or not, was invited with his new wife—a woman from another State and of much wealth and discernment —to stay over a week-end at Brook Meadows. Never having met the Oldnames, she asked something about their house and life in order to decide what type of clothes to pack.

"Oh, it's just a little farmhouse.   Oldname wears a dinner coat, of course; his wife wears—I don't know what—but I have never seen her dressed up a bit!'

"Evidently plain people," thought his wife.   And aloud: "I wonder what evening dress I have that is high enough. I can put in the black lace day dress; perhaps I had better put in my cerise satin——"

"The cerise?" asked her husband, "Is that the red you had on the other night?   It is much too handsome, much! I tell you, Mrs. Oldname never wears a dress that you could notice.   She always looks like a lady, but she isn't a dressy sort of person at all."

So the bride packed her plainest (that is her cheapest) clothes, but at the last, she put in the "cerise."

When she and her husband arrived at the railroad station, *that* at least was primitive enough, and Mr. Oldname in much worn tweeds might have come from a castle or a cabin; country clothes are no evidence.   But her practised eye noticed the perfect cut of the chauffeur's coat and that the car, though of an inexpensive make, was one of the prettiest on the market, and beautifully appointed.

"At least they have good taste in motors and accessories," thought she, and was glad she had brought her best evening dress.

They drove up to a low white shingled house, at the end of an old-fashioned brick walk bordered with flowers.   The visitor noticed that the flowers were all of one color, all in perfect bloom.   She knew no inexperienced gardener produced that apparently simple approach to a door that has been chosen as frontispiece in more than one book on Colonial architecture.   The door was opened by a maid in a silver gray taffeta dress, with organdie collar, cuffs and apron, white stockings and silver buckles on black slippers, and the guest saw a quaint hall and vista of rooms that at first sight might easily be thought "simple" by an inexpert appraiser; but Mrs. Oldname, who came forward to greet her guests, was the antithesis of everything the bride's husband had led her to believe.

To describe Mrs. Oldname as simple is about as apt as to call a pearl "simple" because it doesn't dazzle; nor was there an article in the apparently simple living-room that would be refused were it offered to a museum.

The tea-table was Chinese Chippendale and set with old Spode on a lacquered tray over a mosaic-embroidered linen tea-cloth. The soda biscuits and cakes were light as froth, the tea an especial blend imported by a prominent connoisseur and given every Christmas to his friends. There were three other guests besides the bride and groom: a United States Senator, and a diplomat and his wife who were on their way from a post in Europe to one in South America. Instead of "bridge" there was conversation on international topics until it was time to dress for dinner.

When the bride went to her room (which adjoined that of her husband) she found her bath drawn, her clothes laid out, and the dressing-table lights lighted.

That night the bride wore her cerise dress to one of the smartest dinners she ever went down to, and when they went upstairs and she at last saw her husband alone, she took him to task. "Why in the name of goodness didn't you tell me the truth about these people?"

"Oh," said he abashed, "I told you it was a little house— it was you who insisted on bringing that red dress. I told you it was too handsome!"

"Handsome!" she cried in tears, "I don't own anything half good enough to compare with the least article in this house. That 'simple' little woman as you call her would, I think, almost make a queen seem provincial! And as for her clothes, they are priceless—just as everything is in this little gem of a house. Why, the window curtains are as fine as the best clothes in my trousseau."

The two houses contrasted above are two extremes, but each a luxury. The Oldnames' expenditure, though in no way comparable with the Worldlys' or the Gildings,' is far beyond any purse that can be called moderate.

The really moderate purse inevitably precludes a woman

from playing an important rôle as hostess, for not even the greatest magnetism and charm can make up to spoiled guests for lack of essential comfort. The only exceptions are a bungalow at the seashore or a camp in the woods, where a confirmed luxury-lover is desperately uncomfortable for the first twenty-four hours, but invariably gets used to the lack of comfort almost as soon as he gets dependent upon it; and plunging into a lake for bath, or washing in a little tin basin, sleeping on pine boughs without any sheets at all, eating tinned foods and flapjacks on tin plates with tin utensils, he seems to lack nothing when the air is like champagne and the company first choice.

GUEST ROOM SERVICE

If a visitor brings no maid of her own, the personal maid of the hostess (if she has one—otherwise the housemaid) always unpacks the bags or trunks, lays toilet articles out on the dressing-table and in the bathroom, puts folded things in the drawers and hangs dresses on hangers in the closet. If when she unpacks she sees that something of importance has been forgotten, she tells her mistress, or, in the case of a servant who has been long employed, she knows what selection to make herself, and supplies the guest without asking with such articles as comb and brush or clothes brush, or bathing suit and bath-robe.

The valet of the host performs the same service for men. In small establishments where there is no lady's maid or valet, the housemaid is always taught to unpack guests' belongings and to press and hook up ladies' dresses, and gentlemen's clothes are sent to a tailor to be pressed after each wearing.

In big houses, breakfast trays for women guests are usually carried to the bedroom floor by the butler (some butlers delegate this service to a footman) and are handed to the lady's maid who takes the tray into the room. In small houses they are carried up by the waitress.

Trays for men visitors are rare, but when ordered are carried up and into the room by the valet, or butler. If there are no men servants the waitress has to carry up the tray.

When a guest rings for breakfast, the housemaid or the valet goes into the room, opens the blinds, and in cold weather lights the fire, if there is an open one in the room. Asking whether a hot, cool or cold bath is preferred, he goes into the bathroom, spreads a bath mat on the floor, a big bath towel over a chair, with the help of a thermometer draws the bath, and sometimes lays out the visitor's clothes. As few people care for more than one bath a day and many people prefer their bath before dinner instead of before breakfast, this office is often performed at dinner dressing time instead of in the morning.

TIPS

The "tip-roll" in a big house seems to us rather appalling, but compared with the amounts given in a big English house, ours are mere pittances. Pleasant to think that *something* is less expensive in our country than in Europe!

Fortunately in this country, when you dine in a friend's house you do not "tip" the butler, nor do you tip a footman or parlor-maid who takes your card to the mistress of the house, nor when you leave a country house do you have to give more than five dollars to any one whatsoever. A lady for a week-end stay gives two or three dollars to the lady's maid, if she went without her own, and one or two dollars to every one who waited on her. Intimate friends in a small house send tips to all the servants—perhaps only a dollar apiece, but no one is forgotten. In a very big house this is never done and only those are tipped who have served you. If you had your maid with you, you always give her a tip (about two dollars) to give the cook (often the second one) who prepared her meals and one dollar for the kitchen maid who set her table.

A gentleman scarcely ever "remembers" any of the women servants (to their chagrin) except a waitress, and tips only the butler and the valet, and sometimes the chauffeur. The least he can offer any of the men-servants is two

"IN SMALL HOUSES BREAK-
FAST TRAYS FOR WOMEN
GUESTS ARE CARRIED UP
BY THE WAITRESS."

[Page 426.]

dollars and the most ever is five. No woman gets as much as that, for such short service.

In a few houses the tipping system is abolished, and in every guest room, in a conspicuous place on the dressing-table or over the bath tub where you are sure to read it, is a sign, saying:

"Please do not offer tips to my servants. Their contract is with this special understanding, and proper arrangements have been made to meet it; you will not only create 'a situation,' but cause the immediate dismissal of any one who may be persuaded by you to break this rule of the house."

The notice is signed by the host. The "arrangement" referred to is one whereby every guest means a bonus added to their wages of so much per person per day for all employees. This system is much preferred by servants for two reasons. First, self-respecting ones dislike the demeaning effect of a tip (an occasional few won't take them). Secondly, they can absolutely count that so many visitors will bring them precisely such an amount.

BREAKFAST DOWNSTAIRS OR UP

Breakfast customs are as varied in this country as the topography of the land! Communities of people who have lived or traveled much abroad, have nearly all adopted the Continental breakfast habit of a tray in their room, especially on Sunday mornings. In other communities it is the custom to go down to the dining-room for a heavy American (or English) meal. In communities where the latter is the custom and where people are used to assembling at a set hour, it is simple enough to provide a breakfast typical of the section of the country; corn bread and kidney stew and hominy in the South; doughnuts and codfish balls "way down East"; kippered herring, liver and bacon and griddle cakes elsewhere. But downstairs breakfast as a continuous performance is, from a housekeeper's point of view, a trial to say the least.

However, in big houses, where men refuse to eat in their rooms and equally refuse to get up until they feel like it, a dining-room breakfast is managed as follows:

CONTINUOUS BREAKFAST DOWNSTAIRS

The table is set with a place for all who said they were "coming down." At one end is a coffee urn kept hot over a spirit lamp, milk is kept hot under a "tea cosy" or in a double pitcher, made like a double boiler. On the sideboard or on the table are two or three "hot water" dishes (with or without spirit lamps underneath). In one is a cereal, in the other "hash" or "creamed beef," sausage, or codfish cakes, or whatever the housekeeper thinks of, that can stand for hours and still be edible! Fruit is on the table and bread and butter and marmalade, and the cook is supposed to make fresh tea and eggs and toast for each guest as he appears.

PREPARING BREAKFAST TRAY

The advantage of having one's guests choose breakfast upstairs, is that unless there is a separate breakfast room, a long delayed breakfast prevents the dining-room from being put in order or the lunch table set. Trays, on the other hand, stand "all set" in the pantry and interfere much less with the dining-room work. The trays are either of the plain white pantry variety or regular breakfast ones with folding legs. On each is put a tray cloth. It may be plain linen hemstitched or scalloped, or it may be much embroidered and have mosaic or filet lace.

Every bedroom has a set of breakfast china to match it. But it is far better to send a complete set of blue china to a rose-colored room than a rose set that has pieces missing. Nothing looks worse than odd crockery. It is like unmatched paper and envelopes, or odd shoes, or a woman's skirt and waist that do not meet in the back.

There is nothing unusual in a tray set, every china and department store carries them, but only in "open" stock patterns can one buy extra dishes or replace broken ones; a fact it is well to remember. There is a tall coffee pot, hot milk pitcher, a cream pitcher and sugar bowl, a cup and saucer, two plates, an egg cup and a covered dish. A cereal is usually put in the covered dish, toast in a napkin on a plate, or eggs and bacon in place of cereal. This with fruit is the most elaborate "tray" breakfast ever provided. Most people who breakfast "in bed" take only coffee or tea, an egg, toast and possibly fruit.

THE COURTEOUS HOST

Of those elaborate ceremonials between host and guest familiar to all readers of the Bible and all travelers in the East, only a few faint traces remain in our country and generation. It is still unforgivable to eat a man's bread and remain his enemy. It is unforgivable to criticize your host, or in his presence to criticize his friends. It is unforgivable to be rude to any one under your own roof or under the roof of a friend. If you must quarrel with your enemy, seek public or neutral ground, since quarrels and hospitality must never be mingled.

The Spaniard says to his guest: "All I have is yours." It is supposed to be merely a pretty speech—but in a measure it is true of every host's attitude toward his house guest. If you take some one under your roof, he becomes part of, and sharer in, your life and possessions. Your horse, your fireside, your armchair, your servants, your time, your customs, all are his; your food is his food, your roof his shelter. You give him the best "spare" room, you set before him the best refreshments you can offer, and your "best" china and glass. His bed is made up with your best "company" linen and blankets. You receive your guest with a smile, no matter how inconvenient or troublesome or straining to your resources his visit may be, and on no account do you let him suspect any of this.

KEEPING ONE'S GUESTS OCCUPIED

In popular houses where visitors like to go again and again, there is always a happy combination of some attention on the part of the host and hostess, and the perfect freedom of the guests to occupy their time as they choose.

The host and the men staying in the house arrange among themselves to rest or play games or fish or ride or shoot clay pigeons or swim, etc. The hostess, unless at the seashore where people go bathing in the morning, generally leaves her guests to their own devices until lunch time, though they are always offered whatever diversions the place or neighborhood afford. They are told there is bathing, fishing, golf; and if they want to do any of these things, it is arranged for them. But unless something special, such as driving to a picnic or clambake, has been planned, or there is a tennis tournament or golf match of importance, the hostess makes her first appearance just before luncheon.

This is the same as any informal family meal. If there are thirty guests it makes no difference. Sometimes there are place cards—especially if other people have been invited in—sometimes people find places for themselves.

After luncheon something is usually arranged; perhaps those who play golf go out for their game, and others who do not play go to the country club at the hour the players are supposed to be coming in, so that they can all have tea together. Those who like motoring perhaps go for a drive, or to a neighbor's house for bridge, or neighbors come in for tea. There is always bridge, sometimes there is dancing. In very big houses musicians are often brought in after dinner, and dancing and bridge alternate till bedtime.

A houseful of young people very easily look after their own amusement. As said before, a big house is run very much like a country club, and guests are supposed to look after themselves.

Making an especial effort to entertain a guest who is to stay for a week or longer has gone out of custom in the fashionable world, except for an important personage. A visit from the President of the United States for instance, would necessitate the most punctiliously formal etiquette, no matter how close a friend of the family he may always have been. For such a visitor a hostess would either arrange a series of entertainments or none, according to her visitor's inclination.

A GUEST CAN LOOK AFTER HIS OWN COMFORT

The most trying thing to people of very set habits is an unusual breakfast hour. When you have the unfortunate habit of waking with the dawn, and the household you are visiting has the custom of sleeping on Sunday morning, the long wait for your coffee can quite actually upset your whole day. On the other hand, to be aroused at seven on the only day when you do not have to hurry to business, in order to yawn through an early breakfast, and then sit around and kill time, is quite as trying. The guest with the "early" habit can in a measure prevent discomfort. He can carry in a small case (locked if necessary) a very small solidified alcohol outfit and either a small package of tea or powdered coffee, sugar, powdered milk, and a few crackers. He can then start his day all by himself in the barnyard hours without disturbing any one, and in comfort to himself. Few people care enough to "fuss," but if they do, this equipment of an habitual visitor with incurably early waking hours is given as a suggestion.

Or perhaps the entire guest situation may be put in one sentence. If you are an inflexible person, very set in your ways, don't visit! At least don't visit without carefully looking the situation over from every angle to be sure that the habits of the house you are going to are in accord with your own.

A solitary guest is naturally much more dependent on his host (or her hostess), but on the other hand, he or she is practically always a very intimate friend who merely adapts himself or herself like a chameleon to the customs and hours and diversions of the household.

DONT'S FOR HOSTESS

When a guest asks to be called half an hour before breakfast, don't have him called an hour and a half before because it takes you that long to dress, nor allow him a scant ten minutes because the shorter time is seemingly sufficient. Too often the summons on the door wakes him out of sound sleep; he tumbles exhausted out of bed, into clothes, and down stairs, to wait perhaps an hour for breakfast.

If a guest prefers to sit on the veranda and read, don't interrupt him every half page to ask if he really does not want to do something else. If, on the other hand, a guest wants to exercise, don't do everything in your power to obstruct his starting off by saying that it will surely rain, or that it is too hot, or that you think it is senseless to spend days that should be a rest to him in utterly exhausting himself.

Don't, when you know that a young man cares little for feminine society, fine-tooth-comb the neighborhood for the dullest or silliest young woman to be found.

Don't, on the other hand, when you have an especially attractive young woman staying with you, ask a stolid middle-aged couple and an octogenarian professor for dinner, because the charm and beauty of the former is sure to appeal to the latter.

Don't, because you personally happen to like a certain young girl who is utterly old-fashioned in outlook and type from ultra modern others who are staying with you, try to "bring them together." Never try to make any two people like each other. If they do, they do; if they don't, they don't, and that is all there is to it; but it is of vital importance to your own success as hostess to find out which is the case and collect or separate them accordingly.

THE CASUAL HOSTESS

The most casual hostess in the world is the fashionable leader in Newport, she who should by the rules of good society be the most punctilious, since no place in America, or Europe, is more conspicuously representative of luxury and fashion. Nowhere are there more "guests" or half so many hostesses, and yet hospitality as it is understood everywhere else, is practically unknown. No one ever goes to stay in a Newport house excepting "on his own" as it were. It is not an exaggerated story, but quite true, that in many houses of ultra fashion a guest on arriving is told at which meals he is expected to appear, that is at dinners or luncheons given by his hostess. At all others he is free to go out or stay in by himself. No effort is assumed for his amusement, or

responsibility for his well-being.   It is small wonder that
only those who have plenty of friends care to go there—or
in fact, are ever invited!   Those who like to go to visit the
most perfectly appointed, but utterly impersonal house, find
no other visiting to compare with its unhampering delight-
fulness.   The hostess simply says on his (or her) arrival:

"Oh, howdo Freddie (or Constance)!   They've put you
in the Chinese room, I think.   Ring for tea when you want
it.   Struthers telephoned he'd be over around five.   Mrs.
Toplofty asked you to dinner to-night and I accepted for
you—hope that was all right.   If not, you'll have to telephone and get out of it yourself.   I want you to dinner to-
morrow night and for lunch on Sunday.   Sorry to leave you,
but I'm late for bridge now.   Good-by."   And she is off.

The Newport hostess is, of course, an extreme type that
is seldom met away from that one small watering place in
Rhode Island.

THE ENERGETIC HOSTESS

The energetic hostess is the antithesis of the one above,
and far more universally known.   She is one who fusses
and plans continually, who thinks her guests are not having
a good time unless she rushes them, Cook's tourist fashion,
from this engagement to that, and crowds with activity
and diversion—never mind *what* so long as it is something to see or do—every moment of their stay.

She walks them through the garden to show them all
the nooks and vistas.   She dilates upon the flowers that
bloomed here last month and are going to bloom next.
She insists upon their climbing over rocks to a summer-
house to see the view; she insists on taking them in another
direction to see an old mill; and, again, every one is
trouped to the cupola of the house to see another view.
She insists on every one's playing croquet before lunch, to
which she gathers in a curiously mixed collection of neighbors.   Immediately after lunch every one is driven to a
country club to see some duffer golf—for some reason
there is never "time" in all the prepared pleasures for any
of her guests to play golf themselves.   After twenty min-

utes at the golf club, they are all taken to a church fair.
The guests are all introduced to the ladies at the booth
and those who were foolish enough to bring their purses
with them from now on carry around an odd assortment
of fancy work.   There is another entertainment that her
guests must not miss!   A flower pageant of the darlingest
children fourteen miles away!   Everyone is dashed to that.
On some one's front lawn, daisies and lilies and roses trip
and skip—it is all sweetly pretty but the sun is hot and
the guests have been on the go for a great many hours.
Soon, however, their hostess leaves.   "Home at last!"
think they.   Not at all.   They are going somewhere for
tea and French recitations.   But why go on?   The portrait
is fairly complete, though this account covers only a few
hours and there is still all the evening and tomorrow to
be filled in just as liberally.

THE ANXIOUS HOSTESS

The anxious hostess does not insist on your ceaseless activity, but she is no less persistent in filling your time.   She
is always asking you what you would like to do next.   If
you say you are quite content as you are, she nevertheless
continues to shower suggestions.   Shall she play the phonograph to you?   Would you like her to telephone to a friend
who sings too wonderfully?   Would you like to look at
a portfolio of pictures?   If you are a moment silent, she
is sure you are bored, and wonders what she can do to
divert you!

THE PERFECT HOSTESS

The ideal hostess must have so many perfections of sense
and character that were she described in full, no one seemingly but a combination of seer and angel could ever hope
to qualify.
She must first of all consider the inclinations of her
guests, she must not only make them as comfortable as the
arrangements and limits of her establishment permit, but
she must subordinate her own inclinations utterly.   At the

same time, she must not fuss and flutter and get agitated and seemingly make efforts in their behalf. Nothing makes a guest more uncomfortable than to feel his host or hostess is being put to a great deal of bother or effort on his account.

A perfect hostess like a perfect housekeeper has seemingly nothing whatever to do with household arrangements which apparently run in oiled grooves and of their own accord.

Certain rules are easy to observe once they are brought to attention. A hostess should never speak of annoyances of any kind—no matter what happens! Unless she is actually unable to stand up, she should not mention physical ills any more than mental ones. She has invited people to her house, and as long as they are under her roof, hospitality demands that their sojourn shall be made as pleasant as lies in her power.

If the cook leaves, then a picnic must be made of the situation as though a picnic were the most delightful thing that could happen. Should a guest be taken ill, she must assure him that he is not giving the slightest trouble; at the same time nothing that can be done for his comfort must be overlooked. Should she herself or some one in her family become suddenly ill, she should make as light of it as possible to her guests, even though she withdraw from them. In that event she must ask a relative or intimate friend to come in and take her place. Nor should the deputy hostess dwell to the guests on the illness, or whatever it is that has deprived them of their hostess.

THE GUEST NO ONE INVITES AGAIN

The guest no one invites a second time is the one who runs a car to its detriment, and a horse to a lather; who leaves a borrowed tennis racquet out in the rain; who "dog ears" the books, leaves a cigarette on the edge of a table and burns a trench in its edge, who uses towels for boot rags, who stands a wet glass on polished wood, who tracks muddy shoes into the house, and leaves his room looking as though it had been through a cyclone. Nor are men the only offenders. Young women have been known to commit every one of these offenses and the additional one of bringing a pet dog that was not house trained.

Besides these actually destructive shortcomings, there are evidences of bad upbringing in many modern youths whose lack of consideration is scarcely less annoying. Those who are late for every meal; cheeky others who invite friends of their own to meals without the manners or the decency to ask their hostess' permission; who help themselves to a car and go off and don't come back for meals at all; and who write no letters afterwards, nor even take the trouble to go up and "speak" to a former hostess when they see her again.

On the other hand, a young person who is considerate is a delight immeasurable—such a delight as only a hostess of much experience can perhaps appreciate. A young girl who tells where she is going, first asking if it is all right, and who finds her hostess as soon as she is in the house at night to report that she is back, is one who very surely will be asked again and often.

A young man is, of course, much freer, but a similar deference to the plans of his hostess, and to the hours and customs of the house, will result in repeated invitations for him also.

The lack of these things is not only bad form but want of common civility and decency, and reflects not only on the girls and boys themselves but on their parents who failed to bring them up properly.

THE CONSIDERATE GUEST

Courtesy demands that you, when you are a guest, shall show neither annoyance nor disappointment—no matter what happens. Before you can hope to become even a passable guest, let alone a perfect one, you must learn as it were not to notice if hot soup is poured down your back. If you neither understand nor care for dogs or children, and both insist on climbing all over you, you must seemingly like it; just as you must be amiable and polite to your fellow guests, even though they be of all the people on earth the most detestable to you. You must with the very best dissimulation at your command, appear to find the food delicious though they offer you all of the viands that are especially distasteful to your palate, or antagonistic to your digestion. You must disguise your hatred of red ants and scrambled food, if everyone else is bent on a picnic. You must pretend that six is a perfect dinner hour though you never dine before eight, or, on the contrary, you must wait until eight-thirty or nine with stoical fortitude, though your dinnᵣ. hour is six and by seven your chest seems securely pinned to your spine.

If you go for a drive, and it pours, and there is no top to the carriage or car, and you are soaked to the skin and chilled to the marrow so that your teeth chatter, your lips must smile and you must appear to enjoy the refreshing coolness.

If you go to stay in a small house in the country, and they give you a bed full of lumps, in a room of mosquitoes and flies, in a chamber over that of a crying baby, under the eaves with a temperature of over a hundred, you *can* the next morning walk to the village, and send yourself a telegram and leave! But though you feel starved, exhausted, wilted, and are mosquito bitten until you resemble a well-developed case of chickenpox or measles, by not so much as a facial muscle must you let the family know that your comfort lacked anything that your happiest imagination could picture—nor must you confide in any one afterwards (having broken bread in the house) how desperately wretched you were.

If you know anyone who is always in demand, not only for dinners, but for trips on private cars and yachts, and long visits in country houses, you may be very sure of one thing: the popular person is first of all unselfish or else extremely gifted; very often both.

The perfect guest not only tries to wear becoming clothes but tries to put on an equally becoming mental attitude. No one is ever asked out very much who is in the habit of telling people all the misfortunes and ailments she has experienced or witnessed, though the perfect guest listens with

apparent sympathy to every one else's. Another attribute
of the perfect guest is never to keep people waiting. She
is always ready for anything—or nothing. If a plan is
made to picnic, she likes picnics above everything and proves
her liking by enthusiastically making the sandwiches or the
salad dressing or whatever she thinks she makes best. If,
on the other hand, no one seems to want to do anything,
the perfect guest has always a book she is absorbed in, or
a piece of sewing she is engrossed with, or else beyond
everything she would love to sit in an easy chair and do
nothing.

She never for one moment thinks of herself, but of the
other people she is thrown with. She is a person of sympathy always, and instantaneous discernment. She is good
tempered no matter what happens, and makes the most of
everything as it comes. At games she is a good loser, and
a quiet winner. She has a pleasant word, an amusing story,
and agreeable comment for most occasions, but she is
neither gushing nor fulsome. She has merely acquired a
habit, born of many years of arduous practise, of turning
everything that looks like a dark cloud as quickly as possible for the glimmer of a silver lining.

She is as sympathetic to children as to older people; she
cuts out wonderful paper dolls and soldier hats, always leisurely and easily as though it cost neither time nor effort. She
knows a hundred stories or games, every baby and every dog
goes to her on sight, not because she has any especial talent,
except that one she has cultivated, the talent of interest in
everyone and everything except herself. Few people know
that there is such a talent or that it can be cultivated.

She has more than mere beauty; she has infinite charm,
and she is so well born that she is charming to everyone.
Her manner to a duke who happens to be staying in the
house is not a bit more courteous than her manner to the
kitchen-maid whom she chances to meet in the kitchen
gardens whither she has gone with the children to see
the new kittens; as though new kittens were the apex of
all delectability!

She always calls the servants by name; always says "How

do you do" when she arrives, "Good morning" while there, and "Good-by" when she leaves. And do they presume because of her "familiarity" when she remembers to ask after the parlor-maid's mother and the butler's baby? They wait on her as they wait on no one else who comes to the house—neither the Senator nor the Governor, nor his Grace of Overthere!

This ideal guest is an equally ideal hostess; the principle of both is the same. A ready smile, a quick sympathy, a happy outlook, consideration for others, tenderness toward everything that is young or helpless, and forgetfulness of self, which is not far from the ideal of womankind.

THE GUEST ON A PRIVATE CAR OR YACHT

The sole difference between being a guest at a country house and a guest on a private car or a yacht, is that you put to a very severe test your adaptability as a traveler. You live in very close quarters with your host and hostess and fellow guests, and must therefore be particularly on your guard against being selfish or out of humor. If you are on shore and don't feel well, you can stay home; but off on a cruise, if you are ill you have to make the best of it, and a sea-sick person's "best" is very bad indeed! Therefore let it be hoped you are a good sailor. If not, think very, very carefully before you embark!

CHAPTER XXVI

THE HOUSE PARTY IN CAMP

"Roughing it" in the fashionable world (on the Atlantic coast) is rather suggestive of the dairymaid playing of Marie Antoinette; the "rough" part being mostly "picturesque effect" with little taste of actual discomfort. Often, of course, the "roughing it" is real, especially west of the Mississippi (and sometimes in the East too); so real that it has no place in a book of etiquette at all. In the following picture of a fashionable "camping party" it should perhaps be added, that not only the Worldlys but most of the women really *think* they are "roughing it."

At the same time there is nothing that a genuine dependent upon luxury resents more than to be told he is dependent. It is he who has but newly learned the comforts of living who protests his inability to endure discomfort.

The very same people therefore who went a short time before to Great Estates, women who arrived with their maids and luggage containing personal equipment of amazing perfection and unlimited quantity (to say nothing of jewels worth a king's ransom), and men who usually travel with their own man-servants and every variety of raiment and paraphernalia, on being invited to "rough it" with the Kindharts at Mountain Summit Camp, are the very ones who most promptly and enthusiastically telegraph their delighted acceptance. At a certain party a few years ago, the only person who declined was a young woman of so little "position" that she was quite offended that Mrs. Kindhart should suppose her able to endure discomfort such as her invitation implied.

This year the Worldlys, the Normans, the Lovejoys, the "Bobo" Gildings, the Littlehouses, Constance Style, Jim Smartlington and his bride, Clubwin Doe and young Struthers make up the party. No one declined, not even the Worldlys, though there is a fly in the amber of their perfect satisfaction. Mrs. Kindhart wrote "not to bring a maid." Mrs. Worldly is very much disturbed, because she cannot do her hair herself. Mr. Worldly is even more perturbed at the thought of going without his valet. He has never in the twenty years since he left college been twenty-four hours away from Ernest. He knows perfectly well that Ernest is not expected. But he means to take him—he will say nothing about it; he can surely find a place for Ernest to stay somewhere.

The other men all look upon a holiday away from formality (which includes valeting) as a relief, like the opening of a window in a stuffy room, and none of the women except Mrs. Worldly would take her maid if she could.

THE CLOTHES THEY TAKE

The men all rummage in attics and trunk-rooms for those disreputable looking articles of wearing apparel dear to all sportsmen; oil soaked boots, water soaked and sun bleached woolen, corduroy, leather or canvas garments and hats, each looking too shabby from their wives' (or valet's) point of view to be offered to a tramp.

Every evening is spent in cleaning guns, rummaging for unprepossessing treasures of shooting and fishing equipment. The women also give thought to their wardrobes—consisting chiefly in a process of elimination. Nothing perishable, nothing requiring a maid's help to get into, or to take care of. Golf clothes are first choice, and any other old country clothes, skirts and sweaters, and lots of plain shirt waists to go under the sweaters. An old polo coat and a mackintosh is chosen by each. And for evenings something "comfortable" and "easy to put on" in the way of a house gown or ordinary summer "day dress." One or two decide to take tea gowns in dark color and plainest variety.

All the women who sew or knit take something to "work on" in unoccupied moments, such as the hours of sitting silent in a canoe while husbands fish.

Finally the day arrives. Every one meets at the railroad station. They are all as smart looking as can be, there is no sign of "rough" clothes anywhere, though nothing in the least like a jewel case or parasol is to be seen. At the end of somewhere between eight and eighteen hours, they arrive at a shed which sits at the edge of the single track and is labelled Dustville Junction, and hurrying down the narrow platform is their host. Except that his face is clean shaven and his manners perfect, he might be taken for a tramp. Three far from smart looking teams—two buckboards and an express wagon—are standing near by. Kindhart welcomes everyone with enthusiasm—except the now emerging Ernest. For once Kindhart is nonplussed and he says to Worldly: "This isn't Newport, you know — of course we can give him a bed somewhere, but this is really no place for Ernest and there's nothing for him to do!"

Worldly, for the moment at a loss, explains lamely: "I thought he might be useful—if you could find some corner for him to-night, then we can see—that's all right, isn't it?"

Kindhart as host can't say anything further except to agree. Everyone is bundled into the buckboards (except Ernest who goes on top of the luggage in the express wagon), and a "corduroy" drive of six or eight miles begins.

WHAT THE CAMP IS LIKE

Summit Camp is a collection of wooden shacks like a group of packing cases dumped in a clearing among the pine trees at the edge of a mountain lake. Those who have never been there before feel some misgivings, those who have been there before remember with surprise that they *had* liked the place! The men alone are filled with enthusiasm. The only person who is thoroughly apprehensive of the immediate future is Ernest.

In front of the largest of the shacks, Mrs. Kindhart, surrounded by dogs and children, waves and hurries forward, beaming. Her enthusiasm is contagious, the children look blooming. That the "hardship" is not hurting them, is evident! And when the guests have seen the inside of the camps most of them are actually as pleased as they look. The biggest "shack" is a living-room, the one nearest is the dining camp, four or five smaller ones are sleeping camps for guests and another is the Kindharts' own.

The "living" camp is nothing but a single room about thirty feet wide and forty feet long, with an open raftered roof for ceiling. It has windows on four sides and a big porch built on the southeast corner. There is an enormous open fireplace, and a floor good enough to dance on. The woodwork is of rough lumber and has a single coat of leaf-green paint. The shelves between the uprights are filled with books. All the new novels and magazines are spread out on a long table. The room is furnished with Navajo blankets, wicker furniture, steamer chairs, and hammocks are hung across two of the corners. Two long divan sofas on either side of the fireplace are the only upholstered pieces of furniture in the whole camp, except the mattresses on the beds.

The guest camps are separate shacks, each one set back on a platform, leaving a porch in front. Inside they vary in size; most have two, some have four rooms, but each is merely one pointed-roofed space. The front part has a fireplace and is furnished as a sitting-room, the rear half is partitioned into two or more cubicles, like box-stalls, with partitions about eight feet high and having regular doors. In each of the single rooms, there is a bed, bureau, wash-stand, chair, and two shelves about six or seven feet high, with a calico curtain nailed to the top one and hanging to the floor, making a hat shelf and clothes closet. The few "double" rooms are twice the size and have all furniture in duplicate. There is also a matting or a rag rug on the floor, and that is all!

Each cottage has a bathroom but the hot water supply seems complicated. A sign says your guide will bring it to you when needed. Mrs. Worldly, feeling vaguely uncomfortable and hungry, is firmly determined to go home on the next morning train. Before she has had much time to reflect, Mrs. Kindhart reports that lunch is nearly ready. Guides come with canisters of hot water, and everyone goes to dress. Town clothes disappear, and woods clothes emerge. This by no means makes a dowdy picture. Good sport clothes never look so well or becoming as when long use has given them an "accustomed set" characteristic of their wearer. The men put on their oldest country clothes too. Not their fishing "treasures" to sit at table with ladies! The treasured articles go on in the early dawn, and the guides are the only humans (except themselves) supposed worthy to behold them!

Presently a gong is sounded. The Kindhart children run to the guest houses to call out that "the gong means dinner is ready!" And "dinner" means lunch.

DINING-ROOM DETAILS

In a short while the very group of people who only ten days before were being shown to their places in the World-lys' own tapestry-hung marble dining-room at Great Estates by a dozen footmen in satin knee breeches, file into the "dining camp" and take their places at a long pine table, painted turkey red, on ordinary wooden kitchen chairs, also red! The floral decoration is of laurel leaves in vases made of preserve jars covered with birch bark. Glass and china is of the cheapest. But there are a long centerpiece of hemstitched crash and crash doilies, and there are "real" napkins, and at each plate a birch bark napkin ring with a number on it. Mrs. Worldly looks at her napkin ring as though it were an insect. One or two of the others who have not been there before, look mildly surprised.

Mrs. Kindhart smiles, "I'm sorry, but I told you it was 'roughing it.' Any one who prefers innumerable paper napkins to using a washed one twice, is welcome. But one napkin a day apiece is camp rule!" Mrs. Worldly tries to look amiable, all the rest succeed.

The food is limited in variety but delicious. There are fresh trout from the lake and venison steak; both well cooked in every way that can be devised appear at every meal. All other supplies come in hampers from the city. The head cook is the Kindharts' own, and so is the butler, with one of the chauffeurs (when home) to help him wait on table. They wear "liveries," evolved by Mrs. Kindhart, of gray flannel trousers, green flannel blazers, very light gray flannel shirts, black ties, and moccasins!

The table service, since there are only two to wait on twenty including the children, is necessarily somewhat "farmer style"; ice, tea, rolls, butter, marmalade, cake, fruit, are all on the table, so that people may help themselves.

THE AMUSEMENTS OFFERED

After luncheon Kindhart points out a dozen guides who are waiting at the boat-house to take anyone who wants to be paddled or to sail or to go out into the woods. There is a small swimming pool which can be warmed artificially. Those who like it cold swim in the lake. All the men disappear in groups or singly with a guide. The women go with their husbands, or two together, with a guide. Should any not want to go out, she can take to one of the hammocks, or a divan in the living-room, and a book.

At first sight, this hospitality seems inadequate, but its discomfort is one of outward appearance only. The food is abundant and delicious, whether cooked in the house or by the guides in the woods. The beds are comfortable; there are plenty of warm and good quality, though not white, blankets. Sheets are flannel or cotton as preferred. Pillow cases are linen, towels of the "bath" variety because washing can be done by "natives" near by, but ironing is difficult. Let no one, however, think that this is a "simple" (by that meaning either easy or inexpensive) form of entertainment! Imagine the budget! A dozen guides, teams and drivers, natives to wash and clean and to help the cook; food for two or three dozen people sent hundreds of miles by express!

It is true that the buildings are of the most primitive, and the furnishings, too. The bureau drawers do stick, and there is only "curtained" closet room, and mirrors are few and diminutive, and orders for hot water have to be given ahead of time, but there is no discomfort, except bathing in the cold! The huge fire, lighted early every morning by one of the guides in each guest house, keeps the main part fairly warm but the temperature of one of the bathrooms on a cold morning is scarcely welcoming.

CAMP MANNERS

People do not "dress" for dinner, that is, not in evening clothes. After coming in from walking or shooting or fishing, if it is warm they swim in the pool or have their guides bring them hot water for a bath. Women change into house gowns of some sort. Men put on flannel trousers, soft shirts, and flannel or serge sack coats.

In the evening, if it is a beautiful night, every one sits on steamer chairs wrapt in rugs around the big fire built out doors in front of a sort of penthouse or windbreak. Or if it is stormy, they sit in front of a fire, almost as big, in the living-room. Sometimes younger ones pop corn or roast chestnuts, or perhaps make taffy. Perhaps some one tells a story, or some one plays and everyone sings. Perhaps one who has "parlor tricks" amuses the others—but as a rule those who have been all day in the open are tired and drowsy and want nothing but to stretch out for a while in front of the big fire and then turn in.

The etiquette of this sort of a party is so apparently lacking that its inclusion perhaps seems out of place. But it is meant merely as a "picture" of a phase of fashionable life that is not much exploited, and to show that well-bred people never deteriorate in manner. Their behavior is precisely the same whether at Great Estates or in camp. A gentleman may be in his shirt sleeves actually, but he never gets into shirt sleeves mentally—he has no inclination to.

To be sure, on the particular party described above, Mrs. Worldly wore a squirrel fur cap in the evening as well as the daytime; she said it was because it was so warm and comfortable. It was really because she could not do her hair!

Perhaps some one asks about Ernest? At the end of two days of aloof and distasteful idleness, Ernest became quite a human being; invaluable as baiter of worms for the children's fish-hooks, as extra butler, and did not scorn even temporary experiments as kitchen-maid. In fact, he proved the half-hearted recommendation that he "might be useful" so thoroughly that the first person of all to be especially invited for next year and future years, was—exactly— Ernest.

CHAPTER XXVII

NOTES AND SHORTER LETTERS

In writing notes or letters, as in all other forms of social observance, the highest achievement is in giving the appearance of simplicity, naturalness and force.

Those who use long periods of flowered prolixity and pretentious phrases—who write in complicated form with meaningless flourishes, do not make an impression of elegance and erudition upon their readers, but flaunt instead unmistakable evidence of vainglory and ignorance.

The letter you write, whether you realize it or not, is always a mirror which reflects your appearance, taste and character. A "sloppy" letter with the writing all pouring into one corner of the page, badly worded, badly spelled, and with unmatched paper and envelope—even possibly a blot—proclaims the sort of person who would have unkempt hair, unclean linen and broken shoe laces; just as a neat, precise, evenly written note portrays a person of like characteristics. Therefore, while it can not be said with literal accuracy that one may read the future of a person by study of his handwriting, it is true that if a young man wishes to choose a wife in whose daily life he is sure always to find the unfinished task, the untidy mind and the syncopated housekeeping, he may do it quite simply by selecting her from her letters.

HOW TO IMPROVE A LETTER'S APPEARANCE

Some people are fortunate in being able easily to make graceful letters, to space their words evenly, and to put them on a page so that the picture is pleasing; others are discouraged at the outset because their fingers are clumsy, and their efforts crude; but no matter how badly formed each individual letter may be, if the writing is consistent throughout, the page as a whole looks fairly well.

You can *make* yourself write neatly and legibly. You

448

can (with the help of a dictionary if necessary) spell correctly; you can be sure that you understand the meaning of
every word you use. If it is hard for you to write in a
straight line, use the lined guide that comes with nearly
all stationery; if impossible to keep an even margin, draw
a perpendicular line at the left of the guide so that you
can start each new line of writing on it. You can also
make a guide to slip under the envelope. Far better to
use a guide than to send envelopes and pages of writing
that slide up hill and down, in uncontrolled disorder.

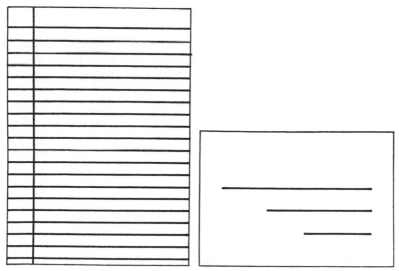

FACSIMILES, REDUCED IN SIZE, OF LETTER AND ENVELOPE GUIDES

CHOICE OF WRITING PAPER

Suitability should be considered in choosing note paper,
as well as in choosing a piece of furniture for a house. For
a handwriting which is habitually large, a larger sized paper
should be chosen than for writing which is small. The shape
of paper should also depend somewhat upon the spacing
of the lines which is typical of the writer, and whether a
wide or narrow margin is used. Low, spread-out writing
looks better on a square sheet of paper; tall, pointed writing
looks better on paper that is high and narrow. Selection
of paper whether rough or smooth is entirely a matter of

personal choice—so that the quality be good, and the shape and color conservative.

Paper should never be ruled, or highly scented, or odd in shape, or have elaborate or striking ornamentation. Some people use smaller paper for notes, or correspondence cards, cut to the size of the envelopes. Others use the same size for all correspondence and leave a wider margin in writing notes.

The flap of the envelope should be plain and the point not unduly long. If the flap is square instead of being pointed, it may be allowed greater length without being eccentric. Colored linings to envelopes are at present in fashion. Thin white paper, with monogram or address stamped in gray to match gray tissue lining of the envelope is, for instance, in very best taste. Young girls may be

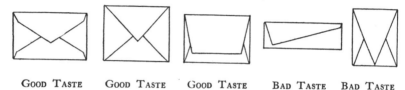

GOOD TASTE   GOOD TASTE   GOOD TASTE   BAD TASTE   BAD TASTE

allowed quite gay envelope linings, but the device on the paper must be minute, in proportion to the gaiety of the color.

Writing paper for a man should always be strictly conservative. Plain white or gray or granite paper, large in size and stamped in the simplest manner. The size should be 5¾ x 7½ or 6 x 8 or 5⅛ x 8⅛ or thereabouts.

A paper suitable for the use of all the members of a family has the address stamped in black or dark color, in plain letters at the top of the first page. More often than not the telephone number is put in very small letters under that of the address, a great convenience in the present day of telephoning. For example:

350 PARK AVENUE
TELEPHONE 7572 PLAZA

DEVICES FOR STAMPING

As there is no such thing as heraldry in America, the use of a coat of arms is as much a foreign custom as the speaking of a foreign tongue; but in certain communities where old families have used their crests continuously since the days when they brought their device—and their right to it—from Europe, the use of it is suitable and proper. The sight of this or that crest on a carriage or automobile in New York or Boston announces to all those who have lived their lives in either city that the vehicle belongs to a member of this or that family. But for some one without an inherited right to select a lion *rampant* or a stag *couchant* because he thinks it looks stylish, is as though, for the same reason, he changed his name from Muggins to Marmaduke, and quite properly subjects him to ridicule. (Strictly speaking, a woman has the right to use a "lozenge" only; since in heraldic days women did not bear arms, but no one in this country follows heraldic rule to this extent.)

THE PERSONAL DEVICE

It is occasionally the fancy of artists or young girls to adopt some especial symbol associated with themselves. The "butterfly" of Whistler for instance is as well-known as his name. A painter of marines has the small outline of a ship stamped on his writing paper, and a New York architect the capital of an Ionic column. A generation ago young women used to fancy such an intriguing symbol as a mask, a sphinx, a question mark, or their own names, if their names were such as could be pictured. There can be no objection to one's appropriation of such an emblem if one fancies it. But Lilly, Belle, Dolly and Kitten are Lillian, Isabel, Dorothy and Katherine in these days, and appropriate hall-marks are not easily found.

COUNTRY HOUSE STATIONERY: FOR A BIG HOUSE

In selecting paper for a country house we go back to the subject of suitability. A big house in important grounds should have very plain, very dignified letter paper. It may be white or tinted blue or gray. The name of the place should be engraved, in the center usually, at the top of the first page. It may be placed left, or right, as preferred. Slanting across the upper corners or in a list at the upper left side, may be put as many addresses as necessary. Many persons use a whole row of small devices in outline, the engine of a train and beside it Ardmoor, meaning that Ardmoor is the railroad station. A telegraph pole, an envelope, a telephone instrument—and

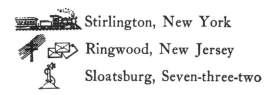

beside each an address. These devices are suitable for all places, whether they are great or tiny, that have different addresses for railroad, post-office, telephone telegraph.

For the Little House

On the other hand, farmhouses and little places in the country may have very bright-colored stamping, as well as gay-lined envelopes. Places with easily illustrated names quite often have them pictured; the "Bird-cage," for instance, may have a bright blue paper with a bird-cage in supposed red lacquer; the "Bandbox," a fantastically decorated milliner's box on oyster gray paper, the envelope

lining of black and gray pin stripes, and the "Doll's House" might use the outline of a doll's house in grass green on green-bordered white paper, and white envelopes lined with grass green. Each of these devices must be as small as the outline of a cherry pit and the paper of the smallest size that comes. (Envelopes 3½ x 5 inches or paper 4 x 6 and envelopes the same size to hold paper without folding.)

It is foolish perhaps to give the description of such papers, for their fashion is but of the moment. A jeweler from Paris has been responsible for their present vogue in New York, and his clientèle is only among the young and smart. Older and more conservative women (and, of course, all men) keep to the plain fashion of yesterday, which will just as surely be the fashion of to-morrow.

MOURNING PAPER

Persons who are in mourning use black-edged visiting cards, letter paper and envelopes. The depth of black corresponds with the depth of mourning and the closeness of relation to the one who has gone, the width decreasing as one's mourning lightens. The width of black to use is a matter of personal taste and feeling. A very heavy border (from ⅜ to 7/16 of an inch) announces the deepest retirement.

DATING A LETTER

Usually the date is put at the upper right hand of the first page of a letter, or at the end, and to the left of the signature, of a note. It is far less confusing for one's correspondent to read January 9, 1920, than 1-9-20. Theoretically, one should write out the date in full: the ninth of January, Nineteen hundred and twenty-one. That, however, is the height of pedantry, and an unswallowable mouthful at the top of any page not a document.

At the end of a note "Thursday" is sufficient unless the note is an invitation for more than a week ahead, in which case write as in a letter, "January 9" or "the ninth of January." The year is not necessary since it can hardly be supposed to take a year for a letter's transportation.

SEQUENCE OF PAGES

If a note is longer than one page, the third page is usually next, as this leaves the fourth blank and prevents the writing from showing through the envelope. With heavy or tissue-lined envelopes, the fourth is used as often as the third. In letters one may write first, second, third, fourth, in regular order; or first and fourth, then, opening the sheet and turning it sideways, write across the two inside pages as one. Many prefer to write on first, third, then sideways across second and fourth. In certain cities—Boston, for instance—the last word on a page is repeated at the top of the next. It is undoubtedly a good idea, but makes a stuttering impression upon one not accustomed to it.

FOLDING A NOTE

As to whether a letter is folded in such a way that the recipient shall read the contents without having to turn the paper, is giving too much importance to nothing. It is sufficient if the paper is folded *neatly,* once, of course, for the envelope that is half the length of the paper, and twice for the envelope that is a third.

SEALING WAX

If you use sealing wax, let us hope you are an adept at making an even and smoothly finished seal. Choose a plain-colored wax rather than one speckled with metal. With the sort of paper described for country houses, or for young people, or those living in studios or bungalows, gay sealing wax may be quite alluring, especially if it can be persuaded to pour smoothly like liquid, and not to look like a streaked and broken off slice of dough. In days when envelopes were unknown, all letters had to be sealed, hence when envelopes were made, the idea obtained that it was improper to use both gum-arabic and wax. Strictly speaking this may be true, but since all envelopes have mucilage, it would be unreasonable to demand that those who like to use sealing wax have their envelopes made to order.

FORM OF ADDRESS

The most formal beginning of a social letter is "My dear Mrs. Smith." (The fact that in England "Dear Mrs. Smith" is more formal does not greatly concern us in America.) "Dear Mrs. Smith," "Dear Sarah," "Dear Sally," "Sally dear," "Dearest Sally," "Darling Sally," are increasingly intimate.

Business letters begin:

Smith, Johnson & Co.,
　20 Broadway,
　　New York.
Dear Sirs:

Or if more personal:

John Smith & Co.,
　20 Broadway,
　　New York.
My Dear Mr. Smith:

THE COMPLIMENTARY CLOSE

The close of a business letter should be "Yours truly," or "Yours very truly." "Respectfully" is used only by a tradesman to a customer, an employee to an employer, or by an inferior, *never* by a person of equal position. No lady should ever sign a letter "respectfully," not even were she writing to a queen. If an American lady should have occasion to write to a queen, she should conclude her letter "I have the honor to remain, Madam, your most obedient." (For address and close of letters to persons of title, see table at the end of this chapter.)

CLOSE OF PERSONAL NOTES AND LETTERS

It is too bad that the English language does not permit the charming and graceful closing of all letters in the French manner, those little flowers of compliment that leave such a pleasant fragrance after reading. But ever since the Eighteenth Century the English-speaking have been busy pruning away all ornament of expression; even the last remaining graces, "kindest regards," "with kindest remembrances," are fast disappearing, leaving us nothing but an abrupt "Yours truly," or "Sincerely yours."

Closing a Formal Note

The best ending to a formal social note is, "Sincerely," "Sincerely yours," "Very sincerely," "Very sincerely yours," "Yours always sincerely," or "Always sincerely yours."

"I remain, dear madam," is no longer in use, but "Believe me" is still correct when formality is to be expressed in the close of a note.

Believe me
                    Very sincerely yours,
or

Believe me, my dear Mrs. Worldly,
                    Most sincerely yours,

This last is an English form, but it is used by quite a number of Americans—particularly those who have been much abroad.

Appropriate for a Man

"Faithfully" or "Faithfully yours" is a very good signature for a man in writing to a woman, or in any uncommercial correspondence, such as a letter to the President of the United States, a member of the Cabinet, an Ambassador, a clergyman, etc.

The Intimate Closing

"Affectionately yours," "Always affectionately," "Affectionately," "Devotedly," "Lovingly," "Your loving" are in increasing scale of intimacy.

"Lovingly" is much more intimate than "Affectionately" and so is "Devotedly."

"Sincerely" in formal notes and "Affectionately" in intimate notes are the two adverbs most used in the present day, and between these two there is a blank; in English we have no expression to fit sentiment more friendly than the first nor one less intimate than the second.

Not Good Form

"Cordially" was coined no doubt to fill this need, but its self-consciousness puts it in the category with "residence" and "retire," and all the other offenses of pretentiousness, and in New York, at least, it is not used by people of taste.

"Warmly yours" is unspeakable.

"Yours in haste" or "Hastily yours" is not bad form, but is rather carelessly rude.

"In a tearing hurry" is a termination dear to the boarding school girl; but its truth does not make it any more attractive than the vision of that same young girl rushing into a room with her hat and coat half on, to swoop upon her mother with a peck of a kiss, and with a "——by, mamma!" whirl out again! Turmoil and flurry may be characteristic of the manners of to-day; both are far from the ideal of beautiful manners which should be as assured, as smooth, as controlled as the running of a high-grade automobile. Flea-like motions are no better suited to manners than to motors.

Other Endings

"Gratefully" is used only when a benefit has been received, as to a lawyer who has skilfully handled a case; to a surgeon who has saved a life dear to you; to a friend who has been put to unusual trouble to do you a favor.

In an ordinary letter of thanks, the signature is "Sin-

cerely," "Affectionately," "Devotedly" — as the case
may be.

The phrases that a man might devise to close a letter
to his betrothed or his wife are bound only by the limit
of his imagination and do not belong in this, or any, book.

THE SIGNATURE

Abroad, the higher the rank, the shorter the name.
A duke, for instance, signs himself "Marlborough,"
nothing else, and a queen her first name "Victoria." The
social world in Europe, therefore, laughs at us for using
our whole names, or worse yet, inserting meaningless
initials in our signatures. Etiquette in accord with
Europe also objects strenuously to initials and demands
that names be always engraved, and, if possible, written
in full, but only very correct people strictly observe this
rule.

In Europe all persons have so many names given them
in baptism that they are forced, naturally, to lay most
of them aside, selecting one, or at most two, for use.
In America, the names bestowed at baptism become in-
separably part of each individual, so that if the name is
overlong, a string of initials is the inevitable result.

Since, in America, it is not customary for a man to
discard any of his names, and John Hunter Titherington
Smith is far too much of a pen-full for the one who signs
thousands of letters and documents, it is small wonder
that he chooses J. H. T. Smith, instead, or perhaps, at
the end of personal letters, John H. T. Smith. Why
shouldn't he? It is, after all, his own name to sign as he
chooses, and in addressing him deference to his choice
should be shown.

A married woman should always sign a letter to a
stranger, a bank, business firm, etc., with her baptismal
name, and add, in parenthesis, her married name. Thus:

Very truly yours,

Sarah Robinson Smith.

(Mrs. J. H. Titherington Smith.)

Never under any circumstances sign a letter "Mr.", "Mrs.", or "Miss" (except a note written in the third person). If, in the example above, Sarah Robinson Smith were "Miss" she would put "Miss" in parenthesis to the left of her signature:

(Miss) Sarah Robinson Smith.

THE SUPERSCRIPTION

Formal invitations are always addressed to Mr. Stanley Smith; all other personal letters may be addressed to Stanley Smith, Esq. The title of Esquire formerly was used to denote the eldest son of a knight or members of a younger branch of a noble house. Later all graduates of universities, professional and literary men, and important landholders were given the right to this title, which even to-day denotes a man of education—a gentleman. John Smith, esquire, is John Smith, gentleman. Mr. John Smith may be a gentleman; or may not be one. And yet, as noted above, all engraved invitations are addressed "Mr."

Never under any circumstances address a social letter or note to a married woman, even if she is a widow, as Mrs. Mary Town. A widow is still Mrs. James Town. If her son's wife should have the same name, she becomes Mrs. James Town, Sr., or simply Mrs. Town.

A divorced woman, if she was the innocent person, retains the right if she chooses, to call herself Mrs. John Brown Smith, but usually she prefers to take her own surname. Supposing her to have been Mary Simpson, she calls herself Mrs. Simpson Smith. If a lady is the wife or widow of "the head of a family" she may call herself Mrs. Smith, even on visiting cards and invitations.

The eldest daughter is Miss Smith; her younger sister, Miss Jane Smith.

Invitations to children are addressed, Miss Katherine Smith and Master Robert Smith.

Do not write "The Messrs. Brown" in addressing a father and son. "The Messrs. Brown" is correct only for unmarried brothers.

Although one occasionally sees an envelope addressed to "Mr. and Mrs. Jones," and "Miss Jones" written underneath the names of her parents, it is better form to send a separate invitation addressed to Miss Jones alone. A wedding invitation addressed to Mr. and Mrs. Jones and family is not in good taste. Even if the Jones children are young, the Misses Jones should receive a separate envelope, and so should Master Jones.

ONE LAST REMARK

Write the name and address on the envelope as precisely and as legibly as you can. The post-office has enough to do in deciphering the letters of the illiterate, without being asked to do unnecessary work for you!

BUSINESS LETTERS

Business letters written by a private individual differ very little from those sent out from a business house. A lady never says "Yours of the 6th received and contents noted," or "Yours to hand," nor does she address the firm as "Gentlemen," nor does she *ever* sign herself "Respectfully." A business letter should be as brief and explicit as possible. For example:

> Tuxedo Park
> New York
>
> May 17, 1922

I. Paint & Co.,
  22 Branch St.,
    New York.

Dear Sirs:

Your estimate for painting my dining-room, library, south bedroom, and dressing-room is satisfactory, and you may proceed with the work as soon as possible.

I find, on the other hand, that wainscoting the hall

comes to more than I had anticipated, and I have decided to leave it as it is for the present.

Very truly yours,

C. R. Town.

(Mrs. James Town)

THE SOCIAL NOTE

There should be no more difficulty in writing a social note than in writing a business letter; each has a specific message for its sole object and the principle of construction is the same:

* Date

Address (on business letter only)

Salutation:

The statement of whatever is the purpose of the note.

Complimentary close,

Signature.

* Or date here

The difference in form between a business and a social note is that the full name and address of the person written to is never put in the latter, better quality stationery is used, and the salutation is "My dear ———" or "Dear ———" instead of "Dear Sir:"

Example:

350 Park Avenue

Dear Mrs. Robinson:

I am enclosing the list I promised you—Luberge makes the most beautiful things. Mower, the dressmaker, has for years made clothes for me, and I think Revaud the best milliner in Paris. Leonie is a "little milliner" who often has pretty blouses as well as hats and is *very* reasonable.

I do hope the addresses will be of some use to you, and that you will have a delightful trip,

Very sincerely,

Martha Kindhart.

Thursday.

THE NOTE OF APOLOGY

Examples:

I

BROADLAWNS

Dear Mrs. Town:

I do deeply apologize for my seeming rudeness in having to send the message about Monday night.

When I accepted your invitation, I stupidly forgot entirely that Monday was a holiday and that all of my own guests, naturally, were not leaving until Tuesday morning, and Arthur and I could not therefore go out by ourselves and leave them!

We were too disappointed and hope that you know how sorry we were not to be with you.

Very sincerely,

Ethel Norman.

Tuesday morning.

II

Dear Mrs. Neighbor:

My gardener has just told me that our chickens got into your flower beds, and did a great deal of damage.

The chicken netting is being built higher at this moment and they will not be able to damage anything again. I shall, of course, send Patrick to put in shrubs to replace those broken, although I know that ones newly planted cannot compensate for those you have lost, and I can only ask you to accept my contrite apologies.

Always sincerely yours,

Katherine de Puyster Eminent.

LETTERS OF THANKS

In the following examples of letters intimate and from young persons, such profuse expressions as "divine," "awfully," "petrified," "too sweet," "too wonderful," are purposely inserted, because to change all of the above enthusiasms into "pleased with," "very," "feared," "most kind," would be to change the vitality of the "real" let-ters into smug and self-conscious utterances at variance with anything ever written by young men and women of to-day. Even the letters of older persons, although they are more restrained than those of youth, avoid anything suggesting pedantry and affectation.

Do not from this suppose that well-bred people write badly! On the contrary, perfect simplicity and freedom from self-consciousness are possible only to those who have acquired at least some degree of cultivation. For flagrant examples of pretentiousness (which is the infallible sign of lack of breeding), see page 61. For simplicity of expression, such as is unattainable to the rest of us, but which we can at least strive to emulate, read first the Bible; then at random one might suggest such authors as Robert Louis Stevenson, E. S. Martin, Agnes Repplier, John Galsworthy and Max Beerbohm. E. V. Lucas has written two novels in letter form—which illustrate the best type of present day letter-writing.

LETTERS OF THANKS FOR WEDDING PRESENTS

Although all wedding presents belong to the bride, she generally words her letters of thanks as though they belonged equally to the groom, especially if they have been sent by particular friends of his.

To Intimate Friends of the Groom

Dear Mrs. Norman:

To think of your sending us all this wonderful glass! It is simply divine, and Jim and I both thank you a thousand times!

The presents are, of course, to be shown on the day of the wedding, but do come in on Tuesday at tea time for an earlier view.

Thanking you again, and with love from us both,

Affectionately,

Mary.

Formal

I

Dear Mrs. Gilding:

It was more than sweet of you and Mr. Gilding to send us such a lovely clock. Thank you, very, very much.

Looking forward to seeing you on the tenth,

Very sincerely,

Mary Smith.

Sometimes, as in the two examples above, thanks to the husband are definitely expressed in writing to the wife. Usually, however, "you" is understood to mean "you both."

II

Dear Mrs. Worldly:

All my life I have wanted a piece of jade, but in my wanting I have never imagined one quite so beautiful as the one you have sent me. It was wonderfully sweet of you and I thank you more than I can tell you for the pleasure you have given me.

Affectionately,

Mary Smith.

III

Dear Mrs. Eminent:

Thank you for these wonderful prints. They go too beautifully with some old English ones that Jim's uncle sent us, and our dining-room will be quite perfect—as to walls!

Hoping that you are surely coming to the wedding,

Very sincerely,

Mary Smith.

To a Friend Who Is in Deep Mourning

Dear Susan:

With all you have on your heart just now, it was so sweet and thoughtful of you to go out and buy me a present, and such a beautiful one! I love it—and your thought of me in sending it—and I thank you more than I can tell you.

Devotedly,

Mary.

Very Intimate

Dear Aunt Kate:

Really you are too generous—it is outrageous of you —but, of course, it *is* the most beautiful bracelet! And I am so excited over it, I hardly know what I am doing. You are too good to me and you spoil me, but I do love you, and it, and thank you with all my heart.

Mary.

Intimate

Dear Mrs. Neighbor:

The tea cloth is perfectly exquisite! I have never *seen* such beautiful work! I appreciate your lovely gift more than I can tell you, both for its own sake and for your kindness in making it for me.

Don't forget, you are coming in on Tuesday afternoon to see the presents.

Lovingly,

Mary.

Sometimes pushing people send presents, when they are not asked to the wedding, in the hope of an invitation. Sometimes others send presents, when they are not asked, merely through kindly feeling toward a young couple on the threshold of life. It ought not to be difficult to distinguish between the two.

I

My Dear Mrs. Upstart:

Thank you for the very handsome candlesticks you sent us. They were a great surprize, but it was more than kind of you to think of us.

Very sincerely,

Mary Smith.

II

Dear Mrs. Kindly:

I can't tell you how sweet I think it of you to send us such a lovely present, and Jim and I both hope that when we are in our own home, you will see them often at our table.

Thanking you many times for your thought of us,

Very sincerely,

Mary Smith.

For a Present Sent After the Wedding

Dear Mrs. Chatterton:

The mirror you sent us is going over our drawing-room mantel just as soon as we can hang it up! It is exactly what we most needed and we both thank you ever so much.

Please come in soon to see how becoming it will be to the room.

Yours affectionately,

Mary Smith Smartlington.

THANKS FOR CHRISTMAS OR OTHER PRESENTS

Dear Lucy:

I really think it was adorable of you to have a chair like yours made for me. It was worth adding a year to my age for such a nice birthday present. Jack says I am never going to have a chance to sit in it, however, if he gets there first, and even the children look at it with longing. At all events, I am perfectly enchanted with it, and thank you ever and ever so much.

Affectionately,

Sally.

Dear Uncle Arthur:

I know I oughtn't to have opened it until Christmas, but I couldn't resist the look of the package, and then putting it on at once! So I am all dressed up in your beautiful chain. It is one of the loveliest things I have ever seen and I certainly am lucky to have it given to me! Thank you a thousand—and then more—times for it.

Rosalie.

Dear Kate:

I am fascinated with my utility box—it is too beguiling for words! You are the cleverest one anyway for finding what no one else can—and every one wants. I don't know how you do it! And you certainly were sweet to think of me. Thank you, dear.

Ethel.

THANKS FOR PRESENT TO A BABY

Dear Mrs. Kindhart:

Of course it would be! Because no one else can sew like you! The sacque you made the baby is the prettiest thing I have ever seen, and is perfectly adorable on her! Thank you, as usual, you dear Mrs. Kindhart, for your goodness to

Your affectionate,

Sally.

Dear Mrs. Norman:

Thank you ever so much for the lovely afghan you sent the baby. It is by far the prettiest one he has; it is so soft and close—he doesn't get his fingers tangled in it.

Do come in and see him, won't you? We are both allowed visitors (especial ones) every day between 4 and 5.30!

Affectionately always,

Lucy.

THE BREAD AND BUTTER LETTER

When you have been staying over Sunday, or for longer, in some one's house, it is absolutely necessary that you write a letter of thanks to your hostess within a few days after the visit.

"Bread and butter letters," as they are called, are the stumbling-blocks of visitors. Why they are so difficult for nearly every one is hard to determine, unless it is that they are often written to persons with whom you are on formal terms, and the letter should be somewhat informal in tone. Very likely you have been visiting a friend, and must write to her mother, whom you scarcely know; perhaps you have been included in a large and rather formal house party and the hostess is an acquaintance rather than a friend; or perhaps you are a bride and have been on a first visit to relatives or old friends of your husband's, but strangers, until now, to you.

As an example of the first, where you have been visiting a girl friend and must write a letter to her mother, you begin "Dear Mrs. Town" at the top of a page, and nothing in the forbidding memory of Mrs. Town encourages you to go further. It would be easy enough to write to Pauline, the daughter. Very well, write to Pauline then—on an odd piece of paper, in pencil, what a good time you had, how nice it was to be with her. Then copy your note composed to Pauline off on the page beginning "Dear Mrs. Town." You have only to add, "love to Pauline, and thanking you again for asking me," sign it "Very sincerely," and there you are!

Don't be afraid that your note is too informal; older people are always pleased with any expressions from the young that seem friendly and spontaneous. Never think, because you can not easily write a letter, that it is better not to write at all. The most awkward note that can be imagined is better than none—for to write none is the depth of rudeness, whereas the awkward note merely fails to delight.

EXAMPLES

From a Young Woman to a Formal Hostess After a House Party

Dear Mrs. Norman:

I don't know when I ever had such a good time as I did at Broadlawns. Thank you a thousand times for asking me. As it happened, the first persons I saw on

Monday at the Towns' dinner were Celia and Donald. We immediately had a threesome conversation on the wonderful time we all had over Sunday.

Thanking you again for your kindness to me,

Very sincerely yours,

Grace Smalltalk.

To a Formal Hostess After an Especially Amusing Week-End

Dear Mrs. Worldly:

Every moment at Great Estates was a perfect delight! I am afraid my work at the office this morning was down to zero in efficiency; so perhaps it is just as well, if I am to keep my job, that the average week-end in the country is different—very. Thank you all the same, for the wonderful time you gave us all, and believe me

Faithfully yours,

Frederick Bachelor.

Dear Mrs. Worldly:

Every time I come from Great Estates, I realize again that there is no house to which I always go with so much pleasure, and leave on Monday morning with so much regret.

Your party over this last week-end was simply wonderful! And thank you ever so much for having included me.

Always sincerely,

Constance Style.

From a Young Couple

Dear Mrs. Town:

We had a perfect time at Tuxedo over Sunday and it was so good of you to include us. Jack says he is going to practise putting the way Mr. Town showed him, and maybe the next time he plays in a foursome he won't be such a handicap to his partner.

Thanking you both for the pleasure you gave us,

Affectionately yours,

Sally Titherington Littlehouse

From a Bride to Her New Relatives-in-Law

A letter that was written by a bride after paying a first visit to her husband's aunt and uncle won for her at a stroke the love of the whole family.

This is the letter:

Dear "Aunt Annie":

Now that it is all over, I have a confession to make! Do you know that when Dick drove me up to your front door and I saw you and Uncle Bob standing on the top step—I was simply *paralyzed* with fright!

"Suppose they don't like me," was all that I could think. Of course, I knew you loved Dick—but that only made it worse. How awful, if you *couldn't* like me! The reason I stumbled coming up the steps was because my knees were actually knocking together! You remember, Uncle Bob sang out it was good I was already married, or I wouldn't be this year? And then—you were both so perfectly adorable to me—and you made me feel as though I had always been your niece—and not just the wife of your nephew.

I loved every minute of our being with you, dear Aunt Annie, just as much as Dick did, and we hope you are going to let us come soon again.

With best love from us both,

Your affectionate niece,

Helen.

The above type of letter would not serve perhaps if Dick's aunt had been a forbidding and austere type of woman; but even such a one would be far more apt to take a new niece to her heart if the new niece herself gave evidence of having one.

After Visiting a Friend

Dear Kate:

It was hideously dull and stuffy in town this morning after the fresh coolness of Strandholm. The back yard is not an alluring outlook after the wide spaces and delicious fragrance of your garden.

It was good being with you and I enjoyed every moment. Don't forget you are lunching here on the 16th and that we are going to hear Kreisler together.

Devotedly always,

Caroline.

From a Man Who Has Been Ill and Convalescing at a Friend's House

Dear Martha:

I certainly hated taking that train this morning and realizing that the end had come to my peaceful days. You and John and the children, and your place, which is the essence of all that a "home" ought to be, have put me on my feet again. I thank you much—much more than I can say for the wonderful goodness of all of you.

Fred.

From a Woman Who Has Been Visiting a Very Old Friend

I loved my visit with you, dear Mary; it was more than good to be with you and have a chance for long talks at your fireside. Don't forget your promise to come here in May! I told Sam and Hettie you were coming, and now the whole town is ringing with the news, and every one is planning a party for you.

David sends "his best" to you and Charlie, and you know you always have the love of

Your devoted

Pat.

To an Acquaintance

After a visit to a formal acquaintance or when some one has shown you especial hospitality in a city where you are a stranger:

My dear Mrs. Duluth:

It was more than good of you to give my husband and me so much pleasure. We enjoyed, and appreciated, all your kindness to us more than we can say.

We hope that you and Mr. Duluth may be coming East before long and that we may then have the pleasure of seeing you at Strandholm.

In the meanwhile, thanking you for your generous hospitality, and with kindest regards to you both, in which my husband joins, believe me,

Very sincerely yours,

Katherine de Puyster Eminent.

AN ENGRAVED CARD OF THANKS

An engraved card of thanks is proper only when sent by a public official to acknowledge the overwhelming number of congratulatory messages he must inevitably receive from strangers, when he has carried an election or otherwise been honored with the confidence of his State or country. A recent and excellent example follows:

EXECUTIVE MANSION

My dear........

I warmly appreciate your kind message of congratulation which has given me a great deal of pleasure, and sincerely wish that it were possible for me to acknowledge it in a less formal manner.

Faithfully,

(*signed by hand*)

An engraved form of thanks for sympathy, also from one in public life, is presented in the following example:

Mr. John Smith
wishes to express his deep gratitude
and to thank you
for your kind expression of sympathy

But remember: an engraved card sent by a private individual to a personal friend, is not "stylish" or smart, but *rude*. (See also engraved acknowledgment of sympathy, pages 406-7.)

THE LETTER OF INTRODUCTION

A letter of business introduction can be much more freely given than a letter of social introduction. For the former it is necessary merely that the persons introduced have business interests in common—which are much more easily determined than social compatibility, which is the requisite necessary for the latter. It is, of course, proper to give your personal representative a letter of introduction to whomever you send him.

On the subject of letters of social introduction there is one chief rule:

Never *ask* for letters of introduction, and be very sparing in your offers to write or accept them.

Seemingly few persons realize that a letter of social introduction is actually a draft for payment on demand. The form might as well be: "The bearer of this has (because of it) the right to *demand* your interest, your time, your hospitality—liberally and at once, no matter what your inclination may be."

Therefore, it is far better to refuse in the beginning, than to hedge and end by committing the greater error of unwarrantedly inconveniencing a valued friend or acquaintance.

When you have a friend who is going to a city where you have other friends, and you believe that it will be a mutual pleasure for them to meet, a letter of introduction is proper and very easy to write, but sent to a casual acquaintance—no matter how attractive or distinguished the person to be introduced—it is a gross presumption.

THE MORE FORMAL NOTE OF INTRODUCTION

Dear Mrs. Marks:

Julian Gibbs is going to Buffalo on January tenth to deliver a lecture on his Polar expedition, and I am sending him a card of introduction to you. He is very agreeable personally, and I think that perhaps you and

Mr. Marks will enjoy meeting him as much as I know
he would enjoy knowing you.

   With kindest regards, in which Arthur joins,

Very sincerely,

Ethel Norman.

   If Mr. Norman were introducing one man to another
he would give his card to the former, inscribed as follows:

   Introducing Julian Gibbs

MR. ARTHUR LEES NORMAN

BROADLAWNS

   Also Mr. Norman would send a private letter by mail,
telling his friend that Mr. Gibbs is coming, as follows:

Dear Marks:

   I am giving Julian Gibbs a card of introduction to
you when he goes to Buffalo on the tenth to lecture. He
is an entertaining and very decent fellow, and I think
possibly Mrs. Marks would enjoy meeting him. If you
can conveniently ask him to your house, I know he would
appreciate it; if not, perhaps you will put him up for a
day or two at a club.

Faithfully,

Arthur Norman.

INFORMAL LETTER OF INTRODUCTION

Dear Claire:

A very great friend of ours, James Dawson, is to be in Chicago for several weeks. Any kindness that you can show him will be greatly appreciated by

Yours as always,

Ethel Norman.

At the same time a second and private letter of information is written and sent by mail:

Dear Claire:

I wrote you a letter to-day introducing Jim Dawson. He used to be on the Yalvard football team, perhaps you remember. He is one of the best sort in the world and I know you will like him. I don't want to put you to any trouble, but do ask him to your house if you can. He plays a wonderful game of golf and a good game of bridge, but he is more a man's than a woman's type of man. Maybe if Tom likes him, he will put him up at a club as he is to be in Chicago for some weeks.

Affectionately always,

Ethel.

Another example:

Dear Caroline:

A very dear friend of mine, Mrs. Fred West, is going to be in New York this winter, while her daughter is at Barnard. I am asking her to take this letter to you as I want very much to have her meet you and have her daughter meet Pauline. Anything that you can do for them will be the same as for me!

Yours affectionately,

Sylvia Greatlake.

The private letter by mail to accompany the foregoing:

Dearest Caroline:

Mildred West, for whom I wrote to you this morning, is a very close friend of mine. She is going to New York with her only daughter—who, in spite of wanting a college education, is as pretty as a picture, with plenty of come-hither in the eye—so do not be afraid that the typical blue-stocking is to be thrust upon Pauline! The mother is an altogether lovely person and I know that you and she will speak the same language—if I didn't, I wouldn't give her a letter to you. Do go to see her as soon as you can; she will be stopping at the Fitz-Cherry and probably feeling rather lost at first. She wants to take an apartment for the winter and I told her I was sure you would know the best real estate and intelligence offices, etc., for her to go to.

I hope I am not putting you to any trouble about her, but she is really a darling and you will like her I know.

Devotedly yours,

Sylvia.

Directions for procedure upon being given (or receiving) a letter of introduction will be found on pages 16 and 17.

THE THIRD PERSON

In other days when even verbal messages began with the "presenting of compliments," a social note, no matter what its length or purport, would have been considered rude, unless written in the third person. But as in a communication of any length the difficulty of this form is almost insurmountable (to say nothing of the pedantic effect of its accomplishment), it is no longer chosen—aside from the formal invitation, acceptance and regret—except for notes to stores or subordinates. For example:

Will B. Stern & Co. please send (and charge) to Mrs. John H. Smith, 2 Madison Avenue,

      1 paper of needles No. 9

      2 spools white sewing cotton No. 70

      1 yard of material (sample enclosed).

January 6.

To a servant:

Mrs. Eminent wishes Patrick to meet her at the station on Tuesday the eighth at 11.03. She also wishes him to have the shutters opened and the house aired on that day, and a fire lighted in the northwest room. No provisions will be necessary as Mrs. Eminent is returning to town on the 5.16.

Tuesday, March 1.

Letters in the third person are no longer signed unless the sender's signature is necessary for identification, or for some action on the part of the receiver, such as

Will Mr. Cash please give the bearer six yards of material to match the sample enclosed, and oblige,

Mrs. John H. Smith.*

THE LETTER OF RECOMMENDATION

A letter of recommendation for membership to a club is addressed to the secretary and should be somewhat in this form:

To the Secretary of the Town Club.

My dear Mrs. Brown:

Mrs. Titherington Smith, whose name is posted for membership, is a very old and close friend of mine. She is the daughter of the late Rev. Samuel Eminent and is therefore a member in her own right, as well as by marriage, of representative New York families.

* A note in 3rd person is the single occasion when a married woman signs "Mrs." before her name.

She is a person of much charm and distinction, and her many friends will agree with me, I am sure, in thinking that she would be a valuable addition to the club.

Very sincerely,

Ethel Norman.

RECOMMENDATION OF EMPLOYEES

Although the written recommendation that is given to the employee carries very little weight, compared to the slip from the employment agencies where either "yes" or "no" has to be answered to a list of specific and important questions, one is nevertheless put in a trying position when reporting on an unsatisfactory servant.

Either a poor reference must be given—possibly preventing a servant from earning her living—or one has to write what is not true. Consequently it has become the custom to say what one truthfully can of good, and leave out the qualifications that are bad (except in the case of a careless nurse, where evasion would border on the criminal).

That solves the poor recommendation problem pretty well; but unless one is very careful this consideration for the "poor" one, is paid for by the "good." In writing for a very worthy servant therefore, it is of the utmost importance in fairness to her (or him) to put in every merit that you can think of, remembering that omission implies demerit in each trait of character not mentioned. All good references should include honesty, sobriety, capability, and a reason, other than their unsatisfactoriness, for their leaving. The recommendation for a nurse can not be too conscientiously written.

A lady does not begin a recommendation: "To whom it may concern," nor "This is to certify," although housekeepers and head servants writing recommendations use both of these forms, and "third person" letters, are frequently written by secretaries.

A lady in giving a good reference should write:

Two Hundred Park Square.

Selma Johnson has lived with me for two years as cook.

I have found her honest, sober, industrious, neat in her person as well as her work, of amiable disposition and a very good cook.

She is leaving to my great regret because I am closing my house for the winter.

Selma is an excellent servant in every way and I shall be glad to answer personally any inquiries about her.

Josephine Smith.

(Mrs. Titherington Smith)
October, 1921.

The form of all recommendations is the same:

.............................has lived with me............. months as....................I
years

have found him .... He
her She

is leaving because........................

(Any special remark of added recommendation or showing interest)
....
(Mrs..................)
Date.

LETTERS OF CONGRATULATION

LETTER OF CONGRATULATION ON ENGAGEMENT

Dear Mary:

While we are not altogether surprized, we are both delighted to hear the good news. Jim's family and ours are very close, as you know, and we have always been especially devoted to Jim. He is one of the finest—and now luckiest, of young men, and we send you both every good wish for all possible happiness.

Affectionately,

Ethel Norman.

Just a line, dear Jim, to tell you how glad we all are to hear of your happiness. Mary is everything that is lovely and, of course, from our point of view, we don't think her exactly unfortunate either! Every good wish that imagination can think of goes to you from your old friends.

Ethel and Arthur Norman.

I can't tell you, dearest Mary, of all the wishes I send for your happiness. Give Jim my love and tell him how lucky I think he is, and how much I hope all good fortune will come to you both.

Lovingly,

Aunt Kate.

CONGRATULATION ON SOME ESPECIAL SUCCESS

My dear Mrs. Brown:

We have just heard of the honors that your son has won. How proud you must be of him! We are both so glad for him and for you. Please congratulate him for us, and believe me,

Very sincerely,

Ethel Norman.

Or:

Dear Mrs. Brown:

We are so glad to hear the good news of David's success; it was a very splendid accomplishment and we are all so proud of him and of you. Please give him our love and congratulations, and with full measure of both to you,

Affectionately,

Martha Kindhart.

CONGRATULATING A FRIEND APPOINTED TO HIGH OFFICE

Dear John:

We are overjoyed at the good news! For once the reward has fallen where it is deserved. Certainly no one is better fitted than yourself for a diplomat's life, and we know you will fill the position to the honor of your country. Please give my love to Alice, and with renewed congratulations to you from us both.

Yours always,

Ethel Norman.

Another example:

Dear Michael:

We all rejoice with you in the confirmation of your appointment. The State needs just such men as you— if we had more of your sort the ordinary citizen would have less to worry about. Our best congratulations!

John Kindhart.

THE LETTER OF CONDOLENCE

Intimate letters of condolence are like love letters, in that they are too sacred to follow a set form. One rule, and one only, should guide you in writing such letters. Say what you truly feel. Say that and nothing else. Sit down at your desk, let your thoughts dwell on the person you are writing to.

Don't dwell on the details of illness or the manner of death; don't quote endlessly from the poets and Scriptures. Remember that eyes filmed with tears and an aching heart can not follow rhetorical lengths of writing. The more nearly a note can express a hand-clasp, a thought of sympathy, above all, a genuine love or appreciation of the one who has gone, the greater comfort it brings.

Write as simply as possible and let your heart speak as truly and as briefly as you can. Forget, if you can, that you are using written words, think merely how you feel—then put your feelings on paper—that is all.

Supposing it is a young mother who has died. You think how young and sweet she was—and of her little children, and, literally, your heart aches for them and her husband and her own family. Into your thoughts must come some expression of what she was, and what their loss must be!

Or maybe it is the death of a man who has left a place in the whole community that will be difficult, if not impossible, to fill, and you think of all he stood for that was fine and helpful to others, and how much and sorely he will be missed. Or suppose that you are a returned soldier, and it is a pal who has died. All you can think of is "Poor old Steve—what a peach he was! I don't think anything will ever be the same again without him." Say just that! Ask if there is anything you can do at any time to be of service to his people. There is nothing more to be said. A line, into which you have unconsciously put a little of the genuine feeling that you had for Steve, is worth pages of eloquence.

A letter of condolence may be abrupt, badly constructed, ungrammatical—never mind. Grace of expression counts for nothing; sincerity alone is of value. It is the expression, however clumsily put, of a personal something which was loved, and will ever be missed, that alone brings solace to those who are left. Your message may speak merely of a small incident—something so trifling that in the seriousness of the present, seems not worth recording; but your letter and that of many others, each bringing a single sprig, may plant a whole memory-garden in the hearts of the bereaved.

As has been said above, a letter of condolence must above everything express a genuine sentiment. The few examples are inserted merely as suggestive guides for those at a loss to construct a short but appropriate note or telegram.

Conventional Note to an Acquaintance

I know how little the words of an outsider mean to you just now—but I must tell you how deeply I sympathize with you in your great loss.

Note or Telegram to a Friend

All my sympathy and all my thoughts are with you in your great sorrow. If I can be of any service to you, you know how grateful I shall be.

Telegram to a Very Near Relative or Friend

Words are so empty! If only I knew how to fill them with love and send them to you.

Or:

If love and thoughts could only help you, Margaret dear, you should have all the strength of both that I can give.

Letter Where Death Was Release

The letter to one whose loss is "for the best" is difficult in that you want to express sympathy but can not feel sad that one who has long suffered has found release. The expression of sympathy in this case should not be for the present death, but for the illness, or whatever it was that fell long ago. The grief for a paralysed mother is for the stroke which cut her down many years before, and your sympathy, though you may not have realized it, is for that. You might write:

Your sorrow during all these years—and now—is in my heart; and all my thoughts and sympathy are with you.

HOW TO ADDRESS

	If you are speaking, you say:	Envelope addressed:	Formal beginning of a letter:
The President	Mr. President And occasionally throughout a conversation, Sir.	The President of the United States or merely The President, Washington, D. C. (There is only one "President")	Sir:
The Vice-President	Mr. Vice-President and then, Sir.	The Vice-President, Washington, D. C.	Sir:
Justice of Supreme Court	Mr. Justice	The Hon. William H. Taft, Chief Justice of the Supreme Court, Washington, D. C.	Sir:
Member of the President's Cabinet	Mr. Secretary	The Secretary of Commerce, Washington, D. C. or: The Hon. Herbert Hoover, Secretary of Commerce, Washington, D. C.	Dear Sir: or Sir:
United States (or State) Senator	Senator Lodge	Senator Henry Cabot Lodge, Washington, D. C. or a private letter: Senator Henry Cabot Lodge, (His house address)	Dear Sir: or Sir:
Member of Congress (or Legislature)	Mr. Bell, or, you may say Congressman	The Hon. H. C. Bell, Jr., House of Representatives, Washington, D. C. or: State Assembly, Albany, New York.	Dear Sir: or Sir:
Governor	Governor Miller (The Governor is not called Excellency when spoken to and very rarely when he is announced. But letters are addressed and begun with this title of courtesy.)	His Excellency The Governor, Albany, New York.	Your Excellency:
Mayor	Mr. Mayor	His Honor the Mayor, City Hall, Chicago.	Dear Sir: or Sir:
Cardinal	Your Eminence	His Eminence John Cardinal Gibbons, Baltimore, Md.	Your Eminence:

IMPORTANT PERSONAGES

Informal beginning:	Formal close:	Informal close:	Correct titles in introduction:
My dear Mr. President:	I have the honor to remain, Most respectfully yours, or I have the honor to remain, sir, Your most obedient servant.	I have the honor to remain, Yours faithfully, or, I am, dear Mr. President, Yours faithfully,	The **President**.
My dear Mr. Vice-President:	Same as for President	Believe me, Yours faithfully,	The Vice-President.
Dear Mr. Justice Taft:	Believe me, Yours very truly, or I have the honor to remain, Yours very truly,	Believe me, Yours faithfully,	'The Chief Justice or, if an Associate Justice, Mr. Justice Holmes.
My dear Mr. Secretary:	Same as above.	Same as above.	The Secretary of Commerce.
Dear Senator Lodge:	Same as above.	Same as above.	Senator Lodge. On very formal and unusual occasions, Senator Lodge of Massachusetts.
Dear Mr. Bell: or Dear Congressman:	Believe me, Yours very truly,	Yours faithfully,	Mr. **Bell**.
Dear Governor Miller:	I have the honor to remain, Yours faithfully,	Believe me, Yours faithfully,	The Governor (in his own state) or, (out of it,) The Governor of Michigan.
Dear Mayor Rolph:	Believe me, Very truly yours,	Yours faithfully,	Mayor Rolph.
Your Eminence:	I have the honor to remain, Your Eminence's humble servant.	Your Eminence's humble servant.	His Eminence.

HOW TO ADDRESS

	If you are speaking, you say:	Envelope addressed:	Formal beginning of a letter:
Roman Catholic Archbiship (There is no Protestant Archbishop in the United States.)	Your Grace	The Most Reverend Michael Corrigan, Archbishop of New York.	Most Reverend and dear Sir:
Bishop (Whether Roman Catholic or Protestant.)	Bishop Manning	To the Right Reverend William T. Manning, Bishop of New York,	Most Reverend and dear Sir:
Priest	Father or Father Duffy	The Rev. Michael Duffy,	Reverend and dear Sir:
Protestant Clergyman	Mr. Saintly (If he is D.D. or LL.D., you call him Dr. Saintly.)	The Rev. Geo. Saintly, (If you do not know his first name, write The Rev. .... Saintly, rather than the Rev. Mr. Saintly.)	Sir: or My dear Sir:
Rabbi	Rabbi Wise (If he is D.D. or LL.D., he is called Dr. Wise.)	Dr. Stephen Wise, or Rabbi Stephen Wise, or Rev. Stephen Wise,	Dear Sir:
Ambassador	Your Excellency or Mr. Ambassador	His Excellency The American Ambassador,* American Embassy, London.	Your Excellency:
Minister Plenipotentiary	In English he is usually called "Mr. Prince," though it is not incorrect to call him "Mr. Minister." The title "Excellency" is also occasionally used in courtesy, though it does not belong to him. In French he is always called *Monsieur le Ministre.*	The Hon. J. D. Prince, American Legation, Copenhagen, or (more courteously) His Excellency, The American Minister, Copenhagen, Denmark.	Sir: is correct but, Your Excellency: is sometimes used in courtesy.
Consul	Mr. Smith.	If he has held office as assemblyman or commissioner, so that he has the right to the title of "Honorable" he is addressed: The Hon. John Smith, otherwise: John Smith, Esq., American Consul, Rue Quelque Chose, Paris.	Sir: or My dear Sir:

*Although our Ambassadors and Ministers represent the United States of America, it is customary both in Europe and Asia to omit the words United States and write to and speak of the American Embassy and Legation. In addressing a letter to one of our representatives in

IMPORTANT PERSONAGES

Informal beginning:	Formal close:	Informal close:	Correct titles in introduction:
Most Reverend and Dear Sir:	I have the honor to remain, Your humble servant,	Same as formal close.	The Most Reverend The Archbishop.
My Dear Bishop Manning:	I have the honor to remain, Your obedient servant, or, to remain, Respectfully yours,	Faithfully yours,	Bishop Manning.
Dear Father Duffy:	I beg to remain, Yours faithfully,	Faithfully yours,	Father Duffy.
Dear Dr. Saintly: (or Dear Mr. Saintly if he is not a D.D.)	Same as above.	Faithfully yours, or Sincerely yours,	Dr. (or Mr.) Saintly
Dear Dr. Wise:	I beg to remain, Yours sincerely,	Yours sincerely,	Rabbi Wise.
Dear Mr. Ambassador:	I have the honor to remain, Yours faithfully, or, Yours very truly, or, Yours respectfully, or very formally: I have the honor to remain, sir, your obedient servant.	Yours faithfully,	The American Ambassador.
Dear Mr. Minister: or Dear Mr. Prince:	Same as above.	Yours faithfully,	Mr. Prince, the American Minister, or merely, The American Minister as everyone is supposed to know his name or find it out.
Dear Mr. Smith:	I beg to remain, Yours very truly,	Faithfully,	Mr. Smith.

countries of the Western Hemisphere, "The United States of America" is always specified by way of courtesy to the Americans of South America.

Foreign persons of title are not included in the foregoing diagram because an American (unless in the Diplomatic Service) would be unlikely to address any but personal friends, to whom he would write as to any others. An envelope would be addressed in the language of the person written to: "His Grace, the Duke of Overthere (or merely The Duke of Overthere), Hyde Park, London"; "Mme. la Princess d'Acacia, Ave. du Bois, Paris"; "Il Principe di Capri, Cusano sul Seveso"; "Lady Alwin, Cragmere, Scotland," etc. The letter would begin, Dear Duke of Overthere (or Dear Duke), Dear Princess, Dear Countess Aix, Dear Lady Alwin, Dear Sir Hubert, etc., and close, "Sincerely," "Faithfully," or "Affectionately," as the case might be.

Should an American have occasion to write to Royalty he would begin: "Madam" (or Sir), and end: "I have the honor to remain, madam (or Sir), your most obedient." ("Your most obedient servant" is a signature reserved usually for our own President—or Vice-President.)

CHAPTER XXVIII

LONGER LETTERS

The art of general letter-writing in the present day is shrinking until the letter threatens to become a telegram, a telephone message, a post-card. Since the events of the day are transmitted in newspapers with far greater accuracy, detail, and dispatch than they could be by the single effort of even Voltaire himself, the circulation of general news, which formed the chief reason for letters of the stage-coach and sailing-vessel days, has no part in the correspondence of to-day.

Taking the contents of an average mail bag as sorted in a United States post-office, about fifty per cent. is probably advertisement or appeal, forty per cent. business, and scarcely ten per cent. personal letters and invitations. Of course, love letters are probably as numerous as need be, though the long distance telephone must have lowered the average of these, too. Young girls write to each other, no doubt, much as they did in olden times, and letters between young girls and young men flourish to-day like unpulled weeds in a garden where weeds were formerly never allowed to grow.

It is the letter from the friend in this city to the friend in that, or from the traveling relative to the relative at home, that is gradually dwindling. As for the letter which younger relatives dutifully used to write—it has gone already with old-fashioned grace of speech and deportment.

Still, people do write letters in this day and there are some who possess the divinely flexible gift for a fresh turn of phrase, for delightful keenness of observation. It may be, too, that in other days the average writing was no better than the average of to-day. It is naturally the letters of those who had unusual gifts which have been preserved all these years, for the failures of a generation are made to die with it, and only its successes survive.

The difference though, between letter-writers of the past and of the present, is that in other days they all tried to write, and to express themselves the very best they knew how—to-day people don't care a bit whether they write well or ill. Mental effort is one thing that the younger generation of the "smart world" seems to consider it unreasonable to ask—and just as it is the fashion to let their spines droop until they suggest nothing so much as Tenniel's drawing in Alice in Wonderland of the cater-pillar sitting on the toad-stool—so do they let their mental faculties relax, slump and atrophy.

To such as these, to whom effort is an insurmountable task, it might be just as well to say frankly: If you have a mind that is entirely bromidic, if you are lacking in humor, all power of observation, and facility for expression, you had best join the ever-growing class of people who frankly confess, "I can't write letters to save my life!" and confine your literary efforts to picture post-cards with the engaging captions "X is my room," or "Beautiful weather, wish you were here."

It is not at all certain that your friends and family would not rather have frequent post-cards than occasional letters all too obviously displaying the meagerness of their messages in halting orthography.

BEGINNING A LETTER

For most people the difficulty in letter-writing is in the beginning and the close. Once they are started, the middle goes smoothly enough, until they face the difficulty of the end. The direction of the Professor of English to "Begin at the beginning of what you have to say, and go on until you have finished, and then stop," is very like a celebrated artist's direction for painting: "You simply take a little of the right color paint and put it on the right spot."

HOW NOT TO BEGIN

Even one who "loves the very sight of your handwriting," could not possibly find any pleasure in a letter beginning:

"I have been meaning to write you for a long time but haven't had a minute to spare."

Or:

"I suppose you have been thinking me very neglectful, but you know how I hate to write letters."

Or:

"I know I ought to have answered your letter sooner, but I haven't had a thing to write about."

The above sentences are written time and again by persons who are utterly unconscious that they are not expressing a friendly or loving thought. If one of your friends were to walk into the room, and you were to receive him stretched out and yawning in an easy chair, no one would have to point out the rudeness of such behavior; yet countless kindly intentioned people begin their letters mentally reclining and yawning in just such a way.

HOW TO BEGIN A LETTER

Suppose you merely change the wording of the above sentences, so that instead of slamming the door in your friend's face, you hold it open:

"Do you think I have forgotten you entirely? You don't know, dear Mary, how many letters I have written you in thought."

Or:

"Time and time again I have wanted to write you but each moment that I saved for myself was always interrupted by—*something.*"

One of the frequent difficulties in beginning a letter is that your answer is so long delayed that you begin with an apology, which is always a lame duck. But these examples indicate a way in which even an opening apology may be attractive rather than repellent. If you are going to take the trouble to write a letter, you are doing it because you have at least remembered some one with friendly regard, or you would not be writing at all. You certainly would like to convey the impression that you want to be with your friend in thought for a little while at least—not that she through some malignant force is holding you to a grindstone and forcing you to the task of making hateful schoolroom pot-hooks for her selfish gain.

A perfect letter has always the effect of being a light dipping off of the top of a spring. A poor letter suggests digging into the dried ink at the bottom of an ink-well.

It is easy to begin a letter if it is in answer to one that has just been received. The news contained in it is fresh and the impulse to reply needs no prodding.

Nothing can be simpler than to say: "We were all overjoyed to hear from you this morning," or, "Your letter was the most welcome thing the postman has brought for ages," or, "It was more than good to have news of you this morning," or, "Your letter from Capri brought all the allure of Italy back to me," or, "You can't imagine. dear Mary, how glad I was to see an envelope with your writing this morning." And then you take up the various subjects in Mary's letter, which should certainly launch you without difficulty upon topics of your own.

ENDING A LETTER

Just as the beginning of a letter should give the reader an impression of greeting, so should the end express friendly or affectionate leave-taking. Nothing can be worse than to seem to scratch helplessly around in the air for an idea that will effect your escape.

"Well, I guess I must stop now," "Well, I must close," or, "You are probably bored with this long epistle, so I had better close."

All of these are as bad as they can be, and suggest the untutored man who stands first on one foot and then on the other, running his finger around the brim of his hat, or the country girl twisting the corner of her apron.

HOW TO END A LETTER

An intimate letter has no end at all. When you leave the house of a member of your family, you don't have to think up an especial sentence in order to say good-by. Leave-taking in a letter is the same:

"Good-by, dearest, for to-day.

Devotedly,

Kate."

Or:

"Best love to you all,

Martin."

Or:

"Will write again in a day or two.

Lovingly,

Mary."

Or:

"Luncheon was announced half a page ago! So good-by, dear Mary, for to-day."

The close of a less intimate letter, like taking leave of a visitor in your drawing-room, is necessarily more ceremonious. And the "ceremonious close" presents to most people the greatest difficulty in letter-writing.

It is really quite simple, if you realize that the aim of the closing paragraph is merely to bring in a personal hyphen between the person writing and the person written to.

"The mountains were beautiful at sunset." It is a bad closing sentence because "the mountains" have nothing personal to either of you. But if you can add "—they reminded me of the time we were in Colorado together," or "—how different from our wide prairies at home," you have crossed a bridge, as it were.

Or:

"We have had a wonderful trip, but I do miss you all at home, and long to hear from you soon again."

Or (from one at home):

"Your closed house makes me very lonely to pass. I do hope you are coming back soon."

Sometimes an ending falls naturally into a sentence that ends with your signature. "If I could look up now and see you coming into the room, there would be no happier woman in the whole State than

Your devoted mother."

LETTERS NO ONE CARES TO READ

LETTERS OF CALAMITY

First and foremost in the category of letters that no one can possibly receive with pleasure might be put the "letter of calamity," the letter of gloomy apprehension, the letter filled with petty annoyances. Less disturbing to receive but far from enjoyable are such letters as "the blank," the "meandering," the "letter of the capital I," the "plaintive," the "apologetic." There is scarcely any one who has not one or more relatives or friends whose letters belong in one of these classes.

Even in so personal a matter as the letter to an absent member of one's immediate family, it should be borne in mind, not to write *needlessly* of misfortune or unhappiness. To hear from those we love how ill or unhappy they are, is to have our distress intensified in direct proportion to the number of miles by which we are separated from them. This last example, however, has nothing in common with the choosing of calamity and gloom as a subject of welcome tidings in ordinary correspondence.

The chronic calamity writers seem to wait until the skies are darkest, and then, rushing to their desk, luxuriate in pouring all their troubles and fears of troubles out on paper to their friends.

LETTERS OF GLOOMY APPREHENSION

"My little Betty ["My little" adds to the pathos much more than saying merely "Betty"] has been feeling miserable for several days. I am worried to death about her, as there are so many sudden cases of typhoid and appendicitis. The doctor says the symptoms are not at all alarming as yet, but doctors see so much of illness and death, they don't seem to appreciate what anxiety means to a mother," etc.

Another writes: "The times seem to be getting worse and worse. I always said we would have to go through a long night before any chance of daylight. You can mark my words, the night of bad times isn't much more than begun."

Or, "I have scarcely slept for nights, worrying about whether Junior has passed his examinations or not."

LETTERS OF PETTY MISFORTUNES

Other perfectly well-meaning friends fancy they are giving pleasure when they write such "news" as: "My cook has been sick for the past ten days," and follow this with a page or two descriptive of her ailments; or, "I have a slight cough. I think I must have caught it yesterday when I went out in the rain without rubbers"; or, "The children have not been doing as well in their lessons this week as last. Johnny's arithmetic marks were dreadful and Katie got an E in spelling and an F in geography." Her husband and her mother would be interested in the children's weekly reports, and her own slight cough, but no one else. How could they be?

If the writers of all such letters would merely read over what they have written, and ask themselves if they could find pleasure in receiving messages of like manner and matter, perhaps they might begin to do a little thinking, and break the habit of cataleptic unthinkingness that seemingly descends upon them as soon as they are seated at their desk.

THE BLANK

The writer of the "blank" letter begins fluently with the date and "Dear Mary," and then sits and chews his penholder or makes little dots and squares and circles on the blotter—utterly unable to attack the cold, forbidding blankness of that first page. Mentally, he seems to say: "Well, here I am—and now what?" He has not an idea! He can never find anything of sufficient importance to write about. A murder next door, a house burned to the ground, a burglary or an elopement could alone furnish material; and that, too, would be finished off in a brief sentence stating the bare fact.

A person whose life is a revolving wheel of routine may have really very little to say, but a letter does not have to be long to be welcome—it can be very good indeed if it has a message that seems to have been spoken.

Dear Lucy:

"Life here is as dull as ever—duller if anything. Just the same old things done in the same old way—not even a fire engine out or a new face in town, but this is to show you that I am thinking of you and longing to hear from you."

Or:

"I wish something really exciting would happen so that I might have something with a little thrill in it to write you, but everything goes on and on—if there were any check in its sameness, I think we'd all land in a heap against the edge of the town."

THE MEANDERING LETTER

As its name implies, the meandering letter is one which dawdles through disconnected subjects, like a trolley car gone down grade off the track, through fences and fields and flower-beds indiscriminately. "Mrs. Blake's cow died last week, the Governor and his wife were on the Reception Committee; Mary Selfridge went to stay with her aunt in Riverview; I think the new shade called Harding blue is perfectly hideous."

Another that is almost akin to it, runs glibly on, page after page of meaningless repetition and detail. "I thought at first that I would get a gray dress—I think gray is such a pretty color, and I have had so many blue dresses. I can't decide this time whether to get blue or gray. Sometimes I think gray is more becoming to me than blue. I think gray looks well on fair-haired people— I don't know whether you would call my hair fair or not? I am certainly not dark, and yet fair hair suggests a sort of straw color. Maybe I might be called medium fair. Do you think I am light enough to wear gray? Maybe blue would be more serviceable. Gray certainly looks pretty in the spring, it is so clean and fresh looking. There is a lovely French model at Benson's in gray, but I can have it copied for less in blue. Maybe it won't be as pretty though as the gray," etc., etc. By the above method of cud-chewing, any subject, clothes, painting the house, children's school, planting a garden, or even the weather, need be limited only by the supply of paper and ink.

THE LETTER OF THE "CAPITAL I"

The letter of the "capital I" is a pompous effusion which strives through pretentiousness to impress its reader with its writer's wealth, position, ability, or whatever possession or attribute is thought to be rated most highly. None but unfortunate dependents or the cringing in spirit would subject themselves to a second letter of this kind by answering the first. The letter which hints at hoped-for benefits is no worse!

THE LETTER OF CHRONIC APOLOGY

The letter written by a person with an apologetic habit of mind, is different totally from the sometimes necessary letter of genuine apology. The former is as senseless as it is irritating:

"It was so good of you to come to my horrid little shanty. [The house and the food she served were both probably better than that of the person she is writing to.] I know you had nothing fit to eat, and I know that everything was just all wrong! Of course, everything is always so beautifully done at everything you give, I wonder I have the courage to ask you to dine with me."

THE DANGEROUS LETTER

A pitfall that those of sharp wit have to guard against is the thoughtless tendency toward writing ill-natured things. Ridicule is a much more amusing medium for the display of a subject than praise, which is always rather bromidic. The amusing person catches foibles and exploits them, and it is easy to forget that wit flashes all too irresistibly at the expense of other people's feelings, and the brilliant tongue is all too often sharpened to rapier point. Admiration for the quickness of a spoken quip, somewhat mitigates its cruelty. The exuberance of the retailer of verbal gossip eliminates the implication of scandal, but both quip and gossip become deadly poison when transferred permanently to paper.

PERMANENCE OF WRITTEN EMOTION

For all emotions written words are a bad medium. The light jesting tone that saves a quip from offense can not be expressed; and remarks that if spoken would amuse, can but pique and even insult their subject. Without the interpretation of the voice, gaiety becomes levity, raillery becomes accusation. Moreover, words of a passing moment are made to stand forever.

Anger in a letter carries with it the effect of solidified fury; the words spoken in reproof melt with the breath of the speaker once the cause is forgiven. The written words on the page fix them for eternity.

Love in a letter endures likewise forever.

Admonitions from parents to their children may very properly be put on paper—they are meant to endure, and be remembered, but momentary annoyance should never be more than briefly expressed. There is no better way of insuring his letters against being read than for a parent to get into the habit of writing irritable or fault-finding letters to his children.

THE LETTERS OF TWO WIVES

Do you ever see a man look through a stack of mail, and notice that suddenly his face lights up as he seizes a letter "from home"? He tears it open eagerly, his mouth up-curving at the corners, as he lingers over every word. You know, without being told, that the wife he had to leave behind puts all the best she can devise and save for him into his life as well as on paper!

Do you ever see a man go through his mail and see him suddenly droop—as though a fog had fallen upon his spirits? Do you see him reluctantly pick out a letter, start to open it, hesitate and then push it aside? His expression says plainly: "I can't face that just now." Then by and by, when his lips have been set in a hard line, he will doggedly open his letter to "see what the trouble is now."

If for once there is no trouble, he sighs with relief, relaxes, and starts the next thing he has to do.

Usually, though, he frowns, looks worried, annoyed, harassed, and you know that every small unpleasantness is punctiliously served to him by one who promised to love and to cherish and who probably thinks she does!

THE LETTER EVERYONE LOVES TO RECEIVE

The letter we all love to receive is one that carries so much of the writer's personality that she seems to be sitting beside us, looking at us directly and talking just as she really would, could she have come on a magic carpet, instead of sending her proxy in ink-made characters on mere paper.

Let us suppose we have received one of those perfect letters from Mary, one of those letters that seem almost to have written themselves, so easily do the words flow, so bubbling and effortless is their spontaneity. There is a great deal in the letter about Mary, not only about what she has been doing, but what she has been thinking, or perhaps, feeling. And there is a lot about us in the letter —nice things, that make us feel rather pleased about something that we have done, or are likely to do, or that some one has said about us. We know that all things of concern to us are of equal concern to Mary, and though there will be nothing of it in actual words, we are made to feel that we are just as secure in our corner of Mary's heart as ever we were. And we finish the letter with a very vivid remembrance of Mary's sympathy, and a sense of loss in her absence, and a longing for the time when Mary herself may again be sitting on the sofa beside us and telling us all the details her letter can not but leave out.

THE LETTER NO WOMAN SHOULD EVER WRITE

The mails carry letters every day that are so many packages of TNT should their contents be exploded by falling into wrong hands. Letters that should never have been written are put in evidence in court rooms every day. Many can not, under any circumstances, be excused; but often silly girls and foolish women write things that sound quite different from what they innocently, but stupidly, intended.

Few persons, except professional writers, have the least idea of the value of words and the effect that they produce, and the thoughtless letters of emotional women and underbred men add sensation to news items in the press almost daily.

Of course the best advice to a young girl who is impelled to write letters to men, can be put in one word, *don't!*

However, if you are a young girl or woman, and are determined to write letters to an especial—or any other—man, no matter how innocent your intention may be, there are some things you must remember—remember so intensely that no situation in life, no circumstances, no temptation, can ever make you forget. They are a few set rules, not of etiquette, but of the laws of self-respect:

Never send a letter without reading it over and making sure that you have said nothing that can possibly "sound different" from what you intend to say.

Never so long as you live, write a letter to a man—no matter who he is—that you would be ashamed to see in a newspaper above your signature.

Remember that every word of writing is immutable evidence for or against you, and words which are thoughtlessly put on paper may exist a hundred years hence.

Never write anything that can be construed as sentimental.

Never take a man to task about anything; never ask for explanations; to do so implies too great an intimacy.

Never put a single clinging tentacle into writing. Say nothing ever, that can be construed as demanding, asking, or even being eager for, his attentions!

Always keep in mind and *never for one instant forget* that a third person, and that the very one you would most object to, may find and read the letter.

One word more: It is not alone "bad form" but laying yourself open to every sort of embarrassment and danger, to "correspond with" a man you slightly know.

PROPER LETTERS OF LOVE OR AFFECTION

If you are engaged, of course you should write love letters—the most beautiful that you can—but don't write baby-talk and other sillinesses that would make you feel idiotic if the letter were to fall into strange hands.

On the other hand, few can find objection to the natural, friendly and even affectionate letter from a young girl to a young man she has been "brought up" with. It is such a letter as she would write to her brother. There is no hint of coquetry or self-consciousness, no word from first to last that might not be shouted aloud before her whole family. Her letter may begin "Dear——" or even "Dearest Jack." Then follows all the "home news" she can think of that might possibly interest him; about the Simpsons' dance, Tom and Pauline's engagement, how many trout Bill Henderson got at Duck Brook, how furious Mrs. Davis was because some distinguished visitor accepted Mrs. Brown's dinner instead of hers, how the new people who have moved onto the Rush farm don't know the first thing about farming, and so on.

Perhaps there will be one "personal" line such as "we all missed you at the picnic on Wednesday—Ollie made the flap-jacks and they were too awful! Every one groaned: 'If Jack were only here!'" Or, "we all hope you are coming back in time for the Towns' dance. Kate has at last inveigled her mother into letting her have an all-black dress which we rather suspect was bought with the especial purpose of impressing you with her advanced age and dignity! Mother came in just as I wrote this and says to tell you she has a new recipe for chocolate cake that is even better than her old one, and that you had better have a piece added to your belt before you come home. Carrie will write you very soon, she says, and we all send love.

"Affectionately,

"Ruth."

THE LETTER NO GENTLEMAN WRITES

One of the fundamental rules for the behavior of any man who has the faintest pretension to being a gentleman, is that never by word or gesture must he compromise a woman; he never, therefore, writes a letter that can be construed, even by a lawyer, as damaging to any woman's good name.

His letters to an unmarried woman may express all the ardor and devotion that he cares to subscribe to, but there must be no hint of his having received especial favors from her.

DON'TS FOR CORRESPONDENCE

Never typewrite an invitation, acceptance, or regret.

Never typewrite a social note.

Be chary of underscorings and postcripts.

Do not write across a page already written on.

Do not use unmatched paper and envelopes.

Do not write in pencil—except a note to one of your family written on a train or where ink is unprocurable, or unless you are flat on your back because of illness.

Never send a letter with a blot on it.

Never sprinkle French, Italian, or any other foreign words through a letter written in English. You do not give an impression of cultivation, but of ignorance of your own language. Use a foreign word if it has no English equivalent, not otherwise unless it has become Anglicized. If hesitating between two words, always select the one of Saxon origin rather than Latin. For the best selection of words to use, study the King James version of the Bible.

CHAPTER XXIX

THE FUNDAMENTALS OF GOOD BEHAVIOR

Far more important than any mere dictum of etiquette is the fundamental code of honor, without strict observance of which no man, no matter how "polished," can be considered a gentleman. The honor of a gentleman demands the inviolability of his word, and the incorruptibility of his principles; he is the descendant of the knight, the crusader; he is the defender of the defenseless, and the champion of justice—or he is not a gentleman.

DECENCIES OF BEHAVIOR

A gentleman does not, and a man who aspires to be one must not, ever borrow money from a woman, nor should he, except in unexpected circumstances, borrow money from a man. Money borrowed without security is a debt of honor which must be paid without fail and promptly as possible. The debts incurred by a deceased parent, brother, sister, or grown child, are assumed by honorable men and women, as debts of honor.

A gentleman never takes advantage of a woman in a business dealing, nor of the poor or the helpless.

One who is not well off does not "sponge," but pays his own way to the utmost of his ability.

One who is rich does not make a display of his money or his possessions. Only a vulgarian talks ceaselessly about how much this or that cost him.

A very well-bred man intensely dislikes the mention of money, and never speaks of it (out of business hours) if he can avoid it.

A gentleman never discusses his family affairs either in public or with acquaintances, nor does he speak more than casually about his wife. A man is a cad who tells anyone, no matter who, what his wife told him in confidence, or describes what she looks like in her bedroom. To impart details of her beauty is scarcely better than to publish her blemishes; to do either is unspeakable.

Nor does a gentleman ever criticise the behavior of a wife whose conduct is scandalous. What he says to her in the privacy of their own apartments is no one's affair but his own, but he must never treat her with disrespect before their children, or a servant, or any one.

A man of honor never seeks publicly to divorce his wife, no matter what he believes her conduct to have been; but for the protection of his own name, and that of the children, he allows her to get her freedom on other than criminal grounds. No matter who he may be, whether rich or poor, in high life or low, the man who publicly besmirches his wife's name, besmirches still more his own, and proves that he is not, was not, and never will be, a gentleman.

No gentleman goes to a lady's house if he is affected by alcohol. A gentleman seeing a young man who is not entirely himself in the presence of ladies, quietly induces the youth to depart. An older man addicted to the use of too much alcohol, need not be discussed, since he ceases to be asked to the houses of ladies.

A gentleman does not lose control of his temper. In fact, in his own self-control under difficult or dangerous circumstances, lies his chief ascendancy over others who impulsively betray every emotion which animates them. Exhibitions of anger, fear, hatred, embarrassment, ardor or hilarity, are all bad form in public. And bad form is merely an action which "jars" the sensibilities of others. A gentleman does not show a letter written by a lady, unless perhaps to a very intimate friend if the letter is entirely impersonal and written by some one who is equally the friend of the one to whom it is shown. But the occasions when the letter of a woman may be shown properly by a man are so few that it is safest to make it a rule never to mention a woman's letter.

A gentleman does not bow to a lady from a club window; nor according to good form should ladies ever be discussed in a man's club!

A man whose social position is self-made is apt to be detected by his continual cataloguing of prominent names. Mr. Parvenu invariably interlards his conversation with, "When I was dining at the Bobo Gildings'"; or even "at Lucy Gilding's," and quite often accentuates, in his ignorance, those of rather second-rate, though conspicuous position. "I was spending last week-end with the Richan Vulgars," or "My great friends, the Gotta Crusts." When a so-called gentleman insists on imparting information, interesting only to the Social Register, *shun him!*

The born gentleman avoids the mention of names exactly as he avoids the mention of what things cost; both are an abomination to his soul.

A gentleman's manners are an integral part of him and are the same whether in his dressing-room or in a ballroom, whether in talking to Mrs. Worldly or to the laundress bringing in his clothes. He whose manners are only put on in company is a veneered gentleman, not a real one.

A man of breeding does not slap strangers on the back nor so much as lay his finger-tips on a lady. Nor does he punctuate his conversation by pushing or nudging or patting people, nor take his conversation out of the drawing-room! Notwithstanding the advertisements in the most dignified magazines, a discussion of underwear and toilet articles and their merit or their use, is unpleasant in polite conversation.

All thoroughbred people are considerate of the feelings of others no matter what the station of the others may be. Thackeray's climber who "licks the boots of those above him and kicks the faces of those below him on the social ladder," is a very good illustration of what a gentleman is *not.*

A gentleman never takes advantage of another's helplessness or ignorance, and assumes that no gentleman will take advantage of him.

SIMPLICITY AND UNCONSCIOUSNESS OF SELF

These words have been literally sprinkled through the pages of this book, yet it is doubtful if they convey a clear idea of the attributes meant.

Unconsciousness of self is not so much unselfishness as it is the mental ability to extinguish all thought of one's self—exactly as one turns out the light.

Simplicity is like it, in that it also has a quality of self-effacement, but it really means a love of the essential and of directness. Simple people put no trimmings on their phrases, nor on their manners; but remember, simplicity is not crudeness nor anything like it. On the contrary, simplicity of speech and manners means language in its purest, most limpid form, and manners of such perfection that they do not suggest "manner" at all.

THE INSTINCTS OF A LADY

The instincts of a lady are much the same as those of a gentleman. She is equally punctilious about her debts, equally averse to pressing her advantage; especially if her adversary is helpless or poor.

As an unhappy wife, her dignity demands that she never show her disapproval of her husband, no matter how publicly he slights or outrages her. If she has been so unfortunate as to have married a man not a gentleman, to draw attention to his behavior would put herself on his level. If it comes actually to the point where she divorces him, she discusses her situation, naturally, with her parents or her brother or whoever are her nearest and wisest relatives, but she shuns publicity and avoids discussing her affairs with any one outside of her immediate family. One can not too strongly censure the unspeakable vulgarity of the woman so unfortunate as to be obliged to go through divorce proceedings, who confides the private details of her life to reporters.

THE HALL-MARK OF THE CLIMBER

Nothing so blatantly proclaims a woman climber as the repetition of prominent names, the owners of which she must have struggled to know. Otherwise, why so eagerly boast of the achievement? Nobody cares whom she knows—nobody that is, but a climber like herself. To those who were born and who live, no matter how quietly, in the security of a perfectly good ledge above and away from the social ladder's rungs, the evidence of one frantically climbing and trying to vaunt her exalted position is merely ludicrous.

All thoroughbred women, and men, are considerate of others less fortunately placed, especially of those in their employ. One of the tests by which to distinguish between the woman of breeding and the woman merely of wealth, is to notice the way she speaks to dependents. Queen Victoria's duchesses, those great ladies of grand manner, were the very ones who, on entering the house of a close friend, said "How do you do, Hawkins?" to a butler; and to a sister duchess's maid, "Good morning, Jenkins." A Maryland lady, still living on the estate granted to her family three generations before the Revolution, is quite as polite to her friends' servants as to her friends themselves. When you see a woman in silks and sables and diamonds speak to a little errand girl or a footman or a scullery maid as though they were the dirt under her feet, you may be sure of one thing; she hasn't come a very long way from the ground herself.

CHAPTER XXX

CLUBS AND CLUB ETIQUETTE

A club, as every one knows, is merely an organization of people—men or women or both—who establish club rooms, in which they meet at specified times for specified purposes, or which they use casually and individually. A club's membership may be limited to a dozen or may include several thousands, and the procedure in joining a club may be easy or difficult, according to the type of club and the standing of the would-be member.

Membership in many athletic associations may be had by walking in and paying dues; also many country golf-clubs are as free to the public as country inns; but joining a purely social club of rank and exclusiveness is a very different matter. A man to be eligible for membership in such a club must not only be completely a gentleman, but he must have friends among the members who like him enough to be willing to propose him and second him and write letters for him; and furthermore he must be disliked by no one—at least not sufficiently for any member to object seriously to his company.

There are two ways of joining a club; by invitation and by making application or having it made for you. To join by invitation means that you are invited when the club is started to be one of the founders or charter members, or if you are a distinguished citizen you may at the invitation of the governors become an honorary member, or in a small or informal club you may become an ordinary member by invitation or suggestion of the governors that you would be welcome. A charter member pays dues, but not always an initiation fee; an honorary member pays neither dues nor initiation, he is really a permanent guest of the club. A life member is one who pays his dues for twenty years or so in a lump sum, and is exempted from dues even if he lives to be a hundred. Few clubs have honorary members and none have more than half a dozen, so that this type of membership may as well be disregarded.

The ordinary members of a club are either resident, meaning that they live within fifty miles of the club; or non-resident, living beyond that distance and paying less dues but having the same privileges.

In certain of the London clubs, one or two New York ones, and the leading club in several other cities, it is not unusual for a boy's name to be put up for membership as soon as he is born. If his name comes up while he is a minor, it is laid aside until after his twenty-first birthday and then put at the head of the list of applicants and voted upon at the next meeting of the governors.

In all clubs in which membership is limited and much sought after, the waiting list is sure to be long and a name takes anywhere from five to more than ten years to come up.

HOW A NAME IS "PUT UP"

Since a gentleman is scarcely likely to want to join a club in which the members are not his friends, he tells a member of his family, or an intimate friend, that he would like to join the Nearby Club, and adds, "Do you mind putting me up? I will ask Dick to second me." The friend says, "I'll be very glad to," and Dick says the same. It is still more likely that the suggestion to join comes from a friend, who says one day, "Why don't you join the Nearby Club? It would be very convenient for you." The other says, "I think I should like to," and the first replies, "Let me put you up, and Dick will be only too glad to second you."

It must be remembered that a gentleman has no right to ask any one who is not really one of his best friends to propose or second him. It is an awkward thing to refuse in the first place, and in the second it involves considerable effort, and on occasion a great deal of annoyance and trouble.

For example let us suppose that Jim Smartlington asks Donald Lovejoy to propose him and Clubwin Doe to second him.   His name is written in the book kept for the purpose and signed by both proposer and seconder:

Smartlington, James

> Proposer: Donald Lovejoy
> Seconder: Clubwin Doe

Nothing more is done until the name is posted—meaning that it appears among a list of names put up on the bulletin-board in the club house.   It is then the duty of Lovejoy and Doe each to write a letter of endorsement to the governors of the club, to be read by them when they hold the meeting at which his name comes up for election.

Example:

Board of Governors,
The Nearby Club.
Dear sirs:

It affords me much pleasure to propose for membership in the Nearby Club Mr. James Smartlington.   I have known Mr. Smartlington for many years and consider him qualified in every way for membership.

He is a graduate of Yalvard, class 1916, rowed on the Varsity crew, and served in the 180th, as 1st Lieut., overseas during the war.   He is now in his father's firm (Jones, Smartlington & Co.).

> Yours very truly,
> Donald Lovejoy.

Lovejoy must also at once tell Smartlington to ask about six friends who are club-members (but not governors) to write letters endorsing him.   Furthermore, the candidate can not come up for election unless he knows several of the governors personally, who can vouch for him at the meeting. Therefore Lovejoy and Doe must one or the other take Smartlington to several governors (at their offices generally) and personally present him, or very likely they invite two or three of the governors and Smartlington to lunch.

Even under the best of circumstances it is a nuisance for a busy man to have to make appointments at the offices of other busy men. And since it is uncertain which of the governors will be present at any particular meeting, it is necessary to introduce the candidate to a sufficient number so that at least two among those at the meeting will be able to speak for him.

In the example we have chosen, Clubwin Doe, having himself been a governor and knowing most of the present ones very well, has less difficulty in presenting his candidate to them than many other members might have, who, though they have for years belonged to the club, have used it so seldom that they know few, if any, of the governors even by sight.

At the leading woman's club of New York, the governors appoint an hour on several afternoons before elections when they are in the visitors' rooms at the club house on purpose to meet the candidates whom their proposers must present. This would certainly seem a more practicable method, to say nothing of its being easier for everyone concerned, than the masculine etiquette which requires that the governors be stalked one by one, to the extreme inconvenience and loss of time and occasionally the embarrassment of every one.

As already said, Jim Smartlington, having unusually popular and well-known sponsors and being also very well liked himself, is elected with little difficulty.

But take the case of young Breezy: He was put up by two not well-known members, who wrote half-hearted endorsements themselves and did nothing about getting letters from others; they knew none of the governors, and trusted that two who knew Breezy slightly "would do." His casual proposer forgot that enemies write letters as well as friends—and that moreover enmity is active where friendship is often passive. Two men who disliked his "manner" wrote that they considered him "unsuitable," and as he had no friends strong enough to stand up for him, he was turned down. A gentleman is rarely "black-balled," as such an action could not fail to injure him in the eyes of the world. (The expression "black ball" comes from the custom of voting for a member by putting a white ball in a ballot box, or against him by putting in a black one.) If a candidate is likely to receive a black ball, the governors do not vote on him at all, but inform the proposer that the name of his candidate would better be withdrawn. Later on, if the objection to him is disproved or overcome, his name can again be put up.

The more popular the candidate, the less work there is for his proposer and seconder. A stranger—if he is not a member of the representative club in his own city—would have need of strong friends to elect him to an exclusive one in another, and an unpopular man has no chance at all.

However, in all except very rare instances events run smoothly; the candidate is voted on at a meeting of the board of governors and is elected.

A notice is mailed to him next morning, telling him that he has been elected and that his initiation fee and his dues make a total of so much. The candidate thereupon at once draws his check for the amount and mails it. As soon as the secretary has had ample time to receive the check, the new member is free to use the club as much or as little as he cares to.

THE NEW MEMBER

The new member usually, but not necessarily, goes for the first time to a club with his proposer or his seconder, or at least an old member; for since in exclusive clubs visitors living in the same city are never given the privilege of the club, none but members can know their way about. Let us say he goes for lunch or dinner, at which be is host, and his friend imparts such unwritten information as: "That chair in the window is where old Gotrox always sits; don't occupy it when you see him coming in or he will be disagreeable to everybody for a week." Or "They always play double stakes at this table, so don't sit at it, unless you *mean* to." Or "That's Double coming in now, avoid him at bridge as you would the plague." "The roasts are always good and that waiter is the best in the room," etc.

A new member is given—or should ask for—a copy of the Club Book, which contains besides the list of the members, the constitution and the by-laws or "house rules," which he must study carefully and be sure to obey.

COUNTRY CLUBS

Country clubs are as a rule less exclusive and less expensive than the representative city clubs, but those like the Myopia Hunt, the Tuxedo, the Saddle and Cycle, the Burlingame, and countless others in between, are many of them more expensive to belong to than any clubs in London or New York, and are precisely the same in matters of membership and management. They are also quite as difficult to be elected to as any of the exclusive clubs in the cities—more so if anything, because they are open to the family and friends of every member, whereas in a man's club in a city his membership gives the privilege of the club to no one but himself personally. The test question always put by the governors at elections is: "Are the candidate's friends as well as his family likely to be agreeable to the present members of the Club?" If not, he is not admitted.

Nearly all country clubs have, however, one open door —unknown to city ones. People taking houses in the neighborhood are often granted "season privileges"; meaning that on being proposed by a member and upon paying a season subscription, new householders are accepted as transient guests. In some clubs this season subscription may be indefinitely renewed; in others a man must come up for regular election at the end of three months or six or a year.

Apart from what may be called the few representative and exclusive country clubs, there are hundreds—more likely thousands—which have very simple requirements for membership. The mere form of having one or two members vouch for a candidate's integrity and good behavior is sufficient.

Golf clubs, hunting clubs, political or sports clubs have special membership qualifications; all good golf players are as a rule welcomed at all golf clubs; all huntsmen at hunting clubs, and yet the Myopia would not think of admitting the best rider ever known if he was not unquestionably a gentleman. But this is unusual. As a rule, the great player is welcomed in any club specially devoted to the sport in which he excels.

In many clubs a stranger may be given a three (sometimes it is six) months' transient membership, available in some instances to foreigners only; in others to strangers living beyond a certain distance. A name is proposed and seconded by two members and then voted on by the governors, or the house committee.

The best known and most distinguished club of New England has an "Annex" in which there are dining-rooms to which ladies as well as gentlemen who are not members are admitted, and this annex plan has since been followed by others elsewhere.

All men's clubs have private dining-rooms in which members can give stag dinners, but the representative men's clubs exclude ladies absolutely from ever crossing their thresholds.

WOMEN'S CLUBS

Excepting that the luxurious women's club has an atmosphere that a man rarely knows how to give to the interior of a house, no matter how architecturally perfect it may be, there is no difference between women's and men's clubs.

In every State of the Union there are women's clubs of every kind and grade; social, political, sports, professional; some housed in enormous and perfect buildings constructed for them, and some perhaps in only a room or two.

When the pioneer women's club of New York was started, a club that aspired to be in the same class as the most important men's club, various governors of the latter were unflatteringly outspoken; women could not possibly run a club as it should be run—it was unthinkable that they should be foolish enough to attempt it! And the husbands and fathers of the founders expected to have to dig down in their pockets to make up the deficit; forgetting entirely that the running of a club is merely the running of a house on a large scale, and that women, not men, are the perfect housekeepers. To-day, no clubs anywhere are more perfect in appointment or better run than the representative women's clubs. In fact, some of the men's clubs have been forced to follow the lead of the foremost of them and to realize that a club in which members merely sit about and look out of the window is a pretty dull place to the type of younger members they most want to attract, and that the combination of the comfort and smartness of a perfectly run private house with every equipment for athletics, is becoming the ideal in club-life and club-building to-day.

GOOD MANNERS IN CLUBS

Good manners in clubs are the same as good manners elsewhere—only a little more so. A club is for the pleasure and convenience of many; it is never intended as a stage-setting for a "star" or "clown" or "monologist." There is no place where a person has greater need of restraint and consideration for the reserves of others than in a club. In every club there is a reading-room or library where conversation is not allowed; there are books and easy chairs and good light for reading both by day and night; and it is one of the unbreakable rules not to speak to anybody who is reading—or writing.

When two people are sitting by themselves and talking, another should on no account join them unless he is an intimate friend of both. To be a mere acquaintance, or, still less, to have been introduced to one of them, gives no privilege whatever.

The fact of being a club member does not (except in a certain few especially informal clubs) grant any one the right to speak to strangers. If a new member happens to find no one in the club whom he knows, he goes about his own affairs. He either sits down and reads or writes, or "looks out of the window," or plays solitaire, or occupies himself as he would if he were alone in a hotel.

It is courteous of a governor or habitual member, on noticing a new member or a visitor, especially one who seems to be rather at a loss—to go up and speak to him, but the latter must on no account be the one to speak first. Certain New York and Boston clubs, as well as those of London, have earned a reputation for snobbishness because the members never speak to those they do not know. Through no intent to be disagreeable, but just because it is not customary, New York people do not speak to those they do not know, and it does not occur to them that strangers feel slighted until they themselves are given the same medicine in London; or going elsewhere in America, they appreciate the courtesy and kindness of the South and West.

The fundamental rule for behavior in a club is the same as in the drawing-room of a private house. In other words, heels have no place on furniture, ashes belong in ash-receivers, books should not be abused, and all evidence of exercising should be confined to the courts or courses and the locker room. Many people who wouldn't think of lolling around the house in unfit attire, come trooping into country clubs with their steaming faces, clammy shirts, and rumpled hair, giving too awful evidence of recent exertion, and present fitness for the bathtub.

THE PERFECT CLUBMAN

The perfect clubman is another word for the perfect gentleman. He never allows himself to show irritability to any one, he makes it a point to be courteous to a new member or an old member's guest. He scrupulously observes the rules of the club, he discharges his card debts at the table, he pays his share always, with an instinctive horror of sponging, and lastly, he treats everyone with the same consideration which he expects—and demands—from them.

THE INFORMAL CLUB

The informal club is often more suggestive of a fraternity than a club, in that every member speaks to every other—always. In one of the best known of this type, the members are artists, authors, scientists, sportsmen and other thinkers and doers. There is a long table set every day for lunch at which the members gather and talk, every one to every one else. There is another dining-room where solitary members may sit by themselves or bring in outsiders if they care to. None but members sit at the "round" table which isn't "round" in the least!

The informal club is always a comparatively small one, but the method of electing members varies. In some, it is customary to take the vote of the whole club, in others members are elected by the governors first, and then asked to join. In this case no man may ask to have his name put up. In others the conventional methods are followed.

THE VISITORS IN A CLUB

In every club in the United States a member is allowed to "introduce" a stranger (living at least fifty miles away) for a length of time varying with the by-laws of the club. In some clubs guests may be put up for a day only, in others the privilege extends for two weeks or more.

Many clubs allow each member a certain number of visitors a year; in others visitors are unlimited. But in all city clubs the same guest can not be introduced twice within the year. In country clubs visitors may always be brought in by members in unlimited numbers.

As a rule when a member introduces a stranger, he takes him to the club personally, writes his name in the visitors' book, and introduces him to those who may be in the room at the time—very possibly asking another member whom he knows particularly well to "look out" for his guest. If for some reason it is not possible for the stranger's host to take him to the club, he writes to the secretary of the club for a card of introduction.

Example:

Secretary,
The Town Club.

Dear Sir:

Kindly send Mr. A. M. Strangleigh a card extending the privileges of the Club for one week.
Mr. Strangleigh is a resident of London.

Yours very truly,
Clubwin Doe.

The secretary then sends a card to Mr. Strangleigh:

The Town Club

Extends its privileges to

Mr. *Strangleigh*

from *Jan. 7.* **to** *Jan. 14.*

Through the courtesy of

Mr. *Clubwin Doe*

Mr. Strangleigh goes to the club by himself. A visitor who has been given the privileges of the club has, during the time of his visit, all the rights of a member excepting that he is not allowed to introduce others to the club, and he can not give a dinner in the private dining-room. Strict etiquette also demands, if he wishes to ask

several members to dine with him, that he take them to
a restaurant rather than into the club dining-room, since
the club is their home and he is a stranger in it. He may
ask a member whom he knows well to lunch with him in
the club rooms, but he must not ask one whom he knows
only slightly. As accounts are sent to the member who
put him up—unless the guest arranges at the club's office
to have his charges rendered to himself, he must be punctilious to ask for his bill upon leaving, and pay it *without
question*.

Putting a man up at a club never means that the member is "host." The visitor's status throughout his stay
is founded on the courtesy of the member who introduced
him, and he should try to show an equal courtesy to every
one about him. He should remember not to obtrude on
the privacy of the members he does not know. He has
no right to criticise the management, the rules or the organization of the club. He has, in short, no actual rights
at all, and he must not forget that he hasn't!

CLUB ETIQUETTE IN LONDON, PARIS AND NEW YORK

"In a very smart London club" (the words quoted are
Clubwin Doe's) "you keep your hat on and glare about!
In Paris you take your hat off and behave with such courtesy and politeness as seems to you an affectation. In
New York you take your hat off and behave as though the
rooms were empty; but as though you were being observed
through loop-holes in the walls."

In New York you are introduced occasionally, but you
may never ask to be introduced, and you speak only to
those you have been introduced to. In London, you are
never introduced to any one, but if the member who has
taken you with him joins a group and you all sit down
together, you talk as you would after dinner in a gentleman's house. But if you are made a temporary member
and meet those you have been talking to when you are
alone the next day, you do not speak unless spoken to.
In Paris, your host punctiliously introduces you to various

members and you must just as punctiliously go the next day to their houses and leave your card upon each one! This is customary in the strictly French clubs only. In any one which has members of other nationalities—especially with Americans predominating, or seeming to, American customs obtain. In French clubs a visitor can not go to the club unless he is with a member, but there are no restrictions on the number of times he may be taken by the same member or another one.

UNBREAKABLE RULES

Failure to pay one's debts, or behavior unbefitting a gentleman, is cause for expulsion from every club; which is looked upon in much the same light as expulsion from the Army. In certain cases expulsion for debt may seem unfair, since one may find himself in unexpectedly straitened circumstances, and the greatest fault or crime could not be more severely dealt with than being expelled from his club; but "club honor"—except under very temporary and mitigating conditions—takes no account of any reason for being "unable" to meet his obligations. He *must*— or he is not considered honorable.

If a man can not afford to belong to a club he must resign while he is still "in good standing." If later on he is able to rejoin, his name is put at the head of the waiting list, and if he was considered a desirable member, he is re-elected at the next meeting of the governors. But a man who has been expelled (unless he can show cause why his expulsion was unjust and be re-instated) can never again belong to that, or be elected to any other, club.

Chapter XXXI

GAMES AND SPORTS

The popularity of bridge whist began a quarter of a century ago with the older people and has increased slowly but steadily until it is scarcely an exaggeration to say that those who do not play bridge, which means "auction," are seldom asked out. And the epidemic is just as widespread among girls and boys as among older people. Bridge is always taken seriously; a bumble puppy game won't do at all, even among the youngest players, and other qualifications of character and of etiquette must be observed by every one who would be sought after to "make up a four."

PEOPLE CHARMING TO PLAY BRIDGE WITH

That no one likes a poor partner—or even a poor opponent—goes without saying.

The ideal partner is one who never criticises or even seems to be aware of your mistakes, but on the contrary recognizes a good maneuver on your part, and gives you credit for it whether you win the hand or lose; whereas the inferior player is apt to judge you merely by what you win, and blame your "make" if you "go down," though your play may have been exceptionally good and the loss even occasioned by wrong information which he himself gave you. Also, to be continually found fault with makes you play your worst; whereas appreciation of good judgment on your part acts as a tonic and you play seemingly "better than you know how."

PEOPLE DISLIKED AT THE BRIDGE TABLE

There is nothing which more quickly reveals the veneered gentleman than the card table, and his veneer melts equally with success or failure. Being carried away by the game, he forgets to keep on his company polish, and if he wins, he becomes grasping or overbearing, because of his "skill"; if he loses he sneers at the "luck" of others and seeks to justify himself for the same fault that he criticised a moment before in another.

A trick that is annoying to moderately skilled players, is to have an over-confident opponent throw down his hand saying: "The rest of the tricks are mine!" and often succeed in "putting it over," when it is quite possible that they might not be his if the hand were played out. Knowing themselves to be poorer players, the others are apt not to question it, but they feel none the less that their "rights" have been taken from them.

A rather trying partner is the nervous player, who has no confidence in his own judgment and will invariably pass a good hand in favor of his partner's bid. If, for instance, he has six perfectly good diamonds, he doesn't mention them because, his partner having declared a heart, he thinks to himself "Her hearts must be better than my diamonds." But a much more serious failing—and one that is far more universal—is the habit of overbidding.

OVERBIDDING

In poker you play alone and can therefore play as carefully or as foolishly as you please, but in bridge your partner has to suffer with you, and you therefore are in honor bound to play the best you know how—and the best you know how is as far as can possibly be from overbidding.

Remember that your partner, if he is a good player, counts on you for certain definite cards that you announce by your bid to be in your hand, and raises you accordingly. If you have not these cards you not only lose that particular hand, but destroy his confidence in you, and the next time when he has a legitimate raise for you, he will fail to give it. He disregards you entirely because he is afraid of you! You *must study the rules for makes* and *never under any circumstances give your partner misinformation;* this is the most vital rule there is, and any one who disregards it is detested at the bridge table. No matter how great the temptation to make a gambler's bid, you are in honor bound to refrain.

The next essential, if you would be thought "charming," is never to take your partner to task no matter how stupidly he may have "thrown the hand."

DON'TS FOR THOSE WHO WOULD BE SOUGHT AFTER

Don't hold a "post-mortem" on anybody's delinquencies (unless you are actually teaching).

If luck is against you, it will avail nothing to sulk or complain about the "awful" cards you are holding. Your partner is suffering just as much in finding you a "poison vine" as you are in being one—and you can scarcely expect your opponents to be sympathetic. You must learn to look perfectly tranquil and cheerful even though you hold nothing but yarboroughs for days on end, and you must on no account try to defend your own bad play—ever. When you have made a play of poor judgment, the best thing you can say is, "I'm very sorry, partner," and let it go at that.

Always pay close attention to the game. When you are dummy you have certain duties to your partner, and so do not wander around the room until the hand is over. If you don't know what your duties are, read the rules until you know them by heart and then—begin all over again! It is impossible to play any game without a thorough knowledge of the laws that govern it, and you are at fault in making the attempt.

Don't be offended if your partner takes you out of a bid, and don't take him out for the glory of playing the hand. He is quite as anxious to win the rubber as you are. It is unbelievable how many people regard their partner as a third opponent.

MANNERISMS AT THE CARD TABLE

Mannerisms must be avoided like the plague. If there is one thing worse than the horrible "post-mortem," it is the incessant repetition of some jarring habit by one particular player. The most usual and most offensive is that of snapping down a card as played, or bending a "trick" one has taken into a letter "U," or picking it up and trotting it up and down on the table.

Other pet offenses are drumming on the table with one's fingers, making various clicking, whistling, or humming sounds, massaging one's face, scratching one's chin with the cards, or waving the card one is going to play aloft in the air in Smart Alec fashion as though shouting, "I know what you are going to lead! And my card is ready!" All mannerisms that attract attention are in the long run equally unpleasant—even unendurable to one's companions.

Many people whose game is otherwise admirable are rarely asked to play because they have allowed some such silly and annoying habit to take its hold upon them.

THE GOOD LOSER

The good loser makes it an invariable rule never to play for stakes that it will be inconvenient to lose. The neglect of this rule has been responsible for more "bad losers" than anything else, and needless to say a bad loser is about as welcome at a card table as rain at a picnic.

Of course there *are* people who can take losses beyond their means with perfect cheerfulness and composure. Some few are so imbued with the gambler's instinct that a heavy turn of luck, in either direction, is the salt of life. But the average person is equally embarrassed in winning or losing a stake "that matters" and the only answer is to play for one that doesn't.

GOLF

Golf is a particularly severe strain upon the amiability of the average person's temper, and in no other game, except bridge, is serenity of disposition so essential. No one easily "ruffled" can keep a clear eye on the ball, and exasperation at "lost balls" seemingly bewitches successive ones into disappearing with the completeness and finality of puffs of smoke. In a race or other test of endurance a flare of anger might even help, but in golf it is safe to say that he who loses his temper is pretty sure to lose the game.

Golf players of course know the rules and observe them, but it quite often happens that idlers, having nothing better to do, walk out over a course and "watch the players." If they know the players well, that is one thing, but they have no right to follow strangers. A player who is nervous is easily put off his game, especially if those watching him are so ill-bred as to make audible remarks. Those playing matches of course expect an audience, and erratic and nervous players ought not to go into tournaments—or at least not in two-ball foursomes where they are likely to handicap a partner.

In following a match, onlookers must be careful to stand well within bounds and neither talk nor laugh nor do anything that can possibly distract the attention of the players.

The rule that you should not appoint yourself mentor holds good in golf as well as in bridge and every other game. Unless your advice is asked for, you should not instruct others how to hold their clubs or which ones to use, or how they ought to make the shot.

A young woman must on no account expect the man she happens to be playing with to make her presents of golf-balls, or to caddy for her, nor must she allow him to provide her with a caddy. If she can't afford to hire one of her own, she must either carry her own clubs or not play golf.

OTHER GAMES AND SPORTS

There are fixed rules for the playing of every game—and for proper conduct in every sport. The details of these rules must be studied in the "books of the game," learned from instructors, or acquired by experience. A small boy perhaps learns to fish or swim by himself, but he is taught by his father or a guide—at all events, some one—how and how not to hold a gun, cast a fly, or ride a horse. But apart from the technique of each sport, or the rules of each game, the etiquette—or more correctly, the basic principles of good sportsmanship, are the same.

In no sport or game can any favoritism or evasion of rules be allowed. Sport is based upon impersonal and indiscriminating fairness to every one alike, or it is not "sport."

And to *be* a good sportsman, one must be a stoic and never show rancor in defeat, or triumph in victory, or irritation, no matter what annoyance is encountered. One who can not help sulking, or explaining, or protesting when the loser, or exulting when the winner, has no right to take part in games and contests.

"PLAYING THE GAME"

If you would be thought to play the game, meaning if you aspire to be a true sportsman, you must follow the rules of sportsmanship the world over:

Never lose your temper.

Play for the sake of playing rather than to win.

Never stop in the middle of a tennis or golf match and complain of a lame ankle, especially if you are losing. Unless it is literally impossible for you to go on, you *must* stick it out.

If you are a novice, don't ask an expert to play with you, especially as your partner. If he should ask you in spite of your shortcomings, maintain the humility proper to a beginner.

If you are a woman, don't ape the ways and clothing of men. If you are a man, don't take advantage of your superior strength to set a pace beyond the endurance of a woman opponent.

And always give the opponent the benefit of the doubt! Nothing is more important to your standing as a sportsman, though it costs you the particular point in question.

A true sportsman is always a cheerful loser, a quiet winner, with a very frank appreciation of the admirable traits in others, which he seeks to emulate, and his own shortcomings, which he tries to improve.

CHAPTER XXXII

ETIQUETTE IN BUSINESS AND POLITICS

A certain rich man whose appointment to a foreign post of importance was about to be ratified, came into the corridor of a Washington hotel and stopped to speak with a lady for a few moments. During the whole conversation he kept his hat on his head and a cigar in the corner of his mouth. It happened that the lady was the wife of a prominent senator, and she lost no time in reporting the incident to her husband, who in turn brought the matter to the attention of certain of his colleagues with the result that the appointment did not go through.

It is not unlikely that this man thinks "politics played against him," whereas the only factor against him was his exhibition of ill-breeding which proved him unsuitable to represent the dignity of his country.

Etiquette would not seem to play an important part in business, and yet no man can ever tell when its knowledge may be of advantage, or its lack may turn the scale against him. The man who remains "planted" in his chair when a lady (or an older man) speaks to him, who receives customers in his shirt sleeves, who does not take off his hat when talking with a lady and take his cigar out of his mouth when bowing or when addressing her, can never be sure that he is not preparing a witness for the prosecution.

ETIQUETTE IN SMOKING

The above does not mean that a gentleman may never smoke in the presence of ladies—especially in the presence of those who smoke themselves—but a gentleman should not smoke under the following circumstances:

When walking on the street with a lady.

When lifting his hat or bowing.

In a room, an office, or an elevator, when a lady enters.

In any short conversation where he is standing near, or talking with a lady.

If he is seated himself for a conversation with a lady on a veranda, in an hotel, in a private house, anywhere where "smoking is permitted," he first asks, "Do you mind if I smoke?" And if she replies, "Not at all" or "Do, by all means," it is then proper for him to do so. He should, however, take his cigar, pipe, or cigarette, out of his mouth while he is speaking. One who is very adroit can say a word or two without an unpleasant grimace, but one should not talk with one's mouth either full of food or barricaded with tobacco.

In the country, a gentleman may walk with a lady and smoke at the same time—especially a pipe or cigarette. Why a cigar is less admissible is hard to determine, unless a pipe somehow belongs to the country. A gentleman in golf or country clothes with a pipe in his mouth and a dog at his heels suggests a picture fitting to the scene; while a cigar seems as out of place as a cutaway coat. A pipe on the street in a city, on the other hand, is less appropriate than a cigar in the country. In any event he will, of course, ask his companion's permission to smoke.

MANNERS AND BUSINESS

If you had a commission to give and you entered a man's office and found him lolling back in a tipped swivel chair, his feet above his head, the ubiquitous cigar in his mouth and his drowsy attention fixed on the sporting page of the newspaper, you would be impressed not so much by his lack of good manners as by his bad business policy, because of the incompetence that his attitude suggests. It is scarcely necessary to ask: Would you give an important commission to him who has no apparent intention of doing anything but "take his ease"; or to him who is found occupied at his desk, who gets up with alacrity upon your entrance, and is seemingly "on his toes" mentally as well as actually? Or, would you go in preference to a man whose manners resemble those of a bear at the Zoo, if you could go to another whose business ability is supplemented by personal charm? And this again is merely an illustration of bad manners and good.

AN ADVANTAGE OF POLISH

One advantage of polish is that one's opponent can never tell what is going on under the glazed surface of highly finished manners, whereas an unfinished surface is all too easily penetrated. And since business encounters are often played like poker hands, it is surely a bad plan to be playing with a mind-reader who can plainly divine his opponent's cards, while his own are unrevealed.

Manners that can by any possibility be construed as mincing, foppish or effeminate are *not* recommended; but a gentleman who says "Good morning" to his employees and who invariably treats all women as "ladies," does not half so much flatter their vanity as win their respect for himself as a gentleman. Again, good manners are, after all, nothing but courteous consideration of other people's interests and feelings. That being true, does it not follow that all customers, superior officers and employees prefer an executive whose good manners imply consideration of his customer's, his company's and his employee's interest as well as merely his own?

PERFECT POLISH THAT IS UNSUSPECTED

The president of a great industry, whose mastery of etiquette is one of his chief assets, so submerges this asset in other and more apparent qualifications, that every plain man he comes in contact with takes it for granted that he is an equally "plain" man himself. He *is* plain in so far as he is straightforward in attitude and simple in manner. No red tape is required apparently to penetrate into this president's private office, whereas many "small" men are guarded with pretentiousness that is often an effort to give an impression of "importance."

In this big man's employ there is an especial assistant chosen purposely because of his tact and good manners.

If an unknown person asks to see Mr. President, this deputy is sent out (as from most offices) to find out what the visitor's business is; but instead of being told bluntly the boss doesn't know him and can't see him, the visitor is made to feel how much the president will regret not seeing him. Perhaps he is told, "Mr. President is in conference just now. I know he would not like you to be kept waiting; can I be of any service to you? I am his junior assistant." If the visitor's business is really with the president, he is admitted to the chief executive's office, since it is the latter's policy to see every one that he can.

He has a courteous manner that makes every one feel there is nothing in the day's work half so important as what his visitor has come to see him about! Nor is this manner insincere; for whatever time one sees him, he gives his undivided attention. Should his time be short, and the moment approach when he is due at an appointment, his secretary enters, a purposely arranged ten minutes ahead of the time necessary for the close of the present interview, and apologetically reminds him, "I'm sorry, Mr. President, but your appointment with the 'Z' committee is due." Mr. President with seeming unconcern, uses up most of the ten minutes, and his lingering close of the conversation gives his visitor the impression that he must have been late at his appointment, and wholly because of the unusual interest felt in his caller.

This is neither sincerity nor insincerity, but merely bringing social knowledge into business dealing. To make a pleasant and friendly impression is not alone good manners, but equally good business. The crude man would undoubtedly show his eagerness to be rid of his visitor, and after offending the latter's self-pride because of his inattentive discourtesy, be late for his own appointment! The man of skill saw his visitor for fewer actual minutes, but gave the impression that circumstances over which he had no control forced him unwillingly to close the interview. He not only gained the good will of his visitor, but arrived at his own appointment in plenty of time.

To listen attentively when one is spoken to, is merely

one of the rules of etiquette. The man who, while some one is talking to him, gazes out of the window or up at the ceiling, who draws squares and circles on the blotter, or is engrossed in his finger-nails or his shoes, may in his own mind be "finessing," or very likely he is bored! In the first case, the chances are he will lose the game; in the second, lots of people are bored, hideously bored, and most often the fault is their own; always they are at fault who show it.

GOOD MANNERS AND "GOOD MIXERS"

When one thinks of a man who is known in politics and business as a "good mixer," one is apt to think of him as a rough diamond rather than a polished one. In picturing a gentleman, a man of high cultivation, one instinctively thinks of one who is somewhat aloof and apart. A good mixer among uncouth men may quite accurately be one who is also uncouth; but the best "mixer" of all is one who adjusts himself equally well to finer as well as to plainer society. Education that does not confer flexibility of mind is an obviously limited education; the man of broadest education tunes himself in unison with whomever he happens to be. The more subjects he knows about, the more people he is in sympathy with, and therefore the more customers or associates or constituents he is sure to have.

The really big man—it makes little difference whether he was born with a gold spoon in his mouth or no spoon at all—is always one whose interest in people, things, and events is a stimulating influence upon all those he comes in contact with.

He who says, "That does not interest me," or "That bores me," defines his own limitations. He who is unable to project sympathy into other problems or classes than his own is an unimportant person though he have the birth of a Cecil and the manners of a Chesterfield. Every gentleman has an inalienable right to his own reserves—that goes without saying—and because he can project sympathy and understanding where and when he chooses, does not for one moment mean that he thereby should break down the walls of his instinctive defenses.

It is not the latter type, but the "Gentleman Limited" who has belittled the name of "gentleman" in the world of work; not so much because he is a gentleman, as because he is not entirely one. He who is every inch a gentleman as well as every inch a *man* is the highest type in the world to-day, just as he has always been. The do-nothing gentleman is equally looked down upon everywhere.

ETIQUETTE IN "REVERSE GEAR"

Etiquette, remember, is merely a collection of forms by which all personal contacts in life are made smooth. The necessity for a "rough" man to become polished so that he may meet men of cultivation on an equal footing, has an equally important reverse. The time has gone by when a gentleman by grace of God, which placed him in a high-born position, can control numbers of other men placed beneath him. Every man takes his place to-day according to born position plus the test of his own experience. And just as an unlettered expert in business is only half authoritative to men of high cultivation, so also is the gentleman, no matter how much he knows of Latin, Greek, history, art and polish of manner, handicapped according to his ignorance on the subject of another's expertness. Etiquette, in reverse, prescribes this necessity for complete knowledge in every contact in life. Through knowledge alone, does one prove one's right to authority. For instance:

A man in a machine ship is working at a lathe. An officer of the company comes into the shop, a gentleman in white collar and good clothes! He stands behind the mechanic and "curses him out" because his work is inefficient. When he turns away, the man at the lathe says, "Who was that guy anyway? What business has he to teach *me* my job?" Instead of accepting the criticism, he resents what he considers unwarranted interference by a man in another "class."

But supposing instead of standing by and talking about inefficiency, the "gentleman" had said, "Get out of there a moment!" and throwing off his coat and rolling up his silk shirt sleeves, he had operated the lathe with a smoothness and rapidity that could only have been acquired through long experience at a bench. The result would be that the next time he came on a tour of inspection that particular man (as well as all those who were witnesses of the former scene) would not only listen to him with respect but without resentment of his "class," because his expertness proved that he had earned his right to good clothes and silk shirts, and to tell those beneath him how work should be done.

The same test applies to any branch of experience: a man who knows as much about any "specialty" as an expert does himself, makes the "expert" think at once, "This man is a wonder!" The very fact that the first man is not making the subject *his* specialty, intensifies the achievement. Everything he says after that on subjects of which the second man knows nothing is accepted without question. Whenever you know as much as the other man, whether you are socially above, or below him, you are on that subject his equal; when you know more than he does, you have the advantage.

THE SELF-MADE MAN AND WORLD-MADE MANNERS

It is not in order to shine in society that grace of manner is an asset; comparatively few people in a community care a rap about "society" anyway! A man of affairs whose life is spent in doing a man's work in a man's way is not apt to be thrilled at the thought of putting on "glad" clothes and going out with his wife to a "pink" tea or a ball.

But what many successful men do not realize is that a fundamental knowledge of etiquette is no less an asset in business or public life, or in any other contact with people, than it is in society.

Just as any expert, whether at a machine bench, an accountant's desk, or at golf, gives an impression of such ease as to make his accomplishment seemingly require no skill, a bungler makes himself and every one watching him uneasy if not actually fearful of his awkwardness. And as inexpertness is quite as irritating in personal as in mechanical bungling, so there is scarcely any one who sooner or later does not feel the need of social expertness. Something, some day, will awaken him to the folly of scorning as "soft," men who have accomplished manners; despising as "effeminate," youths who have physical grace; of being contemptuous of the perfect English of the well-bred gentleman; of consoling himself with the thought that his own crudeness is strong, and manly, and American!

THE "X" MARKERS

But let "success" come to this same inexpert man— let him be appointed to high office, let him then shuffle from foot to foot, never knowing what to do or say, let him meet open derision or ill-concealed contempt from every educated person brought in contact with him, let opprobrium fall upon his State because its governor is a boor, and let him as such be written of in the editorials of the press and in the archives of history! Will he be so pleased with himself then? Does any one think of Theodore Roosevelt as "soft" or "effeminate" because he was one of the greatest masters of etiquette who ever bore the most exalted honor that can be awarded by the people of the United States? Washington was completely a gentleman—and so was Abraham Lincoln. Because Lincoln's etiquette was self-taught it was no less masterly for that! Whether he happened to know a lot of trifling details of pseudo etiquette matters not in the least. Awkward he may have been, but the essence of him was courtesy—unfailing courtesy. No "rough, uneducated" man has command of perfect English, and Lincoln's English is supreme.

One thing that some Men of Might forget is that lack of polish in its wider aspects is merely lack of education. They themselves look down upon a man who has to make an "X" mark in place of signing his name—but they overlook entirely that to those more highly educated, they are themselves in degree quite as ignorant.

SONS OF SELF-MADE MEN

And yet, speak to self-made men of the need of the social graces for their sons, and nine out of ten stampede —for all the world as though it were suggested to put them in petticoats. Do they think a poor unlettered lout who shambles at the door, who stands unable to speak, who turns his cap in his hands, who sidles into the room, and can't for the life of him get out again, well trained for the battle of life?

Picture that Mr. Strong-Man who thrusts his thumbs into his armholes and sits tipped back in his chair with a cigar in the corner of his mouth and his heels comfortably reposing on his solid mahogany desk. This is not in criticism of his relaxation, it is his own desk and certainly he has a right to put his heels on it if he wants to; likewise thumbs and armholes are his own. It is merely a picture that leads to another: Supposing a very great man comes into Mr. Strong Man's office—one whom he may consider a great man, a president perhaps of a big industry or of a railroad, or a senator—and shortly afterwards, Strong Man's own son comes into the room. Would he like to see his son abashed, awkward, spasmodically jerky, like the poor bumpkin who came the other day to ask about removing the ashes, or worse yet, bold and boisterous or cheeky; or would he like that boy of his to come forward with an entire lack of self-consciousness, and as his father introduces him as "My Son!" have him put out his hand in frank and easy and yet deferential friendliness? And then saying quickly and quietly whatever it was he came to say, as quickly and quietly make his way out again? Would he be sorry that the big man thought, "Fine boy that! Ability too!" Why would he think he had ability? Because the ease and dexterity with which he handled the social incident automatically suggests ability to handle other situations!

ETIQUETTE AND BUSINESS AUTHORITY

Another point: Does the self-made man stop to realize that his authority in business would be even greater than it is if he had the hall-marks of cultivation? For instance, when he comes in contact with college graduates and other cultivated men, his opinions gain or lose in weight exactly in proportion as he proves to be in their own "class" or below it.

A man unconsciously judges the authority of others by the standard of his own expert knowledge. A crude man may be a genius in business management, but in the unspoken opinion of men of education, he is in other contacts inferior to themselves. He is an authority they grant, but in limited lines only.

But when a man is met with who combines with business genius the advantage of polished manners and evident cultivation, his opinion on any subject broached at once assumes added weight. Doesn't it?

Chapter XXXIII

DRESS

Clothes are to us what fur and feathers are to beasts and birds; they not only add to our appearance, but they *are* our appearance. How we look to others entirely depends upon what we wear and how we wear it; manners and speech are noted afterward, and character last of all.

In the community where we live, admirableness of character is the fundamental essential, and in order to achieve a position of importance, personality is also essential; but for the transient impression that we make at home, abroad, everywhere in public, two superficial attributes are alone indispensable: good manners and a pleasing appearance.

It is not merely a question of vanity and inclination. In New York, for instance, a woman must dress well, to pay her way. In Europe, where the title of Duchess serves in lieu of a court train of gold brocade; or in Bohemian circles where talent alone may count; or in small communities where people are known for what they really are, appearance is of esthetic rather than essential importance.

In the world of smart society—in America at any rate —clothes not only represent our ticket of admission, but our contribution to the effect of a party. What makes a brilliant party? Clothes. Good clothes. A frumpy party is nothing more nor less than a collection of badly dressed persons. People with all the brains, even all the beauty imaginable, make an assemblage of dowds, unless they are well dressed.

Not even the most beautiful ballroom in the world, decorated like the Garden of Eden, could in itself suggest a brilliant entertainment, if the majority of those who filled it were frumps—or worse yet, vulgarians! Rather be frumpy than vulgar! Much. Frumps are often celebrities in disguise—but a person of vulgar appearance is vulgar all through.

THE SHEEP

Frumps are not very typical of America, vulgarians are somewhat more numerous, but the greatest number of all are the quietly dressed, unnoticeable men and women who make up the representative backbone in every city; who buy good clothes but not more than they need, and whose ambition is merely to be well enough dressed to fit in with their background, whatever their background may be.

Less numerous, but far more conspicuous, are the dressed-to-the-minute women who, like sheep exactly, follow every turn of latest fashion blindly and without the slightest sense of distance or direction. As each new season's fashion is defined, all the sheep run and dress themselves each in a replica of the other, their own types and personalities have nothing to do with the case. Fashion says: "Wear bolster cases tied at the neck and ankle," or "A few wisps of gauze held in place with court plaster," and daughter, mother, grandmother, and all the neighbors wear the same. If emerald green is the fashionable color, all of the yellowest skins will be framed in it. When hobble skirts are the thing, the fattest wabble along, looking for all the world like chandeliers tied up in mosquito netting. If ball dresses are cut to the last limit of daring, the ample billows of the fat will vie blandly with the marvels of anatomy exhibited by the thin. Comfort, convenience, becomingness, adaptability, beauty are of no importance. Fashion is followed to the letter—therefore they fancy, poor sheep, they are the last word in smartness. Those whom the fashion suits *are* "smart," but they are seldom, if ever, distinguished, because—they are all precisely alike.

THE WOMAN WHO IS REALLY CHIC

The woman who is chic is always a little different. Not different in being behind fashion, but always slightly apart from it. "Chic" is a borrowed adjective, but there is no English word to take the place of "elegant" which was destroyed utterly by the reporter or practical joker who said "elegant dresses," and yet there is no synonym that will express the individuality of beautiful taste combined with personal dignity and grace which gives to a perfect costume an inimitable air of distinction. *Une dame élégante* is all of that! And Mrs. Oldname is just such a person. She follows fashion merely so far as is absolutely necessary. She gets the latest model perhaps, but has it adapted to her own type, so that she has just that distinction of appearance that the sheep lack. She has even clung with slight modifications to the "Worth" ball dress, and her "wrapped" or fitted bodice has continued to look the smartest in every ballroom in spite of the Greek drapery and one-piece meal bag and all the other kaleidoscopic changes of fashion the rest of us have been through.

But the average would-be independent who determines to stand her ground, saying, "These new models are preposterous! I shall wear nothing of the sort!" and keeps her word, soon finds herself not at all an example of dignity but an object of derision.

FASHION HAS LITTLE IN COMMON WITH BEAUTY

Fashion ought to be likened to a tide or epidemic; sometimes one might define it as a sort of hypnotism, seemingly exerted by the gods as a joke. Fashion has the power to appear temporarily in the guise of beauty, though it is the antithesis of beauty nearly always. If you doubt it, look at old fashion plates. Even the woman of beautiful taste succumbs occasionally to the epidemics of fashion, but she is more immune than most. All women who have any clothes sense whatever know more or less the type of things that are their style—unless they have such an attack of fashionitis as to be irresponsibly delirious.

To describe any details of dress, that will not be as "queer" to-morrow as to-day's fashions are bound to be, would seem at the outset pretty much like writing about next year's weather. And yet, there is one unchanging principle which must be followed by every woman, man and child that is well dressed—suitability. Nor does suitability mean merely that you must choose clothes suitable to your age and appearance, and that you must get a ball dress for a ball, and a street dress to walk in; it means equally that you must not buy clothes out of proportion to your income, or out of keeping with your surroundings.

DISPROPORTIONATE EXPENDITURE IN BAD TASTE

About fifteen years ago the extravagance in women's dress reached such a high-water mark that it was not unheard of for a New York woman to spend a third of her husband's income on clothes. All women of fashion bought clothes when it would not have occurred to them to buy furniture—when it would have seemed preposterous to buy a piece of jewelry—but clothes, clothes, and more clothes, each more hand-embroidered than the last, until just as it seemed that no dress was fit to be seen if it hadn't a month or two of some one's time embroidered on it, the work on clothes subsided, until now we are at the other extreme; no work is put on them at all. At least, clothes to-day are much more sensible, and let us hope the sense will be lasting.

The war did at least make people realize that luxuries and trimmings could go too far. Ten years ago the American woman who lived in a little cottage, who walked when she went out or took the street car, wore the same clothes exactly that Mrs. Gilding wore in her victoria, or trailed over a Ming rug. The French woman has always been (and the American woman of taste is now) too great an artist to sit in a little room with its cotton-print slip covers, muslin curtains, and geranium pots on the window ledge, in anything strikingly elaborate and expensive. Charming as her dress may be in line and cut and color, she keeps it (no matter how intrinsically good it may be) in harmony with her geranium pots and her chintz.

On the other hand, clothes that are too plain can be

equally out of proportion. Last winter, for instance, a committee of ladies met in what might safely be called the handsomest house in New York, in a room that would fit perfectly in the Palace of Versailles, filled with treasures such as those of the Wallace collection. The hostess presided in a black serge golf skirt, a business woman's white shirt-waist, and stout walking boots, her hair brushed flat and tidily back and fastened as though for riding, her face and hands redolent of soap. No powder, not a nail manicured. Had she been a girl earning her living, she could not have been more suitably dressed, but her millions and her palace background demand that her clothes be at least moderately in keeping.

One does not have to be dowdy as an alternative to being too richly dressed, and to define differences between clothes that are notable because of their distinction and smartness, and clothes that are merely conspicuous and therefore vulgar, is a very elusive point. However, there are certain rules that seem pretty well established.

VULGAR CLOTHES

Vulgar clothes are those which, no matter what the fashion of the moment may be, are always too elaborate for the occasion; too exaggerated in style, or have accessories out of proportion. People of uncultivated taste are apt to fancy distortions; to exaggerate rather than modify the prevailing fashions.

For example: A conspicuous evidence of bad style that has persisted through numberless changes in fashion, is the over-dressed and over-trimmed head. The woman of uncultivated taste has no more sense of moderation than the Queen of the Cannibals. She will elaborate her hairdressing to start with (this is all right, if elaboration really suits her type) and then she will "decorate" it with everything in the way of millinery and jewelry that she can lay her hands on. Or, in the daytime, she fancies equally over-weighted hats, and rich-looking fur coats and the latest edition in the most conspicuous possible foot-wear. And she much prefers wearing rings to gloves. Maybe she thinks they do not go together? She despises sensible clothing; she also despises plain fabrics and untrimmed models. She also cares little (apparently) for staying at home, since she is perpetually seen at restaurants and at every public entertainment. The food she orders is rich, the appearance she makes is rich; in fact, to see her often is like nothing so much as being forced to eat a large amount of butter—plain.

Beau Brummel's remark that when one attracted too much notice, one could be sure of being not well-dressed but over-dressed, has for a hundred years been the comfort of the dowdy. It is, of course, very often true, but not invariably. A person may be stared at for any one of many reasons. It depends very much on the stare. A woman may be stared at because she is indiscreet, or because she looks like a left-over member of the circus, or because she is enchanting to look at.

If you are much stared at, what *sort* of a stare do you usually meet? Is it bold, or mocking, or is it merely that people look at you wistfully? If the first, change your manner; if the second, wear more conventional clothes; if the third, you may be left as you are. But be sure of your diagnosis of this last.

EXTRAVAGANCE NOT VULGARITY

Ostentation is always vulgar but extravagance is not necessarily vulgar—not by any means. Extravagance can become dishonest if carried beyond one's income.

Nearly everything that is beautiful or valuable is an extravagance—for most of us. Always to wear new gloves is an extravagant item for one with a small allowance—but scarcely vulgar! A laundry bill can be extravagant, flowers in one's city house, a piece of beautiful furniture, a good tapestry, each is an extravagance to an income that can not easily afford the expenditure. To one sufficient to buy the tapestry, the flowers are not an extravagance at all.

To buy quantities of things that are not even used

after they are bought is sheer wastefulness, and to buy everything that tempts you, whether you can afford to pay for it or not, is, if you can *not* afford it, verging on the actually dishonest.

DRESSES FOR DINNERS AND BALLS

Supposing, since clothes suitable to the occasion are the first requisite of good taste, we take up a few details that are apart from fashion.

A dinner dress really means every sort of low, or half low evening dress. A formal dinner dress, like a ball dress, is always low-necked and without sleeves, and is the handsomest type of evening dress that there is. A ball dress may be exquisite in detail but it is often merely effective. The perfect ball dress is one purposely designed with a skirt that is becoming when dancing. A long wrapped type of dress would make Diana herself look like a toy monkey-on-a-stick, but might be dignified and beautiful at a dinner. A dinner dress differs from a ball dress in little except that it is not necessarily designed for freedom of movement.

Hair ornaments always look well at a ball but are not especially appropriate (unless universally in fashion) on other occasions. A lady in a ball dress with nothing added to the head, looks a little like being hatless in the street. This sounds like a contradiction of the criticism of the vulgarian. But because a tiara is beautiful at a ball, or a spray of feathers, or a high comb, or another ornament, does not mean that all of these should be put on together and worn in a restaurant; which is just what the vulgarian would do. Whether, to wear a head-dress, however, depends not alone upon fashion but upon the individual. If the type of hair ornament at the moment in fashion is becoming, wear it, especially to balls and in a box at the opera. But if it is not becoming, don't.

Ladies of fashion, by the way, do not have their hair especially dressed for formal occasions. Each wears her hair a certain way, and it is put up every morning just as carefully as for a ball. The only time it is arranged differently is for riding. An informal dinner dress is merely a modified formal one. It is low in front and high in the back, with long or elbow sleeves—or perhaps it is Dutch neck and no sleeves.

When trains are in fashion, all older women should wear them. Fashion or no fashion, no woman who has passed forty looks really well in a cut-off evening dress. An effect of train, however, can very adequately be produced with any arrangement or trimming that extends upon the floor.

The informal dinner dress is worn to the theater, the restaurant (of high class), the concert and the opera. Informal dinner dresses are worn in the boxes at the opera on ordinary nights, such as when no especially great star is to sing, and when one is not going on to a ball afterward, but a ball dress is never inappropriate, especially without head-dress. On gala nights, ball dresses are worn in the boxes and head-dresses and as many jewels as one chooses—or has.

THE TEA-GOWN

Every one knows that a tea-gown is a hybrid between a wrapper and a ball dress. It has always a train and usually long flowing sleeves; is made of rather gorgeous materials and goes on easily, and its chief use is not for wear at the tea-table so much as for dinner alone with one's family.

It can, however, very properly be put on for tea, and if one is dining at home, kept on for dinner. Otherwise a lady is apt to take tea in whatever dress she had on for luncheon, and dress after tea for dinner.

One does not go out to dine in a tea-gown except in the house of a member of one's family or a most intimate friend. One would wear a tea-gown in one's own house in receiving a guest to whose house one would wear a dinner dress.

WHEN IN DOUBT

There is one rule that is fairly safe to follow: When in doubt, wear the plainer dress. It is always better far to be under-dressed than over-dressed. If you don't know whether to put on a ball dress or a dinner dress, wear the dinner dress. Or, whether to wear cloth or brocade to a luncheon, wear the cloth.

ON THE STREET

Your tea-gowns, since they are never worn in public, can literally be as bizarre as you please, and if you are driving in a closed motor, you can also wear an "original" type of dress. But in walking on the street,—if you care to be taken for a well-bred person—never wear anything that is exaggerated. If skirts are short, don't wear them two inches shorter than any one else's; if they are long, don't go down the street dragging a train and sweeping the dirt up on the under-flouncings. (Let us hope *that* fashion never comes back!) Don't wear too much jewelry; it is in bad taste in the first place, and in the second, is a temptation to a thief. And don't under any circumstances, distort your figure into a grotesque shape.

COUNTRY CLOTHES

Nothing so marks the "person who doesn't know" as inappropriate choice of clothes. To wear elaborate clothes out of doors in the country, is quite as out of place as to parade "sports" clothes on the streets in town.

It is safe to say that "sport" clothes are appropriate country clothes—especially for all young people. Elderly ladies, needless to say, should not don "sporting eccentricities" nor wear sweaters to lunch parties; but sensible country clothes, such as have for many decades been worn in England, of homespun or serge or jersey cloth or whatever has replaced these materials, are certainly more appropriate to walk in than a town costume—even for a lady of seventy! Young people going to the country for the day wear sports clothes; which if seen early in the morning in town and again late in the afternoon, merely show you have been to the country. But town clothes in the country proclaim your ignorance of fitness. Even for a lunch party at Golden Hall or Great Estates, every one who is young wears smart country clothes.

SHOES AND SLIPPERS

Sport shoes are naturally adapted to the sport for which they are intended. High-heeled slippers do not go with any country clothes, except organdie or muslins or other distinctly feminine "summer" dresses. Elaborate afternoon dresses of "painted" chiffons, embroidered mulls, etc., are seen only at weddings, lawn parties, or at watering-places abroad.

A SUGGESTION TO THOSE WHO MIND SUNBURN

No advice is intended for those who have a skin that either does not burn at all, or turns a beautiful smooth Hawaiian brown; but a woman whose creamy complexion bursts into freckles, as violent as they are hideous, at the first touch of the sun need no longer stay perpetually indoors in daytime, or venture out only when swathed like a Turk, if she knows the virtue in orange as a color that defies the sun's rays. A thin veil of red-orange is more effective than a thick one of blue or black.

Orange shirt-waists do not sound very conservative, but they are mercifully conserving to arms sensitive to sunburn. Young Mrs. Gilding, whose skin is as perishable as it is lovely, always wears orange on the golf course. A skirt of burnt-orange serge of homespun or linen, and shirtwaists of orange linen or crepe de chine. A hat with a brim and a harem-veil (pinned across her nose under her eyes) of orange marquisette,—which is easier to breathe through than chiffon—allows her to play golf or tennis or to motor or even go out in a sailboat and keep her skin without a blemish.

Constance Style, who also has a skin that the sun destroys, wears orange playing tennis, but for bathing wears a high-neck and long-sleeved bathing suit and "makes her face up" (also the backs of her hands) with theatrical grease paint that has a good deal of yellow in it, and flesh color ordinary powder on top. The grease paint withstands hot sun and water, but it is messy. The alternative, however, is a choice between complexion or bathing, as it is otherwise prohibitive for the "sun afflicted" to have both.

RIDING CLOTHES

The distorted circus-mirror clothes seen on men who know no better, are not a bit worse than the riding clothes seen on actresses in our best theaters and moving pictures—who ought to know better. Nothing looks worse than riding clothes made and worn badly, and nothing looks smarter than they when well made and well put on.

A riding habit, no matter what the fashion happens to be, is like a uniform, in that it must be made and worn according to regulations. It must above all be meticulously trig and compact. Nothing must be sticking out a thousandth part of an inch that can be flattened in.

A riding habit is the counterpart of an officer's uniform; it is not worn so as to make the wearer look pretty! A woman to look well in a habit must be *smart* or she is a sight! And nothing contributes so much to the "sights" we see at present as the attempt to look pretty instead of looking correct. The criticism is not intended for the woman who lives far off in the open country and jumps on a horse in whatever she happens to have on, but for those who dress "for looks" and ride in the parks of our cities, or walk on the stage and before the camera, in scenes meant to represent smart society!

To repeat, therefore, the young woman who wants to look pretty should confine her exercise to dancing. She can also hold a parasol over her head and sit in a canoe—or she can be pretty how and where she will, so long as it is not on a horse in the park or hunting-field. (To mention hunting-field is superfluous; the woman who can ride well enough to follow the hounds is too good a sportswoman, too great a lover of good form to be ignorant of the proper outline necessary to smartness of appearance in the saddle.)

In smartest English society it is not considered best form ,for a young girl to ride astride in the hunting-field or in the park after she is grown. A high-born English girl rides astride as a child, but as soon as she is old enough to be presented at Court, she appears at a Meet or in the "Row" in a lady's habit, trigly perfect in fit, and on a side-saddle. In America this is an extreme opinion, and it is only among the most fashionable that a young girl having all her life ridden in a man's saddle, finds the world a joyless place and parents cruel when she is no longer allowed to ride like a boy. But she becomes, in spite of her protests, "another who looks divine on a horse." And you can look divine too, if you choose! On second thoughts the adjective must be qualified. No one looks divine on a horse who is not thin as a shingle. But since diet produces a shingle shape and every one strong-minded (or vain) enough, can diet, you need only care enough to "count your calories" and be as slim as you please.

Next, the best habit possible. And best habits are expensive, and there are no "second best." A habit is good or it is bad. Whatever the present fashion may be, have your habit utterly conventional. Don't wear checks or have slant pockets, or eccentric cuffs or lapels; don't have the waist pinched in. Choose a plain dark or "dust" color. A night blue that has a few white hairs in the mixture does not show dust as much as a solid dark color, and a medium weight close material holds its shape better than a light loose weave.

You may wear a single white carnation or a few violets in your buttonhole—but no other trimming. Keep the idea of perfect clothes for men in mind, get nothing that the smartest man would not wear, and you can't go wrong. Get boots like those of a man, low-heeled and with a straight line from heel to back of top. Don't have the tops wider than absolutely necessary not to bind, and don't have them curved or fancy in shape. Be sure that there is no elbow sticking out like a horse's hock at the back of the boot, and don't have a corner on the inside edge of the sole. And don't try to wear a small size!

WHEN YOU PUT YOUR HABIT ON

First, hair: Never mind if you look like Mme. Recamier with your hair fluffed and like a skinned rabbit with it tight back, tight, flat back it must go. Brush it smooth as you can, braid it or coil it about level with the top of your ears and wind it in a door mat, not a knob in the back.

If you have a great quantity of hair, you should take all the inner part of it, coil it on top of your head so it will go under your hat out of the way. Then take the outer edge of it and braid or wind it as flat as possible. A large bun at the back of the head is almost as bad as hair drawn over the ears at the side. If you have short hairs likely to blow, you must wear a hunting hair net. And if it is bobbed, it must be drawn back into a silk riding net and made to look trim.

Correct riding clothes are not fashion but form! Whether coat skirts are long or short, full or plain, and waists wasp-like or square, the above admonitions have held for many decades, and are likely to hold for many more.

Gloves must be of heavy leather and at least two sizes bigger than those ordinarily worn.

A hat must fit the head and its shape must be conventional. Never wear a hat that would be incorrect on a man, and don't wear it on the back of your head or over your nose.

Wear your stock as tight as you comfortably can, not *too* tight! Tie it smartly so as to make it flat and neat, and anchor whatever you wear so securely that nothing can possibly come loose.

And if you want to see a living example of perfection in riding clothes, go to the next horse-show where Miss Belle Beach is riding and look at her!

WHAT CLOTHES TO TAKE FOR A WEEK-END

Unless fashion turns itself upside down (which it is, of course, perfectly capable of doing), elaborate clothes, except evening ones, are entirely useless, even in Newport. We have all of us abandoned Paris fashions for country wear in favor of those of England. The Valenciennes insertions and trailing chiffons of some years ago, still seen at watering-places in France, have been entirely superseded by country clothes.

In going to any fashionable house in the country, you should take a dinner dress for each evening, with stockings and slippers to match. You need a country dress for each day, or if the weather is uncertain, a thick one and two thin ones, with a long coat, and a dress suitable for church. This one can perfectly well be a country dress, but not a "sports" one.

If you are not too young and are going to stay in an informal house where you will probably be the only guest, and where it is likely no one will be asked in, a tea-gown or two should be taken.

If you are going especially for a ball, but not given by your hostess, needless to say, you take a ball dress and an evening wrap. In the autumn or winter, a fur coat will do double service for coat and wrap.

Do not take a big trunk full of all the things you don't need. Don't take sports clothes for all occasions if you are not a sportswoman. But if you do ride, or play tennis or golf, or skate or swim, be sure to take your own clothes and *don't* borrow other people's. There are plenty of ingeniously arranged week-end trunks, very compact in size, that have a hat compartment, holding from two to six hats, and plenty of room for a half a dozen dresses and their accessories.

WHEN THE INCOME IS LIMITED

No one can dress well on nothing a year; that must be granted at the outset. But a woman who has talent, taste, and ingenuity can be suitably and charmingly dressed on little a year, especially at present.

First of all, to mind wearing a dress many times because it indicates a small bank account, is to exhibit a false notion of the values in life. Any one who thinks well or ill of her, in accordance with her income, can not be too quickly got rid of! But worthwhile people *are* influenced in her disfavor when she has clothes in number and quality out of proportion to her known financial situation.

It is tiresome everlastingly to wear black, but nothing is so serviceable, nothing so unrecognizable, nothing looks so well on every occasion. A very striking dress can not be worn many times without making others as well as its owner feel bored at the sight of it. "Here comes the Zebra" or "the Cockatoo!" is inevitable if a dress of stripes or flamboyant color is worn often. She who must wear one dress through a season and have it perhaps made over the next, would better choose black or cream color. Or perhaps a certain color suits her, and this fact makes it possible for her habitually to wear it without impressing others with her lack of clothes. But whether her background be black or cerise it should invariably blend with her whole wardrobe, so that all accessories can be made to do double or quadruple service.

Supposing you are a young woman with more beauty than wealth! Let us also suppose you have three evening dresses, a blue, a pink and a green. At the moment you can wear flesh-colored slippers and stockings with everything, which rather weakens the argument—however, a blue fan does not look well with a pink or a green dress, nor do the other combinations. Supposing, however, you had instead a cream-colored dress, a flesh-colored, and an orchid one. Flesh-colored slippers look much better with cream and orchid than with either green or blue, at any rate! A watermelon pink fan is lovely in night-light with all three; so is a cream one. Or perhaps by changing both fan and slippers, a different effect is produced, since the colors of your clothes are background colors.

But nothing really can compare with the utility and smartness of black. Take a black tulle dress, made in the simplest possible way; worn plain, it is a simple dinner dress. It can have a lace slip to go over it, and make another dress. With a jet harness—meaning merely trimming that can be added at will—it is still another dress. Or it can have a tunic of silver or of gold trimming; and fans, flowers and slippers in various colors, such as watermelon or emerald, change it again. In fact, a black tulle can be changed almost as easily as though done with a magician's wand.

To choose daytime clothes that go with the same hats, shoes, parasols, wrist-bags, and gloves, is equally important. A snuff-colored dress and a gray one need entirely different accessories. Russet shoes, chamois gloves, and sand-colored hat go also with henna, raspberry, reds, etc.; but gray must have gray or white shoes, gloves, and hat, which also go with blues, greens and violets.

DON'T GET TOO MANY CLOTHES

Choose the clothes which you must have, carefully, and if you must cut down, cut down on elaborate ones. There is scarcely anywhere that you can not fittingly go in plain clothes. Very few, if any, people *need* fancy things; all people need plain ones.

A very beautiful Chicago woman who is always perfectly dressed for every occasion, worked out the cost of her own clothes this way: On a sheet of paper, thumb-tacked on the inside of her closet door, she put a complete typewritten list of her dresses and hats, and the cost of each. Every time she put on a dress she made a pencil mark. By and by when a dress was discarded, she divided the cost of it by the number of times it had been worn. In this way she found out accurately which were her cheapest and which her most expensive clothes. When getting new ones she has the advantage of very valuable information, since she avoids the dress that is never put on, which is a bigger handicap for the medium-sized allowance than many women realize.

WHAT TO WEAR IN A RESTAURANT

Restaurant dress depends upon the restaurant and the city. Because women in New York wear low-necked dresses and no hats, does not mean that those who live in New Town should do the same, if it is not New Town's custom. But you must *never* wear an evening dress and a hat! And *never* wear a day dress without one. If in the city where you live, people wear day clothes in the evening, you can only very slightly differ from them.

It is never good form to be elaborately dressed in a public place, except in a box at the opera or at a charity ball.

AT A WEDDING, A GARDEN PARTY OR AFTERNOON TEA

These are the occasions when elaborate day dresses are appropriate. But if you have very few clothes, you can perfectly well wear any sort of day dress that may be in fashion. A coat and skirt is not appropriate, since a skirt and shirt-waist is and always has been a utility combination. Unless, of course, the waist is of a color to match the skirt so that it has the appearance of a dress.

You need, however, seldom worry about your appearance because you are not as "dressed" as the others; the time to worry is when you are more dressed than any one else.

For a garden-party a country dress is quite all right; though if you have a very elaborate summer dress, this is the only time you can wear it!

No one has to be told what to wear to church. In small country churches, at the seashore, people go to church in country clothes; otherwise, as every one knows, one puts on "town" clothes, and gloves.

At a formal luncheon in town, one sees every sort of dress from velvet to tailor-made. Certain ladies, older ones usually, who like elaborate clothes, wear them. But younger people are usually dressed in worsted materials or silks that are dull in finish, and that, although they may be embroidered and very expensive, give an effect of simplicity.

One should always wear a simpler dress in one's own house than one wears in going to the house of another.

A FEW GENERAL REMARKS

The fault of bad taste is usually in over-dressing. Quality not effect, is the standard to seek for. Machine-made passementerie on top of conspicuous but sleazy material is always shoddy. Cut and fit are the two items of greatest importance in women's clothes, as well as in men's. But fashion changes too rapidly to make value of material always wise expenditure for one of slender purse. Better usually have two dresses, each cut and made in the whim of the moment, than one which must be worn after the whim has become a freak. In men's clothes the opposite rule should be followed since good style in men's clothes is unchanging.

To buy things at sales is very much like buying things at an auction; if you really know what you want and something about values, you can often do marvellously well; but if you are easily bewildered and know little of values, you are apt to spend your good money on trash. A woman of small means must either be (or learn to be) discriminatingly careful, or she would better have her clothes made at home, or if she is of "model" type, buy them ready-made. The ready-to-wear clothes in the Misses' Department are growing every year better looking; unfortunately and for some inexplicable reason, the usual Women's Department does not compare in good taste in selection of models with the former, and it is unusual to find a dress that a lady of fashion would choose except among the imported models, for which store prices are as a rule higher than those asked by the greatest dressmakers. Evening clothes are still usually unbuyable by the over-fastidious, except for a certain flapper type (and an undistinguished one at that!), and the ultra-smart woman is still obliged to go to the private importers for her débutante daughter's ball-dresses as well as her own— or else into her own sewing-room.

FASHION AND FAT

For years the thin, even the scrawny, have had everything their own way. The woman who is fat, or even plump, has a rather hopeless problem unless fashion goes to Turkey for its next inspiration, which is so unlikely it is almost possible! Two things the fat woman should avoid: big patterns and the stiff tailor-made. Fat women look better in feminine clothes that follow in the wake, never in the advance, of modified fashion. Fat women should never wear elaborate clothes or clothes in light colors or heavily feathered hats.

The tendency of fat is to take away from one's gracility; therefore, any one inclined to be fat must be ultra conservative—in order to counteract the effect. Very tight clothes make fat people look fatter and thin people thinner. Satin is a bad material, since high lights are too shimmeringly accentuated.

Heavy ankles, needless to say, should never be clothed in light stockings and dark shoes; long, pointed slippers accentuate a thick ankle, and so does a short skirt that has a straight hem. A "ragged" edge is most flattering.

Dress, stockings and slippers to match are unavoidable in evening dress, but when possible a thick ankle should have a dark stocking—or at least a slipper to match the stocking.

People should select colors that go with their skin. And elderly women should not wear grass green, or Royal blue, or purple, or any hard color that needs a faultless complexion. Swarthy skin always looks better in colors that have red or yellow in them. A very sallow person in pale blue or apple green looks like a well-developed case of jaundice.

Pink and orchid are often very becoming to older women; and pale blue or yellow to those with fair skin. Because a woman is no longer young is no reason why she should wear perpetual black—unless she is fat.

CLOTHES FOR TRAVELING IN EUROPE

Ideal traveling clothes are those which do not wrinkle or show rain spots; and to find which these are it is necessary to take a sample of each material, sprinkle it with water, and twist it to see how much abuse it will stand. Every woman knows what she likes best, and what she considers suitable. Two alternating traveling dresses at least will be necessary, and two or three semi-evening dresses to put on for dinner. One very simple half-dinner dress of black, that has a combination of trimmings such as described earlier in this chapter, is ideally useful. Tourists do not put on evening clothes except in very fashionable centers, such as London, Paris, Monte Carlo or Deauville, and then only if staying at an ultra fashionable hotel. To be over-dressed is always in bad taste. So that unless you are going to visit or make several-day stops the one black evening dress suggested would answer every possible purpose.

If you intend staying for a long time in one place, you take all of your season's clothes; and if you are going to visit in England, or to stay anywhere in the country, you will need country clothes, but not on ordinary touring. For motoring, space is precious, and clothes should be chosen with the object of packing into small dimensions. Motoring in Europe is cold. A very warm, long wrap is necessary. An old fur one is much the best, and a small, close hat that does not blow.

CLOTHES AND PARIS

It is something like this: You have been hypnotized before, and you vow you won't be again! You make up your mind that you are going to get a black dress and a dark blue—and nothing else.

You enter the lower reception hall and mount the bronze balustraded stairs half way when already Mlle. Marie is aware of your approach. She greets you not only as though you are the only customer she has ever had, but as though your coming has saved—just saved in time— the prestige of the house.

She tells you breathlessly that you are just in time to see the parade of models; she puts you where you may have an uninterrupted view. She then begins her greetings all over again by asking not alone after all the members of your family and an extraordinarily long list of friends, but makes a solicitous inquiry after each dress that she has ever sold you. "Did Madame like her white velvet?" she coos. "Was it not most useful? Was not her black lace charming? And the bisque cloth—surely Madame had found great satisfaction in wearing the bisque cloth?" But your ears are as stone to her blandishments! As a traveling suit, bisque-colored cloth had *not* been serviceable! Black lace with a cerise velvet under petticoat might be effective at Armenonville, but it had seemed queer, to say the least, at the tennis match in August. No, you are at last immune from any of those sudden attacks of new fashion fever that result in loss of judgment. You open your little book and consult your list.

"I should like," you say, "a navy blue serge trimmed with black braid or satin or something like that; a black crêpe de chine absolutely plain; I really need nothing else."

You do not look at Mlle. Marie's crestfallen face, you watch the procession of models. But the old spell works. Besides zebra stripes and gold shot with cerise and purple, you think an emerald green charmeuse is really a perfect substitute for the plain black crêpe de chine you had in mind. You show that you are hypnotized by remarking absently, "It is the color of the grass."

Instantly, Mlle. Marie, the most skillful *vendeuse* in Paris, becomes radiant. "Listen, Madame," she says to you in that insinuating, confidential, yet humbly ingratiating manner of hers. "Let me explain, Madame,—the idea of dress this year is altogether idyllic! Never has there been such charming return to nature. The great originator of our house has taken his suggestion—but yes! from the little animals of the fields and woods—from Nature herself! Our dresses this year are intended to follow the example of all the little animals dressed to match their backgrounds. Is not that thought exquisite?

Is not that delicious? Is an emerald lizard conspicuous in
the tropics? Is a zebra even seen in patches of sun and
shade? And in the snow, think of all the little animals
who put on white coats in winter! Obviously white is the
color intended for winter wear. And for the spring,
green. Emerald green assuredly. It is as Madame herself said, the color of the grass. The emerald charmeuse
on a lawn in summer would be a poem of harmony. The
cerise for afternoons at sunset; this orange shading into
coral embroidery to wear beside the fire. The dark blue
chiffon embroidered in silver is for night. All the colors
that Madame at first found so bright—they are but the
colors of a summer flower garden. What would Madame
wear in a flower garden? Black crêpe de chine? Assuredly not! See this shell pink chiffon, how lovely it would
look under trees of apple blossoms. Blue serge! Oh,
what an escape. And now if Madame will permit me to
suggest?—the green, but assuredly! and the orange and
coral, and the pink chiffon garden dress, and the zebra,
for travelling, and the blue and silver. . . ."

However, to be serious, people do go to Paris and buy
their clothes—beautiful clothes! Of course they do; especially those who go every year. But the woman who goes
abroad perhaps every four or five years is apt to be defi-
cient in a trans-Atlantic sense. "Match backgrounds, like
charming little animals?" Never! Oh, a very big Never
Again! And yet—the next time shall you not find it a
temptation to go just out of curiosity to find out what the
newest artfully enticing little tune of the Pied Pipers of
Paris will be!

CHAPTER XXXIV

THE CLOTHES OF A GENTLEMAN

It would seem that some of our great clothing establishments, with an eye to our polyglot ancestry, have attempted to incorporate some feature of every European national costume into a "harmonicus" whole, and have thus given us that abiding horror, the freak American suit, You will see it everywhere, on Broadway of every city and Main Street of every town, on the boardwalks and beaches of coast resorts, and even in remote farming villages. It comes up to hit you in the face year after year in all its amazing variations: waist-line under the arm pits, "trick" little belts, what-nots in the cuffs; trousers so narrow you fear they will burst before your eyes, pockets placed in every position, buttons clustered together in a tight little row or reduced to one. And the worst of it is, few of our younger men know any better until they go abroad and find their wardrobe a subject for jest and derision.

If you would dress like a gentleman, you must do one of two things; either study the subject of a gentleman's wardrobe until you are competent to pick out good suits from freaks and direct your misguided tailor, or, at least until your perceptions are trained, go to an English one. This latter method is the easiest, and, by all odds, the safest. It is not Anglomania but plain common sense to admit that, just as the Rue de la Paix in Paris is the fountain-head of fashions for women, Bond Street in London is the home of irreproachable clothes for men.

And yet, curiously enough, just as a woman shopping in Paris can buy frightful clothes—or the most beautiful; a man can in America buy the worst clothes in the world —and the best.

The ordinary run of English clothes may not be especially good, but they are, on the other hand, never bad;

whereas American freak clothes are distortions like the reflections seen in the convex and concave mirrors of the amusement parks. But not even the leading tailors of Bond Street can excel the supremely good American tailor —whose clothes however are identical in every particular with those of London, and their right to be called "best" is for greater perfection of workmanship and fit. This last is a dangerous phrase; "fit" means perfect set and line, not plaster tightness.

However, let us suppose that you are either young, or at least fairly young; that you have unquestioned social position, and that you are going to get yourself an entire wardrobe. Let us also suppose your money is not unlimited, so that it may also be seen where you may not, or may if necessary, economize.

FORMAL EVENING CLOTHES

Your full dress is the last thing to economize on. It must be perfect in fit, cut and material, and this means a first-rate tailor. It must be made of a dull-faced worsted, either black or night blue, on no account of broadcloth. Aside from satin facing and collar, which can have lapels or be cut shawl-shaped, and wide braid on the trousers, it must have no trimming whatever. Avoid satin or velvet cuffs, moiré neck ribbons and fancy coat buttons as you would the plague.

Wear a plain white linen waistcoat, not one of cream colored silk, or figured or even black brocade. Have all your linen faultlessly clean—always—and your tie of plain white lawn, tied so it will not only stay in place but look as though nothing short of a backward somersault could disarrange it.

Your handkerchief must be white; gloves (at opera or ball) white; flower in buttonhole (if any) white. If you are a normal size, you can in America buy inexpensive shirts, and white waistcoats that are above reproach, but if you are abnormally tall or otherwise an "out size" so that everything has to be "made to order," you will have to pay anywhere from double to four times as much for each article you put on.

When you go out on the street, wear an English silk hat, not one of the taper crowned variety popular in the "movies." And wear it on your head, not on the back of your neck. Have your overcoat of plain black or dark blue material, for you must wear an overcoat with full dress even in summer. Use a plain white or black and white muffler. Colored ones are impossible. Wear white buckskin gloves if you can afford them; otherwise gray or khaki doeskin, and leave them in your overcoat pocket. Your stick should be of plain Malacca or other wood, with either a crooked or straight handle. The only ornamentation allowable is a plain silver or gold band, or top; but perfectly plain is best form.

And lastly, wear patent leather pumps, shoes or ties, and plain black silk socks, and leave your rubbers—if you must wear them, in the coat room.

THE TUXEDO

The Tuxedo, which is the essential evening dress of a gentleman, is simply the English dinner coat. It was first introduced in this country at the Tuxedo Club to provide something less formal than the swallow-tail, and the name has clung ever since. To a man who can not afford to get two suits of evening clothes, the Tuxedo is of greater importance. It is worn every evening and nearly everywhere, whereas the tail coat is necessary only at balls, formal dinners, and in a box at the opera. Tuxedo clothes are made of the same materials and differ from full dress ones in only three particulars: the cut of the coat, the braid on the trousers, and the use of a black tie instead of a white one. The dinner coat has no tails and is cut like a sack suit except that it is held closed in front by one button at the waist line. (A full dress coat, naturally, hangs open.) The lapels are satin faced, and the collar left in cloth, or if it is shawl-shaped the whole collar is of satin.

The trousers are identical with full dress ones except

that braid, if used at all, should be narrow. "Cuffed" trousers are not good form, nor should a dinner coat be double-breasted.

Fancy ties are bad form. Choose a plain black silk or satin one. Wear a white waistcoat if you can afford the strain on your laundry bill, otherwise a plain black one. By no means wear a gray one nor a gray tie.

The smartest hat for town wear is an opera, but a straw or felt which is proper in the country, is not out of place in town. Otherwise, in the street the accessories are the same as those already given under the previous heading.

THE HOUSE SUIT

The house suit is an extravagance that may be avoided, and an "old" Tuxedo suit worn instead.

A gentleman is always supposed to change his clothes for dinner, whether he is going out or dining at home alone or with his family, and for this latter occasion some inspired person evolved the house, or lounge, suit, which is simply a dinner coat and trousers cut somewhat looser than ordinary evening ones, made of an all-silk or silk and wool fabric in some dark color, and lined with either satin or silk. Nothing more comfortable—or luxurious— could be devised for sitting in a deep easy-chair after dinner, in a reclining position that is ruinous to best evening clothes.

Its purpose is really to save wear on evening clothes, and to avoid some of their discomfort also, because they can not be given hard or careless usage and long survive. A house suit is distinctly what the name implies, and is not an appropriate garment to wear out for dinner or to receive any but intimate guests in at home. The accessories are a pleated shirt, with turndown stiff collar, and black bow tie, or even an unstarched shirt with collar attached (white of course). The coat is made with two buttons instead of one, because no waistcoat is worn with it.

FORMAL AFTERNOON DRESS

Formal afternoon dress consists of a black cutaway coat with white piqué or black cloth waistcoat, and gray-and-black striped trousers. The coat may be bound with braid, or, even in better taste, plain. A satin-faced lapel is not conservative on a cutaway, but it is the correct facing for the more formal (and elderly) frock coat. Either a cutaway or a frock coat is always accompanied by a silk hat, and best worn with plain black waistcoat and a black bow tie or a black and white four-in-hand tie. A gray silk ascot worn with the frock coat is supposed to be the correct wedding garment of the bride's father. (For details of clothes worn by groom and ushers at a wedding, see chapter on weddings.)

Shoes may be patent leather, although black calf-skin are at present the fashion, either with or without spats. If with spats, be sure that they fit close; nothing is worse than a wrinkled spat or one that sticks out over the instep like the opened bill of a duck!

Though gray cutaway suits and gray top hats have always been worn to the races in England, they do not seem suitable here, as races in America are not such full-dress occasions as in France and England. But at a spring wedding or other formal occasions a sand-colored double-breasted linen waistcoat with spats and bow tie to match looks very well with a black cutaway and almost black trousers, on a man who is young.

THE BUSINESS SUIT

The business suit or three-piece sack is made or marred by its cut alone. It is supposed to be an every-day inconspicuous garment and should be. A few rules to follow are:

Don't choose striking patterns of materials; suitable woolen stuffs come in endless variety, and any which look plain at a short distance are "safe," though they may show a mixture of colors or pattern when viewed closely.

Don't get too light a blue, too bright a green, or anything suggesting a horse blanket. At the present moment trousers are made with a cuff; sleeves are not. Lapels are moderately small. Padded shoulders are an abomination. Peg-topped trousers equally bad. If you must be eccentric, save your efforts for the next fancy dress ball, where you may wear what you please, but in your business clothing be reasonable.

Above everything, don't wear white socks, and don't cover yourself with chains, fobs, scarf pins, lodge emblems, etc., and don't wear "horsey" shirts and neckties. You will only make a bad impression on every one you meet. The clothes of a gentleman are always conservative; and it is safe to avoid everything than can possibly come under the heading of "novelty."

JEWELRY

In your jewelry let diamonds be conspicuous by their absence. Nothing is more vulgar than a display of "ice" on a man's shirt front, or on his fingers.

There is a good deal of jewelry that a gentleman may be allowed to wear, but it must be chosen with discrimination. Pearl shirt-studs (real ones) are correct for full dress only, and not to be worn with a dinner coat unless they are so small as to be entirely inconspicuous. Otherwise you may wear enamel studs (that look like white linen) or black onyx with a rim of platinum, or with a very inconspicuous pattern in diamond chips, but so tiny that they can not be told from a threadlike design in platinum—or others equally moderate.

Waistcoat buttons, studs and cuff links, worn in sets, is an American custom that is permissible. Both waistcoat buttons and cuff links may be jewelled and valuable, but they must not have big precious stones or be conspicuous.

A watch chain should be very thin and a man's ring is usually a seal ring of plain gold or a dark stone. If a man wears a jewel at all it should be sunk into a plain "gypsy hoop" setting that has no ornamentation, and worn on his "little," not his third, finger.

IN THE COUNTRY

Gay-colored socks and ties are quite appropriate with flannels or golf tweeds. Only in your riding clothes you must again be conservative. If you can get boots built on English lines, wear them; otherwise wear leggings. And remember that all leather must be real leather in the first place and polished until its surface is like glass.

Have your breeches fit you. The coat is less important, in fact, any odd coat will do. Your legs are the cynosure of attention in riding.

Most men in the country wear knickerbockers with golf stockings, with a sack or a belted or a semi-belted coat, and in any variety of homespuns or tweeds or rough worsted materials. Or they wear long trousered flannels. Coats are of the polo or ulster variety. For golf or tennis many men wear sweater coats. Shirts are of cheviot or silk or flannel, all with soft collars attached and to match.

The main thing is to dress appropriately. If you are going to play golf, wear golf clothes; if tennis, wear flannels. Do not wear a yachting cap ashore unless you are living on board a yacht.

White woolen socks are correct with white buckskin shoes in the country, but not in town.

If some semi-formal occasion comes up, such as a country tea, the time-worn conservative blue coat with white flannel trousers is perennially good.

OTHER HINTS

The well-dressed man is always a paradox. He must look as though he gave his clothes no thought and as though literally they grew on him like a dog's fur, and yet he must be perfectly groomed. He must be close-shaved and have his hair cut and his nails in good order (not too polished). His linen must always be immaculate, his clothes "in press," his shoes perfectly "done." His brown shoes must shine like old mahogany, and his white buckskin must be whitened and polished like a prize bull terrier at a bench show. Ties and socks and handkerchief may go together, but too perfect a match betrays an effort for "effect" which is always bad.

The well-dressed man never wears the same suit or the same pair of shoes two days running. He may have only two suits, but he wears them alternately; if he has four suits he should wear each every fourth day. The longer time they have "to recover" their shape, the better.

WHAT TO WEAR ON VARIOUS OCCASIONS

The appropriate clothes for various occasions are given below. If ever in doubt what to wear, the best rule is to err on the side of informality. Thus, if you are not sure whether to put on your dress suit or your Tuxedo, wear the latter.

FULL DRESS

1. At the opera.
2. At an evening wedding.
3. At a dinner to which the invitations are worded in the third person.
4. At a ball, or formal evening entertainment.
5. At certain State functions on the Continent of Europe in broad daylight.

TUXEDO

1. At the theater.
2. At most dinners.
3. At informal parties.
4. Dining at home.
5. Dining in a restaurant.

A CUTAWAY OR FROCK COAT WITH STRIPED TROUSERS

1. At a noon or afternoon wedding.
2. On Sunday for church (in the city).
3. At any formal daytime function.
4. In England to business.
5. As usher at a wedding.
6. As pall-bearer.

BUSINESS SUITS

1. All informal daytime occasions.
2. Traveling.
3. The coat of a blue suit with white flannel or duck trousers for a lunch, or to church, in the country.
4. A blue or black sack suit will do in place of a cutaway at a wedding, but not if you are the groom or an usher.

COUNTRY CLOTHES

1. *Only* in the country.
To wear odd tweed coats and flannel trousers in town is not only inappropriate, but bad taste.

CHAPTER XXXV

THE KINDERGARTEN OF ETIQUETTE

In the houses of the well-to-do where the nursery is in charge of a woman of refinement who is competent to teach little children proper behavior, they are never allowed to come to table in the dining-room until they have learned at least the elements of good manners. But whether in a big house of this description, or in a small house where perhaps the mother alone must be the teacher, children can scarcely be too young to be taught the rudiments of etiquette, nor can the teaching be too patiently or too conscientiously carried out.

Training a child is exactly like training a puppy; a little heedless inattention and it is out if hand immediately; the great thing is not to let it acquire bad habits that must afterward be broken. Any child can be taught to be beautifully behaved with no effort greater than quiet patience and perseverance, whereas to break bad habits once they are acquired is a Herculean task.

ELEMENTARY TABLE MANNERS

Since a very little child can not hold a spoon properly, and as neatness is the first requisite in table-manners, it should be allowed to hold its spoon as it might take hold of a bar in front of it, back of the hand up, thumb closed over fist. The pusher (a small flat piece of silver at right angles to a handle) is held in the same way, in the left hand. Also in the first eating lessons, a baby must be allowed to put a spoon in its mouth, pointed end foremost. Its first lessons must be to take small mouthfuls, to eat very slowly, to spill nothing, to keep the mouth shut while chewing and not smear its face over. In drinking, a child should use both hands to hold a mug or glass until its hand is big enough so it can easily hold a glass in one.

When it can eat without spilling anything or smearing its lips, and drink without making grease "moons" on its mug or tumbler (by always wiping its mouth before drinking), it may be allowed to come to table in the dining-room as a treat, for Sunday lunch or breakfast. Or if it has been taught by its mother at table, she can relax her attention somewhat from its progress. Girls are usually daintier and more easily taught than boys, but most children will behave badly at table if left to their own devices. Even though they may commit no serious offenses, such as making a mess of their food or themselves, or talking with their mouths full, all children love to crumb bread, flop this way and that in their chairs, knock spoons and forks together, dawdle over their food, feed animals—if any are allowed in the room—or become restless and noisy.

Once graduated to the dining-room, any reversion to such tactics must be firmly reprehended, and the child should understand that continued offense means a return to the nursery. But before company it is best to say as little as possible, since too much nagging in the presence of strangers lessens a child's incentive to good behavior before them. If it refuses to behave nicely, much the best thing to do is to say nothing, but get up and quietly lead it from the table back to the nursery. It is not only bad for the child but annoying to a guest to continue instructions before "company," and the child learns much more quickly to be well-behaved if it understands that good behavior is the price of admission to grown-up society. A word or two such as, "Don't lean on the table. darling," or "pay attention to what you are doing, dear," should suffice. But a child that is noisy, that reaches out to help itself to candy or cake, that interrupts the conversation, that eats untidily has been allowed to leave the nursery before it has been properly graduated.

Table manners must, of course, proceed slowly in exactly the same way that any other lessons proceed in school. Having learned when a baby to use the nursery implements of spoon and pusher, the child, when it is a little older, discards them for the fork, spoon and knife.

THE PROPER USE OF THE FORK

As soon, therefore, as his hand is dexterous enough. the child must be taught to hold his fork, no longer gripped baby-fashion in his fist, but much as a pencil is held in writing; only the fingers are placed nearer the "top" than the "point," the thumb and two first fingers are closed around the handle two-thirds of the way up the shank, and the food is taken up shovel-wise on the turned-up prongs. At first his little fingers will hold his fork stiffly, but as he grows older his fingers will become more flexible just as they will in holding his pencil. If he finds it hard work to shovel his food, he can, for a while, continue to use his nursery pusher. By and by the pusher is changed for a small piece of bread, which is held in his left hand and between thumb and first two fingers, and against which the fork shovels up such elusive articles as corn, peas, poached egg, etc.

THE SPOON

In using the spoon, he holds it in his right hand like the fork. In eating cereal or dessert, he may be allowed to dip the bowl of the spoon toward him and eat from the end, but in eating soup he must dip his spoon away from him—turning the outer rim of the bowl down as he does so—fill the bowl not more than three-quarters full and sip it, without noise, out of the side (not the end) of the bowl. The reason why the bowl must not be filled full is because it is impossible to lift a brimming spoonful of liquid to his mouth without spilling some, or in the case of porridge without filling his mouth too full. While still very young he may be taught never to leave the spoon in a cup while drinking out of it, but after stirring the cocoa, or whatever it is, to lay the spoon in the saucer.

A very ugly table habit, which seems to be an impulse among all children, is to pile a great quantity of food on a fork and then lick or bite it off piecemeal. This must on no account be permitted. It is perfectly correct, how-

ever, to sip a little at a time, of hot liquid from a spoon.
In taking any liquid either from a spoon or drinking ves-
sel, no noise must ever be made.

THE FORK AND KNIFE TOGETHER

In being taught to use his knife, the child should at
first cut only something very easy, such as a slice of
chicken; he should not attempt anything with bones or
gristle, or anything that is tough. In his left hand is put
his fork with the prongs downward, held near the top of
the handle. His index finger is placed on the shank so
that it points to the prongs, and is supported at the side
by his thumb. His other fingers close underneath and
hold the handle tight. He must never be allowed to hold
his fork emigrant fashion, perpendicularly clutched in the
clenched fist, and to saw across the food at its base with
his knife.

THE KNIFE

The knife is held in his right hand exactly as the fork
is held in his left, firmly and at the end of the handle,
with the index finger pointing down the back of the blade.
In cutting he should learn not to scrape the back of the
fork prongs with the cutting edge of the knife. Having
cut off a mouthful, he thrusts the fork through it, with
prongs pointed downward and conveys it to his mouth with
his left hand. He must learn to cut off and eat one mouthful at a time.

It is unnecessary to add that the knife must *never* be
put in his mouth; nor is it good form to use the knife
unnecessarily. Soft foods, like croquettes, hash on toast,
all eggs and vegetables, should be cut or merely broken
apart with the edge of the fork held like the knife, after
which the fork is turned in the hand to first (or shovel)
position. The knife must never be used to scoop baked
potato out of the skin, or to butter potato. A fork must
be used for all manipulations of vegetables; butter for
baked potatoes taken on the tip of the fork shovel fashion,

"IN EATING SOUP THE CHILD MUST DIP HIS SPOON AWAY FROM HIM—
TURNING THE OUTER RIM OF THE SPOON DOWN AS HE DOES SO. . . ."
[Page 573.]

"IN BEING TAUGHT TO USE KNIFE AND FORK TOGETHER, THE CHILD
SHOULD AT FIRST CUT ONLY SOMETHING VERY EASY, SUCH AS A
SLICE OF CHICKEN. . . ." [Page 574.]

"HAVING CUT OFF A MOUTHFUL, HE THRUSTS THE FORK THROUGH
IT, WITH PRONGS POINTED DOWNWARD AND CONVEYS IT TO HIS
MOUTH WITH HIS LEFT HAND. HE MUST LEARN TO CUT OFF AND EAT
ONE MOUTHFUL AT A TIME." [Page 574.]

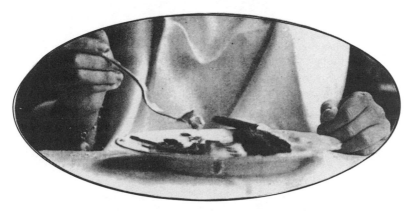

"WHEN NO KNIFE IS BEING USED, THE FORK IS HELD IN THE RIGHT HAND, WHETHER USED 'PRONGS DOWN' TO IMPALE THE MEAT, OR 'PRONGS UP' TO LIFT VEGETABLES." [Page 575.]

"BREAD SHOULD ALWAYS BE BROKEN INTO SMALL PIECES WITH THE FINGERS BEFORE BEING BUTTERED." [Page 583.]

"WHEN HE HAS FINISHED EATING THE CHILD SHOULD LAY HIS KNIFE AND FORK CLOSE TOGETHER, SIDE BY SIDE, WITH HANDLES TOWARD THE RIGHT SIDE OF HIS PLATE. . . ." [Page 575.]

laid on the potato, and then pressed down and mixed with the prongs held points curved up.

When no knife is being used, the fork is held in the right hand, whether used "prongs down" to impale the meat or "prongs up" to lift vegetables.

To pile mashed potato and other vegetables on the convex side of the fork on top of the meat for two or more inches of its length, is a disgusting habit dear to school boys, and one that is more easily prevented than corrected. In fact, taking a big mouthful (next to smearing his face and chewing with mouth open) is the worst offense at table.

When he has finished eating, he should lay his knife and fork close together, side by side, with handles toward the right side of his plate, the handles projecting an inch or two beyond the rim of the plate. They must be placed far enough on the plate so that there is no danger of their over-balancing on to the table or floor when removed at the end of the course.

OTHER TABLE MATTERS

The distance from the table at which it is best to sit, is a matter of personal comfort. A child should not be allowed to be so close that his elbows are bent like a grasshopper's, nor so far back that food is apt to be spilled in transit from plate to mouth. Children like to drink very long and rapidly, all in one breath, until they are pink around the eyes, and are literally gasping. They also love to put their whole hands in their finger-bowls and wiggle their fingers.

A baby of two, or at least by the time he is three, should be taught to dip the tips of his fingers in the finger-bowl, without playing, draw the fingers of the right hand across his mouth, and then wipe his lips and fingers on the apron of his bib.

No small child can be expected to use a napkin instead of a bib. No matter how nicely behaved he may be, there is always danger of his spilling something, some time. Soft boiled egg is hideously difficult to eat without ever getting a drop of it down the front, and it is much easier to supply him with a clean bib for the next meal than to change his dress for the next moment.

Very little children usually have "hot water plates" that are specially made like a double plate with hot water space between, on which the meat is cut up and the vegetables "fixed" in the pantry, and brought to the children before other people at the table are served. Not only because it is hard for them to be made to wait, and have their attention attracted by food not for them, but because they take so long to eat. As soon as they are old enough to eat everything on the table, they are served, not last, but in the regular rotation at table in which they come.

TABLE TRICKS THAT MUST BE CORRECTED

To sit up straight and keep their hands in their laps when not occupied with eating, is very hard for a child, but should be insisted upon in order to prevent a careless attitude that all too readily degenerates into flopping this way and that, and into fingering whatever is in reach. He must not be allowed to warm his hands on his plate, or drum on the table, or screw his napkin into a rope or make marks on the table-cloth. If he shows talent as an artist, give him pencils or modeling wax in his play-room, but do not let him bite his slice of bread into the silhouette of an animal, or model figures in soft bread at the table. And do not allow him to construct a tent out of two forks, or an automobile chassis out of tumblers and knives. Food and table implements are not play-things, nor is the dining-room a playground.

TALKING AT TABLE

When older people are present at table and a child wants to say something, he must be taught to stop eating momentarily and look at his mother, who at the first pause in the conversation will say, "What is it, dear?" And the child then has his say. If he wants merely to launch forth on a long subject of his own conversation, his mother says, "Not now, darling, we will talk about that by and by," or "Don't you see that mother is talking to Aunt Mary?"

When children are at table alone with their mother, they should not only be allowed to talk but unconsciously trained in table conversation as well as in table manners. Children are all more or less little monkeys in that they imitate everything they see. If their mother treats them exactly as she does her visitors they in turn play "visitor" to perfection. Nothing hurts the feelings of children more than not being allowed to behave like grown persons when they think they are able. To be helped, to be fed, to have their food cut up, all have a stultifying effect upon their development as soon as they have become expert enough to attempt these services for themselves.

Children should be taught from the time they are little not to talk about what they like and don't like. A child who is not allowed to say anything but "No, thank you," at home, will not mortify his mother in public by screaming, "I hate steak, I won't eat potato, I want ice cream!"

QUIETNESS AT TABLE

Older children should not be allowed to jerk out their chairs, to flop down sideways, to flick their napkins by one corner, to reach out for something, or begin to eat nuts, fruit or other table decorations. A child as well as a grown person should sit down quietly in the center of his chair and draw it up to the table (if there is no one to push it in for him) by holding the seat in either hand while momentarily lifting himself on his feet. He must not "jump" or "rock" his chair into place at the table. In getting up from the table, again he must push his chair back quietly, using his hands on either side of the chair seat, and *not* by holding on to the table edge and giving himself, chair and all, a sudden shove! There should never be a sound made by the pushing in or out of chairs at table.

THE SPOILED CHILD

The bad manners of American children, which unfortunately are supposed by foreigners to be typical, are nearly always the result of their being given "star" parts by over-fond but equally over-foolish mothers. It is only necessary to bring to mind the most irritating and objectionable child one knows, and the chances are that its mother continually throws the spotlight on it by talking to it, and about it, and by calling attention to its looks or its cunning ways or even, possibly, its naughtiness.

It is humanly natural to make a fuss over little children, particularly if they are pretty, and it takes quite .superhuman control for a young mother not to "show off" her treasure, but to say instead, "Please do not pay any attention to her." Some children, who are especially free from self-consciousness, stand "stardom" better than others who are more readily spoiled; but in nine cases out of ten, the old-fashioned method that assigned children to inconspicuous places in the background and decreed they might be seen but not heard, produced men and women of far greater charm than the modern method of encouraging public self-expression from infancy upward.

CHIEF VIRTUE: OBEDIENCE

No young human being, any more than a young dog, has the least claim to attractiveness unless it is trained to manners and obedience. The child that whines, interrupts, fusses, fidgets, and does nothing that it is told to do, has not the least power of attraction for any one, even though it may have the features of an angel and be dressed like a picture. Another that may have no claim to beauty whatever, but that is sweet and nicely behaved, exerts charm over every one.

When possible, a child should be taken away the instant it becomes disobedient. It soon learns that it can not "stay with mother" unless it is well-behaved. This means that it learns self-control in babyhood. Not only must children obey, but they must *never* be allowed to "show off" or become pert, or to contradict or to answer back; and after having been told "no," they must never be allowed by persistent nagging to win "yes."

A child that loses its temper, that teases, that is petulant and disobedient, and a nuisance to everybody, is merely a victim, poor little thing, of parents who have been too incompetent or negligent to train it to obedience. Moreover, that same child when grown will be the first to resent and blame the mother's mistaken "spoiling" and lack of good sense.

FAIR PLAY

Nothing appeals to children more than justice, and they should be taught in the nursery to "play fair" in games, to respect each other's property and rights, to give credit to others, and not to take too much credit to themselves. Every child must be taught never to draw attention to the meagre possessions of another child whose parents are not as well off as her own. A purse-proud, overbearing child who says to a playmate, "My clothes were all made in Paris, and my doll is ever so much handsomer than yours," or "Is that real lace on your collar?" is not impressing her young friend with her grandeur and discrimination but with her disagreeableness and rudeness. A boy who brags about what he has, and boasts of what he can do, is only less objectionable because other boys are sure to "take it out of him" promptly and thoroughly! Nor should a bright, observing child be encouraged to pick out other people's failings, or to tell her mother how inferior other children are compared with herself. If she wins a race or a medal or is praised, she naturally tells her mother, and her mother naturally rejoices with her, and it is proper that she should; but a wise mother directs her child's mental attitude to appreciate the fact that arrogance, selfishness and conceit can win no place worth having in the world.

CHILDREN AT AFTERNOON TEA

A custom in many fashionable houses is to allow children as soon as they are old enough, to come into the drawing-room or library at tea-time, as nothing gives them a better opportunity to learn how to behave in company. Little boys are always taught to bow to visitors; little girls to curtsy. Small boys are taught to place the individual tables, hand plates and tea, and pass sandwiches and cakes. If there are no boys, girls perform this office; very often they both do. When everybody has been helped, the children are perhaps allowed a piece of cake, which they put on a tea-plate, and sit down, and eat nicely. But as the tea-hour is very near their supper time, they are often allowed nothing, and after making themselves useful, go out of the room again. If many people are present and the children are not spoken to, they leave the room unobtrusively and quietly. If only one or two are present, especially those whom the children know well, they shake hands, and say "Good-by," and walk (not run) out of the room.

This is one of the ways in which well-bred people become used from childhood to instinctive good manners. Unless they are spoken to, they would not think of speaking or making themselves noticed in any way. Very little children who have not reached the age of "discretion," which may be placed at about five, possibly not until six, usually go in the drawing-room at tea-time only when near relatives or intimate friends of the family are there. Needless to say that they are always washed and dressed. Some children wear special afternoon clothes, but usually the clean clothes put on at tea-time go on again the next morning, except the thin socks and house slippers which are reserved for the "evening hour" of their day.

CHILDREN'S PARTIES

A small girl (or boy) giving a party should receive with her mother at the door and greet all her friends as they come in. If it is her birthday and other children bring her gifts, she must say "Thank you" politely. On no account must she be allowed to tell a child "I hate dolls," if a friend has brought her one. She must learn at an early age that as hostess she must think of her guests rather than herself, and not want the best toys in the grab-bag or scream because another child gets the prize that is offered in a contest. If beaten in a game, a little girl, no less than her brothers, must never cry, or complain that the contest is "not fair" when she loses. She must try to help her guests have a good time, and not insist on playing the game she likes instead of those which the other children suggest.

When she herself goes to a party, she must say, "How do you do," when she enters the room, and curtsy to the lady who receives. A boy makes a bow. They should have equally good manners as when at home, and not try to grab more than their share of favors or toys. When it is time to go home, they must say, "Good-by, I had a very good time," or, "Good-by, thank you ever so much."

THE CHILD'S REPLY

If the hostess says, "Good-by, give my love to your mother!" the child answers, "Yes, Mrs. Smith."

In all monosyllabic replies a child must not say "Yes" or "No" or "What?" A boy in answering a gentleman still uses the old-fashioned "Yes, sir," "No, sir," "I think so, sir," but ma'am has gone out of style. Both boys and girls must therefore answer, "No, Mrs. Smith," "Yes, Miss Jones." A girl says "Yes, Mr. Smith," rather than "sir." All children should say, "What did you say, mother?" "No, father," "Thank you, Aunt Kate," "Yes, Uncle Fred," etc.

They need not insert a name in a long sentence nor with "please," or "thank you." "Yes, please," or "No, thank you," is quite sufficient. Or in answering, "I just saw Mary down in the garden," it is not necessary to add "Mrs. Smith" at the end.

ETIQUETTE FOR GROWN CHILDREN

Etiquette for grown children is precisely the same as for grown persons, excepting that in many ways the manners exacted of young people should be more "alert" and punctilious. Young girls (and boys of course) should have the manners of a gentleman rather than those of a lady;

in that a gentleman always rises, relinquishes the best seat and walks last into a room, whereas these courtesies are shown to, and not observed by ladies (except to other ladies older than themselves).

In giving parties, young girls send out their invitations as their mothers do, and their deportment is the same as that of their débutante sister. Boys behave as their fathers do, and are equally punctilious in following the code of honor of all gentlemen. The only details, therefore, not likely to be described in other chapters of this book, are a few admonitions on table manners, that are somewhat above "kindergarten" grade.

THE GRADUATING TESTS IN TABLE MANNERS

A young person may be supposed to have graduated from the school of table etiquette when she, or he, would be able to sit at a formal lunch or dinner table and find no difficulty in eating properly any of the comestibles which are supposed to be "hurdles" to the inexpert.

CORN ON THE COB

Corn on the cob could be eliminated so far as ever having to eat it in formal company is concerned, since it is never served at a luncheon or a dinner; but, if you insist on eating it at home or in a restaurant, to attack it with as little ferocity as possible, is perhaps the only direction to be given, since at best it is an ungraceful performance and to eat it greedily a horrible sight!

ASPARAGUS

Although asparagus may be taken in the fingers, don't take a long drooping stalk, hold it up in the air and catch the end of it in your mouth like a fish. When the stalks are thin, it is best to cut them in half with the fork, eating the tips like all fork food; the ends may then be taken in the fingers and eaten without a dropping fountain effect! Don't squeeze the stalks, or hold your hand below the end and let the juice run down your arm.

ARTICHOKES

Artichokes are always eaten with the fingers; a leaf at a time is pulled off and the edible end dipped in the sauce, and then bitten off.

BREAD AND BUTTER

Bread should always be broken into small pieces with the fingers before being eaten. If it is to be buttered (at lunch, breakfast or supper, but not at dinner) a piece is held on the edge of the bread and butter plate, or the place plate, and enough butter spread on it for a mouthful or two at a time, with a small silver "butter knife." Bread must never be held flat on the palm of the hand and buttered in the air. If the regular steel knife is used, care must be taken not to smear food from the knife's side on the butter. Any food that is smeared about is loathsome. People who have beautiful table manners always keep their places at table neat. People with disgusting manners get everything in a horrible mess.

THE MANAGEMENT OF BONES AND PITS

Terrapin bones, fish bones and grape seed must be eaten quite bare and clean in the mouth, and removed one at a time between finger and thumb. All spitting out of bones and pits into the plate is disgusting.

If food is too hot, quickly take a swallow of water. On no account spit it out! If food has been taken into your mouth, no matter how you hate it, you have got to swallow it. It is unforgivable to take anything out of your mouth that has been put in it, except dry bones, and stones. To spit anything whatever into the corner of your napkin, is too nauseating to comment on. It is horrid to see any one spit skins or pits on a fork or into the plate. The only way to take anything out of your mouth is between first-finger and thumb. Dry grape seeds or cherry pits can be dropped from the lips into the cupped hand. Peaches or other very juicy fruits are peeled and then eaten with knife and fork, but dry fruits, such as apples, may be cut and then eaten in the fingers. *Never* wipe hands that have fruit juice on them on a napkin without first using a finger bowl, because fruit juices make indelible stains.

BIRDS

Birds are not eaten with the fingers in company! You cut off as much of the meat as you can, and leave the rest on your plate.

FORKS OR FINGERS

All juicy or "gooey" fruits or cakes are best eaten with a fork, but in most cases it is a matter of dexterity. If you are able to eat a peach in your fingers and not smear your face, let juice run down, or make a sucking noise, you are the one in a thousand who *may*, and with utmost propriety, continue the feat. If you can eat a napoleon or a cream puff and not let the cream ooze out on the far side, you need not use a fork, but if you can not eat something—no matter what it is—without getting it all over your fingers, you must use a fork, and if necessary, a knife also!

All rules of table manners are made to avoid ugliness; to let any one see what you have in your mouth is repulsive; to make a noise is to suggest an animal; to make a mess is disgusting. On the other hand, there are a number of trifling decrees of etiquette that are merely finical, unreasonable, and silly. Why one should not cut one's salad in small pieces if one wants to, makes little sense, unless one wants to cut up a whole plateful and make the plate messy! A steel knife must not be used for salad or fruit, because it turns black. To condemn the American custom of eating a soft-boiled egg in a glass, or cup, because it happens to be the English fashion to scoop it through the ragged edge of the shell, is about as reasonable as though we were to proclaim English manners bad because they tag a breakfast dish, called a "savory" of fish-roe or something equally inappropriate, after the dessert at dinner.

Many other arbitrary rules for eating food with fork, spoon or fingers, are also stumbling-blocks rather than aids to smoothness. As said above, one eats with a fork or spoon "finger-foods" that are messy and sticky; one eats with the finger those which are dry. It is true that one should not eat French fried potatoes or Saratoga chips in fingers, but that is because they belong to the meat course. Separate vegetable saucers are never put on a fashionable table, neither is butter allowed at dinner. Therefore both must be avoided in company, because "company" is formal, and etiquette is first aid always to formality. But if a man in his own house likes butter with his dinner or a saucer for his tomatoes, he is breaking the rule of fashion to have them, but he is scarcely committing an offense! In the same way, if he likes to eat a chicken wing or a squab leg in his fingers he can ask for a finger-bowl. The real objection to eating with the fingers is getting them greasy or sticky, and to suck them or smear one's napkin is equally unsightly.

ON THE SUBJECT OF ELBOWS

Although elbows on the table are seen constantly in highest fashionable circles, a whole table's length of elbows planted like clothes-line poles and hands waving glasses or forks about in between, is neither an attractive nor (fortunately) an accurate picture of a fashionable dinner table. As a matter of fact, the tolerated elbow-on-table is used only on occasion and for a reason, and should neither be permitted to children nor practised in their presence.

Elbows are universally seen on tables in restaurants, especially when people are lunching or dining at a small table of two or four, and it is impossible to make oneself heard above the music by one's table companions, and at the same time not be heard at other tables nearby, without leaning far forward. And in leaning forward, a woman's figure makes a more graceful outline supported on her elbows than doubled forward over her hands in her lap as though in pain! At home, when there is no reason for leaning across the table, there is no reason for elbows. And at a dinner of ceremony, elbows on the table are rarely seen, except at the ends of the table, where again one has to lean forward in order to talk to a companion at a distance across the table corner.

Elbows are *never* put on the table while one is eating. To sit with the left elbow propped on the table while eating with the right hand (unless one is alone and ill), or to prop the right one on the table while lifting the fork or glass to the mouth, must be avoided.

CHAPTER XXXVI

EVERY-DAY MANNERS AT HOME

Just as no chain is stronger than its weakest link, no manners can be expected to stand a strain beyond their daily test at home.

Those who are used to losing their temper in the bosom of their family will sooner or later lose it in public. Families which exert neither courtesy nor charm when alone, can no more deceive other people into believing that either attribute belongs to them than they could hope to make painted faces look like "real" complexions.

A mother should exact precisely the same behavior at home and every day, that she would like her children to display in public, and she herself, if she expects them to take good manners seriously, must show the same manners to them alone that she shows to "company."

A really charming woman exerts her charm nowhere more than upon her husband and children, and a noble nature through daily though unconscious example is of course the greatest influence for good that there is in the world. No preacher, no matter how saint-like his precept or golden his voice, can equal the home influence of admirable parents.

It is not merely in such matters as getting up when their mother or other older relatives enter a room, answering civilly and having good table manners, but in forming habits of admirable living and thinking that a parent's example makes or mars.

If children see temper uncontrolled, hear gossip, uncharitableness and suspicion of neighbors, witness arrogant sharp-dealing or lax honor, their own characters can scarcely escape perversion. In the same way others can not easily fail to be thoroughbred who have never seen or heard their parents do or say an ignoble thing.

587

No child will ever accept a maxim that is preached but not followed by the preacher. It is a waste of breath for the father to order his sons to keep their temper, to behave like gentlemen, or to be good sportsmen, if he does or is himself none of these things.

In the present day of rush and hurry, there is little time for "home" example. To the over-busy or gaily fashionable, "home" might as well be a railroad station, and members of a family passengers who see each other only for a few hurried minutes before taking trains in opposite directions. The days are gone when the family sat in the evening around the fire, or a "table with a lamp," when it was customary to read aloud or to talk. Few people "talk well" in these days; fewer read aloud, and fewer still endure listening to any book literally word by word.

Railroad station reading is as much in vogue as railroad station bolting of meals. Magazines—"picture" ones— are all that the hurried have time for, and even those who profess to "love reading" dart tourist-fashion from page to page only pausing at attractive paragraphs; and family relationships are followed somewhat in the same way.

Any number of busy men scarcely know their children at all, and have not even stopped to realize that they seldom or never talk to them, never exert themselves to be sympathetic with them, or in the slightest degree to influence them. To growl "mornin'," or "Don't, Johnny," or "Be quiet, Alice!" is very, very far from being "an influence" on your children's morals, minds or manners.

HOME EDUCATION

A Supreme Court Justice whose education had been cut short in his youth by the Civil War, when asked how, under the circumstances, his scholastic attainments had been acquired, answered: "My father believed it was the duty of every gentleman to bequeath the wealth of his intellect, no less than that of his pocket, to his children. Wealth might be acquired by 'luck,' but proper cultivation was the birthright of every child born of cultivated parents. We learned Latin and Greek by having him talk and read them to us. He wrote doggerel rhymes of history which took the place of Mother Goose. He also told us 'bed-time stories' of history, and read classics to us after supper. When there was company, we were brought down from the nursery so that we might profit by the conversation of our betters."

Volumes full of "manners" acquired after they are grown are not worth half so much as the simplest precepts acquired through lifelong habits and through having known nothing else.

THE OLD GRAY WRAPPER HABIT

How many times has one heard some one say: "I won't dress for dinner—no one is coming in." Or, "That old dress will do!" Old clothes! No manners! And what is the result? One wife more wonders why her husband neglects her! Curious how the habit of careless manners and the habit of old clothes go together. If you doubt it, put the question to yourself: "Who could possibly have the manners of a queen in a gray flannel wrapper? And how many women really lovely and good—. especially good—commit esthetic suicide by letting themselves slide down to where they "feel natural" in an old gray flannel wrapper, not only actually but mentally.

The woman of charm in "company" is the woman of fastidiousness at home; she who dresses for her children and "prinks" for her husband's home-coming, is sure to greet them with greater charm than she who thinks whatever she happens to have on is "good enough." Any old thing good enough for those she loves most! Think of it!

A certain very lovely lady whose husband is quite as much her lover as in the days of his courtship, has never in twenty years allowed him to watch the progress of her toilet, because of her determination never to let him see her except at her prettiest. Needless to say, he never meets anything but "prettiest" manners either. No matter how "out of sorts" she may be feeling, his key in the door is a signal for her to "put aside everything that is annoying or depressing," with the result that wild horses couldn't drag his attention from her—all because neither she nor he has ever slumped into the gray flannel wrapper habit.

So many people save up all their troubles to pour on the one they most love, the idea being, seemingly, that no reserves are necessary between lovers.   Nor need there be really.   But why, when their house looks out upon a garden that has charming vistas, must she insist on his looking into the clothes-yard and the ash-can?

She who complains incessantly that this is wrong, or that hurts, or any other thing worries or vexes her, so that his inevitable answer to her greeting is, "I'm so sorry, dear," or "That's too bad," or "Poor darling, it's a shame," is getting mentally into a gray flannel wrapper!

If something is seriously wrong, if she is really ill, that is different.   But of the petty things that are only remembered in order to be told to gain sympathy—beware!

There is a big deposit of sympathy in the bank of love, but don't draw out little sums every hour or so—so that by and by, when perhaps you need it badly, it is all drawn out and you yourself don't know how or on what it was spent.

All that has been said to warn a wife from slovenly habits of mind or dress may be adapted to apply with equal force in suggesting a rule for husbands.   A man should always remember that a woman's regard for him is founded on her impressions when seeing him at his best.   Even granting that she has no great illusions about men in general, he at his best is at least an approximation to her ideal—and it is his chief duty never to fall below the standard he set for himself in making his most cogent appeal.   Consequently he should continue through the years to be scrupulous about his personal appearance and his clothes, remembering the adage that the most successful marriages are those in which both parties to the contract succeed in "keeping up the illusion."   It is of importance also that he refrain from burdening his wife with the cares and worries of his business day.   Many writers insist that the wife should be ready to receive a complete consignment of all his troubles when the husband comes home at the end of the day.   It is a sounder practise for him to save her as much as possible from the trials of his business hours; and, incidentally, it is the best kind of mental training for him to put all business cares behind him as he closes the door of his office and goes home.   When it is said that a husband should not fling all the day's trifling annoyances into the lap of his wife without reflecting that she may have some cares of her own, there is no intention to indicate that a wife should not have a thorough understanding of her husband's affairs.   Complete acquaintance and sympathy with his work is one of the foundation stones of the domestic edifice.

THE FAMILY AT TABLE

Whether "there is company" or whether the family is alone, the linen must be as spotless, the silver as clean, and the table as carefully set as though twenty were coming for dinner.   Sloppy service is no more to be tolerated every day at home than at a dinner party, and in so far as etiquette is concerned, you should live in exactly the same way whether there is company or none.   "Company manners" and "every-day manners" must be identical in service as well as family behavior.   You may not be able to afford quantities of flowers in your house and on your table, or perhaps any, but there is no excuse for wilted flowers or an empty vase that merely accentuates your table's flowerlessness.   There are plenty of table ornaments that need no flowers.   In the same way the compotiers can be filled with candies or conserves of the "everlasting" variety; silver-foiled chocolates or nougat, or gum drops or crystalized ginger or conserved fruits—will keep for months!   But the table must be decorated and a certain form observed at the dinner hour; otherwise gray flannel wrapper habits become imminent.   Letters, newspapers, books have no place at a dinner table.   Reading at table is allowable at breakfast and when eating alone, but a man and his wife should no more read at lunch or dinner before each other or their children than they should allow their children to read before them.

THE TABLE NOT A PLACE FOR PRIVATE DISCUSSION

One very bad habit in many families is the discussion of all of their most intimate affairs at table—entirely forgetting whoever may be waiting on it; and nine times out of ten those serving in the dining-room see no harm (if they feel like it) in repeating what is said. Why should they? It scarcely occurs to them that they were "invisible" and that what was openly talked about at the table was supposed to be a secret!

Apart from the stupidity and imprudence of talking before witnesses, it is bad form to discuss one's private affairs before any one. And it should be unnecessary to add that a man and his wife who quarrel before their children or the servants, deprive the former of good breeding through inheritance, and publish to the latter that they do not belong to the "better class" through any qualification except the possession of a bank account.

Furthermore, parents must never disagree before the children. It simply can't be! Nor can there be an appeal to one parent against the other by a child.

"Father told me to jump down the well!"

"Then you must do it, dear," is the mother's only possible comment. When the child has "jumped down the well," she may pull him out promptly, and she may in private tell her husband what she thinks about his issuing such orders and stand her own ground against them; but so long as parents are living under the same roof, that roof must shelter unity of opinion, so far as any witnesses are concerned.

CHAPTER XXXVII

TRAVELING AT HOME AND ABROAD

To do nothing that can either annoy or offend the sensibilities of others, sums up the principal rules for conduct under all circumstances—whether staying at home or traveling. But in order to do nothing that can annoy or give offense, it is necessary for us to consider the point of view of those with whom we come in contact; and in traveling abroad it is necessary to know something of foreign customs which affect the foreign point of view, if we would be thought a cultivated and charming people instead of an uncivilized and objectionable one. Before going abroad, however, let us first take up the subject of travel at home.

Since it is not likely that any one would go around the world being deliberately offensive to others, it may be taken for granted that obnoxious behavior is either the fault of thoughtlessness or ignorance—and for the former there is no excuse.

ON A RAILROAD TRAIN

On a railroad train you should be careful not to assail the nostrils of fellow passengers with strong odors of any kind. An odor that may seem to you refreshing, may cause others who dislike it and are "poor travelers" to suffer really great distress. There is a combination of banana and the leather smell of a valise containing food, that is to many people an immediate emetic. The smell of a banana or an orange, is in fact to nearly all bad travelers the last straw. In America where there are "diners" on every Pullman train, the food odors are seldom encountered in parlor cars, but in Europe where railroad carriages are small, one fruit enthusiast can make his traveling companions more utterly wretched than

perhaps he can imagine. The cigar which is smolder-
ing has, on most women, the same effect. Certain perfumes that are particularly heavy, make others ill. To
at least half of an average trainful of people, strong
odors of one kind or another are disagreeable if not
actually nauseating.

CHILDREN ON TRAINS

People with children are most often the food-offenders.
Any number not only let small children eat continuously
so that the car is filled with food odors, but occasional
mothers have been known to let a child with smeary
fingers clutch a nearby passenger by the dress or coat
and seemingly think it cunning! Those who can afford
it, usually take the drawing-room and keep the children
in it. Those who are to travel in seats should plan
diversions for them ahead of time; since it is unreasonable to expect little children to sit quietly for hours
on end by merely telling them to "be good." Two little girls on the train to Washington the other day were
crocheting doll's sweaters with balls of worsted in which
were wound wrapped and disguised "prizes." The amount
of wool covering each might take perhaps a half hour
to use up. They were allowed the prize only when the last
strand of wool around it was used. They were then occupied for a while with whatever it was—a little book, or
a puzzle, or a game. When they grew tired of its novelty,
they crocheted again until they came to the next prize.
In the end they had also new garments for their dolls.

LADIES DO NOT TRAVEL WITH ESCORTS

In a curiously naïve book on etiquette appeared a chapter
purporting to give advice to a "lady" traveling for an indefinite number of days with a gentleman escort! That any
lady could go traveling for days under the protection of a
gentleman is at least a novelty in etiquette. As said elsewhere, in fashionable society an "escort" is unheard of, and
in decent society a lady doesn't go traveling around the
country with a gentleman unless she is outside the pale of

society, in which case social convention, at least, is not concerned with her.

. Ladies are sometimes accompanied on short, direct trips by gentlemen of their acquaintance, but not for longer than a few hours.

If a lady traveling alone on a long journey, such as a trip across the continent, happens to find a gentleman on board whom she knows, she must not allow him to sit with her in the dining-car more often than a casual once or twice, nor must she allow him to sit with her or talk to her enough to give a possible impression that they are together. In fact she would be more prudent to take her meals by herself, as it is scarcely worth running the risk of other passengers' criticism for the sake of having companionship at a meal or two. If, on a short trip, a gentleman asks a lady, whom he knows, to lunch with him in the dining-car, there is no reason why she shouldn't.

THE YOUNG WOMAN TRAVELING ALONE

In America, a young woman can go across every one of our thousands upon thousands of railed miles without the slightest risk of a disagreeable occurrence if she is herself dignified and reserved. She should be particularly careful if she is young and pretty not to allow strange men to "scrape an acquaintance" with her. If a stranger happens to offer to open a window for her, or get her a chair on the observation platform, it does not give him the right to more than a civil "thank you" from her. If, in spite of etiquette, she should on a long journey drift into conversation with an obviously well-behaved youth, she should remember that talking with him at all is contrary to the proprieties, and that she must be doubly careful to keep him at a formal distance. There is little harm in talking of utterly impersonal subjects— but she should avoid giving him information that is personal.

Every guardian should also warn a young girl that if, when she alights at her destination, her friends fail to meet her, she should on no account accept a stranger's offer, whether man or woman, to drive her to her destination.   The safest thing to do is to walk.   If it is too far, and there is no "official" taxicab agent belonging to the railroad company, she should go to the ticket seller or some one wearing the railroad uniform and ask him to select a vehicle for her.   She should never—above all in a strange city where she does not even know her direction—take a taxi on the street.

REGISTERING IN A HOTEL

A gentleman writes in the hotel register:

"John Smith, New York."

Under no circumstances "Mr." or "Hon." if he is alone.   But if his wife is with him, the prefix to their joint names is correct:

"Mr. and Mrs. John Smith, New York."

He never enters his street and house number.   Neither "John Smith and Wife" nor "John Smith and Family" are good form.   If he does not like the "Mr." before his name he can sign his own without, on one line, and then write "Mrs. Smith" on the one below.   The whole family should be registered:

John T. Smith,   New York
Mrs. Smith,   "
        and maid
                        (*if she has brought one*)

Miss Margaret Smith,   "
John T. Smith, Jr.,   "
Baby and nurse,   "

Or, if the children are young, he writes:

Mr. & Mrs. John T. Smith, New York, 3 children and nurse.

A lady never signs her name without "Miss" or "Mrs." in a hotel register:

"Miss Abigail Titherington" is correct, or "Mrs. John Smith," never "Sarah Smith."

LADIES ALONE IN AMERICAN HOTELS

If you have never been in a hotel alone but you are of sufficient years, well behaved and dignified in appearance, you need have no fear as to the treatment you will receive. But you should write to the hotel in advance—whether here or in Europe. In this country you register in the office and are shown to your room, or rooms, by a bell-boy—in some hotels by a bell-boy and a maid.

One piece of advice: You will not get good service unless you tip generously. If you do not care for elaborate meals, that is nothing to your discredit; but you should not go to an expensive hotel, hold a table that would otherwise be occupied by others who might order a long dinner, and expect your waiter to be contented with a tip of fifteen cents for your dollar supper! The rule is ten per cent, beginning with a meal costing about three or four dollars. A quarter is the smallest possible tip in a first class hotel. If your meal costs a quarter—you should give the waiter a quarter. If it costs two dollars or more than two dollars, you give thirty or thirty-five cents, and ten per cent on a bigger amount. In smaller hotels tips are less in proportion. Tipping is undoubtedly a bad system, but it happens to be in force, and that being the case, travelers have to pay their share of it—if they like the way made smooth and comfortable.

A lady traveling alone with her maid (or without one), of necessity has her meals alone in her own sitting-room, if she has one. If she goes to the dining-room, she usually takes a book because hotel service seems endless to one used to meals at home and nothing is duller than to sit long alone with nothing to do but look at the tablecloth, which is scarcely diverting, or at other people, which is impolite.

ON THE STEAMER

In the days when our great-grandparents went to Europe on a clipper ship carrying at most a score of voyagers and taking a month perhaps to make the crossing, those who sat day after day together, and evening after evening around the cabin lamp, became necessarily friendly; and in many instances not only for the duration of the voyage but for life. More often than not, those who had "endured the rigors" of the Atlantic together, joined forces in engaging the courier who was in those days indispensable, and set out on their Continental travels in company. Dashing to Europe and back was scarcely to be imagined, and travelers who had ventured such a distance, stayed at least a year or more. Also in those slower days of crawling across the earth's surface by post-chaise and diligence and horseback, travelers meeting in inns and elsewhere, fell literally on each other's neck at the sound of an American accent! And each retailed to the other his news of home; to which was added the news of all whom they had encountered. It is also from these "traveling ancestors" that families inherit their Continental visiting lists. Friends they made in Europe, in turn gave letters of introduction to friends coming later to America. And to them again their American hosts sent letters by later American friends.

But to-day when going to Europe is of scarcely greater importance than going into another State, and when the passenger list numbers hundreds, "making friends with strangers" is the last thing the great-grandchildren of those earlier travelers would think of.

It may be pretty accurately said that the faster and bigger the ship, the less likely one is to speak to strangers, and yet—as always—circumstances alter cases. Because the Worldlys, the Oldnames, the Eminents,—all those who are innately exclusive—never "pick up" acquaintances on shipboard, it does not follow that no fashionable and well-born people ever drift into acquaintanceship on European-American steamers of to-day—but they are at least not apt to do so. Many in fact take the ocean-crossing as a rest-cure and stay in their cabins the whole voyage. The Worldlys always have their meals served in their own "drawing-room" and have their deck chairs placed so that no one is very near them, and keep to themselves except when they invite friends of their own to play bridge or take dinner or lunch with them.

But because the Worldlys and the Eminents—and the Snobsnifts who copy them—stay in their cabins, sit in segregated chairs and speak to no one except the handful of their personal friends or acquaintances who happen to be on board, it does not follow that the Smiths, Joneses and Robinsons are not enlarging their acquaintance with every revolution of the screws. And if you happen to like to be talked to by strangers, and if they in turn like to talk to you, it can not be said that there is any rule of etiquette against it.

DINING SALOON ETIQUETTE

Very fashionable people as a rule travel a great deal, which means that they are known very well to the head steward, who reserves a table, or they engage a table for themselves when they get their tickets. Mr. and Mrs. Gilding for instance, if they know that friends of theirs are sailing on the same steamer, ask them to sit at their table and ask for a sufficiently large table on purpose. Or if they are traveling alone, they arrange to have one of the small tables for two, to themselves.

People of wide acquaintance in big cities are sure to find friends on board with whom they can arrange, if they choose, to sit on deck or in the dining saloon, but most people, unless really intimate friends are on board, sit wherever the head steward puts them. After a meal or two people always speak to those sitting next to them. None but the rudest snobs would sit through meal after meal without ever addressing a word to their table companions. Well-bred people are always courteous, but that does not mean that they establish friendships with any strangers who happen to be placed next to them.

In crossing the Pacific, people are more generally friendly because the voyage is so much longer, and on the other long voyages, such as those to India and South Africa, the entire ship's company become almost as intimate as in the old clipper days.

THE TACTICS OF THE CLIMBER

There are certain constant travelers who, it is said, count on a European voyage to increase their social acquaintance by just so much each trip! Richan Vulgar, for instance, has his same especial table every time he crosses, which is four times a year! Walking through a "steamer train" he sees a "celebrity," a brilliant, let us say, but unworldly man. Vulgar annexes him by saying, casually, "Have you a seat at table? Better sit with me, I always have the table by the door; it is easy to get in and out." The celebrity accepts, since there is no evidence that he is to be "featured," and the chances are that he remains unconscious to the end of time that he served as a decoy. Boarding the steamer, Vulgar sees the Lovejoys, and pounces: "You must sit at my table! Celebrity and I are crossing together—he is the most delightful man! I want you to sit next to him." They think Celebrity sounds very interesting; so, not having engaged a table for themselves, they say they will be delighted. On the deck, the Smartleys appear and ask the Lovejoys to sit with them. Vulgar, who is standing by (he is always standing by) breaks in even without an introduction and says: "Mr. and Mrs. Lovejoy and Celebrity are sitting at my table, won't you sit with me also?" If the Smartlys protest they have a table, he is generally insistent and momentarily overpowering enough to make them join forces with him. As the Smartlys particularly want to sit next to the Lovejoys and also like the idea of meeting Celebrity, it ends in Vulgar's table being a collection of fashionables whom he could not possibly have gotten together without just such a maneuver.

The question of what he gets out of it is puzzling since with each hour the really well-bred people dislike him more and more intensely, and at the end of a day or so, his table's company are all eating on deck to avoid him. Perhaps there is some recompense that does not appear on the surface, but to the casual observer the satisfaction of telling others that the Smartlys, Lovejoys and Wellborns sat at his table would scarcely seem worth the effort.

THOSE ACQUISITIVE OF ACQUAINTANCE

There is another type of steamer passenger and hotel guest who may, or may not, be a climber. This one searches out potential acquaintances on the passenger list and hotel register with the avidity of a bird searching for worms. You have scarcely found your own stateroom and had your deck chair placed, when one of them swoops upon you: "I don't know whether you remember me? I met you in nineteen two, at Countess della Robbia's in Florence." Your memory being wofully incomplete, there is nothing for you to say except, "How do you do!" If a few minutes of conversation, which should be sufficient, proves her to be a lady, you talk to her now and again throughout the voyage, and may end by liking her very much. If, however, her speech breaks into expressions which prove her not a lady, you become engrossed in your book or conversation with another when she approaches. Often these over-friendly people are grasping, calculating and objectionable, but sometimes like Ricki Ticki Tavi they are merely obsessed with a mania to run about and see what is going on in the world.

For instance, Miss Spinster is one of the best-bred, best-informed, most charming ladies imaginable. But her mania for people cannot fail on occasions to put her in a position to be snubbed—never seriously because she is too obviously a lady for that. But to see her trotting along the deck and then darting upon a helpless reclining figure, is at least an illustration of the way some people make friends. It can't be done, of course, unless you have once known the person you are addressing, or unless you have a friend in common who, though absent, can serve in making the introduction.

As said in "Introductions," introducing oneself is often perfectly correct. If you, sharing Miss Spinster's love of people, find yourself on a steamer with the intimate friend of a member of your family, you may very properly go up and say, "I am going to speak to you because I am Celia Lovejoy's cousin—I am Mrs. Brown." And Mrs. Norman, who very much likes Celia Lovejoy, says cordially, "I am so glad you spoke to me, do sit down, won't you?" But to have your next chair neighbor on deck insist on talking to you, if you don't want to be talked to, is very annoying, and it is bad form for her to do so. If you are sitting hour after hour doing nothing but idly looking in front of you, your neighbor might address a few remarks to you, and if you receive them with any degree of enthusiasm, your response may be translated into a willingness to talk. But if you answer in the merest monosyllables, it should be taken to mean that you prefer to be left to your own diversions.

Even if you are agreeable, your neighbor should show tact in not speaking to you when you are reading or writing, or show no inclination for conversation. The point is really that no one must do anything to interfere with the enjoyment of another. Whoever is making the advance, whether your neighbor or yourself, it must never be more than tentative; if not at least met halfway, it must be withdrawn at once. That is really the only rule there is. It should merely be granted that those who do not care to meet others have just as much right to their seclusion as those who delight in others have a right to be delighted—as long as that delight is unmistakably mutual.

STEAMER TIPS

Each ordinary first class passenger, now as always, gives ten shillings ($2.50) to the room steward or stewardess, ten shillings to the dining-room steward, ten shillings to the deck steward, ten shillings to the lounge steward. Your tip to the head steward and to one of the chefs depends on whether they have done anything especial for you. If not, you do not tip them. If you are a bad sailor and have been taking your meals in your room, you give twenty shillings ($5.00) at least to the stewardess (or steward, if you are a man). Or if you have eaten your meals on deck, you give twenty shillings to the deck steward, and ten to his assistant, and you give five to the bath steward. To any steward who takes pains to please you, you show by your manner in thanking him that you appreciate his efforts, as well as by giving him a somewhat more generous tip when you leave the ship.

If you like your bath at a certain hour, you would do well to ask your bath steward for it as soon as you go on board (unless you have a private bath of your own), since the last persons to speak get the inconvenient hours —naturally. To many the daily salt bath is the most delightful feature of the trip. The water is always wonderfully clear and the towels are heated.

If you have been ill on the voyage, some ship's doctors send in a bill; others do not. In the latter case you are not actually obliged to give them anything, but the generously inclined put the amount of an average fee in an envelope and leave it for the doctor at the purser's office.

DRESS ON THE STEAMER

On the *de luxe* steamers nearly every one dresses for dinner; some actually in ball dresses, which is in worst possible taste, and, like all overdressing in public places, indicates that they have no other place to show their finery. People of position never put on formal evening dress on a steamer, not even in the *à la carte* restaurant, which is a feature of the *de luxe* steamer of size. In the dining saloon they wear afternoon house dresses—without hats—for dinner. In the restaurant they wear semi-dinner dresses. Some smart men on the ordinary steamers put on a dark sack suit for dinner after wearing country clothes all day, but in the *de luxe* restaurant they wear Tuxedo coats. No gentleman wears a tail-coat on shipboard under any circumstances whatsoever.

TRAVELING ABROAD

Just as one discordant note makes more impression than all the others that are correctly played in an entire symphony, so does a discordant incident stand out and dominate a hundred others that are above criticism, and therefore unnoticed.

In every country of Europe and Asia are Americans who combine the brilliancy which none can deny is the birthright of the newer world, with the cultivation and good breeding of the old. These Americans of the best type go all over the world, fitting in so perfectly with their background that not even the inhabitants notice they are strangers; in other words they achieve the highest accomplishment possible.

But in contrast to these, the numberless discordant ones are only too familiar; one sees them swarming over Europe in bunches, sometimes in hordes, on regular professionally run tours. This, of course, does not mean that all personally conducted tourists are anything like them. The objectionables are loud of voice, loud in manner; they always attract as much attention as possible to themselves, and wave American flags on all occasions.

The American flag is the most wonderful emblem in the whole world, and ours is the most glorious country too, but that does not mean that it is good taste to wave our flag for no reason whatever. At a parade or on an especial day when other people are waving flags, then let us wave ours by all means—but not otherwise. It does not dignify our flag to make it an object of ridicule to others, and that is exactly the result of the ceaseless flaunting of it by a group of people who talk at the top of their voices, who deliberately assume that the atmosphere belongs to them, and who behave like noisy, untrained savages trying to "show off." In hotels, on excursions, steamers and trains, they insist on talking to everyone, whether everyone wants to talk or not. They are "all over the place"—there is no other way to express it—and they allow privacy to no one if they can help it.

Numberless cultivated Americans traveling in Europe never by any chance speak English or carry English books on railroad trains, as a protection against the other type of American who allows no one to travel in the same compartment and escape conversation. The only way to avoid unwelcome importunities is literally to take refuge in assuming another nationality.

Strangely enough, these irrepressibles are seldom encountered at home; they seem to develop on the steamer and burst into full bloom only on the beaten tourist trails— which is a pity, because if they only developed at home instead, we might be intensely annoyed but at least we should not be mortified before our own citizens about other fellow-citizens. But to a sensitive American it is far from pleasant to have the country he loves represented by a tableful of vulgarians noisily attracting the attention of a whole dining-room, and to have a European say mockingly, "Ah, and those are your compatriots?"

Some years ago, a Russian grand duke sitting next to Mrs. Oldname at a luncheon in a Monte Carlo restaurant, said to her:

"Your country puzzles me! How can it be possible that it holds without explosion such antagonistic types as the many charming Americans we are constantly meeting, and at the same time—" looking at a group who were actually *singing* and beating time on their glasses with knives and forks—"those!"

A French officer's comment to an American officer with whom he was talking in a club in Paris, quite unconsciously tells the same tale:

"You are *liaison* officer, I suppose, with the Americans? But may I be permitted to ask why you wear their uniform?"

The other smiled: "I am an American!"

"You an American? Impossible! Why, you speak French like a Parisian, you have the manner of a great gentleman!" (*un grand seigneur,*) which would indicate that the average American does not speak perfect French nor have beautiful manners. There is much excuse for not speaking foreign languages, but there is no excuse whatever for having offensive manners and riding rough-shod over people who own the land—not we, who seem to think we do.

As for "souvenir hunters," perhaps they can explain wherein their pilfering of another's property differs from petty thieving—a distinction which the owner can scarcely be expected to understand. Those who write their names, defacing objects of beauty with their vainglorious smudges and scribblings, are scarcely less culpable.

In France, in Spain, in Italy, grace and politeness of manner is as essential to merest decency as being clothed. In the hotels that are "used to us" (something of a commentary!) our lack of politeness is tolerated; but don't think for a moment it is not paid for! The officer referred to above, who had had the advantage of summer after summer spent in Europe as a boy, was charged just about half what another must pay who has "the rudeness of a savage."

But good manners are good manners everywhere, except that in Latin and Asiatic countries we must, as it seems to us, exaggerate politeness. We must, in France and Italy, bow smilingly; we must, in Spain and the East, bow gravely; but in any event, it is necessary everywhere, except under the American and British flags, to *bow*— though your bow is often little more than a slight inclination of the head, and a smile—and to show some ceremony in addressing people.

When you go into a shop in France or Italy, you must smile and bow and say, "Good morning, madam," or "Good evening, monsieur," and "Until we meet again," when you leave. If you can't say "Au revoir," say "Good afternoon" in English, but at all events say *something* in a polite tone of voice, which is much more important than the words themselves. To be civilly polite is not difficult—it is merely a matter of remembering. To fail to say "good morning" to a *concierge,* a chambermaid, or a small tradesman in France, treating him (or her) as though he did not exist, is not evidence of your grandeur but of your ignorance. A French duchess would not *think* of entering the littlest store without saying, "Good morning, madame," to its proprietress, and if she is known to her at all, without making enquiries concerning the health of the various members of her family. Nor would she fail to say, "Good morning, Auguste," or "Marie," to her own servants.

EUROPE'S UNFLATTERING OPINION OF US

For years we Americans have swarmed over the face of the world, taking it for granted that the earth's surface belongs to us because we can pay for it, and it is rather worse than ever since the war, when the advantages of exchange add bitterness to irritation.

And yet there are many who are highly indignant when told that, as a type, we are not at all admired abroad. Instead of being indignant, how much simpler and better it would be to make ourselves admirable, especially since it is those who most lack cultivation who are most indignant. The very well-bred may be mortified and abashed, but they can't be indignant except with their fellow countrymen who by their shocking behavior make Europe's criticism just.

Understanding of, and kind-hearted consideration for the feelings of others are the basic attributes of good manners. Without observation, understanding is impossible— even in our own country where the attitude of our neighbors is much the same as our own. It is not hard to appreciate, therefore, that to understand the point of view of people entirely foreign to ourselves, requires intuitive perception as well as cultivation in a very high degree.

AMERICANS IN EUROPEAN SOCIETY

It is only in musical comedy that one can go into a strange city and be picked out of the crowd and invited to the tables of the high of the land, because one looks as though one might be agreeable! To see anything of society in the actual world it is necessary to have friends, either Americans living or "stationed" or married abroad; or to take letters of introduction. Taking letters of introduction should never be done carelessly, because of the obligation that they impose. But to go to a strange country and see nothing of its social life, is like a blind person's going to the theater, and the only way a stranger can know people is through the letters he brings.

Under ordinary circumstances no knowledge whatsoever beyond the social amenities the world over are necessary. A dinner abroad is exactly the same as one here. You enter a room, you bow, you shake hands, you say, "How do you do." You sit at table, you talk of impersonal things, say "Good-by" and "Thank you" to your hostess, and you leave.

The matter of addressing people of title correctly is of little importance. The beautiful Lady Oldworld (who was Alice Town) was asked one day by a fellow countryman, what she called this person of title and that one, and she replied:

"I'm not sure that I know! Why should I call them at all?" which was a perfectly sensible answer. One never says anything but "you" to the person spoken to; and it might be an excellent thing not to know how to speak about anyone with a title, as it would prevent one's mentioning them.

Having gone into the subject thus far, however, it may be added that if at a dinner you are put next to a Duke, if it is necessary to call him anything except "you," you would say "Duke." Unless you are waiting on the table instead of sitting at it, you would not say, "Your Grace" and not even *then* "My Lord Duke." Neither, unless you are a valet or a chambermaid, would you say "Your Lordship" to an Earl! If you are a lady, you call him "Lord Arlington." If you know him really well, you call him "Arlington." To a knight you say, "Sir Arthur," which sounds familiar, but there is nothing else you can call him.

In England a stranger is not supposed to introduce anyone, so that titles of address are not necessary then either; but if you happen to be the hostess and French or Americans are present, who like introductions, you introduce Sir Arthur Dryden to the Duke and Duchess of Overthere, or to Prince and Princess Capri. In talking to her, the latter would be called "Princess" and her husband "Prince Capri" or "Prince" or by those who know him well, "Capri."

PRESENTATION AT COURT

Frequently American men are presented at the British Court at levees held by the King for the purpose. Such men are of course distinguished citizens who have been in some branch of public service, or who have contributed something to art, science, history or progress.

An American lady to be eligible for presentation at a foreign Court should be either the wife or daughter of a distinguished American citizen or be herself notable in some branch of learning or accomplishment.

It is absolutely necessary that such a candidate take letters of introduction to the American Ambassador,* or Minister if in a country where we have a Legation instead of an Embassy. She would enclose her letters in a note to the Ambassadress asking that her name be put on the list for presentation. The propriety of this request is a very difficult subject to advise upon, in that it is better that the suggestion come from the Ambassador rather than from oneself. It is, however, perfectly permissible for one whose presentation is appropriate, but who may perhaps not know the Ambassador or his wife personally, to do as suggested above. It must also be remembered that rarely more than three or perhaps five persons are presented at any one time, so that the difficulty of obtaining a place on the list is obvious.

An American lady is presented by the American Ambassadress (or the wife of the American Minister) or by the wife of the Chargé d'Affaires if the Ambassadress

*In South America alone, where out of courtesy to those who also consider themselves "Americans," the Embassies and Legations of our country are known as those of The United States of America. But in all other countries of the world we are known simply as "Americans"—it is the only name we have. We are not United Staters or United Statians —there is not even a word to apply to us! To speak of the American Minister to this country or that, and of the American Embassy in Paris for instance, is entirely correct.

be absent; or occasionally by the Doyenne of the diplomatic corps at the request of the American Embassy.

It would be futile to attempt giving details of full
court dress or especial details of etiquette, as these vary
not alone with countries, but with time! If you are about
to be presented, you will surely be told all that is necessary by the person presenting you. These details, after
all, merely comprise the exact length of train or other
particulars of dress, the hour you are to be at such and
such a door, where you are to stand, and how many
curtsies or bows you are to make. In all other and essential particulars you behave as you would in any and
every circumstance of formality. In general outline, however, it would be safe to say that on the day of the ceremony you drive to the Palace at a specified hour, wearing specified clothes and carrying your card of invitation
in your hand. Your wraps are left in the carriage (or
motor-car), you enter the Palace and are shown into a
room where you wait, and *wait* and WAIT! until at
last you are admitted to the Audience Chamber where
you approach the receiving Royalties; you curtsy deeply
before them and then back out.

Or else—you stand on an assigned spot while the King
or Queen or both make the tour of those waiting, who
curtsy (or bow) deeply at their approach and again at
their withdrawal.

If you are spoken to at length, you answer as under
any other circumstances, exactly as a polite child answers
his elders. You do not speak unless spoken to. If your
answer is long you need say nothing except the answer;
if short, you add "Sir" to the King and "Madam" to the
Queen. This seemingly democratic title is as a matter
of fact the correct one for all Royalty. "Yes, sir." "Very
much indeed, Madam." "I think so, Madam."

FOREIGN LANGUAGES

In the Latin countries, grace and facility of speech is
an object of life-long cultivation—and no one is considered an educated person who can not speak several lan-

guages well. Those who speak many fluently, by the way, are seldom those who constantly interlard their own tongue with words from another.

Not to understand any foreign languages would be a decided handicap in European society, where conversation is very apt to turn polyglot, beginning in one tongue and going on in a second and ending in a third. So that one who knows only English is often in the position of a deaf person, even though Europeans are invariably polite and never let a conversation run long in a language which all those present do not understand. It might easily happen that a French lady and an American, neither understanding the tongue of the other, meet at the house of an Italian, where there is also an Italian monolinguist, so that the hostess has to talk in three languages at once.

It is unreasonable to expect the average American to be a linguist; we are too far removed from foreign countries. As a matter of fact, if you would make yourself agreeable, it is much better (unless your facility was acquired as a child or you have a talent amounting to genius for accent and construction), to make it a rule when you lunch or dine with Europeans to talk English, since all Latins acutely suffer at hearing their language distorted. English, on the other hand, is not beautiful in sound to the foreign ear; it is a series of esses and shushes, lumped with consonants like an iron-wheeled cart bumping over a cobble-stoned street. The Latin's accent in English is annoying even to us at times, but the English accent in French, Italian or Spanish is murderous! Furthermore, the Latin passionately loves his language in the way the Westerner loves his city; he simply can not endure to have it abused, and execrates the person who does so. And, proportionately, he loves the few who prove they share his love by speaking it creditably.

TO IMPROVE ONE'S ACCENT

If you want to improve your accent, nothing can so help you as going to the theater abroad until your ears literally absorb the sounds! All people are imitative. There are few who do not gradually lose the purity of a good foreign accent when long away from Europe, and all speak more fluently when their ears become accustomed to the sound.

The theater is not only the best possible place to hear correctly enunciated speech, but a play of contemporary life is equally valuable as a study in manners. There is also a suavity of grace in the way Europeans bow and stand and sit, and in the way they speak, that is unconsciously imitated. These "manners" need not—in fact, should not—be gushing or mincing, but you gradually perceive that jerking ramrod motions and stalking into a drawing-room like a grenadier are less impressive than awkward.

THE SPOILED AMERICAN GIRL

The subject of American manners, as they appear to Europeans, cannot be dismissed without comment on a reprehensible type of American girl who flourishes on shipboard, on tours, and in public places generally—but most particularly in the large and expensive hotels of Continental resorts.

If she and her family have a "home," they are never in it, and if they have any object in life other than letting her follow her own unhampered inclinations, it is not apparent to the ordinary observer. Such a girl is always overdressed, she wears every fashion in its extremest exaggeration, she sparkles with jewelry, and reeks of scent, she switches herself this way and that, and is always posing in public view and playing to the public gallery. She generally has a small brother who refuses to go to bed at night, or to stop making the piazza chairs into a train of cars, or to use the public halls as a skating rink. When he is not making a noise, he is eating. And his "elegant" sister looks upon him with disdain.

Sister, meanwhile, jingling with chains and bangles, decked in scarfs and tulle and earrings, leans on or against whatever happens to be convenient, flirting with any casual stranger who comes along. She invariably goes to her meals alone—evidently thinking her parents should be kept apart from her. She is never away from the Kurhaus or Casino, abroad or the hotel lobby in America. She is nearly always alone, and the book she is perpetually reading is always opened at the same page, and she is sure to look up as you pass. She is very ready to be "picked up" and to confide her life's history, past, present and future, to any stranger, especially a young one of the opposite sex. She is rude only to her mother and father. She is also (we know, but Europe doesn't) a perfectly "good" girl. Her lack of etiquette is shocking, but her morals are above reproach. She does not even mean to be rude to her parents, and she has no idea that the things she does are exactly those which condemn her in the opinion of strangers. If she were constantly with, and obviously devoted to her mother, she would make an infinitely better impression, both as to good form and as to heart, than by segregating herself so that she can be joined by any haphazard youth who strolls into view, and thereby cheapening not only herself but the name of the American girl in general.

Curiously enough, if she marries in Europe, she is apt to "settle down" and become an altogether admirable example of American-European womanhood, because she is sound fruit at heart—merely wrapped in tawdry gilt paper trimming by her adoring but ignorantly unwise parents who, in their effort to show her off, disguise the very qualities which should have been accentuated.

LADIES TRAVELING ALONE IN EUROPE.

Europeans can not possibly understand how any lady of social position can be without a maid. A lady traveling alone, therefore, has this trifling handicap to start with. It is a very snobbish opinion, and one who has the temerity to attempt traveling all by herself has undoubtedly the ability to see it through. She need after all merely behave with extreme quietness and dignity and she can go from one end of the world to the other without molestation or even difficulty—especially if she is anything of a linguist.

In going from one place to another, it is wiser to write as long as possible ahead for accommodations—possibly giving the name of the one (if any) who recommended the hotel. But in going far off into Asia or other "difficult" countries, she would better join friends or at least a personally conducted tour, unless she has the mettle of a Burton or a Stanley.

MOTORING IN EUROPE

Motoring in Europe is perfectly feasible and easy. A car has to be put in a crate to cross the ocean, but in crossing the channel between England and France, no difficulty whatever is experienced. All information necessary can be had at any of the automobile clubs, and in going from one country to another, you have merely to show your passports at the border properly viséd and pay a deposit to insure your not selling the car out of the country, which is refunded when you come back.

Garage charges are reasonable, but gasoline is high. Roads are beautiful, and traveling—once you have your car—is much cheaper than by train.

Once off the beaten track, a tourist who has not a working knowledge of the language of the country he is driving through, is at a disadvantage, but plenty of people constantly do it, so it is at least not insurmountable. With English you can go to most places—with English and French nearly everywhere. The Michelin guide shows you in a little drawing, exactly the type of hotels you will find in each approaching town and the price of accommodation, so that you can choose your own stopping places accordingly.

"And etiquette?" you ask. There is no etiquette of motoring that differs from all other etiquette. Except of course not to be a road hog—or a road pig! People who take up the entire road are not half the offenders that others are who picnic along the side of it and leave their old papers and food all over everywhere. For that matter, any one who shoves himself forward in any situation in life, he who pushes past, bumping into you, walking over you, in order to get a first seat on a train, or to be the first off a boat, any one who pushes himself out of his turn, or takes more than his share, anywhere or of anything—is precisely that sort of an animal.

ON A CONTINENTAL TRAIN

Europeans usually prefer to ride backwards, and as an American prefers to face the engine, it works out beautifully. It is not etiquette to talk with fellow passengers, in fact it is very middle-class. If you are in a smoking carriage (all European carriages are smoking unless marked "Ladies alone" or "No smoking") and ladies are present, it is polite to ask if you may smoke. Language is not necessary, as you need merely to look at your cigar and bow with an interrogatory expression, whereupon your fellow passengers bow assent and you smoke.

THE PERFECT TRAVELER.

One might say the perfect traveler is one whose digestion is perfect, whose disposition is cheerful, who can be enthusiastic under the most discouraging circumstances, to whom discomfort is of no moment, and who possesses at least a sense of the ridiculous, if not a real sense of humor! The perfect traveler furthermore, is one who possesses the virtue of punctuality; one who has not forgotten something at the last minute, and whose bags are all packed and down at the hour for the start. Those who fuss and flurry about being ready, or those whose disposition is easily upset or who are inclined to be gloomy, should not travel—unless they go alone. Nothing can spoil a journey more than some one who is easily put out of temper and who always wants to do something the others do not. Whether traveling with your family or with comparative strangers, you must realize that your personal likes and dislikes have at least on occasion to be subordinated to the likes and dislikes of others; nor can you always be comfortable, or have good weather, or make perfect connections, or find everything to your personal satisfaction; and you only add to your own discomfort and chagrin, as well as to the discomfort of every one else, by refusing to be philosophical. Those who are bad sailors should not go on yachting parties; they are always abjectly wretched, and are of no use to themselves or any one else. Those who hate walking should not start out on a tramp that is much too far for them and expect others to turn back when they get tired. They need not "start" to begin with, but having once started, they must see it through.

There is no greater test of a man's (or a woman's) "wearing" qualities than traveling with him. He who is always keen and ready for anything, delighted with every amusing incident, willing to overlook shortcomings, and apparently oblivious of discomfort, is, needless to say, the one first included on the next trip.

Chapter XXXVIII

GROWTH OF GOOD TASTE IN AMERICA

Good taste or bad is revealed in everything we are, do, or have. Our speech, manners, dress, and household goods—and even our friends—are evidences of the propriety of our taste, and all these have been the subject of this book. Rules of etiquette are nothing more than sign-posts by which we are guided to the goal of good taste.

Whether we Americans are drifting toward or from finer perceptions, both mental and spiritual, is too profound a subject to be taken up except on a broader scope than that of the present volume. Yet it is a commonplace remark that older people invariably feel that the younger generation is speeding swiftly on the road to perdition. But whether the present younger generation is really any nearer to that frightful end than any previous one, is a question that we, of the present older generation, are scarcely qualified to answer. To be sure, manners seem to have grown lax, and many of the amenities apparently have vanished. But do these things merely seem so to us because young men of fashion do not pay party calls nowadays and the young woman of fashion is informal? It is difficult to maintain that youth to-day is so very different from what it has been in other periods of the country's history, especially as "the capriciousness of beauty," the "heartlessness" and "carelessness" of youth, are charges of a too suspiciously bromidic flavor to carry conviction.

The present generation is at least ahead of some of its "very proper" predecessors in that weddings do not have to be set for noon because a bridegroom's sobriety is not to be counted on later in the day! That young people of to-day prefer games to conversation scarcely proves degeneration. That they wear very few clothes is not a symptom of decline. There have always been recurring cycles of undress, followed by muffling from shoe-soles to chin.   We have not yet reached the undress of Pauline Bonaparte, so the muffling period may not be due!

However, leaving out the mooted question whether etiquette may not soon be a subject for an obituary rather than a guide-book, one thing is certain: we have advanced prodigiously in esthetic taste.

Never in the recollection of any one now living has it been so easy to surround oneself with lovely belongings. Each year's achievement seems to stride away from that of the year before in producing woodwork, ironwork, glass, stone, print, paint and textile that is lovelier and lovelier.   One can not go into the shops or pass their windows on the streets without being impressed with the ever-growing taste of their display.   Nor can one look into the magazines devoted to gardens and houses and house-furnishings and fail to appreciate the increasing wealth of the beautiful in environment.

That such exquisite "best" as America possessed in her Colonial houses and gardens and furnishings should ever have been discarded for the atrocities of the period after the Civil War, is comparable to nothing but Titania's Midsummer Night's Dream madness that made her believe an ass's features more beautiful than those of Apollo!

Happily, however, since we never do things by halves, we are studying and cultivating and buying and making, and trying to forget and overcome that terrible marriage of our beautiful Colonial ancestress with the dark-wooded, plush-draped, jig-sawed upstart of vulgarity and ignorance. In another country her type would be lost in his, forever! But in a country that sent a million soldiers across three thousand miles of ocean, in spite of every obstacle and in the twinkling of an eye, why even comment that good taste is pouring over our land as fast as periodicals, books and manufacturers can take it.   Three thousand miles east and west, two thousand miles north and south, white tiled bathrooms have sprung like mushrooms seemingly in a single night, charming houses, enchanting gardens, beautiful cities, cultivated people, created in thousands upon thousands of instances in the short span of one generation.   Certain great houses abroad have consummate quality, it is true, but for every one of these, there are a thousand that are mediocre, even offensive.   In our own country, beautiful houses and appointments flourish like field flowers in summer; not merely in the occasional gardens of the very rich, but everywhere.

And all this means?   Merely one more incident added to the many great facts that prove us a wonderful nation. (But this is an aside merely, and not to be talked about to anyone except just ourselves!)   At the same time it is no idle boast that the world is at present looking toward America; and whatever we become is bound to lower or raise the standards of life.   The other countries are old, we are youth personified!   We have all youth's glorious beauty and strength and vitality and courage.   If we can keep these attributes and add finish and understanding and perfect taste in living and thinking, we need not dwell on the Golden Age that is past, but believe in the Golden Age that is sure to be.

INDEX

Acceptance of an invitation, 122-123; to a formal dinner, 187-188; to an informal dinner, 125; to a wedding, 111.

Acknowledgment of Christmas presents, 407-408; of wedding presents, 320; of messages of condolence, 406-408.

Address, forms of. See: Forms of address.

Address, notification of, 180; by bride and groom, 108-109.

Address on envelopes, 460, 486, 488; on letters, 450, 455, 460, 461; on visiting cards, 74-76.

Afternoon parties, chapter on, 165-176.

Afternoon teas. See: Teas.

Ambassador, close of letter to, 456; function of in presentation at court, 609; how to address, 488; how to announce as a guest, 214; how to introduce, 4, 489.

Americans abroad, 604-616.

Announcement of a death, 390; of an engagement, 89, 304-306, 309; of a second marriage, 108; of a wedding, 106-107.

Announcing dinner, 217.

Announcing guests, at afternoon tea, 167; at dinner, 214-215.

Answering the door, 145. See also: "Not at home."

Anthem, national, 23.

Apology, form of, 23-24; letters of, 462-463; at the theater, 41.

Archbishop, close of letter to, 489; how to address, 488; how to introduce, 489.

Argumentativeness, 50.

Arm, etiquette of offering and taking, 30.

Artichokes, how to eat, 583.

Asking for a dance, 267, 270.

Asparagus, how to eat, 582.

Assemblies, 272-275.

Assemblyman, 486, 487.

At home with dancing, invitations to an, 112-116.

Au revoir, avoidance of use of, 19.

Automobiles. See: Motoring; Vehicles.

Baby, clothes for, at a christening, 385; letters of thanks for gifts to, 468; training in table manners, 571.

Bachelor's apartment, tea in, 292; dinner, 230, 336-337, 375; party, 71, 296-298; theater party, 38.

Bachelor girl, 295.

Ball dress, 541, 546-547, 557, 603; in opera box, 37.

Ballroom, etiquette in, 258-262; for an afternoon tea, 167.

Balls, chapter on, 250-275; clothes for, 569; gloves at, 20; hand-shaking at, 20; introductions at, 10, 16; invitations to, 112-116; for a débutante, 276-279; public, 271-275.

Beginning a letter, 492-494.

Behavior, good, fundamentals of, 506-510.

Best man, 331, 344; clothes of, 333; duties of on wedding day, 345-346; during the marriage ceremony, 358, 359, 360; after the marriage ceremony, 361; in rehearsal, 341, 342; at the wedding breakfast, 368.

Best Society, chapter on, 1-3; definition of, 3.

Beverages at afternoon teas, 167, 168, 169, 170, 173, 174; at ball suppers, 257; at formal dinners, 205, 209; at luncheons, 244-245; at wedding breakfasts, 365, 368.

Big dinners, 225-226.

Birds, how to eat, 584, 585.

Bishop, close of letter to, 489; how to address, 488; how to introduce, 5, 489.

Bones, management of, at table, 583-584.

Boots, 551, 568.

Bouquet, bridal, 344, 358, 359; of bridesmaid, 328.

Boutonnière, 334, 344, 354, 357, 551, 563.

Bowing, etiquette of, 20, 21, 23, 24-27, 93, 508; at court, 610.

Bread and butter, how to eat, 583.

Bread and butter letters, 468-470.

Breakfast, invitations to, 238-239; for country house guests, 427-429; wedding, 364-368.

Bridal procession, 339-342, 357-358.

Bridal veil, 350, 351.

Bride, acknowledgment of gifts by, 320-321; acquiring of social position by, 66-68; calls of, 66; calls on, 67-91; gifts of to bridesmaids, 336; gifts to by groom, 344; giving away of, 353, 359; house of on wedding day, 347-350; letters of thanks to relatives-in-law, 471; during the marriage ceremony, 358, 359, 360; in rehearsal, 338-342; at the wedding breakfast, 362, 368; as a chaperon, 289; as a guest of honor, 11.

Bride's going away dress, 370.

Bride's mother, cards left with, 87.

APPLEWOOD BOOKS

More Applewood Titles You Might Enjoy

George Washington's Rules of Civility and Decent Behavior

GEORGE WASHINGTON

The 110 rules that Washington copied into his notebooks and lived by all his life—from such rules as "Spit not in the fire" to "Sleep not when others speak."

ISBN 1-55709-103-x • $9.95
Hardcover • 4¼" x 6¾" • 30pp

Goops and How to Be Them

GELETT BURGESS

"The Goops they lick their fingers, / And the Goops they lick their knives, / They spill their broth on the tablecloth— / Oh, they lead disgusting lives!" The rhymes and drawings in this hilarious introduction to manners for children still amuse and educate 100 years later, providing lessons valuable today and shedding light on turn-of-the-century American morés.

ISBN 1-55709-392-x • $17.95
Hardcover • 6" x 9" • 96pp

The Education of a Daughter

ARCHBISHOP FENELON

Written in 1687 and published in 1847, *The Education of a Daughter* is filled with sound wisdom on the ample subject of rearing both daughters and sons. A constant reminder that good advice gets better with age.

ISBN 1-55709-427-6 • $14.95
Paperback • 5" x 8" • 160pp

Slovenly Betsy

HENRY HOFFMAN

This collection of American poems teaches good and bad behavior through 10 grotesque tales.

ISBN 1-55709-408-x • $7.95
Hardcover • 4" x 5⅜" • 64pp

Publishers of America's Living Past
www.awb.com